THE SUPREME COURT JUSTICES

Illustrated Biographies, 1789-1995

THE SUPREME COURT JUSTICES

Illustrated Biographies, 1789-1995

Second Edition

EDITED BY CLARE CUSHMAN

The Supreme Court Historical Society

FOREWORD BY
CHIEF JUSTICE WILLIAM H. REHNQUIST

CONGRESSIONAL QUARTERLY
WASHINGTON, D.C.

Book design by Kachergis Book Design, Pittsboro, North Carolina.

Printed in the United States of America.

Cover photo: Ken Heinen

LIBRARY OF CONGRESS CATALOGING-IN-PUBLICATION DATA
The Supreme Court justices : illustrated biographies, 1789–1995 / edited
  by Clare Cushman (The Supreme Court Historical Society) ;
  foreword by William H. Rehnquist.—2nd ed.
     p.   cm.
  Includes bibliographical references and index.
  ISBN 1-56802-127-5 (cloth). — ISBN 1-56802-126-7 (pbk.)
    1. Judges—United States—Biography. 2. United States.   Supreme
Court—Officials and employees—Biography. 3. United States.
Supreme Court—History. I. Cushman, Clare. II. Supreme Court
Historical Society.
KF8744.S86 1995
347.73'2634—dc20
[B]
[347.3073534]   95-32634
[B]   CIP

Contents

Foreword

The publication of *The Supreme Court Justices: Illustrated Biographies, 1789–1995* is an important event for the general reader seeking information about the lives of the 106 men and two women who have served on the nation's highest court. The Supreme Court Historical Society, a private nonprofit organization, began developing this manuscript in 1990. It is intended to be an introduction to the lives, careers, and judicial contributions of those who have sat on the Court.

The primary focus of the book is biographical rather than a comprehensive analysis of each justice's jurisprudence. The editors have provided a selected bibliography for those who, after reading the biographies enclosed, wish to study one or more of the justices in greater depth.

Some of the justices portrayed in this volume, such as the great Chief Justice John Marshall, the colorful and quotable Oliver Wendell Holmes, Jr., and the members of the current Court with whom I have the honor to serve, are familiar to the general reader. Others have undeservedly fallen into obscurity and are known only to constitutional law experts and dedicated Supreme Court buffs. A compelling motivation for this project was to make readily available to a broad general audience the story of the justices' private and professional lives and to explore how each contributed to the evolution of the Supreme Court.

Why was the justice selected for appointment by the president? What kind of education and training did the justice have? What were the major constitutional issues faced by the Court during the justice's tenure? This biographical collection attempts to answer these basic questions. It also provides a succinct description of each justice's major opinions and imprint on the Court in terms easily understood by the general reader.

I am delighted that the Supreme Court Historical Society has undertaken this project as part of its mission to expand public awareness and understanding of the Supreme Court of the United States. I also commend Congressional Quarterly Inc. for its part in making this publication available to a wide audience.

WILLIAM H. REHNQUIST
Chief Justice of the United States

Acknowledgments

The Supreme Court Historical Society is indebted to the many individuals whose assistance was crucial to the realization of this book. First and foremost, we gratefully acknowledge the work of all the writers who contributed their time and efforts. We also wish to thank the editorial advisers who provided guidance on the drafts and helped focus and sharpen the discussions of the justices' jurisprudence. The names of these writers and advisers appear on the credits page.

The Society is grateful to all the other editorial consultants who contributed their advice and expertise. They are: Thomas E. Baker, Edward S. Jones, Julie Kimmel, David O'Brien, James O'Hara, and Alice L. O'Donnell. Mrs. Thomas R. Gronlund deserves special mention for helping to revise the biography of her father, Tom C. Clark.

Although many helped shepherd this project to fruition, Kenneth S. Geller and the Society's Publications Committee should be particularly singled out for their efforts. Shelley Dowling and the staff of the Library of the Supreme Court of the United States were also of great assistance. Gail Galloway and the staff of the Curator's Office of the Supreme Court of the United States generously provided access to their extensive illustrations collection. We are indebted to Bernice Loss and Steven Smith of the Harvard Law School Art Collection and Chris Steele of the Massachusetts Historical Society for their help and advice.

The Supreme Court Historical Society gratefully acknowledges its members for their ongoing financial support in its endeavors to educate the public about the Court's history. Similarly, all the individuals, firms, and corporations who contributed to the Society's Endowment Program deserve our appreciation.

Finally, the Society would like to thank Jeanne Ferris and her colleagues at Congressional Quarterly who helped us make this project a reality. Carolyn Goldinger supervised the production of the first edition; Chris Karlsten shepherded the second edition to completion.

THE SUPREME COURT HISTORICAL SOCIETY
SECOND STREET, N.E., WASHINGTON, D.C.

Credits

Editor: Clare Cushman

Illustrations Editors: Jane Alexandra Walsh, Kathleen Shurtleff

Staff Writers: Burnett Anderson, Clare Cushman, David T. Pride, Kathleen Shurtleff

Senior Editorial Researchers: Jennifer M. Lowe, William Reilly

Editorial Researchers: Melissa S. Hardin, Nicholas Birch Harding

Bibliographer: Patricia R. Evans

Editorial Advisers

Richard E. Ellis (pre-Marshall Courts)
  Professor, Department of History
  State University of New York at New York

Herbert Alan Johnson (Marshall Court)
  Hollings Professor of Constitutional Law
  University of South Carolina School of Law

Herman Belz (Civil War and Recovery)
  Professor Emeritus, Department of History
  University of Maryland

Tony A. Freyer (1873–1888)
  University Research Professor of History and Law
  University of Alabama

Charles W. McCurdy (1889–1908)
  Associate Professor of History and Law, Corcoran
  Department of History
  The University of Virginia

Morton Keller (1909–1919)
  Samuel J. and Augusta Spector Professor of History
  Brandeis University

C. Herman Pritchett (1920–1937)
  Professor Emeritus, Department of Political Science
  University of California, Santa Barbara

Lucas (Scot) Powe (Stone and Vinson Courts)
  Anne Green Regents Chair
  School of Law, The University of Texas at Austin

Martin Shapiro (Warren and Burger Courts)
  James W. and Isabel Coffroth Professor of Law
  University of California School of Law (Boalt Hall)

Tony Mauro (Current Court)
  Supreme Court Reporter, *USA TODAY*, Gannett
  News Service Columnist, *Legal Times*

Introduction

Who were Joseph Story . . . Samuel F. Miller . . . Joseph P. Bradley . . . Wiley B. Rutledge? Few Americans know them. Yet each of these men was influential, and ultimately decisive, in establishing, shaping, and guaranteeing the freedoms and rule of law under which this nation is now moving into its third century. Of the 108 chief and associate justices who have served on the Supreme Court of the United States, only a relative few can be called to mind by the larger public, and then only fleetingly.

Charles Evans Hughes, for example, is perhaps better known for his narrow defeat by Woodrow Wilson for the presidency in 1916 than for his seventeen years on the high bench, eleven of them as a distinguished chief justice. Others are remembered for their involvement in great and lasting controversies. Roger B. Taney is cited most often for writing the fateful *Dred Scott v. Sandford* decision of 1857, which helped precipitate the Civil War. His twenty-eight years of devoted service are seldom mentioned, although scholars view his tenure as chief justice as a distinguished and responsible continuation of the tradition of his predecessor John Marshall, the great chief justice.

Some, such as Oliver Wendell Holmes, Jr., and Louis Brandeis, are memorable for their dissents. Another, John Marshall Harlan, earned his niche in history with an eloquent dissent in the Court's 1896 decision estab-

lishing the "separate but equal" doctrine of racial segregation. In 1954 Chief Justice Earl Warren ensured his place in history with a unanimous opinion outlawing racial segregation in the nation's schools, in effect upholding Harlan's dissent.

Often, the Supreme Court of a particular era is identified by the name of the chief justice: the Marshall Court, the Taft Court, the Warren Court, the Burger Court, the Rehnquist Court. This shorthand may be useful, but it overshadows a basic fact. The Supreme Court is a company of genuine equals. Although the chief justice presides over the Court and its conferences and—when in the majority—has the authority to assign which justice writes the Court's opinion, he is still "first among equals." Emphasis should be placed on the word *equals* rather than *first*. The vote of the most junior member of the nine justices, from the moment he or she takes the oath of office, counts for as much as that of the chief justice.

Who are these 108 people who have had the awesome power to decide what the U.S. Constitution means and what it does not mean, who have overruled acts of Congress when they found them in violation of the Constitution, who have on occasion judged and overruled the decisions of every court in the land, including the supreme courts of the fifty states? Where do they come from? What experiences prepared them for their task? How did they come to be chosen by the president as one of the nine or, at various times, six, seven, eight, or ten most important interpreters of American law?

Ultimately each question merits 108 answers, one for each justice. Although they may seem remote and magisterial in their black robes, their lives have the mix of reality and dreams, successes and failures, providence and misfortune, war and peace, to which we are all subject. The following pages are neither a history of the Court nor an examination and evaluation of its judicial decisions. They are an effort to chronicle succinctly the lives of those who have played a role in the establishment and growth of the Supreme Court.

They are all unique individuals, ultimately sharing only their commitment to the rule of law under the Constitution. Yet there are some common threads and similarities. Each was trained in the law. President George Washington established this precedent with his eleven appointments to the high bench, the record number for any chief executive. Eager to bring the former disparate colonies closer together, Washington also established a pattern of geographic distribution. His first six appointments were three northerners and three southerners. By the time Washington finished his two terms, nine of the original thirteen states had achieved representation on the Court. By the early nineteenth century, three of the chairs had become identified as the "New England seat," the "New York seat," and the "Virginia-Maryland seat." As Americans became more mobile, and political and philosophical factors became more important than geographical identification, such representation gradually eroded.

In the early days of the nation, most aspiring lawyers prepared for admission to the bar by "reading law" in the office of an established attorney. What they did was a combination of clerkship, independent study, apprenticeship, and, perhaps, feeding a wood stove and sweeping out the office. It is frequently noted that John Marshall was essentially self-taught, attending only one course of law lectures at the College of William and Mary. But many of his associate justices had no college or university training in the law at all. They read law until they were judged qualified for admission to the city, county, or state bar. This practice changed gradually during the early twentieth century, as Harvard, Yale, Columbia, Virginia, and other colleges and universities began offering specialized studies and degrees in law. Of the justices seated in this century, all but eleven earned a degree from a law school. Some worked their way through, and one, Warren Burger, attended a night law school while holding down a full-time job.

A remarkably large number of the justices showed precocious intellectual powers, and many were top students. James Moore Wayne qualified for enrollment in Princeton at the age of thirteen, but his entrance was delayed a year because of his tender years. Edward T. Sanford took two degrees, B.A. and Ph. B., from the University of Tennessee at the age of eighteen. John A. Campbell was admitted to the Georgia bar at the same age, three years before he could vote. Hughes found first grade in a public school boring and confining. He submitted to his parents the "Charles E. Hughes Plan of Study" to continue his education at home. His parents acquiesced, and at the age of eight Hughes was reading Greek. He graduated from a New York City high school at age thirteen, ranking second in his class.

Most justices came from homes where intellectual pursuits were favored and education was an article of faith. Many were the sons of ministers or lawyers, although some were also sons of farmers. More often than not they were born into comfortable circumstances, but William Johnson, who managed a degree from Princeton in 1790, was the son of a blacksmith. John Catron was born into such humble circumstances that not even his date and place of birth are known for certain, nor where he spent his early childhood. Joseph P. Bradley, oldest of eleven children born to poor farm parents, had become a rural school teacher at the age of sixteen, when a local minister recognized his talents and sponsored his entrance to Rutgers University. Most justices felt called to a law career early, but Samuel F. Miller studied medicine and practiced it for nine years before turning to the bar at the age of thirty-one. He became one of the most accomplished and respected justices of the late nineteenth century. In this century, intellectual prowess is frequently evidenced by brilliance in advanced studies. Phi Beta Kappa, cum laude, magna cum laude, summa cum laude, Rhodes scholar, and head of the class appear repeatedly in the justices' curricula vitae.

Just as they felt called to the law, justices typically also felt called to public service, working through a series of "apprenticeships" in an ascending scale of appointive or elective offices. Many began as a city or county attorney, even as a justice of the peace, and a large number were elected to terms in their state legislatures. They went on to become representatives or senators in Congress, district and circuit judges, judges of the state and federal courts of appeals, judges and chief justices of state supreme courts. Few had as impressive credentials as the first chief justice, John Jay, who served successively as a delegate to the Continental Congress, minister to Spain, chief justice of the New York Supreme Court, and secretary of foreign affairs before he was chosen by President Washington to head the Court. Salmon P. Chase earned his first prominence as an active antislavery Free Soil party member in Ohio and went on to become a U.S. senator, governor of Ohio, and secretary of the Treasury. Willis Van Devanter entered public service as city attorney of Cheyenne, Wyoming, rose to chief justice of the Wyoming Supreme Court, and served seven years on a federal court of appeals before his elevation to the high bench.

Only Chief Justice William Howard Taft apprenticed for the Court as president of the United States.

In the twentieth century, more justices have spent their entire careers within the ranks of the legal system. In 1945 Harold H. Burton was the last sitting U.S. senator to take a place on the Court, and in 1953 Chief Justice Earl Warren was the last state governor to do so. Chief Justice William H. Rehnquist is one of four justices who had their first stint at the Court as law clerks immediately after leaving school. Rehnquist served as clerk to Justice Robert H. Jackson in the 1952–1953 term and was appointed to the Court eighteen years later.

Many factors have played a part in the selection of justices. As the country grew and changed, the Court reflected greater diversity. All the justices had been Protestants until 1835, when President Andrew Jackson appointed Roger B. Taney, a Catholic. Although Woodrow Wilson appointed the first Jew, Louis D. Brandeis, to the Court in 1916, it was Benjamin N. Cardozo's appointment in 1932 that apparently established the tradition of a "Jewish seat," which lasted for almost forty years. The first African-American justice, Thurgood Marshall, was appointed by President Lyndon B. Johnson in 1967. The first woman, Sandra Day O'Connor, broke the gender barrier in 1981. Even before her appointment, the Court had dropped the honorific "Mr.," which had been used for almost two centuries, and "Mr. Justice" became simply "Justice" in the Court's reports and documents. The first Italian-American ascended to the high bench in 1986 with the appointment of Antonin Scalia.

Political party membership has always had important weight in the president's selection of nominees to the Court. Yet nine presidents have chosen justices from opposing parties, beginning with President Abraham Lincoln's appointment of Stephen J. Field, a Democrat, in 1863. More recently, the appointments of William J. Brennan, Jr., and Lewis F. Powell, Jr., crossed party lines. Naturally, presidents look for nominees whose records suggest that they will at least generally support the president's views on how the Constitution should be interpreted. Many times presidents have been disappointed. Appointment to the high bench has often served to liberate justices from some of their earlier, possibly partisan, convictions.

The average tenure of a justice has been just short of sixteen years. The shortest term was that of Thomas Johnson, who had been reluctant to accept the post from his friend George Washington in the first place. William O. Douglas broke a record for longevity on the Court when he resigned in 1975 after thirty-six years and seven months. The previous record was held by Field, who had achieved thirty-four years and nine months when he retired in 1897. Generally, justices have come on the Court in their fifties, with almost all being older than forty. The four exceptions were all in the Court's early years, when William Johnson and Joseph Story were both chosen at age thirty-two, Bushrod Washington at thirty-six, and James Iredell at thirty-eight. The oldest at the time of ascension was Horace Lurton, age sixty-five. (Harlan F. Stone and Hughes were a few years older at the time of their respective elevation and reappointment to the Court as chief justices.)

Aside from the John Marshall Harlan grandfather-grandson relationship, there have been few kinships among the justices. David J. Brewer was Field's nephew, and they sat on the high bench together for nearly six years. Lucius Q. C. Lamar and Joseph Rucker Lamar were cousins.

Unlike the constitutional specifications for election to the presidency or Congress, there are no qualifications for appointment to the Court. There are no age limitations for either appointment or retirement, no residency requirements, no specification even that justices have training or a background in the law. There is no constitutional requirement that justices be native-born, and six of them were not. The Constitution says only that the president shall appoint the members of the Court with the advice and consent of the Senate. They serve "during good Behaviour," and like all civil officers may be removed only "on Impeachment for, and Conviction of, Treason, Bribery, or other high Crimes and Misdemeanors."

Only once has the House of Representatives brought a bill of impeachment against a justice of the Supreme Court, when it voted to bring Samuel Chase, a radical Federalist, to trial in 1804. Historians agree that there were at least improprieties in his behavior. He was ardent in his pursuit of Republican editors under the notorious Alien and Sedition acts, and he heatedly criticized Thomas Jefferson's administration. However, the Senate failed to convict Chase of "high crimes," and he retained his seat.

No matter how involved in politics they may have been before appointment to the Court, today justices generally refrain from partisan activity or party identification once on the high bench. Such reticence was not the case during the nineteenth century. John McLean furnished perhaps the most egregious example of political activity as a sitting justice. He flirted openly with several political parties during his thirty-two years on the Court, consistently seeking but failing to obtain a bid to run for the presidency.

Indeed, over the decades, the range of acceptable outside activities by justices has become increasingly narrow. In the entryway to the justices' dining room there is a handsome clock that was given to Joseph Story for his service as president of a Massachusetts bank from 1815 to 1837. He was already a justice when he accepted the post, which he held for twenty-two years during his tenure on the Court. Today, occupying such a position would be unthinkable.

Members of the Supreme Court have been preponderately family men, and most of those who were widowed prematurely later remarried. Brockholst Livingston and Benjamin R. Curtis each married three times, and each had children by all three wives. Only eight of the justices were bachelors when appointed to the Court, and one of them, Horace Gray, changed his status at the age of sixty-one by marrying the daughter of his colleague Stanley Matthews.

Many of the justices had military records, starting with more than half a dozen who served in the Revolution. Chief Justice Marshall was with General Washington at Valley Forge. Several fought in the Civil War, including Lucius Lamar, a Confederate, and Holmes, who was wounded three times in service to the Union. Chief Justice Rehnquist served during World War II, as did Justices Harlan, Brennan, John Paul Stevens, Arthur Goldberg, Potter Stewart, and Byron White.

Scholars and constitutional authorities generally have concluded that the people of the United States have been fortunate in the selection of their Supreme Court justices. Collectively, the justices have established a record of probity, conscientiousness, and devotion to responsible public service. These standards have been crucial to the survival of the Court and of the nation. The Supreme Court, like the entire judicial branch, has no means of enforcing its decisions. Yet it can tell the president and Congress what they may and may not lawfully do. Its rulings are accepted and executed by the legislative, executive, and judicial branches, and indeed by the people. The legal and moral authority of the Court is essential to maintaining a democratic society.

This authority has grown with the years, since 1803 when Marshall first declared an act of Congress unconstitutional and proclaimed, "It is, emphatically, the province and duty of the judicial department to say what the law is." Although the Court has suffered sporadic declines in its standing relative to the other two branches and in the eyes of the people, its ultimate and final authority rarely has been challenged. It is, without doubt, the most powerful judicial body in any democratic nation. When, in 1974, the Court ruled that the president does not have absolute executive privilege of immunity from court demands for evidence in a criminal trial, President Richard Nixon was forced to comply. When, in 1983, the Court struck down in a single decision more than 200 laws enacted by Congress over a period of fifty years, the lawmakers did not contest the ruling.

The power and prestige of the Supreme Court is due in no small measure to the capabilities and integrity of the individuals who have served and shaped it. Although many are rightly impressed by the phenomenal power and attendant responsibilities of the justices, this examination of their lives serves to remind us that behind the black robes they are simply human beings. Justice Robert Jackson once felt compelled to chide his brethren about both their power and their humanity in his memorable admonition: "We are not final because we are infallible, but we are infallible only because we are final."

LEON SILVERMAN
President, The Supreme Court Historical Society

THE SUPREME COURT JUSTICES

Illustrated Biographies, 1789-1995

John Jay
1789-1795

Source: National Portrait Gallery

JOHN JAY, the first chief justice of the United States and a leader in colonial politics, was unusual among the Founders in that his ancestors were of non-British stock. His mother, Mary Van Cortlandt Jay, was a member of an illustrious New York family of Dutch origin. His father, Peter Jay, was a prosperous merchant descended from French Huguenot refugees. The youngest of eight children, John Jay was born in New York City December 12, 1745, but grew up on a farm in Rye, New York. His mother taught him English and Latin grammar until he left home to be formally tutored for three years at the French Huguenot Church School in nearby New Rochelle.

At age fourteen Jay entered King's College (later renamed Columbia University) and received his diploma with honors in 1764. He then spent nearly two years as a clerk in the law office of Benjamin Kissam, a prominent New York attorney. When the courts closed for several months as a result of the lawyers' strike protesting the Stamp Act of 1765, Jay made good use of the unexpected break. He returned to Rye and studied the

John Jay was already a successful lawyer in 1774 when he married Sarah Van Brugh Livingston, the daughter of William Livingston, a future governor of New Jersey. She sat for this portrait with William and Sarah Louisa Jay, two of her six children, after her husband had resigned as the first chief justice of the United States. *Source: New York State Office of Parks, Recreation and Historic Preservation, John Jay Homestead State Historic Site*

classics, eventually receiving a Master of Arts degree from his alma mater in 1767. Once the Stamp Act crisis ended, Jay became Kissam's chief clerk, and he was admitted to the bar in 1768. He soon became one of the most successful attorneys in New York, first in partnership with an old college classmate, Robert R. Livingston, Jr., and then on his own.

Jay helped form a debating society in 1768 to discuss the burning political questions of the day. The following year he organized a legal debating club. A handsome, cultivated man, he also presided over the social season as manager of the prestigious Dancing Assembly of New York City. Jay married the cousin of his former law partner, Sarah Van Brugh Livingston, in 1774; her father, William Livingston, would later serve as governor of New Jersey during the Revolutionary War. Sarah's brother, Henry Brockholst Livingston, was ap-

pointed to the Supreme Court in 1806, eleven years after John Jay resigned. The Jays had six children, two of whom would follow their father into the law.

A conservative who favored compromise with Britain, Jay only gradually came to support the cause of revolution. Once he committed himself to independence, however, he gave up private practice to devote himself fully to public service. In 1774 Jay represented his state at the First Continental Congress. He did not sign the Declaration of Independence because at the time he was serving as a delegate to the New York Provincial Congress, helping to draft the state constitution.

With the ratification of New York's constitution in 1777, Jay was appointed chief justice of the state's newly formed Supreme Court of Judicature. On the bench he developed a reputation for giving stiff sentences to criminals. His judicial activities ended when he was sent by New York to the Second Continental Congress in November 1778. The following month the Congress elected Jay president—the highest civilian post in the rebelling colonies.

Within the year, however, his colleagues had elected him minister plenipotentiary to Spain and sent him to secure a treaty of alliance and economic aid from the Spanish government. Although the mission met with only modest success, it gave Jay his first taste of international affairs and diplomacy. Shortly thereafter, he was summoned to Paris by fellow peace commissioner Benjamin Franklin to help negotiate the Peace Treaty of 1783, which ended the Revolutionary War with favorable terms for the United States. When Jay returned from Europe he found he had been elected secretary for foreign affairs for the Confederation, a position he held until the new government, under the federal Constitution, was established in 1789.

Once the Constitution had been drafted, Jay used his training as a lawyer, judge, and diplomat to contribute five essays to what became known as *The Federalist Papers*. The essays were intended to persuade the citizens of New York state to ratify the Constitution. He wrote an unsigned pamphlet, "Address to the People of the State of New York," which put forth the case for ratification by exposing the inadequacies of the Confederation both at home and abroad. Jay's international experience gave particular conviction to his arguments on the necessity for the constitutional clause establishing the supremacy of treaties. "[Jay] had as much influence in the preparatory measures in digesting the Constitution, and obtaining its adoption, as any man in the nation," John Adams later claimed.

President George Washington was reportedly willing to consider Jay for any number of high posts in the new government, but on September 24, 1789, he nominated the forty-three-year-old New Yorker to be the nation's first chief justice. Two days later the Senate confirmed the appointment. Jay met with two of the five associate justices for the first session of the Court February 1, 1790, at the Merchants Exchange building in New York City. The required quorum was reached with the arrival of a fourth justice on the second day. Nine days later, the Court adjourned because there were no cases to decide.

As chief justice, Jay voided acts passed by Congress and state legislatures and laid the foundation for a powerful, independent judiciary. His first major Court case, the 1793 *Chisholm v. Georgia* decision, established the right of citizens of one state to sue another state in federal court. Many states feared that economic ruin and loss of sovereignty would result. Responding to these fears, Congress quickly proposed the Eleventh Amendment, which three-quarters of the states ratified by February 1795. Because of delays in certification, the amendment did not take effect until 1798. This amendment, the first since the Bill of Rights, seriously damaged the Supreme Court's prestige; it reversed the Court's decision by barring such suits unless the defendant state consented.

Ranking with *Chisholm* as a landmark case in Jay's career on the Court, *Glass v. The Sloop Betsey* (1794) questioned whether foreign consuls stationed in the United States had authority on American soil. Jay's opinion held that foreign powers on U.S. soil had no jurisdiction over admiralty law, a decision that fortified the sovereignty of the United States in international eyes.

Also in 1793, the year of the *Chisholm* decision, Jay led the Court in establishing an important principle of constitutional law and of federal judicial power. Secretary of State Thomas Jefferson wrote to the Court asking, for himself and President Washington, that the Court advise them as to the constitutionality of measures the government was considering with respect to the European wars. Jay and the other justices respectfully declined the request, pointing out that the Constitution limited federal judicial power to the decision of actual cases and controversies. In their view, the Court had no right to give advisory opinions. But Jay and his colleagues apparently distinguished between formal requests to the Court for advisory opinions, which they would not grant, and informal requests to individual justices for advice, with which they complied. Indeed, throughout his term as chief justice, Jay acted as an unofficial adviser to Washington's administration, and he even helped the president draft the 1793 Neutrality Proclamation and negotiate a treaty in 1794.

In addition to serving on the Supreme Court, all of the justices were required to hold semiannual court sessions in the three circuits (eastern, middle, and southern) created by the Judiciary Act of 1789. Jay complained bitterly about the poor food, uncomfortable accommodations, long distances, and loneliness of circuit riding. He nonetheless used circuit cases as an opportunity to establish the supremacy of the Constitution, federal laws, and the federal judiciary. Finding his circuit-riding duties increasingly "intolerable," Jay did not object to being nominated in 1792 by the New York Federalists as their candidate for governor, although he did not campaign. Longtime incumbent George Clinton won reelection, but by such a narrow margin that the returns were contested.

Two years later President Washington appointed Jay, while still chief justice, to a diplomatic mission to England to ease lingering hostility between the two nations. Southern senators protested Jay's taking on this added role, partly because of his known British sympathies. A Philadelphia political group denounced the assignment as "degrading the Chief Justiceship to partisan uses." The result of the mission was the 1794 Treaty of Amity, Commerce, and Navigation, known as the Jay Treaty, which was widely condemned at home for not extracting enough concessions from the British.

When he returned from Britain, Jay found that once again he had been nominated for governor of New York. This time he won. His immediate resignation from the Supreme Court on June 29, 1795, proved fortunate for its fragile authority, for when news of the Jay Treaty arrived home, the former chief justice was hanged or burned in effigy in several cities. Jay went on to serve as governor of the most populous state for two three-year terms, which were marked by considerable achievements. He revised the criminal code, called for the construction of a model penitentiary, promoted a career civil service, reduced the number of crimes carrying the death penalty, and signed a bill to free New York slaves over a period of time. He declined renomination on November 8, 1800, and retired from public life in 1801.

Chief Justice Oliver Ellsworth had resigned from the Supreme Court in September 1800, leaving a vacancy. President John Adams sent Jay's name, without his knowledge, to the Senate in hopes of reappointing him chief justice. The Senate confirmed him, but Jay declined the position because of his dislike of circuit riding and his disappointment that the Supreme Court was not invested with sufficient authority. Jay explained his reluctance in a letter to Adams. "[T]he efforts repeatedly made to place the Judicial Department on a proper footing have proved fruitless. I left the bench perfectly convinced that under a system so defective it would not obtain the energy, weight, and dignity which was essential to its affording due support to the national government; nor acquire the public confidence and respect which, as the last resort of the justice of the nation, it should possess. Hence I am induced to doubt both the propriety and the expediency of my returning to the bench under the present system."

Sadly, Jay's plans for enjoying a more peaceful life were marred by his wife's death in 1802. He spent his unusually long retirement, which lasted from 1801 until his death on May 17, 1829, in the company of several of his children at his 800-acre estate in Westchester County. There he pursued his interest in agriculture, kept up an extensive correspondence with friends, and

In 1794 President George Washington sent Chief Justice Jay to negotiate with Great Britain, which had been kidnapping American sailors and "impressing" them into service in the British navy. Jay could not persuade Britain to desist, and Americans greeted the resulting "Jay Treaty" with outrage. Jay is represented in this cartoon as a bird riding the British lion and carrying a copy of the unpopular treaty in its beak. The lion is encouraging the devil to pay journalist William Corbett, nicknamed "Porcupine," to write articles in support of Britain's position. *Source: The Historical Society of Pennsylvania*

gave out legal advice. He voiced his opposition to slavery and, as part of a Federalist peace group, opposed the War of 1812. Active in the Episcopalian church, Jay also helped establish the American Bible Society, serving as its president in 1821.

The aristocratic and cultured Jay was more famous for his illustrious career as a statesman and for the wide-ranging extrajudicial activities he carried out while serving on the Court than for his judicial record. His biographer, Richard B. Morris, summed up his tenure on the Court with these words:

He was active neither as a court reformer nor as an expositor of technical branches of law. Indeed, some of his controversial opinions carried scant legal research to bolster them. Instead, he is remembered as a creative statesman and activist Chief Justice whose concepts of the broad purposes of the Constitution were to be upheld and spelled out with vigor by John Marshall. In bringing the states into subordination to the federal government, in securing from the states and the people reluctant recognition of the supremacy of treaties, and in laying the foundation for the later exercise by the Supreme Court of the power to declare acts of Congress unconstitutional, Jay gave bold directions to the new constitutional regime.

John Rutledge
1790-1791, 1795

Source: Library of Congress

JOHN RUTLEDGE's tenure on the Supreme Court was highly unusual: although twice appointed to serve on it, he never attended a formal session of the full Court. He was born in September 1739 in Charleston, South Carolina, to fifteen-year-old Sarah Hext Rutledge, an extremely wealthy South Carolina heiress, and Dr. John Rutledge. His father, a physician who had emigrated from Ireland at a young age, died in 1750. He left his widow, then only twenty-six, with seven children to raise.

An English clergyman took over young Rutledge's tutelage, instructing him in the classics for several years. Rutledge continued his classical education at a Charleston school run by David Rhind, but left after a short time to study law in the office of his uncle, Andrew Rutledge, who was Speaker of the South Carolina Commons House of Assembly. Following his uncle's death in 1755, Rutledge read law under prominent attorney James Parsons before departing for London to study at the Inns of Court, as was the custom of the

6

privileged in colonial South Carolina. After three years of legal training, Rutledge was called to the English bar February 9, 1760.

Within a few months of his return to South Carolina the following year, he was admitted to the state bar and elected to the provincial legislature. Thanks in part to his family's wealth and political connections, he quickly developed a prestigious and lucrative law practice in a colony renowned for the quality of its bar. He did so well that by 1763 he could refuse cases that paid retainers of less than £100 sterling. That year he married Elizabeth Grimke, the daughter of a respected Charleston family. Elizabeth's nieces, Angelina and Sarah Grimke, became South Carolina's most prominent reformers and abolitionists in the 1830s. John and Elizabeth Rutledge produced ten children, including John, Jr., who served in the U.S. House of Representatives from 1797 to 1803.

A powerful public speaker, Rutledge was appointed attorney general of the colony in 1764 by the British governor in a not altogether successful bid to secure Rutledge's allegiance to the king against the rebellious provincial assembly. Rutledge's political career was further advanced ten months later when he was sent with the South Carolina delegation to the Stamp Act Congress in New York. As chairman of the Committee on Resolutions, Rutledge, the youngest delegate, drafted a respectful appeal to the House of Lords for repeal of the burdensome Stamp Act tax. The request was met within the year.

In 1774 Rutledge was elected by the conservative planters of South Carolina to head the state's delegation to the First Continental Congress in Philadelphia. There he united with other conservatives against complete independence from Britain, but spoke out for colonial rights. While most delegates urged a commercial embargo of products to and from the mother country, even though it meant considerable sacrifice, Rutledge stood firm for his home province's economic wel-

Parliament's first direct tax on Americans, the Stamp Act of 1765, was met with widespread defiance. Intended to pay the cost of maintaining British military establishments in the colonies, it drew the wrath of journalists and lawyers, articulate opponents who were most severely burdened by a tax on newspapers, almanacs, and legal documents. Although the tax was quickly repealed, it left a lingering bitterness. *Source: Library of Congress*

fare. In the interest of unanimity, the Congress conceded to Rutledge's demand to exempt from their embargo one commodity—rice—South Carolina's principal export. Rutledge then managed to convince both the irate South Carolina radicals and the indigo growers that his stand had saved the colony from ruin, and he urged rice planters to pay compensation to other growers.

Returned to the Second Continental Congress the following year, Rutledge chaired the Committee on Government and became partially swayed by the movement toward independence. After the Congress adjourned, he helped stabilize conditions in his colony by drafting a new state constitution providing for an independent government. When the new state assembly convened in March 1776, it elected Rutledge the first president of the newly founded Republic of South Car-

Rice, the major export of South Carolina, was the only commodity exempted from the Continental Congress's embargo against Britain, thanks to the efforts of John Rutledge to protect the welfare of his home colony. A planter and a conservative, Rutledge was at first cautious about severing trade with the mother country, but eventually took up the cause of independence. *Source: Library of Congress*

olina. He addressed the assembly at its spring adjournment: "Let it be known that this Constitution is but temporary, till an accommodation of the unhappy difference between Great Britain and America can be obtained; and that such an event is still desired by men who yet remember former friendships and intimate connections, though for defending their persons . . . they are stigmatized and treated as rebels."

Three months after his election, the British navy gathered forces to attack Fort Sullivan, a palmetto log fortification that protected Charleston harbor. Convinced of its strategic importance, Rutledge boldly countermanded the order of General Charles Lee, commander of the Southern Continental Army, to evacuate the vulnerable fort. Firepower from the fort and considerable good luck repulsed the British fleet, driving it from South Carolina's coast for nearly three years. A week after the battle was won, Rutledge's younger brother, Edward, who was a delegate at the Second Continental Congress, signed the Declaration of Independence in Philadelphia.

In March 1778 a new South Carolina constitution called for changing the republic to a state and the president to a governor without veto power over the assembly, as well as the popular election of both houses of the assembly. Rutledge at first opposed it. Averse to simple democracy, he feared that the constitution was too liberal and precluded the possibility of reconciliation with Great Britain. He resigned rather than fight it, but his resignation was short-lived. The onslaught of British troops a year later prompted his election as governor with broad emergency powers.

When the British captured Charleston in 1780, Rutledge and the remnants of South Carolina's government fled to the North Carolina border, where they remained in exile until the summer of 1781. After the British surrendered, Governor Rutledge quickly reestablished order in his state. Unable to succeed himself as governor, he was elected to the Continental Congress in 1782. After a term as South Carolina's representative, the well-respected lawyer got his first exposure to the judicial bench when he was appointed chief judge of South Carolina's new Court of Chancery. He had turned down two congressional appointments, including minister to the Netherlands, because his financial affairs had suffered greatly during the war and needed attention.

Although Rutlege was only one of a group of delegates sent by his state to the 1787 Constitutional Convention in Philadelphia, his vast experience in government gave him a place of honor. William Pierce, a delegate from Georgia, described him as being of "a distinguished rank among the American Worthies . . . a Gentleman of distinction and fortune . . . but too rapid in his public speaking to be denominated an agreeable orator." Rutledge served on the Committee of Detail that proposed the first draft of the Constitution, and, with Oliver Ellsworth, a future chief justice, helped negotiate the compromise between large and small states.

Rutledge's contributions to the convention reflected his wealthy background and his aristocratic nature. He objected to strongly democratic proposals that allowed for direct representation by the people, and he suggested that the number of representatives in the lower house correspond not to population but to "quotas of contribution," or taxes each state paid the national government. He supported property qualifications for elected officials and opposed paying salaries to the upper house so that only the wealthy would serve there. Rutledge fought the ban on the slave trade by saying it was a question of commerce, not morality, and of whether the southern states would remain in the Union. When the final draft was completed, however, Rutledge subordinated his objections, endorsed the Constitution, and helped secure its ratification by a substantial majority in South Carolina.

President George Washington seriously considered Rutledge for the post of chief justice of the United States, but because so many prominent southerners were already in the new government, the seat was offered to John Jay of New York instead. A disappointed Rutledge settled for an appointment as the senior of five associate justices, and he took office February 15, 1790. But, due to a debilitating attack of gout and a lack of cases before the Court, he never attended its first sessions in New York. He did, however, ride the first southern circuit with Associate Justice James Iredell, swearing in lawyers to the federal bar.

Lack of business before the Court, the long-distance travel required of circuit riding, and the lingering resentment at having been passed over for chief justice all conspired to make Rutledge question the wisdom of having left his privileged position in South Carolina. He resigned from the Court in March 1791 to become chief justice of the South Carolina Court of Common Pleas. President Washington immediately made an unusual offer: in a single letter he asked Rutledge's brother Edward and Charles Cotesworth Pinckney, scion of another powerful Charleston family, if either would replace John Rutledge. In a joint reply to the president, both declined.

As the prestige of the Supreme Court increased and

Saint Michael's Church in downtown Charleston, South Carolina, was the site of John Rutledge's professional demise in 1795. The speech he gave there denouncing provisions of the Jay Treaty angered supporters the of protreaty Washington administration. When the Senate convened a few months later, it voted along partisan lines not to confirm Rutledge's nomination as chief justice. *Source: South Carolina Historical Society*

Rutledge grew tired of hearing routine debt and estate cases on the state court, he came to regret his resignation. His wife had died suddenly in 1792, and he suffered serious financial reversal from unwise investments in merchant ships. Anticipating Chief Justice John Jay's imminent resignation from the Court, Rutledge wrote to President Washington June 12, 1795: "[W]hen the office of the Chief Justice of the United States becomes vacant, I feel that the duty which I owe to my children should impel me to accept it, if offered, tho' more arduous and troublesome than my present station, because more respectable and honorable." Washington graciously offered him the appointment, noting that he would get his temporary commission when he arrived in Philadelphia to attend the Supreme Court's term in August. His appointment could not become permanent, however, until Congress reconvened in the fall and the Senate confirmed him.

On July 16, 1795, probably before hearing from the president, Rutledge made a serious political blunder that cost him dearly. In a meeting at St. Michael's Church in Charleston, Rutledge joined other South Carolinians on the speaker's platform and made a lengthy speech denouncing the provisions of the Jay Treaty as being so favorable to British interests that he would rather the president die than sign it. The treaty's outraged partisans exaggerated the reports of Rutledge's political slight to Washington's administration, which backed the treaty, and circulated rumors of his mental unbalance. They demanded Rutledge not be given his temporary commission as chief justice. The president kept his word, however, and Rutledge presided over the August term of the Court as a recess appointee.

When the Senate met in December, it rejected his permanent appointment by a vote of 14-10. The Philadelphia *Aurora*, a Republican newspaper, denounced his rejection as purely political. "It is the first instance in which [the Senate has] differed from [the president] in any nomination of importance, and what is remarkable in this case, is that the minority of the members on the Treaty were the minority on this nomination." Rutledge had become ill while performing circuit duties, and he was in Charleston when news of the Senate vote reached him. He attempted to drown himself by jumping into the bay, but was saved by two passing slaves. The former justice became a recluse and suffered lapses of insanity until he died July 18, 1800.

William Cushing
1790-1810

T HE LONGEST serving of George Washington's six original appointees, William Cushing was the only link between the Court led by Chief Justice John Jay and the Court presided over by Chief Justice John Marshall. Cushing was born March 1, 1732, in Scituate, Massachusetts, into one of the oldest and most powerful families in the colony. His mother, Mary Cotton Cushing, was descended from the Reverend John Cotton, the great seventeenth century Puritan theologian. Both William Cushing's father, John Cush-

ing, and grandfather were members of the Governor's Council and sat as judges on the Superior Court of Judicature for the Massachusetts Bay colony. Josiah Cotton, his maternal grandfather, and Richard Fitzgerald, a teacher at a local Latin school, were responsible for young Cushing's early education.

He was trained in the standard classical curriculum at Harvard College from 1747 to 1751 before teaching for a year at a grammar school in Roxbury, Massachusetts. He then returned to Harvard on a fellowship to study theology. But Cushing eventually changed his mind and, on December 20, 1754, decided to quit his studies to clerk for Jeremiah Gridley, a distinguished Boston lawyer. During his law apprenticeship, Harvard awarded him an honorary M.A. degree; Yale had already done so in 1753. In 1758, after Cushing had spent three years as Gridley's protege, his mentor rewarded him by personally moving for his admission to the bar of the Superior Court of Judicature. Cushing then returned to his hometown of Scituate to set up a law practice, but intense competition for clients made him look around for other opportunities after his practice proved to be unprofitable.

In 1760, attracted by the promise of life on the northern frontier, Cushing and his brother Charles relocated to the town of Pownalborough (now Dresden) in the district of Maine. Before setting off, Charles had secured the post of high sheriff, and William had obtained commissions as justice of the peace and judge of probates for newly created Lincoln County. To augment his modest public servant salary, William Cushing also developed a general legal practice and dabbled in land speculation and the timber business. As one of the few trained lawyers in the district, he was asked to

fill in when the attorney general was away, which further supplemented his income. Cushing also served as counsel for a consortium of wealthy landowners intent on buying title, often by means of court action, to the region's rich timberland. In his duties for the land companies, he occasionally found himself arguing cases against a future U.S. president, John Adams, who represented similar interests.

Cushing returned from Maine in 1771 when his father retired from the Massachusetts Superior Court of Judicature, and he was subsequently chosen, through his father's influence, to replace him. Lack of outside income made Cushing dependent on his judicial salary and, therefore, loyal to the British government, his paymaster. However, a partisan controversy that exploded almost a year after he took office forced him to renounce his loyalty to the Crown. The controversy centered on whether Massachusetts judges, who received their judicial commissions from King George III, should be paid by the British government. To allow judges greater independence and judicial impartiality, many believed the salaries should be appropriated by the Massachusetts legislature.

Cushing kept silent on the issue until revolutionaries

William Cushing sometimes rode his circuit in this one-horse shay. The poor conditions of roads, when there were any, often made it more efficient for him to travel by horseback. *Source: Rudolph Mitchell/Scituate Historical Society*

Before William Cusshing married Hannah Phillips, a Connecticut woman, in 1774, his sister, also named Hannah, traveled with him on circuit. Judge Cushing had special receptacles built into his carriage for the books his wife read to him during their trips.
Source: Independence National Historical Park Collection

started impeachment proceedings against Chief Justice Peter Oliver, who insisted on obtaining his salary from the Crown. To avert impeachment, Cushing chose the legislative appropriation. He was consequently barred from a seat on the Governor's Council and became known as a silent patriot of the revolutionary cause. One observer of his maneuvering noted that Cushing was "remarkable for the secrecy of his opinions: this kept up his reputation through all the ebullitions of discordant parties. He readily resigned the royal stipend, without any observations of his own: yet it was thought at the time that it was with a reluctance that his taciturnity could not conceal. By this silent address he re-

tained the confidence of the Crown faction, nor was he less a favorite among the Republicans."

At the risk of his personal safety, he continued to ride the superior court circuit and to keep the royal courts open until 1775, when all royal officials, including judges, had their commissions revoked. In doing so, he helped maintain the semblance of royal rule long after his colony had started on the path to revolution against Britain. Although Cushing's dedication to the American Revolution seems to have been forged mainly from necessity, he was popular enough to be elected to the Superior Court of Judicature when it was reorganized by the newly formed revolutionary council.

While riding the court circuit, Cushing traveled in a luxurious carriage accompanied by his unmarried sister, Hannah. His slow-paced and relatively comfortable travels often included frequent stops to socialize along the way. In 1774 Cushing wed the Connecticut-born Hannah Phillips, who replaced his sister as his companion on circuit. She read to him from books kept in special receptacles that he had designed for his carriage. A slender man with a fair complexion and blue eyes, Cushing's most distinctive feature was his long nose. He was so sensitive about its shape that he once objected to a portrait that he felt represented his nose too accurately.

Three years after his marriage, Cushing was chosen to replace John Adams as chief justice of Massachusetts's highest court, a position he would hold for twelve years. His opinions on that court are notable for their use of biblical doctrine and Scripture to embellish the written law, which at the time was somewhat sketchy and disjointed.

Cushing's mettle was sharply tested in 1786 during Shays's Rebellion, an uprising by debtors in the western part of the state. Led by Daniel Shays and Jacobb Shattucks, Revolutionary War veterans, dissatisfied farmers protested the Massachusetts legislature's failure to provide debtor relief and increase issues of paper money.

The rioters complained that superior court judges infrequently rode circuit in pairs, the necessary number to hear cases on matters such as the collection of debts. Instead of gaining relief, debtors had to pay even more interest when the court eventually judged their case. Furious, the armed rebels closed down local courts and even the state supreme court, but the uprising soon collapsed. As the judge passing sentence on rebels found guilty by jury verdict, Judge Cushing ordered many of them to be hanged, but ultimately all were pardoned. Despite threats against his person and violence in his courtroom, Cushing managed to maintain order and respect for the law in western Massachusetts.

His experience with regional disorders motivated him to support a strong national government under a federal constitution. There is evidence, however, that Cushing had little interest in the constitutional debates: he passed some of the time at the Massachusetts constitutional convention in 1779 making a list of materials he would need for a new suit. As vice president of the 1788 Massachusetts proceedings to ratify the U.S. Constitution, however, Cushing presided over much of the session because John Hancock, its president, was ill. In a speech he wrote but never delivered, Cushing outlined his thoughts on law and government. He approved of a military clause in the Constitution providing for a standing army because it was consistent with the Massachusetts constitution of 1780. He took issue with a proposal to rotate nationally elected officials every year, saying it would impinge on the people's freedom of choice. Cushing also rejected as superfluous the Constitution's so-called "necessary and proper clause," which expressly gave Congress all the authority it needed to execute the powers assigned to it in the Constitution.

In the first federal election, Cushing, along with the other Massachusetts superior court justices, cast his presidential electoral vote for George Washington. One of the new president's tasks was to appoint judges to the Supreme Court, which was set to convene in New York City. On September 24, 1789, he nominated the entire Court, including Cushing as an associate justice. Cushing was confirmed by a voice vote of the Senate two days later.

When Cushing arrived in New York for the first sitting of the Supreme Court, he kept up his lifelong habit of sporting an old-fashioned judge's wig, although he was one of the last American judges to do so. But he was jeered at on his way to work by groups of children and decided never to wear the professional wig again.

In his twenty-one years on the Court, Cushing wrote only nineteen opinions. His style was modest and straightforward, and his careful, brief opinions reveal little of his judicial philosophy. He was adept at disposing of cases quickly and tersely, but he did so by focusing on one simple issue to resolve the matter. Because of his knowledge of the early jurisprudence of the American states, Cushing was assigned to write decisions on the property rights of colonists who had remained loyal to the British Crown during the War of Independence. As the senior associate justice, he presided over the Court when the chief justice was absent.

In 1794, while still on the Court, Cushing was persuaded to run for governor of Massachusetts against Samuel Adams. He lost by an embarrassing ratio of two to one. This lack of support at home was due both to his reluctance to campaign for the post and to his having joined the majority in the Court's affirmation of the extremely unpopular *Chisholm v. Georgia* case in 1793. In *Chisholm,* its first major case, the Court upheld the right of citizens of one state to bring original suits in the Supreme Court against another state. Worries about the potential economic damage that might result led to adoption of the Eleventh Amendment in 1798.

After Jay resigned and John Rutledge's nomination as chief justice was rejected by the Senate, President Washington nominated Cushing to the center seat on January 26, 1796. Unlike Rutledge, Cushing had de-

Six Loyalists are savagely murdered by three Indians, symbolizing America, in this 1783 cartoon. Colonists who remained loyal to Great Britain during the Revolution often were shunned by their neighbors, and many lost their property either to plunderers or state confiscation. William Cushing wrote many of the opinions for the Supreme Court dealing with the property rights of Loyalists. *Source: Library of Congress*

monstrated conclusively in his 1796 *Ware v. Hylton* opinion that he supported the Federalist agenda. That case involved the 1783 Treaty of Paris with Britain that ended the Revolutionary War and guaranteed the right of British creditors to collect pre-Revolutionary War debts from Americans. The state of Virginia, however, had passed a statute in 1777 making it possible for citizens to pay off those debts by making payments to the Virginia treasury. Subsequently, the U.S. Constitution provided that all earlier debts were still valid and that treaties were the supreme law of the land. When the issue came before the Court, Cushing voted with the majority in overturning the Virginia statute and upholding the provisions of the treaty. He wrote: "To effect the object intended, there is no want of proper and strong language; there is no want of power, the treaty being sanctioned as the supreme law, by the Constitu-tion of the United States, which nobody pretends to deny to be paramount and controlling to all state laws."

The Federalist-dominated Senate rewarded Cushing for his stance by confirming his nomination as chief justice. Cushing kept the commission for a week, during which he attended a presidential dinner party as the new chief justice, but then he declined the appointment because of his "infirm and declining state of health." He kept his seat as associate justice.

In his old age he began to suffer unduly from the tribulations of riding circuit, but he resisted retirement because his long career in public service had left him with no private fortune to fall back on. He wrestled with the decision over whether to retire until he died September 13, 1810, at his home in Scituate. William Cushing, age seventy-eight at the time of his death, was the last of Washington's appointees to leave the bench.

James Wilson
1789-1798

JAMES WILSON was born September 14, 1742, in the village of Carskerdo, in the county of Fife, Scotland. His father, James Wilson, was a farmer and an elder of the Church of Scotland; his mother, Alison Lansdale Wilson, was an equally devout Calvinist. The Wilsons wanted their son to complete his education and become a minister. James finished at the local grammar school at age fourteen and began studies at the University of St. Andrews, which he attended on a scholarship because his family had little money.

The road Wilson traveled from a farm in Carskerdo to a Founder's role in the new republic was indirect. In the spring of 1763, while he was in his fifth year at the university, which he spent at the school of divinity, his father died. As the oldest son among seven children, he was forced to take a job as a tutor to help support his siblings. When his brothers were able to take over some of the financial burden, Wilson traveled to Edinburgh to study accounting and bookkeeping. During the year in Edinburgh, he decided that America held greater promise for someone with his educational background and low social status. In the fall of 1765 Wilson landed in New York with plans to settle in Philadelphia, where his family had relatives.

He secured a tutorship at the College of Philadelphia (later to become the University of Pennsylvania), but soon grew tired of teaching and decided that a career in law would better suit his considerable ambition. In 1766 Wilson found a position reading law in the offices of John Dickinson, a prominent attorney, and within the year began practicing law in Reading, the seat of Berks County. In November 1767 he passed the bar in the adjacent county of Lancaster and soon attracted a sizable clientele. Despite this success, nearly three years later he moved west to the town of Carlisle, where he developed a thriving business practicing land law. Wilson settled down and, after a courtship that lasted several years, married Rachel Bird in 1771. She bore him six children before her death fifteen years later.

Wilson's formal political career began in July 1774 when he was named to head Carlisle's Committee of Correspondence, which organized the town's struggle against Great Britain. Also in 1774, Wilson revised and published a manuscript he had written in 1768, "Considerations on the Nature and Extent of the Legislative Authority of the British Parliament." It espoused the radical notion that Parliament had no power over the colonies, a position that earned him considerable attention at home and abroad.

In 1775 Wilson was elected to the Second Continental Congress, where he cast his vote in favor of independence despite the opposition of several members of the Pennsylvania delegation. On July 4, he became one of two Scots to sign the Declaration of Independence.

Wilson was closely identified with the aristocratic and conservative patriots who opposed Pennsylvania's very democratic constitution of 1776. As a result, an unforgiving Pennsylvania legislature did not return him

the following year as a delegate to the Congress, although he was reelected in 1783.

Wilson moved to Philadelphia, where he made useful business contacts through his lucrative practice of defending Tory businessmen accused of treason. Although this activity did not make him popular, he became enough of a civic leader to serve for a decade as president of the St. Andrews Society, a social and philanthropic club for Scots. He was an ardent supporter of the Bank of North America and wrote an eloquent defense of the institution when it came under attack in 1785. His arguments in favor of the implied powers of Congress anticipated decisions made by the Supreme Court of the United States a quarter century later.

During the 1780s Wilson accelerated the activities in land speculation that were to prove his ultimate downfall. His hunger for wealth led him to become a part-owner of mills on the Delaware River and president of a company that had extensive western land holdings. Borrowing heavily to support his speculation, he believed that his land schemes, in addition to turning a profit, would benefit the country by promoting land settlement in western Pennsylvania.

In 1787 the Pennsylvania legislature chose Wilson to be a delegate to the Constitutional Convention. He and James Madison have been characterized as the most constructive and influential members of the convention. As a member of the Committee of Detail, Wilson participated in preparing the first draft of the Constitution; the treason clause is largely attributable to him and can be traced to his work as an attorney defending Loyalists in treason trials. He developed the concept that two people must testify to witnessing the same overt act of treason as proof of guilt, a safeguard that had not been part of English law.

Despite his image as a conservative, Wilson supported popular election of the executive branch and both chambers of the legislature. He opposed property

Although several future Supreme Court justices played active roles at the 1787 Constitutional Convention in Philadelphia, James Wilson probably had the most influence on the content of the Constitution. As a member of the Committee of Detail, he helped prepare the first draft of the document. Wilson favored popular election of both houses of Congress and the chief executive. He also developed the Article III safeguard for those accused of treason. *Source: Library of Congress*

qualifications for voting and restrictions on admission of new states to the Union. Wilson advocated a strong national government, which in his mind was compatible with the idea of popular sovereignty because the government would be directly elected by the people. He also saw the need for a national judiciary with power over the state courts, a belief that stemmed in part from earlier work as an attorney litigating admiralty cases. Wilson favored the creation of a supreme court with judges appointed by the president. He opposed the Virginia Plan proposal that the judges be appointed by the legislature, arguing, "Experience showed the impropriety of such appointments by numerous bodies. Intrigue, partiality, and concealment were the necessary consequences." Wilson's efforts to get the federal document ratified in his state helped to obtain its passage by a wide margin. He then became the prime mover behind the Commonwealth of Pennsylvania's constitution.

With a long history of contribution to the formation of American democracy, Wilson set his sights on the office of chief justice of the United States. He went so far as to solicit the post in a letter to President George Washington. On September 24, 1789, Washington named him associate justice instead. Some scholars speculate that Wilson was crushed at being passed over, but there is no evidence to support such a view. Others argue that Wilson had offended the president by greedily charging an exorbitant sum to tutor his nephew, Bushrod Washington (a future Supreme Court justice) in 1782. Although Washington realized the fee was lavish, he did not appear to be troubled by it.

In addition to his Court duties, including extensive circuit riding, Wilson found time for other activities. In the winter of 1790 he was chosen to be the first law professor at the College of Philadelphia. His erudition was already well known in Philadelphia society; his knowledge of political theory, history, and philosophy had gained him membership in 1786 to the American Philosophical Society, a prestigious learned society. Wilson's public lectures at the college were the first important discourses on the nature of law in the young republic. His views on society were laid out in his introductory lecture, attended by the president and other notable government leaders. Wilson said, "In free countries . . . law should be studied and taught as a historical science. . . . Every free citizen and every free man has duties to perform and rights to claim. Unless . . . he knows those duties and those rights, he can never act as a just and independent part."

Wilson also made time to court and marry a second wife in 1793, seven years after Rachel's death. Hannah Gray was nineteen years old when they wed, thirty-two years his junior. She often accompanied Wilson on circuit and remained devoted to him during the difficult last year of his life.

The year he remarried, Wilson rendered his most notable legal decision as one of the four majority opinions

Fueled by the education theories of Benjamin Franklin, a group of Philadelphians took over a school for poor children in 1749 and turned it into an academy with a modern curriculum. Rechartered as the College, Academy, and Charitable School of Philadelphia in 1755, the school became the country's first official university in 1791. James Wilson was its first law professor. *Source: The Historical Society of Pennsylvania*

in *Chisholm v. Georgia.* The case arose when citizens of South Carolina sued the state of Georgia to secure compensation for confiscated property. Georgia took the position that a citizen could not sue a sovereign state in federal court. Wilson's opinion adopted an extremely nationalist interpretation of the origins and nature of the Union. He argued that the issue could be reduced to whether a state is subject to the jurisdiction of the U.S. Supreme Court, and he answered in the affirmative.

The Court's decision sent shock waves throughout the country as states feared economic ruin and total subservience to the federal court. Georgia passed a law providing that any agent of the federal government attempting to carry out the decision should be "declared guilty of felony and shall suffer death, without benefit of clergy, by being hanged." The day after the decision, an amendment was introduced in Congress aimed at

making states immune to suits by individuals of another state. In 1798, after revision, it took effect as the Eleventh Amendment to the Constitution.

When John Jay resigned, Wilson was once again passed over for the chief justiceship, and the post went to John Rutledge. Wilson's constant worries over his financial dealings had caused him to miss several circuit court sessions to manage his affairs in Philadelphia, absences that probably had not escaped the president's attention. When the Senate refused to confirm Rutledge, Wilson's hopes must have risen again. Washington instead chose Oliver Ellsworth, and Wilson expressed disappointment. Associate Justice James Iredell wrote at the time that he thought Wilson would resign from the Court. Although he stayed on, the end was near.

Wilson's risky speculation in vast real estate holdings had made his financial situation precarious. At a time when he was in need of funds, the economy fell into

Associate Justice James Wilson, one of the young nation's greatest legal scholars, died in disgrace in Edenton, North Carolina, where he had fled in 1789 to escape his creditors. In 1906 his reputation was restored and his remains transported to Philadelphia for a proper state burial. Chief Justice Melville Fuller and Justice Oliver Wendell Holmes, Jr., led the funeral cortege, and Justice Edward D. White spoke at the ceremonies as the Court's representative. *Source: The Historical Society of Pennsylvania*

depression, and credit grew tighter. Creditors entered judgments against him, and in 1797 Wilson and his wife fled to Bethlehem, Pennsylvania. Continuing on alone, he was arrested in Burlington, New Jersey, where he was jailed because he was unable to post bail. After his son, Bird, managed to come up with the funds to procure his release, he went to North Carolina and stayed at the Horniblow Tavern in Edenton, the hometown of fellow justice James Iredell. Another creditor, former South Carolina senator Pierce Butler, caught up with him there and had Wilson imprisoned for reneging on a $197,000 debt.

Released again through the aid of his son, Wilson was broken in spirit and health. Weak and unable to act, he spent the summer of 1798 sweltering in a room at the dingy Edenton inn, comforted by his young wife who had come to be by his side. He was not aware of the talk of impeachment in Philadelphia that made it unlikely he could return to his Court duties, and was to the end convinced he could find a way out of his predicament.

In July Wilson contracted malaria and the following month suffered a stroke. The man hailed as the greatest judicial mind of the new republic died August 21, 1798, in disgrace. Justice Iredell arranged for his burial at Hayes Plantation, North Carolina, as the Wilson family could not afford to have the body moved to Pennsylvania. The Supreme Court issued no eulogy. In 1906, more than a century later, Wilson's reputation was rehabilitated and his remains were moved to Christ Church in Philadelphia. The dignified ceremony was attended by several members of the Supreme Court.

John Blair, Jr.
1790-1796

Source: Colonial Williamsburg Foundation

APRIVILEGED AND WELL-EDUCATED Virginian, John Blair, Jr., held several important state offices and judgeships before becoming one of President George Washington's original appointees to the Court. Born in Williamsburg in 1732, he was the son of John Blair, Sr., a prominent statesman who served in the House of Burgesses, on the Governor's Council, and as acting governor of Virginia. His mother was Mary Monro Blair, the daughter of the Reverend John Monro of St. John's Parish, King

William County, Virginia. The Blair family had a considerable fortune, including large landholdings in the western part of Virginia, which enabled John, Jr., one of ten children, to obtain the finest education. He graduated with honors in 1754 from the College of William and Mary, which had been established by his great uncle.

The following year he was sent to study law at the Middle Temple in London, where he was a guest of Virginia's former lieutenant governor, Robert Dinwiddie, an old friend of his father. While abroad, he found time to woo Jean Blair, the daughter of a Scottish writer named Archibald Blair. They were married in Edinburgh December 26, 1756, and returned to Williamsburg shortly thereafter.

Once back on Virginia soil, Blair developed a successful legal practice in the colony's General Court. He also launched a political career, and in 1765 the College of William and Mary chose him as its representative to the Virginia House of Burgesses. Then only thirty-three, he was described by a contemporary as preserving "to the last that strict attention to dress which was characteristic of the colonial regime." A political conservative, Blair opposed Patrick Henry's fiery condemnation of the Stamp Act, the first direct tax imposed on the colonies by the British government, and argued for peaceful negotiations with Britain. Four years later, however, Blair participated in the drafting of a nonim-

portation agreement to force the repeal of onerous import taxes. He nonetheless continued to oppose separation from Britain.

Blair resigned his seat in the House of Burgesses in 1771 to become clerk of the Governor's Council, a position his father once held. During this time Blair came to favor independence from Britain. His college alma mater again appointed him delegate, this time to the seminal fifth Virginia convention, which met in May 1776, at Williamsburg, to design a constitution for the new commonwealth. He played an important role at the convention as one of a team of twenty-eight men charged with drawing up a plan of government and a declaration of rights. Upon the constitution's adoption in June 1776, Blair was elected to be a member of the new Governor's Council, another post formerly occupied by his father.

In 1777 Blair got his first experience on the bench

Chartered in 1693, the College of William and Mary educated four Supreme Court justices, including John Blair, Jr., whose great uncle had founded the Williamsburg, Virginia, institution. Top center is the college's oldest structure, the Wren Building, and bottom right is the Governor's Palace. The Capitol building, where the powerful Virginia House of Burgesses convened, is at bottom left.
Source: Library of Congress

John Blair, Jr., was one of the Virginians who drafted a nonimportation agreement at a Williamsburg convention in 1769. This British cartoon mocks the reluctance of many Virginia merchants to sign the agreement to stop trading with Britain. Worried about loss of revenue, some loyalist merchants and farmers signed only under threats from club-wielding colleagues. Bags containing tar and feathers hang from the gibbet in the background—another looming menace. *Source: Library of Congress*

when the state legislature elected him to be one of five judges on the newly created General Court of Virginia, a court set up as part of the establishment of a Virginia judiciary in October of that year. He was promoted to be chief justice of the court two years later. In 1780 Blair was named chancellor of the three-member High Court of Chancery, all the while serving as an ex-officio member of the first Virginia Court of Appeals. Blair and a fellow appeals court judge ruled in *The Commonwealth of Virginia v. Caton et al.* (1782) that their court had the power to review legislative acts and strike them down if they were unconstitutional, a ruling some see as a precedent for the U.S. Supreme Court's historic 1803 *Marbury v. Madison* decision, which asserted the power of judicial review for the high court.

The Virginia legislature chose Blair, along with George Washington, Edmund Randolph, James Madison, George Mason, and George Wythe, as a delegate to the 1787 Constitutional Convention in Philadelphia. Although not a particularly active or vocal participant at the national convention, Blair was one of three Virginians, along with Madison and Washington, to sign the document. In debates, Blair opposed the popular election of a president and instead favored election by the legislature of a ruling council to head the executive branch. His arguments did not persuade the other members of the delegation, and Blair realized that prolonged debate would jeopardize the new Constitution. To ensure the document's final adoption, he accepted a compromise measure by voting with Washington and Madison for the electoral college system.

Returning to his judicial duties in Virginia, Blair also

represented York County at his state's ratifying convention and again urged the U.S. Constitution's passage. In November 1787 the court of appeals on which Blair served heard a landmark case that was appealed from the General Court. *Commonwealth v. Posey* involved a convicted arsonist's claim that he had not been allowed the benefit of consulting a clergyman. On the basis of various English statutes derived from a nearly 200-year-old English precedent called *Powlter's Case*, Posey's claim was rejected. The ruling was significant because Blair and his fellow judges affirmed that old English common law and statutes could serve as precedents for Virginia law.

When the Virginia judicial system was reorganized in the year following the Constitutional Convention, the legislature chose Blair to sit on the Virginia Supreme Court of Appeals. Three months after this new, five-man appeals court held its first meeting in June 1789, President George Washington, much to Blair's surprise, named him to the Supreme Court of the United States. On September 24, 1789, the day that Washington signed the Judiciary Act providing for a Supreme Court, the president also sent the names of six Court nominees—including Blair's—to the Senate for confirmation.

Blair stood nearly six feet tall and was described by a contemporary as "of slight frame, but with an astonishing breadth of brow, particularly between the eyes, which were brown in color, surmounted by a bald forehead fringed with scanty locks of red hair, which fell over his ears." By the time of his appointment he had established a solid reputation for being a kind man and a judge of great integrity. His peers regarded him as "amiable in disposition, blameless and pious, possessed of great benevolence and goodness of heart." Blair missed the first meeting of the Supreme Court, held in New York City, then the nation's capital, on February 1, 1790. He arrived later that day, with Attorney General Edmund Randolph, to join Chief Justice John Jay and Associate Justices William Cushing and James Wilson. Blair's presence constituted the quorum necessary for the Court to conduct its first formal session the following day. After appointing a clerk and admitting attorneys to the bar, the Court adjourned several days later. In its first few terms the Court had a light case load and was occupied mainly with administrative matters.

The Court's slight activity, coupled with his wife's persistent ill health, caused Blair to miss several terms. He did participate in major decisions, most notably *Chisholm v. Georgia* (1793), the first Supreme Court opinion to limit state sovereignty. The *Chisholm* case revolved around the issue of whether a citizen of one state could sue another state in federal court to recover claims compensation. The majority decided that a sovereign state could indeed be sued without its consent, and that the Supreme Court had authority to decide such a case. Each justice outlined his own reasoning in a separate opinion.

Unlike those of his colleagues, Blair's opinion did not rely on political theory or legal precedent. Instead, he found that the provision in the Constitution that gave the federal judiciary jurisdiction over "controversies between a State and Citizens of another State" clearly applied in this case. Others felt that the word order in the clause implied that the Court had jurisdiction only when it was the state that was suing the individual. Blair disagreed. "A dispute between A. and B. is surely a dispute between B. and A.," he argued. He held that the Court should interpret the Constitution literally, and carry out all its provisions. "The constitution of the United States is the only fountain from which I shall draw; the only authority to which I shall appeal," he wrote in the introduction of his opinion. "Whatever be the true language of that, it is obligatory upon every member of the Union." He went on to say that the Constitution requires "the submission of individual states to the judicial authority of the United States."

Less than five years after the Court ruled on the case,

Only three of the six justices were present February 1, 1790, when the Supreme Court met in the Merchants Exchange building, New York City. The Court's first home stood at the intersection of Broad and Water streets, in what is now the financial district. An open-air market was housed under the brick arcades on the first floor, and the courtroom was upstairs. Once a quorum had assembled, the justices' first order of business was to appoint a clerk and admit practicing lawyers to the bar. *Source: Collection of the Supreme Court of the United States*

it was overturned by adoption of the Eleventh Amendment. A popular outcry had condemned the decision as potentially detrimental to the economic well-being of the states. Fearing economic ruin, the states mounted a campaign to get Congress to overturn the decision. The new amendment declared that states could not be sued, without their consent, in federal court by citizens of another state.

Justices Blair and Wilson presided over the middle circuit—one of the three judicial circuits outlined in the Judiciary Act of 1789—which stretched from New Jersey to Virginia. Blair found his circuit duties arduous, and their difficulty was compounded by increasingly persistent spells of headaches. When his wife died in 1792 of a chronic illness labeled "hysteria," a condition that also afflicted their daughters, Blair's health deteriorated further. On June 12, 1795, Blair wrote to his colleague, Justice Cushing, to tell him he would be unable to attend the Court's August term: "A malady which I have had for some years, in a smaller degree, has since I had the pleasure of seeing you increased so

greatly as to disqualify me totally from business. It is a rattling, distracting noise in my head."

Blair resigned from the Court January 27, 1796, citing "a strange disorder of my head, which has lately compelled me to neglect my official duties." He retreated to his home in Williamsburg where he spent his remaining days. On hearing of Blair's retirement, William Plumer, a future New Hampshire senator, wrote: "I consider him as a man of good abilities . . . of firmness, strict integrity, and of great candour."

In a letter to his sister, Blair described the illness that afflicted him periodically during his retirement: "I happened to be involved in some algebraical exercises (of which kind of amusement I was very fond) when all at once a torpid numbness seized my whole face and I found my intellectual powers much weakened and all was confusion. . . . There are intervals when all the distresses abate considerably; but there are times when I am unable to read and am obliged to lay aside a newspaper or whatever else I may happen to be engaged in." The Virginia justice died August 31, 1800.

James Iredell

1790-1799

Source: James Iredell Association

JAMES IREDELL was born October 5, 1751, in Lewes, Sussex County, England, the eldest son in his family. His father, Francis Iredell, was an unsuccessful merchant who had to retire from his business because of a paralytic stroke. His mother was Margaret McCulloh Iredell, whose family connections helped young James secure an appointment as comptroller of customs for Port Roanoke at Edenton, North Carolina. Little is known about Iredell's education or his life before arriving in Edenton late in 1768 at the age of seventeen. The abundant letters and essays he wrote that survive today, however, show that he was well-educated, eloquent, and an astute political observer.

Henry Eustace McCulloh, the customs collector for the port, was absent for long periods, leaving the duties of his office to his young cousin. Iredell also discovered that he was expected to collect rent money and generally oversee the extensive landholdings of the McCulloh family. He mastered his job quickly and performed his duties with skill and dedication beyond his years. A devoted son and a devout Christian, Iredell sent his entire salary to his parents and lived on the meager fees he collected. He earned the respect and friendship of the citizens of Edenton—no small accomplishment for a tax collector of the British Crown in the years preceding the American Revolution.

Soon after moving to Edenton, young Iredell developed a lifelong friendship with the region's most prominent citizen, Samuel Johnston, and began reading law under his tutelage. Not only did Iredell have one of the best lawyers in the area as his teacher, but also he had access to Johnston's library, which was among the finest in the colonies. After finishing his legal apprenticeship in 1773, Iredell married Johnston's sister, Hannah, with whom he had two daughters and a son. James Iredell, Jr., followed his father into public service, eventually serving as governor of North Carolina, U.S. senator, and reporter of the North Carolina Supreme Court.

In 1774 the provincial attorney general appointed Iredell a deputy to prosecute for the Crown in Hertford, Tyrell, and Perquimans counties. That same year his cousin at long last officially transferred the collectorship of customs to him. At the age of twenty-three, Iredell found himself collector of customs, deputy attorney general, and a practicing lawyer all at the same time.

As the controversies between the colonies and the mother country grew more protracted, Iredell at first tried to find some way to preserve the British empire. He was of the opinion that the American colonies should be treated like Scotland prior to the Act of Union—in other words, remain under the British Crown but be governed by its own legislative body. Eventually, he saw that this solution was impossible, and in 1776 he closed the customs office and joined the Revolution, but at a great financial and personal loss.

His uncle, a wealthy Jamaican planter, made good on his threat to remove James as his primary heir if he joined the Revolution. Likewise, he was cut off from his family in England.

Iredell had been expressing his views for some time in his writings. Because he had a slight lisp—but a clear writing style—he communicated more effectively as a writer than as an orator. In 1774 he wrote an anonymous essay, "To The Inhabitants of Great Britain," in which he argued against the supremacy of the British Parliament over the American people. He followed it with "The Principles of an American Whig," and in

This British print depicts John Malcomb, the commissioner of customs at Boston Harbor, in 1774 as he was tarred and feathered for trying to collect custom duties. As a customs collector in North Carolina, James Iredell could have experienced a similar fate. Instead, he won the friendship of the local citizens and eventually closed the customs office to join the Revolution. *Source: Courtesy of the John Carter Brown Library at Brown University*

1777 with an essay renouncing his loyalty to the king and accusing him of bringing on the conflict by his inattention to the pleas of his former subjects in America.

North Carolina established an independent government in 1776, and Iredell was appointed by the legislature to a committee to review and, if necessary, revise all of the state's laws. In 1777 he was elected one of three judges of the Superior Court, which was the highest judicial tribunal in the new state. He accepted the post only reluctantly, however, because he enjoyed his law practice and did not relish the idea of being away from home while he rode circuit throughout the state. After six months he resigned, primarily over differences of opinion with his fellow judges. Iredell felt that Judge Samuel Spencer was not qualified and that Judge Samuel Ashe did not devote enough time or thought to his duties.

Iredell's reputation came to the attention of Gov. Richard Caswell, who in July 1779 appointed him interim attorney general, the state's highest legal officer. He was properly elected to the post in November by the state legislature. As attorney general Iredell was responsible for prosecuting people thought to be guilty of treason against the new government. At one session Iredell wrote that "upwards of eighty persons were indicted and mostly for capital crimes, the greatest number was for high treason." Open conflicts between Loyalists and patriots had reached such a state that officials of the courts had to travel with guards. Thanks to an illness that detained him several days, Iredell narrowly avoided capture by Loyalists at the courthouse in Hillsborough. He nevertheless managed to conduct the courts in a proper and fair manner, opposing the wholesale confiscation of Loyalist property.

When the British surrendered at the end of 1781, Iredell declined to stand for reelection, wishing to be rid of criminal trials and return to private practice. He also felt he would be freer to speak on subjects growing out of the Revolution. It was as a private attorney that Iredell first argued, in *Bayard v. Singleton* (1787), that a court could declare unconstitutional an act of the state legislature found to be in conflict with the state constitution. The court agreed with him, making it the earliest case under a written constitution in which a court exercised the power of judicial review. That same year the legislature appointed Iredell to revise all the state laws; the new laws were codified in 1791.

After the war Iredell emerged as a leader of the Federalist movement in North Carolina. When delegates met in Hillsborough to consider adoption of the U.S. Constitution in 1788, Iredell led the floor fight in favor of ratification. Although anti-Federalist sentiment at the convention prevailed, Iredell continued to be diligent in his defense of the work of the Constitutional Convention. Because of his efforts, the state legislature named a new North Carolina county for Iredell. The following year a second state convention held at Fayetteville adopted the Constitution, and North Carolina joined the Union.

When Robert H. Harrison, one of President George Washington's six original nominees to the newly established Supreme Court of the United States, declined to serve, the president considered Iredell for the position. His prominence in North Carolina, his fight for the ratification of the Constitution, and his standing in the legal profession all made him an attractive candidate. Washington also was aware that no North Carolinian had been appointed to an important federal office. The president nominated Iredell February 8, 1790, and he was unanimously confirmed by the Senate two days later. Iredell was thirty-eight at the time, making him the youngest of Washington's appointees. The nomination was a pleasant surprise to Iredell, who had expected instead to be named a federal district court judge.

Iredell first sat with the Supreme Court in August, at its second session in New York, the temporary seat of

Isaac Weld drew this American stagecoach during his journey through North America in the late 1790s. He shared the stage to Philadelphia with a Supreme Court justice, probably either Samuel Chase or James Iredell. John Marshall was among the southern lawyers who accompanied them. Traveling by stagecoach, boat, and horseback to preside over circuit courts, the justices considered this duty particularly burdensome because transportation was slow and accommodations were primitive. *Source: New York Public Library*

government, where Iredell moved his family. Just as at the first session, there was little business and the Court adjourned after two days. When the federal government moved to Philadelphia in 1790, Iredell uprooted his family once again, this time to the pleasure of his wife who did not like New York. Her stay in Philadelphia, however, was short. Because of the frequent yellow fever epidemics, Iredell took his family back to their old home in Edenton in 1793.

The Judiciary Act of 1789 stipulated that the circuit courts consist of two Supreme Court justices and a district court judge. Iredell was assigned to the southern circuit, the largest, which required that the justices ride some 1,800 miles to attend all the courts. It was first be-

lieved that there would be a rotation in circuits among the justices, but at the February 1791 sitting of the Court the justices decided to make permanent assignments of the circuits. Dismayed, Iredell immediately wrote to Chief Justice John Jay stating that he thought it impossible to attend the circuit courts in the South and be expected to attend two yearly sittings of the Court. Although they might have agreed, it took a great deal of letter writing from Iredell not only to members of Congress but also to the president to correct the situation. Relief came in 1792 in the form of an amendment to the Judiciary Act of 1789 stating that a justice would not be required to ride the faraway southern circuit twice in a row unless he agreed.

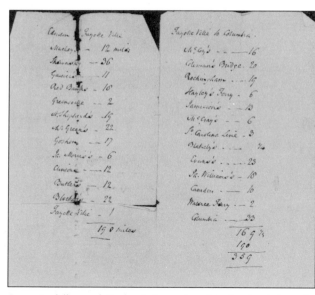

James Iredell complained at being assigned to the dreaded southern circuit, which required traveling some 1,800 miles to attend the courts. Nonetheless, he rode this circuit five times between 1790 and 1794, keeping track of the many stops he made between Edenton, North Carolina, and Columbia, South Carolina. *Courtesy of North Carolina Division of Archives and History*

Nevertheless, Iredell rode the long and tiresome southern circuit five times between 1790 and 1794. On one occasion he reported being forced to share a bed with a man who was "of the wrong sort"; on other nights he tried to sleep in rooms where men were drinking, gambling, and swearing all night. He suffered accidents along the way as well. Once his horse bolted, causing his coach to hit a tree, throw him out, and run over his leg.

The most important case the Court decided while Iredell was a member was *Chisholm v. Georgia* (1793). The majority ruled in favor of two citizens of South Carolina who had sued the state of Georgia for recovery of confiscated property. Georgia refused to appear in federal court because it did not recognize the Supreme Court's jurisdiction, even though the Constitution explicitly gave the Court the right to settle disputes between a state and citizens of another state. Iredell, in probably his finest legal writing, dissented. He denied that the Framers of the Constitution or the Judiciary Act intended to give such extended authority to the federal government. Iredell argued that a sovereign state could not be sued except with its consent.

Despite the fact that Iredell's opinion represented the belief of most Americans at the time, the majority opinion became the binding opinion of the Court—but not for long. The decision set off an uproar, with states foreseeing economic ruin if individuals were allowed to sue them. To most Americans, the Court's ruling represented an extreme nationalistic viewpoint. The day following the announcement of the decision, Congress introduced legislation, which was in basic agreement with Iredell's dissent, to reverse the ruling. The legislation was eventually adopted as the Eleventh Amendment and marked the first time a decision of the Court was overturned by a constitutional amendment.

In another important case, *Calder v. Bull* (1798), the Court interpreted certain provisions of the Constitution as prohibiting state legislatures from extending *ex post facto* laws, which are laws affecting matters that happened before their enactment, to apply to criminal cases. Iredell's opinion expressed support for overturning federal as well as state laws that conflict with the Constitution. "If any act of Congress, or of the Legislature of a state, violates . . . constitutional provisions, it is unquestionably void," he wrote.

During the summer of 1799 Iredell's health began to fail. The hardship of riding circuit was taking its toll. For a number of years he had complained of feeling fatigued and of having headaches, but he kept up his strenuous schedule. He was on his way to Philadelphia for the fall term when he became seriously ill and had to return to Edenton. Although doctors were unable to fashion a cure for his ailments and he grew worse, he continued to give legal advice to clients and to write cheerful letters. On October 20 James Iredell died at the age of forty-eight, at the height of his career.

Thomas Johnson
1792-1793

Thomas Johnson was born November 4, 1732, in Calvert County on the Chesapeake Bay in southern Maryland. His grandfather, Thomas Johnson, was a fervent royalist who had come to America in 1690 from Yarmouth, a port town on the Isle of Wight. Johnson's father, also named Thomas, was a gentleman farmer and country squire who served in the Maryland Assembly. The future justice's mother, Dorcas Sedgwick Johnson, was from a Maryland family of English origin that had prospered in land acquisition and water mills.

Although the Johnsons were financially comfortable, they had twelve children to support, and Thomas's early education therefore was conducted privately at home rather than at a prestigious but expensive school abroad. As a young man, he went to Annapolis, the colonial capital, to work as a court clerk and to read law under the supervision of Stephen Bordley, a distinguished former attorney general of the province. Johnson subsequently began his own legal career in Annapolis and by the age of twenty-nine, when he was elected to the Provincial Assembly, he was already a leading member of the bar.

Even in his youth Johnson was involved in land acquisition and development. In 1761 he bought land in Frederick County, Maryland, as an investment, and quickly became fascinated by the potential of the Potomac River as a commercial waterway. A decade earlier, the young surveyor George Washington had recognized that potential, and he too had seen that the problems—rapids, shoals, and falls—were surmountable if clearing, dredging, and canal construction could be financed and engineered. Around 1770 they began a correspondence about river navigation, and their acquaintance ripened into warm friendship and respect, becoming a profound influence on Johnson's life.

The years prior to the Revolution witnessed Johnson's continued growth in prestige. His legal practice prospered, and he assumed greater legislative responsibility in the lower house of the Assembly. He promoted a

colonial Maryland lottery and served on the council overseeing construction of the Maryland State House. In 1766 Johnson married Ann Jennings, daughter of his first employer. Their marriage was happy, and they were parents of eight children, five girls and three boys. A portrait painted about this time shows Johnson was a man of medium stature, with reddish brown hair, not handsome, but with pleasing features. A contemporary found him "a most pleasant, joyous, companionable man."

Johnson led the Maryland opposition to the 1765 Stamp Act, which was the first direct tax levied by the British Parliament on the American colonies. His law office became a meeting place for many activists and intellectuals, but his chief associates were William Paca, Samuel Chase, and Charles Carroll of Carrollton, all of whom would be signers of the Declaration of Independence. Johnson was particularly close to Chase, a business associate in land speculation and a future Supreme Court justice, and to Carroll, one of the richest men in America, who became his client.

The Stamp Act was promptly, if reluctantly, repealed

As early as 1770 George Washington and Thomas Johnson began corresponding about the possibilities of making the Potomac River fit for commercial traffic. The two friends formed the Potowmack Company, which explored ways to construct a canal to skirt obstacles such as falls and rapids. By 1850 the land to the right of this 1798 view, three miles from Georgetown, would be the site of the Chesapeake and Ohio Canal. *Source: Maryland Historical Society, Baltimore*

Thomas and Ann Johnson and three of their eight children in an elegant family portrait by Charles Willson Peale. Johnson is better remembered for his participation in the revolutionary politics of his native Maryland and his three years' service as governor than for his fourteen-month tenure on the Supreme Court. *Source: Baltimore Museum of Art*

only a year after its passage, but Parliament insisted on its right to raise moneys in the colonies. This struggle between the mother country and its colonies intensified through the next decade, with political sentiment in Maryland echoing that of Massachusetts and Virginia. And whenever there was patriotic activity in Maryland, Johnson and his friends were in the thick of it. When Maryland's governor, Sir Robert Eden, imposed duties on tea, glass, paper, and other imports, Johnson led the fight to rescind. When Massachusetts pleaded for assistance from the other colonies after the Boston Tea Party, Johnson helped to form Maryland's Committee of Correspondence. When Maryland chose its delegates to the First Continental Congress, not surprisingly, Johnson was one of them.

The Continental Congresses provided him a new and larger stage. Already a friend of George Washington, he came to know John Jay, Benjamin Franklin, John Adams, Samuel Adams, and the other important revolutionary leaders. John Adams recorded in his diary in October 1774 that "Johnson of Maryland has a clear

and a cool head, an extensive knowledge of trade as well as law." He found Johnson "deliberating . . . but not a shining orator," a man of "reason and penetration," but not "rhetoric." Johnson served on a number of major committees in the First and Second Continental Congresses, but his most important contribution was to nominate Washington to be commander in chief of the Continental Army. Although he did not sign the Declaration of Independence, Johnson was a political whirlwind at home. He was a participant when Maryland declared its own independence July 6, 1776. He served as a member of the Council of Safety; he became a broker of supplies and arms; he raised a regiment of 1,800 men, which he headed personally with the rank of brigadier general; and he helped to draft Maryland's first constitution.

When the new and independent state legislature convened in February 1777, its first constitutional task was to choose a governor. Johnson was elected overwhelmingly, but the times were so difficult that his administration was hard pressed to attend to the usual duties of government. Twice, the state was threatened by British invasion, once by land and once when a flotilla of English ships entered the Chesapeake Bay; there were also pockets of Tory disloyalty and insurrection. The greatest problem of all, however, was finding the arms, powder, food, clothing, and bedding for his own militia and in response to the incessant requests of the federal government. The governor appointed collectors, with instructions to fan out through the state, gathering and purchasing goods for the troops who were suffering from hunger and exposure. The letters between General Washington and Governor Johnson continued during the war, the general begging for help and the governor frantically striving to supply it.

The Maryland Constitution provided for a one-year gubernatorial term, with no more than three consecutive terms. Johnson was elected unanimously for each of the next two years. He left office in late 1779, less than two years before the end of the war, and decided not to return to Annapolis, but to settle on his land in Frederick. He built Richfields, a large colonial house, and settled down to what he undoubtedly hoped would be serene retirement. He declined a seat in Congress, but did agree to return to the state legislature, where he urged Maryland's ratification of the Articles of Confederation.

After ratification, Johnson returned to legal practice and began also to pursue his old prewar interest in the Potomac River. With Washington, he organized the Potowmack Company to engage in the financing and construction of a canal to skirt the rapids and falls. Their idea was a failure until—at a later date and built by someone else—the Chesapeake and Ohio Canal became a reality.

In the late 1780s Johnson joined in the effort to ratify the Constitution, and when that task was accomplished, to work for Washington's election as president. Once again in 1790 he attempted to settle down to the private life he truly sought. He had declined to serve

While representing Maryland at the Continental Congress, Thomas Johnson nominated his friend George Washington to be commander in chief of the Continental Army. In 1790 John Trumbull painted a victorious General Washington receiving the French troops after they helped defeat the British at Yorktown.
Source: Courtesy of Winterthur Museum

again as governor when the office was offered two years before. He declined now to serve in the Electoral College that selected Washington as president, and he declined to serve when Washington asked him to become the first U.S. district judge for Maryland. He did agree to become chief judge of the General Court, the most important state court under the Maryland Constitution of 1776, perhaps because the duties, while requiring detailed understanding of state law and a willingness to interpret the new federal Constitution, were not burdensome. Johnson believed, no doubt, that his family and business interests would not suffer.

Once again, however, there was an intrusion, this time by the president. In early 1791 Washington asked

Johnson to chair the Board of Commissioners of the Federal City, a body established by Congress to purchase the land and provide the buildings for the new District of Columbia. Johnson agreed. The new capital was not far from home and located on his beloved Potomac. Moreover, Daniel Carroll, an old Maryland friend and a signer of the state constitution, was one of the other commissioners. Johnson even looked forward, as a labor of love, to the design of the new city and of its principal buildings.

But a few months later, on July 14, Washington wrote again, asking "with frankness, and in the fullness of friendship" if the former governor would agree to an appointment as associate justice of the Supreme Court, succeeding John Rutledge, who had resigned. Johnson was very reluctant. He was almost sixty and did not want the responsibilities of circuit travel, particularly in the vast southern circuit over which Rutledge had presided. So his initial reply to Washington on July 27 was noncommittal, mentioning his concern about the travel. A second response written three days later still did not agree to the appointment; this time Johnson added worried comments about his health and family interests. But Washington sent the temporary commission anyway, saying that he had conferred with Chief Justice John Jay. The circuit problems could be worked out, Washington said, and besides, he continued, the next Congress would be reviewing "alterations" in the judicial system, "among which this [circuit duty] may be one." When Congress met later that year, the nomination was forwarded to the Senate, and Johnson was confirmed November 7.

Once Johnson took office, all of his anxieties were realized. He presided in the circuit court at Richmond in November and December of 1791, but was indisposed when the Supreme Court met in Philadelphia for its 1792 February term. His health prevented his hearing cases in the spring circuit of 1792, but he did attend the Court's August term in Philadelphia, where his com-

mission was read and he was duly qualified. During the fall circuit that year, he became ill in Charleston in October, but in November was able to preside for a few days over a circuit court in Augusta, Georgia. He was a conscientious man and would not retain the office if he could not perform its duties. On January 16, 1793, he sent his resignation to the president, noting ruefully, "The office and the man do not fit."

Johnson's service of fourteen months on the Court was the shortest in the Court's history, and most of his judicial record involved only routine business. He sat in Richmond at a preliminary stage of a landmark case, *Ware v. Hylton,* where the lawyers included Patrick Henry and John Marshall, but the trial was continued until the next session. He also took part in the first Supreme Court case in which written opinions were filed—*Georgia v. Brailsford.* But this case was also in a procedural stage, and the issues were not argued until later. Johnson seems to have been moderate, rational, and temperate, not unlike Justice William Paterson who succeeded him.

Following the laying of the cornerstone of the Capitol in September 1793, Johnson also resigned from the board of the federal city. But he was not to enjoy his longed-for tranquillity at Richfields, because his wife died November 22, 1794, after twenty-eight years of marriage. The retired governor moved to nearby Rose Hill, the estate of his daughter, Ann Grahame. He remained active in his business ventures, but determined not to accept any public office—even declining Washington's offer of service as secretary of state. In the last years of his life he befriended a young lawyer named Roger B. Taney, a future chief justice of the United States, who had opened a Frederick office and served as a witness to Johnson's will. Johnson was active in service to All Saints Episcopal Church until he died peacefully at Rose Hill October 26, 1819, only ten days before his eighty-seventh birthday.

William Paterson

1793-1806

WILLIAM PATERSON, one of only six foreign-born Supreme Court justices, was born December 24, 1745, in County Antrim, Ireland. His father, Richard, was a tin plate worker, and little is known of his mother, Mary. In 1747 the family sailed from Londonderry and landed in Newcastle, Delaware. Over the next few years the Patersons moved to New York, then Connecticut, before settling permanently in Princeton, New Jersey.

Once in Princeton the family opened a general store catering to the students and faculty of the College of New Jersey (now Princeton University). The family business doomed William to hours of menial tasks but gave him early exposure to the intellectual environment of a major university. He was accepted at the college in 1759 after doing preparatory work to prove his proficiency in Latin and Greek at a school run by Aaron Burr. His father's shrewd investments in real estate helped finance his education.

After his graduation in 1763, Paterson entered a mas-

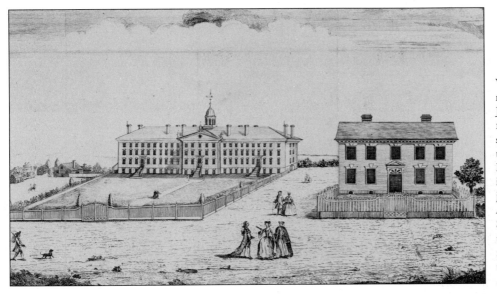

William Paterson was already familiar with the College of New Jersey when he matriculated in 1759; his father ran a general store in Princeton that catered to students and faculty. Young Paterson shared classes with Oliver Ellsworth, whom he later joined in drafting the Judiciary Act of 1789, creating the U.S. Supreme Court. After service in the Senate, the former classmates were both appointed to the Supreme Court. *Source: Library of Congress*

ter's degree program and apprenticed himself to Richard Stockton to study law. He earned the master's degree in 1766. Paterson was admitted to the bar three years later and relocated to New Bromley, some thirty miles away, to establish a practice. Impatient at times with the slow growth of his legal business, he sought a position in government.

In 1775 Paterson was selected as a delegate from Somerset County to the First Provincial Congress of New Jersey and served as assistant secretary. He eventually became secretary of the Congress, helped draft the New Jersey Constitution, and earned a reputation as a leading architect of the state's independence. In 1776 he was named the first attorney general of the state and actively prosecuted Loyalists. He retired from the post in 1783 to devote his full time to the practice of law.

In 1777 he met Cornelia Bell, the daughter of a Somerset County landowner, whom he described as "the sweetest pattern of female excellence." They married in February 1779. Cornelia died in childbirth four years later, leaving him with two small children to raise. In 1784 he married his wife's best friend, Euphemia White.

Paterson represented New Jersey at the Constitutional Convention of 1787, which was held in Philadelphia. His name is immortalized as the architect of the Paterson Plan, or New Jersey Plan, as it is also known. The new Republic had been governed since its independence by the Articles of Confederation, but this loose association proved too weak for the continued existence of a cohesive union. The Constitutional Convention was an attempt to restructure the government. Headed by James Madison, the Virginia delegation proposed a bicameral legislature, calling for popular election of the first house with the second house selected by the first. Paterson proposed a single chamber in which each state had an equal vote regardless of its population or wealth. The delegates from Delaware, Connecticut, Maryland, and North Carolina supported his plan. The Virginia and New Jersey plans were consolidated to form the American legislative scheme, with a lower house proportioned by population and the Senate consisting of two members from each state and chosen by the state legislatures.

His contribution made, Paterson wrote to his wife July 17, "The business is difficult, and unavoidably takes up much time, but I think we shall eventually

William Paterson was a staunch Federalist in the U.S. Senate and was instrumental in organizing the judicial branch. The Senate chose him to tally the electoral votes to certify the presidential election of George Washington, shown here at his first inaugural, April 30, 1789, on the balcony of Federal Hall in New York. *Source: The Bettmann Archive*

agree upon and adopt a system that will give strength and harmony to the Union and render us a great and happy people." In November 1788 the New Jersey legislature named Paterson one of its senators. He had second thoughts about accepting the nomination, in part because he feared that the job would force him to give up much of his legal practice. In March 1789 he arrived in New York City, then the capital of the United States, ready to begin work. However, the necessary quorum of twelve senators failed to arrive for almost three weeks. Paterson complained about the time wasted during those three weeks in "idle ceremony and show." The Senate finally began its work on April 6, certifying the electoral ballots so that George Washington could be inaugurated. On behalf of the Senate, Paterson tallied the votes and was subsequently appointed to help prepare the certificate of election for President George Washington and Vice President John Adams.

Next, the Senate organized the judicial branch of the federal government. In Article III of the Constitution the Framers had provided only for a Supreme Court; lower courts were discretionary and required legislation by Congress. On April 7 Paterson and the other senators began this process, eventually passing the Judiciary Act of 1789, which was drafted by Paterson and his old college classmate, Sen. Oliver Ellsworth of Connecticut, a future chief justice of the United States. The act created a three-tiered system consisting of the Supreme Court, circuit courts, and district courts. However, it provided for only two kinds of federal judges—members of the Supreme Court, of which there were to be six, and thirteen district court judges. Because no separate circuit judges were appointed, it was mandated that two Supreme Court justices, riding circuit, along with a district court judge would preside over the circuit courts.

The following year Paterson served on committees that established the census, framed copyright laws for "the encouragement of learning," and drafted "a bill defining the crimes and offences that shall be cognizable under the authority of the United States and their punishment." As a senator, Paterson was a strong voice for a centrally controlled economic structure. He supported Secretary of the Treasury Alexander Hamilton's

Federalist policies with such enthusiasm that a hostile critic described him as a member of Hamilton's "gladiatorial band."

In July 1790 Paterson's friend William Livingston, the governor of New Jersey, died, and Paterson was unanimously elected by the legislature to complete his term. Paterson resigned his seat in the Senate. Leaving New York was no burden because he would be closer to his family and, in his own words, "Gay life has never been my wish: my disposition is naturally pensive." He was reelected governor of New Jersey for three consecutive one-year terms, during which time he codified the state laws and made court proceedings more efficient. With his friend Hamilton he planned an industrial city on the Passaic River, with the proposed name of Paterson.

On March 4, 1793, George Washington appointed Paterson to the U.S. Supreme Court. The president had written to him February 20: "I think it necessary to select a person who is not only professionally qualified to discharge that important trust, but one who is known to the public, and whose conduct meets their approbation. I shall have the satisfaction to believe that our country will be pleased with and benefited by the acquisition." This appointment carried with it prestige and a salary of $3,500, but there were associated burdens. As the newest appointee to the Court, Paterson was assigned to the vast southern circuit. Once a year Paterson had to travel from New York to attend trials in North Carolina, South Carolina, and Georgia, a round trip of several thousand miles. Riding the circuit was no joy for Paterson: the roads were bad, the lodgings were uncomfortable, and transportation was slow and unpredictable.

While on the Court, Paterson participated in several of the most famous and important cases in American jurisprudence. The first of these, and the one for which he was best known in his lifetime, was *Van Horne's Lessee v. Dorrance* (1795), a circuit court case. It invalidated a Pennsylvania statute as being in conflict with the federal and state constitutions because it violated the rights of property. Paterson used this case to deliver a lecture on the nature of constitutional governments.

What is a Constitution? It is a form of government, delineated by the mighty hand of the people, in which certain first principles of (or?) fundamental laws are established. The Constitution is certain and fixed; it contains the permanent will of the people, and is the supreme law of the land; it is paramount to the power of the Legislature, and can be revoked or altered only by the authority that made it. . . . What are Legislatures? Creatures of the Constitution; they owe their existence to the Constitution; they derive their power from the Constitution; It is their commission; and, therefore, all their acts must be conformable to it, or else they will be void. The Constitution is the work or will of the People themselves, in their original, sovereign, and unlimited capacity. Law is the work or will of the Legislature in their derivative or subordinate capacity. The one is the work of the Creator, and the other of the Creature. The Constitution fixes limits to the exercise of legislative authority and prescribes the orbit within which it must move. In short, gentlemen, the Constitution is the sun of the political system, around which all Legislative, Executive, and Judicial bodies must revolve. Whatever may be the case in other countries, yet in this there can be no doubt, that every act of the Legislature, repugnant to the Constitution, is absolutely void.

Paterson's *Van Horne* opinion served as an important precedent for *Marbury v. Madison* (1803), probably the most glorified and celebrated Supreme Court opinion in American history. *Marbury* established the right of the judicial branch to review and void acts of the executive and legislative branches if the acts violate the Constitution. In his *Marbury* opinion, Chief Justice John Marshall paraphrased Paterson's opinion in *Van Horne*. Paterson had written: "There can be no doubt, that every act of the Legislature, repugnant to the Constitution, is absolutely void." Eight years later, Marshall wrote these substantially similar words: "that an act of the legislature, repugnant to the constitution, is void." As to the Court's right to review statutes, Paterson had said, "I take it to be a clear position; that if a legislative act oppugns [contradicts] a constitutional principle, the

A federal tax on carriages, such as those awaiting their passengers outside the Capitol, was the subject of *Hylton v. United States* (1796), an important Supreme Court decision. The carriage tax was sustained, after a debate about the revenue-raising power of the new national government. *Source: Library of Congress*

former must give way, and be rejected on the score of repugnance. I hold it to be a position equally clear and sound, that, in such case, it will be the duty of the Court to adhere to the Constitution, and declare the act null and void." Marshall restated this principle in these words: "So if a law be in opposition to the constitution . . . the court must determine which of these conflicting rules governs the case. This is the very essence of the judicial duty."

In 1796 Paterson wrote one of the separate majority opinions in *Hylton v. United States.* In that case the Supreme Court considered whether in taxing carriages Congress had unconstitutionally enacted a "direct tax," which the Constitution required be apportioned among the states by population. Paterson's discussion in this case relied on both the Framers' intent and economist Adam Smith's definition of a direct tax as a tax ei-

ther on population or on land. Because carriages did not fit into these categories, he argued that taxing them constituted an indirect tax. Almost 100 years later this opinion proved pivotal when the Court declared the federal income tax unconstitutional. The Sixteenth Amendment was passed and ratified in 1913 to dispense with the requirement of apportionment.

In 1803 Paterson was severely injured when his coach went off the road and rolled down a ten-foot embankment. He never fully recovered, but continued on the Court until his death on September 9, 1806, while he was traveling to his daughter's home in Albany, New York. William Paterson was successful in each role offered to him—lawyer, senator, governor, statesman, and jurist. Along the way, the emigré from County Antrim amassed a sizable fortune, won fame, and made many influential friends.

Samuel Chase
1796-1811

SAMUEL CHASE was born April 17, 1741, in Somerset County, Maryland, on the east side of the Chesapeake Bay. His father, Thomas Chase, was a British-born clergyman of the Church of England. His mother, Matilda Walker Chase, the daughter of a Somerset County family, died when Samuel was born. Reverend Chase and his son moved to Baltimore in 1744, where Samuel received a good classical education studying under his father's supervision.

The Chases seemed always to be short of money, even though a clergyman was considered to be a gentleman. As a result, Samuel Chase developed some rather contradictory attitudes. On the one hand, he had considerable sympathy for the problems of the common man and rather crude manners. On the other hand, he accepted the idea that a responsible elite should govern. Chase believed that membership in such an elite should be based on merit, not birth or political patronage. But he always wanted to achieve landed wealth and be accepted as one of the colony's elite.

In 1759 Samuel Chase began his legal training in the office of John Hall, an Annapolis, Maryland, attorney. After a slow start Chase built his own successful practice and later represented Annapolis in Maryland's colonial legislature. The domed building at center is the State House, where the legislature convened. *Courtesy of the Hammond-Harwood House Association*

Chase studied law in the Annapolis office of attorney John Hall from 1759 until his admission to the bar in 1763. He had difficulty getting business from the upper class and at first mainly defended debtors. Eventually, he built a successful practice in Annapolis, the colonial and state capital, where he remained until 1786, when he moved to Baltimore. In 1762 Chase married Ann Baldwin, the daughter of a bankrupt farmer. They had seven children, three of whom died in infancy. Ann died some time between 1776 and 1779. In 1784 Chase was remarried to Hannah Kitty Giles of Kentbury, Berks, England, who bore him two daughters.

Chase won election to the lower house of Maryland's colonial legislature in 1764 and represented Annapolis or Anne Arundel County there until the American Revolution. By the early 1770s he had become one of the colony's foremost political leaders, both as a gifted legislator and as a fiery leader of crowds protesting the British policies that led to the Revolution. Other demonstrations he led against the city government caused the Annapolis mayor and aldermen to condemn him as a "busy, restless incendiary, a ringleader of mobs, a foul-mouthed and inflaming son of discord."

One of the first prominent Marylanders to endorse independence, Chase represented his state at the First and Second Continental Congresses, 1774–1778. He served on as many as thirty committees and urged that the colonies unite in an economic boycott of England. With Benjamin Franklin and Charles Carroll, Chase participated in an unsuccessful mission to Montreal to persuade Canada to join the colonies in their revolt against Great Britain. In 1776 Chase signed the Declaration of Independence and successfully gathered support for the document in Maryland.

Chase was one of the authors of the Maryland Constitution of 1776. He wanted to design a state government that would keep power in the hands of gentlemen of property, yet make sure that those gentlemen governed responsibly for the common good and were ultimately answerable to the wishes of the majority of voters. He was generally pleased with the final document.

Serving in the Maryland House of Delegates for all but a year and a half from 1777 to 1788, Chase proposed more important legislation than any other Maryland politician during those years. Repeatedly, however, his proposals met with strong opposition in the independent, elitist Senate that Chase had helped to design. Increasingly, Chase reverted to the role he had played before independence, that of champion of the common man against an allegedly selfish ruling elite. The climax came in the 1786–1787 term, when Chase led an unsuccessful campaign for state paper money and debt relief laws to help debtors who were in danger of losing all their property during those years of economic depression.

He failed again in 1788 when he opposed Maryland's ratification of the U.S. Constitution in a newspaper article signed "Caution" and as a delegate to the state ratifying convention. He thought the Constitution concentrated too much power in the central government, where the common man would have little influence and liberty would be endangered. Chase's stand against the Constitution cost him his seat in the state legislature.

Out of office in 1788, Chase was also bankrupt. He had always lived beyond his means, going into debt to buy large amounts of land. He had been dismissed from the Continental Congress for two years for allegedly attempting to corner the flour market through speculation in 1778. Investments in war-supply businesses and coal and iron operations during the war also had fared poorly. From 1778 on, constant (and sometimes true) charges that he used his political position for his own gain damaged his reputation. Chase's failure to secure debt relief legislation in 1786 and 1787 meant the end of his dreams of landed wealth.

At this point the aging Chase sought a position of honor and financial security. He became a local judge in Baltimore County in 1788 and was named chief judge of the Maryland General Court in 1791. Irked that Chase held two judgeships simultaneously, and annoyed by his overbearing manner on the bench, the Maryland assembly tried to strip him of his judicial posts, but not enough votes could be mustered to force him out.

Increasingly, Chase aligned himself with the emerging Federalist party. He feared that the radical ideas of the French Revolution would spread to America, putting social order and religion in danger. Again, as in 1776, he began to favor a strong government led by an elite to preserve order and liberty.

President George Washington nominated Samuel Chase to the Supreme Court January 26, 1796, and the Senate unenthusiastically confirmed the nomination the next day. Washington had several reasons for choosing Chase—his great legal ability, his services during the Revolution, his recent conversion to the Federalist party, and the urging of Maryland Federalist leader James McHenry. Another important consideration was that it was difficult to find qualified lawyers who would take the job. The Supreme Court was not yet very powerful, nor did it pay well. And justices had to endure the physical strain of riding long distances to preside over the circuit courts as well.

By 1800 Justice Chase had made clear his belief that the Supreme Court was the final authority on the constitutionality of state and federal laws, a position considered controversial at that time. But he also advocated judicial restraint: the Court should uphold acts of the legislative branch unless they were very clearly in conflict with the Constitution. Chase thought that the Constitution should be interpreted strictly. The U.S. government had only those powers the Constitution expressly gave it. He was ahead of his time in insisting that the federal courts should adopt uniform procedural rules, rather than following

The Sedition Act, which made it a crime to criticize the U.S. government or its leaders, became law in 1798 and was repealed in 1801. Of the twenty-five people arrested under the act, one was Rep. Matthew Lyon of Vermont, shown in this contemporary cartoon attacking a fellow member of Congress. Samuel Chase's enthusiastic support for the Sedition Act was one reason for his impeachment. *Source: Library of Congress*

the practice of the state where each case arose or was tried.

Chase's first Supreme Court opinion, in *Ware v. Hylton* (1796), has been called a masterpiece of legal reasoning. It struck down a Virginia law regarding the payment of debts owed to Britons that was contrary to the 1783 Treaty of Paris. His opinion gave teeth to the constitutional provision that treaties were the supreme law of the land. In *Hylton v. United States* (1796), Chase upheld the constitutionality of a national excise tax on carriages and provided a definition of direct taxes under the Constitution that was accepted until 1895. His definition of the constitutional meaning of *ex post facto* laws, which are laws affecting matters preceding their enactment, in *Calder v. Bull* (1798) is still accepted today. He held that the constitutional prohibition of *ex post facto* laws applied only to criminal trials, not to cases in which one person sued another. In the circuit court case of *United States v. Worrall* (1798), Chase voiced but eventually withdrew the opinion that the English common law could not be enforced in U.S. federal courts, an unusual position for Federalists at the

time, but one that the Supreme Court accepted in 1812.

Justice Chase became most widely known for his zealous enforcement of the Sedition Act of 1798. That law prohibited "false, scandalous, and malicious" attacks on the government, the president, or Congress. It was an attempt to curb outspoken criticism of the administration of President John Adams by journalists and politicians of the rival Democratic-Republican party during an undeclared naval war with France that Republicans opposed. Chase had long believed that freedom of the press had its limits, and he now thought that the often vicious attacks on the nation's leaders that were being made by Republican editorialists exceeded those limits. He presided over several highly publicized sedition trials in the circuit courts in 1799 and 1800. In those cases, and in the 1800 treason trial of Pennsylvania riot leader John Fries, Chase appeared eager to see the defendants convicted. Republicans accused him of obvious bias and unusual procedures that made the trials unfair.

Chase's conduct, and possibly his personality, made him a major target after the Republicans won the election of 1800. He was tall, stout, red-faced (some called him "Old Bacon Face"), and physically imposing. Fiery and impulsive, he often attacked political opponents without restraint. His was not a judicial temperament.

Conflict mounted between President Thomas Jefferson and the Republican Congress on the one hand, and the Federalist judges on the other. In 1803 Chase told a federal grand jury in Baltimore that Maryland's new state law abolishing property qualifications for voting would lead to the destruction of liberty and property rights. Reportedly he also made a political attack on Jefferson from the bench. In fact, he probably did not, but the incident provoked Jefferson to suggest that the

The efforts of Rep. John Randolph of Roanoke, Virginia, to prosecute Samuel Chase in his 1805 impeachment trial before the Senate were no match for the defense, and Chase was acquitted. The House of Representatives had earlier voted to impeach Chase, a Federalist, for showing bias against Democratic-Republican defendants in circuit court trials. *Source: National Portrait Gallery*

House of Representatives consider Chase's impeachment, although the president took no subsequent part in it.

In 1804 the House voted to impeach Chase on eight charges. Seven charges accused him of procedural errors and bias in the Fries trial and the sedition cases. The eighth in effect accused him of seditious criticism of Jefferson in the 1803 Baltimore grand jury charge. When Chase was tried before the U.S. Senate in 1805, his chief prosecutor, Rep. John Randolph of Roanoke, Virginia, bungled the prosecution. Chase's lawyers did a fine job of presenting his conduct in the best possible light, and he was acquitted. Some Republican senators came to believe that any misconduct on Chase's part was not serious enough to justify his conviction and removal from office. Others hesitated to convict him in the belief that his impeachment was motivated more by party politics than by any real offense on Chase's part. Chase's acquittal helped establish that impeachment would be used sparingly in the future. Judges and other officials could not be successfully impeached just because they took positions that were politically unpopular.

Despite his troubles with his fellow politicians, Chase did not hold personal grudges once a political battle was over. He was basically warm-hearted and sympathetic to those in distress. People who were not repelled by his often gruff manner or his politics found him sociable, talkative, and a very pleasant companion.

It is impossible to say how much Chase contributed to the Supreme Court's decisions after John Marshall became chief justice in 1801. Marshall wrote all the Court's major opinions, and one can only guess at Chase's influence behind the scenes. Despite declining health, including attacks of gout that periodically kept him off the bench, Chase continued to serve on the Supreme Court. He died from "ossification of the heart" in Baltimore on June 19, 1811.

Oliver Ellsworth
1796-1800

Source: Independence National Historical Park

OLIVER ELLSWORTH was born April 29, 1745, in the Connecticut farming village of Windsor, where his great-grandfather had settled after emigrating from England nearly a century earlier. He was one of seven children of Capt. David Ellsworth and Jemima Leavitt Ellsworth. Oliver studied with a minister in Bethlehem, Connecticut, before entering Yale at seventeen. He was forced to leave Yale at the end of his sophomore year when a number of mischievous incidents resulted in his dismissal, but soon found himself back in school—this time at the College of New Jersey (later Princeton). There he established a debating society with fellow student William Paterson, whom he would later join on the Supreme Court.

After graduation in 1766, Ellsworth returned to Windsor where, at the urging of his father, he began theological training. A year later, he abandoned theology for the law, taking prominent Connecticut lawyer Matthew Griswold as his mentor. Griswold's fees proved too costly, however, and Ellsworth left him for the less prominent but more affordable Jesse Root. In 1771 he gained admission to the Connecticut bar.

The following year Ellsworth married sixteen-year-old Abigail Wolcott, the niece of former Connecticut governor Roger Wolcott. The connections his marriage brought would help set the course of his political and economic fortunes. The young couple rented a farm near Windsor from Ellsworth's father and earned their primary income from Ellsworth's wood-cutting business. He managed to cultivate a few legal clients, but collected only paltry fees. When court opened at Hartford, ten miles away, Ellsworth would walk the distance to drum up any stray legal business not taken by the leaders of the town's bar.

Eventually, his law business blossomed, and he moved to Hartford to be closer to the courts and clients. By 1779 his reputation had grown significantly. His law clerk that year, the future lexicographer Noah Webster, reported that Ellsworth was actively engaged in more than 1,000 cases.

His political career also progressed. Elected to represent Windsor in the Connecticut General Assembly in

1773, he became justice of the peace for Hartford County the following year and soon thereafter a member of the Committee of the Pay Table, which supervised the state's Revolutionary War expenditures. Other appointments came in rapid succession. In 1777 he became state's attorney for Hartford County, a position that did not interfere with his law practice or other legislative duties.

His debut in national politics came in 1777 when he was selected to represent Connecticut at the Continental Congress. Although he served on any number of committees, boards, and commissions, two committee memberships foreshadowed his appointment to the Supreme Court and later his service as minister plenipotentiary to France. As a member of the Committee on International Treaties, he became familiar with international and admiralty law. More important, his membership on the Committee of Appeals gave him judicial responsibilities in the nation's first established court of appeals.

During the years he represented Connecticut in the Continental Congress, Ellsworth continued to rise in

Ralph Earl finished painting this portrait of Oliver Ellsworth and Abigail Wolcott Ellsworth in 1792, four years before Ellsworth became chief justice. The couple is seated in the library at Elmwood, their home in Windsor, Connecticut, which is cleverly pictured through the open window. Ellsworth holds the Constitution in his left hand.
Source: Wadsworth Atheneum, Hartford, Connecticut. Gift of the Ellsworth heirs.

state politics. He found time to represent Hartford County in the state's General Assembly, serve on the powerful Council of Safety, and participate in the Governor's Council. His success in Connecticut politics earned him a seat on the bench of the Supreme Court of Errors and a year later a judgeship on the state's superior court.

With the apparent failure of the Articles of Confederation, the states called a constitutional convention in Philadelphia in 1787. Connecticut selected Ellsworth as one of its three delegates. Within days of the opening of the convention, the explosive issue of representation was on the floor, embodied in the Virginia Plan, which called for states to be represented in both houses of the national legislature on the basis of population. The small state delegations feared that a national government whose legislature was apportioned by population would go against their interests. They proposed instead a unicameral legislature with representation by states, a scheme known as the Paterson plan.

By mid-June, with small state delegations at loggerheads with large state delegations, the convention was poised, in the words of one delegate, "on the verge of dissolution, scarce held together by the strength of a

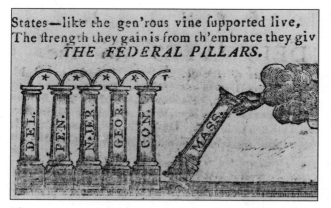

This 1788 cartoon, entitled "United They Stand, Divided They Fall," shows a hand reaching from a cloud to set Massachusetts in line with states that had already agreed to ratify the Constitution. Sen. Oliver Ellsworth's compromise plan of government appealed to both large and small states. *Source: Library of Congress*

hair." At this point, the Connecticut delegation put forth another idea. Ellsworth's colleague, Roger Sherman, previously had proposed that each state be accorded an equal vote in the Senate with representation in the lower house proportional to population. Ellsworth joined Sherman and proposed "a general government partly federal and partly national," a principle that, while reflecting a unified government, could lead to a compromise.

Why not, Ellsworth asked, create a national legislature composed of two bodies: the first branch of the legislature (the House) could be based on proportional representation, thus favoring the most populous states and satisfying the national principle; the second branch (the Senate) could be based on equal representation for each state, thus favoring the less populous states and comporting with the federal principle. Ellsworth's proposal outlined the scheme of the new government of the United States and helped to avoid a dissolution of the convention and with it the Union. Although he had to leave the convention before signing the document, Ellsworth worked diligently to ensure the ratification of the Constitution in Connecticut. His efforts were rewarded when he was selected to be a U.S. senator in 1789. His reputation as a coalition builder and leader quickly propelled him to the forefront of the Senate leadership, and he became one of the administration's chief spokesmen.

Ellsworth was appointed to head the important Senate Rules Committee, and he pursued his duties with vigor. By the second session of the First Congress he was serving on thirty-six committees, on many of them as chairman, while his colleagues each averaged eleven committee memberships. Ellsworth suggested a trade embargo of Rhode Island to force it into the Union. He worked with others to organize the army and the post office and to establish a national census. He served on the committee that considered Alexander Hamilton's plan for funding the national debt and for incorporating the Bank of the United States, and he quickly became one of Hamilton's most ardent proponents. He helped draft the bill that allowed for North Carolina's admission to the Union and wrote the legislation that inaugurated the consular service.

Of all the committees Ellsworth chaired, perhaps none was as important as the Senate Judiciary Committee. As the principal author of the Judiciary Act of 1789 (sections 10 through 23 of the original draft are in Ellsworth's hand) he gave life to Article III of the Constitution that called for the "judicial Power of the United States . . . [to] be vested in one supreme Court, and in such inferior Courts as the Congress may from time to time ordain and establish."

Ellsworth was described as a physically "robust man" with "broad shoulders," who stood six feet, two inches tall, with blue eyes and a high forehead. His personal appearance was "always scrupulously elegant—he invariably wore a white, ruffled shirt, silk stockings, and silver knee-buckles." He had the habit of consuming great quantities of snuff and harbored an intense hatred of correspondence. During his Senate service, his wife Abigail gave birth to twins. William Ellsworth would follow in his father's footsteps, becoming a lawyer, member of Congress, and governor of Connecticut.

When the Senate rejected South Carolinian John Rutledge as chief justice of the United States, President George Washington nominated Ellsworth. The appointment met with immediate and widespread approval. New Hampshire representative Jeremiah Smith voiced his approval to a colleague. "No appointment in the U.S. has been more wise or judicious than this: He is a very able lawyer, a very learned man, a very great Politician, and a very honest man; in short he is every thing one would desire." John Adams described Ellsworth as having "the Stiffness of Connecticut; though his Air and Gait are not elegant; though he can not enter a Room nor retire from it with the Ease and Grace of a Courtier: yet his Understanding is as sound,

his Information as good and his heart as Steady as any Man can boast." During Ellsworth's four years as chief justice, he tried to persuade the Court to hand down *per curiam* opinions (single decisions representing the will of the entire Court) as opposed to *seriatim* decisions (a series of separate opinions by individual justices), a change that would be pursued with greater vigor and success by John Marshall.

Ellsworth participated in fewer than a dozen opinions and in none of the landmark cases that were decided during his service. The decisions in which Ellsworth did participate mostly revolved around the scope of the judiciary's power. In *United States v. La Vengeance* (1796) Ellsworth set out the boundaries of federal admiralty jurisdiction under Section 9 of the Judiciary Act, which he and his associate William Paterson had drafted. The case is significant because subsequent Courts cited it as the first that extended federal admiralty jurisdiction beyond the confines of British law. Ellsworth further defined the judiciary's boundaries in his one-page opinion in *Turner v. Bank of North America* (1799), upholding congressional power to determine the jurisdiction of the federal courts under Article III of the Constitution.

In *Moodie v. Ship Phoebe Anne* (1796) the validity of the Franco-American Treaty of 1778 was tested before the Court. The attorney representing British interests argued the "impolicy and inconveniency" of allowing French privateers to equip in American ports. Ellsworth, speaking for the Court, responded that "suggestions of policy and conveniency cannot be considered in the judicial determination of a question of right." The treaty with France, the chief justice pointed out, allowed French vessels to enter American ports for emergency repairs and therefore no violation of neutrality took place.

In July 1798 the Federalist-dominated Congress passed the first of a series of acts designed to stifle freedom of speech rights of pro-French and anti-adminis-

In 1796 the Supreme Court was asked to decide whether French ships, such as the two depicted here in New York Harbor in 1794, had the right to equip themselves in American ports. At a time when relations between the two countries were hostile, the Supreme Court dismissed questions of politics and upheld the validity of the Franco-American Treaty of 1778, which allowed French privateers to stop along American shores for emergency repairs. *Source: Museum of the City of New York*

tration critics. The justices in support of the president and Congress began delivering pointed charges to grand juries in all judicial circuits, calling for them to seek out and bring to the bar persons violating the statutes. In this context Ellsworth issued a charge to the grand jury attacking the anti-Federalists' opposition to the idea of the United States adopting the English common law. For Ellsworth, the common law "as brought from the country of our ancestors, with here and there an accommodating exception, in nature of local customs, was the law of every part of the union at the formation of the national compact." The notion that the Founders intended a "discontinuance" of the common law "is not to be presumed; and is a supposition irreconcilable with those frequent references in the constitution, to the common law, as a living code."

The August 1799 term was Ellsworth's last as a presiding chief justice. The previous February, President John Adams had appointed him minister plenipotentiary to France in an attempt to head off war with that country. For the remainder of 1799, Ellsworth waited for the president's call. In November it came, and he and two colleagues embarked on their mission, leaving behind the court he had worked so hard to create. Ellsworth's negotiations over reparations for French seizures of American merchant ships resulted in temporarily patched-up relations between France and the United States. At home, however, the treaty was not well received by the Federalists, who were hoping for a complete failure of the mission.

On October 16, 1800, Ellsworth, now fifty-five years old, wrote to President Adams that the constant affliction of "the gravel, and the gout in my kidneys, the unfortunate fruit of sufferings at sea, and by a winter's journey through Spain," combined to prevent his return to the Court. He spent the remainder of the winter recuperating in the restorative waters of Bath, England.

The following spring he returned to a life of semiretirement, serving on the Governor's Council. He later accepted, but then declined because of ill health, the chief justiceship of the state supreme court. He died at his farm in Windsor November 26, 1807.

Ellsworth's contemporaries provided a lasting description of the nation's third chief justice. Sen. William Maclay of Pennsylvania described him as "all-powerful and eloquent in debate," while diplomat William Vans Murray "profoundly admired the neatness and accuracy of his mind."

Bushrod Washington

1799-1829

BORN JUNE 5, 1762, in Westmoreland County, Virginia, Bushrod Washington was the son of John Augustine Washington, a delegate to the Virginia legislature, and Hannah Bushrod Washington, the daughter of an illustrious Virginia family. Present on the day of Bushrod's birth was his uncle, George Washington, the future first president of the United States. Having no children of his own, George Washington would take a special interest in the career and well-being of his "favorite nephew."

Young Bushrod was privately tutored in the classics at the home of Richard Henry Lee and graduated from the College of William and Mary at age sixteen. He returned to his alma mater in the spring of 1780 to study under George Wythe, the first professor of law in the United States. Washington shared classes with John Marshall, and the two future justices were elected to the Phi Beta Kappa Society, then a secret fraternity. Marshall left the school after a short time, but Washington remained at William and Mary through the fall, ob-

The first law professor to teach in an American college, George Wythe boasted two future Supreme Court justices, Bushrod Washington and John Marshall, among his students at the College of William and Mary. Wythe's concept of the law also influenced other future leaders such as Henry Clay, Thomas Jefferson, and James Monroe. *Source: National Portrait Gallery*

taining a far more extensive formal education than most American law students of the day.

When Lord Cornwallis's army invaded Virginia, Washington volunteered for duty in the Continental Army and joined a cavalry unit under the command of Col. John Francis Mercer. Serving as a private of dragoons, Washington was involved in the final stages of the War of Independence, seeing action at Green Spring and later witnessing the surrender of Cornwallis at Yorktown.

Washington received further legal training by study-

ing for two years in Philadelphia under prominent attorney James Wilson, a signer of the Declaration of Independence. Washington would succeed Wilson as an associate justice on the Supreme Court of the United States sixteen years later.

Completing his tutelage at twenty-one, Washington began his law practice in Westmoreland County, Virginia, before moving to Alexandria, Virginia, where he specialized in chancery cases. In 1785 he married Julia Ann Blackburn, a music lover and the daughter of an aide de camp of his illustrious uncle. Julia Washington's physical and mental health would prove poor throughout her life, and the couple had no children. Despite her frailty, she often accompanied her husband on the arduous trips he made as a circuit judge.

Bushrod Washington's interest in politics soon got him involved in the Patriotic Society, a political club of tidewater-area Virginians, and he began to aspire to elective office. In 1787 Washington successfully ran for election to the Virginia House of Delegates, where he joined his old classmate John Marshall. Both men also served as active members of the Virginia convention to ratify the U.S. Constitution. Following the victory over ratification, Washington established a successful law practice in Richmond, where he sometimes faced John Marshall as an adversary before the Virginia Court of Appeals—then the nation's highest court. Between 1792 and 1796 he was involved in nearly one-quarter of the cases heard by that court, finally earning himself enough money to hire law clerks. He kept careful notes of cases brought before the court, and published them as a two-volume work, *Reports of Cases Argued in the Court of Appeals of Virginia.*

A serious student of the law, Washington was avid in his pursuit of legal knowledge. In evaluating him as a candidate for the Supreme Court, Secretary of State Thomas Pickering would later remark on the toll Washington's studiousness had taken on his health: "[His] indefatigable pursuit of knowledge and the business of his profession has deprived him of the sight of one eye, it will be happy if the loss does not make him the perfect emblem of justice." Despite high praise for his abilities, one Philadelphia attorney would find fault in Washington's singular focus on his profession, noting that "[his] literary reading was so limited that it is questionable whether he ever knew who was the author of *Macbeth*." If Washington's boundless enthusiasm for studying the law had distracted him from pursuing a broader education, this same diligence, and the deep understanding of legal principles it fostered, made him an excellent teacher of the law. Many aspiring attorneys sought to study under him, including Henry Clay, perhaps his most famous student.

Washington enjoyed a close relationship with George Washington, who had considerable influence on his early career. He had financed Bushrod's legal apprenticeship under James Wilson, and in 1798 he urged him to run for a seat in the Virginia legislature. Bushrod followed his uncle's advice reluctantly, because he had grown weary of politics and preferred practicing law. It did not make it easier that George Washington, who scorned nepotism, insisted his nephew make his own way in politics. In several instances he bent over backwards to give the appearance of fairness. As president, Washington refused Bushrod's request to be appointed U.S. attorney for the District of Virginia.

When Justice Wilson's death opened up a seat on the Court in 1798, the former president refrained from using his influence to secure his nephew's appointment. In any case, President John Adams was determined to place either Bushrod Washington or John Marshall on the Court in order to reestablish Virginia's representation, which had lapsed with the resignation of John Blair in 1796. Both men were eminently qualified, but Adams instructed Secretary of State Timothy Pickering to offer the seat to Marshall, who had seniority at the bar. Marshall, who preferred to run for Congress, declined the nomination and recommended Bushrod

Julia Ann Blackburn Washington's father was an aide de camp to Gen. George Washington, Bushrod Washington's illustrious uncle. At Mount Vernon, the estate Bushrod inherited from his childless uncle, Julia showed her love for music by staging concerts. *Source: Portrait of Julia Ann Blackburn Washington attributed to Chester Harding, Collection of the Supreme Court of the United States*

Washington. As his own bid for Congress was half-hearted at best because of his preference for the law over politics, Washington gladly quit the campaign trail a few months before the Virginia congressional election to accept a temporary recess appointment to the high court.

Easily confirmed by the Federalist-dominated Senate December 20, 1798, Washington had by then already

Former classmates John Marshall and Bushrod Washington often crossed paths in Richmond's hallways of power. Both served in Virginia's House of Delegates and maintained prestigious legal practices, sometimes finding themselves opponents in the Virginia Court of Appeals. This 1798 watercolor by Benjamin Latrobe shows Richmond from the South; on a hill in the distance, to the left, can be seen a house once owned by Bushrod Washington. *Source: Maryland Historical Society, Baltimore*

attended, as a recess appointee, a November circuit court session in Augusta, Georgia, which marked his first experience as a judge. A short, untidy man who liked snuff and suffered from ill health, Washington was nonetheless meticulous and well organized about his work. His tenure on the Court coincided largely with the service of his old friend John Marshall, who accepted appointment as chief justice in 1801. During that time, Marshall enhanced the Court's prestige by capably massing it to speak with a single voice, thanks in no small part to Washington, who was Marshall's strongest supporter and a cohesive force on the Court. Because he preferred to defer to Marshall, Washington wrote only seventy majority opinions in his thirty-one years on the bench and formally dissented only once. Justice Joseph Story, himself a strong supporter of Marshall, once credited Washington with persuading him to suppress a dissent by expressing his view that "delivering dissenting opinions on ordinary occasions weakens the authority of the Court, and is of no public benefit." Although Washington disagreed only three times with Marshall during their twenty-nine years together

on the bench, it was Washington who forced the chief justice into his only dissenting role on a constitutional question. In *Ogden v. Saunders* (1827) Washington broke a tie on the Court with a vote in favor of state insolvency laws.

Despite his deference to Marshall, Washington was a well-respected judge with considerable backbone. While riding circuit in Philadelphia, he courageously ignored threats on his life and sentenced a Pennsylvania militia general to jail for obstructing federal process. Washington's experiences in the Pennsylvania circuit court made him an authority on admiralty law, and Chief Justice Marshall often asked his advice on difficult issues in this field.

Washington's otherwise admirable reputation has been tarnished by his slave-holding practices. When George Washington died, he bequeathed his Mount Vernon estate to Bushrod with instructions that he was to free the slaves upon the death of his wife, Martha Washington. Many of the slaves had already been liberated by the time she died in 1802, and Bushrod dutifully freed the remainder. However, he subsequently

Sea captain and shipbuilder Paul Cuffee (in silhouette) was an influential and wealthy freedman from Massachusetts. In 1816 he took a group of American blacks to colonize Sierra Leone because he believed they would never be completely accepted by a white society. This experiment inspired prominent slaveholders, such as Bushrod Washington, to found the American Colonization Society, which persuaded Congress to purchase territory for black Americans in Africa. *Source: Library of Congress*

brought his own slaves to Mount Vernon in an attempt to return the seriously dilapidated property to a profitable operation. But, lacking farming experience, Washington pushed the estate even deeper into debt. Rising insubordination among the slaves, including arson and several escapes, along with growing evidence that a large slave contingent could not support itself at Mount Vernon, prompted Washington to sell more than half of the Mount Vernon slaves in 1821. He made a deliberate but only partially successful attempt to ensure that families would not be separated on the auction block.

When the news broke, abolitionists charged that he should have followed his uncle's example and freed his slaves. Washington contended that they were his property to do with as he saw fit. He did believe, however, that slavery should be gradually eliminated. As the lifetime president of the American Colonization Society, he supported efforts to encourage the voluntary emancipation and resettling of free blacks in Africa—a movement not generally favored by abolitionists. Indeed, the most outspoken critics of Washington's sale of his slaves were no doubt covertly trying to discredit the American Colonization Society.

Justice Washington died November 26, 1829, while on circuit court business in Philadelphia; his heart-broken wife died while bringing his body back to Mount Vernon for burial three days later. Justice Story, who shared the bench with Washington for many years, eulogized him with these words:

He was a learned judge. Not that every-day learning which may be gathered up by a hasty reading of books and cases; but that which is the result of long-continued laborious services, and comprehensive studies. He read to learn, and not to quote; to digest and master, and not merely to display. He was not easily satisfied. If he was not as profound as some, he was more exact than most men. But the value of his learning was, that it was the keystone of all his judgments. He indulged not the rash desire to fashion the law to his own views; but to follow out its precepts, with a sincere good faith and simplicity. Hence, he possessed the happy faculty of yielding just the proper weight to authority; neither, on the one hand, surrendering himself to the dictates of other judges, nor, on the other hand, overruling settled doctrines upon his own private notions of policy or justice.

Alfred Moore
1800-1804

Source: Etching of Alfred Moore by Albert Rosenthal, Collection of the Supreme Court of the United States

ALFRED MOORE was born May 21, 1755, in the town of Brunswick in New Hanover County, North Carolina. His birthplace is in the southeastern part of the state near the coastal city of Wilmington and less than twenty miles from the mouth of the Cape Fear River. His parents, Judge Maurice Moore and Anne Grange Moore, had three children, Alfred, Maurice, and Sarah, all of whom lived to adulthood.

The extended Moore family was part of the gentry class of Carolina landowners who made their fortunes in naval stores, lumber, and planting. The family's political influence matched its wealth: Alfred's great uncle, James Moore, served as governor of the province of South Carolina, and his grandfather had donated 320 acres from his more than 83,000-acre holdings to create Brunswick.

Following the death of his mother and his father's remarriage, Alfred was sent to Boston at age nine for his formal education. There, according to family lore, he caught the attention of the commander of a British garrison, who offered the thirteen-year-old an ensign commission. The boy turned him down.

Returning to North Carolina, Moore studied law under the direction of his father. In 1775 he was admitted to the bar and married Susanna Elizabeth Eagles, also of Brunswick. The same year he took up arms against the British. With his brother, Maurice, Moore joined the First North Carolina Regiment of the Continental Line, which was commanded by their uncle, Col. James Moore. As captain and company commander, Moore fought in the battle of Moore's Creek Bridge and later served under his cousin, Maj. Gen. Robert Howe, at the battle of Charleston.

Despite their wealth and political influence, the Moore family paid dearly in the quest for American independence. Not long after the Moore's Creek Bridge campaign, Maurice died in a skirmish. Six months later his father and uncle were killed on the same day. Sarah Moore's husband, Francis Nash, took over the command from Colonel Moore and fell at the battle of Germantown.

The series of tragedies that befell the twenty-three-year-old Moore and his family prompted him to resign his commission and return to manage the family plantation, Buchoi, on Eagles Island near Wilmington. The respite from the battlefield was short-lived, however, and Moore took command of the local militia, who were busily harassing British lines around Wilmington. The British retaliated by burning his plantation buildings, carrying off his slaves, and destroying his crops. Following the British retreat from Wilmington in 1781, Moore served out the remainder of the war as a judge advocate of the North Carolina forces.

With the coming of peace, Moore returned to law and soon became one of the leaders of the state's bar. During this time he also represented Brunswick in the state legislature. In May 1782 the General Assembly appointed him to succeed his friend James Iredell (whom

Two of the brightest lawyers in North Carolina, William R. Davie and his friend Alfred Moore, dominated the bar in the state's formative years. They successfully campaigned to get the state to ratify the Constitution and collaborated in establishing the University of North Carolina. Elected governor in 1798, Davie resigned the following year to go to France on a peace mission. *Courtesy of North Carolina Division of Archives and History*

he would later succeed on the U.S. Supreme Court) as attorney general. In his eight-year tenure, Moore shaped the office and defined its function.

As the state's chief law officer, he often found himself at the bar opposite his friends Iredell and William R. Davie. Together, they constituted the best legal minds of the state. Moore also worked with Davie to establish

A satiric look at the plight of Loyalists after the Revolution shows a hapless Tory dangling from a "liberty pole." North Carolina sought a more practical form of revenge by passing a law upholding the state's right to confiscate and resell land seized from Loyalists during the Revolution. Alfred Moore and James Iredell, friends and fellow North Carolina lawyers, found themselves on opposing sides in an important state court case that struck down the confiscation statute.
Source: Library of Congress

the University of North Carolina and served as a trustee to the university for nearly the remainder of his life. In 1785 the state honored Moore, age thirty, by naming a county after him.

In 1787 Moore and Iredell met headlong over the now-famous case of *Bayard v. Singleton*. The case grew out of an act passed by the state legislature that required its courts to dismiss, upon petition by defendant, any claim made by Tories to land confiscated by North Carolina during the Revolution and subsequently

resold. In 1785 a suit was brought by the daughter of Samuel Cornell, a wealthy Tory and former resident of the state, who had left for England at the outbreak of the Revolution. Eight days before a confiscation bill passed the legislature, Cornell willed his daughter the land. The defendant and present owner of the land claimed title by virtue of a deed from the state superintendent of confiscated estates.

Moore moved for a dismissal under the confiscation statute, while Iredell, joined by his brother-in-law

Samuel Johnston, argued that the act violated the due process clause of the state constitution, which guaranteed trial by jury. The court, hoping that the legislature would repeal the act, deferred action only to be answered by an enraged Assembly, which clamored for their heads and began an inquiry into their near-treasonous behavior. Despite the political storm, the judges were exonerated. Emboldened, they ruled that the confiscation statute was unconstitutional and vague. The plaintiffs, however, lost before a jury who had little sympathy for the cause of Loyalists. The case was the first in which a court declared a legislative act unconstitutional. As such it provided a precedent for the doctrine of judicial review adopted by the Supreme Court in its landmark *Marbury v. Madison* (1803) decision.

Moore's political activities were not hindered by his attorney generalship. Appointed by the legislature to represent the state at the Annapolis Convention in 1786, he stood for election to the first state ratifying convention, but his Federalist orientation lost him the post. Following the failure of the state to ratify the Constitution, Moore again fought for a delegate's slot. This time he succeeded and, joined by friends Davie and Iredell, pushed ratification through.

He continued as attorney general until January 1791, when he resigned in protest of the legislature's creation of a solicitor general's office. He viewed the new position as an incursion on his own powers. In 1792 Moore returned to the state legislature and three years later made an unsuccessful bid for the U.S. Senate, losing by only one legislative vote to Democratic-Republican Timothy Bloodworth. Moore's Federalist loyalties drew the attention of President John Adams, who appointed him, in January 1798, one of three commissioners to conclude a treaty with the Cherokee Nation. He withdrew from negotiations, however, before the treaty was signed, and soon began service on the North Carolina Superior Court.

When Associate Justice James Iredell died, Adams considered appointing Davie to fill the Supreme Court seat, but he had just been made diplomatic envoy to France. Instead, the president once again turned to Moore, nominating him to the Supreme Court on December 4, 1799. He was confirmed by the Senate six days later and took the oath of office April 21, 1800, at the Circuit Court of the District of Georgia in Savannah.

Moore's five years on the Court were for the most part unremarkable. He delivered only one opinion, but it caused an outburst of criticism and condemnation from anti-Federalists. The 1800 case, *Bas v. Tingy,* came at a time when partisan feelings were running at a fever pitch. The Court held that a state of "limited partial" war existed between the United States and France. The decision buttressed the Federalist anti-French policy, both foreign and domestic. Democratic-Republicans, already incensed over the passage and enforcement of the Alien and Sedition Acts, which were hostile to foreigners and imposed stiff penalties for criticizing the government, exploded in rage. Calls for impeachment of the entire Court appeared in anti-Federalist newspapers throughout the country.

The *Bas* case was to be Moore's only contribution to jurisprudence. The remainder of his career became a story of missed opportunities. He missed the biggest case, *Marbury v. Madison,* because of a delay in traveling from his circuit-riding assignment on the southern circuit. He arrived in time to hear only a final witness and did not participate in the decision.

Moore's biographers and contemporaries describe him as a man who appeared "so small in stature that at first glance he seemed only a child, for his height was about four feet five inches, and he was proportionately slender." One contemporary noted that "probably he weighted [*sic*] about 80 or 90 pounds. His head was large for his body, after the manner of dwarfs, and his face . . . was fine-featured, good-humored and dark-eyed."

Samuel F. B. Morse executed this huge painting in oils in 1822. Measuring almost eleven feet wide and more than seven feet high, the painting depicts an evening session at the House of Representatives. The justices of the Supreme Court are seated on the dais on the far side of the chamber. *Source: Corcoran Gallery of Art, Museum Purchase*

Following his resignation from the Court January 26, 1804, because of ill health, Moore returned to North Carolina to continue his work building the university. He died six years later on October 15, 1810, at the Bladen County home of his daughter Anne and her husband Maj. Hugh Waddell. Judicial circuit riding and supervising plantations had taken their toll on the fifty-five-year-old former justice. He left his property and estates to his two sons, Alfred, Jr., and Maurice, and to his daughters, Anne and Sarah. Still a minor, Sarah was also provided with money for her education and for "a piano and proper music books." Moore willed his library and "philosophical and nautical instruments" to Alfred, Jr., who carried on the family's political tradition by becoming Speaker of the North Carolina House of Representatives and mayor of Wilmington.

By all accounts, Moore numbered among the leaders of the North Carolina bar of his generation. A brilliant lawyer, with a profound knowledge of criminal law, he had "a keen sense of humor, a brilliant wit, a biting tongue, a masterful logic, [which] made him an adversary at the bar to be feared." His "judgment . . . was almost intuitive. His manner of speech was animated, and he spoke with ease and with force enlivened with flashes of wit."

Despite the promise of his career at the bar, his service on the bench was eclipsed by that of his brethren and, in the words of one biographer, made "scarcely a ripple in American judicial history."

John Marshall

1801-1835

Source: Library of Congress

JOHN MARSHALL was born on the frontier near Germantown, Virginia, September 24, 1755. He was the eldest of fifteen children of Thomas Marshall, a member of the gentry, who served in the House of Burgesses from Fauquier County and as the county's representative to the Virginia Provincial Convention of 1775. Marshall's mother, Mary Randolph Keith Marshall, was the daughter of an Anglican minister, and through her the family was related to the large and prominent Randolph family, which included Thomas Jefferson. Young Marshall was tutored at the Westmoreland County academy conducted by Rev. Archibald Campbell; a fellow student was future president James Monroe. Subsequently, Marshall received instruction from James Thompson, an Anglican minister assigned to Fauquier County.

When hostilities broke out in Virginia following the battles of Lexington and Concord, Marshall, at age twenty, was chosen as lieutenant in the Culpeper Minute Men and fought in the battle of Great Bridge.

Sent on a mission to France to reduce hostilities and avert war, John Marshall, Elbridge Gerry, and Charles Cotesworth Pinckney were asked by agents of Talleyrand, the foreign minister, for a $250,000 bribe and a $10 million loan to France before they would even consider holding talks. This anti-French cartoon depicts the insulted Americans refusing to pay the five-headed French Directory, while French revolutionaries feast on frogs in the shadow of a guillotine.
Source: Huntington Library and Art Gallery

Returning home he was appointed lieutenant in the Eleventh Virginia Continental Regiment. Although his company participated in a number of regimental re-alignments, Marshall, who was promoted to captain, served with many of the same men, leading them in the battles of Brandywine, Germantown, and Stony Point.

After his war service Marshall went back to Virginia and studied law under George Wythe for three months in 1780 at the College of William and Mary. He was admitted to Phi Beta Kappa and, after returning to his native Fauquier County, to the Virginia bar. Marshall moved to Richmond in 1783, drawn to the capital city by his desire to practice in the central courts and the highest court, the Court of Appeals. Richmond was also the home of Mary Willis Ambler, the daughter of the state treasurer, whom Marshall had courted for several years. They were married in January 1783, and had ten children, raising six to adulthood in their relatively modest town residence near the state capitol complex. Polly, as Mary Marshall was called, suffered from nervous disorders and chronic illness most of her life.

Marshall's account books document a steady expansion in the size of his law practice, which increasingly centered around arguing appeals in the General Court, the High Court of Chancery, and the Court of Appeals. With the ratification of the federal Constitution in 1788, new legal business developed from the collection of pre-Revolutionary commercial debts owed to British mercantile firms by prominent Virginia planters. Marshall became one of the leading attorneys defending Virginians in the U.S. District Court of Virginia, and as a consequence he was selected to be lead counsel in arguing the landmark case, *Ware v. Hylton,* at the 1796 term of the U.S. Supreme Court. This case resulted in a ruling that Virginians could not be protected from actions brought by their British creditors that were based, in part, upon the provisions of the 1783 and 1794 treaties with Great Britain.

Before 1797 Marshall's political career was closely tied to his residence in Richmond. Perennially he held legislative office, either as a member of the Virginia House of Delegates or as a member of the Governor's Council of State. From July 1785 to March 1788 he was recorder of the Richmond City Hustings Court, his only judicial office before his appointment to the Supreme Court. Elected to the Virginia convention that ratified the federal Constitution in June 1788, he played only a limited role in supporting the ratification cause, but his speech on the judiciary did much to allay local fears of a federal court system.

After resisting a number of attempts to appoint him to federal office, Marshall accepted President John Adams's assignment to join Charles Cotesworth Pinckney and Elbridge Gerry on a diplomatic mission to revolutionary France. The French Directory insisted upon receiving a gift of tribute before they would negotiate with the American envoys. Pinckney and Marshall, having rejected the demands presented by three emissaries, designated Messrs. X, Y, and Z in diplomatic dispatches, returned home to publish their correspondence with the French. Public resentment against France made Marshall's name well known nationally and led former president George Washington to ask him to campaign as a Federalist for the Richmond seat in the U.S. House of Representatives. Marshall won the election and took his seat early in December 1799. For the next six months, Marshall was prominent in floor debates, his most important contribution being a defense of President Adams's decision to allow the extradition of one Jonathan Robbins, who had been accused of murder and mutiny by the British authorities.

When Adams decided to reorganize his cabinet in May 1800, he appointed Marshall secretary of state. Marshall conducted American foreign relations for nine months. He also was closely involved in making appointments to federal offices, and, during the president's extended absences from Washington, he handled the day-to-day administration of the government. This dedicated and loyal service put Marshall in a strong position to replace Oliver Ellsworth as chief justice in 1801. However, the office was first offered to former chief justice John Jay, who declined. Moreover, the president was under strong pressure to elevate Associate Justice William Paterson of New Jersey. Resisting the pleas of Paterson's supporters, on January 20 Adams

"Midnight appointee" William Marbury, whose suit against James Madison led to a landmark Supreme Court case in 1803. John Marshall's opinion in *Marbury v. Madison* established the Court's authority to review the constitutionality of acts of Congress. *Source: Maryland Historical Society, Baltimore.*

turned to the younger man who had served him well as secretary of state. The Senate confirmed the nomination January 27.

Political tempers were high when President Thomas Jefferson took office in March 1801. First on the agenda of his Democratic-Republican party was the repeal of the Judiciary Act of 1801, which had created a series of federal circuit courts, and with them a bonanza of judgeships for Federalist lawyers. The subsequent repeal of the 1801 act displaced all of these newly appointed circuit judges, and it fell to Marshall's Court to decide in *Stuart v. Laird* (1803) that the repeal was constitutional and that Supreme Court justices would once more be required to preside at the various circuit courts.

During the same term, Marshall and his colleagues heard argument and decided the landmark case, *Marbury v. Madison,* which involved the "midnight appointments" of Federalist justices of the peace for the

District of Columbia. Through Marshall's oversight as secretary of state, a number of these commissions had not been delivered, and the appointees asked the Supreme Court to order the new secretary of state, James Madison, to do so. After a careful discussion of the appointment process and concluding that the would-be justices of the peace had a property right in their new offices, Marshall proceeded to inquire whether the Supreme Court had authority to order Secretary Madison to deliver the commissions. This question required him to compare the jurisdiction of the Supreme Court, as outlined in the Constitution, with the authority supposedly conferred by the Judiciary Act of 1789. Failing to find the constitutional provisions to support the powers conferred by the Judiciary Act, Marshall denied the petition of William Marbury, one of the appointees. Although this decision limited the power of the Supreme Court, it also served to establish the Court's authority to review the constitutionality of acts of Congress. The doctrine of judicial review, hitherto applied by state courts and some of the federal circuit courts, became a cardinal principle of U.S. constitutional law.

Chief Justice Marshall delivered 519 of the 1,215 opinions of the Supreme Court during his thirty-four-year tenure and probably wrote most of those he delivered. As a result, historians have tended to view Marshall as a dominant presence on the Court, although it has become apparent that his influence varied considerably. In the years before 1812 the advanced age of his associate justices, coupled with their willingness to concur in Marshall's opinions, permitted the chief justice to become preeminent in opinion delivery. In addition, the Court switched from the *seriatim* practice, under which each justice wrote and read his own views, to adopting the "opinion of the Court" approach, a form that remains predominant to the present day.

The second phase of the Marshall Court, from 1813 to 1818, was initiated by the arrival in 1812 of Associate Justice Joseph Story, whose conservative economic views greatly influenced Marshall. During these years the Court divided sharply over prize ship cases generated by the War of 1812. There were numerous dissents and concurring opinions, and new appointees were of Jeffersonian political persuasion and more active in their participation in the work of the Court than the aged associate justices of the first period.

The third period, from 1819 through 1822, can be termed the "golden age" of Marshall's tenure, for it was during this critical period that economic growth and diversification sparked rapid development and westward expansion. His great nationalist decisions, *McCulloch v. Maryland* (1819), *Dartmouth College v. Woodward* (1819), and *Cohens v. Virginia* (1821), date from this period, and the encyclopedic Commerce Clause decision, *Gibbons v. Ogden* (1824), came initially before the Court in 1821.

Marshall's declining influence is apparent in the last period of his tenure. The arrival of Jacksonian jurists on the Supreme Court fractured the working consensus Marshall had developed with most of his Democratic-Republican colleagues. Marshall's only dissent in a constitutional case was delivered in *Ogden v. Saunders* (1827), a case in which the majority upheld the validity of a state insolvency law. In *Willson v. Blackbird Creek Marsh Company* (1829) Marshall set forth an expanded view of state police powers that can be seen as a retreat from the broad view he had taken of the Commerce Clause in his *Gibbons v. Ogden* decision. It was also in this time period that the Court had a major confrontation with the executive branch over Indian treaty rights (*Cherokee Nation v. Georgia*, 1831, and *Worcester v. Georgia*, 1832), concluding with executive refusal to implement Marshall's opinions recognizing the civilized tribes as "dependent, sovereign nations." Politically, this was a period of rising states' rights, coupled with widespread demands for greater economic freedom and mobility. With his strong personal belief in the sanctity of

The lawsuit of one-time business partners Thomas Gibbons, left, and Aaron Ogden, right, led to a landmark Commerce Clause decision in 1824. John Marshall's opinion for the Court defined commerce and stated that Congress has the power to regulate interstate commerce. *Source: (Gibbons) Georgia Historical Society; (Ogden) Courtesy of the New York Historical Society*

private property and his devotion to a strong federal government, the aging and ailing chief justice was in a distinct minority—on his Court and in the general population.

Marshall and his colleagues were responsible for shaping the federal government into the form it would take until the end of the Civil War. This pattern included a commitment to according the federal government preeminent authority in foreign affairs, in the exercise of war powers, and in the control of interstate and foreign commerce. In addition, the Marshall Court before 1815 began to lay the foundations for the Supreme Court's own powerful position in the development of constitutional and international law, which was accomplished through the selective assertion of jurisdiction, not only on its own behalf but also for the lower federal courts.

In economic matters, Marshall has rightly been identified as a protocapitalist. He understood the need for predictability in commercial transactions. His thinking is apparent not only in his development of the Contract Clause to defend property rights (*Fletcher v. Peck,* 1810, and *Dartmouth College*), but also in the efforts he made to resolve embarrassing and conflicting rules of negotia-

bility in the District of Columbia. Marshall recognized the danger that state-based mercantilism would pose for the nation's future economic growth, and a theme running through many opinions stresses the "common market" philosophy of those who wrote and fought to ratify the Constitution. Finally, the chief justice viewed realistically, but with trepidation, the industrial potential of the United States. Unlike his distant cousin, Thomas Jefferson, he did not develop an agrarian preference, but rather hoped that legal institutions would protect America from the environmental ills and class conflict inherent in an urban industrial society.

Marshall's last years were marked by loneliness and painful illness. In 1831 he underwent surgery for bladder stones and survived that ordeal only to suffer the death of his "Dearest Polly" later in the same year. His final illness was an intestinal blockage, but he persisted in attending the February 1835 term before seeking medical assistance in Philadelphia. There he died on July 6, 1835, three months before his eightieth birthday, mourned by friend and political foe alike. His humble demeanor, robust sense of humor, and devotion to the nation he loved and served so well, marked him as one of the preeminent statesmen of the Republic.

William Johnson
1804-1834

Source: Portrait of William Johnson by unknown artist, Collection of the Supreme Court of the United States

WILLIAM JOHNSON, the first great dissenter on the Supreme Court, was born December 27, 1771, in Charleston, South Carolina. He was the second of eleven children of William Johnson, Sr., a blacksmith who had moved to Charleston in the early 1760s, and Sarah Nightingale Johnson, who soon inherited considerable wealth from her father. Extremely active in politics, the elder Johnson served in South Carolina's state legislature for nearly two decades. During the struggle for independence, he was the leader of South Carolina's Liberty Tree party and a strong critic of Britain's efforts to administer the unrepresented colonies through Parliament. When the British laid siege to and captured Charleston during the American Revolution, Johnson was sent to Florida for detention. He was ultimately freed through a prisoner exchange, but nearly two and a half years passed before he was reunited with his family

William Johnson read law under Charles Cotesworth Pinckney, a respected lawyer and political leader in Charleston, South Carolina, who played a prominent role in drafting the U.S. Constitution. He was successful in opposing a religious test for holding office, but not in his appeal that slaves be counted equally with whites in determining representation in the U.S. House. Pinckney served with John Marshall on the ill-fated diplomatic mission to Paris in 1796 and was the Federalist nominee for president in 1804 and 1808. *Source: Library of Congress*

at their South Carolina plantation. These events gave his son a deep reverence for the right to challenge government authority.

Despite the adversity war brought to his family, young William was a good student and graduated first in his class at the College of New Jersey (now Prince-

ton) in 1790. Returning to Charleston, he read law under the tutelage of Charles Cotesworth Pinckney, a well-regarded attorney and a leader of the Federalist party. Pinckney, who had studied law at the Inns of Court in England, left a deep impression on his young protégé, who later attributed to him "every quality that can render man amiable and estimable." Johnson was admitted to the bar in 1793.

The following year he married the sister of his political crony, Thomas Bennett, a future governor of South Carolina. Sarah Bennett Johnson gave birth to eight children, but six died in childhood. The couple later adopted two refugee children from Santo Domingo. The year he wed, Johnson also began his political career, departing from Pinckney's Federalist teachings to enter South Carolina's House of Representatives as a Democratic-Republican. He joined with his mentor's young cousin, Charles Pinckney, to establish Thomas Jefferson's new party in South Carolina and to promote his own budding career.

Johnson served three consecutive two-year terms in the state legislature, becoming its Speaker in 1798. As a legislator Johnson gained considerable experience on a broad range of issues, including judicial reform. He secured an appointment to be one of three judges on the Court of Common Pleas in 1799 and spent the next four years riding circuit. Most of the cases he ruled on involved the limits of state versus federal power. Owing to the Republican majority in South Carolina's legislature, the seats of the state's high bench were awarded mainly to members of Johnson's party, a contrast to the situation in which he would later find himself on the Supreme Court of the United States.

Jefferson's victory in the presidential election of 1800, accompanied by major gains for the Democratic-Republicans in Congress, set the stage for a series of confrontations between his administration and the Federalist-dominated Supreme Court. Among these was the

1804, and he was confirmed two days later by the Senate's Republican majority.

If Johnson's tendency toward judicial independence figured prominently in Jefferson's decision to nominate him, the president soon discovered his independent nature to be a two-edged sword. Seeking to avert American entry into the Napoleonic Wars, Jefferson had secured passage of a trade embargo to stop further seizures of American ships bound for English or French ports. Denying material aid to both of the warring parties was thought to be a practical means of avoiding charges of favoritism as well as punishing the two antagonists for ignoring U.S. neutrality laws. Subsequently, in an attempt to tighten the law's numerous loopholes, the U.S. Treasury authorized port collectors to detain in port any vessel they even suspected was preparing to violate the embargo.

When his vessel was embargoed in Charleston after he applied for clearance to carry a load of cotton and rice to Baltimore, Adam Gilchrist petitioned Justice Johnson, then making his circuit court rounds, for its release. Johnson boarded the vessel and personally issued sailing orders to its captain in defiance of Jefferson's administrative decree. He then proceeded to other similarly detained ships and instructed the captains of each to set sail. His circuit opinion in *Gilchrist v. Collector of Charleston* (1808) asserted that it was not Congress's intention to set such restraints upon commerce and that the detentions could not be justified simply under the guise of obeying an executive order. Jefferson was incensed at this apparent betrayal by his appointee and directed Attorney General Caesar A. Rodney to publish a legal opinion publicly repudiating the *Gilchrist* decision. A heated exchange followed in the press. Not until more than a decade after Jefferson left office was the rift with Johnson healed when, in 1822, they began a cordial exchange of correspondence.

When Johnson served on South Carolina's Court of Common Pleas, its judges expressed their individual

Thomas Jefferson, who appointed William Johnson and two others to the Supreme Court. *Source: Library of Congress.*

watershed case of *Marbury v. Madison* (1803). The *Marbury* decision so outraged Jefferson and Republican leaders that they became determined to gain a toehold in the Court, which they viewed as the last bastion of Federalist power. An opportunity arose when the ailing Alfred Moore submitted his resignation, giving President Jefferson his first Court vacancy to fill. Recognizing the persuasive powers of Chief Justice John Marshall and the peer pressure that could be brought to bear by the Court's other four Federalist justices, Jefferson sought a replacement of strong intellect and independent character. Aside from Johnson's considerable judicial experience, his political credentials were impeccable and he received a hearty endorsement from South Carolina's Republican delegation in Congress. Jefferson placed Johnson's name in nomination on March 22,

opinions in cases, issuing them serially. At the time of the Supreme Court's inception in 1789, the justices also had reported their opinions in this fashion, called *seriatim,* in reverse order of seniority. As a result, the Court's first reported opinion produced considerable confusion because it was a dissent from the majority, and all of the opinions had to be considered to even determine what the majority stance was. When John Marshall became chief justice in 1801 he was determined to change this situation. Guided by a broad view of the Court's role under the Constitution, he sought to suppress the practice of issuing *seriatim* opinions and dissents, both of which he felt undermined the Court's prestige and stability. Instead, he often persuaded his brethren to permit him to give a single majority opinion for the Court, so as not to make their internal differences public. Marshall's approach increased the importance of bargaining and persuasion among the justices.

Before Marshall had succeeded in his efforts to unify the Court behind his own powerful leadership, he was challenged by Justice Johnson, who issued the first real dissenting opinion on the Court in *Huidekoper's Lessee v. Douglass* (1805). During the remainder of his thirty-year tenure on the bench, Johnson would account for nearly half of the seventy dissenting opinions recorded. In doing so, he established a tradition of dissent in Supreme Court procedure and became the first great Court dissenter.

Many of his brethren were appalled at Johnson's practice of publicly airing the Court's differences of opinion about the law. Johnson later recounted his colleagues' scorn: "Some case soon occurred in which I differed from my brethren, and I thought it a thing of course to deliver my opinion. But during the rest of the session, I heard nothing but lectures on the indecency of judges cutting each other." Throughout his career, Johnson was pressured to subordinate his independence to the interests of the Court as an institution. Preserving his independence was especially difficult for him because he was only thirty-two when he joined the Court, and his concurring opinions and dissents often were viewed

President Thomas Jefferson got Congress to pass an embargo act in 1807 forbidding any ships from leaving American ports for the purpose of overseas trade. Intended to hurt the warring nations of Great Britain and France by cutting off U.S. raw materials, the embargo put Americans out of work and encouraged smuggling. This cartoon shows a turtle, symbolizing the embargo, snapping at a smuggler carrying a keg of New England rum to a British ship, while the smuggler curses the "ograbme" (embargo spelled backwards). Justice William Johnson defied the embargo in a circuit court decision, angering Jefferson. *Source: New York Public Library*

not only as divisive, but also as a challenge to the wisdom of his elder brethren. It did not help that his colleagues considered him hot-tempered and somewhat mercurial.

Johnson's position became even more tenuous in 1812 when Joseph Story joined the high bench. Like Johnson, Story came to the Court at the young age of thirty-two, and he had been active in Democratic-Republican politics prior to his appointment. But, unlike Johnson, Story embraced Chief Justice Marshall's belief in the importance of a unified bench and a powerful national judiciary. In particular, Story held a more nationalist view than Johnson on the issue of jurisdiction of federal courts in admiralty matters. He also differed sharply from him on the important issue of federal common law. Johnson wrote the majority opinion in *Hudson v. Goodwin* (1812), holding that there was no federal common law—a landmark decision that limited the scope of federal criminal law to those matters that would be treated by statute.

In 1822 Thomas Jefferson, now retired but still the Democratic-Republican party's philosophical mentor, wrote to Johnson to complain of how many in his party had fallen under the political influence of Federalists like John Marshall and had forsaken Republican ideals. Jefferson strongly criticized Marshall's practice of speaking for the Court as a whole. By then, however, Johnson had modified his views on the subject and replied: "At length I found that I must either submit to circumstances or become such a cypher in our consultations as to effect no good at all." In his last eleven terms, he delivered only nine of eleven concurring opinions and eighteen of forty-two dissents.

During his last years on the Supreme Court, Johnson lived full time in New York City. He was forced out of Charleston in part because of the strong nationalist position he had taken against South Carolina's Negro Seamen Act. Passed in response to a rebellion by slaves and free blacks against white rule in Charleston, the act required black seamen to be jailed until they were claimed by a ship captain or, failing that, sold into slavery. In his 1823 circuit court opinion *Elkison v. Deliesseline,* Johnson held that the act violated the federal commerce power, which he believed to be "paramount and exclusive," and could not be restricted by the state. Because the act was challenged by a black sailor who was a British subject, it also called into question the right of states to interfere with foreign commerce. Johnson reasoned that the commercial treaty guaranteeing the British access to American ports was supreme and that for a state to restrict it would be perilous to the Union.

Throughout his life, the South Carolina justice expressed great interest in literature and education. A longtime member of the American Philosophical Society, he was also instrumental in founding the University of South Carolina. Jefferson wrote to congratulate Johnson in 1822 on the publication of his acclaimed two-volume biography of Revolutionary War general Nathanael Greene, a project undertaken by Johnson in part to reply to Marshall's Federalist polemics in his biography of George Washington. Four years later, Johnson would write *Eulogy of Thomas Jefferson* in tribute to the man who appointed him to the Court.

During the conflicts of his early tenure on the high bench, Johnson had attempted at least twice to secure an executive appointment so that he might abandon the Court for other pursuits. Buoyed by occasional victories, interesting cases, and a raise in judicial salaries in 1819, Johnson stayed on the Court until his death. At age sixty-two, with thirty years of service to the Court, Johnson was stricken with a jaw infection and died August 4, 1834, following surgery.

Henry Brockholst Livingston

1807–1823

Source: Courtesy of the New York Historical Society

Henry Brockholst Livingston was born November 25, 1757, in New York City, but his family moved to an estate near Elizabethtown, New Jersey, when he was in his teens. His father, William Livingston, served as governor of New Jersey during the American Revolution and was active in revolutionary politics; his mother was Susanna French Livingston. The extended Livingston family was socially prominent and a powerful political force in colonial New York. Their forebear, Robert Livingston, emigrated from Scotland to New York in the seventeenth century and became a fur trader and a power in the affairs of the colony. He settled in Albany, where he married the daughter of a wealthy Dutch patroon and set up an estate that ultimately consisted of 160,000 acres spread throughout Dutchess and Columbia counties.

Livingston graduated in 1774 from the College of New Jersey (now Princeton), where he was a classmate of James Madison. That same year, his sister, Sarah Van Brugh Livingston, married John Jay, who would become the first chief justice of the United States. Jay was already closely aligned with the family as he practiced law in partnership with an illustrious cousin, Robert R. Livingston, Jr., who went on to help draft the Declaration of Independence and serve as chancellor of New York.

With the outbreak of the Revolutionary War, Livingston served as a captain on Gen. Philip Schuyler's staff when the British took Fort Ticonderoga, and he participated in the battle of Saratoga as an aide to Benedict Arnold. By the age of nineteen he had achieved the rank of major and subsequently was promoted to lieutenant colonel. His military career ended when Jay went to Spain to serve as the American minister and took his brother-in-law along as his private secretary.

The post not only provided Livingston an honorable removal from the military arena, but also the beginning of a political career and a chance to travel and study. Initially the relationship between the Jays and Livingston was congenial, but it soon deteriorated. This problem may have been the result of the younger man's difficulty in making the transition from being Colonel Livingston (his sister referred to him as "the Colonel" in her letters) to a situation in which his conduct and finances were monitored by his brother-in-law. The irritation may also have come from living in a foreign country with few associations outside the family circle. Sarah Jay suggests in a letter that another secretary at the embassy, William Carmichael, incited Livingston against Jay because he feared Jay would promote Livingston to Carmichael's detriment. "I'm well persuaded he [Carmichael] has in the most artful manner endeavored all along to make Mr. Jay and the Colonel disatisfyed with each other," she wrote.

As relations between the Jays and Livingston worsened, Sarah wrote a long letter to her father on June 24, 1782, complaining about her sibling's behavior: "My brother's temper I always knew to be irritable to an unhappy excess, but I flattered myself that that generosity

As a young man Henry Brockholst Livingston dropped his first name to avoid confusion with two cousins. Born into a distinguished, but divided, New York family, he led the Manor branch of the Livingstons in litigation against the rival Clermont branch. A noted wit, Livingston published *Democracy: An Epic Poem* under the pseudonym of Aquiline Nimble Crops when he was a young lawyer and politician. *Source: Courtesy of the New York Historical Society*

of disposition which I had remarked with pleasure in our family would secure us from impoliteness except at times when his passions were not under the influence of his reason and which I would readily have pardoned. But I was mistaken. A constant captiousness and sulkiness has without ceasing marked his conduct." Family letters reveal that Livingston threatened to leave Europe on several occasions, but Jay persuaded him it would damage his reputation and political future. He stayed in Spain for the duration of the mission, but he developed a lifelong antipathy to Jay and was frequently a conspicuous and vocal critic of his brother-in-law.

The diplomatic delegation broke up when Jay was sent to Paris to negotiate a treaty with the British. Livingston left Madrid February 7, 1782, and sailed from Cadiz early in March carrying dispatches to Congress. His ship was captured by a British frigate April 25, but Livingston managed to destroy the dispatches before he was taken prisoner. The British brought him to New York, where he was detained in jail for carrying messages to Congress. Ironically, Livingston's cell mate in New York was John Jay's brother, Sir James Jay. He was probably planted in Livingston's cell in an attempt to obtain information that could be used to gain an advantage in negotiations with Congress. Adding to the discomfort surrounding his imprisonment, Livingston was considered a potential hostage against the life of a British officer who had been condemned to death in retaliation for a wrongful execution by the British of an American officer.

Finally paroled, Livingston decided to go to Albany and study law under an attorney named Peter Yates. Livingston gained admittance to the bar in 1783, after which he settled in New York City. At this time he officially dropped the "Henry" in his name, having preferred to be called Brockholst all his life. He may also have wished to avoid being confused with two cousins in New York who were also named Henry Livingston.

Livingston became a respected practitioner of the law and a speculator in banking and securities. Not surprisingly, he also began a career in politics. Livingston was elected in 1786 to the New York Assembly for a term and eventually served that body for two more terms. During the early years of his law practice he was associated with Alexander Hamilton and Aaron Burr, serving with both as co-counsel for the defense in a sensational case referred to as "the Manhattan well mystery." The case involved the discovery of the body of a young woman in a well and the subsequent trial of her fiancé for her murder.

Livingston's dislike for John Jay came to the surface

When John Jay returned from London in 1795 with a disappointing treaty that elicited few concessions from the British, Americans hanged and burned his effigy in several cities. Jay's brother-in-law, Brockholst Livingston, was present at one such occasion in New York. Livingston made no secret of his dislike for Jay; he had even campaigned against Jay's bid for governor of New York. *Courtesy of the New York State Historical Association, Cooperstown*

again when Jay ran for governor of New York in 1795. Livingston circulated highly critical unsigned pamphlets attacking Jay and systematically campaigned against him. Although these efforts cost him critical votes, Jay won the election. Swiftly on the heels of that skirmish came the controversy over the treaty Jay had negotiated with the British in 1794, commonly referred to as the Jay Treaty. Many were outraged over the terms, which they considered too favorable to the British, and Jay was maligned throughout the country. In New York he was hanged in effigy on at least one occasion at which Livingston was present.

Perhaps as a result of his animosity toward Jay, or because of his early association with Madison, Livingston, along with members of one branch of the Livingston family, switched loyalty from the Federalist party to the Democratic-Republican party. He became associated with De Witt Clinton and Aaron Burr and worked with them to promote the Jefferson-Burr presidential ticket in 1800, the Democratic-Republican candidate's victory in the 1801 New York gubernatorial campaign, and Clinton's senatorial campaign in 1802. Allied with the victors, Livingston was rewarded with an appointment to the New York Supreme Court in 1802.

Livingston developed a reputation as an independent and energetic judge. He wrote 149 opinions in only

Ambitious and ruthless, De Witt Clinton served ably as mayor of New York for five terms before becoming the state's reformist governor in 1817. A Democratic-Republican, Clinton formed an alliance with Brockholst Livingston, who abandoned the Federalist party in the 1800 presidential election of Thomas Jefferson. *Source: Library of Congress*

four years, and, in a time when individual opinions were unusual, he led the court in the largest number of independent expressions. As New York was a developing commercial city with a major port, Livingston became increasingly involved in deciding maritime and prize ship litigation, as well as commercial litigation. These areas would be of great interest to him throughout his judicial career. Livingston kept his hand in the political arena during his time on the bench, and there are indications that he was considered for the position on the U.S. Supreme Court that went to William Johnson in 1804. Two years later, on September 9, 1806, Associate Justice William Paterson of New Jersey died, and President Thomas Jefferson offered Livingston the vacancy on December 13. The Senate confirmed the nomination five days later.

Livingston took his place on the Supreme Court bench for the February 1807 term. He fit in well with the early Court's customs of congeniality and collegiality. He particularly enjoyed the camaraderie between the justices as they lived and worked together in a boarding house during the Court term. In 1808 a young lobbyist named Joseph Story, who was to become a colleague and a great friend of Livingston on the Court, described him as having "a fine Roman face; an aquiline nose, high forehead, bald head, and projecting chin, [which] indicate deep research, strength, and quickness of mind. I have no hesitation in pronouncing him a very able and independent judge. He evidently thinks with great solidity, and seizes on the strong points of argument. He is luminous, decisive, earnest and impressive on the bench. In private society he is accessible and easy, and enjoys with great good humor the vivacities, if I may coin a word, of the wit and the moralist."

Story's description of Livingston is consistent with other contemporary accounts, which show that, despite his occasional flares in temper, Livingston was a cultured, genial man. He was married three times, to

The *Planter,* an American ship, beats off a French privateer in this 1799 battle. The United States waged an undeclared naval war with France from 1798 to 1800, after Congress authorized American ships to prey on French commerce in retaliation for the insulting treatment of American envoys during the French Revolution. As a New York lawyer, Brockholst Livingston developed an expertise in French prize ship litigation that later proved useful on the Supreme Court. *Source: Library of Congress*

Catharine Keteltas, Ann Ludlow, and Catharine Kortright, was widowed twice, and had a total of eleven children. He was an accomplished classical scholar and active in public service. Motivated by a concern for elementary education, he played an important role in organizing the New York public school system. He was a cofounder and officer of the New York Historical Society and served as a trustee and treasurer of Columbia University from 1784 until his death. He also had a violent streak and fought several duels, including one in 1798 in which he killed his opponent. An attempt was made on his life in 1785.

Livingston's legal writing was remarkable. His style was crisp, factual, and less florid than many of his contemporaries, making it seem almost modern by comparison. In his seventeen years on the Court he wrote a total of fifty-two opinions: thirty-eight for the majority, six concurrences, and only eight dissents. He was markedly less independent than he had been on the New York court, probably because of Chief Justice John

Marshall's persuasive personality and desire to have a united Court. Livingston seemed to revert to the federalism of his earlier years, again most likely because of Marshall's strong influence. While he participated in many of the great landmark cases of the Marshall Court, most of the opinions were written by the chief justice. Drawing on his experience as a judge in New York, where he had performed his more substantive work, Livingston left his mark on the high court in the eight opinions he wrote concerning prize ship cases.

In early 1823 Livingston developed pleurisy; he died March 18 in Washington, D.C. The Court's eulogy, probably written by his close friend Justice Story, notes his contributions to the law: "His genius and taste had directed his principal attention to the maritime and commercial law; and his extensive experience gave to his judgments in that branch of jurisprudence a peculiar value, which was enhanced by the gravity and beauty of his judicial eloquence."

Thomas Todd

1807–1826

Source: Portrait of Thomas Todd by Matthew H. Jouett, Collection of the Supreme Court of the United States

Thomas Todd, the first justice to be appointed from a state west of the Appalachians, was born January 23, 1765. He was the second son of Richard Todd and Elizabeth Richards Todd of King and Queen County, Virginia, and a descendant of Thomas Todd, a wealthy Virginia landowner who had purchased thousands of acres of land in 1669. Much of that land was passed down to young Thomas's father, who served as the high sheriff of Pittsylvania County.

He died, however, when Thomas was only eighteen months old.

As was customary, Richard Todd willed his sizable estate not to his widow, but to his eldest son, William. Elizabeth Todd and Thomas eventually moved to Manchester, Virginia, where Elizabeth ran a successful boarding house and saved money for her son's education. She died, however, within a year of arriving in Manchester, leaving Thomas an orphan at age eleven.

George Caleb Bingham's 1851 painting, "Daniel Boone Escorting Settlers Through the Cumberland Gap," glorifies the pioneers who migrated westward to settle the land. Boone's contemporary, Thomas Todd, had made the same trip across the Appalachian mountains in 1784, settling in Danville, where he worked for Kentucky County's admission to the Union as a separate state. *Source: Washington University Gallery of Art, St. Louis. Gift of Nathaniel Phillips, Boston, 1890*

He was put under the guardianship of a family friend and physician, who squandered his ward's modest inheritance. Before the money ran out, however, the guardian saw that Todd received a good classical education.

When the British Army invaded Virginia, Todd, at sixteen, joined the Continental Army as a substitute for another draftee. He served six months as a private, which provided him with some income. After the war Todd enrolled at Liberty Hall (now Washington and Lee University), a Presbyterian institution in Lexington, Virginia, which placed great emphasis on mathematics

and the classics. He received his degree in 1783 after one year of study. Following graduation, Todd was invited to live with his late mother's cousin, Harry Innes, a distinguished Virginia lawyer and legislator. In exchange for room, board, and a legal education, Todd tutored Innes's daughters.

Active in the movement to make Kentucky a separate state from Virginia, Innes introduced Todd to politics. When Innes was asked to set up a district court of Kentucky in 1784, he moved his family, including Todd, across the Appalachians to Danville, in what would become the state of Kentucky. Beginning that year, Innes chaired the first of five conventions organized to petition the newly created federal government for Kentucky's admission to the Union as a separate state. Todd served as the secretary-clerk at all five conventions.

In 1788 Todd was admitted to the bar of Virginia and quickly developed a thriving practice specializing in land and title claims. Confusing Virginia land laws and westward migration to the frontier caused many legal disputes over property titles and gave Todd ample business. He rapidly gained a reputation for fairness and superior legal skills. The year he was admitted to the bar, Todd married Elizabeth Harris, with whom he would have five children. Their second son, Charles Stewart Todd, was named minister to Russia in 1841, a post he held for four years.

With Kentucky's admission to the Union in 1792, Todd became secretary of its new legislature, while continuing to sustain his private practice. The original draft of Kentucky's constitution, written in 1792, is in Todd's hand. When the Kentucky Supreme Court was created in 1799, he was chosen to be its chief clerk. The first three justices to sit on the bench were seasoned veterans, providing the newly established court with a stable beginning and a sound reputation. In 1801 the state legislature decided to create a fourth judgeship, with the intention of infusing the bench with new blood. At age thirty-six Todd was selected by Gov. James Garrard to be the fourth judge, and he moved his family from Danville to Frankfort, the state capital. Five years later when the chief justice, George Muter, retired, Todd was elevated to fill his seat. The state of Kentucky reneged on its pension obligations to Muter, so Todd took him in and cared for him until his death. In a display of gratitude, Muter willed him his vast estate.

In 1807 Congress amended the Judiciary Act of 1789 to create a seventh federal judicial district out of Tennessee, Kentucky, and Ohio, thereby adding a seventh seat to the U.S. Supreme Court. In filling the new posi-

Thomas Todd's sister-in-law, Dolley Madison, was a great asset to her husband, President James Madison. Not only did she counterbalance his bland public persona, but also she made their home the center of Washington social life. Her Wednesday evening parties for politicians, diplomats, and the public helped to soothe tensions between Federalists and Democratic-Republicans. *Source: Library of Congress*

tion, President Thomas Jefferson did not follow convention by appointing someone with whom he was personally acquainted. Rather, Jefferson asked the advice of members of Congress from those states, almost all of whom named Todd as either their first or second choice. Taking their advice, Jefferson announced February 28, 1807, that he was nominating Todd for the seat. On March 3 the Senate confirmed the Kentucky judge's nomination by voice vote, and he became an associate justice at the age of forty-two. Jefferson met his appointee for the first time at the investiture.

The first wedding to take place in the executive mansion was organized by Dolley Madison, wife of President James Madison, for her sister Lucy Payne. Overcoming her initial reluctance, Lucy had agreed to become widower Thomas Todd's "second prey" in 1812. That year war broke out with Great Britain, and the president's residence was burned in a raid two years later. *Source: Library of Congress*

Todd sat on the Court during the February term of 1808, but missed the 1809 term due to poor travel conditions. "I set out for the Federal City," Todd wrote to his son, Charles Stewart, "but owing to the extreme high freshlets which had removed every bridge between Lexington & Chillicothe & almost every bridge & causeway between the latter place and Wheelin, I went no farther than to Chillicothe. Your Mama's ill health when I left her had considerable influence to induce me to return." His wife died in 1811.

The following year Todd courted Lucy Payne, a sister of Dolley Madison, President James Madison's wife. Lucy was also the widow of George Steptoe Washing-ton, the first president's nephew. When she refused his marriage proposal, Todd left for Kentucky. Lucy soon changed her mind and sent him a note by a special messenger on horseback, who caught up to Todd's carriage at Lancaster, Pennsylvania. The note said she was willing "to be a second prey," and Todd returned to Washington immediately. Some ten days later they were married in the president's mansion, the first wedding to be held there. Like her sister, Lucy Payne was raised a Quaker, but she had since given up her faith and the ceremony was Episcopalian.

Illness and personal business kept Todd from sitting on the Court during the 1813, 1815, 1819, and 1826 terms. During his nineteen-year tenure, the Court decided well over 600 opinions, of which Todd wrote just fourteen. His first opinion was his only dissent: five lines in a land title case arguing that a plaintiff was not entitled to financial compensation if he had not originally sought monetary redress in his suit. Of the eleven majority opinions Todd wrote, ten resolved land or title claims. Typical of these was his 1816 decision in *Preston v. Browder,* upholding North Carolina's right to maintain the sanctity of Indian treaties by restricting land claims within the boundaries of Indian territory. These sparse accounts say little, however, of Todd's judicial philosophy.

In addition to his frequent absences, Todd left a light imprint on the Court because it was dominated during his tenure by the dynamic leadership of Chief Justice John Marshall. Believing in a strong federal government, Marshall aimed to strengthen the national judiciary. He persuaded his brethren to issue unanimous opinions that gave the Court one clear and powerful voice. Despite being appointed by President Jefferson, a political rival of Chief Justice Marshall, Todd supported Marshall almost without fail. While the other Jefferson appointees to the Supreme Court, Associate Justices William Johnson and Brockholst Livingston, occasionally disagreed with the chief justice, Todd fully supported Marshall's conservative economic agenda and his efforts to limit the power of the states.

"[H]is support for the Constitution was unwavering," recalled a contemporary of Justice Todd about his demeanor on the high bench. "He had an uncommon patience and candour in investigation . . . he was not ambitious of innovations upon the settled principles of the law; he was content with the more unosentatious [*sic*] path of jurisdiction . . . hence he listened to arguments for the sake of instruction, and securing examination; and not merely for that of confutation or debate." Other contemporary accounts credit him with good looks, a kind heart, and good judgment.

By the end of his life, Todd had amassed more than 7,000 acres of Kentucky real estate in addition to his residence in the city of Frankfort. His wealth permitted him to invest in public improvements in his adopted state. As a charter member of the Kentucky River Company, he sought to promote navigation of Kentucky's waterways. The Kentucky Turnpike, one of the first public highways west of the Allegheny Mountains, and the Frankfort toll bridge, which spanned the Kentucky river, were two of the public works in which he chose to invest.

Justice Todd died February 7, 1826, in Frankfort, Kentucky, while the Supreme Court was in session. Even after his estate provided for his eight children (he had an additional three with his second wife), and their numerous offspring, there was still more than $70,000 remaining, a considerable sum for that era.

Gabriel Duvall

1811-1835

GABRIEL DUVALL, who sat for nearly a quarter century on the Supreme Court, was born December 6, 1752, at Darnall's Grove, the family plantation in Prince Georges County, Maryland. He was the sixth of ten children of Benjamin and Susannah Tyler Duvall, who were first cousins. Both were grandchildren of Mareen Duvall, a Huguenot who had fled France about 1650—possibly because of persecution for his Protestant faith. He settled in Maryland, and his enterprise won him great prosperity as a merchant and landowner. The family was large, and by the time Gabriel was born his relatives owned vast tracts stretching from Frederick in central Maryland to Annapolis on the Chesapeake Bay. Gabriel's birthplace, itself more than 3,000 acres, was located in what is now the suburbs of Washington, D.C. (It should be noted that family members used various spellings for the name Duvall, and these variations, sometimes using a capital "V" or a single "l," have raised questions about the appropriate spelling of the justice's surname. All of his signatures and most contemporary citations use the lower case "v" and the double "l.")

Little is known about the young man's education, but the conjecture is that he was tutored, as were many boys of his social standing, in mathematics, grammar, and the classics. His tutors were probably members of the Anglican clergy, the family having joined that church in the absence of a French Protestant congregation in Maryland.

When the time came for Duvall to study law, residence at the London Inns of Court was ruled out because of the growing tension between England and the colonies. He went instead, it appears, to the colonial capital of Annapolis. Historical accounts do not identify his tutor, but the events of the day became his principal teacher. While he was still a student—not yet twenty-three—shots were fired at Lexington, and the American Revolution began.

Duvall was caught up in revolutionary activity: he was elected mustermaster and commissary of stores for the Maryland army. When the call went out for volunteers to the state militia, Duvall joined up. He also served as clerk for the Maryland convention that assumed authority after the collapse of British rule in 1775 and as clerk for the council of safety, its executive arm. He undertook the same role for the convention that drafted Maryland's original constitution, and then became clerk of the lower house of the first elected legislature. In the last years of the war, Duvall was one of the commissioners responsible for protecting Loyalist property. During that time, two of his younger brothers were killed in battle. Even though wartime activities interfered with the routine of study, Duvall was admitted to the bar in 1778.

After the war, the young lawyer began his practice in Annapolis and gradually rose in prestige and prominence. In 1782 he was elected to the Maryland State Council and, five years later, to the state House of Delegates. On April 23, 1787, he was chosen to represent

Thomas Jefferson appointed Albert Gallatin, a brilliant Swiss-born financier living in Pennsylvania, to serve as secretary of the Treasury. Gallatin introduced a modern itemized budget and, at Jefferson's suggestion, tried to trim government waste. He used 70 percent of the federal revenue to pay off the national debt and halved the budget for the army and navy. Gabriel Duvall served as Gallatin's comptroller from 1802 to 1811. *Source: Library of Congress*

Maryland at the Constitutional Convention in Philadelphia, but along with four other delegates elected that day, he declined. Historians have speculated on the political rationale for this mass refusal to serve. Duvall's reasons were almost wholly personal, for on July 24, 1787, while the Philadelphia Convention was still in session, Gabriel Duvall married Mary Brice, the daughter of a wealthy and well-connected Annapolis family.

Mary Duvall died three years later, shortly after the birth of their only child, a son.

In 1794 Duvall, now a distinguished leader of the bar, was elected as a Democratic-Republican to the U.S. House of Representatives to fill the unexpired term of John Francis Mercer, who had resigned. His service in the House was brief, but it was probably there that he met for the first time two colleagues who would substantially influence his career, the illustrious James Madison of Virginia and the brilliant Swiss-born Albert Gallatin of Pennsylvania. During Duvall's two years in Congress, he also remarried. His second wife, Jane Gibbon, was from Philadelphia; the marriage lasted until her death almost forty years later.

Duvall resigned from Congress in 1796 to become a judge of the General Court of Maryland, succeeding Samuel Chase, who had been elevated to the U.S. Supreme Court. By modern standards, the General Court was an anomaly because it was both a trial court and an appellate court. The court heard criminal and civil appeals from the county courts and had original jurisdiction in suits where the parties were from different counties. Technically, it was not Maryland's highest court, for some of its decisions could be carried to the Court of Appeals, but in public esteem it was regarded as the state's principal court. Its docket was filled with important, though routine, cases involving debts, land titles, estates, and common law criminal offenses. Duvall seemed happy in his judicial position and for the next six years faithfully heard cases in Annapolis and across the Chesapeake Bay on Maryland's Eastern Shore.

Roger B. Taney, a future chief justice of the United States, tried his very first case as a young lawyer before Judge Duvall. Taney later recalled that the judge's "manner was kind and encouraging," even if he had a "grave face and dignified deportment."

Duvall got his first taste of national politics when he agreed to serve as an elector for the 1796 and 1800 elections. The victor in 1800, Thomas Jefferson made two appointments that were of major importance for Duvall: James Madison became secretary of state, and Albert Gallatin became secretary of the Treasury. Midway in Jefferson's first term, on December 15, 1802, Duvall was appointed to serve as comptroller of the Treasury, a deputy to Gallatin.

In those days, the Treasury Department had a staff of more than 1,000 employees scattered throughout the country, many of them customs agents and excise tax agents, but the Washington office had fewer than a hundred. Secretary Gallatin's style was to address policy matters himself and to rely on subordinates for daily operations. Comptroller Duvall had complete responsibility for certification of accounts payable and for management of major department activities in Washington. He continued in this position when Madison became president in 1809. The comptroller was highly regarded by Congress, and when Secretary Gallatin did battle with the Senate, a fairly regular occurrence, both sides tended to rely on Duvall for accurate factual information.

When Justice William Cushing died in 1810, President Madison had great difficulty selecting a suitable replacement. His first choice, former attorney general Levi Lincoln, declined because of failing eyesight. The next nominee, Alexander Wolcott of Connecticut, was overwhelmingly rejected by the Senate. The president then selected the universally respected John Quincy Adams, who was serving as minister to Russia, and the Senate quickly confirmed him. Several months later—the usual time for correspondence to Russia and back—the president learned that Adams did not want the post. Meanwhile, Justice Chase also had died, compounding Madison's problem. He now had to fill two seats when he had already taken more than a year to fill one without success.

Finally, on November 15, 1811, Madison nominated Gabriel Duvall and Joseph Story to the two vacancies.

They were confirmed three days later, with Duvall out-ranking Story in seniority because Duvall was older. It is easy to speculate that Madison was persuaded by Duvall's calmness, his quiet competence at Treasury, his loyal friendship, and his expressed "horror" at the partisan severity of the Federalist judges a decade earlier. At the time of his appointment, Duvall was almost sixty years old.

Duvall sat on the Supreme Court for more than twenty-three years, his entire tenure occurring during John Marshall's chief justiceship. Although appointed by a Democratic-Republican president, Duvall was a staunch supporter of Marshall's nationalist interpretation of the Constitution. Like Marshall, he advocated a strong central government in cases relating to federal power. Duvall backed Marshall in nearly all the well-known cases in which the Court asserted the power of the federal government over the states. He even sided with Marshall and Story against the overriding majority in *Ogden v. Saunders,* an 1827 case involving the constitutionality of applying a state insolvency law to a preexisting contract.

Measured by written opinions, Marshall clearly dominated the Court for more than three decades. Duvall seldom wrote an opinion either for the Court or in concurrence or dissent. Yet historians have now come to understand that decisions of the Marshall Court were joint efforts, the result of discussion and debate not only in formal conferences but also in informal give-and-take, an inevitable side effect of the justices' boarding together during their meetings in Washington. It is therefore difficult to trace the individual contributions of members of the Court such as Bushrod Washington, Brockholst Livingston, Thomas Todd, Robert Trimble, or Gabriel Duvall.

Only in the celebrated *Dartmouth College v. Wood-*

In 1814 the British burned the original Treasury building, in which Gabriel Duvall had worked for nine years as comptroller, to avenge the burning of York (Toronto) by American forces. This building was constructed in 1817. *Source: New York Public Library*

"An overseer doing his duty. Sketched from life near Fredericsburg," 1798, by Benjamin Latrobe. Despite having numerous slaves on his own Maryland plantation, Gabriel Duvall's Supreme Court opinions were strongly antislavery. *Source: Maryland Historical Society, Baltimore*

ward (1819) case, where the majority voted to limit state legislative power, did Duvall oppose Marshall. Unfortunately, he did not write a dissenting opinion, so his reasoning cannot be analyzed. In slavery cases, Duvall, a slave-holding plantation owner, took positions that, for the day, were surprisingly advanced. In *Mima Queen and Child v. Hepburn* (1813) a slave suing for freedom sought to produce hearsay evidence that her mother had been free. The Court would not allow the evidence, but Justice Duvall dissented. "It will be universally admitted that the right to freedom is more important than the right of property," he argued. In *LeGrand v. Darnall* (1829) Duvall wrote for the unanimous Court that a master leaving property to a slave was, in effect, freeing the slave.

As Duvall aged, his hearing declined sharply, and he was frequently absent from the bench. A contemporary account, describing the justice in 1827 when he was seventy-five, calls Duvall "the oldest-looking man on the Bench. His head was white as a snowbank, with a long white cue hanging down to his waist." Seven years later, lawyer Charles Sumner noted that Duvall "is so deaf as to be unable to participate in conversation."

Finally, after being told that President Andrew Jackson intended to appoint Roger B. Taney, a fellow Marylander, to succeed him, Gabriel Duvall admitted his infirmities and agreed to step down. Jane Duvall's death the year before may also have been a factor in his decision to retire. He left the Court January 14, 1835, secure in his knowledge that his successor would not be "too much of a politician." When Taney was rejected by the Senate, however, Philip Barbour, a states' rights Virginian, turned out to be his replacement.

He lived for another nine years in retirement. Although almost completely deaf, Duvall carried on a correspondence indicating a lively interest in his ancestry and lands. He died peacefully March 6, 1844, at Marietta, the manor house he had built on the estate of his birth. He was ninety-two years old. Justice Story, at the Court's memorial meeting after Duvall's death, did not dwell on his colleague's slight judicial contributions. He remembered only the man, "his irbanity [*sic*], his courtesy, his gentle manners, his firm integrity and undependence [*sic*], and his sound judgment."

Joseph Story
1812–1845

Source: Portrait of Joseph Story by George P. A. Healy, Collection of the Supreme Court of the United States

JOSEPH STORY, one of the most influential legal scholars in American history, was born September 18, 1779, in Marblehead, Massachusetts. He was the eighth of eighteen children of the two marriages of Elisha Story, a prominent local physician. His mother, Mehitable Pedrick Story, captivated Joseph's imagination with stories of how his maternal grandfather, John Pedrick, had daringly foiled a would-be British raid on the Salem, Massachusetts, arsenal in 1771. Young Joseph was also impressed with the successful career of his pa-

ternal grandfather, William Story, who had served as assistant deputy registrar of the British Vice Admiralty Court in Boston and as clerk of the American Navy Board. But Story's greatest admiration was reserved for his father, who, in addition to being a respected physician, had distinguished himself through his participation in the Boston Tea Party.

In Joseph's last year at Marblehead Academy, a local private school, he was severely disciplined for brawling with a fellow student. Feeling the punishment was unjust, Story left the academy and sought early admission to Harvard. By diligently studying on his own, he was able to enroll in 1795. Story graduated second in his class in 1798, but such devotion to his studies had detrimental effects on his health, and he emerged balding and sickly.

His health improved when he moved back to Marblehead and read law under a distinguished attorney, Samuel Sewall, a future chief justice of the Massachusetts Supreme Court. When Sewall was appointed to a judgeship, Story completed his apprenticeship under Samuel Putnam in the thriving city of Salem. Under his tutelage, Story was admitted to the bar in 1801.

Although he was a diligent law student, Story's personal inclination was to devote himself to reading and writing poetry. His florid compositions were poorly received, although "the poet of Marblehead," as he was known, did succeed in having poems published in the local papers. His most substantial work was *The Power of Solitude,* a 1,500-line poem written in heroic couplets and published as a book in 1805. Disheartened by his poetry's limited critical and public appeal, Story decided to concentrate seriously upon the law and to write poetry in his spare time.

This decision coincided with the death of his father, whose professional reputation had been sullied by an unfortunate incident. Because many parts of the country had suffered from outbreaks of smallpox, Dr. Story sought to protect the citizens of Marblehead by inoculating them with a newly developed serum from England. Tragically, the serum sent to Story was mislabeled; it proved to be not a vaccine, but live smallpox, resulting in numerous deaths and a local quarantine. Although Dr. Story ultimately was exonerated, many of those who had lost family members held him accountable. These events may have pushed Story to excel in his profession and salvage his family's honor. His father's death in 1805 was preceded by the death of Mary Story, young Story's wife of only seven months and his

collaborator in writing poetry. Devastated at losing his wife, Story bought up all the copies of *The Power of Solitude* he could find and destroyed them.

Story opened his own law practice, but at first attracted few clients. Federalist newspapers, which dominated in the county, openly attacked his Republican politics and his conversion to the Unitarian religion, and on one occasion Story was assaulted and beaten. Discouraged, he considered moving to Baltimore for a time. Through his close association with Salem's fledgling Democratic-Republican party, headed by shipping magnate Jacob Crowninshield, Story's law practice slowly began to expand. His considerable success, in both local courts and the Massachusetts Supreme Court, attracted more clients and impressed even his Federalist antagonists.

In 1805 Story was elected to the first of three terms in the Massachusetts House of Representatives. His election was a testament to the increased vigor of the Democratic-Republican party, an organization he had helped to build. Yet, his emergence as a local party leader coincided with a growing detachment from partisan loyalties. Story spent much of his tenure in the legislature promoting measures for judicial reform and greater judicial independence. His absences from legislative roll calls, due mainly to time spent litigating cases, coupled with his nearly perfect attendance on the legislature's judiciary committee, suggest that Story's political ambitions had already succumbed to his growing interest in the courts.

He became acquainted with the nation's highest court and its members in 1808 when he was retained by a group of New England land speculators to appear as their counsel in Washington. He sought financial redress for his clients in the notorious Yazoo land fraud case, *Fletcher v. Peck,* which came before the Supreme Court in 1810. The speculators sought to reverse the Georgia legislature's invalidation of the corrupt public land sale of an enormous tract of land (extending into

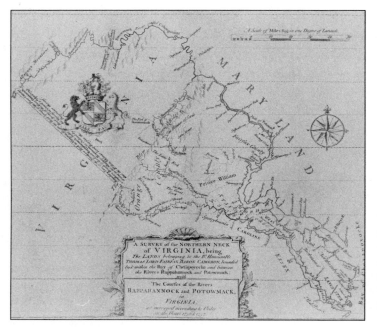

The complicated case of *Martin v. Hunter's Lessee* (1816) involved a parcel of land in the northern neck of Virginia that the state had confiscated from Thomas Lord Fairfax, a Loyalist, during the American Revolution. Joseph Story's landmark opinion established the Supreme Court's authority to reverse state court decisions involving federal laws or constitutional rights. *Source: Virginia State Library and Archives*

Alabama and Mississippi) made by the previous legislature, since voted out of office. Unanimously accepting Story's argument, the Court struck down Georgia's revoking act, obliging the state to uphold its contract, although corrupt, and eventually pay restitution to the speculators. The decision marked the first time the Court relied upon its implied powers to overturn state laws it held contrary to the Constitution.

Story's role in the Yazoo land fraud controversy brought him national prominence. He had been elected in 1808 to finish out the congressional term of his old political ally, Jacob Crowninshield, who had died in office. While in the U.S. Congress, Story broke with party leadership to oppose President Thomas Jefferson's foreign trade embargo. The decision was a difficult one for Story, and it earned him powerful political enemies in Washington, including the president. Disgusted with political chicanery and wanting to resume his law practice, Story returned to Massachusetts. He was once again elected to the state legislature and served briefly as Speaker of the Massachusetts House of Representatives in 1811.

Despite his hectic professional life, Story found time to court Sarah Waldo Wetmore, and they married in 1808. A distant relative of his first wife, and the daughter of a judge of the Boston Court of Common Pleas, Sarah fulfilled the hopes for home and family that had been dashed three years earlier by Mary Story's sudden death. The second marriage was a happy match, but it too was touched by tragedy. Only two of the couple's seven children survived childhood. A son, William Wetmore Story, became a prominent lawyer and, reversing his father's progression from art to law, became an artist and sculptor of world renown.

The death of Associate Justice William Cushing in September 1810 created a vacancy on the Supreme Court that Joseph Story would fill for almost thirty-four years. But his path to this high office was neither easy nor certain. At thirty-two, he was considered by many to be too young and inexperienced to serve on the nation's highest bench. His political enemies argued that Story's record of loyalty to the Democratic-Republicans, also the party of President James Madison, made him overly partisan. Ironically, many Democratic-Republicans, including Jefferson, questioned Story's allegiance. Nevertheless, after three unsuccessful attempts to fill the seat, including a refusal from John Quincy Adams, then ambassador to Russia, the president sent Story's nomination to the Senate on November 15, 1811. Story was confirmed three days later, becoming one of the youngest appointees ever to sit on the high bench. Gabriel Duvall was confirmed on the same day, but Story, because he was younger, ranked behind Duvall in seniority.

On the Court, Story followed Chief Justice John Marshall's lead and gradually embraced an expansive federalist view on the authority of the Supreme Court as a coequal third branch of government. To promote this view, Story successfully worked to expand the jurisdiction of federal courts to protect the supremacy of federal law. His opinion in *Martin v. Hunter's Lessee* (1816) established the Court's power to reverse the decisions of state courts and ensure that federal law was interpreted uniformly throughout the nation. He advocated the establishment of a federal common law of crimes to expand the scope of federal criminal law. He also sought to exert federal admiralty jurisdiction as widely as possible.

Story supplied the intellectual reasoning behind many of the Court's opinions. According to tradition, Marshall is said to have remarked after reading his opinions: "These seem to be the conclusions to which we are conducted by the reason and spirit of the law. Brother Story will furnish the authorities." Although their beliefs on the Court's constitutional role in government were similar, Story differed from Marshall in several instances, notably in his views on corporations. *Dartmouth College v. Woodward* (1819) questioned whether the New Hampshire legislature, having granted Dartmouth College a corporate charter, could later rewrite that charter without impairing a contract, an action expressly forbidden by the Constitution. Marshall found no reason to exempt private charters from constitutional protection, but Story made clear in his separate opinion that states could retain the power to make future modifications in contracts without violating the Constitution if such a provision is written into the charter.

Story provoked strong reactions in others. Many adored him, but others, such as his colleague and adversary William Johnson, found him impetuous and garrulous. He was indeed known to monopolize the justices' discussions. Johnson also resented Story's close friendship with Henry Wheaton, the Supreme Court's reporter of decisions.

Even if Story had not served on the Supreme Court, he might have left a lasting mark on the nation's legal system. He was one of the nation's greatest legal schol-

A Harvard University graduate, Joseph Story moved back to Cambridge, Massachusetts, in 1829 to teach while continuing to perform his Supreme Court duties. He became an influential professor who contributed enormously to Harvard Law School's success and to legal education in general. Dane Hall, built in 1832, housed Harvard's law school for more than a century. *Source: Harvard Law Art Collection*

ars, and his commentaries are still cited as legal authority. In 1829 Harvard Law School finally persuaded
Story, after several entreaties, to move from Salem to
Cambridge, Massachusetts, and join the law faculty. By
then his ties to the university were already well established; he had become a Harvard overseer in 1819 and a
fellow of the Harvard Corporation in 1825.

While continuing as associate justice, Story wrote a
series of nine works clarifying the philosophical and
legal bases of law. The series demonstrated the remarkable breadth of Story's legal knowledge. Although all
the books were well received and widely read, his landmark *Commentaries on the Constitution,* published in
three volumes in 1833, was so successful that it was
eventually translated into French, Spanish, and German. A one-volume abridgment of that work became a
popular text in law schools. By 1844 money from his
book royalties was more than twice his judicial salary,
and the influence of his writings was widespread.

With the election of Andrew Jackson as president
in 1828, Story contemplated retirement from the Court
to devote himself entirely to academic life. Jackson's
victory, heralding a new era of populism, prompted
Story to observe cynically that "the reign of 'King
Mob' seemed triumphant." One by one, death
claimed Story's colleagues, including, in 1835, his great
friend and longtime ally, John Marshall. Jackson
balked at appointing Story—the obvious and popular
choice—to fill the chief justice's chair and selected
Roger B. Taney instead. By 1837 Jackson had replaced
five of the justices on the seven-member bench, but,
despite widespread speculation, Story did not retire. He
spent the next nine years conducting a rear guard defense of the Marshall Court's record of jurisprudence.
Significantly, many of the radical reforms expected of
the Jacksonian appointees did not materialize, perhaps
in part because of Story's participation. While Story
often disagreed with his new colleagues on various is-

A popular and forceful president, Andrew Jackson was caricatured
by his opponents as a despotic monarch because he expanded the
powers of the president at the expense of the legislature. This cartoon charges that Jackson exceeded his authority by vetoing the
1832 bill to recharter the National Bank. *Source: Library of Congress*

sues, he did not often dissent. Dissents, he felt, should
be used sparingly because they weakened the institution
whose authority he had spent a lifetime trying to build.

Story's energy began to wane in the early 1840s, and
he was absent from the 1843 term due to illness. He
struggled through the 1844 term, and in 1845 he commenced his circuit duties with the intention of retiring
as soon as a successor could be named. Before he could
tender his resignation, Story became gravely ill, and on
September 10, 1845, he died.

Smith Thompson

1823-1843

Source: Portrait of Smith Thompson by unknown artist, Collection of the Supreme Court of the United States

S MITH THOMPSON was born January 17, 1768, in Amenia, in eastern Dutchess County, New York, to Ezra and Rachel Smith Thompson. Ezra Thompson, a well-to-do farmer, land speculator, and lead mine developer, was also prominent in politics. He was elected one of the anti-Federalist delegates from Dutchess County to the state convention to ratify the Constitution, which met in Poughkeepsie in June 1788. The future justice's connections to the anti-Federalist forces at the convention also included a maternal uncle, Melancton Smith, and his future father-in-law and law partner, Gilbert Livingston. Although Smith and Livingston were two of the most articulate opponents of ratification, they ultimately voted vote in favor; the count was 30–27. Ezra Thompson was ill at the time of the vote.

Young Smith Thompson went to common schools before attending the College of New Jersey (now Princeton), from which he graduated in 1788. He returned to Dutchess County and, after teaching school for a few months, began a three-year legal apprentice-ship in the firm of James Kent and Gilbert Livingston. Kent, who was largely responsible for supervising whatever legal training Thompson received, would become one of the most influential figures in nineteenth century American law. Completing his clerkship in 1793, Thompson was admitted to the bar. That same year he succeeded Kent as partner when Livingston and Kent, a Federalist, could no longer paper over their political differences.

The new partnership was further strengthened in 1794 when Thompson married Gilbert Livingston's daughter, Sarah. The Livingstons were particularly doting parents and grandparents—the Thompsons had two daughters and two sons—and Thompson seems to have profited from his father-in-law's support. Al-

After supervising Smith Thompson's legal studies, James Kent became one of the most respected and influential justices on the New York Supreme Court, gaining the chief justiceship in 1804. Thompson replaced him in 1814 when Kent was named to the court of chancery. As chancellor Kent established the principles upon which American equity law is based. *Source: Library of Congress*

though he has been mistakenly identified as a member of the powerful Clermont branch of the Livingston family, which included state chancellor Robert R. Livingston, Gilbert Livingston actually belonged to a less prominent branch of the clan. Yet his connections with the Democratic-Republican party's Clintonian faction—led by Gov. George Clinton—made it possible for Thompson to serve one term in the New York Assembly in 1800 and as a member of the New York Constitutional Convention of 1801, which made some minor adjustments in the state constitution. That same year he declined appointment as district attorney for the middle district of New York, but when named to the New York Supreme Court the following year he accepted, beginning forty-one consecutive years of public service.

The court's membership was noteworthy. Appointed the same year were the chief justice, Morgan Lewis, who would be elected governor in 1804, and Brockholst Livingston, whom Thompson would eventually succeed on the U.S. Supreme Court. Ultimately, the court's most influential member would be Thompson's former mentor, James Kent, particularly after Livingston's appointment to the nation's highest court in 1807. Thompson and his brethren did not lack ability and independence, but they found it convenient to defer to Kent's industry and erudition in crafting opinions. When Kent, who had succeeded Lewis in 1804, left to become chancellor of the state in 1814, Thompson replaced him as chief justice, a position he held for four years. During his sixteen years on the state court, Thompson developed the jurisprudence that he would use throughout his twenty years on the U.S. Supreme Court. It emphasized adherence to legal precedent and deference to the legislative branch of government.

Among the more interesting precedents Thompson helped set was a formula for determining legislative intent in *People v. Utica Insurance Co.* (1818), in which he was aided by Attorney General Martin Van Buren's ef-

In 1807 genius inventor Robert Fulton put a steam engine in the *Clermont* and proved that boats could be powered by something other than wind and manpower. New York State granted Fulton and his partner Robert Livingston a monopoly to operate steamboats on the Hudson River. The monopoly was contested, and the resulting case, *Gibbons v. Ogden,* became an important test of Congress's right to regulate interstate commerce. While serving on the New York Supreme Court, Thompson had set a precedent by upholding the states' regulation. *Courtesy of the New York Historical Society*

fective argument. Thompson's formula is still in use today. He also broke ground in the matter of civilians not being subject to military jurisdiction (*Smith v. Shaw,* 1815), with reasoning that was put to good use a half century later by Justice David Davis in his opinion, *Ex parte Milligan* (1866). Not surprisingly, because of its burgeoning economic development, New York was the site of the first interpretation of the federal Commerce Clause. The case was *Livingston v. Van Ingen* (1812), and Thompson and Kent, in separate opinions, were the first American judges to enunciate the "concurrent position," that until an actual conflict occurred between state and federal laws, a state regulation of commerce—in this instance the Livingston and Fulton steamboat monopoly—was valid.

Thompson and his New York brethren were closely involved in politics as well as law. This entanglement was partly institutional. The New York Supreme Court judges, along with the governor and chancellor, comprised the Council of Revision, a body that had veto power over all legislative bills. In 1805 New York members of the Democratic-Republican party were divided on a bill to charter the Merchant's Bank, and this divi-

sion extended to the Council of Revision. Apparently, because of a lifelong belief in the need to expand the currency supply, Thompson and Governor Lewis joined the Federalists on the council in supporting the bank, and they were subsequently ostracized by the Republican majority—comprised of supporters of De Witt Clinton. With opposition to Clinton marking the rest of his political career, Thompson joined with a rising politician from Columbia County named Martin Van Buren. Leader of the Bucktails, the anti-Clintonian faction of the New York Republican party, Van Buren came to be known as the "Little Magician" for his adroitness in politics. So close was the friendship between Van Buren and Thompson that the Van Burens named their fourth son Smith Thompson Van Buren. Thompson become important enough in Van Buren's Bucktail faction to be its leading candidate for federal patronage.

Thus, in 1818, when it was rumored that the lucrative collectorship of the Port of New York was to become vacant, Thompson's name was advanced to President James Monroe and was consequently "available" when a real vacancy, the position of secretary of the Navy, oc-

Martin Van Buren was called the Little Magician for his diminutive stature and his dexterity at manipulating New York's political machine. Blond and dapper, he was elected to the U.S. Senate in 1821 after leading the Bucktails, a faction of the Democratic-Republican party in the New York Senate. Strong friends, Smith Thompson and Van Buren had a falling out when Thompson accepted a seat on the Supreme Court that Van Buren coveted. In 1836 Van Buren was elected president. *Source: Library of Congress*

curred. Relatively innocent of naval matters, perhaps overmatched by his more illustrious colleagues (Secretary of State John Quincy Adams, Secretary of War John C. Calhoun, Secretary of the Treasury William H. Crawford, and Attorney General William Wirt), and more attuned to New York patronage than national policy, Thompson took his cabinet seat on January 1, 1819.

In the course of four years, however, he succeeded in ingratiating himself so fully with Monroe that the presi-

dent literally refused to appoint any other New Yorker to the Supreme Court in 1823, when Brockholst Livingston's death created a vacancy in the "New York seat." (Because Supreme Court justices rode circuit, it was traditional to make appointments from a particular circuit. Livingston came from the Second Circuit—Vermont, Connecticut, and New York—which for political reasons meant the appointment came from New York.) Although the appointment was limited to New York, there was no dearth of candidates, including Van Buren, now a U.S. senator, and James Kent, now retired. Monroe's insistence on Thompson for the seat led to a rupture in the friendship between Thompson and Van Buren because of what Van Buren saw as Thompson's duplicity. Thompson finally succumbed to Monroe's entreaties and was confirmed by the Senate on December 19, 1823, by voice vote.

The Court appointment, however, was but one in a series of differences between them. Most notable was a split over which presidential candidate to support in the election of 1824. Van Buren and the Bucktails backed William Crawford, while Thompson favored any candidate but Crawford because of his perceived hostility toward the Monroe administration, despite his position as Monroe's secretary of the Treasury. In short, Thompson had switched his primary allegiance from Van Buren's Bucktails to the Monroe administration, to the extent that he let his name be used as a candidate in a vain effort to divide Crawford's Bucktail support.

The timing of Thompson's twenty-year Supreme Court tenure makes him a transitional figure between the Court led by John Marshall and that of his successor Roger B. Taney, which differed in not only constitutional doctrine, but also in the way the Court conducted its business. Unanimity was the operative word for the Marshall Court, with the justices even boarding together. Sarah Thompson had accompanied her husband on his arduous New York judicial travels and had stayed in Washington while he served as head of the

Navy. Subsequently, she succeeded in breaking up Marshall's boardinghouse arrangement.

More important, Justice Thompson was more inclined to join William Johnson in following an independent course on the Court than was his predecessor, Livingston. Thus, in 1827, Thompson's vote helped push "the Great Chief Justice" into his only constitutional dissent (in *Ogden v. Saunders*) because Marshall believed that a New York bankruptcy law violated the Constitution's Contract Clause. For Thompson, such laws had always been part of the normal way of doing business, a view that Livingston had shared, but had been less inclined to express. Similarly, in what would be his best remembered area of constitutional contribution—the Commerce Clause—Thompson continued to adhere to the concurrent approach he had advanced on the New York court in *Livingston v. Van Ingen*. While the concurrent position remained a minority one on the Marshall Court, there was considerable support for it on the Taney Court, and after Thompson died his concurrent approach became the basis for a compromise settlement called "selective exclusiveness," in *Cooley v. Board of Wardens of the Port of Philadelphia* (1852).

Another major contribution to constitutional development, which also reflected his New York background, was Thompson's *Cherokee Nation v. Georgia* (1831) dissent. The Cherokees sought an injunction against the state of Georgia's assumption of control over them. For the Court to hear the case, the justices would have to recognize the Indians as a sovereign nation. A majority of the Court was not prepared to do so in 1831, but Thompson's wide-ranging dissent advanced what became known as the "Cherokee doctrine"—that despite being vanquished, the Cherokees retained their sovereignty. The following year in *Worcester v. Georgia*, Chief Justice Marshall, who had uncharacteristically suggested that Thompson produce his *Cherokee Nation* dissent, accepted Thompson's reasoning. The sovereignty doctrine was revived in the 1970s when Native Americans turned to the courts to win the return of their lands. The notes for Thompson's *Cherokee Nation* dissent are the only surviving manuscripts from his Court years, and they, as well as the opinion itself, show a close reliance on an 1823 opinion written by his former mentor, James Kent.

Since Thompson's Court tenure ended before the slavery controversy burst fully on the Court, he was able to exercise his general adherence to self-restraint and states' rights (both traits in contrast to his *Cherokee Nation* opinion), with less controversy. In general, Thompson's slavery jurisprudence sustained the "peculiar institution," and was remarkably similar to that of his successor to the New York seat, Samuel Nelson.

Thompson's political activities during the presidential campaign of 1824 were repeated in 1828. Convinced that his gubernatorial candidacy against Van Buren would aid the reelection campaign of John Quincy Adams, Thompson ran, but unsuccessfully. And although it can be said that he ran in name only, he did not resign his seat on the Court. Ironically, eight years earlier Van Buren had unsuccessfully tried to persuade Thompson, then secretary of the navy, to quit his post and run for the governorship against their arch political foe, De Witt Clinton, with the idea of his resigning the governorship after he won, and returning to the cabinet.

Thompson, a Presbyterian, served for many years as a vice president of the American Bible Society. As secretary of the Navy, he had seen to it that Bibles were readily available to sailors.

Halfway through Thomson's high court tenure, his wife died. Two years later Thompson married her cousin, Eliza Livingston, whom Kent described as "very young & flountingly gay." They had two daughters and a son. Ironically, Thompson's last residence, "Rust Plaets" (Resting Place), where he died on December 18, 1843, would later become the Poughkeepsie Rural Cemetery.

Robert Trimble

1826-1828

Source: Library of Congress

LITTLE IS KNOWN about the life of Robert Trimble, in large part because a fire at the family home some years after his death destroyed his letters, papers, and possibly a diary he may have kept. Most likely Trimble was born in Berkeley County, Virginia, not Augusta County, as some sources indicate. The confusion comes from the creation of new Virginia counties out of previously existing subdivisions. Although the date of his birth is often given as simply the year 1777, the impressive monument his family erected over his grave indicates that it was November 17, 1776. His father, William Trimble, was descended from a Scot who came to America with his four brothers in 1732 so that they might freely practice their Presbyterian religion. Robert's mother, Mary McMillan Trimble, was the daughter of a Scottish-born school teacher and a woman of similar ancestry whose family had been in the colonies for several generations.

In the fall of 1779 the Trimbles left Berkeley County for Boonesboro, Kentucky, to join relatives already there. Along the way another daughter was born. The family was attacked by Indians, and, at his own request, an injured uncle was left alone on the trail to die. The family's destination was land on Howard's Creek in Clark County, Kentucky, and there they prospered. In addition to farming the land, young Trimble hunted game and scouted Indians. His grandfather served as his first tutor, teaching him land surveying and Greek and making him read the Bible. He then attended organized schools on the Kentucky frontier, paying his tuition in pork, as was the custom. Trimble briefly taught school himself to provide funds for his schooling. He supplemented attendance at school by making good use of the resources, although meager, in his neighborhood library.

Trimble entered Bourbon Academy in 1795 but was forced to leave after less than a year because of an attack of "bilious fever." He became a member of a class of nineteen law students organized under the auspices of Transylvania University in Woodford County, Kentucky. George Nicholas, the first attorney general of Kentucky, taught the class, and after his death James Brown, later United States minister to France, took over. It was most likely 1803 when Trimble was admitted to the bar and began his practice in Paris, Kentucky, a town that was to be his residence until his death.

Trimble was a success in his new profession. *The American Jurist* magazine later recounted his accomplishments at the bar: "His great candor and fairness secured him the attentive ear of the court; and his sound judgment, which was his most distinguishing characteristic, generally saved his client from being deceived or disappointed. His arguments in court, though less brilliant than those of some others, were sound, logical, forcible and interesting." On August 18, 1803, the same year he began his legal career, Trimble married Nancy P. Timberlake. They had at least ten children. The four sons did not live to maturity, but several of the daughters survived.

In 1802 Trimble was elected to represent Bourbon County in the lower branch of the Kentucky legislature. This position was his first taste of politics and also his last. He did not enjoy the hectic life of a politician and thereafter refused to be a candidate for political office. On two occasions he could have been chosen a U.S. senator; only his consent was necessary to secure his election. Once, in 1812, no other candidate was considered until it had been determined that he would not serve, and even then there were those who insisted on naming him anyway.

James Brown migrated to Lexington, Kentucky, from Virginia in 1789 and became the frontier state's first secretary of state three years later. He taught law to future justice Robert Trimble and eighteen other students at Transylvania University, the first American college west of the Allegheny Mountains, before moving to Louisiana in 1812 and serving as a U.S. senator for several terms. *Source: The Filson Club*

This aversion to public office did not extend to judicial posts; after considerable urging, he accepted a judgeship on the Kentucky Court of Appeals. He was commissioned on April 13, 1807. Although his work was well regarded, Trimble resigned from the bench at the close of the fall term of 1808, giving as his reason his inability to support his large family on the meager annual salary of $1,000.

During the following seven years he diligently applied himself to his law practice. It flourished, and he was able to afford a number of slaves. He also found time for civic duties, becoming a founder of the first public library in his town and a boundary commissioner to settle disputes between Kentucky and Tennessee. He served as a trustee at Transylvania University for a number of years, but refused offers to become a law professor. In the election years 1808, 1812, and 1816 he was a presidential elector, twice voting for James Madison and once for James Monroe. Trimble was also president of his county agricultural society and had a strong interest in improved farming methods.

When he was appointed chief justice of Kentucky in 1810, Trimble declined the position because he did not want to give up his lucrative law practice for a small judicial salary. He did, however, accept the part-time post of Kentucky district attorney in 1813. And when President Madison nominated him to the post of U.S. judge for the District of Kentucky in 1817, he immediately accepted. He was confirmed three days later, on January 31.

The position did not prove to be particularly comfortable. In the years following his appointment, the government of Kentucky was often at odds with federal authorities over matters such as control of waterways and state laws protecting settlers who had made improvements on disputed lands. Kentucky also took offense at federal rulings upholding the activities of the Bank of the United States. Judge Trimble was a supporter of a strong national government, with power over the states; consequently he found his written opinions often opposed popular sentiment in Kentucky. When he ruled in 1821 that a Kentucky law delaying judgments against debtors was not binding on federal courts, he was pointedly reminded by the local press of the impeachment proceedings against Justice Samuel Chase of the U.S. Supreme Court. These controversies involving state versus federal power would last beyond the lifetime of the judge.

Although as a judge he favored a strong national goverment, politically, Trimble was a "Thomas Jefferson Republican." As such, he supported the more conservative wing of the Democratic-Republican party, which believed a democracy should be based on an agricultural society of educated landholders. After Trimble's death, Joseph Story, who sat on the Supreme Court bench with him, said: "In politics, he was a firm and undeviating Republican" while in "constitutional law, he belonged to that school [federalism] of which Mr. Chief Justice Marshall is the acknowledged head and expositor." It is difficult to imagine a Jeffersonian Federalist, but by the time Trimble arrived on the federal bench, let alone the Supreme Court, a number of people both on and off the courts were managing to reconcile the once totally opposite philosophies. A centrist approach to some old issues was being forged, and Trimble was one of those who could willingly support the results.

On February 7, 1826, Associate Justice Thomas Todd died. It was said that before his death he had made known that he wished Trimble, his friend and fellow Kentuckian, to succeed him on the Supreme Court. At that moment Congress was considering the expansion of the Court to ten members. President John Quincy Adams waited for the outcome of the proposal, which failed, before naming Todd's successor. Trimble's name was finally sent to the Senate on April 11, 1826. Kentucky senator John Rowan fought the appointment, partly for political and partly for personal reasons. The

Senate tabled the issue temporarily, but took it up again on May 9 and confirmed Trimble by a 27–5 vote. At twenty-eight days, his confirmation proceedings had taken much longer than those of earlier justices, which generally averaged two days. Trimble was Adams's only appointment to the Supreme Court.

In relation to his colleagues, Justice Trimble was later described as being a "comparatively young man . . . , to all appearances of a robust and strong constitution. He looked as if he would be one of the last to be called away, and yet he was one of the first." Age fifty when he joined the Court, Trimble served only two years before his death in 1828.

During his brief service, the number of cases decided by the high court totaled forty-eight the first term and fifty-five the next. Chief Justice John Marshall dominated the Court at the time, although somewhat less than in earlier decades, and he wrote a large share of the opinions himself. Trimble, however, outmatched the output of the next most prolific justices—Joseph Story and William Johnson—in the 1827 and 1828 terms. The first year he wrote nine majority opinions, and the second year, seven. Given Marshall's domination of the Court, this number was surprisingly large for a new justice. A majority of these opinions involved matters relating to land, probably because of Trimble's experience with land litigation in Kentucky.

Although generally a strong supporter of Chief Justice Marshall's views on the power of the federal judiciary, Trimble disagreed with Marshall in *Ogden v. Saunders* (1827). The case involved the question of the respective powers of the states and the federal legislature over bankruptcy jurisdiction, and final arguments before the justices had been delayed until Trimble took his seat. Several justices wrote majority opinions, including Trimble; Marshall dissented. In his writing, the Kentucky justice remembered his Jeffersonian roots and upheld the rights of states to legislate their own bankruptcy laws.

Trimble had not yet joined the Supreme Court when the famous case involving *The Antelope,* a ship engaged in the international slave trade, was originally decided. He did, however, speak for the Court in approving the methods that had been used in settling the ownership of the slaves found on the ship, thus closing the case.

In his first opinion for the Court, *Montgomery v. Hernandez* (1827), Trimble spelled out procedural matters that are still followed by the Court today. He argued that "the appellate jurisdiction of [the Supreme Court], in cases decided in state courts, is very special and limited in its character." To obtain a hearing in the Supreme Court for a violation of federal rights, he reasoned, one must have first raised that issue in a trial in the state court. A secondary issue, regarding limits on the length of time after a crime allegedly has been committed that a case may be prosecuted, also remains law to this day.

Following the adjournment of the 1828 Supreme Court term, Justice Trimble returned to his home in

Although officially a Democratic-Republican, as a district judge Robert Trimble tended to favor a strong national government. His Federalist leanings led him to support the power of the federal government against the wishes of Kentucky farmers. Trimble's opinions regarding the rights of settlers who made improvements on disputed lands made him particularly unpopular among his fellow frontiersmen. *Source: Library of Congress*

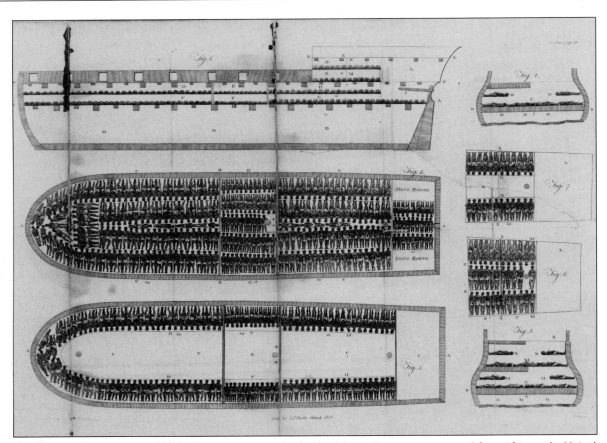

Shackled together by twos and crammed tightly into the dank holds of ships, slaves were transported from Africa to the United States to be sold at auction. In *The Antelope* (1825) the Court heard its first case involving slavery and determined that the institution, although immoral, was not illegal under international law. The case involved the question of how to "dispose of" human cargo brought to the United States by an American revenue cutter, which had captured *The Antelope,* a foreign ship bound from Africa. *Source: Library of Congress*

Kentucky. In August he was stricken by a recurrence of "bilious fever." He died at home August 25, and was buried in the Paris Cemetery. A local Kentucky newspaper noted: "The public has lost an upright, able, and faithful judge, society a useful, benevolent, and excellent citizen; his family a most affectionate and kind husband, a tender, provident, and indulgent parent, a mild, attentive, and excellent master." Privately, Chief Justice Marshall wrote to Kentucky senator Henry Clay: "I need not say how deeply I regret the loss of Judge Trimble. He was distinguished for sound sense, uprightness of intention, and legal knowledge. His superior can not be found. I wish we may find his equal."

Had Trimble lived a decade or so beyond his fifty-two years, he might well have been one of the outstanding members of the Supreme Court. Instead the most that can be said of him is that he showed promise. In the brief two years he served on the Court he did much more work than expected of a new member, and he did it in an impressive manner.

John McLean

1830-1861

Source: *Portrait of John McLean by John Wesley Jarvis, Collection of the Supreme Court of the United States*

JOHN MCLEAN was born March 11, 1785, in northern New Jersey, but in a series of moves by his family to western Virginia, Kentucky, and finally in 1797 to a farm near the town of Lebanon, Ohio, he became a westerner. At the age of eleven he traveled with his father to stake out the land that was to become the family farm. Throughout his career he was identified politically and geographically with the West.

McLean's Scotch-Irish ancestry has been traced back to the twelfth century. His father, born Fergus McLain, emigrated to New Jersey in 1775; he was a weaver by trade and a Presbyterian by conviction. He married Sophia Blackford of Middlesex County, New Jersey, and they had several children. Their son John was able to obtain an education in the raw frontier environment of his teenage years: he attended a nearby school in Warren County, Ohio, and later studied with two schoolmasters who were Presbyterian ministers, paying them with money he earned working as a farm hand. He was only nineteen when he began to study law, obtaining a two-year contractual apprenticeship with John S. Gano, a Cincinnati lawyer who was also clerk of the Court of Common Pleas of adjoining Hamilton County. Simultaneously he read law with a second attorney, Arthur St. Clair, Jr.

In 1807 McLean was admitted to the bar. He had just passed his twenty-second birthday when he married Rebecca Edwards of Newport, Kentucky, a union that was to produce four daughters and three sons. The need to support a wife, and soon a family, was undoubtedly a major factor in McLean's decision to open a printing office in Lebanon at the end of his apprenticeship and go into business. He established a weekly newspaper, the Lebanon *Western Star,* which, like virtually all the papers of the era, was partisan. McLean's newspaper supported the Jeffersonian party. By 1810 he was able to turn the newspaper and printing business over to his brother Nathaniel and work full time at the law.

In 1811 he was appointed examiner of the U.S. Land Office in Cincinnati, the first in a series of increasingly important political posts. The same year he underwent a religious experience that was to exert a tremendous influence throughout his life. A persuasive evangelist named John Collins converted McLean and his brother to Methodism. In time John McLean became the leading Methodist layman in the country. He wrote a series of articles on the Bible, and in 1849 was named honorary president of the American Sunday School Union.

The year following his conversion to Methodism, McLean won election, at age twenty-seven, to the U.S. Congress from one of the six Ohio districts. He had campaigned as a supporter of national unity and of President James Madison's vigorous prosecution of the War of 1812. McLean won reelection two years later, and became chairman of the House committee on accounts. He supported finance bills made necessary by the war and other nationalist measures, but also demonstrated sensitivity to egalitarian politics. Although he had voted for an earlier bill to establish a sec-

ond Bank of the United States, in 1816 he opposed the legislation that actually created the bank because the law permitted holders of depreciated government scrip to buy bank stock with it at an unequal exchange rate. On a pensions and compensation bill following the War of 1812, he pushed unsuccessfully for compensation based on loss, rather than military rank.

Members of Congress were ill-paid for their service. The lack of money and a desire to be closer to his growing family persuaded McLean to retire from his seat in 1816, but only after he had laid the base for a future political claim by working hard in the Democratic-Republican political caucus for James Monroe's presidential nomination. Back in Ohio, the legislature elected McLean one of four judges of the state supreme court. It was not an easy post; circuit riding was a huge burden, with a minimum of two members of the court sitting at least once a year in each county of Ohio. Rendering justice on circuit was particularly difficult. McLean was often without access to a law library, and resorting to postponements could delay resolution for as much as a year.

Most of the rulings and opinions of his state supreme court years were of only local interest. However, forty years later in the landmark *Dred Scott v. Sandford* case, a whole nation had good reason to remember a decision read by Judge McLean during his second year on the bench. A Kentucky slave named Richard Lunsford had been sold to a Cincinnati resident, who employed him in the free state of Ohio by day, but had him return to slavery in Kentucky each night. McLean ruled that Lunsford should be discharged from custody as a slave on the grounds that if a master used slave labor in a free state "by such act he forfeits the right of property in slaves." He did not go so far as to say that any slave introduced into free territory by his master was automatically freed, but used the decision to air a revealing personal bias. In the abstract, McLean said, he would lean toward emancipating all slaves "according to the im-

John McLean was appointed postmaster general in 1823 and served for six years. His tenure at the General Post Office, pictured here in about 1846, saw the expansion of the postal system throughout the country and a return to profitability. By 1828 the service had become the largest department in the government, with many employees appointed as a result of political loyalty to the party in power. *Source: Library of Congress*

mutable principles of natural justice." An institution that has "its origin in usurpation and fraud can never be sanctified into a right. But as a judge I am sworn to support the Constitution of the United States."

In 1822 McLean lost a bid in the state legislature to be elected to the U.S. Senate. But shortly thereafter his advocacy six years earlier for James Monroe, now president, brought its first reward. Monroe appointed him commissioner of the booming General Land Office in Washington, D.C., tripling his previous salary, and the following year elevated him to the position of postmaster general.

For the next six years McLean proved to be an exceptionally able administrator, popular with his employees. He greatly expanded the number of routes and deliveries, established more than 3,000 new post offices, and earned a reputation for hard work, fairness, and efficiency. He converted an operational loss of more than $150,000 a year when he took office to a net profit of $100,000 by 1827. The service became the largest department of government, employing almost 27,000 people by 1828.

McLean began to harbor aspirations for the presidency, an ambition that would persist until his death in 1861. By this time, he was demonstrating a remarkable talent for survival in the shifting landscape of nineteenth century American politics. McLean had managed to survive as postmaster general following the election of President John Quincy Adams in 1824, despite having been a strong original supporter of Adams's rival, John C. Calhoun.

However, it eventually became clear to Adams that McLean was using his power of appointment to cultivate ties to Andrew Jackson, the only serious contender to threaten Adams's reelection. By the last year of his presidency, Adams was convinced that McLean was a "double-dealer," but complained that he "plays his game with so much cunning and duplicity that I can fix upon no positive act that would justify the removal of him." McLean's "duplicity" was quickly rewarded following Jackson's election in 1828. On March 7, 1829, he was named to succeed Robert Trimble of Kentucky in the so-called "western seat" on the Supreme Court, and he was confirmed the same day.

Ascent to the Court did not diminish McLean's aspirations for the presidency, however, and his political activities while on the high bench are perhaps unparalleled in the history of the Court. McLean carried on successive flirtations for the presidential nomination with several political parties, quickly breaking his political ties with the president who had appointed him. His name was often presented to more than one national party convention, and usually withdrawn before the voting began. He first put himself forward as a moderate Democrat and then affiliated himself with the anti-Masons. In 1848 he was a potential nominee of the Free Soil party, but was overtaken by Martin Van Buren. He was also in the ring for the Whig party's nomination in 1848, but nothing came of it. By 1854 McLean had become a member of the newly formed Republican party and received 196 first ballot votes, compared to John

C. Fremont's 359, at the party's 1856 convention in Philadelphia before once more withdrawing his name. Only a year before his death, at the historic Republican convention of 1860 that nominated Abraham Lincoln, McLean once again figured among the nominees.

During his thirty-two-year tenure on the Court, McLean shifted from supporting a Jacksonian view of constitutional law to a nationalist one. He developed a close relationship with Justice Joseph Story, who persuaded him of the merits of strengthening the powers of the federal government. After Story's death in 1845, McLean became the senior associate justice and presided over the Court with ability and efficiency during Chief Justice Roger B. Taney's frequent absences due to ill health.

McLean wrote his most important majority opinion in the 1834 case of *Wheaton v. Peters,* which involved a dispute between two of the Supreme Court's reporters of decisions. To increase sales and make money, Richard Peters, Jr., decided to revise and republish the decisions recorded by his predecessor, Henry Wheaton. Fearing that the public would no longer need to buy the old decisions from him, and that he would receive correspondingly fewer profits from their sales, Wheaton sued Peters. The Court found that the opinions were public domain and that there was no violation of copyright.

McLean is recorded in history above all for his dissent in the fateful *Dred Scott* case of 1857 in which Scott, a slave, sued his master for freedom in a Missouri court after having been taken to live for several years on free soil. The dissenting opinions of McLean and his colleague Benjamin Curtis helped prod the majority to go beyond disposing of the case on the narrow, less inflammatory ground that Scott's fate must be determined by Missouri law. In his dissent McLean insisted that Congress had the power to exclude slavery from the territories and to liberate blacks voluntarily brought into free states. His argument led the five majority justices to go to the heart of the issue, holding that blacks

While a sitting justice, John McLean (middle row, second from right) joined various political parties in an effort to fulfill his presidential ambitions. His last bid for the White House came in 1860, a year before his death, when he was one of the Republican party's candidates for nomination. *Harper's Weekly* pictured the leading Republican candidates on the eve of the convention, placing William H. Seward, the favorite, in the center. In an unexpected and dramatic climax, Abraham Lincoln (bottom row, second from left) won the nomination. *Source: National Portrait Gallery*

Henry Wheaton, the Supreme Court's first official reporter of decisions, was appointed in 1816. *Source: Portrait of Henry Wheaton by Robert Hinckley, Collection of the Supreme Court of the United States*

Richard Peters, Jr., became the Court reporter in 1828. *Source: Portrait of Richard Peters, Jr., by Robert Hinckley, Collection of the Supreme Court of the United States*

could not be citizens and that Congress could not pass legislation to prevent the spread of slavery to the territories.

Dred Scott fanned the fires that eventually led to the Civil War. When the war was won, McLean's dissent was virtually written into the Constitution as the Fourteenth Amendment. Thus, a single dissenting opinion from his pen may have done more to direct the course of American history than his three decades of casting in the troubled political waters of presidential politics for a prize that forever eluded him.

Large in size and aloof in manner, McLean was often criticized for his cold demeanor but praised for his financial generosity to friends and family in need. His seventy-six years were not without their personal tragedies. Between 1834 and 1841, three of McLean's four daughters died, as did his parents. In 1839 his brother William died from consumption; and the responsibility of taking care of his nephews increased McLean's already heavy financial burdens. Then came the death of his wife in 1840. Three years later McLean married Sarah Bella Garrard, daughter of a distinguished Cincinnati family and the widow of a prominent lawyer. They had one son, Ludlow, who died a few weeks after his birth in the summer of 1846. The second Mrs. McLean was an advocate of abolition and may have reinforced her husband's antislavery views.

McLean was showing evidence of failing strength as early as 1859, but he managed to serve through the 1860–1861 session of the Court. In March he returned to his home near Cincinnati, going into the city nearly every day before his death on April 3, 1861.

Henry Baldwin

1830-1844

Source: Portrait of Henry Baldwin by Thomas Sully, Collection of the Supreme Court of the United States

H ENRY BALDWIN came from a remarkable New England family. Born January 14, 1780, in New Haven, Connecticut, he was the son of Michael and Theodora Wolcot Baldwin. Michael Baldwin was a blacksmith, a respectable occupation in his day, who married Theodora after his first wife died. The family produced a number of prominent children. Abraham, who was Henry's half brother, represented Georgia in the Constitutional Convention of 1787 and in the U.S. Senate. His sister Ruth and her fa-

mous husband, poet Joel Barlow, lived at Kalorama, a Washington, D.C., mansion where presidents and dignitaries were entertained. Brother Michael, also a lawyer, settled in Ohio and helped write its constitution.

That Henry was to enroll at Yale was a foregone conclusion because his brothers had gone there. His classmate, Lyman Beecher, who became a noted evangelist, believed the college at that time was in a "most ungodly state," with student skepticism, intemperance, profanity, gambling, and licentiousness commonplace. He may have had Baldwin in mind when he described the seedy side of his college days, for Baldwin was not exactly a model student. Another classmate, Thomas Day, recalled that Baldwin's reputation was that of a "light-headed boy, who neither aimed at, nor attained to, much distinction as a scholar."

Still, Day remembered him as someone whose mental powers developed after his graduation in 1797 while attending the law lectures of Tapping Reeve at his school in Litchfield, Connecticut. Arguing hypothetical cases before a moot court was more to Baldwin's liking than the uninspiring lectures at Yale. His Litchfield stay also helped shape his early political convictions. The Federalist politics of Reeve and his assistant, James Gould, convinced Baldwin that he belonged in the opposite camp, that of the Jeffersonian party.

After Litchfield, Baldwin clerked in the law offices of Philadelphia's Alexander James Dallas, an outstanding lawyer and a clever strategist for the Jeffersonians. His apprenticeship prepared him both professionally and politically. Once he was admitted to the bar, Baldwin moved to Meadville, Pennsylvania, to begin his duties as deputy attorney general (the title was later changed

to district attorney). His political appointment was part of a revamping of the state following the 1799 election of Thomas McKean as governor. With Dallas's help, the new governor and the Jeffersonians broke up the huge Federalist county of Allegheny into many new counties, including Crawford, in which Meadville is located.

In a few years Baldwin moved to Pittsburgh. Opportunities were much greater in this promising manufacturing town. Congenial, talented, and handsome, he soon became one of Pittsburgh's most respected lawyers and civic-minded residents. With his colleague, Tarlton Bates, and his law partner, Walter Forward, he also provided leadership for a Jeffersonian faction and its newspaper, the *Tree of Liberty*. The political scene at this time was so intense that differences were sometimes settled with dueling pistols. Bates was killed in a duel; and the story goes that in another duel Baldwin was spared when a silver dollar in his pocket stopped a bullet from entering his chest.

In 1802 Baldwin married Marianna Norton, a distant cousin. The following year she died after giving birth to his only child, Henry, who would also become a lawyer. Baldwin then married Sally Ellicott, the daughter of Andrew Ellicott, the famous surveying engineer. The

Demand was so great for Tapping Reeve's law lectures that he built a one-room schoolhouse next to his house to accommodate more students and his law library. In 1798 Reeve took on a partner, former student James Gould, to share the teaching load. Gould continued the school after Reeve's death in 1823, but declining enrollments and competition forced it to close its doors in 1830. Among the more than 1,000 graduates were three Supreme Court justices, Henry Baldwin, Levi Woodbury, and Ward Hunt. *Courtesy of the Litchfield Historical Society, Litchfield, Connecticut*

marriage was not a particularly happy one, and they spent much time apart.

A successful practice made Baldwin a pillar in the business community and enabled him to invest in several mills, turnpike companies, and land. Some of these investments were rewarding; most were not. The purchase of more than 600 land warrants in northwestern Pennsylvania for $90,000, for example, proved disastrous.

A favorite with Pittsburgh's manufacturing class, Baldwin ran for Congress in 1816 and was elected as a coalition candidate. The campaign issues were less political than economic. Faced with hard times following the War of 1812, the moneyed groups in Pittsburgh, notably the manufacturers, demanded that their interests be well represented in Congress. And no one in the House of Representatives spoke more convincingly for protecting American industry than Baldwin. His revised tariff bill got through the House with ease, but died in the Senate. Southerners and mercantile interests feared that protectionism would lead to a reduction in trade, higher prices, and a deeper slump in the economy.

During debate over Missouri's admission to the Union, Baldwin criticized northern attempts to restrict slavery in that territory. If Missourians want slavery, he argued, that is their choice. Although he disliked slavery, he questioned the constitutionality of its restriction and cautioned against the abuse of federal powers. Should northerners continue to expand these powers, he feared the federal system would collapse.

Nothing he did in Congress affected his career more than his defense of Andrew Jackson's conduct in the Seminole War. Raiding parties of Indians and runaway slaves had crossed into Georgia to pillage American settlements before fleeing back to their Florida sanctuaries. General Jackson marched across the border, destroyed property, punished the Indians, and executed two British subjects. Some in government were out-

raged and demanded that Jackson be court-martialed for these acts, but Baldwin disagreed. Confining his remarks to the legal aspects of the affair, he said Jackson had acted properly and had not violated the Constitution, for it was never intended to protect renegades.

Jackson eluded a court-martial and never forgot how Baldwin had stood up for him while others were knotting the noose. It was the beginning of a long friendship; Jackson often sought Baldwin's counsel. After his resignation from Congress in 1822 because of ill health, Baldwin campaigned for a Jackson presidency. With Baldwin's help, Jackson mania spread throughout Pennsylvania, and the general achieved victory in 1828.

Jackson's election opened the door for Baldwin's eventual appointment to the Supreme Court. At first, he expected to be named secretary of the Treasury, a position that Jackson had intended to offer him; but Pennsylvania supporters of Vice President John C. Calhoun did not like Baldwin and persuaded the president to appoint another Pennsylvanian, Samuel Ingham, instead. Visibly shaken, Baldwin vented his hostility against those "blacklegs" and "reptiles" who surrounded the president. Jackson had disappointed him. After years of loyalty and service, "I am regarded of as much consequence as a candlesnuffer at a court-house meeting," he wrote a friend. "It was my misfortune to have been the friend of the General." Jackson offered Baldwin three foreign missions, all of which he refused.

Baldwin sulked, feeling sorry for himself. But his appointment to the nation's highest court following the death of Bushrod Washington revived his faith in his fellow man, or at least in Jackson. Only the two senators from Calhoun's South Carolina voted against his confirmation on January 6, 1830. Mixed feelings greeted the news of Baldwin's appointment, but the majority of the opinions expressed were favorable.

Baldwin's judicial tenure got off to a bad start. So unhappy was he with what he regarded as an untenable extension of the Court's powers that he considered re-

The Seminole Indians of Spanish Florida angered their northern neighbors by siding with the British in the War of 1812 and attacking American villages and army posts, as depicted here. After several such raids into Georgia, Gen. Andrew Jackson and his troops crossed into Florida in 1818 to retaliate. Many in Congress thought Jackson's brutal measures, especially the execution of two Britons, cause for court-martial, but Rep. Henry Baldwin argued that Jackson had not violated the law, thus winning Jackson's gratitude. *Source: Library of Congress*

signing, but Jackson talked him out of it. During the 1831 term he dissented so often and his conduct became so irascible and unconventional that word circulated that his mind had become unhinged. Unpredictable, intemperate, and antagonistic—and virtually oblivious to the negative feelings he stirred in others—Baldwin certainly did not fit the image of a typical austere jurist. One learned judge of Philadelphia was sure Baldwin was insane simply because he had coffee and cakes brought to him on the bench. By nineteenth century standards, perhaps he was, but those who knew him best insisted that his accusers were unaccustomed to his independence, peculiarities, and strange humor. He carried candy in his pockets to pass among children, played silly pranks on his friends, and, as a judge, once shocked observers by strutting down a street carrying a ham by the hock.

Many of his judicial views, Baldwin admitted, were not in the mainstream, which was one reason he was appointed. Jackson hoped some braking action might be applied to the Supreme Court's continuing efforts to strengthen the roles of Congress and the federal judiciary. The president wanted Baldwin to alter the direction of the Court, but Baldwin's independence made him an unreliable follower of administration policy.

The two men were at odds over the legitimacy of the United States Bank and over *United States v. Arrendondo* (1832), a case regarding land titles. Jackson was furious with Baldwin for that landmark opinion, which forced the government to have greater respect for treaties.

Baldwin was unlikely to bend the Constitution to accommodate anyone. Abstract notions, sentimentality, or pleas for compassion did not soften him. He ruled out public opinion as a factor in judicial proceedings. Public feelings for the Indian and slave did not budge Baldwin from his commitment to constitutional restraint. In two 1830s cases involving the state of Georgia and the Cherokees, he showed little sympathy for the Indians. With respect to slavery, he stated in *Groves v. Slaughter* (1841) that slaves were "property" as well as "persons" and therefore subject to congressional regulation in interstate commerce. Baldwin did not care what the abolitionists had to say. Slaves were property: it was the law of the land. In *Johnson v. Tompkins and Others* (1833) and *Prigg v. Pennsylvania* (1842) he upheld fugitive slave laws.

After the death of Chief Justice John Marshall, with whom he disagreed but whom he greatly admired, Baldwin remained no less independent on the Court of

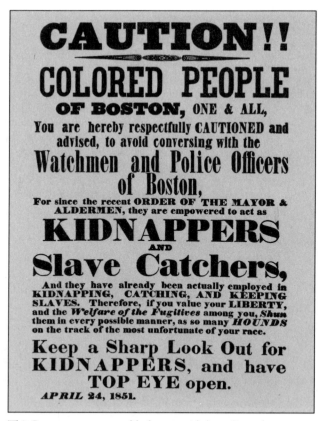

This Boston poster warns blacks to avoid the police, who, as a result of the Fugitive Slave Act of 1850, were empowered to kidnap alleged fugitive slaves and return them to owners in another state. The act was passed partly in response to the Supreme Court's decision in *Prigg v. Pennsylvania* (1842), which denied that the states had the authority to enact fugitive slave laws, prompting the South to clamor for a tougher federal law. *Source: Library of Congress*

Roger B. Taney. Aware of his "peculiar views," he decided to publish his separate opinions on several cases in the 1837 term. The result was *A General View of the Origin and Nature of the Constitution and Government of the United States*. More significant than his opinions, however, was his concern with the extremism he felt was motivating certain jurists and lawmakers. At one end was the nationalist school, which sought to extend the authority of the federal government through the "implied powers" of the Constitution; at the other was

the strict or narrow constructionist school, which wanted to inflate the reserved powers of the states under the Tenth Amendment. Neither faction was good for the federal system, he concluded. He supported a third view: the Constitution was a grant of the sovereign people of each state and must be interpreted according to the "expressed intention" of its Framers. Jurists and lawmakers must not read meaning into the document. If change is necessary or desired, it must be brought about through amendment.

Baldwin's years on the bench were not happy. Financial and physical problems were in part responsible. Prior to his appointment he had filed for bankruptcy, and in the winter of 1832–1833 he suffered a serious breakdown that hospitalized him and caused him to miss one Court term. He had good days and days when his disposition was totally disagreeable. He seemed to perform better on circuit than in Washington, where his mannerisms upset those with whom he worked, particularly Richard Peters, the Court reporter.

His eccentricity tainted his reputation as a jurist. At best, he played the devil's advocate by combating every idea that appeared to him repugnant to the Constitution. His tenacity was important at a time when that document was being twisted to validate one view or another regarding the very nature of the Union. By defending the rights of states against federal intervention, he was sustaining a principle unpopular with many Americans, but he did not care.

Baldwin died in Philadelphia April 21, 1844. He had had little chance to enjoy the comforts of the beautiful mansion he built in Meadville. Burdened with debt, his widow had no choice but to sell it. Earlier, he had made arrangements with Taney to sell part of his library, one of the finest in the country. Baldwin was remembered as a political maverick, a controversial and disruptive jurist, an indifferent businessman, and an unyielding champion of the Constitution and the federal system.

James M. Wayne

1835-1867

ONE OF only twelve justices to serve on the Supreme Court more than thirty years, James Moore Wayne joined the Court when John Marshall was chief justice and served until the end of the Civil War. He was born sometime in 1790, in Savannah, Georgia, the twelfth of thirteen children. His father, Richard Wayne, had come to America from England in 1759 as a junior major in the British army. He settled in Charlestown, South Carolina, prospered as a commission merchant, and married Elizabeth Clif-

ford, a member of an old and influential South Carolina family.

Richard Wayne showed his sympathies with the American revolutionary cause by enlisting in the South Carolina Regiment of Volunteer Militia. Later, after being taken prisoner by British troops and paroled, he had a change of heart and joined the British militia. Five years after the end of the Revolutionary War, Richard Wayne moved with his family to Savannah, then only a village, where James was born. By the time

James was four years old his family was prominently established in Savannah's social and commercial life.
Richard Wayne owned plantations and rice fields, with
nearly 100 slaves; his wharf and store were prospering,
and his commerce included trade in slaves.

James began his education with an Irish tutor, who
came to Savannah to live with the family. The boy
made such rapid progress that he qualified for enrollment in the College of New Jersey (now Princeton) at
the age of thirteen. His tutors held him back a year because of his youth, and he entered the college in 1804.
Wayne was bored by the classical curriculum and
tended to neglect his assignments in favor of outside
reading. This interest in books was the beginning of a
lifelong devotion to reading that would later make him
a familiar sight at the Library of Congress during his
Washington years. He managed to graduate in 1808,
but not without first being expelled temporarily for
participating in a student rebellion.

Wayne returned to Savannah to read law under a
local attorney and then was accepted for instruction by
Judge Charles Chauncy of New Haven, a distinguished
lecturer on the law. Wayne performed well, but returned to Savannah when his father died in 1810 to settle the estate. He continued his legal studies in the office of his brother-in-law, Richard Stites, who had become his legal guardian on his father's death. Following
an examination in open court, Wayne was admitted to
the bar in January 1811. Wayne began his legal career in
partnership with a young lawyer named Samuel M.
Bond. The firm was dissolved in 1816, and for the next
three years Wayne practiced independently. However,
there was much to distract him from the law during
this period.

With the outbreak of the War of 1812, Wayne enlisted
in a newly formed company of cavalry, the Chatham
Light Dragoons. Two years later he was elected captain.
In 1813 Wayne married eighteen-year-old Mary Johnson
Campbell, daughter of a distinguished Richmond, Virginia, attorney. The marriage lasted until Wayne's death
fifty-four years later and produced three children, of
whom the first-born, James Alexander Wayne, died in
1818 at the age of four.

The Waynes were popular in social circles, so much
so that Judge Chauncy wrote to his former pupil that
attending balls and dinners was no way to become a
lawyer. Wayne later admitted that Chauncy was "more
than half right." Savannah had developed an active social scene, with balls, theater, a literary society, card
games, golf, and horse racing. Opulent houses were
being built, and in 1821 the Waynes moved into a handsome Regency residence complete with three cooks and
five other servants.

During this period Wayne began his political career
as one of five candidates to represent Chatham County
in the Georgia legislature. His campaign platform included "a limitation of the action of the Government to
the text of the constitution—the best and only security
for the perpetuity of the Union." Wayne received 460
out of 557 votes cast in the 1815 election, and he was reelected the following year by a similarly wide margin.
His first speech in the legislature was published and circulated around the state, beginning his reputation as an
orator.

Meanwhile, Wayne had become an alderman of the
city of Savannah, and in 1817, at the age of twenty-
seven, he was elected mayor. He wrestled with stubborn
fiscal problems, including an expenditure of $80,000
for an effort to decrease malaria-breeding wetlands. But
if malaria was decreased, yellow fever continued to rage
and, in Wayne's words, to bring the hearse "to every
man's door."

Wayne resigned as mayor after two years to resume
his law practice, this time in partnership with a young
lawyer named Richard R. Cuyler. Later that year Wayne
was elected judge of a newly created court of common
pleas for the city of Savannah, with jurisdiction in mis-
demeanor and minor civil cases. His salary was small,

As a representative from South Carolina, James M. Wayne led the cry for nullification of the 1828 "tariff of abominations," which placed a duty on manufactured goods. Angry at having to purchase goods from northern manufacturers at higher prices, the South rebelled. This cartoon shows England's delight as "The Union Pie" begins to crumble and South Carolina threatens secession if the federal government forces it to collect the hated tariff. Opposition was the most vigorous in South Carolina because the depression of 1819 had caused cotton prices to plummet. *Courtesy of the New York Historical Society*

but he was able to continue with his law practice on the side. His firm soon built up a substantial practice in most of the state and federal courts of eastern Georgia.

After an unsuccessful candidacy in 1821, the following year Wayne was elected superior court judge for Georgia's eastern circuit by the legislature. There was no lack of work: a typical workload for a term consisted of 129 cases covering a wide variety of legal issues.

Wayne left the bench to run for the U.S. Congress in 1828 and was elected without difficulty. During his first term, he was challenged to a duel by William C. Daniell, a well-known Savannah physician. Daniell was angered by Wayne's role in initiating a federal investigation of efforts to clear the Savannah River of certain obstructions, a project Daniell supervised. Although actively opposed to dueling, Wayne could not walk away from the challenge. Daniell refused, however, to accept Wayne's choice of weapons—broad swords and rifles—and the affair ended.

In Congress, Wayne, elected as a Democrat, supported most of the policies of President Andrew Jackson. He backed Jackson's refusal to accept the creation of a Cherokee Indian nation within Georgia's boundaries, a position popular with the majority of Wayne's

As the numbers of immigrants streaming into U.S. ports increased dramatically in the mid-1840s, coastal states began to worry about how to accommodate the new arrivals. Unlike those disembarking from this relatively elegant ship in 1855, many immigrants were poor and illiterate. When states passed laws taxing all newcomers to help support the indigent ones, the Supreme Court struck down the laws as violations of the commerce power of the federal government. *Museum of the City of New York*

constituents. He was at least as opposed as Jackson to the centralized Bank of the United States.

Wayne was reelected to Congress in 1830, 1832, and 1834. There was passionate opposition in the South to the "tariff of abominations" of 1828, which imposed costly duties on a number of raw materials and manufactured goods imported from overseas. South Carolina had declared the tariff unconstitutional and in 1832 moved to have it "nullified" or revoked. The state forbade the collection of duties within South Carolina, threatening secession if the federal government resorted to force. Wayne sought a middle ground, opposing both the tariff and nullification. He was the only member of the Georgia delegation to support President Jackson's "force bill," which gave the president authority to use federal troops to collect tariffs. Wayne constantly sought to find a compromise between his unwavering

support for the Union and mounting dissatisfaction in the South with federal policies.

Associate Justice William Johnson of North Carolina died in 1834, creating a vacancy on the Supreme Court. To maintain regional balance on the Court, Jackson needed to appoint another southerner; he nominated Wayne, his supporter, on January 6, 1835. Three days later the Senate confirmed the appointment of the Unionist southerner by voice vote. He took his seat on the bench only five months before the death of Chief Justice John Marshall.

Wayne was just short of forty-five years of age when he became an associate justice. A visitor to the Court in 1850 described him "as an exceedingly handsome man—about 5 feet 10 inches high, of stout but graceful figure, muddy complexion, fine teeth and clustering wavy hair, now mixed with gray." Another called him "the model of an elegant, cultivated and courtly gentleman."

On the Court, Wayne was a strong nationalist, an unusual position for a southern justice. He opposed the exercise of state power in the *Passenger Cases* (1847), which involved state attempts to regulate immigration by taxing newcomers, because he thought it violated Congress's power under the Commerce Clause of the Constitution. In the 1852 case, *Cooley v. Board of Wardens of the Port of Philadelphia,* he expressed a similar view of sovereignty and commerce in a nationalist dissent. His views on commerce extended to supporting the rights of corporations and opposing state attempts to remove their tax exemptions.

His lack of sympathy for state sovereignty led him to be surprisingly unsupportive, for a southerner, of slavery. The first case assigned to him at the 1835 term involved a slave's freedom. Wayne ruled that the right of a slave given his freedom in his owner's will was superior to the claim of a creditor, so long as there were sufficient property assets to meet the debts of the owner's estate. He did, however, support the broad sweep of the *Dred Scott v. Sandford* decision of 1857. Indeed, it was Wayne who persuaded Chief Justice Roger B. Taney to tackle the issue of the constitutionality of the congressional attempt to prohibit slavery from the territories head on, instead of ruling on narrower issues. Such a decision, he said, "could put an end to all further agitation of the subject of slavery in the territories."

Instead, three years later the Civil War broke out, and Wayne saw his only son, Maj. Henry C. Wayne, resign his commission in the United States Army and return home to fight for Georgia. Throughout the war he stayed with the Georgia state troops, refusing high-ranking commissions in the Confederate Army. Henry Wayne ended the war as a general in command of the last military resistance to Union general William Sherman's victorious march to the sea. Although he supported his son's decision to return to Georgia, Justice Wayne stayed in Washington.

Unlike his colleague, John Campbell of Alabama, Wayne refused to resign his seat, and remained a strong supporter of the Union throughout the war. He believed the Court needed "a judicial voice in behalf of the South and her Constitutional rights." His decision was not without agonizing results. Justice Wayne's citizenship was repealed in 1862 by a Georgia court, which branded him an enemy alien and seized his property. Said a southern newspaper: "Georgia does not claim him, and he is no more of us." The northern press praised him, however, for his decision to stay on the bench. By remaining on the Court he was able to affirm his lifelong faith in the Union and the Constitution by consistently voting to uphold the contested war measures of the administration of Abraham Lincoln.

As soon as the war ended, Wayne took passage on a ship to Georgia, arriving in Savannah in May 1865. A local paper reported his arrival and said his "numerous friends" would be pleased to see him. By special authority of President Andrew Johnson, Gen. Henry Wayne was allowed to visit Washington the following September and be reunited with his parents, his wife, and his children.

Both during and after the war, Justice Wayne used his influence to assist his southern compatriots. He even obtained a pardon for the judge of the court that had ruled him an enemy alien. In 1867 Wayne cast the deciding vote in a Supreme Court ruling that invalidated the federal and state loyalty oaths that had prevented ex-Confederates from pursuing their vocations. He opposed measures designed to punish the South and refused to perform his circuit court duties in Southern states under military rule by the federal government.

In the hot Washington summer of 1867, Wayne contracted typhoid fever. He died July 5, at age seventy-seven, bringing to a close thirty-two years of service to the Court.

Roger B. Taney
1836-1864

ROGER BROOKE TANEY, the fifth chief justice of the United States, was born in Calvert County, Maryland, March 17, 1777. His father, Michael Taney, owned a tobacco plantation and was a member of a prominent Roman Catholic family whose ancestors had settled in the tidewater area of Maryland in the 1660s. After attending a local school and being tutored by a Princeton College graduate, Roger Taney entered Dickinson College in Carlisle, Pennsylvania, at the age of fifteen. Elected class valedictorian, he graduated in 1795.

As his father's second son, Taney did not stand to inherit the family plantation, so he moved to Annapolis, where he studied law for three years under Judge Jeremiah Chase of Maryland's General Court. Taney was a zealous student who read "for weeks together . . . twelve hours in the twenty- four." While in Annapolis he became acquainted with Francis Scott Key, the illustrious attorney who wrote the words to "The Star-Spangled Banner." Key became his lifelong friend, and in time, his brother-in-law. Taney was admitted to the bar in 1799.

The same year Taney went into the practice of law, he also entered politics. A member of the Federalist party, he served for one year in the Maryland House of Delegates but lost his seat in the anti-Federalist tide brought on by Thomas Jefferson's election as president in 1800. He then moved to the town of Frederick, Maryland, where he practiced law for more than two decades. He would never stray far from his native Maryland, and there is no record that he ever made a journey of any consequence, either north or south, on his own volition. His provincialism, although concealed by the urbanity of his manners, was a distinctive element of his character.

In 1806 Taney married Anne Phoebe Carlton Key, the beautiful daughter of a wealthy farmer, John Ross Key, and sister of Francis Scott Key. Although Taney was a devout Roman Catholic, he agreed to raise their six daughters in the Episcopalian faith of his wife. Under the couple's pact, a son, who died in infancy, would have been raised a Catholic. Taney, who suffered poor health throughout his life, was described in his youth as a "tall, gaunt fellow, as lean as a Potomac herring, and as shrewd as the shrewdest." His marriage to Anne was likened to the "union of a hawk with a skylark," because of their contrasting appearances. Taney had a passion for flowers and nature, which his wife shared.

While continuing his profitable legal practice, Taney remained active in politics, although he became something of a political maverick. When the Maryland Federalist party split into factions over the War of 1812 controversy, the section of the party that supported the war was soon named the "Coodies," and Taney, the faction's leader, became known as "King Coody." Although he

backed Federalist concerns, such as a national bank, he also believed in states' rights—particularly on the issue of slavery. Taney had freed the slaves he inherited, but he still believed the federal government had no right to limit the institution of slavery and that questions involving slavery should be resolved by individual states.

Due to a change in the political climate, Taney regained Federalist support and was elected to the Maryland Senate in 1816. After serving his five-year term, he settled in Baltimore in 1823. He continued to be successful in his law practice and in party politics, and was elected attorney general of Maryland in 1827.

Abandoning the Federalists, Taney became a staunch supporter of Andrew Jackson and the Democratic party and threw himself into partisan politics with zeal. He was rewarded for leading Maryland's effort in behalf of Jackson's successful 1828 presidential campaign by being named U.S. attorney general in 1831. Taney became Jackson's confidant and for a brief time acted as secretary of war in addition to his duties as attorney general.

When Taney came into the cabinet, Jackson was already embroiled in a battle with the Senate over the rechartering of the national Bank of the United States. The bank's charter was due to expire in 1836, and Jackson, who disliked banks in general and particularly feared a centralized one, was determined the charter would not be renewed. In July 1832 Congress passed a bill to recharter the bank and sent it to the president for approval. Jackson vetoed the bill and returned it to Congress with a vehement attack against the "moneyed Monster." The conflict became so bitter that Vice President Martin Van Buren was forced to wear pistols to preside over the Senate when it debated the bank's future.

Enraged over actions that had been taken to ensure the bank's survival, Jackson demanded that Secretary of the Treasury William J. Duane withdraw all federal funds. Duane refused to carry out the order or to resign

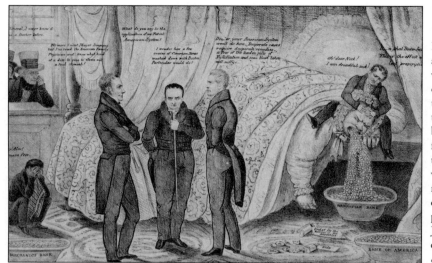

President Andrew Jackson was determined to shut down the Bank of the United States, which he thought had a privileged monopoly of the government's business. In 1833 Secretary of the Treasury Roger B. Taney ordered the bank's funds moved to smaller state banks, clearing out its coffers three years before its charter was due to expire. This cartoon depicts the bank as an obese woman vomiting coins into basins marked with the names of state banks. Bank president Nicholas Biddle is holding her head, while supporters Henry Clay, Daniel Webster, and John Calhoun are lampooned as doctors discussing various political remedies. *Source: Library of Congress*

his position. In desperation, Jackson fired Duane and replaced him with his loyal supporter, Taney, who, upon taking office, ordered the removal of federal funds, thereby sealing the bank's fate.

As secretary of the Treasury, Taney oversaw the creation of a network of depository state banks designed to substitute for the national bank. He named the Union Bank of Maryland as one of these "pet banks." When the news came out, however, that Taney had previously been employed at the Union Bank as an attorney, and that he owned some of its stock, questions of conflict of interest were raised. Because of the tense political climate, Jackson had delayed sending Taney's name to the Senate for approval for the Treasury post as long as possible. When he finally did, the Senate rejected Taney's nomination, although by then it was June 1834 and Taney had already held the position for nine months. He was the first cabinet nominee to be rejected by the Senate.

Taney returned to private practice in Baltimore, but in 1835 Jackson nominated him to replace Gabriel Duvall on the Supreme Court. By postponing its decision indefinitely after a close vote, the Senate again refused to confirm Taney's appointment to a federal post. Nearly ten months later, Jackson nominated him to succeed John Marshall, whose death had left the chief justice's seat vacant. The Senate confirmed his appointment, by a vote of 29–15, on March 15, 1836. Believing him much too radical, the Whigs, then the opposition party, were furious and claimed that Taney's political connections would prejudice his judicial role.

The Maryland justice became the first non-Protestant and first Roman Catholic to sit on the high bench. It is ironic to note that Taney, the aristocrat, introduced the custom of wearing ordinary trousers instead of formal knee breeches under judicial robes. Taney also changed the way the Court issued opinions. Chief Justice Marshall had delivered the vast majority of the Court's constitutional decisions in order to give an appearance of unanimity and increase the Court's power. Taney initiated the practice of assigning important opinions to associate justices to write—a custom that has continued ever since.

The tradition of living together in a boardinghouse was abandoned during Taney's tenure as the justices began to bring their wives with them to Washington. Despite the divisions caused by sharp ideological and personal differences, the persuasive and well-respected chief justice was remarkably able at getting the Court to work together.

Taney was a man who held seemingly contradictory views. He adhered to the Jacksonian principle of "divided sovereignty," which held that the states and the national government should share powers. In Taney's view it was up to the Supreme Court to decide which powers should be shared and which should be assigned as state or federal domain. Many worried that Taney would break with the nationalism of the Marshall Court by granting the states autonomy on significant issues. While his Court did indeed transfer some powers to the states, particularly in the realm of commerce, it refined but did not dismantle his predecessor's federalist vision.

One controversial modification, however, pertained to Marshall's view of the sanctity of business contracts. Many were outraged by Taney's opinion in *Charles River Bridge v. Warren Bridge* (1837), the first assertion by the Court that private property had a social responsibility and that contracts made by the legislature should be construed in the public interest. In addition to establishing the modern doctrine on contracts,

Taney was progressive in many other areas of constitutional law.

Despite his modernizing influence on the Court, the chief justice's reactionary stance on slavery has tended to cloud his reputation. In his notorious *Dred Scott v. Sandford* (1857) opinion, Taney ambitiously and unwisely tried to settle the issue of slavery once and for all. He thought that by issuing a clear decision on slavery, the Court could save the Union from the sectional strife that was tearing it apart. Unfortunately, the decision had the opposite result. It struck a serious blow to the reputation of the chief justice and the Court and hastened the outbreak of the Civil War.

Taney ruled in *Dred Scott* that the Framers of the Constitution had considered slaves to be so inferior that they possessed no legal rights, hence they could neither become citizens of the United States nor have standing in federal courts. The judgment further declared the Missouri Compromise unconstitutional because Congress was bound by Article V of the Constitution to protect personal property and, because the Constitution recognized slaves as property, Congress was bound to protect slavery in the territories.

The monopoly of this chartered toll bridge, built in the 1780s to link Boston with Cambridge, Massachusetts, was later challenged by a rival bridge. The result was one of the landmark Supreme Court decisions, *Charles River Bridge v. Warren Bridge* (1837). The owners of the Charles River Bridge claimed that their state charter gave them exclusive right to traffic across the river, but Chief Justice Roger B. Taney ruled that the state had the authority to approve construction of a second bridge because it was in the public interest. *Source: Library of Congress*

News of the controversial *Dred Scott v. Sandford* decision commanded the nation's attention in 1857. The Supreme Court determined that Congress was powerless to restrict slavery in the territories and that blacks were not citizens. The case was based on Missouri slave Dred Scott's appeal for freedom because his owner, an army surgeon, had taken him to live for several years in free territory. Although Scott, pictured here with his wife, Harriet, lost the suit, his owner freed him. *Source: Library of Congress*

Taney's opinion in the *Dred Scott* case came some thirty-five years after he had spoken out against slavery while arguing the case of a northern Methodist minister accused of inciting slaves to rebellion. During the course of that trial he had said: "A hard necessity, indeed, compels us to endure the evil of slavery for a time; yet while it continues it is a blot on our national character." This view appears to be Taney's true personal stand, that of the southern aristocrat who voluntarily freed his own slaves before the law required. Pensioning his older slaves and freeing the rest had been a considerable financial sacrifice for Taney, because, although well born, he was not wealthy.

The *Dred Scott* decision split the Court in bitter debate, causing Justice Benjamin Curtis to resign. Public condemnation of Taney for his opinion followed not long after he had suffered a personal blow: the loss of his wife and youngest daughter in an 1855 yellow fever epidemic.

Taney was never afraid of being unpopular. During the Civil War, he challenged President Abraham Lincoln's constitutional authority to implement several extraordinary emergency measures. While presiding over a circuit court, Taney ruled that a Baltimore military commander must bring before the court a civilian named John Merryman, who had been imprisoned for his anti-Union activities. The commander refused to comply on the grounds that the president had authorized some military commanders to suspend the privilege of the "writ of habeas corpus," the instrument used to investigate whether the government's detention of an individual is justified. In an extraordinary expansion of executive power, Lincoln had suspended the privilege in border states to make it easier to stem support for the Confederacy. Taney ruled that only Congress had the authority to suspend the privilege, and that the president's actions were unconstitutional. In his circuit court opinion, which he sent to Lincoln, the chief justice ordered the president to uphold the law of the land and the courts. Lincoln ignored Taney's directive, and the president's supporters denounced him as "an apologist for treason" because of his apparent preference for civil liberties over the preservation of the Union.

Taney did not live to see the end of the war. He died October 12, 1864, at the age of eighty-seven, having ably served his country as chief justice for twenty-eight years. Two years later, after the wartime emergency had passed and he and Lincoln were dead, the Supreme Court upheld Taney's position in the Merryman case in *Ex parte Milligan*.

Philip P. Barbour
1836-1841

Source: Library of Congress

B ORN MAY 25, 1783, into an old Virginia family with diminished financial resources, Philip Pendleton Barbour was raised a member of the Tidewater gentry. His grandfather was a Scottish merchant who settled in Virginia in the late 1600s. His father, Thomas Barbour, was an Orange County planter who served in the Virginia House of Burgesses and, after the Revolution, in the General Assembly. His mother, Mary Pendleton Thomas, was the daughter of a wealthy planter and was related to the region's most distinguished jurists and political leaders.

Thomas Barbour's financial situation was less secure than that of many of his social peers, and he was frequently in debt. As a result, Philip did not receive the private education typical of sons of Virginia's aristocracy, but instead attended a local school. He showed great aptitude as a student, mastering Romance languages and reading the classics. He also received reli-

Sen. James Barbour, Philip P. Barbour's older brother, did not share his belief in states' rights. Instead, he argued before the Senate that the national government had the power to use $1.5 million of the new Bank of the United States to finance "internal improvements" such as canals and turnpikes. President James Madison vetoed the so-called Bonus Bill, agreeing with Philip Barbour that the Constitution did not explicitly give the federal government such authority. *Source: Library of Congress*

gious instruction from an Episcopal clergyman, Rev. Charles O'Neil, whose strict discipline included severe whipping. Although they may have instilled in Barbour a respect for hard work and well-maintained order, O'Neil's methods perhaps also explain his notable indifference to matters of the church.

In 1800, eager to prove himself, the seventeen-year-old left eastern Virginia and traveled to Kentucky with the hope of establishing himself in his own law practice. But Barbour's self-taught legal education left him unprepared for the challenge. Within a year he returned to Virginia, borrowed some money, and enrolled at the College of William and Mary in Williamsburg. After completing one term, he left the school to set up prac-

tice again, this time in Virginia. Such limited legal training was not uncommon at the time.

By 1804 Barbour had prospered sufficiently to marry Frances Todd Johnson and start a family that would in time include seven children. His wife was the daughter of Benjamin Johnson, a prosperous Orange County planter whose family was already connected with the Barbours. The oldest Johnson daughter had married Philip's older brother, James, twelve years earlier.

At the age of twenty-nine, Philip Barbour followed in the footsteps of his father and brother by being elected to the Virginia House of Delegates from Orange County. His reputation as a skillful lawyer and his family's prominence in state politics gained him important assignments on the judiciary and finance committees. After a short two years in the state legislature, Barbour was elevated to national politics when he was elected to the U.S. House of Representatives in 1814.

By the time he arrived in Washington, Barbour had already begun to deviate from his brother's political views. James was now serving in the U.S. Senate and increasingly favored a strong national government. Philip opposed this nationalist trend, associating himself with a conservative group of Virginians. Known as the Richmond Junto, they worried about the declining dominance of Virginia in national politics (the White House having been occupied for all but four years since 1789 by sons of Virginia). Only if states' rights were vigorously defended could Virginia be assured prosperity, they reasoned, even if that prosperity was based upon institutions such as slavery. As the spokesman for his political clique, Barbour argued that restrictions on slavery in states being admitted to the Union were unconstitutional.

In 1817 Philip openly broke with his brother over legislation known as the Bonus Bill. The bill would have authorized the federal government to subsidize the construction of roads and canals, in particular a so-called "national road" from Buffalo to New Orleans. Opposed to what he viewed as the unwarranted encroachment of the national government on state powers, Barbour attacked the legislation, labeling it "a bill to construct a road from the liberties of the Country by way of Washington to despotism." The bill was passed over Philip Barbour's opposition in the House and with James Barbour's support in the Senate, but was vetoed by President James Madison, who endorsed the younger Barbour's argument that the Constitution did not grant the national government the authority to finance such projects.

Philip Barbour again rose to debate a controversial motion before the House when he opposed the censure of Gen. Andrew Jackson in 1819. Jackson, whose victory over the British at the Battle of New Orleans in 1815 established him as a national hero, had shocked Congress by his zealous management of a military campaign in Spanish Florida against the Seminole Indians. In particular, Jackson had ordered the execution of two British agents for inciting and aiding insurrection against the United States. Barbour's eloquent defense of Jackson was persuasive, and the censure motion was defeated by the House.

In 1821 Barbour served as counsel for Virginia in the landmark Supreme Court case, *Cohens v. Virginia*. Arguing that the Constitution provided the defendant no right of appeal from the decision of the state court to the federal judiciary, Barbour forcefully opposed the implied extension of federal jurisdiction by the Supreme Court. In a blow to states' rights, Chief Justice John Marshall's Court was not persuaded by these arguments. As a result of his concern over the growing power of the high court, Barbour unsuccessfully introduced a bill in 1829 requiring the concurrence of five of the seven justices in any case or controversy involving a constitutional question.

The same year as the *Cohens* case, Barbour defeated John W. Taylor of New York for the position of Speaker of the House. Taylor, who had been elected Speaker

after a decade of distinguished leadership by Henry Clay, was voted out by southerners upset by his strong support for the abolition of slavery. During Barbour's two-year tenure as Speaker, competition with his two predecessors in the chair frequently extended into vigorous floor debates over tariffs, domestic improvements, and the growing jurisdiction and power of the federal judiciary. In 1823, after a shift in the political composition of the House, Clay regained the Speaker's chair.

Perhaps as a result of the strain of his years of legislative leadership, Barbour did not stand for reelection to

This 1828 wood engraving criticizes Gen. Andrew Jackson's exploits in the campaign against the Seminole Indians ten years earlier. Jackson had court-martialed and executed two Englishmen who sided with the Seminoles against his militia. Like Henry Baldwin, Virginian Philip P. Barbour spoke in defense of Jackson when a censure motion was brought before the House of Representatives. Although Jackson was grateful for helping him avoid punishment, he did not view Barbour as a loyal supporter. *Source: Woodcut, Artist unknown*

his House seat in 1824, choosing instead to return to private life. Thomas Jefferson, now retired to his home in Monticello, quickly obtained for his neighbor and friend a law professorship at the newly founded University of Virginia, but Barbour turned it down. Instead, he accepted appointment to the Virginia General Court for the Eastern District, serving as a state judge for the next two years.

Barbour's decision to retire from public life may also have been affected by the prominent position—secretary of war—that his brother James held in the new administration of John Quincy Adams. Despite his disdain for the Adams administration, Philip Barbour was ultimately persuaded by his friends that he still had a role to play in Washington. In 1827 he ran unopposed for his old seat in Congress. He immediately became a candidate for Speaker but was defeated in a three-way race against his old enemy John Taylor and fellow Virginian Andrew Stevenson, the compromise candidate and ultimate victor. Although Barbour failed to regain the Speaker's chair, he remained the legislative leader of the House's conservative, states' rights wing. He sought to make the government's part ownership and business dealings with the Bank of the United States a political issue, introducing a bill to sever the government's involvement with what he considered a private commercial enterprise. His attempt proved premature, and the bill was soundly defeated. But the matter was not forgotten by Andrew Jackson, who soon made it an important part of his Democratic platform.

In 1829 Barbour was elected to succeed the ailing James Monroe as president of the Virginia Constitutional Convention. An assembly of distinguished statesmen, the convention struggled to resolve issues that would divide Virginia, and the nation, three decades later. Barbour identified himself with the state's conservative eastern slaveholders. Representatives from Virginia's western counties, which included what would become the separate state of West Virginia, opposed

legislative apportionment based on census figures that included slaves. Barbour endorsed a "compound ratio" based on white population and "property" (slaves) combined. He also regarded land ownership as an essential qualification for the right to vote. Although he believed that all men are created free and equal in their natural rights, he denied that all men are entitled to an equal share of political power. Barbour maintained, however, that the abundant availability of property gave any hard-working man the opportunity to buy land and become eligible to vote.

When Jackson became president in 1829, Barbour's name was frequently mentioned as a possible cabinet appointee because he had by then aligned himself with the Jacksonian forces within the Democratic party. Although grateful for Barbour's support, Jackson did not view the Virginian as one of his most loyal supporters; and he appointed him not to a cabinet position but to a judgeship on the U.S. District Court for Eastern Virginia.

In the 1832 presidential election, Jackson clearly favored Martin Van Buren as a running mate and likely successor. Van Buren's candidacy displeased southern conservatives, who considered him unreliable on the slavery issue. Southern leaders organized a Jackson-Barbour movement to defeat Van Buren's nomination. Fearing a split in the party, influential Democrats eventually persuaded Barbour to withdraw from the campaign. Barbour's decision not to oppose Jackson's vice presidential candidate was a wise one. By stepping aside, he ensured the president's reelection and strengthened his own position within the party. His support for Jackson also increased the likelihood that he would be considered again for higher office.

Barbour's name had been mentioned frequently as a possible candidate to the Supreme Court. Predictably, his political opponents dreaded the thought of a Barbour appointment. John Quincy Adams was particularly concerned that the aged chief justice, John Mar-

The ship's cook reprimands unruly passengers for being late with their breakfast in this 1824 sketch of the *Acasta*. More worrisome were passengers carrying contagious diseases or holding prison records, particularly for the state authorities where the newcomers disembarked. To ensure the health and safety of its citizens, New York began requiring ships to file reports of their passengers, a right that was upheld by Philip P. Barbour in *Mayor of New York v. Miln* (1837). *Source: Chicago Historical Society*

shall, might retire, and "some shallow-pated wild-cat like Philip P. Barbour, fit for nothing but to tear the Union to rags and tatters" might be nominated to replace him. Adams's fears were realized, but only partly. On July 6, 1835, Chief Justice Marshall died in Philadelphia, but Associate Justice Gabriel Duvall's resignation earlier in the year had provided President Jackson with another opening on the Court. The same day he nominated Roger Taney to succeed Marshall, Jackson sent Barbour's name to the Senate as Duvall's successor. The appointment of the chief justice drew more attention and more fire than that of Barbour, who was confirmed March 15, 1836, by a 30–11 vote.

On the Court, Barbour backed Taney in softening the Marshall Court's most expansively nationalistic opinions. He did not, however, have time to make much of a mark in his five short years on the bench. Barbour's most important opinion, *Mayor of New York v. Miln* (1837), vigorously upheld the authority of the

state of New York to protect the health, safety, and welfare of its citizens, in this case by requiring ship masters entering the port of New York from another country or state to provide a description of their passengers. Applying his states' rights views to constitutional law, Barbour concluded that "the authority of a state is complete, unqualified and exclusive."

On February 24, 1841, Barbour attended a conference of the justices that lasted late into the evening. He was found dead of a heart attack in his home the following morning. Writing to his wife shortly after his colleague's death, Justice Joseph Story, whose judicial philosophy was at odds with Barbour's, remembered him as "a man of great integrity, of a very solid and acute understanding, of considerable legal attainments, (in which he was daily improving,) and altogether a very conscientious, upright, and laborious Judge, whom we all respected for his talents and virtues, and his high sense of duty."

John Catron

1837-1865

Source: Collection of the Supreme Court of the United States

LITTLE IS KNOWN about John Catron's early years. His birth date is variously reported between 1779 and 1786, and questions remain as to whether he was born in Pennsylvania or Virginia. It is known that his father, Peter Catron, was the son of a German immigrant who settled in Pennsylvania. The Catrons were poor but had experience working with horses, and in the early 1780s Peter Catron relocated to Virginia to work on one of the state's renowned horse farms. He moved again to Kentucky in 1804, with the

hope of establishing his own horse farm. The family's humble social position would eventually account for the political and philosophical distance that developed between the future justice and the South's ruling elite, and may explain why Catron, although a southerner in many respects, sided with the Union during the Civil War.

John Catron was a bright student with an exceptional memory, but he was unable to afford the considerable expense of private education. While helping to support his family by working various odd jobs, such as herding cattle and grooming horses, he found time to read the classics and acquire basic academic skills. He was unusually well-read in history and geography for someone lacking a formal education.

Around 1812 John Catron moved to Sparta, a town in the Cumberland Mountain region of Tennessee. The tall, dark-haired southerner married Matilda Childress about this time; the couple had no children. He read law briefly in Sparta under the guidance of George W. Gibbs, but interrupted his studies to join a local corps of volunteers called to avenge the massacre of the Fort Mims garrison by the Creek Indians. The unit, known as the Second Tennessee Regiment, eventually joined Gen. Andrew Jackson's army in Alabama and participated in various campaigns during the War of 1812. Some accounts indicate that Catron was promoted on the battlefield to the rank of sergeant major, and he

most likely fought in the famous Battle of New Orleans.

Following the war, Catron returned to the Cumberland Mountain area, exhausted and ill. He resumed his legal studies and was admitted to the state bar in 1815. During this time he became a close friend of Isaac Thomas, a prominent local attorney. When Thomas was elected to Congress in 1815, Catron took over his friend's practice.

During the years of his military service, Catron had come to know and respect General Jackson, with whom he corresponded on a regular basis. In 1818 Jackson suggested to Catron that he move to Nashville, a frontier city that Jackson believed had tremendous potential for growth. Catron had acquired a considerable reputation for land title law, which comprised a significant part of the litigation before state courts during Tennessee's early years. The young attorney decided to take Jack-

Tennessean John Catron left his law studies in 1814 to join the Second Tennessee Regiment in a revenge attack against the Creek Indians. As depicted here, the southeastern tribe massacred 517 of the 533 settlers at Fort Mims, in what is now the state of Alabama. Shortly after, the Creeks were defeated by Gen. Andrew Jackson and his army in the Battle of Horseshoe Bend and forced to relinquish the better part of their land. *Source: The Granger Collection, New York*

This 1852 cartoon pokes fun at a hypocritical temperance advocate disposing of his empty jugs in anticipation of one of the many state liquor laws passed during that reform-minded era. In 1847 the rights of states to require licensing regulation on all sales of alcohol within the state's borders, including foreign imports, came before the Supreme Court, which decided that the regulations were a valid exercise of state police power. *Source: Library of Congress*

son's advice, and he quickly developed a lucrative law practice in Nashville, the hub of Tennessee's expanding economy.

By 1824 Catron's mastery of land title law and his political skill earned him election to the newly expanded bench of Tennessee's highest court, the Court of Errors and Appeals. When he took his seat, the court was bogged down in litigation resulting from conflicting land claims in the rapidly developing region. Catron helped impose order upon this chaotic situation by establishing legal principles for the resolution of title conflicts. During this time, Catron, with financial help from his brother and a third partner, invested in Tennessee's fledgling iron industry by purchasing the Buffalo Iron Works. Catron owned and operated the profitable company from 1827 to 1833; when he sold his interest in the company, he earned $20,000 for his share.

A strong supporter of Jackson and the Democratic party, Catron saw his loyalty rewarded in 1831 when he was appointed to the new position of chief justice of the Court of Errors and Appeals. The appointment reflected Catron's reputation as a politically reliable jurist of high moral character. He opposed gambling, drunkenness, and the wasteful destruction of men through the practice of dueling, which he characterized as "wicked and willful murder." His scathing journalistic attacks on the Bank of the United States, published in June 1829, predated and anticipated the assault on the bank by his friend—now president—Andrew Jackson.

As a judge Catron generally upheld states' rights and consistently supported the institution of slavery. In *Fisher's Negroes v. Dabbs* (1834), he held that the state reserved the right to approve contracts of emancipation between slave and owner, because, he argued, freed slaves in a slaveholding region frequently had a bad influence on the unemancipated labor force. He wrote that freed slaves should be required to relocate to the colony of Liberia, a notion that enjoyed wide acceptance within his party and state during the 1830s.

A new state constitution, passed in 1834, reorganized Tennessee's judiciary and abolished the Court of Errors and Appeals. Catron returned to private practice, but remained active in Democratic politics, directing Martin Van Buren's 1836 presidential campaign in Tennessee. Catron's service to the party and his respected record as a judge did not go unrewarded. On his last day in office, March 3, 1837, President Jackson sent Catron's name to the Senate to fill one of two new seats on the Supreme Court created by the Judiciary Act of 1837.

When news of his nomination became known, the *New York Commercial Advertiser* pronounced him "a well-informed, industrious man, and a tolerably good lawyer, but not exactly the person to be put on the bench of the Supreme Court. He is, however, a favorite of the Hero [President Jackson]— that is enough." Five days after his name was proposed, the Senate confirmed the Tennessean by a 28–15 vote. Chief Justice Roger B. Taney viewed him as "a most valuable acquisition to the Bench of the United States."

Like the chief justice, Catron supported balancing the rights of states against federal authority. As a Jacksonian Democrat, he was critical of corporations when they interfered with state sovereignty. In *Piqua Branch Bank v. Knoop* (1854) the Court found in favor of an Ohio bank that refused to pay a state tax because it had been chartered under a law that permitted it to pay a certain percentage of its profits in lieu of taxes. Catron dissented, calling the power to tax "a political power of the highest class" that should not be taken away from the state because of a contract entered into by one legislature.

When it came to deciding cases involving the Com-

Chief Justice Roger B. Taney administering the presidential oath of office to James Buchanan in 1857. Hoping to announce a settlement of the question of territorial slavery at his inauguration, Buchanan had asked Justice John Catron, a political supporter, how the Supreme Court intended to rule in the *Dred Scott* case. When Catron informed him that Robert Grier might not support Taney's majority opinion, Buchanan persuaded Grier to give the Court a more decisive majority. *Source: Library of Congress*

merce Clause of the Constitution, Catron also leaned toward state powers. In the *License Cases* of 1847, which involved state laws seeking to limit the importation of liquor from abroad and from other states, he ruled that the states had a right to regulate the flow of liquor. He argued that the federal commerce power was not exclusive, and that if the national government had failed to regulate a particular commercial activity, the states had a right to do so.

In 1857 Catron wrote a separate opinion (as did all the justices in the majority) concurring with Taney's infamous *Dred Scott v. Sandford* decision. The chief justice's opinion, considered the Court's official decision, held that as a slave Dred Scott was not a citizen and therefore could not bring a law suit to federal courts.

Taney's damaging opinion went even further by over-turning the Missouri Compromise of 1820 and denying Congress the authority to exclude slavery from the territories. Catron's opinion took a more moderate view than Taney's on the question of whether blacks were citizens.

President-elect James Buchanan, anxious to announce a resolution to the slavery controversy at his inauguration address, had earlier sent a letter to Catron, a political supporter, seeking information about how the Court intended to rule on the case. In a breach of judicial tradition and common sense, Catron informed Buchanan that a decision was almost ready, but advised the president-elect that Justice Robert Grier was undecided on the issue of excluding slavery from the territories. In the hope of settling the slavery conflict through a decisive opinion by the Court, Buchanan persuaded Grier, a fellow Pennsylvanian, to support Chief Justice Taney's opinion. It is not surprising that amidst the angry outcry that met the Court's controversial 7–2 decision, at least one northern newspaper singled out Catron for particular criticism.

Despite his southern background and "southern" views on slavery, when the prospect of the South seceding from the Union loomed in March 1861, Catron, a Union supporter, returned to Nashville with the hope of restoring federal authority in the region. The border states of Kentucky, Missouri, and Tennessee, which comprised Catron's judicial circuit, were in a state of rebellion and seriously considering secession, although only Tennessee would ultimately join the Confederacy. When the justice arrived in Nashville, the Tennessee legislature had already pledged military assistance to the southern cause, and the local marshals refused to provide any police protection for Catron. They warned that his life might be in danger should he attempt to hold his circuit court, and they cautioned him not to discuss his pro-Union views. After holding a brief session of court in St. Louis, during which he boldly de-

nounced the Confederate cause, Catron returned to Nashville, where he again attempted to hold court. This time he was greeted by an ugly mob demanding either his resignation or his immediate departure from the city. Catron was forced to withdraw under a military escort, leaving behind his ailing wife—who subsequently rejoined him in Washington—and an estate valued at more than $100,000.

An unexpectedly strong political supporter of the national government throughout the war, Justice Catron wrote an opinion refusing to order a defendant's release if there was evidence that he was a Confederate sympathizer. In this respect he differed from Chief Justice Taney, who angered military authorities by insisting on a proper civilian trial. In Catron's reasoning, the suspension of a defendant's constitutional rights was justified by the wartime state of emergency.

Despite his expansive view of the federal government's war powers, Catron nevertheless dissented from the majority decision in the 1863 *Prize Cases*. The majority ruling upheld President Abraham Lincoln's order to blockade southern ports and seize vessels carrying goods to and from the rebelling states. Because the order was issued prior to a declaration of war by Congress, Catron viewed it as an overreach of presidential authority.

During the war Catron worked hard to uphold federal authority in the Eighth Circuit, where he continued to preside until the judicial districts were reorganized in 1862. He was then assigned to the newly constituted Sixth Circuit, which included Tennessee, Arkansas, Louisiana, Texas, and Kentucky. In his remaining three years on the Supreme Court, Catron traveled the circuit, remaining in close contact with President Lincoln to ensure that vacancies on federal benches in his circuit were filled rapidly to avoid potential disruption. Justice Catron died May 30, 1865, in Nashville, not long after the South surrendered.

John McKinley
1838-1852

JOHN MCKINLEY was born May 1, 1780, in Culpeper County, Virginia. His parents were Andrew McKinley, a physician, and Mary Logan McKinley. When he was a child, his family moved to Lincoln County, on the Kentucky frontier, where his mother's family was prominent. Nothing is known of his early education. He read law on his own and was admitted to the Kentucky bar in 1800.

McKinley set up practice in Frankfort, the state capital, and Louisville, a bustling commercial city on the Ohio River. In 1818 he moved to Alabama, then just on the verge of statehood. He lived in Huntsville until nearly the end of the next decade, when he moved to the other side of the Tennessee River Valley, to the new town of Florence, Alabama. He married first Juliana Bryan, then Elizabeth Armistead, but little is recorded about his personal life.

McKinley had not settled long in Alabama before he entered politics. He held seats in the state legislature, representing Tennessee River Valley constituents intermittently from 1820 to 1837. In 1824 he backed Henry Clay for president. When Clay was handily defeated in Alabama by Andrew Jackson, McKinley publicly announced that he would bow to the popular will and became a Jackson supporter. If only for political self-interest, he became a Democrat. He was elected to the U.S. Senate in 1826 by a margin of three votes in the legislature, and served until 1831. Two years later, he won a seat in the House of Representatives but returned to the state legislature in 1836 after one term.

In Congress, McKinley favored the reform of federal land policies. He wanted more land made available to the small purchaser rather than the large-scale land speculator. He advocated transferring public land from the federal government to the states for economic development. The land should be made available to the public, he argued as a democrat, and under the control of the states, he argued as a defender of states' rights.

In the state legislature, he drew up a petition to Congress denouncing the Bank of the United States and endorsed Jackson's attempts to dismantle it. He refused to join fellow southerner John C. Calhoun's movement either on the tariff nullification issue or in opposition to Vice President Martin Van Buren's succeeding Jackson.

McKinley was amply rewarded for his support of Jackson and Van Buren. At the end of Jackson's second term, Congress increased the number of justices on the Supreme Court from seven to nine. After Van Buren became president, he appointed McKinley to fill one of the two new seats. The Senate confirmed McKinley's nomination on September 25, 1837, by a voice vote. Although he had been reelected to the Senate that year, McKinley accepted the Court appointment before the new Congress convened and did not serve any part of his second Senate term. The fifty-seven-year-old justice was assigned to the newly created Ninth Circuit, which encompassed Alabama, Mississippi, Louisiana, and Arkansas. He moved back to Louisville, so that he would be located between his circuit and Washington.

The new justice was quick to get the people's attention. In the circuit court in Alabama, in three related cases known collectively as the *Alabama Bank Cases,* he

Alabaman John McKinley championed the rights of settlers and small farmers. As a senator, McKinley urged the federal government to grant land to the states for economic development. He believed the states would then sell small parcels to poor settlers, who, unlike land speculators, would improve the land and live on it. This pioneer cabin was sketched by an itinerant Frenchman in 1826. *Source: Library of Congress*

While riding circuit, Justice John McKinley heard a group of important cases affecting Alabama's banks and corporations, such as those depicted on this busy thoroughfare in downtown Montgomery. The *Alabama Bank Cases,* which were appealed to the Supreme Court in 1839, involved Alabama's right to regulate the exchange of bills in the state by out-of-state banks. *Source: Library of Congress*

ruled in favor of Alabama's power to prohibit out-of-state banks from buying and selling of bills of exchange there. As his fellow justice, Joseph Story, put it, McKinley "frightened half the lawyers and all the corporations of the country out of their proprieties." Nicholas Biddle, president of one of the banks involved in the litigation, the state-chartered United States Bank of Pennsylvania, warned that if McKinley's opinion was upheld, it would "shake the whole foundations of intercourse between the States." He asked the great advocate Daniel Webster to take up the appeal to the Supreme Court and "to show that this is really a Union—not a mere string of beads with a rotten thread to hold them together." Webster had said he envisioned "neither limit nor end to the calamitous consequences" that would come of McKinley's opinion. The decision was "in its principle, anti-commercial and anti-social, new and un-

heard of in our system, and calculated to break up the harmony among the states and people of this Union." Webster accepted the case.

In 1839 the Supreme Court heard the appeal, reported as *Bank of Augusta v. Earle.* The occasion was momentous for the economy of the new republic. If McKinley's circuit opinion was upheld, the ability of corporations to engage in interstate economic activity would be greatly restricted. Webster argued that the corporations in these cases were similar to citizens of one nation who did business in other nations through a kind of international law known as the "comity of nations." The law of comity can best be described as the operation of one nation's laws within the boundaries of another, with either the latter's consent or the absence of the latter's restrictions against the operation of foreign laws. Chief Justice Roger B. Taney gave the majority opinion. Partially accepting Webster's argument, Taney declared that there was a comity that applied to the American states. By the law of comity, out-of-state banks could buy and sell bills of exchange in Alabama just as they could elsewhere.

McKinley was the lone dissenter. He did not believe that international law applied in the case. The states were not nations. He made an interesting point while taking a states' rights position—defending a state's control over banking inside its territory—against a more nationalist position taken by the Court. His point brought out the irony that the Court was using the South's extreme state sovereignty doctrine, that states were nations, a doctrine that would fuel the cry for secession and trigger the Civil War. McKinley reminded the Court that the states had ceased to be nations when they ratified the Constitution. He was also disturbed that the majority of the Court went beyond the Constitution and congressional statute to find authority for its jurisdiction in these cases in international law.

Taney's opinion in the *Alabama Bank Cases,* however, did allow each state to legislate specific exceptions to the general law of comity that applied within the state. This practice was similar to commercial law. For the most part, states found that having rules similar to those of other states and nations attracted business and was generally good for economic development. Yet, the state could make exceptions where it wished. McKinley was receptive to this logic, and in the 1846 opinion he wrote for the Court in *Musson v. Lake,* he accepted Taney's balance between interstate commercial development and states' rights.

McKinley's dissenting opinion in *Lane v. Vick* (1845) is significant in revealing his jurisprudence. As he understood the Constitution, the federal courts had appellate jurisdiction over the state courts only in certain specific areas established by the Constitution and federal statutes, particularly the Judiciary Act of 1789. When a case came before it, was the Court confined to interpreting federal questions, or could it deal with all questions raised in the case? Southern states' rights proponents were vehement in denying the Court's authority to do the latter. McKinley gave a capable statement of this position in his dissenting opinion. He noted that the *Lane v. Vick* case was a common law suit dealing with a property dispute. No federal question was raised, and no comity of nations or commercial law was involved. On what basis could the Court rule against a state supreme court's interpretation of the common law in that state? McKinley endeavored to keep the Court within its proper jurisdictional bounds. If the Court was going to decide all questions on all cases brought before it, what would the consequences be? If two sets of courts formulated common law rules for the states, the result would be a conflict between federal and state law, and a contest between the federal and state courts. "To avert such a contest," he stated, was "of great importance to the peace and harmony of the people of the United States." Chief Justice Taney concurred in McKinley's opinion.

If McKinley had a positive agenda as a justice, and as a politician, it was to get the federal government to grant land to the states for economic development and for land sales to small farmers. He supported legislation that would encourage the poor to emigrate to the new states and become landholders. His most significant contribution was in writing the opinion of the Court in *Pollard's Lessee v. Hagan* (1845). It provided a legal basis for opening America's land. The original states had not been territories and owned all their public land. In new states, made from federal territories, the federal government held public land, which, he argued, made those states inferior to the original thirteen. To maintain a necessary equality between the states, the federal government should hold public land only as a trust. When a territory became a state, the public land was rightfully the state's. McKinley was looking after not only the interest of the states, but also the economic development

A statement shewing the number of miles which each judge of the Supreme Court has to travel, in attending the Courts of the circuit allotted to him and in attending the Supreme Court of the United States.

Names of the judges.	Number of miles
Roger B. Taney	458
Henry Baldwin	2000
James M. Wayne	2370
Philip P. Barbour	1498
Joseph Story	1896
Smith Thompson	2590
John McLean	2500
John Catron	3464
John McKinley	10000

The number of miles traveled by each justice while on circuit was recorded in this 1839 list, which shows that John McKinley rode 10,000 miles, more than three times the distance covered by most of his colleagues. Despite his and other justices' complaints Congress did not abolish the practice until late in the century. *Source: Collection of the Supreme Court of the United States*

of the country. This opinion contributed to the Taney Court's balance between general economic development and states' rights.

McKinley was noted for his simple and unassuming manner, honesty, and devotion to his duties. He had the longest distance to travel each year of all the circuit-riding justices, about 10,000 miles from Washington through the Gulf states and back. His docket of circuit court cases was also the largest; in addition, he had to deal with Louisiana's unique mix of civil law and common law. Congress in 1842 reduced part of his caseload by relieving him of circuit court duties in Mississippi and Arkansas, but later added Kentucky because he was living in Louisville. The burden of his circuit duties contributed to his poor health, which prevented him from playing an active role in the second half of his fifteen-year tenure on the high bench.

McKinley made significant contributions to the Court during his active, healthy years, when he served well the southern states' rights cause, not as an extremist but as a moderate. Unlike Justice Peter Daniel, he did not play the part of the stalwart states' rights dissenter. McKinley generally voted with the majority, and he delivered several opinions for the Court overruling state court decisions. He could also be a swing vote, as in the 1849 *Passenger Cases* when he concurred with the majority against the states' rights position. Generally, McKinley tried to find the proper balance between states' rights and federalism. No one could accuse him of being an ideologue. Indeed, his major concern was keeping the peace rather than being an advocate. And there was general respect for his efforts to avoid conflict by keeping federal courts in their proper bounds and by preserving the line between federal and state jurisdiction. But, in reality, the line was never clear, which is why there was so much debate over federalism preceding the Civil War. As Webster put it in answering McKinley's circuit court opinion in the *Alabama Bank Cases*, Americans will never be "able to define and describe the orbit of each sphere in our political system with such exact mathematical precision. There is no such thing as arranging these governments of ours by the laws of gravitation, so that they will be sure to go on forever without impinging." Yet McKinley kept trying to exercise "mathematical precision" because, unlike Webster, he worried that if the federal and state governments collided, the states would lose in the conflict.

Chronic health problems limited McKinley's activities during his last seven years on the Court. During his time on the high bench he wrote only nineteen majority opinions, as well as four dissents and two concurrences. Justice McKinley died in Louisville July 19, 1852. Taney remembered him as "a sound lawyer, faithful and assiduous in the discharge of his duties while his health was sufficient to undergo the labor."

Peter V. Daniel

1842-1860

Source: Collection of the Supreme Court of the United States

PETER VIVIAN DANIEL was born on a farm in Stafford County, Virginia, about halfway between Richmond and what is now Washington, D.C. His birth date, April 24, 1784, is roughly three years after the end of the American Revolution and three years before the writing of the U.S. Constitution. He was born into a venerable Virginia family with considerable landholdings, including the Crow's Nest, the estate where Daniel grew up.

After being tutored privately, Daniel went to college at Princeton in 1802 and stayed for one year. He then moved to Richmond, where he studied law in an office headed by Edmund Randolph, President George Washington's attorney general and a significant figure in the preparation and ratification of the Constitution. At age twenty-four, Daniel fought a duel and killed his adversary; no one has ever explained why. The episode is worth mentioning only because it illustrates the most conspicuous facet of Daniel's personality—he never backed away from a fight. The following year, 1809, Daniel married Randolph's daughter, Lucy. It was a happy marriage and lasted until her death in 1847.

The year he married, Daniel was elected to the Virginia House of Delegates. He served there until 1812 when he became a member of the Virginia Counsel of State, a part of the governor's office that also acted as a kind of judicial body. As the War of 1812 drew closer, Daniel belonged to the faction that wished to fight both England and France. The war progressed badly, and Daniel strongly supported the creation of a special

Although Edmund Randolph had been a reluctant signer of the Constitution because he believed it concentrated too much power in the executive, George Washington appointed the Virginia governor his attorney general in 1789. As such, he attended the second day of the first session of the Supreme Court in New York. Randolph's daughter Lucy married Peter V. Daniel after he clerked in her father's law office. *Source: Virginia State Library and Archives*

state army for Virginia in the belief that the federal government's defenses were insufficient. During this period he became part of the Richmond Junto, an informal alliance of strong political figures who ruled the state of Virginia. He was chosen lieutenant governor of Virginia in 1818, keeping his position on the Counsel of State, and held both posts until 1835.

Daniel's political activities extended beyond Virginia, taking on a more national role. He became a regular correspondent of Martin Van Buren, then the governor of New York, and what came to be thought of politically as an Albany-Richmond axis developed, pulling two of the major states of the country into a political alliance. This axis supported Andrew Jackson for the presidency of the United States. In 1832 Van Buren became vice president for Jackson's second term; four years later he succeeded Jackson as president.

There were political rewards for this alliance with Van Buren and Jackson. Daniel was offered the position of attorney general in Jackson's cabinet, but declined it, essentially because the salary was inadequate. Never in his life did Daniel have sufficient income to do comfortably even the modest things he wished to do. In 1835 he was the leader of the Virginia delegation to the Democratic National Convention, which nominated Van Buren as president. This support would cost him his positions as counselor of state and lieutenant governor. In March 1836, however, President Jackson appointed Daniel a U.S. district judge for Virginia with the endorsement of another Virginian, former president James Madison. The appointment marked Daniel's switch from state government to a judicial career.

The ethics of that time permitted Daniel to serve both as a district judge and as a strong and continuous political supporter of President Van Buren. In 1840, when Van Buren was renominated for the presidency, Daniel presided over the Democratic state convention. The platform at the convention articulated the basic

To avenge President Martin Van Buren's eleventh-hour appointment of Peter V. Daniel to the Supreme Court, the incoming party rearranged the trial circuits, assigning Daniel the states that were hardest to reach. Bumpy stage coaches were the uncomfortable lot of justices, who had to endure hazardous conditions and long stretches away from their families while riding circuit. *Source: Library of Congress*

beliefs Daniel would soon carry to the Supreme Court, namely an absolute support of states' rights and a belief that the federal government should be limited to the exact powers spelled out by the Constitution. Like his party, Daniel did not support internal improvements, such as the building of roads and canals, and opposed any kind of protective tariff.

Daniel's advancement to the Supreme Court came as a result of a fluke. Van Buren lost his bid for a second term and was to leave office March 4, 1841. On February 25 a vacancy was created on the Court with the death of Justice Philip Barbour. On February 27, only a week before the end of his term, Van Buren appointed Daniel to the Court, and the Democratic-controlled Senate confirmed him March 2.

The Whigs, the new party in power, immediately took their revenge. At that time, Supreme Court justices still sat as trial judges in parts of the country assigned to them. The Whigs rearranged the circuits for trial service, assigning Daniel to the region of Arkansas and Mississippi—difficult states to reach in 1841. For a time he had to cross the Appalachians by carriage, but by 1850 he could get to Wheeling, West Virginia, by a very uncomfortable train. He could then take a boat down the Ohio River to reach Arkansas, where in Little

Rock the only hotel was an abandoned boat drawn up on the beach. Typically, it took him twelve days of this kind of travel to get from Washington to Arkansas. The conditions were often filthy.

The work in Washington was more comfortable, as well as more congenial. Roger B. Taney of Maryland, a fellow Jacksonian who was already Daniel's friend, was chief justice. In those days, the justices commonly took their meals together at a boardinghouse. Those who lived nearby, as did both Daniel and Taney, could occasionally contribute something from home to the common table. For example, Daniel was delighted when Taney, not much a man for vegetables, enjoyed the asparagus from the Daniel farm outside Richmond.

On the Supreme Court, Daniel advocated an agrarian philosophy. He believed in a society in which agriculture was king. He did not believe in the modern capitalist system. His will, for example, provided that none of his estate could be put into "stocks or bonds of banks, railroads, or corporation or joint stock companies of any kind." For his entire period of service, he never agreed that corporations should be allowed to either sue or be sued in the federal courts; he did not want the legal system to recognize them at all. Daniel's point of view was prevalent in American thought between 1790 and 1810, his formative years. Corporations were not in common use during that time, and banking structures were still being formed. Daniel's attitude was, in the history of American ideas, early Jeffersonian. Because he lived a long life and was singularly inflexible, Daniel became a Jeffersonian who outlasted Thomas Jefferson.

For example, in Daniel's youth, ocean-going ships were a common form of transportation, even between New York and Richmond. Admiralty law applied to these ships. At that time the internal rivers of the country were not heavily used for transportation, and the Great Lakes, the country's vast inland seas, were not being used for commerce. During the mid-nineteenth century, admiralty law was expanded to inland waterways to help the shipping industry as a transportation system. In 1851 even Chief Justice Taney concluded that admiralty law should be extended to the great rivers and lakes of America. But Daniel, the lone dissenter, never agreed to this. In his view, the jurisdiction in admiralty of the federal courts needed to be forever frozen where it was when the Constitution was written. The notion that the Constitution might grow and that the institutions of government might be adapted to change as the American republic moved off the East Coast and spread across the continent, was not a concept Daniel could accept.

Daniel was never willing to grant the federal government any more power than it absolutely had to have. The Constitution provides, for example, that the federal government could make bankruptcy laws. In Daniel's view, so could the states. There are some who thought that only the federal government should regulate interstate commerce. Not Daniel; he was for letting the states regulate freely. Chief Justice John Marshall had made it difficult for states to modify corporate charters in the famous *Dartmouth College* case in 1819. Daniel had no problem with state regulation of corporations, even if such regulation required a modification of the corporation's charter. For example, he believed that a state could not give up the power to tax a bank no matter what the state may have said when it granted the charter.

Daniel was dissenting from the economic and constitutional current of his times. As a result, not much of his work has held up over time. One exception is his opinion in *West River Bridge Company v. Dix* (1849). The question was whether a state, which had chartered a bridge company to build and operate a bridge, could take ownership of the bridge by paying for it. Daniel accepted the fact that a corporate charter was a contract, but, he said, any such charter is subject to the limitation that the state must have the capacity of "guarding its own existence, and of protecting and pro-

"No conversation is forbidden, and nothing which goes to cause cheerfulness, if not hilarity. The world and all its things are talked of." So wrote abolitionist Charles Sumner in 1834 of his dinner with the justices in their boardinghouse. Most justices lived and took meals together at Brown's Indian Queen Hotel in the early 1800s, a cozy situation that bred camaraderie and courtesy. *Source: Library of Congress*

Reference books displaying charts of New York Harbor and directions of how to navigate safely into port began appearing in the early nineteenth century. Justice Peter V. Daniel believed that Congress had the right to regulate ocean-going commerce but, unlike his brethren, he did not find it had authority over commerce in the inland waterways and Great Lakes because the Constitution had not anticipated such activity.
Source: New York Public Library

moting the interests and welfare of the community at large." During the Great Depression in the 1930s, it was to this passage that the Supreme Court returned in upholding the power of the states to relieve farmers of mortgage payments.

Daniel served until the eve of the Civil War, so the greatest single issue during his tenure was slavery. A dedicated spokesman for a slave state, he had no qualms about the institution of slavery. As sectionalism divided the country, Daniel quickly became one of the earliest and most extreme secessionists. During his early political life, Daniel had been a bridge between the North and South and a major southern ally of Van Buren. But in the 1840s, when Van Buren became a Free Soiler, adopting the view that the territory acquired after the Mexican war should be barred to slavery, that personal friendship ended. Daniel became a fanatic, resolving never to travel north of Maryland again.

He was a strong upholder of slavery in every case that came before the Court in the nineteen years he was on the bench. He supported the rigorous enforcement of the Fugitive Slave Law of 1850. The *Dred Scott v. Sandford* case of 1857, which questioned whether Scott, a slave, had become free when he was taken into free territory, was a disaster, needlessly impelling the nation toward civil war. The case could have been resolved without deciding whether the Missouri Compromise, as the division of the country into free and slave areas in 1820 was called, was constitutional. In Daniel's blunt opinion, members of the "African Negro race" were always regarded "as subjects of commerce or traffic." The slave, he said, "is himself strictly property, to be used in subserviency to the interests, the convenience, or the will, of his owner." An owner might free a slave, Daniel acknowledged, but he could not make him a citizen. He thought the Missouri Compromise was unconstitutional; no act of Congress could prevent a slave owner from taking his slaves wherever he wished. The *Dred Scott* decision, he thought, would "finally put to rest" the entire problem of federal control over slavery. Within eight years, and after hundreds of thousands of deaths in the Civil War, the issue *was* finally put to rest, but differently.

On May 31, 1860, Daniel died. He was survived by his two children from his second marriage, to Elizabeth Harris, who died in a tragic fire several years after he married her in 1853. As the last old Jeffersonian on the high court, Daniel was a firm representative, even in his own lifetime, of principles that had become obsolete. But some of what Daniel believed has endured, particularly his views on the Contract Clause of the Constitution. His efforts to preserve public lands, his loyalty to the jury system, and his insistence on basic fairness in criminal law enforcement all still have their followers.

Samuel Nelson

1845-1872

Source: Collection of the Supreme Court of the United States

SAMUEL NELSON was born in the town of Hebron, in upstate New York, November 11, 1792. His parents, John Rogers Nelson and Jean McArthur Nelson, were farmers. His grandparents were Scotch-Irish who had emigrated to America thirty-two years before his birth. Young Samuel attended local schools and proved to be such a good student that his parents urged him to become a minister. They sent him to private academies for three years before he enrolled at Middlebury College, in Vermont, as an eighteen-year-old sophomore. His father helped finance his tuition through the sale of a slave girl.

Upon graduation from Middlebury in 1813, Nelson decided against religious training in favor of the study of law. He returned to New York State, where he clerked in the law office of Savage and Woods in Salem. When Woods left to set up his own practice in Madison County, Nelson went with him and eventually became his partner. He was admitted to the bar in 1817 and married Pamela Woods, his partner's daughter, in

1819. The marriage was short-lived; she died three years later after giving birth to a son.

After two years with Woods, Nelson struck out on his own in the small town of Cortland. As the county seat, Cortland provided him with plenty of business, and he quickly gained prominence. In 1820 he was appointed postmaster, a position he held for three years. Nelson was also named a presidential elector, and showed his loyalty to the Democratic-Republican party by voting for James Monroe in the 1820 election. The following year he represented his county at the state constitutional convention and helped to revise state laws. Nelson closely identified with Martin Van Buren's Bucktails, a dissident faction of New York's Democratic-Republican party, and voted with them at the convention to extend voting rights to men without property. The convention also substantially reorganized the judiciary, dividing the state into circuits so that state supreme court justices would not have to do trial duty.

In 1823 Nelson embarked on what was to become a fifty-year judicial career. He was thirty-one at the time of his first judicial appointment and had begun practicing law only six years earlier. The post was on the Sixth Circuit of New York, one of eight judicial circuits created at the convention. During his eight years as circuit judge, Nelson made a new home for himself in Cooperstown, where he married Catherine Ann Russell, the daughter of a prominent doctor. They had two daughters, and a son, Rensselaer P. Nelson, who became a U.S. district court judge in Minnesota.

Gov. Enos Throop appointed Samuel Nelson to the state supreme court in 1831. His former law tutor, John Savage, was then serving as chief justice, and the two sat on the bench together for six years. When Savage retired, Gov. William L. Marcy, a Democrat, elevated Nelson to the chief justiceship, a position he held for nearly eight years. As chief justice, Nelson also was entitled to sit as a member of the Court of Errors, the state's court of last resort. He was by all accounts a wise

and able judge, respected for his logic and common sense. A 1907 biographer acknowledged that his "opinions were read and admired for their terseness, directness, lucidity, and practical comprehension of the cases under consideration, by members of the bench and bar throughout the country." Under his capable guidance, the New York Supreme Court furthered its reputation as one of the best courts in the country and avoided becoming politicized.

Despite Nelson's distinguished service on the New York bench, his appointment to the Supreme Court was wholly unexpected. By the time Smith Thompson's death created a vacancy in 1843, President John Tyler had abandoned his party, the Whigs, and was suffering from a severe strain in his relations with Congress. A lame duck president with no hope of being reelected by his party, Tyler would distinguish himself by having more nominees to the Court not confirmed by the Senate than any other president. His first nominee, Secretary of the Treasury John Spencer, was rejected, and his second nominee, Chancellor of New York Reuben Walworth, withdrew in the face of opposition. A number of other prominent jurists declined to be considered for the seat because of party politics. After months of delay, Tyler finally tendered the nomination to Nelson with an eye to perpetuating the "New York seat" vacated by Thompson, a New Yorker. Nelson accepted, and the Senate confirmed the able, uncontroversial judge with relief on February 14, 1845. Nelson's easy confirmation was all the more impressive considering how disinclined the Senate was to honor the choice of an unpopular president so near the end of his term.

Nelson charted a steady course on the Court, working hard and writing precise opinions. He was "very courteous in manner, and dignified yet easy in deportment," according to a newspaper account written a decade after he joined the Court. "His apprehension is not rapid, but he thinks clearly and reasons strongly. . . . He is not suspected of ulterior political

This 1850s view of St. Louis shows the white-domed courthouse (at right) where *Dred Scott v. Sandford* was first tried. When the case reached the Supreme Court, Justice Samuel Nelson urged his brethren to let stand the Missouri court's ruling that as a slave Scott was prohibited from suing in federal court. *Source: Chicago Historical Society*

views, and his integrity and independence are not doubted." During his twenty-seven year tenure, Nelson maintained a low profile and generally went along with the majority of the Court in deciding cases. He did not contribute significantly to constitutional law.

Nelson's most visible moment came during the deliberations over the infamous *Dred Scott v. Sandford* case. Scott, a Missouri slave whose master had taken him to live for several years in Illinois and Wisconsin, territories made free by the Missouri Compromise of 1820, sued for freedom upon returning with his master to Missouri, still a slave state. The Missouri Supreme Court ruled that since Scott and his family had kept their home in Missouri, they were subject to state law, which enforced their status as slaves. Scott then sued for his freedom in federal court, which held that he did not have the right to sue in federal court because as a slave he was not considered a U.S. citizen. When the case reached the Supreme Court in 1856, Nelson joined

the majority in trying to dispose of the case as being a "question exclusively of Missouri law, which, when determined (as it had been) by that state, it is the duty of federal courts to follow it." He wanted to resolve the matter without going into the question of whether Congress had the authority to enact the Missouri Compromise or whether blacks were considered citizens.

However, the justices were split on a number of the technical issues presented, and Nelson, fearing that their disagreement might be used in the upcoming political campaign, suggested a reargument. The case was duly reargued the next term, with Nelson urging his colleagues to resolve it around two specific issues: whether the Missouri court had jurisdiction over the case, and whether Scott was a citizen of Missouri. Nelson consequently prepared an opinion upholding the lower court's ruling on those narrow issues.

Meanwhile, other justices came to believe that the

Court should tackle the larger political questions raised by the case, including whether Congress had the power to exclude slavery from some territories as it had done in the since-repealed Missouri Compromise. Nelson was told that each justice would now write a separate opinion. He stuck to his original draft opinion, submitting what would have been the Court's opinion (it used the pronoun "we") as his separate opinion. It said that "the law of the State is supreme over the subject of slavery within its jurisdiction," and that the Illinois law granting Scott freedom did not have jurisdiction in Missouri.

Chief Justice Roger B. Taney's opinion, considered the official view of the Court, declared that blacks were not citizens under the Constitution. The ruling instantly drew the anger of Republicans and northern Free-Soilers and severely damaged the Court's reputation. Had Nelson's opinion, limiting the scope of the debate, been issued instead, the Court would likely have spared itself a loss of prestige. Nevertheless, Nelson's original opinion also came under attack, and he was accused of ducking the opportunity to stand up against slavery. This criticism was not unwarranted; in general Justice Nelson leaned toward slavery at every

opportunity. His reputation remained sufficiently intact in some quarters, however, for him to be considered as a presidential nominee at the Democratic convention in 1860.

As the nation appeared to be tearing apart over the slavery issue, Nelson despaired. A constitutionally conservative Democrat, he thought the Republican administration of Abraham Lincoln should be willing to make concessions to the South to avoid civil war. In a 1860 letter to Benjamin Curtis, he said: "The Republican leaders are unyielding, and, I think, there is no hope for an adjustment through them. If the Union can be saved, it must be by the masses of the people." A despondent Nelson decided to take action. In March 1861 he joined with fellow justice John Campbell of Alabama to act as intermediary between William Seward, the new secretary of state, and a delegation of southern commissioners who had come to Washington seeking recognition of the Confederacy. The two justices dutifully relayed to the Confederates a message from Seward that the Union army would evacuate Fort Sumter in South Carolina. Realizing, however, that Seward had no intention of fulfilling his promise, Nelson withdrew, leaving Campbell to con-

Although South Carolina had seceded from the Union on December 20, 1860, Fort Sumter in Charleston Harbor was one of two outposts in Confederate territory that remained in Union hands. Rebel forces bombarded the fort on April 12 and 13, 1861, signifying the beginning of the war. "The first gun that spat its iron insult at Fort Sumter smote every loyal American full in the face," angrily declared a young Yankee named Oliver Wendell Holmes, Jr. *Source: Library of Congress*

Lingering grievances from the Civil War included the so-called *Alabama* claims, which sought reparations from Great Britain for the 257 Union ships destroyed by Confederate vessels built in Britain. The *Alabama* alone was responsible for sinking sixty merchant ships. In 1871 the negotiators, including Justice Samuel Nelson, submitted the matter to an arbitration court in Geneva, Switzerland. The international panel allowed the United States to clip $15.5 million from the British lion in compensation. *Source: Library of Congress*

tinue negotiating with Seward until war erupted a few days later.

Although by no means disloyal to the Union, Nelson never supported the Lincoln administration in its use of force to save it. He grew increasingly melancholy about the war as it dragged on. His refusal to accept the necessity of the war was echoed when the Court heard the *Prize Cases* in 1863. The cases ruled on the constitutionality of President Lincoln's blockade of southern ports between the time hostilities broke out in April 1861 and Congress's authorization of war when it convened three months later. The majority opinion upheld the president's actions, arguing that during a war the government has the right to seize ships and take their cargoes as prizes. Writing for the dissenters (Taney, John Catron, and Nathan Clifford), Nelson replied that until Congress officially declared it a war, such actions by the executive were illegal. He argued that "the President does not possess the power under the Constitution to declare war or recognize its existence . . . and thus change the country and all its citizens from a state of peace to a state of war. . . . [T]his power belongs exclusively to the Congress." Naturally, Nelson enforced the majority's ruling in the *Prize Cases* while sitting on cir-

cuit courts, but he was careful to examine each case's merits so as not to give the government a free hand in seizing ships.

Nelson's lack of support for the government's actions did not prevent President Ulysses S. Grant from asking him to be one of five U.S. members of the 1871 Alabama Claims Commission. The commission's task was to present claims against England for the damage caused during the Civil War by British-built warships, especially the *Alabama,* for the Confederate government. Despite deteriorating health, including recurrent insomnia, the seventy-nine-year-old justice accepted. He was eager to apply his expertise in admiralty law, his demonstrated specialty on the Supreme Court, to set up an international tribunal to resolve differences between the United States and Great Britain.

Greatly weakened by his work on the commission, Nelson retired from the Court November 28, 1872. His infirmity had caused him to miss some important cases and most likely prodded Congress into passing an act in 1869 providing retirement benefits for justices, making it easier for them to step down whepn their health declined. Nelson spent a quiet year at home in Cooperstown before he died December 13, 1873.

Levi Woodbury

1845-1851

LEVI WOODBURY was born December 2, 1789, in Francestown, New Hampshire, the same year that the U.S. Constitution came into effect and George Washington assumed the presidency. A product of the New England frontier, Woodbury could trace his family's origins back seven generations to the earliest Puritan migration to New England. He was a direct descendant of John Woodbury, who came to Cape Ann in 1623 and became one of the "old planters" of Salem Village in Massachusetts. Levi's mother, Mary, also a Woodbury, traced her line back to a brother of John Woodbury. The Woodbury family fervently supported the American Revolution: both of Levi Woodbury's grandfathers were revolutionaries who came to New Hampshire just before the crisis with Great Britain broke.

Woodbury's father, Peter, settled his family on a farm in Francestown, which is located in the hill country between the Connecticut and Merrimack rivers, some twenty miles from Concord. Levi's youth was spent in

146

this farming and trading community as a member of a large and fairly prosperous family. His father developed a small retail trade as a sideline and participated in local politics, serving as a selectman and state representative. Because Levi was the eldest son, his education was a matter of some importance to his parents. The local "free school" provided him with a basic education. However, unlike the sons of most yeoman farmers, he was sent on to Atkinson Academy to prepare for his eventual entry at Dartmouth College.

Beginning with his student days at Dartmouth, Woodbury developed what would become a lifelong habit of writing periodic examinations of conscience, inventories of his personal habits, and successes and failures. All through his life he would continue to write a running commentary on his actions and innermost thoughts. Very rarely did he mention names and specific details, but he used this method to direct his very considerable energies. In his early years, he expressed almost a fanatical desire to excel, and he became an unusually hard worker. At Dartmouth he also decided on his career objective: "The study of law and politics and politeness."

After graduating with honors in 1809, he spent a term studying at a law school set up by Judge Tapping Reeve in Litchfield, Connecticut. He gravitated back to the traditional apprenticeship system, however, when he entered the law office of Samuel Dana in Boston. Not caring for Boston society, he ended up in the office of one of New Hampshire's leading jurists, Jeremiah Smith, in the state capital of Exeter.

Woodbury's political career began in 1812, the same year he became a member of the bar. Returning to Francestown, he was admitted to the bar of the state circuit court at Hopkinton, a nearby town, and set up practice. Meanwhile, as an active supporter of the administration of President James Madison, he was invited to deliver an address at Amherst, a town just to the south, to the assembled Jeffersonian Republicans.

He mounted the rostrum and delivered a stirring patriotic call to war with England. The county Republicans asked the twenty-two-year-old hawk to draft a series of resolutions expressing full support for President Madison and a denunciation of England and all who supported her.

Woodbury's public career coincided with a major change in New Hampshire politics. The Democratic-Republicans had always had a significant voice in state politics, but the dominant political establishment was Federalist. The disintegration of this Federalist establishment allowed Woodbury a rapid political rise. In 1816 he attained his first political office as clerk of the New Hampshire Senate. He became a protégé of the new and able Republican governor, William Plumer. Woodbury was quickly appointed by the governor to the new Board of Trustees of Dartmouth College, which the state of New Hampshire had recently taken over as a solution to a complicated political, religious, and academic feud and renamed Dartmouth University. In 1817 Plumer appointed the twenty-seven-year-old to the state superior court.

That three-member court heard the controversial case brought by the old Dartmouth College trustees against William H. Woodward, who had turned over all records, seals, and the charter to the new, public university. Woodbury had resigned from the university board and seems to have participated in the case and its decision upholding the trustees' position. Ultimately, the case was taken on appeal to the Supreme Court, where Chief Justice John Marshall rendered his historic *Dartmouth College v. Woodward* decision in 1819.

The year 1819 was a crucial one for the young judge. After a two-year courtship, Woodbury, now of Portsmouth, New Hampshire, married Elizabeth Williams Clapp of Portland, Maine. Portland was the leading seaport in the soon-to-be state, and Elizabeth Clapp was the daughter of Asa Clapp, a Jeffersonian Republican and the richest merchant north of Boston. Clapp

When New Hampshire converted Dartmouth College into a university in 1816, William H. Woodward, Dartmouth's secretary-treasurer, was responsible for turning over the original charter. He was sued by the school's trustees, who were unhappy with the changes initiated by the state, in particular its decision to enlarge the number of trustees. Judge Levi Woodbury resigned from the board of trustees and participated in the case when it came before the superior court on which he served. *Source: Dartmouth College*

became a major supporter of his son-in-law's political career. The couple had one son and four daughters, two of whom married men who served in Abraham Lincoln's administration.

A solidly built man who stood nearly six-feet tall, Woodbury was self-disciplined and puritanical. His dedication to his work was intense and often kept him away from home. His absences were a source of tension with his wife, who complained of loneliness. Even Woodbury's hobbies were studious and methodical: he enjoyed collecting statistical and archaeological information and studying engineering and experimental farming techniques.

Judge Woodbury remained on the bench of the state's highest court until 1823, when he became a fusion candidate—he was supported by some factions of Republicans and Federalists—for governor. He served a one-year term as governor, then was defeated in 1824; but he came back the next year to win a seat in the New Hampshire House and was elected Speaker. Shortly thereafter, Woodbury was elected to the U.S. Senate by the legislature and began his national career.

In Washington, the young senator found himself drawn into the conservative Republican camp of Martin Van Buren, and thus he became an opponent of President John Quincy Adams and a supporter of Andrew Jackson. However, Woodbury was also drawn to the Virginia Republicans and to John C. Calhoun's southern coterie. In Concord, New Hampshire's new state capital, another voice, Isaac Hill, a sometime political rival but now an ally of Woodbury, also began an anti-Adams campaign in his newspaper, the *Concord Patriot*. The Hill-Woodbury axis came to dominate New Hampshire politics from the election of 1828 to the election of 1860.

Three years after his 1828 presidential victory, Andrew Jackson reorganized his cabinet and appointed Levi Woodbury secretary of the navy. Another newcomer was Roger B. Taney, who received the post of attorney general. The careers of these two men became intertwined, and their complementary characteristics and political beliefs made for an effective working alliance. Taney tended to express his political views in an open and frank manner, while Woodbury never committed himself until absolutely necessary. Justice John Catron later noted this behavior on the Supreme Court: "My Brother Woodbury has never in word or motion shown any symptoms as to what side he is on . . . and is the most valuable example of prudence, in the Court, or in all society I think." Taney described Woodbury's manner in the cabinet similarly in his memoir about the national bank controversy: "Mr.

In 1819 John Marshall wrote the decision in *Dartmouth College v. Woodward*, which forbade the New Hampshire legislature to alter the charter of the college (pictured here in 1793) because the charter was a "contract." According to the Constitution, states can not "pass any law impairing the obligation of contracts." Marshall's decision enabled businesses to rely on their charters, without worry of legislative interference, and to invest more confidently. *Source: Dartmouth College*

Woodbury was a trained politician. . . . But he was a singularly wary and cautious man, unwilling to commit himself upon any opinion upon which he was not obliged immediately to act and never further than that action required."

And yet when the veto message on the Bank of the United States was being drafted in 1832, the only cabinet member besides Taney who assisted in the effort was Woodbury. Again, in 1833 when Taney, who by then had an interim appointment as secretary of the Treasury, was preparing for the removal of deposits from the Bank of the United States, he sent a note to Woodbury asking him to help in those arrangements. Woodbury was noncommittal in word, but reliable in action. After Taney's appointment was rejected by the Senate, it was Woodbury who replaced him as secretary of the Treasury in 1834, serving through Van Buren's presidency until 1841, when William Henry Harrison and the Whigs took office.

When Woodbury's ten-year cabinet service ended, the New Hampshire legislature again elected him to the U.S. Senate. In 1844 the National Democratic Convention unexpectedly nominated James K. Polk for president. One of the names that surfaced at this convention was Woodbury's, and, after Polk's nomination, Woodbury was seriously considered as a possible vice presidential candidate. In May 1845 Polk offered Woodbury the post of minister to Great Britain, which he refused. Less than ten days after Justice Joseph Story's death in September 1845, Polk gave Woodbury a recess appointment to the Supreme Court. The Senate confirmed his nomination by voice vote January 3, 1846.

Reunited with Taney, his old political ally, Woodbury served only five years on the Court. His name was associated with no great precedent or case, but his solid reasoning and hard work made him a useful and respected member of the Court. His position as a conservative, states' rights Jacksonian sometimes led contemporaries to label him a "doughface," that is, a northerner with southern principles. This reputation was reinforced by his refusal to accept the antislavery attitudes that undermined the constitutional recognition of the institution

This denunciation of Daniel Webster's support for the Fugitive Slave Act of 1850 shows the Massachusetts senator helping a slave catcher chase a woman fleeing with her child. Longtime admirers and abolitionists were disappointed in Webster, although his support for the act was mainly a compromise gesture to the South to protect the Union. Levi Woodbury dismissed such political compromises in a 1847 Supreme Court opinion involving an earlier fugitive slave law, which he found constitutionally valid. *Source: Worcester Art Museum, Worcester, Massachusetts*

of slavery. In fact, this opinion was unjust. Woodbury was neither prosouthern nor proslavery. Rather, he was a Jeffersonian Republican who believed in the integrity of state power and saw the Constitution as a limitation on federal power to be closely read and applied. This attitude, expressed both politically and judicially, put him in harmony with the southern states' rights position.

In *Jones v. Van Zandt* (1847) Woodbury upheld the validity of the national fugitive slave law, despite arguments by abolitionist lawyers intended to discredit it on both technical and moral grounds. In his majority opinion Woodbury said: "Whatever may be the theoretical opinions of any as to the expediency of some of those [constitutional] compromises, or of the right of property in persons which they recognize, this Court has no alternative while they exist, but to stand by the Constitution and laws with fidelity to their duties and their oaths. The path is a straight and narrow one."

This opinion and his public support for such a straight and narrow path made Levi Woodbury acceptable in the South.

His ability to bridge the widening gap between North and South made him a leading candidate for the Democratic presidential nomination in 1848. The nomination went instead to Lewis Cass, who lost to Zachary Taylor and the Whigs. After the election, Woodbury spoke out in favor of sectional understanding and hailed the Compromise of 1850. He had decided to make a dedicated effort to obtain the Democratic nomination in 1852, but died suddenly at his home in Portsmouth, September 4, 1851. A major figure in New Hampshire politics, Woodbury served in many capacities and in all three branches of government on the state and national level. While the law and the courts were important to him, his political ambition was predominant.

Robert C. Grier
1846-1870

Source: Collection of the Supreme Court of the United States

ROBERT COOPER GRIER was born March 5, 1794, in Cumberland County, west of Harrisburg, Pennsylvania, on the Susquehanna River. That same year the family moved a considerable distance north, to Lycoming County, on the banks of the West Susquehanna. His father, Isaac Grier, was a Presbyterian minister who made his living by a combination of preaching, farming, and conducting a grammar school. His mother, Elizabeth Cooper Grier, was the daughter of Rev. Robert Cooper, also a member of the Presbyterian clergy. In 1806, when Robert Grier was twelve years old, his father accepted an offer to head a private school and the pastorate of three churches, so the family moved southeast to the town of Northumberland.

Young Robert was an apt and diligent scholar under his father's able tutelage. He had completed the usual preliminary course of Latin and Greek by the age of twelve, and to the end of his life he read his Bible in Greek. Dickinson College in Carlisle, Pennsylvania, admitted him as a junior in 1811, at the age of seventeen, and graduated him the following year. In addition to excelling in the classical languages, he received "valuable instruction" in chemistry from an inspiring teacher.

Grier spent an additional year at Dickinson as an instructor before returning to Northumberland to assist his father in running the academy, which had been chartered as a college. When he was little more than twenty years old, Grier was appointed president of the school; he taught mathematics, astronomy, chemistry, Latin, and Greek, and, according to one chronicler, went fishing, all while studying law on the side. In 1815 his father died, and Grier began to study law with Charles Hall in the nearby town of Sunbury. Through Hall, Grier was admitted to the bar only two years later. He began his practice in Bloomsburg, Pennsylvania, but in 1818 moved to nearby Danville, the county seat, and remained there until he was appointed to a judicial post. Fees from his law practice were sufficient to help him support his mother and ten younger brothers and sisters.

Marriage to Isabella Rose in 1829 further improved his finances. His wife's father was an immigrant Scotsman who had achieved wealth and influence. He owned an extensive estate on Lycoming Creek, near Williamsport, Pennsylvania, which eventually came into Grier's possession. There Grier exercised his fly rod each summer in the company of good friends.

Ironically, Grier's judicial career began because he was expected to decline an appointment to the bench. Gov. George Wolfe of Pennsylvania offered him the post in 1833 as part of a complicated political intrigue over the selection of the judge for a newly created district court in Allegheny County. Grier's unexpected acceptance of the judgeship for the district court disappointed the governor and his supporters. Grier consequently had a difficult time when he took his seat on the bench in Pittsburgh. His reception there was anything but cor-

dial, even though his legal and personal credentials were fully acceptable. Although by this time Grier had become a successful county seat attorney and an established Jacksonian Democrat, he was hardly a political force, and was perceived as an outsider from the dominant eastern part of the state. However, the passage of time, along with Grier's easy personality and professionalism, soon overcame the original hostility. He stayed in the post for thirteen years and developed a reputation as a knowledgeable and hard-working judge.

"Judge Grier is a man of large proportions; upwards of six feet high; apparently of great muscular power, and iron constitution, and somewhat corpulent; of sanguine temperament; ruddy complexion, and a most agreeable and good-natured face." This description was given in 1856 by a prominent fellow member of the Pennsylvania bar, David Paul Brown, who also noted Grier's occasional roughness of manner and harshness of voice.

Although Grier was certainly qualified for elevation to the nation's highest court, political patronage and geography were the decisive factors in his nomination to the Supreme Court. The "Pennsylvania justice," Henry Baldwin, died in 1844 after fourteen years on the Court. President John Tyler was in the last year of a chaotic administration, and several of his Court nominees had been rejected. A future president, James Buchanan, then a senator from Pennsylvania, could have had the seat, but he declined. Grier was then among a half dozen or so other Pennsylvanians whose names were put forth. The seat was still vacant when President James Polk took office in March 1845.

Polk's first choice was George Woodward, a state judge, but the Senate rejected him, presumably because of his sympathies with the anti-Catholic and anti-immigrant movement. The door was again opened to Buchanan, but he declined. An exasperated Polk finally nominated Grier on August 3, 1846, and the Senate confirmed him the following day. He was fifty-two

In 1836 Congress established a new system for granting patents that put responsibility for reviewing requests in the hands of a patent commissioner and his staff. Previously, the secretary of state had routinely granted all requests for patents. Although the U.S. Patent Office (pictured here in the 1840s) was empowered to decide which inventions "promote the Progress of Science and useful Arts," the Supreme Court increasingly became the arbiter of standards used to assess the validity of patents. *Source: Library of Congress*

years old. Until 1867, when he was stricken with partial paralysis, Grier never missed a session of the Court.

His influence among the nine justices on the Court was substantial. Grier was generally considered a supporter of federal power in the tradition of John Marshall and Roger B. Taney. The extensive record of his opinions, concurrences, and dissents makes clear that he did not simply follow strong leadership but made his own analysis of the cases. In 1847 Grier concurred in the *License Cases* decision upholding the use of a state's police powers to curb the flow of liquor. Two years later, in the *Passenger Cases,* he joined a majority that made it clear that state police powers were not unlim-

ited and in certain instances they must give way to the commerce power of the federal government. Specifically, the decision struck down state laws that taxed passengers arriving by ship at a U.S. port, the revenue from which was intended to support indigent immigrants.

Grier drew praise for his clarity and command of "judicial English," perhaps partly a product of his early training in the classical languages. In 1854 he wrote an important majority opinion in *Marshall v. Baltimore and Ohio Railroad Company,* a corporate case concerning federal jurisdiction over disputes between states. Grier's decision established that for jurisdiction purposes corporate stockholders are considered citizens of the state where the enterprise is incorporated. He also spoke for the Court in several patent cases, protecting manufacturers and promoting accessibility to technical information.

Also notable is Grier's participation in the succession of tortured maneuvers that eventually produced a majority ruling in the 1857 case of *Dred Scott v. Sandford*, issued in separate opinions by each justice. He initially favored judicial restraint, settling the case without touching the explosive constitutional questions—whether blacks were citizens of the United States and whether the Missouri Compromise of 1820 was unconstitutional because it deprived persons of their property, namely slaves. However, Grier changed his mind after a discussion with President-elect James Buchanan about

Patent examiners, such as these pictured at work in 1846, saw an enormous increase in the number of patents registered in the mid-nineteenth century. Patent cases eventually swamped the Supreme Court's docket as the high court was asked by manufacturers to help them protect their inventions and to resolve patent disputes.
Source: Library of Congress

how he would rule in the case. Buchanan had been persuaded to approach Grier directly, and he succeeded in getting him to promise that he would vote with Chief Justice Taney and Justice James Wayne, who favored confronting the larger constitutional questions. Although such discussions between justices and a president are now seen as violations of judicial ethics in confidentiality, notions of judicial propriety were far different in that era.

Grier kept his word to the president with a brief opinion stating that blacks were not citizens, and therefore not entitled to sue in federal court, and that the Missouri Compromise was unconstitutional. The opinion drew its share of criticism from abolitionists, as had Grier's earlier insistence on proper enforcement of the fugitive slave law. Some of the criticism acknowledged that Grier was not actually proslavery even though he was opposed to abolition.

With the onset of the Civil War, it quickly became clear that Grier did not accept the South's secession. He was visiting a son-in-law in Frankfort, Kentucky, when war broke out and was sorry to learn, he said, that the younger man "was a secessionist as insane as the others." Following the Union's early defeat at the battle of Bull Run, he told Justice Nathan Clifford that "the result of this great battle will make a long war of this. We must conquer this rebellion or declare our republican government a failure, if it should cost 100,000 men and 1,000 millions of money." He affirmed this position judicially from the circuit bench in October 1861, when he held that those in rebellion were traitors and could not plead that they acted lawfully under authority of the Confederate government and the rules of war.

In 1863 Grier wrote the majority opinion in the *Prize Cases,* upholding the legality of President Abraham Lincoln's blockade of southern ports in April 1861, three months before Congress formally authorized war. It was not essential that a declaration of war be made by Congress for the president to enact the blockade, Grier

When the Union blockade sealed off southern ports during the Civil War, it also blocked cotton exports destined for Great Britain and France. The ensuing slump in European textile production greatly angered Henri Mercier, the French minister to Washington, who threatens Uncle Sam with intervention if the blockade is not lifted. The legality of the blockade in the period before Congress officially authorized the war was the subject of the *Prize Cases,* a landmark decision by the Supreme Court in 1863. *Source: Library of Congress*

ruled, for "a civil war is never solemnly declared; it becomes such by accident. . . . The President was bound to meet it in the shape it presented itself, without waiting for Congress to baptize it with a name; and no name given to it by him could change the fact." The Lincoln administration obtained everything it needed in Grier's decision to continue prosecution of the war: the national power had been sustained, the conflict had been declared a war, and Confederate sovereignty had still been denied.

Only a year later, in 1864, there was a report that Grier's health was failing. By that time he had already ceased riding the judicial circuit because of illness. He suffered a form of paralysis in 1867. Two years later his disability was alluded to on the floor of Congress, with a reference to an eminent member of the Court "who is not able today to reach the bench without being borne to it by the hands of others." Yet he was also reported to have gone fishing as late as the summer of that year.

An old friend and colleague from the Philadelphia bar, George Harding, made a special trip to Washington in the fall of 1869 in an effort to persuade a senile Grier to step down, but without success. The justice's resolve was probably strengthened by the knowledge that he could not resign before a new retirement bill took effect and still qualify for his benefits, the first ever provided by Congress. Under the law, justices with ten years or more of service could retire at age seventy and draw full pay for life. Grier's salary at this time was $6,000 annually, up from the $4,500 he had received during his first nine years of service.

"The Chief [Salmon P. Chase] and Judge [Associate Justice Samuel] Nelson waited on Pa this morning to ask him to resign," reads a letter written three weeks after Harding's visit by Sarah Grier Beck, one of Grier's two married daughters, with whom he resided when the Supreme Court was in session. All Grier's colleagues now joined in asking him to step down. Reluctantly, he did so in December 1869, with the resignation to take effect in February 1870. A letter from President Ulysses S. Grant acknowledging his resignation cited "the great service which you were able to render to your country in the darkest hour of her history by the vigor and patriotic firmness, with which you upheld the just powers of the government and vindicated the right of the nation under the constitution to maintain its own existence." Grier died on September 25, in the Philadelphia home he had occupied during his years on the Court.

Benjamin R. Curtis

1851-1857

Source: Collection of the Supreme Court of the United States

BENJAMIN ROBBINS CURTIS is best known for having resigned from the Supreme Court in the aftermath of the divisive *Dred Scott v. Sandford* decision. He was born November 4, 1809, in Watertown, Massachusetts. His father, Benjamin Curtis III, a ship's captain, died on a voyage to Chile when Curtis was only five years old, leaving Benjamin's mother, Lois Curtis, to care for him and his brother. She supported them by starting a dry goods business and a circulating library.

An apt and dedicated student, Curtis qualified for admission to Harvard, entering at age fifteen. His tuition was paid by his mother, who moved to Cambridge to run a boardinghouse for undergraduate students. Graduating in 1829 with highest honors, Curtis decided to continue his studies. Perhaps due to the influence of his half-uncle, Harvard professor George Ticknor, Curtis enrolled in Harvard Law School. At that time the school was under the direction of Joseph Story, the Supreme Court justice. Curtis briefly interrupted his studies to prepare financially for marriage by working for a law firm in the town of Northfield, Massachusetts. He finished his studies in 1832 and was admitted to the bar.

In 1834 Curtis joined his distant cousin Charles Pelham Curtis in his Boston law practice and quickly achieved standing in the profession. He was noted for his powerful legal arguments, which Story praised in 1836 for their "learning, research and ability" and for being as "thorough and exact" as any he had ever heard. Curtis cut to the heart of a case, avoiding corollary issues that might deflect attention from the most vital points and give the opposition material that could accidentally prove useful. He limited his practice so that he was confident he could research each case exhaustively.

Curtis specialized in commercial, maritime, insurance, and bankruptcy law. He was also one of the foremost patent attorneys in the United States. He argued more than 100 cases before the Supreme Judicial Court of Massachusetts and almost as many before the First Circuit Court of the United States in Boston. Testament to his reputation and standing was Curtis's appointment at the age of thirty-six as a fellow of the Harvard Corporation to replace Justice Story, who had died. He was an active member of the Boston community, supporting its civic institutions and contributing generously to charities from his growing income.

Curtis married three times and had twelve children. His first wife, Eliza Maria Woodward, was a cousin. They were married from 1833 to 1844 and had five children before she died of tuberculosis. Eliza's death was a serious blow to Curtis. Eighteen months later he married Ann Wroe Curtis, a distant cousin and the daughter of his law partner. They had three children and were married fourteen years before she died. A year after Ann's death, Curtis wed Maria Malleville Allen from Pittsfield, Massachusetts, with whom he had four children. Throughout his life Curtis placed great importance on his family and friends. He was by nature sedate and sober, and, although generous and warm with family and close friends, he maintained a certain detachment and distance from outsiders.

One of Curtis's great achievements was the passage of legal reforms while he was serving in the Massachusetts legislature from 1849 to 1851. After introducing legislation to create a commission for judicial reform, he was subsequently appointed its chairman. Curtis proposed framing a new, more efficient code of court procedure to simplify issues and speed up trials. His work became the basis for the Massachusetts Practice Act of 1851, bringing Curtis fame and moving Massachusetts to the forefront of states working for legal reform.

When Justice Levi Woodbury died in 1851, President Millard Fillmore was determined to replace him with a member of the Whig party to counteract the preponderance of southern Democrats on the Supreme Court. Fillmore wanted to nominate a candidate of "vigorous constitution with high moral and intellectual qualifications, a good judicial mind, and such age as gives a prospect of long service." He nominated Curtis, a Whig, on December 11, and the Senate confirmed him by voice vote December 20.

One of the most important opinions Curtis wrote during his six years on the Court concerned the interpretation of the Commerce Clause of the Constitution as it applied to the federal government's jurisdiction over interstate commerce. In *Cooley v. Board of Wardens of the Port of Philadelphia* (1852) Curtis advocated the doctrine of "selective exclusiveness." He argued that where the federal government had exercised its power to regulate interstate or foreign commerce, the states could not impose their own regulations, but that in those areas where there was no federal regulation, the states could regulate. Curtis reasoned that commerce could be either local or national in character and that regulation should be determined on that basis. He also thought that it was important to give some latitude for future interpretation by leaving many of the undefined

Philadelphia's ordinance regulating the use of pilots in the city's harbor (viewed here from the South Street Bridge) was challenged as an infringement on the commerce power of the federal government. Justice Benjamin R. Curtis upheld the ordinance in 1852, stating that some commerce was essentially local and could be regulated locally if Congress had not already passed contradictory laws. This decision, *Cooley v. Board of Wardens of the Port of Philadelphia*, made room for a less categorical approach to the recurring question of state versus federal control over commerce. *Source: Library of Congress*

areas ambiguous, to be clarified at such time as it became necessary.

"During the first term after his appointment, [Curtis] took rank with the first on the bench, for sureness of judgment, keenness of analysis and accuracy of legal research," noted an observer. Others implied that Curtis's oratorical skills were more impressive than his writing skills. It was the opinion of several justices that "if in those days there had been a stenographer in the conference room to take down his language his great reputation would have been founded not so much on his reported opinions" as on his remarks in the justices' private conferences.

Curtis's areas of speciality were commercial and admiralty law. His opinion in *Steamboat New World v.*

King (1853) expanded federal jurisdiction to include inland rivers based on their navigability rather than the ebb and flow of the ocean tide. The decision also updated the law by discussing what constitutes negligence for steamboat carriers, in addition to sailing vessels.

Curtis found living in a Washington boardinghouse disagreeable; he missed his family and the comforts of his Boston home. For the first few terms he tried bringing his wife and family to Washington with him, but he hated to subject them "to a kind of vagrant life in boarding houses." His financial obligations were sizable: Curtis supported a large family and maintained homes in Boston and the Berkshire mountains. With an annual salary of only $4,500, his financial problems were critical. Even though the salary was increased by one-third in 1855, it was not adequate to his needs. He edited an edition of Supreme Court decisions to supplement his income.

In addition to his financial problems, Curtis became disenchanted with his life as a public servant, despite his admiration for the Court. He found himself the target of public criticism, particularly in New England where he presided over the First Circuit. Many of his opinions there concerned the constitutionality of the Fugitive Slave Act of 1850. Although he found the act abhorrent, he felt it was his duty to uphold it. As a consequence, Curtis was attacked by the press and dubbed "the slave-catcher judge." Curtis performed his circuit duties ably, streamlining and regularizing the proceedings, but none of these accomplishments defused the criticism.

The slavery issue rocked the Supreme Court in 1857 when it decided the controversial case of *Dred Scott v. Sandford.* The resulting decision not only caused personal trauma for Curtis, forcing him to resign his seat, but history has judged it a disaster that degraded the Court and the Constitution and precipitated the Civil War. The case involved Dred Scott, a Missouri slave, who claimed that he should be liberated because his master had taken him to live on soil made free by the Missouri Compromise of 1850.

Congress and the president urged the Court to make a firm statement on the slavery issue, and Chief Justice Roger B. Taney, in response, covered unnecessarily broad ground in his opinion for the Court. Taney built his argument on three major points: that, as a black, Scott was not a citizen and therefore could not sue in federal court; that the Missouri Compromise was unconstitutional because Congress had no right to infringe on the property rights of slaveowners; and that, despite temporary residence in Illinois and Louisiana Purchase territory, only Scott's state of permanent residence, Missouri, could determine his status.

Although each justice found it necessary to write a separate opinion outlining his reasoning, Curtis and John McLean were the lone dissenters. Curtis's dissent contradicted several of Taney's assertions, starting with the contention that under the Constitution blacks were not and could not be citizens. Curtis pointed out that

The *Dred Scott v. Sandford* decision set the tempo for the 1860 presidential contest. The four presidential candidates of the battered national parties dance with members of their respective constituencies in this campaign cartoon. Clockwise from upper left are southern Democrat John C. Breckinridge, Republican Abraham Lincoln, Constitutional party candidate John Bell, and Democrat Stephen A. Douglas. *Source: Library of Congress*

in 1787 blacks in five states were granted not only the rights of citizenship, but voting rights as well. He also noted that federal compacts did not deny blacks their citizenship, and that under the Articles of Confederation and the Constitution citizens of a state were accorded citizenship in the United States with all of its attendant rights and privileges, including the right to sue in federal court.

Curtis further argued that residence on free soil entitled a slave to freedom. He concluded that Congress had the right to prohibit the spread of slavery under the Missouri Compromise, citing the language in Article V of the Constitution granting Congress the power to make "all needful rules and regulations."

Although Curtis certainly did not intend to ignite a crusade for freedom, the one-time "slave-catcher" judge was quickly proclaimed a hero by the antislavery movement, which was outraged by the Court's decision. When the Court adjourned March 6, 1857, Curtis immediately filed his dissent with the clerk of the Court and then forwarded it to a Boston newspaper. He then left town and, following a vacation, arrived in Boston to find that the other opinions had not been published. He heard a rumor that the chief justice was revising his opinion to refute each of the points Curtis had raised in his dissent.

Curtis wrote to the clerk of the Court requesting a copy of Taney's written opinion in the case, but his request was denied, and he was told that a new rule had been adopted that prohibited the distribution of opinions prior to their being officially printed. There followed several weeks of bitter correspondence in which Taney refused to show the revision and accused Curtis of inciting public opinion against the Court's ruling by publishing his opinion before the majority ruling was printed. Curtis denied the charges, but the normally even-toned Taney wrote Curtis a scathing letter saying that this was the first instance in the history of the Court when "the assault [on the Court] was commenced by the publication of the opinion of a dissenting Judge" and accusing him of violating judicial decorum and propriety. The rift, which might have been bridged had it concerned a less weighty issue, greatly disturbed Curtis.

On September 1, 1857, Curtis wrote a letter of resignation to President James Buchanan. After having struggled for six years to support his family on an inadequate salary, he resumed his lucrative legal practice in Boston. Curtis argued more than fifty cases before the Supreme Court for clients, including the first *Legal Tender Case,* which reviewed Congress's decision to issue paper money during the Civil War. He lost that case, but had many other triumphs in his postjudicial career. In 1868 the former justice presented the opening argument in President Andrew Johnson's successful defense at the Senate's impeachment trial. Curtis later declined President Johnson's offer to become attorney general.

Over the next few years Curtis's health deteriorated, although as late as 1874 he was nearly elected to the Senate. Curtis finally suffered a brain hemorrhage, and died September 15, 1874, at the age of sixty-four.

John A. Campbell
1853-1861

Source: Collection of the Supreme Court of the United States

JOHN ARCHIBALD CAMPBELL, a southerner who resigned from the Supreme Court at the outbreak of the Civil War, was born June 24, 1811, near Washington, Georgia. He was given the name of his paternal Scotch-Irish grandfather, who was a Revolutionary War officer on the personal staff of Gen. Nathanael Greene. Campbell's father was a highly successful lawyer and legislator. His mother also had Revolutionary War antecedents as the daughter of a lieutenant colonel in a famous Georgia regiment.

Campbell was brought up in intellectual and prosperous circles and soon showed himself to be a child prodigy. He graduated in 1825 from Franklin College (now the University of Georgia) with first honors at the age of fourteen and was then appointed to West Point Military Academy by John C. Calhoun, a friend of his father. His record there was less impressive: he ranked in the lower third of his class. In 1828 he was forced to resign when his father died suddenly. At the time of his death, the elder Campbell was on the verge of being

Daniel Webster was one of the nation's most talented advocates. Although he won less than half his cases, he probably had the greatest influence on the Supreme Court and its work of any advocate in the nineteenth century. *Source: Library of Congress*

elected governor of Georgia, but his estate was heavily encumbered with debt. To help pay it off, young John taught school for a year in Florida.

Returning to Georgia, he took up the study of law with two uncles, John W. Campbell and John Clarke, a former governor of the state. In 1829, by special act of the state general assembly, he was admitted to the Georgia bar at the unusually young age of eighteen. For the next twenty-three years Campbell practiced law, with ever-increasing success. Within a year he moved to Montgomery, the capital of Alabama, which was then still a small city. There he met and married Anna Esther Goldthwaite, a New Hampshire native who had settled in the South with her two brothers. The couple had one son and four daughters.

Campbell laid the foundations of what became a great law library, boasting volumes in several languages. He mastered the intricacies of land titles, which were often based on obscure and complex Spanish land grants. Elected to the state legislature in 1836, Campbell moved the following year to Mobile, Alabama, to expand his professional field. He had already been offered a seat on the state supreme court, but declined it as he did a second offer some years later. He served a second term in the state legislature in 1843, this time from Mobile.

By the 1840s Campbell had become the leading attorney of Alabama, widely regarded as a brilliant advocate without peer in his arguments before the state supreme court. He was dedicated to his work, and a contemporary described him as "cold, taciturn, not the least suggestion that he courts society, absorbed in thought, with heavy brow, yet unassuming expression of countenance. At times he is pleasant, and always respectful when it becomes necessary for him to converse."

Before he was forty years old, Campbell gained a national reputation for his arguments before the U.S. Supreme Court. He argued six cases in the 1851 term, including one, *Gaines v. Relf,* in which celebrated advocate Daniel Webster was the opposing counsel. Although Campbell lost the long-fought case in a split decision, it was reversed by the Court ten years later, under the name *Gaines v. Hennin.*

During this time, the careers of American public figures were increasingly being defined by their position on the heated issue of slavery. In 1850 Campbell was chosen by the legislature as a delegate-at-large to a convention at Nashville, Tennessee, convened to protect southern rights against antislavery pressures from the North. There he counseled patience and compromise, introducing sixteen resolutions that were relatively moderate and conciliatory in nature. He and others managed to defeat the extreme secessionists. The final resolutions were essentially those brought forward by Campbell.

When President Franklin Pierce, a Democrat, was inaugurated in 1853, there was a vacancy on the Supreme Court that his Whig predecessor, Millard Fillmore, had been unable to fill because of Senate rejections. In an unprecedented action, Chief Justice Roger B. Taney and the associate justices unanimously requested that the president appoint Campbell, a states rights Jacksonian Democrat. Pierce obliged on March 21, 1853, and four days later Campbell was confirmed by a unanimous Senate.

On the Court, Campbell demonstrated a broad knowledge of the law, notably in setting guidelines for maintaining charities, determining corporate liability, drawing boundary lines between the states, and deciding who had jurisdiction of rivers. In 1857 he concurred in the damaging *Dred Scott v. Sandford* decision, but would have preferred to settle it on narrower grounds, neither asking nor answering the question of whether Congress had authority to limit slavery in the territories.

On the question of slavery Campbell was a gradualist. "My observations were that slavery ought not to form a cause for the dissolution of the union," he wrote in February 1861, "that it was a transitory institution and would necessarily be modified or abrogated in the process of time; that it had regularly been receding to the South and Southwest since the adoption of the Constitution, and now more rapidly than at any time before." Campbell had freed his own slaves eight years earlier when he took his seat on the high bench and thereafter hired only free blacks as servants.

As the secessionist fever spread following the election of President Abraham Lincoln in November 1860, Campbell publicly warned southerners against dissolving the Union. When commissioners of the newly created Confederacy arrived in Washington, Secretary of State William H. Seward refused to respond to their request for a meeting for fear of recognizing a secessionist government. Campbell was persuaded to intervene with Seward and, for more than than two weeks, tried vainly to get conversations started. The effort ended when the North moved to reinforce its troops at Fort Sumter in South Carolina and the ensuing bombardment began the Civil War.

Believing that he had been tricked by Seward and that the southern judicial circuit he represented was no longer within the Supreme Court's jurisdiction, Campbell resigned April 26, 1861. He was denounced in the North for his decision to return to Alabama, but he was also rejected in the South, where his efforts to negotiate peace had been grossly misrepresented. When he returned to Mobile in May, he was threatened with lynching; he chose to move to the more tolerant climate of New Orleans and set up a law practice.

The hostility to Campbell gradually abated, and in October 1862 he accepted an appointment as assistant secretary of war with the special duty of administering the law drafting Confederate soldiers. He found the work distasteful and, as the war dragged on and defeat for the South loomed nearer, he became more interested in peace. As early as 1864 he made several overtures to the North for negotiation through his old friend, Associate Justice Samuel Nelson.

In January 1865 Jefferson Davis, the president of the Confederacy, named Campbell to a three-member peace commission that met fruitlessly with President Lincoln and Secretary of State Seward in Hampton Roads, Virginia, for a four-hour discussion. When Richmond was evacuated and taken by Union forces, Campbell was the only high-ranking Confederate official to remain there, at some physical danger to himself. Lincoln visited Richmond April 5, and Campbell obtained an interview with him. The result was formal permission by Lincoln for a session of the Virginia legislature to consider the president's terms of surrender. But Gen. Robert E. Lee surrendered at Appomattox only four days later, and the permission was withdrawn. Five days later, Lincoln was assassinated.

When the Confederate government evacuated its capital, Richmond, Virginia, on April 3, 1865, John A. Campbell was the only high-ranking Confederate official to remain in the city. Risking his life, he stayed to receive the victors. So that ammunition would not fall into enemy hands, arsenals and armories were blown up. Fires quickly broke out and massive looting ensued. *Source: Library of Congress*

In the anger following the president's death, the War Department ordered Campbell's arrest on a charge of having misrepresented Lincoln's views and having misled the commanding general in Richmond, Maj. Gen. G. Weitzel. Campbell was imprisoned at Fort Pulaski, Georgia. Benjamin Curtis and Samuel Nelson, his former fellow justices, persuaded President Andrew Johnson to release him four months later.

Campbell was one of the first southerners to accept the peace terms. He petitioned for amnesty under President Johnson's general pardon, took an oath of loyalty to the Union, and endorsed the Emancipation Proclamation. Nonetheless, at the age of fifty-four Campbell found himself bankrupt. His home and all his property in Mobile had been destroyed, and public office and the polls were now closed to him under the Reconstruction Acts.

He returned to New Orleans and formed a law partnership with his son, Duncan, and former Louisiana Supreme Court judge Henry Spofford. Campbell's op-

portunities were circumscribed at the start as his practice was limited to the disorganized and intermittently functioning state courts. Congress had passed a law barring from practice in the federal courts lawyers of the secessionist states who would not take an oath that they had not taken part in the war. The Supreme Court declared the act unconstitutional in January 1867 in the landmark case *Ex parte Garland.*

Again Campbell was to become one of the nation's outstanding advocates. He averaged six cases a year before the U.S. Supreme Court until his retirement from full-time practice in 1884. For the second time, he assembled a superb library. In 1873 he was involved in the most significant legal argument of his lifetime, as leading counsel in the famous *Slaughter House Cases.* Scholars have judged it the most brilliant work of his career.

The cases questioned the constitutionality of a Louisiana statute that granted a monopoly to a single corporation for butchering animals in New Orleans, depriving more than 1,000 other butchers of their occu-

After the Civil War, southerners were asked to swear allegiance to the Constitution. If only 10 percent of a former Confederate state's voters agreed to take the oath, President Lincoln promised that the government would recognize the state and let the people rule themselves. Congress also imposed a more specific "test oath" for those wishing to practice law in federal courts, which required them to affirm their loyalty—past and present—to the Union. In 1867 the Supreme Court found the test oath unconstitutional in *Ex parte Garland*. *Source: New York Public Library*

pation. This case was the first interpretation of the Equal Protection and Due Process clauses of the Fourteenth Amendment, which guarantees the privileges and immunities of U.S. citizenship. As attorney for the butchers, Campbell argued that the slaughtering monopoly violated the Fourteenth Amendment by restricting his clients' rights to practice their trade. He maintained that the federal government was obligated by the amendment to protect the butchers' rights even if those rights were not protected by state law. His presentation, although masterful, did not prevail, and the Court found that the right to do business was not a privilege of U.S. citizenship and could therefore be abridged at the state level. In succeeding decades, however, Campbell's interpretation was in effect adopted and was used to protect blacks from having their civil rights restricted by the states.

In 1882 Duncan Campbell died prematurely, and two years later the former justice's wife died. At age seventy-three, he moved his residence once more, to Baltimore, Maryland, where two of his daughters lived. He gave up his general practice, but continued to accept and argue cases in the Supreme Court as they came to him. A Washington reporter described Campbell as he argued his last case before the Court as follows:

He is a very old man. His form is thin and bent, his skin is in the parchment state, and his hair is as white as the driven snow; but a great mind looks out through his keen eye and a great soul controls his fragile body. He is a lawyer to the core—in some respects one of the wisest, broadest, deepest, and most learned in the United States. He has neither the presence, voice, nor tongue of the orator, but when he speaks in his thin, measured tones, never wasting a word, the Supreme Court of the United States listens as it listens to almost no other man.

Campbell died in Baltimore March 12, 1889, after a long illness attributed to old age.

Nathan Clifford
1858-1881

Source: Collection of the Supreme Court of the United States

NATHAN CLIFFORD was born in Rumney, New Hampshire, August 18, 1803, into a family whose English ancestors had come to America in 1644. The oldest child and only son among seven children, Nathan spent much of his youth working on the family's small farm alongside his parents, Nathaniel and Lydia Simpson Clifford. His parents insisted there was neither time nor money for a formal education, but Nathan managed to receive some schooling by attending Haverhill Academy, where he earned his tuition by teaching and giving singing lessons to the school's younger students.

Although poorly educated, young Clifford was extremely industrious, and he was able to persuade a prominent local attorney, Josiah Quincy, to take him on as an apprentice. In 1827 he passed the bar and moved to Newfield, in the western part of Maine, where he opened a law office. There he met and married Hannah Ayer, the daughter of an influential family whose local connections brought him a substantial real estate practice. Despite a steady flow of clients from the lumber business, mostly involved in land claim disputes, money remained tight, as it would throughout his life. Much of the family budget went to maintaining a household of six children. Aside from fishing, his favorite pastime, Clifford spent most of his leisure time enjoying his close-knit family.

Clifford's modest means and rural background led him early on to support the principles of Jacksonian democracy. He soon gained the respect of local organizers in the Democratic party, and at age twenty-seven he was elected to Maine's House of Representatives on the Democratic ticket. He did well enough to be voted Speaker of that legislative body, a position he held until the legislature appointed him state attorney general in 1834. During his four-year tenure in that office, Clifford unsuccessfully sought a seat in the U.S. Senate. He rebounded from the defeat by winning a Democratic seat in the U.S. House of Representatives in 1838.

While in Congress, Clifford staunchly opposed high tariffs and a federal banking system and showed loyal support for the policies of President Martin Van Buren. At the same time, Clifford criticized the movement to abolish slavery and supported compromises over the issue. Political opponents quickly labeled him a "doughface"—a northern Democrat with southern sympathies. Congressional redistricting divided Clifford's political base in 1843, costing him his reelection to a third term in Congress.

In 1846 President James Polk appointed Clifford, a loyal supporter, to be his attorney general. Polk did so in part to round out his cabinet with a representative from New England. Shortly before his Senate confirmation hearings, Clifford, concerned that his legal training might prove inadequate for litigating federal cases before the Supreme Court, had a crisis of confidence and asked Polk to relieve him of his post. Polk's faith in his appointee remained unshaken, however, and he persuaded Clifford to stay. His confidence proved well-founded, as Clifford's subsequent performance before the Court impressed the Senate enough to earn him unanimous confirmation.

Despite Clifford's early reticence, he turned out to be a hard-working, competent attorney general who grew in confidence. His most famous case, *Luther v. Borden* (1849), was more notable, however, for the controversy that surrounded it than for Clifford's involvement. The case involved a large group of Rhode Island citizens, led by Thomas Dorr, and their attempt to expand the number of people eligible to vote in the state. To accomplish their goal, they established a new state government with less restrictive voting requirements. The original government, acting under a modified colonial charter dating back to 1663, refused to accept as legitimate a public referendum calling for a new government, and violence ensued. Clifford, arguing on behalf of the federal government, supported the claimants' position that the charter government had violated the people's constitutional right to a republican form of government and had illegally arrested and imprisoned its opponents. The Supreme Court, however, agreed with Daniel Webster, Clifford's able opponent, and ruled that the issue was essentially political in nature and therefore outside the Court's jurisdiction.

In addition to his duties as attorney general, Clifford was also given the role of trouble-shooter for the Polk administration's policy in Mexico. He supported Polk's aggressive prosecution of the Mexican-American War, which had begun in 1846. One of Clifford's important contributions as a member of the cabinet was to mediate between Polk, who sought to pursue the war vigorously, and James Buchanan, his more cautious secretary of state. Buchanan respected and trusted Clifford and, when he became president, would appoint Clifford to the Supreme Court.

When the Mexican government asked for a settlement, Polk asked Clifford to resign from the cabinet to serve as his emergency peace commissioner. Clifford ar-

Attorney General Nathan Clifford argued the government's position in *Luther v. Borden* (1849). At issue was whether the state of Rhode Island acted legitimately in imposing martial law to suppress a rebellion, sparked by the actions of attorney Thomas Wilson Dorr. The unorganized efforts of the rebels to take over the public arsenal had failed quickly. The Supreme Court ruled that the complaint against the state was a "political question." *Source: Courtesy of the Rhode Island Historical Society*

rived in Mexico City in April 1848 and ultimately secured the government's ratification of a treaty highly favorable to America's expansionist ambitions in the West. In recognition of that success, Polk asked Clifford to remain as his minister there. Staying in the post until September 1849, Clifford risked bodily harm as the American representative; he was twice assaulted in his coach by local bandits and once robbed at gunpoint. At first insensitive to Mexico's difficulties and critical of its economic problems, Clifford eventually came to see the need for the United States to aid its neighbor by supporting Mexico's progressive reform movement.

His efforts were cut short, however, by the election of 1848 and his recall by Zachary Taylor, the new president. The Democrats' electoral loss eliminated Clifford's chances of securing a new appointment. He decided to return to Maine, where he established a law partnership with John Appleton in the prosperous city of Portland. Private practice did not hold his interest for long, however, and Clifford spent much of his time trying to restore his political career. He was unsuccessful in bids for a Senate seat in 1850 and 1853, even though the Democrats recaptured the presidency in 1852. His party finally recognized him when his old political ally, James Buchanan, became president and appointed him to the Supreme Court December 9, 1857.

The Court vacancy had been created by the resignation of Benjamin Curtis, who had stepped down in the wake of the divisive *Scott v. Sandford* decision. The selection of Clifford, a quiet, massive man, had been a difficult choice for Buchanan. To retain the Court's geographic balance, it was necessary to appoint a New Englander, but the vacancy came at a time when the political infighting over the admission of Kansas to the Union and the issue of fugitive slaves was near its peak.

Buchanan's own Democratic party was being torn apart over these issues, and the nomination of a Yankee abolitionist or a proslavery southerner would most likely have split the president's support in the Senate, making confirmation impossible. Clifford was a logical compromise, as he was a New Englander with southern sympathies whose party loyalty was beyond question. Even with such strong credentials, his confirmation process became entangled in a heated debate that reflected the nation's political turmoil. Following weeks of discussion about his legal qualifications and criticism of his lack of political independence, Clifford was confirmed January 12, 1858, by a 26–23 vote.

The political sectionalism that had colored Clifford's confirmation hearings continued during his twenty-three years on the Court. His unpopular Democratic party affiliation drew critical scrutiny of his jurisprudence during five successive Republican administrations. As much as one-fifth of all his writings for the Court were dissents. Although he wrote more opinions than his colleagues, he tended to be long-winded and was almost never assigned to write opinions on major constitutional questions. Still, diligence and exhaustive research helped him overcome the handicaps of his mediocre legal training to achieve a measure of competence as a jurist. Yet his advocacy of a narrowly conservative interpretation of the Constitution, his anti-abolitionist views, and his preoccupation with the dangers of centralized power, at a time when the Court was moving toward expansion of federal authority, overshadowed any contributions he may have made to the Court.

Although Clifford frequently opposed Republican attempts to expand federal authority at the expense of the states, he considered the Union itself sacred and condemned the idea of secession as a "wicked heresy." During the Civil War he supported the government in cases involving the issuance of paper currency used to finance the war effort. By voting with the majority in *Ex parte*

Vallandigham (1864) he upheld the government's extensive use of martial law during wartime. Clifford, however, took exception to the Lincoln administration's conduct of the war in one instance. He dissented in the *Prize Cases* of 1863 because he believed that the federal government did not have the power to blockade southern ports without Congress's formal authorization of war.

After the Civil War, when the survival of the Union was no longer at stake, Clifford's opposition to the policies of the Republicans became far more evident. He consistently dissented from Court opinions upholding the power of the federal government to confiscate property during wartime. When the issue of the legality of paper money reappeared before the Court in the early 1870s, this time Clifford objected to the government's policy of paying prewar contracts with postwar paper currency, since devalued. Almost mechanical in his strict interpretation of judicial power, Clifford consistently argued that the Court had the power to strike down only those laws expressly prohibited by the Constitution, and not "on the vague ground that they think it opposed to a general latent spirit supposed to pervade or underlie the Constitution."

Although Clifford was willing to support an imperiled Union in time of crisis, he opposed extending federal authority to support the government's policies of Reconstruction. Thus, he became a loyal critic of the federal government, with northern roots and southern sentiments. These seemingly contradictory traits exposed him to criticism from both political parties throughout most of his career. The two traits also made him the logical choice to preside over the electoral commission established in 1877 to resolve the hotly disputed Rutherford B. Hayes–Samuel J. Tilden presidential election.

Tilden, the Democratic candidate, had won a majority of the popular vote, and, had the commission certified only one of the electoral votes in his favor in any of

To resolve the disputed returns in the presidential election of 1876, Congress created an electoral commission, shown here deliberating by candlelight. Made up of five senators, five members of the House of Representatives, and five Supreme Court justices, the commission voted 8–7 to give Republican candidate Rutherford B. Hayes the disputed electoral votes. Commission members voted strictly along party lines, causing Justice Nathan Clifford, a Democrat, to question Hayes's legitimacy and to later refuse to appear at White House functions. *Source: Library of Congress*

the three states with disputed returns, he would have been president. The Republican-dominated committee found, however, that Hayes had beaten Tilden in all three states and that Hayes had won the election, 185-184. Clifford dutifully reported the commission's findings to Congress and signed the order certifying the election of Hayes as president. He acted patriotically in agreeing to serve on the electoral commission and by not trying to contest the pro-Republican results. But Clifford never considered Hayes a legitimate president. Hayes later acknowledged that his victory was the result of "a strictly party vote" that demonstrated "the strength of party ties." Clifford declined the invitation to attend Hayes's inauguration, and he refused to accompany the other justices on traditional visits to the White House during the Hayes presidency.

Hayes's election fueled Clifford's determination to remain on the bench until a Democratic president could name his successor. His final years on the Court were marred by frequent absences resulting from a steady deterioration in his health. In 1880 he suffered a severe stroke that left him physically and mentally impaired. After a long absence from the bench, he was visited by Justice Samuel Miller, a former physician, who reported Clifford's mental condition to be extremely poor. Although Clifford insisted that he would return to his duties, the amputation of a foot compounded his health problems and prevented him from doing so. The election of Republican James Garfield in 1880 ended his hopes for a Democratic president. Clifford died July 25, 1881, in Cornish, Maine, bringing to an end twenty-three tumultuous years of service on the Court.

Noah H. Swayne
1862-1881

Source: *Library of Congress*

NOAH HAYNES SWAYNE'S first American ancestor was Francis Swayne, who emigrated from England in 1710 to the Quaker colony founded by William Penn, and settled on a farm near Philadelphia. Noah's parents, Joshua Swayne and Rebecca Smith Swayne, both strict Pennsylvania Quakers, moved to a farm in Frederick County, in northern Virginia, where Noah Swayne was born December 7, 1804, the youngest of nine children. Four years later Joshua

Swayne died, leaving his widow to support and rear their large family.

Noah attended a local school until the age of thirteen and then was sent to Jacob Mendenhall's academy in Waterford, Virginia, a highly regarded Quaker school. After two years, he moved to Alexandria, Virginia, to study medicine with George A. Thornton, a respected physician and the owner of a small apothecary's store. Swayne's budding medical career, which next would have taken him to a Philadelphia hospital, ended after only a year, when his teacher died. Swayne then turned his career hopes to the law, and he entered an academy in Alexandria to prepare for college. He gained some grounding in the classics before learning that his guardian would be unable to finance a college education. He plunged at once into reading law in the office of John Scott and Francis P. Brooks in Warrenton, Virginia, and was admitted to the bar in 1823 at the age of nineteen.

A pivotal decision in Swayne's life, to move to the free state of Ohio, was driven by his hatred of slavery, a conviction no doubt influenced by his Quaker religion and by the example of his antislavery parents. Traveling more than 300 miles by horseback, he settled in the town of Zanesville, east of Columbus, for the preliminary year of residence required before out-of-state attorneys could practice in Ohio. In 1825 he moved north to Coshocton, some sixty miles east and a bit north of the capital city of Columbus. He was immediately successful and within a year was appointed prosecuting attorney of Coshocton County.

Other avenues of opportunity quickly opened to the young attorney. In 1829 he was elected to the state legislature as a Jacksonian Democrat from Coshocton County. The following year, President Andrew Jackson appointed him U.S. attorney for the District of Ohio, persuading him to turn down another offer, nomination for a seat in Congress. His new official duties took him to Columbus, the state capital, where he was elected city councilman in 1834. He was again elected to the state legislature in 1836, this time from Franklin County, his new home. All the while Swayne continued to serve as U.S. attorney for Ohio, a post he held until 1841.

In 1832 Swayne married Sarah Ann Wager of Harper's Ferry, Virginia, a union that produced four sons and one daughter. The marriage brought several slaves into Swayne's possession, but in agreement with his new wife they were immediately freed.

While serving in the state legislature and as U.S. attorney for Ohio, he continued to practice law. Over the years he gained a distinguished reputation as a trial lawyer and counsel to many of the area's businesses and corporations. Swayne formed a law partnership with James Bates in 1839 that lasted until 1852, and a subsequent one with Llewellyn Taber that continued for another seven years.

One of his most sensational cases was tried in 1853 in the U.S. circuit court in Columbus. Owners of the steamboat *Martha Washington* were charged with burning the vessel to collect the insurance. Swayne won a verdict of not guilty by what was described as four days of shrewd cross-examination, further adding to his growing reputation. During the same period a boundary dispute with the state of Michigan threatened to erupt into violence when armed men crossed the border from Michigan. With two others, Swayne was sent by the Ohio governor to Washington to seek a peaceful resolution. They were successful, and the disputed region remained with Ohio.

While practicing law, Swayne found time for a range of unpaid public service to Ohio. State finances had broken down in the panic of 1837, and Swayne was one of three members of a special commission appointed to take charge of reducing the outstanding debt and financing public works. Both problems were successfully resolved within three years. In 1840 he was appointed to another three-member commission, this time to survey the condition of the blind in Ohio, an evaluation later extended to the deaf and the mentally impaired. Among the results was the establishment of a school for the blind. He continued his volunteer contributions as a trustee of several similar institutions.

Swayne's support of Jacksonian democracy eroded over the Democrats' proslavery position. When the an-

In 1862 President Abraham Lincoln authorized military officials to arrest civilians suspected of "disloyalty," even in areas far from combat. The military arrested, tried, and convicted Clement L. Vallandigham, a Confederate sympathizer, in Ohio, even though civilian courts were open. He pressed his case all the way to the Supreme Court. In an argument based largely on a legal technicality, the Court ruled in 1864 that it had no jurisdiction over the case, effectively allowing Lincoln's policy to continue. *Source: Library of Congress*

tislavery Republican party was formed in the 1850s, Swayne made the switch. He became a strong and active supporter of John C. Fremont, the 1856 Republican presidential nominee, who ran on a platform upholding congressional authority to exclude slavery from the territories. With the advent of the Civil War, Swayne firmly backed President Abraham Lincoln, the Republican party, and the Union.

Lincoln nominated Swayne to the Supreme Court on January 21, 1862, the first of his appointments to the high bench. Despite his lack of judicial experience or national reputation, Swayne enjoyed strong support from all the members of Ohio's congressional delega-

tion, and the governor, William Dennison, journeyed to Washington to lobby for him. Justice John McLean, Swayne's predecessor on the Court and a fellow Ohioan, former colleague, and close friend, had made it known to Lincoln that he wanted Swayne to succeed him. The fifty-eight-year-old attorney campaigned on his own behalf, as well, even traveling to Washington to solicit support. The Senate confirmed him, 38–1, three days after his nomination, and his appointment was praised by the press. Swayne was assigned to the Sixth Circuit, comprised of Ohio, Indiana, Illinois, and Michigan, and enjoyed instant popularity.

On the Supreme Court bench, Swayne fulfilled the

hopes of President Lincoln and the Republican party by supporting the emergency actions of the federal government during the Civil War. He joined the majority in the critical *Prize Cases* of 1863, which upheld the constitutionality of Lincoln's prosecution of the war before Congress had given him formal authorization. Swayne was also in the majority when the Court upheld the legality of the wartime issuance of paper money, which had been used to finance the war. Again, he was with the majority in *Ex parte Vallandigham* in 1864, a decision that permitted Union military commanders to continue carrying out arrests far beyond Union lines of citizens who threatened national security.

Swayne's patriotic zeal did not, however, drive him to blind partisanship. He tried unsuccessfully to persuade President Lincoln to free a Confederate spy condemned to death; he also intervened with the president in the arbitrary military arrest of a civilian. Swayne himself freed a man charged with treason on the grounds of insufficient evidence, remarking that "causeless and wicked as this rebellion is . . . it is not the less our duty to hold the scales of justice . . . with a firm and steady hand." Swayne and the Court resisted treating the Confederate rebels as traitors and instead conceded them rights befitting insurgents. This distinction was later spelled out in Swayne's 1869 opinion in *Hickman v. Jones,* which held that "the pretended government of the Confederacy" was not sovereign and that "in the eye of the law" the war should be treated as an insurrection.

Swayne wrote the 1864 majority decision in *Gelpcke v. Dubuque,* the first of several cases in which he sided with the nation's growing railroads. The case involved municipal bonds issued by the city of Dubuque to underwrite railroad construction, an action the Iowa court held valid under state law. After widespread mismanagement of the railroads led to financial collapse, however, public sentiment against financing them induced the Iowa court to reverse its position. When the case reached the Supreme Court, Swayne held that the contract obligations must be upheld and that the law and the bonds were still valid. He proved to be a strong ally of business, particularly the powerful railroad interests, during his nineteen years on the bench. This tendency won Swayne the undying opposition of his colleague, Samuel Miller, who labeled him a mediocre jurist.

An 1875 stock certificate for the Dubuque & Sioux City Rail Road Company. Fierce competition for railroads sometimes led cities into financial difficulties. When Dubuque issued railroad bonds that exceeded the debt limits set by the state constitution, a reform-minded state supreme court eventually reversed earlier rulings that found the bonds valid. In *Gelpcke v. Dubuque,* Noah Swayne wrote the opinion rejecting the Iowa court's last ruling. He held that the Supreme Court could interpret a state constitution in view of the state supreme court's inconsistency. *Source: State Historical Society of Iowa*

Noah Swayne's active support for the Fifteenth Amendment in his adoptive state of Ohio was crucial to getting it passed by the state senate, and helped to secure its eventual ratification in 1870. The amendment enabled black men to cast their votes for the first time. A decade later, however, blacks found themselves effectively barred from polls as white leaders used intimidation and legal maneuvers to keep them from voting. *Source: Library of Congress*

The nationalism Swayne showed during the Civil War continued into the Reconstruction era. He generally supported the postwar amendments to the Constitution, which were intended to improve the status of blacks. Swayne endorsed the Thirteenth Amendment, which abolished the institution of slavery, as "an act of grace and justice" and the only way to end the practice. He dissented sharply from the majority in the landmark *Slaughter House Cases* of 1873, which restricted the scope of the Fourteenth Amendment's guarantee of the privileges and immunities of U.S. citizens. The Court's narrow interpretation opened the way for states to curtail the civil liberties of blacks. Swayne's dissent anticipated the broad reach that future Courts would take in interpreting the amendment, and it sharply criticized Justice Miller's opinion as diverging from the intent of the legislature in passing the amendment to protect blacks.

Swayne pushed hard for passage of the Fifteenth Amendment, which says that the right to vote cannot be denied on the basis of race, color, or previous condition of servitude. When its ratification was in doubt, Swayne's adopted state of Ohio played a decisive role. Gov. Rutherford B. Hayes asked him for help in 1870, and Swayne used all his influence to rally support. The ratification forces carried the Ohio Senate by one vote

and the House by two votes, thereby assuring the Fifteenth Amendment's eventual passage.

When Chief Justice Roger B. Taney died in 1864, Swayne mounted a campaign to succeed him. He mustered considerable support, although his backers' primary motivation may have been opposition to Salmon P. Chase, who was secretary of the Treasury and President Lincoln's anticipated choice for the post. Several members of Lincoln's cabinet supported Swayne, as did some of his brethren. The many arguments Lincoln heard against Chase were unpersuasive, however, and in December 1864 Chase received the nomination. When Chase died in 1873, Swayne, then almost sixty-nine, made a desperate second effort for the position. He was again disappointed, this time by Morrison Waite's appointment.

By 1877 Swayne was showing signs of failing health. In 1881, with a promise from President Hayes to appoint his friend and fellow Ohioan Stanley Matthews as his successor, Swayne resigned on January 25, at the age of seventy-six. His wife died the following year. Swayne, in ill health, moved to New York City to be with his son, Wagner Swayne, a practicing lawyer, and died there June 8, 1884.

Samuel F. Miller
1862–1890

Source: Collection of the Supreme Court of the United States

SAMUEL FREEMAN MILLER was born April 5, 1816, in Richmond, Kentucky. The location of the Miller farm was known locally as Poosey's Ridge, where, according to one resident, "nobody was rich and nobody poor; there were very few slaves." Samuel was the eldest of Frederick and Patsy Freeman Miller's eight children. His father was of Pennsylvania-German stock. His mother, one of thirteen children, was the daughter of Samuel Freeman, who had come to Kentucky from North Carolina in the late 1700s. In a letter written about his mother in later life, Miller remarked, "How much of the success which has attended my life I attribute to her example, her instruction, and the qualities I have inherited from her." He went on to explain that he helped her with the family responsibilities: "Owing to my father's habits I was at a very early age taken into her confidence as a substitute, and the care of my younger sisters and my brother were a joint affair."

Until he was fourteen Miller attended schools in

Richmond, including a respected academy where he was at the head of his class. He left school to work in a local drug store owned by a relative of his mother. Miller began to develop an interest in medicine, studying it on his own and taking two lecture courses in the medical department of Transylvania University at Lexington. The records of the college, now the University of Kentucky, show that he submitted a twenty-three-page manuscript on cholera, passed his exams, and received an M.D. degree on March 9, 1838, at the age of twenty-one.

For the next nine years Miller practiced the primitive medicine of the day in the hamlet of Barbourville, a settlement of only a few hundred inhabitants near the Tennessee and Virginia borders and the seat of Knox County. The life of a lone country doctor was difficult, and he spent his days—and nights—riding his horse along rugged mountain roads with a bag full of medical supplies. His office was a log cabin shared, significantly, with a young lawyer named Silas Woodson.

Frustrated at being unable to alleviate much of the suffering he confronted and bored with his continual rounds, Miller turned his attention to the Barbourville Debating Society, which he had helped organize in 1837. The group debated the public policy issues of the day and was remarkable for the number of its members who eventually attained high state and federal office. Seeds of later decisions on the circuit and Supreme Court bench have been found in Miller's arguments. Five times he argued that there was no moral justification for capital punishment, demonstrating an antipathy to taking human life later reflected in his reluctance to impose or confirm a death sentence.

Miller was physically impressive, standing well over six feet in height and weighing more than 200 pounds. He was energetic and unpretentious and loved to sing and tell stories. His politics were fairly progressive, and he was a Unitarian. On November 8, 1842, Miller married Lucy L. Ballinger, the daughter of locally promi-

nent parents who had come from North Carolina. The couple had three children before Lucy Miller's death from consumption at an early age.

Miller got his first experience in public affairs in Barbourville when he was sworn in as a justice of the peace in 1844 and took his seat as a member of the county court. He soon abandoned the medical profession and began reading law in his shared office. In 1847 he was admitted to the bar of the Circuit Court of Knox County, on the motion of his office mate and debating partner, Woodson. For three years Miller practiced his new profession in the same community, long enough to aspire to a seat in the Kentucky Constitutional Convention of 1849 as an advocate of the emancipation of slaves. He withdrew, however, when his friend Woodson entered the race, so as not to split the antislavery vote.

The attempt to do away with slavery in Kentucky failed completely. Miller, whose aversion to the institution went back to his childhood and the memory of seeing his black nursemaid flogged, resigned himself to the fact that slavery would never be voluntarily abolished in a slave state such as Kentucky. After a tour of the Northwest in the fall of 1849, he decided to move to Iowa, a free state. He arrived in Keokuk by riverboat in May 1850, with his wife and children. He also brought his slaves and freed them. Now almost thirty-five years old, but still a fledgling lawyer, Miller was able to enter into a partnership with an already prominent attorney, Lewis Reeves, who had a large practice in land title, steamboat, and commercial law. Almost at once, Miller was heavily engaged in a profitable practice and within a year had become known throughout the state.

In 1854 Miller suffered the death of his wife and the death of his law partner. He formed a new partnership with another leading Keokuk lawyer, John Rankin, which lasted until Miller's appointment to the Supreme Court. Two and a half years after his wife's death he married Eliza Winter Reeves, the widow of his first law partner. Described as high-spirited and warm-hearted, she bore him two children and survived him by ten years. It was said at the time that "the old firm of Reeves and Miller was renewed under a different contract."

There is impressive evidence of Miller's success as a lawyer. In a communication of 1856, he speaks of some 300 cases in which he was engaged and awaiting trial in the next term of court. He appeared frequently before the Iowa Supreme Court, his name figuring in seventy of the reported cases from 1851 to 1862. He was also emerging as a political force in the new Republican party and in 1856 was chosen chairman of the first Republican organization in Keokuk. Later that year he was nominated for the state senate, but, as expected, was not elected. In 1861 he lost the Republican nomination for governor to Samuel Kirkwood, the incumbent.

Miller continued to denounce slavery as evil "to both the white man and the black." He called it "the most stupendous wrong, and the most prolific source of human misery, both to the master and the slave, that the sun shines upon in his daily circuit around the globe." Despite his strong views, he condemned the ex-

tremists on both sides, abolitionists and proslavery Democrats alike. He opposed the extension of slavery into free territory, argued against secession, recognized states' rights, and strongly favored the gradual emancipation of slaves and the preservation of the Union at all costs. His position was similar to that of Abraham Lincoln, whom he supported enthusiastically for the Republican presidential nomination. Once the Civil War came, Miller backed his words with deeds: he gave his own money to raise and arm troops.

As a small-town attorney with no formal legal education and little judicial experience, Miller was not an obvious candidate for an appointment to the U.S. Supreme Court. The Iowa lawyer's chances would increase dramatically, however, if Congress were to create a new judicial circuit embracing only the states west of the Mississippi River. After pressure from Iowa and its neighboring states, and six months of intricate political maneuvers on Capitol Hill, the new circuit was created. Within a day of its establishment, Miller's supporters were able to present President Lincoln with petitions for his appointment signed by twenty-eight of the thirty-two senators then in Congress and by 129 mem-

Convinced that his native Kentucky would never voluntarily end the practice of slavery, abolitionist Samuel F. Miller decided to move to the free state of Iowa. In May 1850 the Miller family, with their slaves, came by riverboat to Keokuk, viewed from the Mississippi River. There Miller freed his slaves, became a successful lawyer, and was chosen chairman of the town's first Republican party organization. *Source: Library of Congress*

One of the earliest group photographs of the Supreme Court shows its members in 1865: (seated, left to right) Justices David Davis, Noah Swayne, Robert Grier, James M. Wayne, Chief Justice Salmon P. Chase, Justices Samuel Nelson, Nathan Clifford, Samuel Miller, and Stephen J. Field. Miller, appointed in 1862, became a dominant force on the Court during his twenty-eight-year tenure, writing a large share of the opinions on constitutional issues. *Source: Library of Congress*

bers of the House, some three-fourths of the membership. Lincoln sent Miller's nomination to the Senate the evening of July 16, 1862, and it was confirmed within a half-hour without reference to committee. Miller was sworn in five days later, becoming the first member of the Court appointed from west of the Mississippi River. He was also the first justice born west of the Appalachians.

Miller was concerned about joining a Court that had rendered decisions that were detestable to a westerner and an opponent of slavery. Although he had never met him, Miller said he "hated" Chief Justice Roger B. Taney for attempting to shut down the Bank of the United States and for being the Court's chief spokesman in the controversial *Dred Scott v. Sandford* case, which ruled that blacks were not citizens of the United States. "But from my first acquaintance with him, I realized that these feelings toward him were but the suggestions of the worst elements of our nature; for before the first term of my service in the Court had passed, I more than liked him," Miller later remarked of Taney, further adding that "conscience was his guide and sense of duty his principle." Taney fully reciprocated Miller's respect and affection and predicted he

would "maintain and advance the high traditions of the Court" and have "a career of great usefulness and honor."

Taney's prediction was borne out in the succeeding twenty-eight years. Soon Miller was being assigned twice the normal share of cases in which the Constitution was to be interpreted. He wrote the opinion of the Court in 616 cases, more than any previous justice, 95 of them on constitutional issues. He became, in the words of the next chief justice, Salmon P. Chase, "beyond question the dominant personality . . . upon the bench, whose mental force and individuality are felt by the Court more than any other." Miller commented in later years that he had been the "organ of the Court" in constitutional cases. Miller's opinions show that he found a balance between the Constitution's protections of federal and state power. He wrote the Court's dissenting opinion in seventy-eight cases, thirty-one of them interpreting the Constitution, and he lived to see some of his dissents accepted by the Court in later decisions. His arguments were persuasive because of their logic, common sense, and boldness.

Perhaps Miller's most significant opinion for the Court was in the landmark *Slaughter House Cases* of

When Louisiana granted the Crescent City Live Stock Landing and Slaughter House Company a twenty-five year monopoly on livestock-butchering in New Orleans, it forced every butcher to use the facility and to pay for the use. The butchers sued, basing their 1873 case before the Supreme Court on the Fourteenth Amendment, which forbids states to pass laws that "abridge the privileges or immunities" of U.S. citizens. Samuel Miller wrote the Court's opinion, upholding the Louisiana law. *Source: Historic New Orleans Collection*

1873. Louisiana butchers seeking to protect their businesses brought the suit after the state had granted a particular corporation a monopoly on the slaughtering trade in New Orleans. They argued that the clauses of the Fourteenth Amendment that provided for the privileges and immunities of U.S. citizenship, equal protection of laws, and due process guaranteed them the right to practice their trade. In upholding the Louisiana statute, Miller wrote that the right to do business did not derive from one's U.S. citizenship and was therefore not protected by the amendment. He reasoned, narrowly, that the amendment protected but did not expand the rights an individual possessed under federal citizenship and that it did not refer to rights under state citizenship. He did not want the Court to be in a position of "perpetual censor" over state legislation regarding the civil rights of its citizens.

Years later, Miller wrote the decision in *Wabash, St. Louis and Pacific Railway Co. v. Illinois* (1886), holding that states could not set rates for railroads that were part of an interstate network without infringing on federal control of interstate commerce. The ruling paved the way for the Interstate Commerce Act of 1887, the first major piece of regulatory legislation.

Miller sat on the fifteen-man commission to settle the disputed 1876 presidential election results, and he voted with the Republican majority to give Rutherford B. Hayes the election. He was considered for the position of chief justice in 1873 and 1888 by two presidents, Ulysses S. Grant and Grover Cleveland, but both were reluctant to promote from the bench. His name was also mentioned for the presidency in 1880 and 1884, but he never mustered enough support.

Miller presided over a circuit court in St. Louis, Missouri, on October 2, 1890. It would be his last time on the bench. The seventy-four-year-old justice returned to Washington for the Supreme Court term. On his way home from a visit to the Court October 13, he suffered a stroke and died a few hours later.

David Davis
1862-1877

Source: Library of Congress

DAVID DAVIS was born of Welsh ancestry in Cecil County, Maryland, March 9, 1815. He was named after his father, a doctor, who had died some eight months earlier. A teenage widow, Ann Mercer Davis had returned to her father's Maryland plantation, where her son was born. David was nursed by a slave, and his first playmates were the children of slaves.

In 1820 his mother married Franklin Betts, a bookseller and stationer in Baltimore. The couple set about having children of their own and sent David to live with his uncle, Henry Lyon Davis, in Annapolis. Reverend Davis was rector of St. Anne's Episcopal Church and served as president of St. John's College. He became a surrogate father to young David and eventually carried on a bitter legal struggle over custody of the boy with his stepfather, David's legal guardian. Henry Davis charged that Betts was diverting funds from the estate David had inherited from his father to pay his debts; Betts countered that Davis drank to excess. Betts won

181

The earliest known photograph of Abraham Lincoln was taken in 1846, when he was an obscure Whig representative from Illinois. Lincoln's opposition to the Mexican War made him unpopular among his constitutents, and he only served one term. He returned to his law practice in Illinois, where he often argued cases before Judge David Davis. *Source: Library of Congress*

the legal battle, retrieved David, and in 1826 sent him off again, this time to the New Ark Academy in Delaware.

In 1828, at age thirteen, Davis entered Kenyon College in Ohio. Betts chose Kenyon because the tuition, at seventy dollars per year, was half the amount charged by Yale, his initial preference. Davis helped pay his way by working on the college farms and buildings during his vacations. After graduating in 1832, Davis went to study law at the office of Henry W. Bishop in Lenox, Massachusetts. In 1834 he entered the New Haven Law School, which was associated with Yale. The prescribed

course of study lasted for two years and did not result in a degree. Davis attended for less than a year before being admitted to the Illinois bar.

Davis moved to Pekin, Illinois, where he established a law practice and soon had some level of success. A month after his arrival, he was elected a member of a delegation charged with securing a charter for a railroad to run from Pekin to the Wabash River. While serving in this capacity, he met a number of influential political figures. Davis also met a lanky, disheveled young member of the Illinois legislature named Abraham Lincoln, who became a lifelong friend and had an enormous impact on his life.

In almost no time, however, Davis's fondness for Pekin faded. He complained in a letter that there was "absolutely nothing to do [in Pekin] but quarrel among one another and wrangle all the time." Furthermore, in the summer of 1836, he contracted a serious case of malaria. Later that year he moved to Bloomington, Illinois, where he maintained his residence for the remainder of his life.

On October 30, 1838, Davis married Sarah Walker, whom he had met in Lenox and courted for several years. Sarah's father, Judge William Walker, had been slow in giving his consent and, upon their marriage, her family lamented that she was being taken as far west as Illinois.

Davis had political ambitions, but in these early years they were not much satisfied. In 1839 he campaigned (rather half-heartedly) for the position of district attorney for the state's newly established Eighth Judicial Circuit. Lincoln lent him some assistance, but he lost anyway. In 1840 Davis campaigned as Whig candidate for the Illinois Senate, again without success. Under the circumstances, such a setback was hardly surprising. Davis was only twenty-five years old, and his opponent, John Moore, was an experienced politician. Moreover, during the course of the campaign David and Sarah lost their first child, a son, who died at birth. Davis took time away from the race to care for Sarah, and his absence almost certainly contributed to his defeat.

After these losses, Davis's fortunes slowly began to improve. Although Illinois was struggling, he steadily built a solid law practice. He also became an adept land speculator. In 1842 Sarah gave birth to a healthy son, whom they named George Perrin Davis. (Two subsequent children died in infancy.)

Davis's political career also began to move. In 1844 he won a seat in the Illinois legislature and was appointed to serve on its education committee. After a term in the state House, he was elected a member of the state constitutional convention of 1847. At the convention he was instrumental in changing the judicial system, advancing reforms so that judges were elected by the people rather than by the legislature.

His own judicial career started in 1848, when he was elected circuit judge on the Illinois Eighth Circuit. This position, which he held for fourteen years, had its drawbacks: his circuit covered a vast territory; he was often away from his wife; and the food and accommodations left much to be desired. But the position also

had its benefits and improved with time. In 1852 and 1857 the territory within the circuit was narrowed, and the courthouses eventually became accessible by rail. Most important, riding circuit gave Davis the opportunity to travel with his good friend Lincoln, who often appeared before him in court. It is a tribute to Davis's impartiality that, despite his close friendship with Lincoln, he ruled for the opposing party in forty-seven of the eighty-seven nonjury cases that Lincoln tried before him.

As the Whig party disintegrated in the 1850s, both Davis and Lincoln joined the newly formed Republican party. Davis enthusiastically campaigned for Lincoln in his two losing bids for the U.S. Senate and, later, when he sought the presidential nomination of the Republican party. Davis was the primary architect of the strategy to nominate Lincoln at the 1860 Republican convention. The plan was to obtain pledges from each state to support Lincoln as its second choice. This tactic would not antagonize any of the front-runners, but, by the same token, would provide Lincoln with a secure position from which he could advance. The device

David Davis stumped for his close friend Abraham Lincoln in two unsuccessful Senate campaigns before becoming his campaign strategist in his 1860 bid for the Republican presidential nomination. Lincoln and his running mate, Hannibal Hamlin, ran on a platform declaring that slavery was morally wrong. Their victory proved that the North was populous enough to elect a minority party that had no support in the South. *Source: Library of Congress*

Copperheads, the derisive term for northern Democrats who opposed the Civil War, are shown menacing the Union cause in this 1863 cartoon. Confederate sympathizer Lambdin P. Milligan and other Copperheads plotted to liberate Confederate prisoners held in northern camps and arm them. David Davis wrote in *Ex parte Milligan* (1866) that civilians could not be tried by a military court, even during emergency war conditions. *Source: Library of Congress*

worked brilliantly, and, in the course of the convention, Lincoln dramatically progressed from the long-shot candidate to the leader. When Lincoln's nomination was finally announced, an exhausted Davis broke into tears.

Davis was also intimately involved in Lincoln's presidential campaign. He advised Lincoln on campaign strategy and went, as Lincoln's emissary, to the critical states of Pennsylvania and Indiana. Indeed, Davis was so involved in campaigning that it sometimes distracted him from his duties on the bench. When Lincoln was elected, Davis continued to advise him, notably in the delicate process of assembling a cabinet. He read and criticized a draft of Lincoln's inaugural address and fielded the deluge of postelection requests for appointments and offices. It is ironic that, when this flurry of activity subsided, Davis had not secured a position for himself. Almost two years passed before he received any

meaningful recognition for his efforts on Lincoln's behalf. In October 1862 Lincoln gave Davis a recess appointment to the U.S. Supreme Court. Davis was confirmed by a voice vote December 8. He replaced Justice John Campbell, an Alabaman who had resigned to help the Confederate cause.

Davis must have been an imposing Supreme Court justice. He weighed more than 300 pounds and sported long gray mutton chops that joined his close-cropped beard. Although usually courteous and charming, at times he was headstrong and let his temper show.

As a judge in Illinois, he had presided over cases tried by some of the nation's leading advocates; he was also probably the president's best friend. Under the circumstances, it might seem logical that Davis would thrive in his position, would assume a powerful leadership position on the Court, and would have a significant influence on the Court's jurisprudence. The reverse was true. Davis sorely missed the excitement of the political arena. He had more interest in leading the country than in leading on the Court and wrote few noteworthy opinions. His tenure was also marred by the assassination of President Lincoln on April 14, 1865—an event that was, in his case, a tragedy of both national and personal dimensions. Davis was appointed to serve as the administrator of his old friend's estate.

Although Davis never expressed much interest in legal scholarship, his opinion in *Ex parte Milligan* (1866) is sufficient to secure his place in the history of American constitutional law. The case involved Lambdin P. Milligan, a civilian who was tried by an Indiana military court and convicted of conspiracy during the Civil War. Milligan was sentenced to death for his involvement in a plot to release and arm Confederate prisoners so they could participate in an invasion of Indiana. By a series of fortunate events, Milligan managed to escape hanging. He petitioned a lower federal court for relief from his "unlawful imprisonment" and, when relief was refused, appealed to the Supreme Court.

Davis's opinion in the case is a tribute to the principles of liberty and justice. Acknowledging that "the temper of the times [during the Civil War] did not allow that calmness in deliberation and discussion so necessary to a correct conclusion of a purely judicial question," Davis vowed to decide the case fairly now that public safety was assured. He argued that constitutional rights do not cease to exist during wartime: "The Constitution of the United States is a law for rulers and people, equally in war and in peace, and covers with the shield of its protection all classes of men, at all times, and under all circumstances." That Milligan's actions had occurred during wartime did not affect the legitimacy of the inquiry over whether his constitutional rights were violated by the military trial.

Davis concluded that Milligan's rights had indeed been infringed when he was tried by a court that was not "ordained and established by Congress." Moreover,

those rights were further infringed when he was denied his right to trial by jury—a right, Davis emphasized, that "is not held by sufferance, and cannot be frittered away on any plea of state or political necessity." His opinion held that the president had no power to mandate that civilians be tried by military commission in areas where civilian courts continued to operate.

Davis was sharply criticized for his opinion in *Milligan*. One newspaper wrote that "the hearts of traitors will be glad that treason, vanquished upon the battlefield and hunted from every other retreat, has at last found a secure shelter in the bosom of the Supreme Court." Davis weathered the controversy well, telling his brother-in-law, "Cowardice of all sorts is mean, but judicial cowardice is the meanest of all . . . I abide the judgment of *time*."

Eventually, Davis could no longer resist the lure of politics. Disenchanted with the Republicans, he flirted with nomination as a presidential candidate of two splinter groups during the conventions of 1872. Finally, in 1877, he resigned from the Supreme Court after the Illinois legislature elected him to the U.S. Senate. He was hailed in the Senate as a true independent, unaffiliated with any party, and a man of conscience and self-reliance. From 1881 until 1883, when he retired, he served as president pro tempore of the Senate. As such, under the succession law in effect, he was next in line for the presidency should anything happen to President Chester A. Arthur.

Upon retiring, Davis married Adeline Burr, a young woman who had nursed his first wife before her death in 1879. They returned to Bloomington where, diagnosed with diabetes, Davis died June 26, 1886. Although he has been described as a public figure of the second rank, the friendship and guidance he gave Lincoln, and the opinion he wrote in *Milligan,* secured for him an important place in the history of American liberty.

Stephen J. Field
1863-1897

THE SIXTH CHILD OF David Dudley Field and Submit Dickinson Field, Stephen Johnson Field was born November 4, 1816, in Haddam, Connecticut. His father was a stern Congregationalist minister, and both parents were descended from old Puritan families of New England. At age thirteen, Field accompanied his eldest sister and her husband to what is now Turkey, where they lived for two and a half years. The trip broadened his horizons and enabled him to learn several foreign languages, prompting speculation that he might become a language professor.

Field graduated at the top of his class from Williams College in 1837 and began to study law with his eldest brother, David Dudley Field, Jr., a successful New York attorney. He continued his legal studies in the Albany office of state attorney general John Van Buren. Field was admitted to the bar in 1841 and practiced law in partnership with his brother for seven years. After touring Europe, which was undergoing widespread political turmoil, he returned to New York in October 1849. Excited by the news that gold had been discovered in California, a restless Field booked passage on a ship to San Francisco. He was ferried in a canoe across Panama and eventually reached his destination in late December, with only $10 in his pocket and no immediate prospect of a job.

Unlike many of his traveling companions, Field had no intention of breaking his back in search of gold. He hoped to establish a lucrative legal practice in the rapidly expanding San Francisco area, but after a month there Field realized that his expectations had been unrealistic. He decided to move inland, traveling about 100 miles by boat up California's Sacramento and Feather rivers to a settlement called Marysville. He found the town's 600 or so residents living in tents, shacks, and a few small adobe buildings. He also found a man displaying a map marked off in lots that people were buying for $250 each. On asking the consequences of signing up for a lot and deciding not to take it, Field was informed that no penalty would be imposed. Although he had only about $20, Field signed up for sixty-five lots—worth a total of $16,250. The townspeople assumed that he was a wealthy capitalist from San Francisco and held a dinner to honor the new "benefactor." Field persuaded his dinner companions of the necessity of electing a local government, and his eloquence secured his own election as the town's first "alcalde."

A judicial office originating in Spanish law, the alcalde was the only form of legitimate local authority that had survived Mexican cession of California. Field promptly established a police force to maintain order by taxing the local gambling tables. At the outset, he found himself in somewhat of a predicament in providing justice for serious offenses, as there was neither a jail nor any funds to build one. The penalty for theft and other crimes had been lynching, which Field strongly opposed, so he devised other forms of punishment. Field also served as an informal arbiter of land disputes, directed the grading of the river banks to ease landings by river traffic, and performed various administrative services for the town.

Field's duties as alcalde ended in May 1850 with the installation of local officials under the newly ratified California state constitution. Relations between Field and his successor, California District Court judge William R. Turner, were openly hostile from the beginning, motivated by mutual jealousy and political differences. Field's first appearance before Turner produced a heated verbal exchange that earned the former alcalde a $500 fine, two days imprisonment in the judge's chambers, and expulsion from the California bar. Field immediately secured a ruling from the California Supreme Court overturning the decision, but he also petitioned the governor for Turner's suspension. Failing in the latter effort, Field engaged Turner in a running exchange of editorial criticism throughout the summer of 1850 in the local newspapers. One such attack, signed by Field, so enraged Judge Turner that he ordered Field brought before him and demanded that he show cause why he should not again be expelled from the bar. Once in court, Field characteristically unleashed an assault on his adversary's personal character and judicial competence.

Reinstated once again to the bar by the California Supreme Court, Field decided upon a different tack, and in the fall of 1850 he ran a successful campaign for a seat in the California Assembly, the lower house of the legislature. There he introduced a variety of judicial reforms, one of which succeeded in banishing Judge Turner to a newly created district in the extreme northwest of the state. Poor relations between the two men continued for many years and nearly resulted in a shoot-out on the floor of the Assembly in 1851. As his political career progressed, Field's opponents frequently tried to exploit the Field-Turner battles to discredit and embarrass him.

Despite these efforts, Field's career advanced. While serving in the California legislature, he was primarily responsible for turning California's tangle of Spanish law, frontier practices, and American legal precedents into a single body of civil and criminal state law that could be generally applied. His inspiration for writing the code was drawn from his experience a few years earlier when he assisted his brother in a similar task for New York State. His substantial legal training, tempered by a frontier practicality, proved well-suited for California's early years of statehood, and his contribution to the state's legal system laid a foundation that would become a model for codification in neighboring states in the years to come.

In the summer of 1851 Field hoped to advance his legislative career by running for California's state Senate, and he collected a sufficient number of proxies from delegates unable to attend the Democratic convention in Sacramento to assure his nomination. Upon his arrival, he distributed the proxies to several of his cronies to be voted on his behalf. To Field's dismay, his supposed friends promptly traded away the votes for political favors. After losing the nomination by two votes, Field furiously vowed to take revenge.

Field returned to private practice until 1857, when he made another unsuccessful bid, this time for the Democratic nomination to the U.S. Senate. His exuberant confidence in his victory over his opponent was shared by few of his political allies, but Field's campaign in the Senate primary gained him considerable attention. As a result, he was elected to the California Supreme Court in 1857.

At that time, the California Supreme Court was interpreting a constitution that was only seven years old and dealing with a number of novel legal issues. Land titles were complicated by a treaty with Mexico, which required that existing property rights be recognized as they were under Mexican law. Even more complex were questions involving water and mineral rights. Because of the vast fortunes that hung in the balance, Field often found himself under attack from the public, which was quick to charge him with corruption, although there was never any substantiation for the claim.

In June 1859, at age forty-two, the bearded, spectacled judge put his bachelor days behind him and married Sue Virginia Swearingen. The marriage lasted until Field's death forty years later, but the couple had no children. His wife's calming influence greatly helped further Field's judicial career.

The year they wed, California's chief justice, David S. Terry, resigned his position to challenge a political adversary, David C. Broderick, a U.S. senator, to a duel. Field was promoted to take Terry's place as chief justice. Unfortunately, Broderick, who had been Field's close friend, was fatally wounded in the duel. His death began a bitter feud between Field and the volatile Terry that would erupt into an enormous national scandal nearly thirty years later.

In 1863, as the Civil War dragged on, Republicans in Congress made a provision to increase support for the Union on the U.S. Supreme Court by authorizing the addition of a tenth seat. This plan promised the added advantage of pulling Oregon and California firmly onto the Union side by providing the Pacific states with their own federal circuit and representation on the high court. Because of the many California cases dealing with land use and mineral rights, westerners urged that someone familiar with those issues be appointed. Not surprisingly, Field was unanimously recommended by the California and Oregon delegations.

A strong, outspoken supporter of the Union, Field also satisfied the need to appoint someone who could be expected to uphold the legality of the emergency measures taken during the Civil War. Field was a Democrat, but President Abraham Lincoln crossed party lines to appoint him on March 6, 1863. Unlike his Radical Republican supporters, Lincoln was looking toward the war's end, when a Democrat might prove more sympathetic to reconstruction plans than a member of his own party. Field was confirmed four days later.

Upon their arrival in Washington, the Fields quickly became regular participants at the capital city's social functions, where Justice Field's colorful life in California and his unlimited capacity for exaggeration provided an abundance of entertaining anecdotes. He also kept a hand in politics, serving on the electoral commission that decided the contested presidential election of Rutherford B. Hayes in 1876 and voting on the losing Democratic side. Field himself would make unsuccessful bids for the Democratic presidential nomination in 1880 and 1884. When Chief Justice Morrison Waite died in 1888, Field sought the seat, but President Grover Cleveland chose Melville Fuller instead.

Field may have been passed over because of his tendency to hold grudges and feud with enemies. The nation was reminded of his hot-headed behavior in 1888, when his feud with his former colleague from the California bench, David Terry, came to a climax. The episode involved an appeal to a federal circuit court in California, where Field was presiding, in which Terry's new wife, Sarah, claimed that she had been secretly married to William Sharon, a Nevada tycoon and former U.S. senator, and was therefore entitled to a divorce settlement. Upon hearing Field's unfavorable ruling, Sarah Terry accused him of taking a bribe, and the couple made such a commotion in the courtroom that they were sentenced to jail.

David Terry, who was known for his violent temper and habit of carrying a weapon, threatened Field's life, and the justice was provided the protection of a deputy U.S. marshal named David Neagle for his western travels. By coincidence, the Terrys crossed Field's path one day in a station restaurant in Lathrop, California. Terry

When Sarah Althea Hill sought to prove that she was entitled to a divorce settlement from William Sharon, a wealthy Nevada mine-owner, she engaged David S. Terry as one of her attorneys. Terry, an old enemy of Justice Stephen J. Field since their days together on the California Supreme Court, fell in love with his client and married her. The highly publicized case landed in Field's circuit court, and he ruled that Sarah Terry had never been married to Sharon. Incensed by the verdict, David Terry threatened Field's life. *Source: Bancroft Library*

struck Field and was fatally shot by Neagle, but turned out to be unarmed. Field then arranged to get the murder trial moved to the federal circuit court in San Francisco. The accomplice charges against Field were dropped, and Neagle was cleared. The circuit court's decision was upheld in 1890 by the Supreme Court (Field did not vote), and the whole incident brought the California justice great notoriety.

On the high bench, Field wrote blunt, weighty opin-

When David S. Terry threatened to kill Justice Stephen J. Field, the attorney general ordered an armed federal marshal, David Neagle, to protect Field during his circuit court travels in California. In a railroad station restaurant, Terry accosted Field and slapped him. Thinking Terry was armed, Neagle shot him and was charged with murder. Neagle contended that the state could not hold him for actions taken in the course of duties carried out under federal law. The Supreme Court ordered Neagle's release when it heard the case, absent Field, in 1890. *Source: Bancroft Library*

ions that left no doubt where the Court stood on the issues. He firmly believed that private business should not be subject to regulation if it was not eligible for public subsidy. He consistently opposed the income tax and wrote a concurring opinion in 1895 striking down the government's first effort to impose one. He attacked the mildly progressive tax as an "assault on capital" that would lead to a political "war between the poor and the rich." He objected to the tax's graduated rates because they violated his strong belief in uniformity and equal treatment. Field was joined in this view by his nephew, Associate Justice David Brewer, who shared the bench with him for eight years.

As Field entered his fourth decade on the Court, his growing infirmity strained relations with his nephew and other Court members. By 1895 he was in constant pain as a result of a poorly healed knee injury, which limited his mobility and taxed his patience. By the 1896 term Field's powerful physique had long since given way to his years, and his failing mental powers had become a source of public concern. Field stayed on the Court through November 30, 1897, just long enough to set a new record of service by surpassing Chief Justice John Marshall's thirty-four-year tenure. He died April 9, 1899, in his eighty-fourth year.

Salmon P. Chase
1864-1873

Source: Collection of the Supreme Court of the United States

THE EIGHTH OF eleven children, Salmon Portland Chase was born January 13, 1808, in Cornish, New Hampshire. The Chase family, which had emigrated from England to Massachusetts in the 1600s, moved to Cornish forty-five years before Salmon's birth and became well established in the community. His father, who operated a local tavern and a glass factory, died when Salmon was nine years old. Although faced with financial hardship, Chase's mother saw that he received a good education, both in district schools and with a private tutor.

At age twelve Chase moved to Ohio to work on the farm of his uncle, Philander Chase, who had recently been made bishop of Ohio for the Episcopal Church. When his uncle assumed the presidency of Cincinnati College, Chase went with him and finished the college's two-year curriculum, which was not particularly challenging, in a year's time. Returning to his family in

New Hampshire, Chase prepared for Dartmouth College. He graduated Phi Beta Kappa from that institution in 1826.

Leaving his rural state for the nation's capital, Chase found work as a teacher at a classical school, where he taught the sons of several prominent politicians, including Attorney General William Wirt. Chase discovered that his interest was in the law; he persuaded Wirt to oversee his legal studies and came to enjoy a close relationship with him. He passed the bar and returned to the rapidly growing city of Cincinnati to set up a practice. At first, Chase also turned his attention to writing and lecturing, and he tried to establish a literary magazine. Eventually he was forced to devote all his energies to developing his commercial law practice into a successful enterprise.

Tall, broad-shouldered, and handsome, Chase was popular with women. He married three society belles, but each marriage was cut short by death. His first wife, Katherine Jane Garniss, died tragically in 1835 after less than two years of a happy marriage. The second, Eliza Ann Smith, bore him a daughter, Kate, who would prove to be an important political adviser to her father. In 1852 Chase's third wife, Sarah Ludlow, gave him another daughter, Nettie. Sarah Chase died of tuberculosis and left Chase a widower after almost six years of marriage. He spent the rest of his life alone, except for the close companionship of his two daughters. To compensate for these tragedies in his life, he threw himself into his work and political activities.

In the 1830s Chase took an active stance against slavery, the burning issue of the era. A deeply religious man who read Scripture daily, he was morally outraged by the treatment of slaves. He defended abolitionists who had protected fugitive slaves escaping to Ohio and Illinois from proslavery Kentucky, arguing one case up to the Supreme Court. His actions earned him the derisive nickname "Attorney General for Runaway Negroes." Chase accepted the title with pride, acknowledging that

he "never refused . . . help to any person black or white; and liked the office nonetheless because there were neither fees nor salary connected with it." He developed effective legal arguments against slavery that were pragmatic, procedural, and based on federal-state relations rather than abstract principles or moral philosophy.

Chase's antislavery sentiment soon led him to politics, and he joined the Liberty party in the early 1840s. In 1848 he switched to the Free-Soil party and helped articulate its platform of keeping the new states in the West free from slavery. The following year, as a result of a pact by the Free-Soilers to help Ohio Democrats organize the state legislature, Chase was elected a U.S. senator on the Free Soil ticket. In the Senate he and his close friend, Charles Sumner, quickly became leaders of the antislavery movement. He opposed expansion of slavery into the territories and voted against the Compromise of 1850 and the 1854 Kansas-Nebraska bill. While Chase opposed the spread of slavery, he was not, however, as radical as the abolitionists who advocated an immediate end to the practice.

Neither a supporter of the Democrats' agenda nor of the policies of the other ruling party, the Whigs, Chase helped to create the antislavery Republican party. In 1855 he was elected governor of Ohio, with Republican backing, in a close and bitter campaign. As governor, Chase fostered bills to promote education, reform the prison system, establish insane asylums, and promote women's rights.

Considered but passed over in 1856 for the Republican presidential nomination, he was again supported by the more fervent abolitionists in the party for the 1860 presidential election. In contrast to William Seward, his chief rival for the nomination, Chase was not good at organizational politics and managed his campaign poorly. Despite being an early front-runner, he did not inspire his supporters to action, and he continued to be tagged—as he was throughout his life—as an opportunist who put his personal ambitions above all else.

On July 22, 1862, Abraham Lincoln gave the first reading of the Emancipation Proclamation to the members of his cabinet. Seated, left to right, Secretary of War Edwin M. Stanton, President Lincoln, Secretary of the Navy Gideon Welles, Secretary of State William H. Seward, Attorney General Edward Bates. Standing, left to right, Secretary of the Treasury Salmon P. Chase, Secretary of the Interior Caleb B. Smith, Postmaster General Montgomery Blair. When Lincoln delivered the proclamation in public several months later, he officially tied the struggle for a political Union to a crusade against slavery, thus delighting Chase and other abolitionists. *Source: Library of Congress*

Moreover, Chase refused to modify his antislavery stance to appease the moderates who dominated the party. On the crucial third round of balloting, Chase's supporters switched their votes to Abraham Lincoln, who won the party nomination and the election.

In deference to his party's leaders, President Lincoln appointed Chase and Seward to his cabinet, as secretary of the Treasury and secretary of state, respectively. To take up the Treasury post, Chase resigned the Senate seat he had won in the 1860 election, after only two days on the job. In the critical early months of the Civil War, due partly to the ineffectiveness of Edwin M. Stanton, the secretary of war, Chase was largely in charge of organizing the North's effort. He was also re-

sponsible for financing the war, which he did mostly through large short-term loans. This policy has been criticized because the resulting debt service considerably increased the expense of the war. At the time, however, Chase was told by Union generals that the conflict would not last long, and increasing taxes was not an easy alternative.

Although he opposed the idea at first, Chase reluctantly came to see the necessity for the government to issue paper money to use as legal tender, in addition to "hard money"—gold or silver coin—to pay debts. He saw "greenbacks" only as a temporary, emergency measure, to be phased out after the war. Chase was more skilled as a politician than as a financier, but Lincoln was confident enough in his abilities to leave economic questions almost entirely in his hands.

Although near victory in 1864, the Union government had been shaken to its foundations by the war. A split in the Republican party threatened to deny Lincoln renomination because of his moderate views on the abolition of slavery and what some considered his inadequate management of the war. A faction of abolitionists drafted Chase as their candidate in the 1864 presidential election. When news of Chase's candidacy was made public that spring, he offered to resign his cabinet post, but Lincoln saw no reason to accept his resignation and risk offending the liberal wing of his party.

The radicals' efforts to substitute Chase as the Republican nominee could not overcome Lincoln's popularity, however, and a disappointed Chase withdrew his name. During the summer he once again offered to resign his Treasury post, this time because of a minor dispute with Lincoln over a political appointee. Chase had previously made threats to resign if he did not get his way on patronage issues, but Lincoln preferred to compromise rather than allow him to quit. This time, however, the president accepted the resignation, saying he no longer felt obliged to "continue to beg him to take it back, especially when the country would not go to destruction in consequence." After stepping down, Chase turned his energies to supporting Lincoln's presidential campaign, partly in hopes of securing a new appointment.

Once reelected, Lincoln nominated Chase to the Supreme Court to fill the vacancy left by the death of Chief Justice Roger B. Taney. Chase was confirmed the same day as his nomination, December 6, 1864, by a voice vote. Public esteem for the Court was low when Chase took his seat as chief justice, and the war had badly divided the justices. War-related controversies, such as the draft, the emancipation of slaves, and the is-

suance of paper money to pay debts, had subjected the government to harsh criticism from opposing political factions. Lincoln's nomination of Chase to the Court was based partly on his belief that he would uphold the extraordinary measures the federal government had taken during the war.

Chase's fellow justices viewed his political ambitions and lack of judicial experience with suspicion, but his firm leadership and commitment to hard work won them over and helped to unify a Court that was divided over Reconstruction issues. During his nearly eight-year tenure, Chase wrote more than his share of opinions—but few dissents—and helped the Court regain some of the prestige it had lost in the wake of his predecessor's damaging *Dred Scott v. Sandford* decision. He successfully steered the Court away from challenging Congress on the political aspects of Reconstruction.

In the spring of 1865 Chase personally surveyed the South and issued eyewitness reports to Lincoln's successor, Andrew Johnson. He urged President Johnson to seize the initiative in bringing about a successful Reconstruction by giving blacks the right to vote. While continuing to support suffrage for blacks, Chase questioned the Radical Republicans' insistence on military government in the South. He antagonized his supporters by seeking a pardon for former Confederate leaders and a faster restoration of the southern states in the Union. When the Radical-dominated Congress sought to impeach President Johnson in 1868 for his similarly moderate stance on Reconstruction, Chase used his position as chief justice to fight for a fair trial in the Senate. His admirable insistence on sticking to legal procedure and his determination not to give in to Republican political pressure probably saved President Johnson from impeachment.

Now alienated from the Republican party, Chief Justice Chase encouraged the efforts of Democrats to promote his candidacy in the 1868 election. Although they

WE HAVE POLKED them in 44 | WE HAVE PIERCED them in 52 | WE HAVE BUCKED them in 56 | WE WILL CHASE them in 68

Having split with the Radical Republicans over their insistence on maintaining a military occupation of the South, Chief Justice Salmon P. Chase encouraged the efforts of some Democrats to get him the presidential nomination in 1868. This cartoon shows Chase vanquishing the "Radicals" while Democrats remind viewers of earlier Democratic victories. Despite wooing Democrats by modifying his support of black voting rights, Chase did not win the nomination. *Source: Library of Congress*

were uncomfortable with his support of voting rights for blacks, Democrats found his stance against military occupation of the South and in favor of a general amnesty appealing. Chase consequently modified his position on black voting rights, suggesting that the issue be left up to the individual states. His daughter Kate, envisioning herself as "the presiding lady at the White House," pushed hard, but ultimately without success, for Chase's nomination as the Democratic party's candidate.

Although frustrated yet again in his quest for the presidency, Chief Justice Chase remained active on the bench. In *State of Mississippi v. Johnson* (1867), he rejected a state claim that the president stop enforcing provisions in the Reconstruction Acts, which had divided the South into five districts and put them under military control. The following year he wrote an important opinion in *Texas v. White,* which defined the status of former Confederate states and gave the Court's approval to Congress's Reconstruction program. He also wrote the majority opinion declaring the unconstitutionality of the Legal Tender Acts in 1869. Chase's deci-

sion came as a surprise because he had implemented the issuance of paper money as a means of financing the war when he was secretary of the Treasury. As a judge, however, Chase argued that the acts were an improper way for Congress to exercise its war powers. When the Court reversed itself on this issue in 1871 after a change in membership, Chase maintained his position in a dissenting opinion.

A series of crippling strokes began in 1870, forcing Chase to slow his pace and preventing him from writing effectively. Despite his precarious health, he let his daughter and other admirers mount yet another presidential campaign in 1872. Less driven than in past efforts, Chase was markedly less disappointed at not securing the nomination.

The chief justice died May 7, 1873, while visiting his daughter Nettie in New York City. Although his fellow justices had often complained of his excessive political ambition, their assessments of his leadership and judicial abilities at the time of his death were complimentary.

William Strong

1870-1880

Source: Portrait of William Strong by Robert Hinckley, Collection of the Supreme Court of the United States

WILLIAM STRONG was born May 6, 1808, the eldest of eleven children of William Lighthouse Strong and Harriet Deming Strong. His father was a Presbyterian minister whose ancestors had emigrated from England in 1630 and settled in Dorchester, Massachusetts. One branch of the family moved to Connecticut, where the future justice's grandfather was an eminent lawyer. William was born and raised on a small farm in Somers, Connecticut.

Young Strong attended the local public school and studied mathematics and the classics under his father's direction. He was sent for a year to preparatory academies in Monson and Plainfield, Massachusetts, and entered Yale College at the age of fifteen. He graduated in the class of 1828.

Strong taught school in New Jersey for three and a half years to pay off his student debts; he also studied law with a local attorney. He then returned to Yale and entered the law school. Strong received a master's degree in law in 1832 and was admitted to the bar in both Connecticut and Pennsylvania the same year.

After consulting experienced friends, Strong settled in the industrial town of Reading, Pennsylvania, and opened his own law office. The advantage of Pennsylvania Dutch country was its booming economy. Strong found, however, that the town and county were populated largely by German immigrants, and many of his clients spoke no English. He set about learning the local German dialect, and soon spoke and wrote it fluently. Professional success came quickly, and his law practice flourished. Within ten years Strong became a member of the city council and the board of education, a director of the Farmer's Bank and the Lebanon Valley Railroad, and counsel to the Philadelphia and Reading Railroad Company.

Strong was sociable, athletic, and fond of outdoor sports and hunting. He married Priscilla Lee Mallery, the daughter of the presiding judge of the judicial district, in 1836. She bore him two daughters and a son before her premature death in 1844. Six years later Strong married Rachel Davies Bull, widowed daughter of a former representative to Congress. The couple had two daughters and two sons.

Strong, a Democrat, won election as an antislavery candidate to Congress in 1846. Future presidents Abraham Lincoln and Andrew Johnson were among his colleagues in the House of Representatives. He was reelected in 1848 and served as chairman of the Committee on Elections, but declined to run for a third term and returned to the practice of law full time. Strong was generally acknowledged to be the head of the bar in his Pennsylvania county and district.

In 1857, still a Democrat, Strong was elected a judge of the Pennsylvania Supreme Court for a fifteen-year term. An antislavery advocate and an unwavering supporter of the Union, he switched his allegiance to the Republican party between his election and the outbreak of the Civil War in 1861. On the bench, Strong also supported the Union cause. He voted with the majority to uphold the wartime acts of the federal government. His ruling on one of these laws, the controversial Legal Tender Act of 1862, which provided for the issuing of paper money to pay debts and finance the war, would become a decisive factor in Strong's future appointment to the U.S. Supreme Court. The Pennsylvania court was one of fifteen state supreme courts that ruled the act constitutional, with Strong concurring in the opinion.

When Chief Justice Roger B. Taney died in 1864, President Abraham Lincoln stated frankly that he wanted a successor who would "sustain what has been done in regard to emancipation [of slaves] and the legal tenders," and that a man of known opinions must be chosen. President Lincoln considered nominating Strong as Taney's successor, but instead chose his political rival, Salmon P. Chase, who had just resigned his post as secretary of the Treasury. Chase had been responsible for the passage by Congress of the legal tender acts of 1862 and 1863 and was expected to sustain their constitutionality.

Meanwhile, Judge Strong, after eleven years on the Pennsylvania Supreme Court, resigned to reestablish his law practice and repair his sagging finances, this time in Philadelphia. His services were immediately in demand and he developed a lucrative legal business.

Justice Robert Grier submitted his resignation from the U.S. Supreme Court, December 15, 1869, citing his advanced age and infirmity. The resignation was to be effective on February 1, 1870. A second president, Ulysses S. Grant, now favored Strong for appointment to the Supreme Court. Once again, however, other considerations took supremacy. There was great sentiment in Congress for Edwin M. Stanton, former secretary of war. A large majority of both houses signed a petition for Stanton, and Grant yielded to their demands. The Senate confirmed Stanton's appointment on December 20.

The selection of Stanton aroused immediate partisan criticism across the country, but the outcry proved unnecessary. Stanton died suddenly four days later, before taking the oath of office and achieving official status as an associate justice. Now President Grant let it be known that he would nominate Strong, but not until after Grier's official day of retirement. The president wanted, according to a contemporary newspaper report, to avoid "the curious spectacle of a Judge dead and buried in state while his predecessor [Grier] sits on the Bench and goes to the funeral." Unfortunately, Grant's delay would eventually contribute to an even more serious charge.

Because of their importance, when the legal tender acts first came before the Supreme Court in 1867, they were held for reargument in 1868. The justices decided the case in November 1869, striking down the acts as unconstitutional, but they did not officially announce their decision. Contrary to expectations, Chief Justice Chase condemned his own actions as secretary of the Treasury by voting with the majority. The minority unsuccessfully tried to persuade Chase to postpone issuing his majority opinion until the two empty seats on the Court (a second vacancy remained since 1868) were filled.

On February 7, 1870, six days after Grier's official retirement, President Grant submitted the names of William Strong and Joseph P. Bradley of New Jersey to fill the two vacancies. Hours later, Chief Justice Chase announced that the Court had found the legal tender acts unconstitutional by a 4–3 vote. The Court ruled that all contracts made after 1862, when the paper currency was first issued, were illegal, and therefore debts and other obligations incurred after that date would have to be paid in silver or gold coin, rather than depreciated paper money. The amount of money at stake was

Edwin M. Stanton, appointed secretary of war by Abraham Lincoln in 1862, was kept in that post by Andrew Johnson, who later fired him and almost lost the presidency as a result. Although in ill health, Stanton accepted Ulysses S. Grant's nomination to the Supreme Court. The Senate confirmed him December 20, 1869, but he died before he could take the oath of office. *Source: Library of Congress*

enormous, and the coincidental timing of the two new appointments led to an immediate charge that Grant was trying to "pack" the Court with justices who would help overturn Chase's decision. The nominations were further criticized in the Senate by southern Republicans who wanted at least one seat to go to a southerner. Nonetheless, Strong's appointment was confirmed February 18, and Bradley's a month later.

Although Strong and Bradley were eminently quali-

The Treasury first issued paper money in 1862 to pay off debts and finance the Civil War. Because the notes were printed with green ink, they became known as greenbacks. When the Supreme Court found the issuance of paper currency unconstitutional, the government faced having to repay all obligations incurred since 1862 in gold and silver coin. President Grant filled two vacancies on the Court with William Strong and Joseph P. Bradley, justices Grant hoped would help overturn the decision. *Source: Library of Congress*

fied for the high bench, the Court-packing allegation cast a cloud over their appointments. The charge gained credence when the Court overruled the legal tender decision only fifteen months later, in May 1871. Thanks to its two new members, the Court did an about-face and found the acts to be a valid use of Congress's war powers. Justice Strong wrote the historic 5–4 decision establishing paper money as legal currency.

The charge that Grant tried to pack the Court was unfair. Strong had been considered for nomination well before the 4–3 decision was made known, although Grant probably had knowledge of the case's outcome indirectly from Chase two weeks in advance. Further, it would have been difficult for President Grant to have found a Republican nominee who would have ruled otherwise. Of more than sixty judges who dealt with the issue in state courts, all but one of the Republicans held the legal tender laws valid. Nevertheless, Charles Evans Hughes, the future chief justice, described the quick reversal as damaging to the Court's prestige. He called the turnaround the second of the Court's "self-in-

flicted wounds," the first being the 1857 *Dred Scott v. Sandford* decision. "Stability in judicial opinions," he said, "is of no small importance in maintaining respect for the court's work."

In his eleven years on the Court, Strong was regarded as an able judge and a skilled and articulate opinion writer. He wrote an important constitutional opinion stating that blacks had a constitutional right not to be discriminated against in the selection of jurors. In general, however, he was assigned relatively few constitutional cases, and the bulk of his work dealt with patents, common law matters, taxes, and shipping rights—the routine business of the Court in those days. As the Court heard more and more cases involving commerce, Strong generally sided with the pro-business wing of the Court that opposed government regulation.

Unlike some of his colleagues, Strong avoided politics while on the bench. He was a very reluctant member of the commission appointed in 1877 to decide between Rutherford B. Hayes and Samuel J. Tilden in the disputed election for president. Consistently voting with

"The art of war is simple enough," said Gen. Ulysses S. Grant. "Find out where your enemy is. Get at him as soon as you can. Strike him as hard as you can, and keep moving on." As president, Grant pursued politics in a less straightforward manner than war, and his administration was marked by corruption and scandal. The charge that Grant tried to "pack" the Supreme Court with justices chosen exclusively to reverse the ruling invalidating the legal tender acts was, however, unfair. *Source: Library of Congress*

the other Republicans in support of Hayes, Strong was condemned by Democratic partisans.

Strong's departure from the Court at the peak of his ability was an effort to set an example for those justices whose increasing infirmities were a burden to the Court. Nathan Clifford, Ward Hunt, and Noah H. Swayne were frequently absent from the bench due to illness, but they gave no evidence of intention to leave. Strong persuaded Swayne to join him in retirement, and they so informed their colleagues. Strong retired December 14, 1880. Swayne stalled but followed suit only a few weeks later. Clifford died the following July, and Hunt held out until early 1882. One of Strong's daughters later recalled that Strong, still physically vigorous and in full command of his faculties, would not have stepped down if the retirement of the others could have been effected without his example. She added that her father thought it was better to leave while people would exclaim "Why does he?" rather than wait until they asked "Why doesn't he?" Justice Samuel F. Miller said that Strong's departure was a heavy loss to the Court, that other justices could have been spared instead.

Strong continued to live in Washington and was to make one more contribution to the Court. A year after his resignation he wrote an article for the *North American Review* on the needs of the Supreme Court. Several of his proposals for relieving the excessively heavy workload of the justices were incorporated into law ten years later.

Long an active member of the Presbyterian church, Strong spent his time and energies in retirement continuing his activities in religious affairs. During the Civil War he had presided over a "National Association to secure certain religious amendments to the Constitution." The purpose was to recognize "the Lord Jesus Christ as the ruler of all nations, and his revealed will as the supreme law of the land." Strong served as a vice president of the American Bible Society from 1871 to 1895, as president of the American Tract Society from 1873 to 1895, and as president of the American Sunday School Union from 1883 to 1895.

After a brief illness, Strong died at Lake Minnewaska, New York, August 19, 1895, at the age of eighty-seven.

Joseph P. Bradley

1870-1892

Source: Library of Congress

JOSEPH P. BRADLEY was born in the town of Berne, near Albany, New York, March 14, 1813. He was the eldest of twelve children. The middle initial "P" did not stand for anything: he adopted it in his youth, perhaps in tribute to his father, whose name was Philo. His early years were typical of large farm families, filled with "plowing . . . clearing land and burning wood, carting bark to the tanneries, and peddling charcoal at Albany," the state capital. Apparently finding this routine "an irksome life," at the age of eighteen Bradley decided to go to New York City to work. However, the future justice never reached his destination. Apparently, the boat he planned to take departed a few minutes early because of freezing temperatures. Indeed, the river froze before morning, leaving Bradley temporarily stranded in Albany, where he spent a few days listening to debates in the state legislature. Had he been able to get on the boat, he later recalled, "he would have become a grocer in New York."

Recognizing Bradley's potential, a former teacher

At age eighteen Joseph P. Bradley decided to leave the family farm outside Albany, New York, and work in New York City. He missed his boat and was forced to spend a few days in the state capital (pictured here in the mid-1850s). Listening to debates in the state legislature inspired Bradley to stay in school and eventually study law. *Source: Library of Congress*

arranged for a local minister to sponsor his admission in 1833 to Rutgers College in New Jersey. He graduated in two years and was later described by another scholar as "a desperately serious young man." Note Bradley's solemn pledge: "I will not, by any means, or on any account whatever, except it be from absolute necessity, call at any of the public houses of this city for the purpose of getting refreshment, refectory, or trash of any kind except oysters, during my collegiate course."

Shortly after graduation, he decided to study law—largely with himself as the instructor. He did some of his reading in the office of Archer Gifford, collector of the port of Newark, New Jersey. He read all the usual law volumes and must have been rigorous in his preparation. One entry in his notes cites five different sources, one in Latin, two in French, and two in English. He studied Roman law, admiralty (shipping law)

and maritime jurisdiction, besides doing intensive work on the origins and contents of the common law.

Bradley passed the bar in 1839 and for the next thirty years centered his life and legal career around the city of Newark. But he did more than practice law. For a time, he served as a legislative correspondent. He also took a job with a newly established insurance company—Mutual Benefit Life—as an actuary, remaining with the firm for twelve years. In 1844 he married Mary Hornblower, the daughter of the chief justice of the New Jersey Supreme Court, and the couple had seven children. Slowly, his law practice expanded, as did his acquaintance with numerous leaders of Newark's business and legal community. Eventually, Bradley became a prominent attorney who specialized in patent, corporate, and commercial law, and counted the powerful Camden and Amboy Railroad as one of his clients.

Conservative in viewpoint, Bradley agreed to run for Congress as a Republican in 1862, a hopeless contest, considering the very strong Democratic leanings in the district. He lost, but, given some of his later opinions as a justice, his position on the South during the Civil War is of interest. Many Republicans, including Abraham Lincoln, had no difficulty in supporting the demise of slavery and the survival of the federal Union, while at the same time foreseeing little change in racial attitudes toward blacks. It was perfectly consistent, according to this view, to be pro-Union, antislavery, and antiblack all at the same time. Thus, as a congressional candidate, Bradley failed to endorse freedom for the slaves, let alone racial equality. "We were," he insisted, "always willing to concede to the South all their just rights—the entire control and regulation of their own affairs."

By 1869 Bradley was a legitimate choice for nomination to the Supreme Court, a position he openly desired. Although he had no judicial experience, he was at the height of a successful career as an attorney and was able to gather support from a broad spectrum of political figures. However, with two seats on the Court open, the new president, Ulysses S. Grant, chose to nominate Attorney General E. Rockwood Hoar and Lincoln's former secretary of war, Edwin M. Stanton. Hoar's nomination failed due to senatorial machinations, while Stanton, who breezed through confirmation, fell ill, a victim of the strains caused by lingering tensions of war and the turmoil of Reconstruction. He died four days after being confirmed. Again Grant had two vacancies open, and on February 7, 1870, one of them went to Bradley. Senate confirmation followed five weeks later by a vote of 46 to 9.

Justice Bradley served on the Court for almost twenty-two years. Seven years after taking his seat he became the center of public controversy when he was named the fifteenth and final member of the commission to decide the contested presidential election of 1876. He was chosen after Justice David Davis, an independent, had declined to serve; Bradley was considered the next least partisan justice. He cast the deciding vote in favor of the Republican candidate, Rutherford B. Hayes, giving him the presidency. Condemned by the Democratic press, Bradley insisted that he had made the decision on constitutional, not partisan, grounds.

Bradley brought to his judging a tough mind, free of sentiment. In 1873 the Supreme Court decided the case of *Bradwell v. Illinois*. It involved the efforts of a woman, Myra Bradwell, to gain admittance to the Illinois bar. Rebuffed by the Illinois Supreme Court in a

Having studied the law with her husband, a judge, Myra Bradwell edited and published the *Chicago Legal News,* the most important legal publication in the Midwest. Although Bradwell passed the bar examination, the Illinois Supreme Court refused her admittance to the state bar because of her sex. She appealed to the U.S. Supreme Court in 1873, arguing that the Fourteenth Amendment protected her right to practice law. The Court ruled against her, having just the day before restricted the scope of the Fourteenth Amendment's protections in the *Slaughter House Cases. Source: Library of Congress*

graceful yet condescending decision, she turned to the high court. There she argued that the newly adopted Fourteenth Amendment prevented Illinois from abridging her "privileges and immunities," one of which was her right to practice her chosen calling. The Court, Bradley included, disagreed.

Because Bradley had vigorously dissented in the *Slaughter House Cases,* decided the day before, the question of inconsistency arises. If he thought that a group of butchers had a constitutionally protected right to practice their profession, why did he not think a woman qualified to practice law had a similar right? The answer lay in Bradley's old-fashioned but deeply felt beliefs concerning "the peculiar characteristics, destiny and mission of woman," which was "to fulfill the noble and benign offices of wife and mother. This is the law of the creator." His opinion, according to one contemporary newspaper, "seemed to cause no little amusement upon the Bench and on the Bar."

In 1875 Congress passed the Civil Rights Act, making it illegal to deny any person access to inns, theaters, and other public places (not including, it should be noted, public schools) based on race. In his copybook, Bradley sharply distinguished between a legal, political right and a matter of social preference. He wrote of the new statute that "to deprive white people of the right of choosing their own company would be to introduce another kind of slavery. . . . It can never be endured that the white shall be compelled to lodge and eat and sit with the negro. . . . The antipathy of race cannot be crushed and annihilated by legal enactment." When he spoke for the Court in 1883, declaring the 1875 Act unconstitutional, Justice Bradley simply repeated views he had espoused as early as 1862 when he ran for Congress. While the Fourteenth Amendment did indeed ban state action, private discrimination seemed permissible to him. For many of Bradley's time, the abolition of slavery and the tools to maintain it did not imply or require abolition of racial prejudices.

When it concerned power to regulate the railroads and expand the scope of the Commerce Clause of the Constitution, Bradley was much more sympathetic to federal authority. A former railroad lawyer, he did not hesitate to denounce these often poorly managed corporations as "absolute monopolies of public service." Although his colleague, Chief Justice Morrison Waite, spoke for the Court in 1877 affirming state power to regulate private enterprise in the public interest (*Munn v. Illinois*), the doctrine was probably formulated for Waite by Bradley. Indeed, Harvard law professor Felix Frankfurter, who became a Supreme Court justice, wrote of Bradley: "He who by his previous experience would supposedly reflect the bias of financial power, was as free from it as any judge, and indeed much more radical."

Bradley demonstrated an impressive sensitivity in interpreting the Commerce Clause so as to support the effectiveness of the federal government. In several cases, he skillfully explored the controversial boundaries between federal regulation of interstate commerce and the state taxing power. As far as the former went, he said, "The United States are but one country, and are and must be subject to one system of regulation, and not to a multitude of systems."

Bradley was one of the strongest intellects on the bench. He brought added strength to his decisions through his practical experience in the world of business and his knowledge in fields such as mathematics, philosophy, and natural science. His interest in steam engines led him to research and publish a pamphlet on the history of their development. He invented a calendar that determined on which day of the week any given date in history had fallen. He enjoyed tracking a legal doctrine as far back as he could. His private library contained some 16,000 volumes, and he often "spiced up" his opinions with scholarly footnotes and citations. In one case, for example, he traced a legal principle back to the era of Justinian, the great sixth century

Pragmatic and decisive, Joseph P. Bradley was a strong intellect on the Supreme Court. His many extrajudicial pursuits included writing the history of steam engines and inventing a calendar to determine on which day of the week a particular day in history had fallen. He is shown here in his study toward the end of his career, when, according to a colleague, he was full of "vinegar." *Source: Library of Congress*

Byzantine emperor, and he cited French, Latin, and Spanish sources, including a footnote in French.

He was equally at home expounding on a fair rate of return for a railroad or discussing the incredibly intricate issues of patent litigation, an area on which he often spoke for the Court. An old friend noted that Bradley had a compulsion "not only to be but to know." If, wrote one of his fellow justices, "there is a principle on which a case can be decided that no one else has thought of, it has for that reason a charm for him." On the other hand, "he had little or no deference for the mere opinion of others."

Bradley seems to have been a somewhat irascible person. "He was," wrote one of the jurist's oldest friends, "amusingly petulant—naturally eccentric." Toward the end of his life, he was described by a contemporary observer of the Supreme Court as "a little dried-up anatomy of a man. . . . His skin hangs in wrinkles and all of his fat has long since gone to figures and judicial decisions. He is seventy-seven years old, but there is a fair chance for his lasting at least twenty-three years longer. There is not much of him to die, and when his soul is disembodied, it will not be much freer than it is now."

Bradley was an outstanding technician of the law, and his greatest opinions in terms of influence on the development of constitutional law were in the field of commercial regulation. But in other realms of law, such as civil rights, areas that are now considered more important than interstate commerce, Bradley—with his own understandable but still unfortunate biases concerning sex and race—was unable to transcend the limits of his own time. Yet, he believed passionately in both progress and the perfectibility of man. He died January 22, 1892, while still in service to the Court. The obituary in the *Washington Post* fittingly praised him as a "man of profound and varied learning, legal acumen, and moral rectitude."

Ward Hunt

1873-1882

WARD HUNT was born June 14, 1810, in Utica, New York, then a village of 1,600 inhabitants. His parents, Montgomery and Elizabeth Stringham Hunt, were well known within their small community because Ward's father worked as a cashier at the First National Bank of Utica for many years. The Hunts were descended from a New England settler, Thomas Hunt, who lived in Stamford, Connecticut, as early as 1650.

Ward Hunt began his education at the local Oxford and Geneva academies. After attending Hamilton College in Clinton, New York, for one year, he transferred to Union College in nearby Schenectady, where he graduated with honors at the age of eighteen. In 1829 he went to study law at the Tapping Reeve School, a private academy run by Judge James Gould in Litchfield, Connecticut. Supreme Court justices Henry Baldwin and Levi Woodbury had also attended this school. Hunt returned to Utica to serve as a clerk for a local judge, Hiram Denio, and was admitted to the bar in 1831.

Compelled by poor health to spend a winter in New Orleans, Hunt returned to enter a law partnership with Judge Denio. Hunt established his office in his old family home and soon developed a large and lucrative practice. Once comfortably settled into his profession, Hunt devoted himself to starting a family. In 1837 he married Mary Ann Savage, daughter of a prominent judge. The Hunts had three children, one of whom died in childhood. His wife died in 1845, and Hunt remained a widower for eight years before marrying Marie Taylor, who survived him.

His reputation as a successful lawyer helped Hunt win a seat in 1838 in the New York state legislature, where he served for one term as a representative of Oneida County. In 1844 Hunt was elected mayor of Utica, which had been incorporated as a town in 1832 and had grown to a population of more than 9,000.

Hunt won these positions as a Jacksonian Democrat; however, in the late 1840s his opposition to the extension of slavery and to the annexation of Texas compelled him to loosen his ties with the Democratic party. As the slavery issue became increasingly bitter, Hunt moved away from the Democrats, supporting Martin Van Buren and the Free-Soil party in the presidential campaign of 1848. Hunt completed his break with the Democrats in 1856 when he threw himself into organizing the Republican party in New York State. During this time he formed an alliance with fellow Utica native Roscoe Conkling, who became the boss of New York's Republican political machine and who would ultimately be responsible for Hunt's nomination to the U.S. Supreme Court.

Hunt's zealous support for the Republican party and his vigorous efforts at organizing won him prominence in the ranks of the young organization. In 1857 the Re-

publican caucus in Albany actively considered him as a candidate for the U.S. Senate. Hunt's eventual decision to withdraw from the race was motivated by his desire to preserve harmony within the party as well as his ambivalence about running for political office.

Less interested in politics than jurisprudence, Hunt had early ambitions for judicial office. A few years after he served as mayor, Hunt had sought a position on the New York Court of Appeals. His defeat was allegedly due to Irish hostility inspired by Hunt's successful de-

When Ward Hunt switched to the Republican party in 1856, he befriended Roscoe Conkling, who was active in establishing the party in New York. Conkling moved quickly up the political ranks, becoming a U.S. senator and the boss of the New York Republican machine. He pressured President Grant to appoint his friend Ward Hunt to the Supreme Court, but in 1882 declined a seat on the Court to pursue presidential ambitions. *Source: Library of Congress*

fense of a policeman who had been charged with the murder of an Irishman. In 1853 he ran for the same office again on the Democratic ticket and lost, probably because of his defection to the Free-Soilers in the presidential election several years earlier.

Hunt's decisive switch to the Republican party and his success within it improved his chances of becoming a judge. During the Civil War, Hunt gained visibility when he served as temporary chairman of the 1863 Republican Union Convention in Syracuse, New York, as it rejoiced over the latest Union army victories at Vicksburg and Gettysburg. In 1865 Hunt was finally elected as a Republican to the New York Court of Appeals, the state's highest court, where he succeeded Judge Denio, his former law partner. Three years later he was elevated to chief justice of the court of appeals. Following a judi-

cial reorganization effected by constitutional amendment in 1869, he was retained as commissioner of appeals.

In the fall of 1872 Conkling, who had been elected a senator from New York in 1866, persuaded President Ulysses S. Grant to nominate his old ally to succeed Justice Samuel Nelson on the U.S. Supreme Court. As a result, Hunt won out over several better known figures who had been considered for the vacancy. He was confirmed by the Senate December 11, by a voice vote, and took his seat January 9, 1873. During his five years of active service on the Court, Justice Hunt would craft few opinions on significant constitutional issues, and would write only seven dissents.

Hunt made his most noteworthy and enduring contribution in his dissent in *United States v. Reese* (1876).

Despite adoption of the Fifteenth Amendment, making it illegal to bar citizens from voting because of their color, blacks were turned away from polls by a combination of Ku Klux Klan harassment, intimidation, and various legal gimmicks. Ward Hunt was the lone dissenter in *United States v. Reese* (1876), a Supreme Court decision that weakened the government's power to impose stiff penalties for interfering with the rights of blacks to vote. *Source: New York Public Library*

By invalidating parts of the Enforcement Act of 1870, the *Reese* decision weakened any chance for the application of the Fifteenth Amendment to protect black voting rights. In response to the outbreak of Ku Klux Klan intimidation of southern blacks, Congress had passed the Enforcement Act, which guaranteed voting rights for black males and imposed severe penalties for interfering with the right to vote. The *Reese* case began when two inspectors at a municipal election in Kentucky were indicted for refusing to accept and count the vote of William Garner, a black. The trial court dismissed the indictment, and the Supreme Court later affirmed that decision by a vote of 8 to 1. Hunt was the lone dissenter.

For the majority, Chief Justice Morrison Waite declared that "the Fifteenth Amendment does not confer the right of suffrage upon anyone"; rather, it merely "prevents the States, or the United States . . . from giving preference, in this particular, to one citizen of the United States over another on account of race, color, or previous condition of servitude." Furthermore, he found that in the Enforcement Act of 1870 Congress had not limited the penalty provisions to illegal refusals of voters because of their race. In a far-reaching dissent, Hunt argued that while the two sections of the Enforcement Act that discussed penalties and alternate voting procedures did not include the word "race," both sections contained such references as "the wrongful act or omission aforesaid of the person or officer." Hunt argued that "aforesaid" obviously referred to the prohibitions against racial discrimination mentioned in the preceding sections. Despite Hunt's contention, the majority dismissed the indictment, sending the message to Congress that unless it crossed every "t" and dotted every "i," the Court would not sustain its civil rights legislation.

Although he seemed to support black civil rights in the *Reese* case, Hunt was not as progressive when it came to women's rights. In 1872 women's suffrage advocate Susan B. Anthony voted in an election in Rochester, New York. Because the state constitution limited suffrage to males, Anthony acted in violation of Section 19 of the Enforcement Act of 1870 by "knowingly . . . voting without having a lawful right to vote." Anthony was indicted, and Hunt served as circuit judge at her trial in June 1873. He refused to instruct the jury that proof of the defendant's belief in good faith that she had a right to vote would render her not guilty. Hunt reasoned that since the court was supposed to acquit if there was not sufficient evidence to warrant conviction, then likewise, the court should deliver a verdict of guilty when the facts constituting guilt were undisputed. Anthony, Hunt said, "intending to do just what she did . . . had knowingly voted, not having a right to vote, and . . . her belief did not affect the question." He fined Anthony $100. Nine years later, circuit court judge C. J. McCrary overturned the reasoning Hunt had used in *United States v. Anthony,* saying that "the court erred in charging the jury to find the defendant guilty."

Justice Hunt is chiefly remembered for his refusal to resign from the Court for three years after suffering an incapacitating stroke. In 1877 Hunt's health began to fail, and he missed several sessions of the Court because of gout. In January 1879 Hunt had a stroke that left his right side paralyzed. Although he regained some mobility, the minutes record that he sat on the bench only one more time, on November 29, 1881.

More than three years behind with its docket, the Supreme Court was overwhelmed. In addition to Hunt, Justice Nathan Clifford was also permanently disabled. Despite many gentle hints from Chief Justice Waite, Hunt refused to resign. He had not met the requirement of the Judiciary Act of 1869, which granted a lifetime salary to any judge of any court of the United States who had served ten years and had reached the age of seventy. Furthermore, Senator Conkling, who was feuding with President Rutherford B. Hayes over the

Susan B. Anthony, a leader of the women's rights movement, helped persuade New York State to pass laws giving women control over their own property, a share in the guardianship of their own children, and the right to sue. But her pursuit of the right to vote for women, which lasted a half-century, was less successful. In 1872 Anthony voted in a New York election to test the legality of women's suffrage, and Justice Ward Hunt, sitting as circuit judge, fined her $100. *Source: Library of Congress*

president's reform of the "spoils system" of political patronage, urged Hunt not to give Hayes the opportunity to appoint his successor. In January 1882, prompted by Sen. David Davis, Hunt's former colleague on the Court, Congress passed a special retirement bill for Hunt, granting him a pension. He retired the day the bill became law, and, in an unusual twist, President Chester A. Arthur nominated Conkling, who had recommended Hunt for a seat on the Court, as his successor. Conkling was confirmed but declined the seat because he harbored presidential ambitions.

Although obscured by the strong personalities of Justices Samuel F. Miller, Stephen J. Field, and Joseph P. Bradley, Hunt was a well-liked and respected member of the bench. He was a hard-working judge who researched carefully and wrote clear decisions. Like most of his colleagues, Hunt averaged about twenty-five majority opinions per year during his five years of active service. Justice Miller, usually critical and sharp, described his colleague as one of the "most agreeable men on the bench." He conceded that while Hunt was "not a very strong man in intellect," he considered him to be a "cultivated lawyer and gentleman." Hunt died in Washington, D.C., on March 24, 1886, four years after his retirement.

Morrison R. Waite

1874-1888

MORRISON REMICK WAITE, the seventh chief justice of the United States, was born November 27, 1816, in Lyme, Connecticut. The Waite family had come to the New World in the late 1600s and gained prominence in Connecticut politics. Ancestors on both sides of his family served as officers in the Continental Army during the Revolutionary War, notably Col. Samuel Seldon, who died as a British prisoner following his capture in the Long Island campaign. Morrison was the eldest son of Henry Matson Waite, a judge and gentleman farmer, who encouraged him to enter the legal profession. His father's eventual appointment as chief justice of the Connecticut Supreme Court bound young Waite even closer to the world of law.

Like many of his forebears, Waite attended Yale College, graduating in the class of 1837. Because his father was too busy to train him in law, Waite struck out for northwest Ohio in 1838 and settled in Maumee City near Toledo. He studied with a distinguished lawyer,

Samuel D. Young, eventually becoming his partner. Through diligence and a reputation for integrity and compassion, Waite became one of Ohio's most prominent lawyers. He built his practice by carrying a sizable caseload of minor land and property disputes, but eventually his firm came to represent a number of railroad companies during that industry's boom, earning Waite a reputation as a "railroad lawyer." His unwillingness to charge his clients anything but moderate fees gave Waite a comfortable, but relatively modest, income for a lawyer of his stature.

Two years after arriving in Ohio, Waite married Amelia C. Warner, a second cousin from Lyme. A decade later the couple moved to Toledo, where they raised their five children. A well-liked and respected member of the community, Waite was generous with his time and money. He became a director of the Bank of Toledo and president of the Young Men's Association.

Politically active in the Whig party, Waite ran unsuccessfully for Congress on his party's ticket in 1846. Three years later, he won a term in the Ohio General Assembly. His opposition to slavery got him involved in organizing the Republican party in his state, although his fairly conservative politics set him apart from the radicals within that party. Throughout the Civil War, Waite made speeches and drafted petitions in support of the Union in an effort to lift public morale and rally his state's support for the war. In 1862 he ran again for Congress, this time as an independent Republican, but lost. Waite threw his political weight into campaigning for John Brough, a pro-Union gubernatorial candidate, and was offered a seat on the Ohio Supreme Court in return for his efforts when Brough won. The future chief justice refused the position, however, in favor of an informal advisory role to the governor.

Waite was catapulted to national attention when, at the suggestion of Secretary of the Interior Columbus Delano, a fellow Ohioan, President Ulysses S. Grant named him one of three U.S. representatives to the Geneva Arbitration in 1871. The appointment of the obscure Ohio lawyer surprised the public because of the enormous gravity of the case. The arbitration was to settle compensation claims, primarily between the United States and Great Britain, resulting from the Civil War. Waite's dogged compilation of the pertinent facts in the case helped the government demonstrate that Britain had violated the rules of neutrality by allowing Confederate ships to be outfitted in British ports during the war. Waite's part in the successful arbitration, which resulted in the United States being awarded $15.5 million, made something of a national hero of the modest lawyer from Toledo.

Upon his return to the United States, Waite was elected to the Ohio Constitutional Convention of 1873 and was subsequently chosen its president. One of the issues that particularly interested him was the burdensome caseload of the Ohio Supreme Court. While he was presiding over the convention, a telegram arrived informing him that President Grant had nominated him to be chief justice of the United States. Waite was as surprised by the news as the rest of the nation. The Senate confirmed him unanimously January 21, 1874, thereby ending an arduous campaign by the Grant administration to fill the post Salmon P. Chase had vacated the year before.

President Grant had approached at least five men prior to Waite. Political patronage, widely practiced by politicians in those days, was used by the Grant administration with little regard for the appointee's character or competence. Consequently, many of the president's nominees were either unsuitable or plainly corrupt. One nominee had withdrawn after his involvement in a major financial scandal was disclosed. Another was seventy-four years old and had little hope of gaining confirmation. In a last-ditch effort to extricate himself from a seven-month political debacle, Grant chose Waite because he was not one of the president's cronies. But

Members of the Supreme Court in 1876: (left to right) Joseph P. Bradley, Stephen J. Field, Samuel F. Miller, Nathan Clifford, Chief Justice Morrison R. Waite, Noah H. Swayne, David Davis, William Strong, and Ward Hunt. In interpreting the Civil Rights Amendments, the Waite Court was reluctant to increase the federal government's power to enforce individual rights or to expand the list of rights that it protected. *Source: Collection of the Supreme Court of the United States*

Grant also saw in him two important attributes that his earlier choices did not have. First, Waite was relatively new to national politics and had yet to acquire many political enemies. Second, the small measure of national prominence that Waite had attained in Geneva was entirely favorable.

When Waite took his seat on the bench in March 1874, at age fifty-seven, he had no judicial experience and had never argued a case before the Court. Because of his judicial inexperience, he was not warmly received by his colleagues, who patronized him at first for his lack of familiarity with court procedure. But Chief Justice Waite soon took the reins of leadership and steered a course of moderation and stability. He proved to be a good manager whose humility and friendliness won over his colleagues. Through the force of his personality he succeeded in keeping harmony among his brethren. Justice Samuel Miller, by nature a tough critic, acknowledged that Waite possessed a "kindliness of heart rarely if ever excelled." Waite was remarkably industrious, setting an example by taking on the largest share of opinions to write himself and by assuming the work of his colleagues when they were ill. He issued 872 opin-

ions in his fourteen years on the Court, a remarkably high number, although his writing may have lacked inspiration.

President Grant had signaled a change of national attitude in his 1869 inaugural address when he proclaimed, "Let us have peace." Reconciliation with the South gained increasing momentum throughout Grant's first term. But the unreconstructed South was plagued with outbreaks of violence, and the ongoing domestic strife resulting from the assimilation of large numbers of free blacks hampered agricultural production and stifled economic recovery. By 1875 many prominent northern politicians were in favor of a new era of reconciliation in order to foster a better business climate. As the Reconstruction era's civil rights legislation came under the Waite Court's careful scrutiny, the Court's decisions reflected this new attitude, even if it meant sacrificing some of the rights granted black citizens in the aftermath of the Civil War.

Under Waite, the Court remained reluctant to interpret the Civil War Amendments (the Thirteenth, Fourteenth, and Fifteenth) as having expanded the federal government's power to enforce civil rights in the states.

This 1866 view of the Chicago River shows, at right, the grain storage elevator operated by Ira Munn and George L. Scott. Convicted of charging storage rates that exceeded those set by the state, Munn argued that the regulatory laws reduced the value of his grain elevator, depriving him of his property without due process of law. In *Munn v. Illinois* (1877) Chief Justice Morrison R. Waite upheld the state laws, saying that some private property was so closely tied to the public interest that states could use their police powers to regulate it. *Source: Library of Congress*

In *United States v. Reese* (1876) Waite wrote the majority opinion establishing that the Fifteenth Amendment, which forbids the states from denying an individual the right to vote based on his race, color, or previous condition of servitude, did not guarantee anyone the right to vote. He ruled that Congress therefore could not penalize state officials who did not let blacks vote by refusing to count their votes, obstructing their ability to vote, or simply denying them the right. Waite reasoned that the right to vote was granted under state law, and therefore the Fifteenth Amendment could protect from racial discrimination only those who wished to exercise a right to vote where that right already existed under state law. During that same term, Waite wrote the unanimous opinion in *United States v. Cruikshank,* which de-

termined that the case against Louisiana citizens accused of using violence and fraud to prevent blacks from voting should be dismissed because the indictments did not charge them with racial discrimination and the acts of fraud and violence were not federal offenses. "We may suspect," Waite wrote, "that race was the cause of the hostility but it is not so averred."

In the many landmark cases dealing with economic and business issues, Waite showed an increasing tolerance for states' rights. The Court faced an important controversy in this area in an 1877 case, *Munn v. Illinois,* in which Waite spelled out the rights of business against those of society. *Munn* typified a series of cases, called the *Granger Cases,* concerning the power of state and local governments to regulate commerce when it was deemed "affected with a public interest." Ira Munn and George L. Scott, operators of a Chicago-based grain elevator company, were appealing a conviction for operating without a license and for charging rates in excess of those set by the 1871 Illinois Warehouse Act. They argued that by limiting the rates they could charge for storing grain, the state reduced the value of their property and was therefore violating the Fourteenth Amendment's Due Process Clause. In writing the Court's opinion, Waite rejected this challenge to state regulation, in this case, laws setting maximum rates for grain storage. He determined that in the absence of a conflict with a federal law, states had the power to regulate private property dedicated to public use.

In contrast to his predecessor, Salmon P. Chase, Waite carefully steered clear of national politics. He refused to let his name be considered for the 1876 Republican presidential nomination, writing to a nephew that his "duty was not to make [his post] a stepping-stone to something else, but to preserve its original purity." He also served his position well by declining appointment to the electoral commission to determine the outcome of the bitterly disputed 1876 presidential race between his close friend Rutherford B. Hayes and Samuel J. Tilden, who had been his classmate at Yale.

Cases concerning commerce and property increasingly dominated the Court's docket during the last part of Waite's fourteen-year tenure and helped swell the number of petitions and appeals to more than 1,500 cases a year by the end of the 1880s. In 1850 that figure had been closer to 250. This tremendous increase in the workload took its toll on Waite. In 1885 he suffered an illness that briefly kept him off the bench. In addition to extreme physical exhaustion, his relatively meager salary of $10,500, coupled with the increasingly costly social obligations of his office, completely depleted his financial resources and left him nearly bankrupt.

On March 5, 1888, he completed the Court's opinion in the *Telephone Cases,* which involved a number of hotly disputed patent claims. The opinion climaxed the longest and perhaps most complex case in the first 100 years of the Court's history. Exhausted and suffering from a severe case of pneumonia, Waite insisted on appearing in Court for fear that his wife, who was vacationing in California, would read of his absence in the press and be alarmed. He came to the Court on March 20 to read the *Telephone Cases* opinion, but was too ill to do so. Waite died three days later, at the age of seventy-one. A collection had to be raised to ensure that his widow would end her days in comfort.

The costly social obligations of his post and the meager $10,500 annual salary depleted whatever savings Morrison R. Waite (shown with his son and grandson) had when he was appointed chief justice, leaving him nearly bankrupt. Despite passage in 1869 of a pension bill, which made it easier for justices to retire, Waite, overworked and ill, dutifully remained on the Court until his death in 1888. *Source: Collection of the Supreme Court of the United States*

John Marshall Harlan
1877-1911

Source: Library of Congress

Although no longer frontier territory, rural Kentucky was a comparatively primitive area in 1833 when, on June 1, John Marshall Harlan was born in Boyle County. James Harlan, his father, was a small-town lawyer and, like all the Harlans, a strong southern Whig. His mother was Eliza Davenport Harlan. At that time Whigs had two idols: Kentucky's own Henry Clay and John Marshall, the chief justice of the United States. An older son was already named for Clay, and it was natural that another would be christened John Marshall, although his parents could hardly have known that the squalling infant would in his turn become a renowned Supreme Court justice.

The Harlans were of largely English ancestry, having migrated to Delaware in 1687 and gradually moved west, arriving in Kentucky in 1774. James Harlan, born in 1800, became a prominent lawyer in the growing state, serving as a Whig member of Congress for two terms and as Kentucky's attorney general for several terms. Young John was raised in Harrodsburg and Frankfort, the state capital, and received a good classical education at Centre College in Danville before proceeding to law school at Transylvania University in 1851. After admission to the bar in Frankfort, Harlan practiced law with his father and entered Kentucky politics. He was elected city attorney of Frankfort and then served as a county judge for a year—his only judicial experience prior to his appointment to the Supreme Court.

After the Whig party died, Harlan spent some years searching for a political home that would be congenial to his proslavery Whig inheritance and yet allow some chance for an electoral win. A failed bid for Congress in 1859 indicated his lack of success in this endeavor.

When the Civil War broke out, Harlan, although a slaveholder and a southern aristocrat, became a leader of Kentucky's pro-Union majority that fended off an attempt in the legislature to follow Tennessee into the Confederate camp. He also volunteered as an officer for the northern army, becoming a colonel of the Tenth Kentucky Volunteer Infantry and acting brigade commander in several only partially successful campaigns to repel Confederate cavalry raids. Upon his father's death in 1863, however, Harlan resigned from the army and returned to his legal practice. He was almost immediately drawn back into politics when he was elected the state's attorney general on a Union ticket.

His Unionism did not mean that Harlan supported President Abraham Lincoln. In fact, he opposed both the Emancipation Proclamation and the embattled president's reelection in 1864. He also opposed the adoption of the postwar Reconstruction Amendments, which attempted to guarantee the rights of blacks, and he continued to own a few household slaves until the Thirteenth Amendment was ratified. His political position became increasingly difficult, as his state was moving into the Democratic camp. The consequence was his failure to be reelected attorney general and the gen-

Malvina Shanklin Harlan's northern background and abhorrence of slavery may have influenced John M. Harlan, a Southern aristocrat, to join the Republican party in 1867. Intelligent and supportive, "Mallie" Harlan has been described as an "ideal wife for a Supreme Court justice." *Source: Library of Congress*

eral failure of his party, the so-called Conservative Unionists, in state elections once hostilities ceased. He would, in fact, never hold another elective office.

In 1856 Harlan had married Malvina F. Shanklin of Evansville, Indiana, and they had an ideal marriage. Of their six children, the three sons all achieved distinction: Richard Davenport Harlan became a prominent Presbyterian clergyman and college president; James Shanklin Harlan was one of the first members of the Interstate Commerce Commission; and John Maynard Harlan was a successful Chicago lawyer and Republican—he served a term as a reform city councilman, and ran unsuccessfully both for mayor and for governor of

Longtime friend and law partner to John M. Harlan, Benjamin H. Bristow became his rival for a seat on the Supreme Court in 1877. An outspoken member of the reform wing of the Republican party, Bristow lost out to Harlan because President Rutherford B. Hayes considered Bristow a political competitor whose appointment would greatly anger the conservative Stalwarts in the party. *Source: Library of Congress*

Illinois. His son, named John Marshall after his grandfather, became a Supreme Court justice in 1955.

It is possible that "Mallie" Harlan, a northerner who had been brought up to believe slavery was wrong, influenced her husband's decision to turn finally to the Republican party in 1867. Never one for half-hearted attachments, Harlan was soon supporting all the Radical Republican policies he had previously opposed. He was an inveterate and highly skilled campaigner and a great orator in the florid style of those days, and quickly became, with his law partner, Benjamin H. Bristow, the moving force in the state party. Even though he lost both times, his campaigns for governor helped greatly to build Republicanism in Kentucky into a respectable opposition force.

Having moved to Louisville, Harlan was now a Republican power broker siding with the reformers in the party against the corruption-ridden Stalwart wing. He had a great impact on national politics when he led the Kentucky delegation to the Republican National Convention in 1876 and organized the campaign for the presidential nomination of his old friend Bristow—now secretary of the Treasury. At a crucial time, seeing that Bristow was certain to lose, he swung the delegation to support Rutherford B. Hayes of Ohio, another reformer, who secured the nomination and ultimately the presidency. This service to Hayes was followed by Harlan's thankless task of serving on the Louisiana Commission in 1877; the results enabled President Hayes to withdraw federal troops from occupying that state. While his participation did not endear Harlan to the Stalwarts, it cemented his standing with Hayes.

As an element in his policy of reconciliation with the South, Hayes wanted to appoint a southerner to the Supreme Court vacancy that existed when he came into office. Prominent southern Republicans were hard to find, but among them, Harlan certainly stood out. Although as both a recent convert to Republicanism and a reformer, he had Stalwart opposition, Harlan was confirmed by the Senate and took the oath of office December 10, 1877.

At age forty-four, Harlan was a fine physical specimen, even if he was beginning to lose his youthful slenderness. He was tall—two inches over six feet—and probably weighed more than 200 pounds. With red-blonde hair and an erect carriage, he made an impressive-looking judge. He also had a lively temperament and sense of humor, and he liked to deliver his opinions in the old-fashioned style, without using a prepared text. A lifelong Presbyterian, Harlan's faith is attested by the fact that he taught Sunday school throughout his

"TO THINE OWN SELF BE TRUE."

This sentimental 1875 engraving depicts Columbia (the United States) passing the Civil Rights Act of 1871 to the hands of black Americans. The act protected blacks from discrimination by state and city governments and prohibited private businesses, such as inns and theaters, from denying blacks access. When the legislation came before the Supreme Court in the *Civil Rights Cases* (1883), only John M. Harlan upheld the federal government's power to legislate against acts of discrimination by private businesses. *Source: New York Public Library*

adult life and was elected vice-moderator of the national Presbyterian church.

During his tenure of nearly thirty-four years, Harlan participated in the gradual transition of the Supreme Court from a body that handled primarily private law cases to a great public law court. In the 1880s the Court reviewed only a few constitutional cases each year, but many appeals in private cases and suits against states or the national government. By the time of Harlan's death, the Court was fully established as a body that decided major public policy issues referred to it under constitutional claims. Harlan's reputation was established as the judges "felt" their way into this new role, and, as it happened, his status was based largely on his disagreements with most of his colleagues.

An illustration of this changing role is the string of cases in which the Court was asked by private businesses to protect them from the growing number of state and federal regulations passed to curb some of the excesses of capitalism. The Court could—and did—use the Constitution's Commerce Clause to achieve some degree of protection for these businesses. With Harlan dissenting, the Court limited the power of Congress by interpreting the idea of interstate commerce narrowly. In *United States v. E. C. Knight Co.* (1895), for example, the Court held that a new antitrust law did not apply to manufacturing companies because manufacturing is not commerce—an idea that Harlan alone opposed.

The Court also found wanting state laws regulating commerce, either because they interfered with interstate commerce—as in the 1886 *Wabash, St. Louis & Pacific Railway Co. v. Illinois* case involving state regulation of railroad rates (a case that found Harlan in the majority)—or because they violated a somewhat mystical concept of due process of law stemming from the Fourteenth Amendment. The latter development was accepted in principle by Harlan, although he sometimes disagreed with the majority's application of it. He argued that the Court was wrong in *Lochner v. New York* (1905) when it struck down a New York law limiting the hours of work in bakeries; in fact, Harlan found ample justification for such a limitation.

Harlan also found himself opposed to the rest of the Court in several important cases that questioned the reach of the Due Process Clause in cases involving state criminal law procedures. In general, Harlan felt that the Bill of Rights ought, after the adoption of the Fourteenth Amendment, to protect citizens against state acts in the criminal procedures field as fully as it had always done for federal action. These beliefs were most fully and finally spelled out in his dissent in *Twining v. New Jersey* (1908). He argued that if the majority argument were pursued, the Constitution would pose "no obstacle whatever in the way of a state law [allowing the] rack or thumbscrew, censorship, unreasonable search, or double jeopardy."

But Justice Harlan's enduring reputation rests mostly on his dissents in cases involving questions of racial discrimination. He believed very strongly that the words "equal protection" in the Fourteenth Amendment meant full equality in all government dealings with blacks. He thought—and none of his colleagues agreed with him—that states could neither require nor permit unequal practices such as segregation by race, and that Congress could block such actions. His dissenting opinions show his belief in a "color-blind" Constitution. In the *Civil Rights Cases* (1883), for example, Harlan argued that congressional power under the Fourteenth Amendment reached even private actions not regulated by states. He claimed that the Court's majority—in striking down congressional acts prohibiting racial segregation in private accommodations—proceeded upon "grounds entirely too narrow and artificial," sacrificing the "substance and spirit" of the amendment "by a subtle and ingenious verbal criticism." To lend strength to this basic argument, he developed the doctrine that the actions of private companies such as railroads or hotels, since they are common carriers that have always been regulated by government, are really state acts and as such are covered by the amendment. In its day this argument was strikingly innovative; it was not accepted by the Court until the mid-twentieth century.

Harlan was perhaps on stronger constitutional ground when he dissented in *Plessy v. Ferguson* (1896). The Court majority upheld a Louisiana law requiring separate cars for blacks and whites on railroad trains, so long as the cars were "equal." Harlan would have none of such verbal subterfuge, knowing as a southerner and former slaveholder that such laws were inspired only by ideas of white supremacy. He asserted that the amendment does not permit states to "know the race" of those entitled to its protection.

Harlan wrote once more on this subject in *Berea College v. Kentucky* (1908), in which the Court upheld a Kentucky law barring integration in private schools: "Have we become so inoculated with prejudice of race that an American government . . . can make distinctions between . . . citizens in the matter of their voluntary meeting for innocent purposes, simply because of their respective races?"

Harlan died rather suddenly, apparently of pneumonia, October 14, 1911, only a few days after attending the opening session of the Court's 1911 term. He was a judicial activist for what he regarded as right, and his reputation endures because what his heart told him ought to be in the Constitution has become what modern society views as right. Although he could not lead his colleagues, he alone was able, perhaps accidentally, to predict the course of future constitutional interpretation.

William B. Woods
1881-1887

WILLIAM BURNHAM WOODS was born August 3, 1824, in the city of Newark in the central part of Ohio. His father, Ezekiel Woods, a farmer and a merchant, had migrated there from Kentucky; his mother, Sarah Burnham Woods, was a New Englander.

After attending Western Reserve College for three years, Woods graduated from Yale College in 1845 as valedictorian of his class. He returned to his hometown to read law with a prominent local attorney, S. D. King, and was admitted to the Ohio bar in 1847. He then joined King's firm as a partner, rising to prominence in Newark, the county seat of Licking County. In 1855 he married Anne E. Warner, and they had a son and a daughter.

Politics was Woods's major involvement prior to the Civil War. Initially a member of the Whig party, Woods soon switched his affiliation to the Democrats.

He was elected mayor of Newark in 1856 and the following year was chosen for the state legislature, becoming Speaker in his second term. When the Republicans became the majority party in 1859, Woods became the minority leader. An ardent Democrat, he opposed the rise of the newly formed Republican party and the administration of President Abraham Lincoln. With the secession of the South and the Civil War, however, Woods came to support the Union cause and Lincoln's war policies.

Woods entered the Union army as a lieutenant colonel of the Seventy-sixth Ohio Regiment in 1862. He participated in the battles of Shiloh and Vicksburg, and marched with Gen. William Sherman through Georgia. Promoted to brigadier general, Woods rode through Washington, D.C., in the Grand Review of the Union Troops at the close of the war. His brother, Charles Robert Woods, was a highly regarded field general in the Union army. William, however, had more staff experience. More important, he had the confidence of Sherman and two other generals, Ulysses S. Grant and John A. Logan, all of whom supported his promotion to brevetted major general.

At war's end Woods was assigned to Mobile, Alabama. In February 1866 he was released from the army but stayed on in Alabama. The fact that his wife's brother, Willard Warner, had recently been elected a U.S. senator from the state was probably a strong motivation for settling there. Woods, now a member of the Republican party, became a cotton planter, invested in iron works, and practiced law. Within two years, he was elected on the Republican ticket as a chancellor to Alabama's southern chancery court.

With the election of General Grant to the presidency in 1868, Congress passed legislation creating nine circuit judgeships. Grant was blessed with an outstanding attorney general in Ebenezer Hoar, who sought to appoint men of merit and integrity to the judicial positions. Woods was appointed to the Fifth Circuit, which covered Georgia, Florida, Alabama, Mississippi, Louisiana, and Texas. There is scant information concerning the appointment, yet having served with Grant, being a Republican, and having a brother-in-law in the Senate all no doubt proved beneficial.

Woods served eleven years as U.S. circuit court judge, riding long distances between the states to hear federal cases. At first he maintained his residence in Alabama, but in 1877 he moved to Atlanta, Georgia. He also acted as the reporter for the federal courts' decisions, having them published to be read by practicing lawyers. When the landmark *Slaughter House Cases* were tried in his circuit court, he sat with Justice Joseph P. Bradley listening to former justice John Campbell argue for the state of Louisiana. It was probably one of the few times when a sitting justice of the Supreme Court, a former justice, and a future justice were involved in the same case.

Despite his northern upbringing and his service in the Union army, Judge Woods succeeded in gaining the confidence and respect of members of the southern bench and bar and of the communities where he presided. He administered the law to ensure that the federal courts would not seem alien to southerners and would protect their rights and deliver justice fairly.

On March 4, 1877 Rutherford B. Hayes became president, after a tumultuous election that needed a commission to determine its outcome. The same day, a vacancy opened on the Supreme Court when David Davis resigned to begin a term in the U.S. Senate. While concessions were made to the South in consideration of its assistance in helping Hayes win the White House, no specific commitment has been documented concerning the filling of vacancies on the Court by southern judges. Nonetheless, of the twenty-four men proposed to fill the seat, only one could be characterized as a northerner. A Kentuckian, John Marshall Har-

William B. Woods earned the respect of Gen. William T. Sherman, commander of the Union forces in the West, by distinguishing himself at the battles of Shiloh and Vicksburg. When Woods was being considered for nomination to the Supreme Court in 1877, Sherman urged his brother, Secretary of the Treasury John Sherman, to present letters of support for Woods to President Rutherford B. Hayes. *Source: Library of Congress*

lan, soon became the odds-on favorite and was ultimately the president's choice. Yet, the consideration of Woods as a possible appointee merits discussion because it played an important role in his eventual appointment three years later, in 1880.

Justice Samuel Miller, a man with a keen political eye, recorded several observations on potential appointees. Miller considered his brother-in-law, William Ballinger, as a possible candidate for the Davis seat. Ballinger was reluctant and instead suggested that Campbell be reappointed, citing Woods as his second

choice. Miller considered Campbell, at age seventy-five, too old, complaining that there was enough infirmity on the Court. But in truth, Miller had never forgiven Campbell for resigning from the Court at the advent of the Civil War.

Campbell's interest in the Supreme Court was not for himself but for Woods. He became, along with federal district judge Edward C. Billings, Woods's major supporter, if not campaign manager. Campbell was able to enlist the support of the most notable son of the Confederacy then serving in Congress, Lucius Q. C. Lamar. Writing to Campbell, Lamar stated: "It will give me pleasure to do what I can to promote your views in regard to the appointment of Judge Woods to the Supreme Court Bench. I will state to the President your favorable estimate of his qualifications and express the opinion that his appointment would be more acceptable to our people than any of those most likely to get the position."

While Harlan made a personal approach regarding his nomination by writing directly to members of the executive branch, Woods did nothing himself. Campbell and Billings had the reins and obtained more written endorsements for Woods than were filed in behalf of Harlan. District judges, southern Republicans, southern politicians, carpetbaggers, and confederate veterans signed the eighty-one petitions in support of Judge Woods. In addition, Woods's connections to Ohio and to Sherman, his former commanding officer, earned him support. General Sherman's brother, John, was secretary of the Treasury and received and forwarded to President Hayes endorsements for Woods from Alabama senator John A. Morgan, the Mobile Bar Association, and Ohio representative James A. Garfield. Chief Justice Morrison Waite and Associate Justice Noah Swayne, both from Ohio, also supported Woods.

Harlan's ultimate appointment must be attributed, in part, to his extensive support for Hayes during the elec-

When William B. Woods (standing, left) joined the Supreme Court in 1880, he found it swamped with cases. In the 1860 term the Court—then the only federal appeals court—had reviewed 310 cases; in 1890 that figure was 1,816. Relief came in 1891 with the creation of the circuit courts of appeals, federal courts designed to hear the appeals of routine cases lacking constitutional implications. *Source: Library of Congress*

tion. Still, his confirmation was a long hard fight that took about six weeks of debate in the Senate. The setback for Woods put him in a strong position for the next vacancy.

Associate Justice William Strong submitted his resignation from the Supreme Court on December 14, 1880. Because it was speculated that Sen. Stanley Matthews of Ohio would fill the vacancy, few remarked on the significance of the chief justice's administrative reassignment of Justice Bradley from the southern Fifth Circuit, where Woods sat, to the northern Third Circuit. This action indicated that a judge from the Fifth Circuit would be elevated to the high court. Miller believed the president already favored Woods. Swayne, ill and anticipating his own retirement, was trying to condition his resignation on Woods's appointment.

Such a complex deal was not necessary. The day after Strong resigned, President Hayes sent Woods's nomination to the Senate. Chief Justice Waite had apparently backed him, but, most important, Hayes believed he needed an appointee who would help reconcile North and South. As a Union veteran and Ohio native whose professional interests lay in the South, Woods was the kind of "southerner" Hayes found easy to appoint. Although his earlier supporters, including the southern senators, all continued to back Woods, there was some indignation in the region that he was not a true Georgian. A fuss also arose over the large number of Ohioans (Waite, Swayne, and Salmon Chase) who had served recently on the Court, but this complaint largely reflected the Democrats' political frustration. Woods was confirmed six days later, on December 21, by a 39–8 vote, making him the first justice appointed from a Confederate state since 1853.

The Court Woods joined was swamped with work. Its jurisdiction was overly broad during this time and ran the gamut from cases involving constitutional interpretation to the mundane, with the latter being the norm. Moreover, the caseload had increased significantly, and the Court was short-handed. Two ailing justices were not participating in deliberations yet would not vacate their seats for another two years. Joining a five-member Court (Swayne having resigned shortly after Woods was appointed), Woods found the case backlog triple the Court's annual disposition rate. The Court would not be up to full strength until 1883, when new justices were appointed. The caseload problem would not be solved until 1891, with the creation of the circuit courts of appeal.

Woods was a diligent worker, and wrote more opinions—159—during the six and a half years he sat on the Court than any other associate justice. Although the quantity was significant, the subject matter mirrored the general legal nature of the Court's jurisdiction at the time. Most opinions dealt with nothing more than routine legal disputes. Real property disputes, patent litigation, commercial matters, and estate and trust cases monopolized the docket, with the remainder pertaining to corporations, taxes, and municipal law.

Only a few of his opinions touch on constitutional issues. In *United States v. Harris* (1883) Woods, writing for a majority of eight justices, held that the Fourteenth Amendment did not give Congress authority to enact laws that punished individuals for depriving other individuals of their civil rights. He joined Harlan in his dissent in *Elk v. Wilkins* (1884), in which the Court held that Indians were not citizens within the meaning of the Fourteenth Amendment. Speaking for a unanimous Court in *Presser v. Illinois* (1886), Woods determined that a state law seeking to regulate private military organizations did not violate the Constitution. His opinion held that the Second Amendment's guarantee of the right to bear arms was applicable only to the federal government, not to the states.

Woods clearly should be characterized with the majority of the Court. He dissented only eight times during his tenure on the Court, and four of his dissents occurred in 5–4 decisions. His contributions have been overshadowed, however, by those of Waite, Miller, Harlan, and Stephen Field—all justices who served much longer than he.

Woods became ill suddenly in the spring of 1886. An extended recuperation in California failed to restore his health, and he died in Washington May 14, 1887. After his death, the South's wish for a "real representative" was fulfilled when Woods's former supporter, Lucius Lamar, a Confederate veteran, was appointed to his seat. At the time of Woods's death, it appeared the newspapers were more interested in his successor than in discussing his contributions to the Court.

Since Woods's personal papers, in the main, have not been found, the basis and extent of his personal and political influence are obscure. What has been determined is that he was a private person noted for his sincerity, abhorrence of pretension, and hard work. Probably the best statement reflecting his commitment came from the chief justice of Georgia: "We are proud of him because he is identified with us, and while serving as a judge in our midst has known nothing but the law, and has been loyal to nothing but the law."

Stanley Matthews
1881-1889

THOMAS STANLEY MATTHEWS was born in Cincinnati, Ohio, July 21, 1824, to Thomas J. Matthews and Isabella Brown Matthews. He dropped "Thomas" from his name in adulthood. Stanley was the first of eleven children of his father's second marriage. An educator, engineer, and inventor, Thomas Matthews was a remarkable man, but Isabella Matthews, who maintained a household of sixteen children, must have been at least as extraordinary.

Educated primarily by his father, Matthews grew up in Cincinnati and Lexington, Kentucky. He was admitted as a junior (a common practice) to Kenyon College in June 1839 and graduated with honors in July of the following year. Among the acquaintances Matthews made at Kenyon, none was so significant as a future U.S. president, Rutherford B. Hayes.

After briefly studying law in Cincinnati, Matthews moved to Columbia, Tennessee, because Ohio required lawyers to be twenty-one before they could be admitted to the bar, and he was only eighteen. In addition to practicing law, Matthews edited the *Tennessee Democrat,* which backed Democrat James K. Polk. In 1843 Matthews married Mary Ann ("Minnie") Black, the daughter of a prominent Whig politician.

In 1844 Matthews's family moved to Cincinnati, where, on reaching age twenty-one, he was admitted to the bar. Matthews was caught up in both the burgeoning commercial activity that drove the young city, and the antislavery controversy gripping the country. He gravitated toward political abolitionism and succeeded Gamaliel Bailey as editor of the antislavery *Morning Herald.* Matthews wrote an editorial criticizing the Supreme Court for its proslavery *Jones v. Van Zandt* (1847) decision, and the piece drew a response from Ohio's "representative" on the Court, John McLean. A prominent antislavery lawyer in the case was the future chief justice, Salmon P. Chase, one of Matthews's Ohio mentors.

The Ohio legislature selected Matthews as its clerk in 1848. Three years later, Matthews was elected to Hamilton County's court of common pleas, but he resigned after two years because of the inadequate salary. In 1855 Matthews was elected to the state senate and served until 1858.

Matthews also kept his legal career moving forward, appearing before the Supreme Court as early as 1858. He served as counsel to the Cincinnati, Hamilton & Dayton Railroad, the construction of which coincided with the development of Glendale, a suburban village Matthews helped found in 1855.

Accompanying this prosperity was a moderating of Matthews's antislavery views. Although in the late 1840s he had joined Chase as a Free-Soil Democrat, by the time of his service in the Ohio Senate he had become a mainstream Democrat. Indicative of his (short-lived) party regularity, was Matthews's appointment as U.S. attorney for the Southern District of Ohio in 1858 by President James Buchanan. As U.S. attorney he demonstrated his commitment to law and order when in 1859

he successfully prosecuted newsman W. B. Connelly for violating the Fugitive Slave Act of 1850 by helping two slaves escape. The reporter was popular, and the law was unpopular, but Buchanan's Justice Department was firmly committed to enforcing it. In Matthews's defense, even the leader of the local underground railroad understood his dilemma.

Perhaps Matthews was distracted by more pressing personal matters. In March 1859 a scarlet fever epidemic ravaged the Matthews household, claiming four of their six children. Although Minnie had four more children in the next eight years, the couple was devastated by the deaths, and, while previously inclined to religious freethinking, they now sought solace in the more stable tenets of "old school" Presbyterianism.

With Abraham Lincoln's election, Matthews resigned his post as U.S. attorney. At the outbreak of the Civil War, he and Hayes, being of one mind on the rightness of the conflict, enlisted together in the Twenty-third Ohio Infantry, Matthews as a lieutenant-colonel and his fellow Cincinnati lawyer as a major. In the latter part of 1862 Matthews was promoted to colonel in the Fifty-first Ohio Volunteers. His service must have been troubling. Separated from Minnie only two years after their children's tragic deaths, bypassed for further promotion, and beset by a persistent and painful case of hemorrhoids and a severe battlefield injury that kept him out of Murfreesboro—the only major battle in which he might have participated—Matthews succumbed to the blandishments of Ohio Republican leaders and resigned his commission to successfully run for the Cincinnati Superior Court in April 1863.

Matthews remained on the bench until 1865, when he returned to his practice as a premier railroad lawyer. Active at various levels as a Presbyterian layman, Matthews drafted the church's formal condemnation of slavery at its 1864 General Assembly. He had to resign as a Presbyterian elder in 1869, however, when he accepted the controversial case of *Minor v. Board of Edu-*

Chief Justice Morrison R. Waite administers the oath of office to Rutherford B. Hayes on March 4, 1877, while Stanley Matthews (right) looks on. Perhaps as a reward for skillful campaign advice, Hayes secured for Matthews the Senate seat of John Sherman, an Ohioan who was named to the cabinet. *Source: Library of Congress*

cation. The case concerned the Cincinnati Board of Education, which, in response to the city's diverse population, ordered cessation of the regular morning Scripture reading. Irate parents immediately sued the board, and Matthews became one of its counsel. He and his associates won the case before the Ohio Supreme Court. Particularly memorable was Matthews's ringing phrase at the trial, "Toleration—I hate that word." What he meant is that all religions should be equal before the law, that tolerance should be automatic.

Evidence of Matthews's independence continued to surface. He had served as a Republican presidential elector in 1864 and 1868, but was unhappy with the cor-

ruption of President Ulysses S. Grant's first term. Matthews's commitment to the objectives of reconciliation with the South led to his involvement in the Liberal Republican movement. The party conveniently met in Cincinnati in the summer of 1872, designating Matthews temporary chairman. But when the convention decided on protectionist Horace Greeley as its candidate, Matthews, who was particularly devoted to free trade, disavowed his connection with the infant party and supported Grant in the election.

It was, however, Matthews's ties to Hayes that had the most influence on his career. Matthews's efforts for his friend (they had also become related through the marriage of one of Matthews's sisters to a brother of Lucy Webb Hayes) in the 1876 election included an unsuccessful run for Congress from the Ohio Second District, in which his past unpopular actions—enforcement of the Fugitive Slave Act, defense of the ban on Bible reading, and involvement in the Liberal Republican movement—were used against him. Matthews became one of Hayes's principal campaign advisers and was deeply involved in negotiating the end of Reconstruction and Hayes's presidential election.

When the hotly contested Hayes-Tilden election of 1876 came before an electoral commission for resolution, Matthews was one of Hayes's counsel. The contest focused on the validity of the electoral votes of Florida, Louisiana, and South Carolina (states still under Reconstruction), and Oregon. The point to be made, which Matthews did with what has been called "admirable precision," was that the commission could not go beyond the recorded tally of a state. That the commission's vote of eight Republicans to seven Democrats to elect Hayes tainted the result as political should not detract from Matthews's lawyerly skills in providing the line of reasoning for the eight Republicans to follow.

Whether as a reward or because he needed his services in the Senate, Hayes used his influence with the Ohio legislature in March 1877 to secure Matthews's election to replace John Sherman, who had been appointed secretary of the Treasury. Although a Hayes ally in the Senate, Matthews nevertheless had his differences with the president, most notably over monetary policy. Hayes remained staunchly committed to the gold standard, while a resolution to repay the federal debt in silver bore Matthews's name, a difference Hayes still remembered at the time of Matthews's death. "He did not show political wisdom . . . on grave questions like the currency," Hayes said.

In December 1880, as Hayes was leaving the presidency, Justice Noah Swayne retired from the Supreme Court, and the president appointed Matthews to fill the vacancy. The Senate failed to act, however, and Hayes's term concluded. But the new president, James A. Garfield, resubmitted Matthews's name March 14, 1881. Although fellow Ohioans, Garfield and Matthews were not on particularly friendly terms; indeed, Matthews had obtained his Senate seat at Garfield's expense. Yet, even though the "cronyism" charge was removed with Hayes's departure, opposition to the appointment did not abate, and the arguments used against Matthews in his 1876 congressional bid were renewed. Also not forgotten was his successful argument before the Electoral Commission. In addition, his service as attorney for "robber baron" Jay Gould of the Erie Railroad led to the charge that he would continue on Gould's retainer while on the Court. Finally, after exhaustive and often vitriolic debate in the Senate and the nation's press, and despite a 7–1 vote against the nomination by the Judiciary Committee, the Senate approved Matthews's nomination on May 12, by a vote of 24–23.

Matthews did not leave a significant imprint on constitutional jurisprudence, partly because he spent fewer than eight years on the Court. Because his appointment coincided with that of several other new justices, however, small but significant shifts occurred in a number of areas. In a question involving the Eleventh Amendment, which expresses the immunity of states against law suits, Matthews reasoned that states were not exempt from adherence to the Constitution's Contract Clause, and, consequently, state officials could be sued as individuals for enforcing invalid acts, despite the Eleventh Amendment. Specifically, in *Poindexter v. Greenhow* (1885) a railroad sought to pay its taxes in bond coupons, as allowed by a state law of 1871, but rescinded by a later statute. Matthews and the rest of the five-justice majority that found against the state may have been influenced by the fact that the railroad bringing the suit faced financial ruin if it could not pay its taxes with bond coupons.

Naturally, much of the Court's work of the 1880s reflected the thinking of that era, and a number of its decisions seem unfortunate from a later perspective. An example is Matthews's opinion for the Court in *Hurtado v. California* (1884), which involved the conviction for murder and death sentence of one Joseph Hurtado. Because the prosecution had been based on an information (a formal accusation by the prosecutor detailing the nature and circumstances of the charge) rather than a grand jury indictment, Hurtado claimed that the Fourteenth Amendment's Due Process Clause had been violated. The Court's majority, with John Marshall Harlan dissenting, held that a grand jury indictment was not necessary to protect a defendant's liberty, and Matthews maintained that the Constitution "was made for an undefined and expanding future," including new devices like an information rather than an indictment.

And those who would read too much into Matthews's argument in support of separating church and state in the *Minor* case should also take into account his opinion for the Court in *Murphy v. Ramsey* (1885), sustaining the Edmunds Act of 1882, which disenfranchised polygamists. Matthews validated the law, in part, because of its support for matrimony, "the sure foundation of all that is stable and noble in our civilization."

He struck down a San Francisco ordinance requiring

In 1886 Stanley Matthews wrote the Court's opinion in *Yick Wo v. Hopkins,* striking down a fire ordinance that was written in a racially neutral way but enforced in a discriminatory manner against Chinese laundry owners. *Source: Library of Congress*

laundries not housed in brick or stone buildings to obtain permits from the board of supervisors in his 1886 opinion for the Court in *Yick Wo v. Hopkins.* All 200 Chinese-owned laundries in wooden buildings had been denied permits. All but one of the eighty non-Chinese applications for a permit had been granted. In finding that the ordinance in its operation violated the Fourteenth Amendment's Equal Protection Clause, Matthews wrote, "Though the law itself be fair on its face . . . yet if it is applied and administered by public authority with an evil eye and an unequal hand . . . the denial of justice is still within the prohibition of the Constitution."

Minnie Matthews had died in 1885, and, despite the objections of his children, Matthews had married Mary Theaker in 1887. Although in his sixties, Matthews was in full vigor when he contacted a mysterious rheumatic illness as a result of being trapped in New York City during the great blizzard of 1888. He showed signs of recovery during the next few months, but died at his Washington home March 22, 1889.

Understandably, because of his role in elevating Matthews to the Court, Hayes readily endorsed Justice Harlan's eulogy: "A great judge, a heavy loss to the court; a rapid worker; wise and able; growing all the time." Undoubtedly, there was hyperbole customary for such occasions in Harlan's words, but none can doubt the subject's skill as a lawyer.

Horace Gray

1882-1902

Source: Collection of the Supreme Court of the United States

H ORACE GRAY was born March 24, 1828, into a wealthy and prominent family of merchants and shipbuilders in Boston. His grandfather, William Gray, the son of a poor New England shoemaker, had built the family fortune by developing trade with Russia, China, and India, and he served two terms as lieutenant governor of Massachusetts. Horace Gray, Sr., father of the future justice, married Harriet Upham, the daughter of a distinguished lawyer and member of the House of Representatives.

She died when her first child, Horace, Jr., was only six years old. His father remarried after a few years, and the second marriage produced John Chipman Gray, who was to become a renowned professor of law at Harvard University.

Young Horace was prepared for college in Boston area private schools. From early childhood he was abnormally tall, reaching his full height of six feet, six inches, by the time he was thirteen and entered Harvard. His father, fearing that the young man's size was outpacing his physical strength, limited the number of hours he could spend in the library. The elder Gray gave his son a gun and turned him out of doors. This youthful activity was the beginning of Gray's habit of taking long walks in the nearby countryside and his fondness for hunting and shooting for sport.

By all accounts Gray's undergraduate years at Harvard were interesting, but undistinguished. He was given no part in the commencement exercises when he was graduated in 1845 at age seventeen, indicating that he was not in the upper half of his class. Fascinated with natural history and insects, Gray took courses with the great naturalist Louis Agassiz and became especially knowledgeable about birds. He preferred modern languages to the classics and gained enough language proficiency to become an acknowledged critic of light French and Italian prose in later life.

As with other well-placed young men, Gray was in no hurry to enter a profession. His father, who had taken over the family business interests, was an exceedingly wealthy man. However, when Gray was on a leisurely tour of Europe, he received word from his father that the business had failed and the family was penniless. Faced with choosing a serious and lucrative profession, Gray enrolled in Harvard Law School in 1848. Unlike his undergraduate approach, he threw himself into his studies with industry and enthusiasm and excelled in his work. Although he had never expressed an interest in law, Gray did not have to look far for notable precedents in his ancestry. His father's brother, Francis Calley Gray, had earned a permanent place in the annals of jurisprudence with his discovery of the original version of New England's first legal code, "Liberties of the Massachusetts Colony in New England," adopted in 1641.

Even at Harvard the course of study for law in Gray's day was a far cry from the modern three-year curriculum. No examinations were required either for admission or graduation; there were no grades; and residence at the law school for a year and a half, attested only by receipted payment of three term bills, entitled a student to the diploma. Gray, together with a fellow student named John Felton, contributed to a major change in the American teaching of law. Felton was an innovator, choosing what was then an unusual approach to research, the case study method, which their classmate George Hoar described as examining "a legal principle in historic order, going back to the first case where it was announced and tracing it down through the re-

As an undergraduate at Harvard University, Horace Gray studied with Louis Agassiz, a Swiss-born zoologist and geologist. Renowned for his inspired teaching, Agassiz was a great promoter of scientific study in the United States. Gray developed a strong interest in the study of birds from Agassiz's courses in natural history. *Source: Library of Congress*

ports, making no use of the text books." Gray not only fell in with Felton's method but helped pass it on to a new student, Christopher Langdell, later famed as the dean of the Harvard Law School who established the case study method. Gray graduated in 1849 and continued his legal education by reading law with John Lowell and clerking for the firm of Sohier and Welch. In 1851 he was admitted to the bar.

Striking out on his own as a lawyer, he was in full-time practice only a few months when his penchant for records and scholarship was rewarded. Luther S. Cushing, reporter of decisions for the Massachusetts Supreme Court, had become ill, and he engaged the young Gray to follow the court on circuit and do the reporting. When Cushing's health worsened, Gray took on more and more of the work, preparing the entire last volume of Cushing's reports. With the support of the most prominent members of the state bar, he was appointed at age twenty-six to the position of reporter, the youngest person ever to occupy that office. The position at that time was one of great prestige, ranking only below membership on the state supreme court itself. Further, the reporter was allowed to continue his legal practice to the extent time permitted. From 1854 to 1864 Gray argued thirty-one cases before the Massachusetts Supreme Court, some of them on constitutional grounds, winning twenty-four and losing seven.

He also flirted briefly with politics and attempted unsuccessfully to obtain the Republican nomination for state attorney general. At the same time, however, his reporting work and independent writing was earning him a remarkable reputation for legal and historical research. His close friend from college, George Hoar, who became an influential U.S. senator, wrote of him: "He had already acquired a great stock of learning for a man of his age. Even then a wonderful capacity for research, the instinct which, when some interesting question of law was up, would direct his thumb and finger to some obscure volume of English reports of law or eq-

At Harvard Law School, Horace Gray learned an innovative approach to the study of law—the case method—from classmate John Felton. Gray passed this method, which emphasizes formulating legal principles from the study of specific court decisions, to Christopher Langdell, above, who introduced it to the curriculum of Harvard Law School when he served as dean from 1870 to 1895.
Source: Harvard Law Art Collection

uity, was almost like the scent of a wild animal or bird of prey."

Two published manuscripts of his vast scholarship were on slavery, to which he was opposed. The first, *Slavery in Massachusetts,* covered in fifty pages the entire history of the institution in all the New England states. The second, written in collaboration with the editor of the *Monthly Law Review,* was an elaborate summary and evaluation of the notorious *Scott v. Sanford* case, which had determined that blacks were not citizens of the United States. Typical of Gray's thoroughness was his subsequent discovery that in 1807 three black men taken off an American ship by a British man-of-war had been described by President Thomas Jefferson as "native citizens of the United States." Gray found and verified the source, and the additional evidence establishing Negro citizenship was added in a note for a later edition.

Gray's elevation to associate justice of the state supreme court in 1864 made him the youngest appointee ever named to that court. Nine years later, after the resignation of several senior justices, he became the chief justice, employing a young Harvard student, future Supreme Court justice Louis D. Brandeis, as his law clerk. Gray was a prolific writer of opinions, producing 515 as an associate justice and 852 as chief justice. Because he believed dissents weakened the effectiveness of the court, he endeavored to persuade colleagues to come to agreement on a disputed point. He dissented only once in seventeen years. None of his decisions for the state court was overruled during his lifetime.

In addition to his judicial duties, Gray became a counselor to the governor on legal and constitutional questions, particularly the thorny issues arising from the Civil War. Meanwhile, he had found time to accept election to the state historical society and take an active part in its affairs as a member of the governing body and as a historian. He also became a member of Boston's Trinity Church and attended services regularly.

Gray was appointed associate justice of the Supreme Court by President Chester A. Arthur on December 19, 1881, shortly after the assassination of James A. Garfield, who had been considering naming Gray to the Court. Aside from his obvious qualifications for the post, he was strongly supported by lifelong friends in the Senate, led by Hoar. Gray was confirmed the following day by a 51–5 vote. His confirmation was generally hailed by the press, in part because the selection appeared to be devoid of political partisanship, cronyism, or machine politics. As he was throughout his judicial life, Gray had been meticulous in his avoidance of any appearance of office-seeking or political partisanship; he had even refused to select for the president copies of some of his "best opinions."

Although he produced more than 450 opinions on the Supreme Court, it is difficult to pinpoint his judicial philosophy. He is best remembered as a great legal and historical scholar and as an exponent of history and precedent as the ultimate determinants of the law. An example is his dissent in *Budd v. New York* (1892), in which the majority affirmed a New York statute that fixed the rates companies could charge for grain storage. Gray's dissent drew on historical authorities such as a colonial Virginia statute and a 1709 act of Parliament regulating coal prices to show that "the prices of necessary articles were controlled by the legislature, in England and America, at the time of the adoption of the State and National Constitutions."

He was a strong nationalist—although he became more moderate with the passage of years—and firm in his interpretation of the sovereignty of the federal government. Ironically, when he finally had his chance to voice the majority opinion on national sovereignty, in the last of the controversial *Legal Tender Cases,* he had difficulty finding enough legal precedents for the precise issue, the power of the government to issue paper money as legal tender. Reaching to Austro-Hungarian history for precedent, he aroused a stinging dissent from Justice Stephen J. Field. Gray's opinion was the most sweeping on the extent of congressional power up to that time.

A bachelor for sixty years, Gray fell in love with Jane Matthews, the daughter of his friend and colleague, Justice Stanley Matthews. Matthews was four years older than he, and Jane thirty years younger. After a brief courtship, they married June 4, 1889.

Horace Gray's passion for historical scholarship, widely reflected in his Supreme Court opinions, made him one of the great intellectuals of his day. As such, he was asked to join the Saturday Club, a Boston-based group of distinguished writers and thinkers. This painting of contemporary literary giants depicts several members of the club: Oliver Wendell Holmes, Sr., second row, second from left; Henry Wadsworth Longfellow, first row, fifth from left; Nathaniel Hawthorne, second row, seventh from left; Richard Henry Dana, first row, sixth from right; James Russell Lowell, second row, third from right. *Source: National Portrait Gallery*

Gray's love of historical scholarship, his extensive library, and his encyclopedic and accurate memory brought him into the company of many of the great minds of his time. He became a member of Boston's famed Saturday Club shortly after its founding. The early members included distinguished writers such as James Russell Lowell, Henry Wadsworth Longfellow, Ralph Waldo Emerson, Richard Henry Dana, and Oliver Wendell Holmes, Sr. During Gray's two decades of membership, novelist Nathaniel Hawthorne, noted politician Charles Sumner, and Charles William Eliot, the president of Harvard, also joined.

An ailing Justice Gray missed a good part of the 1894 term of the Court. Starting in 1896 his share of the work dropped off; the quality never faltered, but he was able to accomplish less. He sat in Court for the last time on February 3, 1902, and in the evening suffered a paralytic stroke. The sea air off the Massachusetts shore failed to produce hoped-for improvement, and he sent his resignation to President Theodore Roosevelt July 9, 1902, to take effect on the appointment of a successor. He died September 15 in Nahant, Massachusetts, before his successor could be chosen. His replacement on the high bench, Oliver Wendell Holmes, Jr., was the same judge who had succeeded him on the Massachusetts bench.

Samuel Blatchford

1882-1893

S AMUEL BLATCHFORD, one of the hardest-working and most productive justices ever to sit on the Supreme Court bench, was born March 9, 1820, in New York City. His paternal grandfather, a dissident English clergyman, had immigrated to Lansingburg, New York, in 1795. Blatchford's father, Richard Milford Blatchford, was born three years later in Stratford, Connecticut, into a family of seventeen children. As a young man, Richard Blatchford moved to New York and graduated from Union College. After teaching school and studying law, he began a successful law practice in New York City in 1820 and specialized in matters of mercantile law and finance. He married Julia Ann Mumford, the daughter of the well-known publicist, John R. Mumford, a man of some social standing and prestige. Blatchford subsequently became counsel and financial agent for the Bank of England and the Bank of the United States, invested his money well, and was elected to the New York legislature as a member of the Whig party.

New York governor William Seward, a family friend, asked Samuel Blatchford to be his private secretary and then to join his law firm, teaching him both politics and law. Seward became an outspoken opponent of slavery, served as secretary of state under Abraham Lincoln and Andrew Johnson, and was instrumental in securing the purchase of Alaska from Russia in 1867. *Source: National Portrait Gallery*

Despite his family's wealth and prominence, young Samuel was raised to appreciate frugality and industry. He attended William Forrest's school in Pittsfield, Massachusetts, before entering an academy in New York City. There he was a pupil of Dr. Charles Anthon, a well-known educator who stressed classical studies. At the age of thirteen Blatchford entered Columbia College, and he graduated four years later at the top of his class. Already on his way to a good career, Blatchford was to achieve early success, but not entirely without the advantages provided by his father's prestige and position. He began studying law in his father's New York office, but was invited by one of his father's closest friends, William Seward, to serve as his private secretary. Seward, a powerful Whig leader and astute politician, was governor of New York at the time. The daily contact and intimacy that developed between the governor and his bright young secretary afforded Blatchford unusual opportunities for professional development by giving him the chance to learn about public policy, not just the ordinary practice of law.

In 1842 Blatchford was admitted to the bar, and for the next three years he practiced with his father in New York City. He married Caroline Appleton of Lowell, Massachusetts, in 1844. Seward, his former mentor, was temporarily out of public office and invited Blatchford to join him and Christopher Morgan as a partner in their country law practice in Auburn, New York. Once again, Blatchford had a chance to develop his substantial talents. Working side-by-side with two seasoned veterans, he benefited from the advantages of a country practice. In addition to the variety of cases and causes handled by the Auburn firm, the slower pace of business provided the time for reading and research not enjoyed by successful New York City lawyers. Unquestionably, Blatchford's association with Seward, first as his private secretary and then as his law partner, contributed greatly to the young man's subsequent success.

After nine years in the Auburn partnership, Blatchford and Seward's nephew (and adopted son) established a new partnership, Blatchford, Seward, and Griswold, in New York City. Blatchford turned down a seat on the state supreme court in 1855 to devote himself fully to his admiralty and international law practice. During his legal career Blatchford undertook the laborious task of reporting federal court decisions, then uncollected in any continuing series. He began his reporting in 1852 with the first volume of *Blatchford's Circuit Court Reports,* a series that consisted mainly of admiralty cases—which involved shipping and maritime law—decided in New York's Second Circuit since 1845.

A New York City lawyer, Samuel Blatchford specialized in cases involving admiralty and maritime law. The industrious attorney collected all the decisions in the federal and district courts for New York and published them in a series. These cases mainly involved prize ship claims and commercial shipping, issues vital to a city that relied on the business of its busy port. The Brooklyn Bridge can be seen in the background of this 1887 view of New York Harbor. *Source: Library of Congress*

Ultimately publishing twenty-four volumes, Blatchford continued reporting his series even after being appointed a judge. He also published *Blatchford's and Howland's Reports,* an 1855 volume of admiralty cases decided between 1827 and 1837 in the District Court for the Southern District of New York, and *Blatchford's Prize Cases,* which covered prize cases in circuit and district courts of New York from 1861 to 1865. Blatchford's reporting provided an important addition to published admiralty law cases and substantially increased the practicing lawyer's access to the rapidly growing body of federal cases.

On May 3, 1867, Blatchford was appointed district judge for the Southern District of New York, succeeding Judge Samuel R. Betts. A distinguished admiralty judge, Betts had in his later years become taxed by the great questions of public law that flooded the courts during the Civil War and Reconstruction. It was hardly a secret that for some years Judge Betts had relied heavily upon Blatchford for assistance. As a consequence, Blatchford's appointment was received with great satisfaction and some relief by both the legal profession and the business community. The same year he was named to the bench, Blatchford was also appointed a trustee of his alma mater, Columbia University, a position he would hold until his death.

In 1872 Blatchford was appointed judge for the Second Circuit (the southern part of New York State). He quickly became known as one of the most industrious judges on the circuit, working long hours to keep up with the court's increasing case volume. As one colleague would later comment, "No yeoman on the banks of the Connecticut ever followed his plough with more patience than did Justice Blatchford labor." He expanded his expertise to include the evolving field of patent law, and his decisions generally stood the test of appeal to the U.S. Supreme Court.

After fifteen years of service in the federal judiciary, Blatchford seemed to many a logical choice for the Supreme Court seat vacated when Ward Hunt of New York announced his retirement in 1882. As a lifelong New Yorker, Blatchford was considered an appropriate choice to fill the "New York seat," so designated because an unbroken succession of New Yorkers had served on the Court since 1806. Moreover, Blatchford was a moderate Republican with excellent connections to the state's political and business elite. President Chester A. Arthur's first choice for the vacancy, however, was Roscoe Conkling, a New York politician and Arthur's political crony. Confirmed by the Senate, Conkling refused the appointment because he had presidential ambitions. The president's second choice, Sen. George F. Edmunds of Vermont, declined the nomination for personal reasons. On March 13 President Arthur finally turned to Blatchford, a quiet, modest man, who was easily confirmed in the Senate two weeks later by voice vote. He took his seat on the Court April 13, 1882, having been promoted into the serene atmosphere of the high court after "the constant collisions and the hand-to-hand conflicts," as one trial lawyer put it, of a trial judge.

An austere man with few interests outside the law, Blatchford was short of stature and sported a narrow white beard that framed his face. As a political and ju-dicial moderate, he consistently supported the opinions of the Court, writing only two dissents during his tenure. Blatchford wrote an impressive total of 430 majority opinions, although few dealt with major constitutional issues. Noted New York trial lawyer Joseph H. Choate said that on the Supreme Court Blatchford "exhibited that sweetness of temper, that uniform serenity and courtesy, which had always been inherent to his character." Blatchford became known for his particular encouragement of younger members of the legal profession. He showed courtesy to lawyers presenting oral arguments by not reading cases while they spoke.

During Blatchford's tenure, the Supreme Court was flooded with cases, deciding between 250 and 300 per term. A substantial number of these were admiralty and patent cases, and Blatchford proved invaluable to the Court by contributing his considerable expertise in those areas. Although the Court members were all overworked, Blatchford became known as a "workhorse," taking on 20 percent more than his fair share of the workload. One leading member of the Court's bar contended that "the power of labor in Justice Blatchford, from beginning to end, was unsurpassed and hardly [equaled] in any instance that I have ever known. No man that I have ever seen could take a great record in print or in manuscript and so soon pluck from it the vital facts of the case and the questions that had to be disposed of. He seemed to have only to turn it over to draw out the matters that were to be passed upon by himself." Even Chief Justice Melville Fuller observed that "the discharge of duty was an impulse, and toil a habit." There was only one instance in which Blatchford avoided work; he generally deferred to his brethren in matters affecting the administration of criminal justice, having found criminal cases particularly unsettling when he served on the lower bench.

After eight years of working in relative obscurity, Blatchford was thrust into the national spotlight when he was criticized for his interpretations of the Due Process Clause of the Fourteenth Amendment. In 1890 he wrote the pivotal opinion for *Chicago, Milwaukee and St. Paul Railway Co. v. Minnesota,* striking down an 1887 statute that established a railroad commission with power to establish the maximum rates that the railways could "reasonably" be allowed to charge to protect the public interest. He called the statute unconstitutional on the grounds that it did not allow a court to review the "reasonableness" of the commission's rates and therefore violated the railway's right to due process. Less than two years later, however, Blatchford ruled in *Budd v. New York* that the legislature could indeed set rates for businesses that affect the public interest. This decision seemed to contradict his previous thinking that the reasonableness of rates ultimately should be determined by the judiciary, not the legislature. Taken together, the two opinions drew fire from business and regulatory interests alike.

Blatchford was more successful with his cleverly crafted opinion for *Counselman v. Hitchcock* (1892), a rare nineteenth century case interpreting the Bill of Rights that would have lasting influence. In *Counselman,* Blatchford broadly interpreted the Fifth Amendment's right against self-incrimination, a ruling that gave individuals increased protection against federal authority.

After eleven years on the Court, Justice Blatchford died in Newport, Rhode Island, on July 7, 1893, following a short illness. At a memorial service, Attorney General Richard Olney called him the "model of a competent, well-trained, laborious, conscientious, and above all, modest public servant," who "bore his high honors so . . . quietly and unostentatiously as to attract to himself but slight notice from the public he so faithfully served." Blatchford's death ended the long tradition of the New York seat. At the time of his death, the two senators from New York were so antagonistic to President Grover Cleveland that they objected to both of the candidates from their state whom he proposed to fill the vacancy. The president was finally forced to abandon candidates from New York, choosing instead a Louisiana senator, Edward D. White, who was easily confirmed by his colleagues.

Lucius Q. C. Lamar
1888–1893

Source: Library of Congress

LUCIUS QUINTUS CINCINNATUS LAMAR, whose nomination in 1888 ended the Republican party's quarter-century monopoly on U.S. Supreme Court appointments, was born September 17, 1825, in Eatonton, Georgia. Descended from French Huguenots, his family owned extensive plantations in Georgia, dating from the mid-seventeenth century, and a large number of slaves. At the time of Lucius's birth, the Lamar family ranked among the elite landed aris-tocracy. His uncle, Mirabeau Buonaparte Lamar, served as the second president of the Republic of Texas. His father, for whom Lucius was named, was a circuit court judge in Georgia whose brief judicial career ended trag-ically in 1834 when, following months of depression, he committed suicide. Only the support of his close-knit family softened the emotional blow of this experience for Lucius, who was then nine years old.

His mother, Sarah Bird Lamar, moved to Covington

and placed Lucius, the fourth of her eight children, in the Methodist-run Georgia Conference Manual Labor School. In later years Lamar complained of the drudgery he endured at the school, but acknowledged the benefits of its mixture of strenuous academic study and farm labor. He graduated in 1841 and continued his Methodist education at Emory College, taking his degree four years later. Emory's president, Rev. Augustus B. Longstreet, had a profound influence on young Lamar's political philosophy. Longstreet, a strong advocate of states' rights and southern sectionalism, had lost his only son many years earlier and quickly took on the role of mentor to the fatherless student. Two years after graduation, Lamar married Longstreet's daughter Virginia. The couple had one son and three daughters.

Lamar studied law in his uncle's firm for two years in Macon, Georgia, before returning to Covington and opening a successful law office. In 1849 Longstreet became president of the University of Mississippi, in Oxford, and hired his son-in-law to teach mathematics. Encouraged by Longstreet, Lamar developed an interest in Mississippi politics and at the age of twenty-six he substituted for Sen. Jefferson Davis at an important public debate concerning the Compromise of 1850. Reports of Lamar's able performance against pro-compromise senator Henry Foote substantially advanced his political reputation.

Lamar's interest in politics continued when he returned to Covington in 1852 to establish with Robert Harper, a close friend, what quickly became a thriving law practice. A little more than a year later Lamar won a Democratic seat in the Georgia legislature from a county dominated by the Whig party. His law partnership dissolved shortly thereafter, and a restless Lamar moved to Macon to open a new office. Although his legal practice continued to prosper, if more modestly, Lamar's failure to win the Democratic nomination to Congress, together with his family responsibilities, per-

suaded him to return to Mississippi in 1855. He purchased numerous slaves and a large plantation he called Solitude, determined at age thirty to withdraw from public life.

This self-imposed exile did not last long. In 1856 he ran successfully for election to the U.S. House of Representatives on an extreme states' rights platform. Lamar's first speech on the floor of the House was a powerful defense of southern sectionalism. The speech won the praise of many southerners, but drew criticism from the Democratic party's national leaders for encouraging party disunity.

Lamar became a strong supporter and confidant of Davis, who sent him to the Democratic National Convention in April 1860 to urge the southern delegates to use moderation and adopt compromise measures. Despite this mission, when Stephen Douglas's moderate coalition won the party's support, Lamar protested by leading the Alabama and Mississippi delegations out of the convention hall. The resulting split within the Democratic party ensured the election of the Republican candidate, Abraham Lincoln. Had Lamar been willing to negotiate, he might have used his political influence to win a compromise within the party. In any case, Lamar took no pleasure from the party infighting or from the threat of war that resulted from his action. Confused, he again withdrew from politics, resigning from Congress in January 1861 after accepting a teaching post at the University of Mississippi.

Following Lincoln's election, Lamar showed a growing sense of loyalty to the southern cause. Although he continued to support compromise with the North, seeking either the creation of a southern republic or a constitutional amendment to safeguard southern rights, he became increasingly identified with the movement to secede from the Union. When Mississippi's secession convention met January 7, 1861, Lamar drafted the state's secession ordinance. His outspoken support for secession may have influenced his cousin, Justice John

Lucius Q. C. Lamar's participation in Mississippi politics led to his friendship with Sen. Jefferson Davis (above). During the Civil War, Lamar served briefly as an aide to Davis, who had been chosen president of the Confederate States of America. *Source: National Portrait Gallery*

Campbell, who resigned from the Supreme Court on April 30, shortly after the outbreak of the Civil War.

Lamar served as a lieutenant colonel of the Nineteenth Mississippi Regiment and fought at the Battle of Williamsburg in May 1862. Attacks of apoplexy, an illness he had suffered since childhood, forced him to withdraw from combat. In November he received an appointment as special commissioner to Russia to seek diplomatic recognition for the Confederacy. The continental European powers avoided granting such recognition, and a discouraged Confederate Senate soon recalled its foreign envoys. Lamar, whose appointment had never been made official, traveled between London and Paris hoping to achieve a diplomatic breakthrough,

but returned home in 1863 without ever having reached Russia. He spent the remainder of the war as an aide to Jefferson Davis and as a judge advocate for the Army of Northern Virginia.

The war proved disastrous for Lamar. He lost two brothers and most of his property. Many of his friends were either dead or in jail, and he was disqualified from holding public office. He sought refuge at the University of Mississippi in September 1866, assuming the position of professor of ethics and metaphysics that he had earlier accepted but never occupied because of the war. The following term he became a professor of law, which he found more compatible with the legal practice he had since resumed. In 1870, when his political enemies gained control of the university's governing board, Lamar resigned from the faculty and devoted himself to expanding his law practice.

Although the old southern aristocracy had lost power, Lamar won an easy victory in the congressional election of 1872. The House granted him a special pardon for his role in the Confederacy and allowed him to take his place with the Mississippi delegation. In Congress, Lamar repeatedly expressed his acceptance of the war's outcome and advocated reconciliation. He also sought to restore political control by the Democratic party in Mississippi. The Radical Republicans in Congress continued to oppose Lamar, but among more moderate politicians in both parties he earned increasing respect.

Lamar's springboard to national prominence was his eloquent address in memory of the leader of the Radical Republicans, Sen. Charles Sumner of Massachusetts, delivered in 1874. The speech, considered one of the finest orations ever delivered in the House, praised Sumner's achievements and emphasized the need for reconciliation and a renewed spirit of unity between North and South. The memorial won Lamar national acclaim as the "great pacificator." It also provoked sharp criticism from southern supporters who charged him with betraying the ideals they stood for during the war.

However, Lamar was not sacrificing his intense loyalty to the South in advocating reconciliation and nationalism. Instead, he had come to view the strengthening of the Union as the best way to serve southern interests.

Despite criticism from former Confederates, Lamar's shrewd political maneuvers gained him enough control of Mississippi politics to win election to the U.S. Senate in 1876. He occasionally broke with Mississippi party leaders and the wishes of his constituents, notably in his unsuccessful opposition to legislation authorizing the free coinage of silver. Despite his independence, Lamar's deep-rooted political support enabled him to win a successful bid for reelection to the Senate in 1881.

When Grover Cleveland, a Democrat, became president in 1885, he appointed Lamar as his secretary of the interior to balance his cabinet geographically and gain southern support for his administration. Lamar resigned from the Senate and accepted the post to show that the South was interested in serving "the best and highest interests of a common country." He was an honest and efficient administrator, who oversaw the stricter enforcement of land laws that resulted in the government reclaiming millions of acres of public lands. Lamar also began a new Indian policy that encouraged individual landholding and citizenship. In addition, his support for the Interstate Commerce Act of 1887 helped the administration to enact it.

Lamar ended his lonely isolation after the death in 1884 of his wife of thirty-seven years by marrying Henrietta Dean Holt in 1887. Also that year, Justice William B. Woods of Georgia died, creating a vacancy on the Supreme Court. Impressed by Lamar's abilities, President Cleveland decided to take the political risk of nominating the first Democrat to the high bench since the end of the Civil War, nearly twenty-five years before. Republican opponents rallied in an attempt to defeat the nomination, but a handful of Republican senators from western states, who felt the rejection would imply a ban on all Confederate veterans, joined with southern Democrats to confirm Lamar January 16,

Grover Cleveland (seated third from right) appointed Lucius Q. C. Lamar (fourth from right) his secretary of the interior in 1885. The only representative of the South in the cabinet, Lamar took pride in his efficiency and honesty as an administrator. He implemented a new policy that awarded U.S. citizenship to Indians and divided up reservation land to give each Indian family a 160-acre farm. Unfortunately, this "Americanization" policy, intended as humane, tended to destroy Indian culture and reduce Indian landholdings by half. *Source: Library of Congress*

As the nation industrialized, the Supreme Court often faced issues involving the extent of the federal government's power to regulate interstate commerce. Lucius Q. C. Lamar's opinion in *Kidd v. Pearson* (1888) defined commerce narrowly and made it more difficult for the government to regulate manufacturing, such as the making of cans (shown here) for use in meatpacking. *Source: Library of Congress*

1888, in a close, 32–28 vote. He took his oath of office two days later, at age sixty-two.

Lamar's five-year tenure on the bench was uneventful. His first few months were spent learning procedures because, as those who opposed his appointment had pointed out, he had no judicial experience. As a result, his style was humble: "I would be an impostor," he wrote a friend in 1889, ". . . if I were to allow you to believe that I am doing anything useful or even with moderate ability." As the years went by, however, he made more important contributions to the Court, relying now and then on his colleague, Justice Joseph P. Bradley, for advice.

Lamar's declining health, made worse by the Court's heavy workload, severely challenged his productivity. Despite physical weakness, however, Lamar kept up with an immense caseload, writing as many opinions—primarily dealing with land boundaries and titles—as all but the most productive justices. Lamar consistently voted to uphold the rights of business. In one of his most noted opinions, *Kidd v. Pearson* (1888), he narrowly defined commerce to exclude manufacturing: "Manufacture is transformation—the fashioning of raw materials into a change of form for use. The functions of commerce are different . . . the buying and selling . . . and transportation [of goods]." This legal distinction made it more difficult for Congress to regulate

manufacturing under the antitrust laws, which had the power to regulate only what was defined as commerce.

In another precisely reasoned opinion, *McCall v. California* (1890), Lamar protected interstate commerce from state interference. The case involved a license tax on a San Francisco agency that advertised, but did not sell, tickets on the company's railroad line from Chicago to New York. Lamar held that California's license tax on the agency was illegal because its business was exclusively concerned with interstate commerce. The state argued that because the agency conducted no commerce in California the state tax was unrelated to interstate commerce and was therefore legal. Lamar easily rejected this argument in his logical style: "To state such an argument is to refute it: for if the clause in question prohibits a state from taxing interstate commerce as it passes through its own territory, [then] the prohibition will extend to such commerce when it does not pass through its territory." The decision led to the protection of agencies engaged in interstate commerce from state taxes.

Following a series of apoplectic strokes, Justice Lamar died in Macon, Georgia, January 23, 1893, not far from where he was born. Of his departed friend, Chief Justice Melville Fuller said, "His was the most suggestive mind that I ever knew, and not one of us but has drawn from its inexhaustible store."

Melville W. Fuller
1888-1910

Source: Library of Congress

Born February 11, 1833, Melville Weston Fuller, the eighth chief justice of the United States, was the second son of Frederick A. Fuller, a successful lawyer who achieved a degree of prominence in his law practice, and Catherine Weston Fuller of Augusta, Maine. His father came from a distinguished old New England family that boasted an ancestor who signed the Mayflower Compact.

Despite this heritage, young Melville would scarcely benefit from his father's status and professional reputa-

tion. Two months after his birth, his parents separated, and his mother subsequently won a divorce from her husband on the grounds of adultery. She took custody of the two small boys and returned to live with her parents, giving piano lessons to help pay for her children's support. She remarried when Melville was eleven, but her sons continued to live with her father, a justice of the Maine Supreme Court.

In 1839 Frederick Fuller also remarried. The obligations of his new family left him either unable or unwilling to provide any substantial financial assistance to Melville or his brother. Financial insecurity and the social ramifications of a broken home were factors that significantly affected Fuller's childhood.

Politically, the Weston and Fuller families were Jacksonian Democrats in an area where Federalists and Whigs predominated. Although the Jacksonians carried much of the country in the presidential election of 1832, they were still a minority viewed with disdain in conservative Federalist Maine. Political antipathy was probably responsible for a rift within the South Parish Congregational Church, which eventually forced Fuller's mother and her parents to resign their membership when Melville was seven. The families then joined a local Episcopal church.

At the age of sixteen Fuller entered Bowdoin College in Brunswick, Maine. He received a strong classical education, became active in politics, and was elected to Phi Beta Kappa upon graduating in 1853. His most notable achievement at Bowdoin was not to be revealed in public honors, however, but in the records of the Athenaean Society, a literary club on campus. During his four years at college, Fuller read more books in the society's 5,000-volume library than any other student. As a child Fuller had shown a strong interest in reading and literature, and his grandfather's library had provided a ready supply of challenges. Although his earliest works are now best forgotten, Fuller was also a prolific poet. When his mother died in 1854, a grief-stricken son expressed his sorrow in verse.

After graduating from Bowdoin, Fuller read law in the office of an attorney in Bangor, Maine, and attended lectures for six months at Harvard Law School. This postgraduate experience would make Fuller the first chief justice of the United States to have any law school training. He was admitted to the Maine bar in 1855 and returned to Augusta to practice law. In keeping with his passion for politics, he also took a position as an editor at *The Augusta Age*, a Democratic newspaper

run by his father's brother. Just twenty-two years old, he was appointed city solicitor for Augusta and elected president of the Common Council. A year later, dejected over a broken engagement to a young woman, Fuller left Maine to seek his fortune in the West.

Settling in Chicago, Fuller joined the law firm of Pearson and Dow and practiced real estate and commercial law. Through a peculiar set of circumstances, Fuller became Dow's partner the following year. Pearson had been living for some time in a boardinghouse operated by a woman who eventually sued him for failing to pay his bills. Fuller represented the landlady and won a judgment in her behalf, despite Pearson's defense that he had been living with the claimant with her consent, and for her "accommodation, edification, entertainment and benefit." Deeply in debt, Pearson left the firm and moved to Springfield, Illinois, where he was later fatally shot by a policeman during a street brawl.

For the next several years Fuller devoted little of his time to his law practice. Instead, he became an active participant in local Democratic party and Chicago politics. Although he was opposed to slavery, he rejected the position of abolitionists as dangerous and socially divisive. He witnessed firsthand the civil strife that resulted from passage of the Kansas-Nebraska Act of 1857 while serving briefly as a correspondent for the *New York Herald*. In 1858 Fuller joined the political entourage of Stephen Douglas, who was campaigning for reelection to the U.S. Senate against a relatively unknown Republican candidate named Abraham Lincoln. Following Douglas's victory, Fuller turned his attention once again to the practice of law, but his heart was not really in it. He was constantly in debt, and the partnership with Dow was dissolved in 1860. Two years later he played an influential role at the Illinois Constitutional Convention and was elected in 1863 to the Illinois House of Representatives, serving for a year.

Fuller paused briefly from his political activities in 1858 to marry Calista Ophelia Reynolds. In the next few

Melville W. Fuller made his early career in the burgeoning city of Chicago, at first mainly in Democratic politics. He not only developed a successful legal practice but also was invited to join the Chicago Literary Club in 1877, having demonstrated a flair for writing and lecturing. His speculation in Chicago real estate reaped huge profits as the city, shown in this 1890s photograph, experienced a boom in population and industry. *Source: Library of Congress*

years he became the father of two daughters and was faced with growing responsibilities. In 1862 Fuller formed a new partnership with Charles H. Ham, which got off to a rocky start. The Civil War disrupted business, and Fuller went deeper into debt. In 1864 his wife died of tuberculosis, leaving him to raise his two young daughters by himself. Responding to this crisis, Fuller threw himself into his work, devoting his considerable energies for the first time to establishing himself as a legal practitioner. He quickly built a reputation and gained a new level of prominence and financial security.

Fuller's luck further improved in 1866 when he married Mary Ellen Coolbaugh, the daughter of one of Chicago's most distinguished bankers. The marriage was happy, and the couple had eight children, seven of whom survived childhood. Because of his new familial connections and his skill in meeting the legal needs of Chicago's leading businessmen, Fuller's practice flourished during the next decade. The city of Chicago chose him to litigate over its rights to property along Lake Michigan's shore. His own real estate investments in that area had begun to turn a handsome profit, and his earnings reached as high as $30,000 a year by the mid-1880s.

In a case that drew national attention, Fuller, a high Episcopalian, defended a dissident Episcopalian minister accused of "low church practices" by a church tribunal. Fuller's arguments on behalf of the defendant helped bring the Reformed Protestant Episcopal church in America into being. Fuller also gained a reputation during this period for his literary accomplishments. Joining the Chicago Literary Club in 1877, he met many of the intellectual leaders of his day and was frequently asked to address this distinguished group of local literati. Fuller was a cultivated man who enjoyed the theater and had a personal library of more than 6,000 volumes.

An influential Democrat, Fuller attended four Democratic national conventions and befriended Grover Cleveland. When Cleveland was elected president in 1884, he solicited Fuller's advice, especially concerning various appointments. Despite the president's efforts to press him into public service, Fuller declined offers to be chairman of the Civil Service Commission or solicitor general, pleading that the demands of his family and practice precluded his accepting a position in government. On April 30, 1888, Cleveland finally prevailed upon his friend to accept a position that even Fuller could not refuse—chief justice of the United States. The Republican-dominated Senate debated Fuller's war record (he had supported the Union with words but not with military service) and his ties to big corporations, but his nomination was confirmed by a vote of 41 to 20 July 20, 1888. His appointment corrected a geographic imbalance: there had not been a representative of the burgeoning Seventh Circuit, comprising Illinois, Indiana, and Wisconsin, on the Court since Justice David Davis had stepped down eleven years earlier.

In Washington, Fuller purchased an immense brick mansion to house his large family. His house frequently served as the site of the justices' conferences, as it was far more comfortable than the Court's inadequate accommodations in the Capitol. Although Fuller made friends easily by virtue of his gracious manner and subtle wit, he found it difficult to contend with the demands of Washington society. As a result of the Court's growing caseload and his considerable administrative responsibilities, Fuller withdrew from active participation in the social life of the capital. Such self-imposed seclusion has characterized the lives of many of the justices ever since.

Throughout his tenure on the Court, Chief Justice Fuller served with subtle diplomacy and quiet dignity. To promote harmony among his colleagues, he instituted the practice of having the justices shake hands with each other at the beginning of their private conferences and before going into the courtroom. An able lawyer of diverse experience, he did not seek personal fame, assigning opinions in the most prominent and important cases to his colleagues. Fuller was a gifted conciliator, respected by his fellow justices for his capable leadership and administrative skill. Justice Samuel F. Miller, who had served with three previous chief justices, and Justice Oliver Wendell Holmes, Jr., who went on to share the bench with three subsequent chief justices, both found Fuller to be the most successful chief justice they had known.

Fuller was a dapper man, with a large white mustache and a slight build. He was so short he had to have his seat elevated at the bench. He presided over the Court as the nineteenth century gave way to a new century and society underwent a massive transformation. Rapid industrialization, urbanization, and breakthroughs in science and technology not only modernized society but brought a host of new issues before the Court. Faced with enormous change, the Court maintained a general conservatism.

The Fuller Court, however, issued several decisions that revolutionized constitutional interpretation in the realm of economic development. Chief Justice Fuller

Melville W. Fuller presided over the Supreme Court when it decided a series of cases determining the strength of the Sherman Antitrust Act, which Congress had passed to break up monopolies. When President Theodore Roosevelt dissolved the Northern Securities Company, which held the stock of three major railroads and enjoyed a monopoly over transportation in the Northwest, the Court upheld his action. It ruled that stock transactions were within the realm of interstate commerce, which the federal government is allowed to regulate. The *Northern Securities* decision gave teeth to the antitrust act and unsettled the business community. *Source: Harlan Papers, University of Louisville*

Photographed in his Supreme Court chambers, Chief Justice Melville W. Fuller introduced the practice of having the justices shake hands with each other before meeting in conference or going on the bench. The custom, which continues today, is intended to remind the justices that they are pursuing a common goal despite whatever differences they may have. *Source: Library of Congress*

wrote the majority opinion in *United States v. E. C. Knight Co.* (1895), which held that the Sherman Antitrust Act of 1890 did not outlaw monopolies in manufacturing—in this case a company that refined 90 percent of the sugar sold in the United States. The decision substantially weakened the government's ability to enforce antitrust legislation. The same year Fuller wrote the opinion striking down the first general tax on personal income enacted by Congress. In 1908 he wrote the unanimous decision ruling that "secondary" boycotts (a union's attempt to organize workers in one factory while simultaneously boycotting the same company's products in other states) violated antitrust laws.

Fuller was also instrumental in securing passage of the Circuit Court of Appeals Act of 1891. He did it by inviting legislators to dinner to hear justices complain about their workload. The act finally relieved the justices of the burdensome duty of sitting as judges on the circuit courts and had the effect of cutting down their workload significantly.

When Cleveland was reelected to the White House in 1893, he offered his friend the position of secretary of state. Fuller declined to switch to a cabinet post because he thought doing so might lower the status of the Supreme Court. But he was interested in treaties and international law and was asked in 1897 to serve on the Venezuela-British Guiana commission that resolved a border dispute. The following year he was appointed to the Permanent Court of Arbitration in the Hague, on which he served for a decade while still continuing to fulfill his duties as chief justice.

As the years went by, the strain of his demanding schedule began to take its toll. He never fully recovered from the shock of losing his second wife in 1904; after her death his health was uneven, and his energy sapped. His physical condition deteriorated considerably in 1909, and it became obvious to Fuller and to the other members of the Court that he was beginning to fail noticeably under the strain of the Court's demanding pace. He served almost twenty-two years—the third-longest tenure of any chief justice—before dying of a heart attack July 4, 1910, at his summer home in Sorrento, Maine. Noting that Fuller had outlived most of his contemporaries, Justice Holmes accurately assessed the nation's response to his death: "I think the public will not realize what a great man it has lost. . . . He turned off the matters that daily called for action, easily, swiftly, with the least possible friction, with inestimable good humor that relieved any tension with a laugh."

David J. Brewer
1890–1910

Source: Portrait of David J. Brewer by Robert Lea MacCameron, Collection of the Supreme Court of the United States

DAVID JOSIAH BREWER was born June 20, 1837, in Smyrna, Asia Minor, in what is now Izmir, Turkey. His father, Rev. Josiah Brewer, was fresh from divinity training at Yale when he went to Asia Minor in 1836 to staff a school for women recently established by the Ladies Greek Association of New Haven. He was accompanied by his bride, Emilia Field Brewer, and her thirteen-year-old brother, Stephen J. Field.

The Brewer family stayed abroad for two and a half years before Reverend Brewer was named chaplain of St. Francis Prison in Wethersfield, Connecticut. Young David developed friendships with the inmates while playing on the grounds of the penitentiary. His parents imparted to him a strong moral, religious, and intellectual heritage, and he remained a member of the Congregational church and a supporter of missionary work throughout his life.

Emilia Brewer was the daughter of David Dudley Field of Stockbridge, Massachusetts, a distinguished

New England clergyman who reared a remarkable family. One of Emilia's brothers, Cyrus W. Field, was a successful paper manufacturer and merchant who promoted the first trans-Atlantic telegraph cable in 1866. Another was David Dudley Field, Jr., an eminent New York lawyer who was commissioned by the New York legislature in 1847 to prepare a code of civil procedure to modernize the common law. The Field Code, ultimately adopted by twenty-three states, became the basis of reformed procedure in U.S. federal courts and in England. Stephen Field, the brother who accompanied Emilia to Asia Minor, became chief justice of the California Supreme Court in 1859 and played an active role in the codification of California law before his appointment to the U.S. Supreme Court in 1863. He would sit on the high court for thirty-four years, eight of them with his nephew, David Brewer. Emilia's fourth brother, Henry Martyn Field, was a noted writer, editor, and clergyman. This extraordinary family had considerable influence on David Brewer's successful career.

At the age of fifteen, Brewer began his collegiate training at Wesleyan University in Middletown, Connecticut. He stayed there two years before enrolling at Yale University, his father's alma mater. He graduated with high honors in 1856. After college, Brewer entered the law office of his uncle, David Field, to study under his supervision. He also completed a one-year course at Albany Law School, graduating in 1858, and was admitted to the New York bar. Although urged to stay in New York, he followed the example of his Uncle Stephen and headed west. He tried his hand at prospecting for gold in Colorado and then moved to Leavenworth, Kansas, in September 1859.

Brewer worked briefly for a law firm, but then opened an office with a partner in the booming frontier town of Leavenworth. There he met Louise R. Landon of Burlington, Vermont, and they married in 1861. That same year, at age twenty-four, Brewer began his judicial career. He did so only reluctantly, however, having first set his sights on a seat in the legislature. He was initially appointed U.S. commissioner of the Circuit Court for the District of Kansas, an administrative position. The following year he was elected judge of the probate and criminal courts of Leavenworth County. In 1864 he won election as a judge of the First Judicial District. At the expiration of his term in 1868, Brewer was elected Leavenworth County attorney. Two years later, at age thirty-three, Brewer was elected to serve on the Kansas Supreme Court. He was reelected in 1876 and 1882.

Brewer's decisions during his fourteen years on the Kansas court, while well within the conventions of the time, exhibit an individualistic, even progressive, instinct. One of his cases was *Monroe v. May*, an 1872 decision that spelled out the rights of married women who owned money prior to marriage or earned it subsequently. This decision also defined a woman's interest in the family homestead. Brewer's interest in improving the legal status of women entering fields dominated by men is evident in *Wright v. Noell* (1876), in which he held that a woman, although not eligible to vote, could nonetheless hold the office of county superintendent of public instruction in Kansas. It was one of the pioneer decisions articulating the rights of women.

Another of his opinions brought him national recognition and foreshadowed decisions that would cause him to be remembered as one of the most property conscious justices in Supreme Court history. In *State v. Mugler* (1883) the defendant had been convicted for selling and manufacturing beer after Kansas passed a prohibition law. Brewer concurred in the conviction for selling the contraband, but thought the defendant should be compensated $7,500 for the depreciation of his brewing equipment because the state had arbitrarily decided to prohibit the manufacture of beer.

On March 31, 1884, Brewer resigned from the Kansas Supreme Court to accept President Chester A. Arthur's appointment to the Eighth Judicial Circuit. Five years later, when Stanley Matthews, an associate justice of the

Old Man Prohibition receives a cold reception from barmaids whose establishments are named for various states in this 1889 cartoon. As a judge on the Kansas Supreme Court, David J. Brewer upheld in 1883 the conviction of a beer manufacturer for continuing to sell his product after Kansas passed a prohibition law, but ruled that the defendant should be compensated for the depreciation in value of his brewing equipment due to state regulation.

Source: Library of Congress

U.S. Supreme Court, died, Republican senators Preston B. Plumb and John J. Ingalls of Kansas urged President Benjamin Harrison to appoint Brewer to the vacancy. The president received a letter from Brewer, however, recommending the appointment of Henry Billings Brown, a Michigan district judge and a former classmate at Yale. Brewer's generous praise for his friend so impressed the president that he nominated Brewer instead. Although his appointment was opposed by some prohibitionists, he was confirmed by the Senate, December 18, 1889, by a vote of 53 to 11.

The Court Brewer joined was grappling with issues arising from the change from a slow-moving, rural nation to a modern industrialized state. The resulting social unrest brought some highly controversial cases before the Court. Within four years of his appointment, the Court began using broad concepts of "life, liberty, and property" as a basis for invalidating the income tax, weakening the Sherman Antitrust Act, and permitting the use of the judicial injunction as a weapon against organized labor. Because of these decisions, Brewer has traditionally been considered a conservative stalwart

and the member of the Court most sympathetic to business interests and the rights of property.

His constitutional philosophy, however, was more complex than this label indicates. He hated the excess and greed of capitalism and respected man as an individual. According to Brewer, the individual, free and independent, must be protected from whatever seems to harm his liberty, whether corporation, union, government, or the individual himself. Brewer's early decisions on the Kansas Supreme Court indicate that his natural sympathies lay with the rugged settlers and homesteaders who settled the frontier, rather than with the adventurers and speculators who came later and sought government assistance to make their fortunes. The themes that show up in the early Brewer decisions—concern and admiration for the individual, the right of private capital to be unhampered by government regulations, the appeal to frontier values of self-denial and thrift, the references to Christian and biblical virtues—all attest to the strong religious and frontier influence that formed his judicial philosophy.

He favored the idea of limited government and of

limited state intervention into the economy. He reluctantly accepted that the federal and state governments had the power to regulate the rates charged by businesses, provided the regulation was fair, reviewable by courts, and limited to those enterprises that had received favors from government and thereby voluntarily incurred an obligation. The principle he supported for determining fairness was that regulation should neither deprive the company of profit nor burden it with unreasonable operating expenses.

In general, Brewer believed that "men should be able to take care of themselves and not be coddled by protection." Hence, he consistently dissented from opinions affirming *Munn v. Illinois,* a case decided just before his appointment. The decision had allowed the state legislature to regulate businesses dedicated to public use or serving the public interest. Brewer's dissenting opinions in two subsequent cases expressed the minor-

When Oregon imposed a sixty-hour maximum work week for women, laundry owner Curt Muller (with arms folded) argued that the law violated his rights. Writing the 1908 opinion for a unanimous Supreme Court that upheld the validity of state maximum working hour laws, David J. Brewer accepted sociological arguments about the effects of long hours on women's health and reproductive systems. *Courtesy Mrs. Neill Whismont and the Portland Chamber of Commerce*

ity view that the "public interest" doctrine of *Munn* unlawfully and unreasonably interfered with private enterprise. However, when it came to the biggest monopolies of the day—the trusts and holding companies—Brewer consistently voted with the majority to uphold regulation.

Cases involving a state's use of its police power to regulate business seemed to give Brewer the most difficulty. He had no objection to a state regulating goods deemed harmful, such as alcohol, but he continued to follow the reasoning that he expressed in *State v. Mugler* that compensation should be paid for all value destroyed by regulation. Because such compensation was often impossible as a practical matter, Brewer carefully examined the necessity of regulation in each case.

Brewer is most remembered by constitutional scholars for his 1908 opinion in *Muller v. Oregon,* a case that tested the constitutionality of a law imposing a sixty-hour maximum work week for women employed in laundries and factories. Three years earlier, in the *Lochner v. New York* bakery case, the Court had determined by a narrow majority that a state law setting maximum working hours was unconstitutional. To distinguish *Muller* from *Lochner,* Louis D. Brandeis, the special counsel for Oregon, knew he would have to deal less with literal issues of law and more with issues of economics and sociology. Therefore, the famous "Brandeis brief"—more than 100 pages long—used statistical studies to show that long hours of labor had direct and undesirable effects on the health, safety, and morals of working women, evils that could be remedied only by statutes limiting their working hours. Brandeis's argument was just the sort of reasoning that appealed to Justice Brewer, who had shown receptiveness to such social and economic arguments in prior cases. Writing for a unanimous Court, Brewer said that Brandeis's studies were not "technically speaking, authorities, and in them there is little or no discussion, of the constitutional question presented to us for determination, yet

A strong peace advocate, David J. Brewer (first row, left) was elected president of the commission empowered to arbitrate the boundary dispute between British Guiana and Venezuela that had been lingering for more than half a century. Chief Justice Melville W. Fuller (first row, second from right) was also a member of the commission, photographed in Paris in 1899, after negotiating a settlement that generally favored Great Britain's claim.
Courtesy of the New York Historical Society

they are significant of a widespread belief" that a woman is entitled to special legislative protection because "the performance of maternal functions place[s] her at a disadvantage."

During his twenty years on the Court, Brewer spoke out passionately on a variety of political issues. He supported causes such as education, charities, women's voting rights, and residency rights for Chinese aliens in America. He lectured on American citizenship at Yale University and corporate law at Columbian (now George Washington) University, and he was a prolific writer of books, pamphlets, and articles. Brewer also edited collections of the world's finest speeches and essays.

A staunch and outspoken advocate of peace, Brewer was appointed in 1895 to the congressional commission to oversee the disputed boundary between Venezuela and British Guiana. The commission, which elected him as its president, brought about a successful arbitration with Great Britain, calming fears of war. In 1907 Brewer became one of the founders of the American Society of International Law, an organization that fa-

vored arbitration to settle international disputes. During the Spanish-American War, Brewer said that America's strength lay "not so much in its army and navy as its public schools" and cautioned against "the dazzle of military glory." He criticized his country's seizure of Puerto Rico and the Philippines, former Spanish possessions, in the imperialist aftermath of the war, but reasoned that the liberation of Cuba had justified the conflict with Spain.

Brewer was physically large and vigorous and notoriously clumsy with mechanical gadgets. He played cards and read detective stories for relaxation and was widely known as a storyteller. He was considered by his colleagues and contemporaries a clear and profound thinker, and he was admired for his warm personal qualities, affability, patience, and ability to deal with people. Brewer's first wife died in 1898, and he married a Washington woman named Emma Miner Mott three years later.

While still on the Court, Justice Brewer died suddenly of a stroke March 28, 1910, at his home in Washington, D.C.

Henry B. Brown
1891–1906

Source: Harvard Law Library

"I WAS BORN of a New England Puritan family in which there has been no admixture of alien blood for two hundred and fifty years," was the way Henry Billings Brown introduced himself in his autobiographical memoir. The date of his birth was March 2, 1836, and the place was the small village of South Lee, Massachusetts. His father, Billings Brown, ran flour and saw mills in the village, and Henry remembered with pleasure the time he spent at his father's businesses. He speculated that he enjoyed being around the machinery so much he probably would have taken up the work for his own career if his father had not sold his holdings and moved to the nearby town of Stockbridge in 1845. Four years later the family moved again, to Ellington, Tolland County, Connecticut.

The move from South Lee gave Henry Brown much greater educational opportunities. He went to the local private academy, where he began his study of Latin, which he believed "should be the foundation of the intellectual equipment of every educated man." In any case, he was better at languages than at mathematics. His parents, though not well educated themselves, placed high value on schooling for their naturally bright son, who was reading before he was five. His precocious reading probably advanced his education, but it also may have contributed to his eye trouble. While he was still very young, he developed a severe eye inflammation, the results of which troubled him throughout his life. His mother, Mary Tyler Brown, was devoutly religious, read literature avidly, and excelled at painting and drawing. Because of her, Henry was a regular attendant of the Protestant church in his youth.

Brown was sent to an academy in Monson, Massachusetts, for two years before he entered Yale University in 1852. He was only sixteen, and because of his immaturity it took him about two years to find himself and settle down to serious work. Unlike most incoming freshmen, he did not have to make up his mind about a career; his father had already decided upon the law as a suitable profession. "I felt," Brown wrote later, "that my fate was settled, and had no more idea of questioning [his father's decision] than I should have had in impeaching a decree of Divine Providence." He graduated in 1856 with "respectable," though not high, standing in

his class, which included David Brewer, who later became his colleague on the Supreme Court.

As a graduation present Henry's father gave him a year's trip to Europe. He was much distressed by the working conditions of the sailors on his ship, but viewed his overseas travel as his single most valuable educational experience.

When he returned in 1857, Brown began the study of law in Ellington, Connecticut, but he found the revivalist environment created by the local church authorities unacceptable. He transferred his study of the law first to Yale and subsequently to Harvard, where he spent six happy months. He would have liked to finish his law studies at Harvard, but decided instead to begin his career, not in New England, but in the West. In 1859 he moved to Detroit, a growing city of 45,000 inhabitants. Although he found the people "extremely hospitable," he confessed that his "prejudices are still in some respects in favor of the East."

After finishing his legal apprenticeship in the summer of 1860, Brown received his first political appointment, as U.S. deputy marshal for Detroit. This post had an important effect on his later career because it put him in contact with men in the shipping business who came

Henry B. Brown was appointed U.S. deputy marshal for Detroit in 1860. The experience he gained in the legal problems of the shipping business led Brown to specialize in admiralty law when he became a partner in a local law firm. Already a bustling harbor, Detroit is viewed here from the Canadian shore in 1836, the year before Michigan became a state. *Source: New York Public Library, Stokes Collection*

to the office with their legal problems. Detroit was a busy port city, and Brown developed an interest in shipping law. In 1863 he was promoted to assistant U.S. attorney for the Eastern District of Michigan, a position that further broadened his contacts and laid the foundation for a successful legal practice.

The Civil War had little effect on Brown. He hired a substitute to perform his military service, which was not an unusual practice for a man of means. He was not a proponent of emancipation, but he was a loyal Republican and a strong supporter of the Union and Abraham Lincoln. The most important event of the period was his marriage in 1864 to Caroline Pitts, the daughter of a wealthy Detroit family. When her father died in 1868, she inherited much of the family fortune. This inheritance made Brown financially independent and able to accept appointment to a prestigious but low-paying position as judge of Wayne County Circuit Court. He failed to win his bid for a full term, however, in the November 1868 election.

Brown then formed a law partnership with John S. Newberry and Ashley Pond, specializing in shipping cases. He had time to participate in Detroit politics, including a failed attempt to win the Republican nomination for Congress from Detroit in 1872. Three years later, President Ulysses S. Grant appointed him a U.S. district judge for Eastern Michigan, a position he came to greatly enjoy.

During his fourteen years as a federal judge, Brown earned a national reputation as an expert on shipping law, technically known as admiralty law. He also enjoyed teaching regularly at the law school of the University of Michigan, where a student publication praised him for being "so conversant with his subject" and for his "kindly manner."

On December 26, 1890, Brown wrote President Benjamin Harrison to thank him for "a magnificent Christmas gift"—appointment to the U.S. Supreme Court. He told the president the position was "the culmination of all my earthly ambitions." Brown filled the vacancy left by the death of Justice Samuel Miller. It seems clear that Brown wanted the post and worked to win it. He gave much of the credit for his successful quest to his good friend Judge Howell Jackson of Tennessee, who personally made Brown's case with the president. At Brown's urging, Harrison named Jackson to the Court when Lucius Q. C. Lamar died.

Both in Washington and Detroit, Brown's appointment was a surprise, but the public response was favorable. The *Washington Post* headlined its story, "Appointed on His Record Only," and the *Detroit Free Press,* a strongly Democratic paper, captioned its story, "A Good Man For the Place," and warmly praised him. Not surprisingly, he had no trouble being confirmed December 29, 1890.

At the time of his appointment, Brown was fifty-four years old. He was a little above medium height, solidly built, and, unlike the president and most of his colleagues, cleanshaven. He was seen as a warm person who enjoyed a busy social life and foreign travel. His wife was active in the Presbyterian church, but Brown was not greatly interested in theological questions or organized religion. Although he liked Detroit, he looked forward to moving to Washington, which he recognized offered him a much richer professional and social life.

In his fifteen years on the Court, Brown generally took on the role of the centrist judge who avoided dissents and tried to find a compromise solution to difficult issues. His associates on the Court saw him as fairminded, willing to listen to the arguments presented and to be convinced by them. Justice William Day said Brown "had an admirable judicial style" and described him as

one of the most agreeable of colleagues . . . absolutely free from all jealousy and bitterness. He always came to the consultation room acquainted with the cases from careful attention to the arguments and full consideration of the

To protect mine workers, Utah passed a law limiting their employment to eight hours a day; a mine owner challenged the regulation. Henry B. Brown recognized in *Holden v. Hardy* (1898) that the statute abridged the employer's freedom to contract workers, but he ruled that the state had the right to protect the health of its citizens. *Source: Utah State Historical Society*

records and briefs. He took a personal part in the discussions at the conference table at all times, earnest in the statement of his views, but at the same time good tempered and courteous in their expression. He was particularly helpful in the Court in patent and admiralty cases, in both of which branches of law he had experience before coming to Washington.

Justice Brown saw himself as moderately conservative, and he usually stood with the majority of his colleagues in their view of government and the Constitution. Writing for the Court in *Holden v. Hardy* (1898), Brown upheld states' rights to regulate labor conditions; his argument expressed great concern for the hazards posed by the mining industry for its workers. He was, however, also in the majority in *Lochner v. New York* (1905), which held invalid a maximum hours law for bakers. In his view, the liberty to make contracts was such a fundamental right that it could be abridged by the government only for a good reason. He did not see the regulation of bakers' hours as a true health and safety issue, as he had for miners.

In another case, Brown's strongly worded dissent argued with passion to uphold the legality of the federal income tax. "I hope," Brown wrote, "it [the decision] may not prove the first step toward the submergence of the liberties of the people in a sordid despotism of wealth. . . . I cannot escape the conviction that the decision of the court in this great case is fraught with immeasurable danger to the future of the country, and that it approaches the proportions of a national calamity."

The most significant case associated with Brown was his majority opinion in *Plessy v. Ferguson,* an 1896 decision clearly reflecting the conventional viewpoint. The case originated when Homer Plessy, a black Louisiana resident, took a seat in a railway coach reserved for whites. He was arrested and ultimately convicted of violating a Louisiana statute that required separating the races in railroad cars. Plessy's lawyers challenged the constitutionality of the law on the grounds that it conflicted with both the Thirteenth and Fourteenth Amendments to the Constitution. Brown, speaking for the Court, concluded that there was no violation of the Constitution, and that the Fourteenth

JIM CROW LAW.

UPHELD BY THE UNITED STATES
SUPREME COURT.

Statute Within the Competency of
the Louisiana Legislature and
Railroads—Must Furnish Separate Cars for Whites and
Blacks.

Washington, May 18.—The Supreme
Court today in an opinion read by Justice Brown, sustained the constitutionality of the law in Louisiana requiring the railroads of that State to provide separate cars for white and colored passengers. There was no interstate commerce feature in the case
for the railroad upon which the incident occurred giving rise to case—Ples-
sey vs. Ferguson—East Louisiana
railroad, was and is operated wholly
within the State, to the laws of Congress of many of the States. The
opinion states that by the analogy of
the laws of Congress, and of many of
states requiring establishment of separate schools for children of two races
and other similar laws, the statute in
question was within competency of
Louisiana Legislature, exercising the
police power of the State. The judgment of the Supreme Court of State
upholding law was therefore upheld.
Mr. Justice Harlan announced a very
vigorous dissent saying that he saw
nothing but mischief in all such laws.
In his view of the case, no power in
the land had right to regulate the enjoyment of civil rights upon the basis
of race. It would be just as reasonable and proper, he said, for states to
pass laws requiring separate cars to
be furnished for Catholic and Protestants, or for descendants of those of
Teutonic race and those of Latin
race.

Attorney and equal rights activist Albion Tourgée argued the
case of Homer Plessy, a black
man who tested Louisiana's Jim
Crow laws by riding in a railroad
car reserved for white passengers.
Rejecting Tourgée's arguments,
Justice Henry B. Brown wrote
the decision in *Plessy v. Ferguson*
(1892) and established the separate but equal doctrine that
would persist for more than sixty
years. "The Constitution is col-
orblind," the celebrated phrase
from John M. Harlan's lone dissent, was suggested by Tourgée's
brief. *Source: National Geographic Society*

Amendment protected only political, not social, equality.

Separation, the Court pointed out, did not mean inequality. Brown's opinion further reasoned that powers
to separate races "have been generally, if not universally
recognized" as falling within the police power of states,
and it cited school segregation as the most common example. The Court saw the main weakness in Plessy's defense to be the assumption that enforced separation of
the two races stamped blacks as inferior. "If this be so,
it is . . . solely because the colored race chooses to put
that construction upon it," Brown wrote.

The decision was in keeping with the times, and only
one justice, John M. Harlan, dissented. It received very
modest press attention. The reaction is not surprising,
for during this time in American history legislatively
imposed segregation was expanding and widely accepted in the South and the border states. Brown's separate-but-equal doctrine was not overturned until 1954.

During his tenure, Brown enjoyed a good personal
and professional relationship with Chief Justice
Melville Fuller. He wrote to Fuller, for example, to tell
him of his grief after the unexpected death of his wife
in the summer of 1901 while the Browns were traveling
abroad. In 1904, at the age of sixty-seven, Brown married Josephine E. Tyler, his cousin's widow.

As he grew older, Brown became totally blind in one
eye and largely blind in the other. Eye problems made
his work on the Court increasingly difficult. Believing
that "the country was entitled to the services of judges
in the full possession of their faculties," he submitted
his resignation on his seventieth birthday. After his retirement, he traveled abroad before settling in Bronx-
ville, New York, where he died September 4, 1913.

George Shiras, Jr.
1892-1903

Source: Portrait of George Shiras, Jr., by A. L. Dahlberg, Collection of the Supreme Court of the United States

GEORGE SHIRAS, JR., the only justice with no judicial or political experience prior to his appointment to the Supreme Court, was born January 26, 1832, in Pittsburgh, Pennsylvania. His mother, Eliza Herron Shiras, was the daughter of a Presbyterian minister. The Shiras family was of Scotch ancestry and had lived in America since 1765. Shiras's grandfather, a judge for whom he was named, migrated to western Pennsylvania with the militia to suppress the Whiskey Rebellion, a 1794 uprising against the government's enforcement of a whiskey tax. He started Pittsburgh's first brewery and passed the thriving business on to his son. Shiras's father made enough money to quit the brewery business in his early thirties and buy farmland on the banks of the Ohio River, some twenty-two miles from Pittsburgh. It was there that Shiras and his two brothers spent their early years, helping out on the farm.

Converters make Bessemer steel in this 1886 wood engraving of a Pittsburgh factory. An attorney in Pittsburgh for more than thirty years, George Shiras benefited enormously from the city's steel manufacturing boom and counted industrial tycoons among his many corporate clients. *Source: Library of Congress*

Shiras attended Ohio University in Athens, Ohio, from 1849 to 1851 and then transferred to Yale University. Greek was his favorite course at Yale, which may account for his noted ability to write clearly and persuasively. He earned his B.A. in 1853, picking up a Phi Beta Kappa key along the way. Shiras went on to study law at Yale, but left before receiving his degree. In 1883 he would be awarded an honorary doctorate of law from Yale, the first alumnus to be so honored.

Shiras read law in the Pittsburgh office of Judge Hopewell Hepburn. He was admitted to the Allegheny County Bar in 1855, but moved to Dubuque, Iowa, to practice law with his brother, Oliver Perry Shiras, who later became a federal district judge in northern Iowa.

On New Year's Eve 1857, Shiras married Lillie E. Kennedy, the daughter of a Pittsburgh manufacturer. The couple had two sons, both of whom followed their father into the legal profession. The eldest, George Shiras III, would serve from 1903 to 1905 as a U.S. representative from Pennsylvania. After marrying, Shiras returned to Pittsburgh to become Judge Hepburn's law partner.

When Hepburn died in 1862, Shiras carried on the lucrative practice independently. He remained in his native city, practicing law, until his appointment to the Supreme Court thirty years later. His major clients were Pittsburgh's great industrial corporations, which were reaping enormous profits from the mining of coal and the manufacture of steel and iron. At this time, the railroads also were developing into enormously profitable enterprises, and Shiras tapped into this wealth by representing the powerful Baltimore and Ohio Railroad. As a result, he developed close social ties with the leading business magnates and steel barons who were building their industrial empires. In spite of the success of his legal career, he remained indifferent to money. Once he presented a bill to a client, he did not follow up if payment was not received.

Much of his success came from his reputation as an able practitioner with good judgment and complete integrity. A modest, quiet man, Shiras had a dignified yet unpretentious manner. Politically, he was a moderate Republican who was not involved in party politics. In 1881 Shiras refused the Pennsylvania legislature's offer of a U.S. Senate seat. He did, however, agree to serve as a presidential elector in 1888.

On July 19, 1892, when Shiras was sixty years old, President Benjamin Harrison nominated him to the U.S. Supreme Court to replace Justice Joseph P. Bradley of New Jersey, who had recently died. This office was the first public post held by Shiras, who had spent thirty years in private practice and had no judicial experience. Indeed, the president selected Shiras precisely because he was a capable lawyer who had stayed out of his state's Republican political machine. Shiras had been recommended to the president by Secretary of State James Blaine, Shiras's cousin.

At first, Shiras's appointment was vigorously opposed by his state's two U.S. senators, James Donald Cameron and Matthew S. Quay, who were members of Pennsylvania's Republican political establishment. President Harrison had not practiced the usual courtesy of consulting them before sending Shiras's name to the Senate. However, once they realized that Shiras commanded the support of the Pennsylvania bar, the press, Rep. John Dalzell of Pennsylvania, prominent business leaders such as steel magnate Andrew Carnegie, and many of Shiras's influential Yale classmates, Cameron and Quay withdrew their opposition. Their stance had been purely political and reflected the anger of the state Republican machine at the appointment of an independent Republican to the nation's highest court without its consent. Shiras was confirmed by voice vote a week after his name was submitted.

Although not thought of as a particularly colorful man, Shiras was, in many ways, a nonconformist. He had bushy whiskers that he refused to clip, despite occasional derogatory comments. He never smoked or used the telephone, and he avoided Washington's social whirl, even refusing to attend weddings and funerals. He loved wildlife and was an avid fisherman. He enjoyed playing card games with friends and devoted much of his time to reading history, theology, and the works of British novelists Charles Dickens and William Thackeray. According to a contemporary, Shiras was regarded by his associates and friends as engaging, whimsical, and unpretentious.

Shiras's nearly eleven years on the Court showed him to be a capable, if undistinguished, justice. Like the majority of his brethren, he was considered conservative, and many of his opinions were based on precedent. He wrote only fourteen dissenting opinions because he believed that, whenever possible, the Court should be unanimous. He carried his full weight on the Court, writing 259 majority opinions, considered a reasonable number. Most were on procedure, although he also wrote a number of opinions on constitutional law and property. He was an expert legal technician, and his opinions were respected for their logic and analysis. The cases in which he was involved were not particularly notable, but they concerned basic issues of importance to the public.

Justice Shiras's highest profile moment on the Court came in the celebrated income tax case of 1895, when he allegedly switched his vote on reargument and brought about the death of the income tax in a 5–4 decision. The case, *Pollock v. Farmers' Loan & Trust Co.* (1895), involved the constitutionality of the first national peace-time tax on personal income, which resulted from passage of the Wilson-Gorham Tariff Act during President Grover Cleveland's administration. The Court held that tax on real estate income was unconstitutional unless it was levied in the manner required for a direct tax—that is, apportioned according to state population. As to

Fear of an influx of cheap labor led to anti-Chinese rallies, such as this late nineteenth century gathering by the Workingmen's party in San Francisco. Congress passed a number of laws excluding Chinese immigrants and denying Chinese-Americans basic rights. Although in *Wong Wing v. United States* (1896) the Supreme Court unanimously struck down an act of Congress, most turn-of-the-century restrictions of the rights of Chinese-Americans were upheld. *Source: Library of Congress*

other forms of income, the Court was evenly divided. With Justice Howell Jackson not voting because of illness, the decision rendered on April 8, 1895, was 4–4. A reargument was then ordered, and a second decision was reached May 20, in which Jackson did participate. By a vote of 5–4, the Court held the entire tax invalid. This decision resulted in bitter attacks on the Court and was followed, in 1913, by Congress adopting the Sixteenth Amendment, which provided for a national income tax.

In the 5–4 vote, Justice Jackson voted with the minority, which meant that one of the justices who found the tax constitutional during the first case changed his mind for the second vote. Because there was no opinion written and no breakdown of the vote in the earlier 4–4 decision, it is not known who switched his vote. Many believe it was Shiras. In 1928, however, Chief Justice Charles Evans Hughes suggested that Shiras was not the one who changed his vote; some Supreme Court scholars think either Justice Horace Gray or Justice David Brewer changed his mind.

An examination of his opinions shows that Shiras supported challenges to new extensions of national power that were said to imperil states' rights or individual rights. In addition to voiding the income tax, he tended to support curtailing the power of the Sherman Antitrust Act in regulating monopolies and limiting the effectiveness of the Interstate Commerce Act. He joined the unanimous decision in *Wong Wing v. United States* (1896), which held that a congressional act mandating stiff penalties for illegal Chinese aliens was unconstitutional. He proved himself a defender of civil liberties in the independent stance he took in his dissent in *DeLima v. Bidwell* (1901), where he argued that full constitutional rights should be extended to residents of American territories.

In three major cases Shiras voted with the majority to uphold government regulation against challenges from the states, relying on the Due Process Clause of the Fourteenth Amendment to restrict private enterprise in the public interest. In *Brass v. North Dakota* (1894) Shiras joined the Court in sustaining government price regulation. He voted with the majority in *Holden v. Hardy* (1898), which validated a maximum working hours statute for miners in the state of Utah to protect them from the hazardous conditions in underground mines. Three years later, in *Knoxville v. Harbison,* Shiras voted to sustain a Tennessee statute that barred payment of wages in company store scrip.

He also provided one of the eight majority votes in *Plessy v. Ferguson* (1896), which established the separate but equal doctrine of racial segregation.

In general, Shiras is remembered as an impartial judge and an independent thinker. He enjoyed good relations with the other members of the Court and was particularly fond of Chief Justice Melville Fuller. The two shared a love for Dickens's novels, and, when attorneys argued cases before the bench, Fuller and Shiras would often exchange notes designating them as various characters from the books. A contemporary reported that Shiras "is said to be the liveliest spirit on the bench, although a spectator would think him about ready to expire with ennui, so grave and unmoving is his countenance."

Shiras had long said that he would retire from the Court after ten years of service. True to his word, he submitted his resignation February 23, 1903. President Theodore Roosevelt appointed William R. Day to replace him. Shiras lived twenty-one years in retirement, considered a record for Supreme Court justices during that time. Most justices had either died while still serving on the bench or retired because of ill health. Shiras enjoyed his last years in his typical low-key fashion, surrounded by his family. He split his time between his home in Florida and a summer home on the Michigan side of Lake Superior. He had one last moment of fame when the Sixteenth Amendment was adopted in 1913 and newspaper accounts focused attention on the question of the switched vote in the 1895 income tax case.

The former justice died in Pittsburgh, August 2, 1924, at the age of ninety-two. His death was caused by a fall followed by pneumonia. No particular notice had been taken at his retirement, and his death attracted little attention. His son George began a biography of his father. When he died at age eighty-three, his nephew, Winfred Shiras, completed the book. *Justice George Shiras, Jr., of Pittsburgh* was published in 1953.

Howell E. Jackson
1893–1895

Source: Collection of the Supreme Court of the United States

HOWELL EDMUNDS JACKSON was born April 8, 1832, in Paris, Tennessee, a small town just south of the Kentucky border in the western part of the state. He was the eldest child of Alexander Jackson, a university-trained doctor, and Mary Hurt Jackson, the daughter of a Baptist minister. Descended from old Virginia families, the Jacksons migrated west from their native state two years before Howell's birth. In 1840 the family relocated southwest to the town of Jackson in Madison County. Dr. Jackson was elected as a Whig to two terms in the state legislature before serving as Jackson's mayor from 1854 to 1856. Young Howell attended the local preparatory school, where a schoolmate remembered him as serious and hardworking except "when the skating was good."

Jackson studied Greek and Latin, the traditional curriculum, at Western Tennessee College. After graduating in 1850, he followed his father's wishes and continued his education at the University of Virginia. Two years later, he graduated with high honors. Jackson re-

266

turned to Tennessee to clerk with two distinguished lawyers, Judge A. W. O. Totten of the Tennessee Supreme Court and former U.S. representative Milton Brown. Then followed a year at Cumberland Law School in the city of Lebanon. Jackson received his law degree in 1856, passed the bar, and returned to his hometown to set up a legal practice. His extensive education made him better trained than most attorneys of his time.

Despite his formal training and his father's local prominence, Jackson was unable to attract sufficient clients in such a small town. In 1858 he moved to the growing city of Memphis, where he formed a partnership with David M. Currin, a well-established attorney fifteen years his senior. Currin was an active Democrat whose firm represented corporations and railroads. One of their clients was a local banker whose daughter, Sophia Malloy, caught Jackson's fancy. They were married in 1859 and had six children, two of whom died in infancy.

When the Civil War broke out, Jackson opposed Tennessee's secession from the Union. Unlike his younger brother William, who became a brigadier-general in the Confederate Army, he did not enter military service. Nonetheless, as did many southern Whigs, Howell remained loyal to the South. He served the Confederacy by acting as a receiver of property confiscated from Unionists, which involved commandeering the sequestered property, selling it at auction, and delivering the proceeds to the state treasury. Further proof of his loyalty to the Confederate cause was his unsuccessful effort in 1863 to secure a post as a military judge in a Confederate court, even though the army was by then demoralized and nearing defeat. He wrote to a friend, "I am exceedingly anxious to get the appointment, as it is in the line of my profession [and] suited to my tastes." Jackson's considerable judicial aspirations would not be met until 1875.

At war's end, he took the oath of allegiance to the Union, which enabled him to resume practicing law in Memphis, this time with a new partner, Bedford M. Estes. Their firm prospered, representing prominent banks, businesses, and railroad companies, including many northern interests. Jackson became a Democrat and, in the words of his friend Sen. George Hoar, "was anxious to have the South take her place as a great manufacturing community."

The same year that the Panic of 1873 triggered an economic depression, epidemics of smallpox, cholera, and yellow fever crippled Memphis. Jackson's wife died in the epidemic, and he was left to care for his children. He returned to Jackson, where he eventually entered into a partnership with Gen. Alexander Campbell. Because the town was only one-eighth the size of Memphis and offered fewer corporate clients, Jackson began to take on criminal cases.

He married again the following year. Mary E. Harding was the daughter of Gen. W. G. Harding of Nashville, who owned a magnificent 3,000-acre plantation and stock farm, which he split into two parts. West Meade was given to Mary, Howell, and their seven children (they had three daughters together), while the main estate, Belle Meade, was retained by Selene, Mary's sister and the wife of Jackson's brother William. The two brothers enjoyed the sporting life—fox-hunting and raising thoroughbreds. The marriage not only gave Howell Jackson's children a mother, but also afforded him social connections to many prominent Tennesseans. Despite his professional and social successes, he complained of the difficulty in collecting legal fees from his clients and resulting financial worries. The splendor of his wife's estate gave many the false impression that he was wealthy.

Jackson's judicial career began when he was appointed a special judge to the Madison County chancery court. This position was followed in 1875 by an appointment to the Court of Arbitration for Western Tennessee, a temporary court designed to assist the

Howell E. Jackson applied the expertise in patent law he had gained on the Sixth Federal Circuit Court to the many cases involving patents for inventions meeting the criteria of novelty and utility, such as this lifeboat. When patent disputes reached the Court, the justices were particularly supportive of pioneering inventions of great social utility such as the telephone or electric lamp. *Source Library of Congress*

state supreme court in disposing of the accumulated backlog of war-related cases. When the court was disbanded, Jackson allowed his name to be placed before the Democratic nominating committee for a seat on the state supreme court. He lost by a single vote.

Jackson's ambitions were judicial rather than political, a preference that reflected the growing professional-

ism of his field. Nevertheless, he became involved in the "state-credit" wing of the Democratic party, which believed that Tennessee had an obligation to pay off its debts, in contrast to the "low-tax" Democrats, who favored virtual repudiation of the debts. His stand in the controversy, the burning issue of the day, resulted in his election to the state legislature in 1880, even though he had made little effort to seek the office. The following year he was elected to the U.S. Senate, having won the support of many Republicans in addition to the state-credit Democrats. One Republican justified his crossover vote by describing Jackson as "an unprovincial, unsectional, broad, liberal, Federal Democrat."

During his five years in the Senate, Jackson served on the post office, pension, claims, and judiciary committees and earned a reputation as a tireless worker, skilled debater, and master of legislative detail. On the Senate floor he was seated next to a Republican senator from Indiana, Benjamin Harrison, and the two developed a friendship that would prove fortuitous for Jackson. Jackson also befriended President Grover Cleveland and faithfully supported the administration's tariff policies. In 1887, a year before the end of Jackson's Senate term, Cleveland asked him to recommend candidates to replace a Tennessean on the Sixth Federal Circuit Court. The President ignored the advice and chose the adviser instead. An embarrassed Jackson was reluctant to resign his Senate seat and abandon his constituents, but Cleveland insisted that he accept the appointment.

Jackson heard a broad range of cases in his seven years as a circuit court judge, including a large number of patent cases. His diligence and patience in sorting out the details of cases were again evident. Jackson's duties took him to Michigan, where he stayed in the home of his friend Henry Billings Brown, a federal district judge on the Sixth Circuit. When a vacancy opened on the Supreme Court in 1889, Jackson went to Washington to lobby his old friend and former colleague Harrison, now president, to appoint Brown to

Stricken with tuberculosis a year after his appointment to the Supreme Court, Howell E. Jackson went to California in 1894 to try to regain his health. He posed (second from right) in Monterey, California, with his wife (right) and family members and friends who accompanied him. His brother, William H. Jackson (third from left), asked Chief Justice Melville W. Fuller to persuade Congress to pass a special retirement bill so that Jackson might resign. The request was dropped when Jackson briefly returned to his duties. *Source: Private collection of W. Ridley Wills II*

the Court. Although Brown was passed over for that particular appointment, Harrison named him to the Court the following year. Jackson received a promotion of his own in 1891, when the circuit court of appeals was established and he was made presiding judge.

Justice Lucius Q. C. Lamar, a former Confederate, died in 1893, and President Harrison, only two months away from leaving office, was determined not to let his successor have the opportunity to appoint "another secessionist" to the Court. Although he wanted to replace Lamar with a southerner, Harrison realized that the Democratic-controlled Senate would not confirm a Republican nominee by an outgoing president. Returning his friend's favor, Justice Brown urged Harrison to appoint Jackson as an acceptable southern Democrat. The nonpartisan nomination was announced February 2, 1893, and confirmed unanimously by the Senate sixteen days later.

Jackson at age sixty brought considerable experience in patent law to a Court clogged with cases of that nature. In the two years he served on the Court, during which time he spent only fifteen months on the bench, Jackson wrote forty-six opinions and four dissents. However, he was absent for most of the important cases, and wrote few opinions on weighty matters.

Although in good health at the time of his appointment, Jackson was stricken with tuberculosis just one year later. In October 1894 he left the Court to seek the restorative climate of the West. After several months there his brother wrote to Chief Justice Melville Fuller asking whether Congress might pass a special retirement bill for Jackson, who had no independent wealth to fall back on, thus enabling him to resign. In February 1894 Jackson, feeling better, returned to Tennessee and asked that the retirement bill be dropped because he was hoping to take up his duties again in the fall.

In one of the most dramatic moments in Supreme Court history, Jackson managed to return to the Court, but only to cast his vote in one last case, on the constitutionality of a national income tax. Because the eight justices, absent Jackson, had previously been evenly divided on the tax case, when it was reargued in May it

Although social reformers favored a federal income tax to reduce disparities of wealth arising from the rapidly industrializing economy, most individuals and businesses argued it was unconstitutional. This 1895 cartoon throws its weight against the tax, agreeing with the Supreme Court's majority. In his dissent, Howell E. Jackson called the Court's decision a "disastrous blow" to the power of Congress. It was reversed in 1913 with passage of the Sixteenth Amendment to the Constitution. *Source: Library of Congress*

became essential that the full Court be present to settle the issue conclusively. Unwilling to resign and let a new justice decide the outcome, Jackson opted to make the trip to Washington.

The suit had been brought as a challenge to the federal income tax passed by the Senate in August 1894, which provided for a 2 percent tax on all annual incomes exceeding $4,000. The measure was supported by southerners and midwesterners as a way to reapportion the tax burden, which had been mainly derived from tariffs. The bill was vilified by wealthy easterners who saw it as socialistic and a threat to private property.

On the first argument of the case, the Court debated the legality of taxes on different forms of income. It made no distinction between taxes on land and taxes on income from land, calling them both "direct taxes." Under the Constitution, direct taxes are permissible only if they are apportioned by state according to population. On the matter of whether taxes on other kinds of income constituted direct taxes, the Court reached a stalemate.

Haggard and frail, Jackson drew national attention with his arrival for the reargument. One reporter noted: "He interests the crowd more than all the rest of the bench; that his life can last but a short time and that it will probably be shortened by the effort which he has made to attend the hearing." Although the attorneys mostly directed their arguments at Jackson, and speculation over how he would vote was rampant, his vote was not the tie-breaker. In a 5–4 vote the Court found the income tax unconstitutional; Jackson, however, had voted with the minority, indicating that one of the other justices switched his vote. Delivering a separate dissenting opinion, punctuated by coughing fits, he decried the decision as "the most disastrous blow ever struck at the Constitutional power of Congress. It strikes down an important portion of the most vital and essential power of the government in practically excluding any recourse to incomes from real and personal estate for the purpose of raising needed revenue to meet the government's wants and necessities under any circumstances." He argued that income from some forms of property were not subject to the apportionment rule and that the invalid portion of the law should not void the rest.

On August 8, 1895, less than three months after delivering his dissent, the dedicated Tennessean died at home in Nashville. Eighteen years later, the Sixteenth Amendment to the Constitution gave Congress the power to enact a national income tax.

Edward Douglass White

1894-1910, 1910-1921

Source: Collection of the Supreme Court of the United States

EDWARD DOUGLASS WHITE was the first associate justice to be directly elevated to the position of chief justice. The second Catholic named to the Court, he was the only justice appointed from Louisiana—a state whose unique legal code is based on French civil law rather than English common law. White was born into an illustrious Louisiana family November 3, 1845, in Lafourche Parish. His great-grandfather, an Irish Catholic, emigrated to America in the 1730s and became a prosperous Philadelphia mer-

chant. His grandfather, James White, was a physician who moved to Tennessee, where he became a territorial representative to Congress in 1794. Eventually settling in southwest Louisiana, James established himself as a prominent member of the local landed gentry by securing an appointment as a U.S. district judge.

James White's death in 1809 left his son Edward, the future chief justice's father, financially secure and politically well connected. Edward White put his father's legacy to good use, serving as a city judge, a five-term representative to Congress, and governor of Louisiana. In 1847 he died suddenly on his 1,600-acre sugar-beet plantation in Thibodaux, Louisiana, leaving behind a wife and five children. The revenues from the plantation provided them with financial security.

Catholicism was such an important part of the White family heritage that when Edward turned six he was sent to be raised at a convent school in New Orleans. At age eleven he traveled north to Emmitsburg, Maryland, to enter Mount Saint Mary's, a preparatory school run by Jesuits. After a year he enrolled at another Jesuit institution—Georgetown College (now University) in Washington, D.C. Although not an honor student, White did fairly well at Georgetown until his education was disrupted by the outbreak of the Civil War. Like hundreds of other young southerners enrolled in northern schools, he returned home in 1861.

Although White initially planned to continue his studies in Louisiana, he enlisted in the Confederate Army before the end of the year. Because of his relative youth and good education, White served for the first eighteen months of the war behind the lines as an aide-de-camp. In July 1863 he and thousands of other rebel troops were trapped by the Union siege of Port Hudson, Louisiana, on the Mississippi River. After enduring weeks of attack without relief, the out-gunned southerners surrendered a bloody battlefield to Gen. Nathaniel Banks's forces. Ill and emaciated, White was released after a brief period of detention and returned to the plantation in Thibodaux, where he spent the remainder of the war.

At war's end, White went to New Orleans to study law. He took classes at the University of Louisiana, a Jesuit institution that later became Tulane University, and read law under the direction of Edmund Bermudez, a highly regarded local attorney. Passing the Louisiana bar in 1868, White began to practice law.

In 1874 he was elected to the state Senate, and his support in 1877 for the successful Democratic guberna-torial candidate, Francis T. Nicholls, earned him an appointment to the Louisiana Supreme Court the following year. As a consequence of a dispute within the party, Nicholls's successor tried to force White out by passing a minimum age requirement for judges. White, then only thirty-five years old, lost his seat on the court and returned to private life.

During the next several years, White strengthened his reputation and standing in the legal community through a series of successful associations with the most prominent and influential law firms in New Orleans. He also devoted himself to a number of important civic projects, including the establishment of Tulane in 1884. White's fluency in French and comfortable income allowed the portly lawyer to enjoy the cultural and culinary charms of the New Orleans French Quarter, where he resided.

White turned his attention to Louisiana politics once again by serving as campaign manager in 1888 for his old friend Nicholls in his successful campaign to regain the governor's office. Nicholls rewarded White by appointing him to fill a vacancy in the U.S. Senate. White served only three years, but he enjoyed enormous respect and influence among his fellow senators from the South. He repeatedly and vigorously took the floor in defense of states' rights against the federal government's powers. He did, however, make exceptions. Most notably, he rejected limitations on the power of the federal government to establish tariffs protecting sugar farmers, who numbered among his constituents, from foreign competition.

In February 1894, in the midst of an unusually stiff Senate debate over a tariff reform bill, White was called to the White House by President Grover Cleveland. Although White had been generally supportive of the president's legislative initiatives, he was clearly opposed to Cleveland's attempt to lower the tariff barriers that protected southern agricultural products, such as his own sugar beets. White arrived at the White House ex-

Edward D. White's 1,600-acre sugar plantation in Louisiana grew beets rather than the sugar cane shown in this 1875 engraving. As a senator, White approved restrictions on the federal government's powers in every area but one—tariffs protecting sugar farmers, who made up a sizable portion of his constituents. He openly clashed with Grover Cleveland on tariffs, making his nomination to the Supreme Court in 1894 a surprise.
Source: Library of Congress

pecting an argument over the tariff bill, but departed, much to his surprise, with a nomination to the Supreme Court of the United States.

Cleveland had twice been rebuffed by the Senate in his attempt to fill the seat left vacant by Justice Samuel Blatchford's death in July 1893. The president's choices—both from Blatchford's home state of New York—had been rejected on the recommendation of New York's two senators, who actively opposed the president and his policies. A frustrated Cleveland guessed correctly that the Senate would approve their popular colleague from Louisiana. But if the president thought the nomination would thin the ranks of those opposed to the tariff bill, he was mistaken. White remained in the Senate for several weeks following his appointment and confirmation, both of which took place February 19, 1894, and led the battle against the president's tariff reform legislation. Not only was Cleveland's bill defeated, but opposing senators succeeded in passing their own legislation, which substantially increased the existing tariffs.

With this impressive victory for his constituents and for the South, White left the Senate in March to take his place, at age forty-eight, on the Court. A few months later, he achieved another important victory. After an intermittent twenty-year courtship, set back by numerous rebuffs and her marriage to another man, Virginia Montgomery Kent agreed to become his wife in November 1894. Although he never had any children of his own, White adored them and often carried candy in his pockets to comfort children in distress.

For much of his seventeen-year service as associate justice, White continued to oppose the federal government's intrusions on the power of the states to regulate their own economies. He dissented in *Lochner v. New York,* a 1905 case in which the Court overturned a state law limiting the number of hours bakery employees could work, on the grounds that the statute infringed on states' rights. White also dissented when the Court struck down the 1895 act of Congress imposing the nation's first general tax on personal income. Congress (and the public) agreed with White's dissenting views and in 1913 passed the Sixteenth Amendment, which followed White's reasoning in permitting such a tax.

In the first few years of the twentieth century, the Court dealt with issues relating to the aftermath of the

Spanish-American War. The United States had gained extensive overseas possessions in the war, and serious legal questions were raised with regard to whether the U.S. Constitution followed the American flag. White was persuasive at convincing his colleagues that the Constitution applied to the territories if Congress had chosen to incorporate them.

When Chief Justice Melville Fuller died in July 1910, President William Howard Taft appointed White to fill his seat. Among the other candidates given serious consideration for the post was Charles Evans Hughes, a former governor of New York and friend whom Taft had put on the Court only a few months earlier. Taft had made no secret of his own aspirations to sit in the center chair and had often remarked that he would have preferred to be chief justice rather than president. Undoubtedly, the ages of the two leading contenders played a role in Taft's decision—White was sixty-five and Hughes only forty-eight. If the president was indeed positioning himself for the chief justiceship, it was more strategic to elevate one of the Court's elderly justices rather than its youngest and newest member. Taft also may have wished to appoint a Catholic southerner to quell lingering anti-Catholic and anti-South sentiments and to win support from those constituencies in the next election. Whatever his rationale, on December 12, 1910, Taft nominated White, and the Senate confirmed him the same day. White took the oath of office as the ninth chief justice of the United States a week later, the first associate justice confirmed to that office.

The most lasting legacy of White's ten years as chief justice was the Court's adoption of the "rule of reason" in judging antitrust cases. The rule was developed in response to the Court's efforts to interpret the Sherman Antitrust Act of 1890, which distinguished between legal and illegal business combinations. Specifically, it arose out of the Court's 1911 decision breaking up the Standard Oil Company on the grounds that it had unduly restrained trade and was therefore an "unreason-able" combination. White's majority opinion asserted, however, that not all monopolies were illegal. The Court's role was to restrict only those it judged to be "unreasonable" or conspiratorial in their restraint of trade. Two weeks after the Standard Oil decision, White ruled in another case that the American Tobacco Company was engaged in "reasonable" restraint of trade and therefore did not need to be dissolved.

Justices Oliver Wendell Holmes, Jr., and John Marshall Harlan generally opposed the rule of reason, arguing that the Court was taking on legislative powers reserved for Congress. Nevertheless, White persuaded the rest of the Court to favor selective application of antitrust legislation—thereby ushering in a time when many businesses, particularly mammoth conglomerates, would flourish. For most of the twentieth century the rule of reason continued to be applied in cases in which corporations were charged with monopolistic behavior.

Chief Justice White was much beloved for his warmhearted and approachable manner. Although not a talented administrator, he was able to foster a spirit of cooperation among his colleagues. White demonstrated this skill in 1915 when he rallied unanimous support for his opinion striking down the discriminatory "grandfather clauses" that prevented many blacks from voting. His decision challenged an Oklahoma law imposing a literacy test on potential voters but exempting those whose ancestors had voted in elections in 1866. The law was intended to penalize blacks, who had not been allowed to vote prior to passage of the Fifteenth Amendment in 1870. White found that the law violated the Fifteenth Amendment's guarantee that states could not deny citizens the right to vote because of their race. The case exemplified the former Confederate soldier's efforts to use his position as chief justice to reconcile North and South.

When the United States entered World War I, White's considerable patriotic zeal led him to take an

The Standard Oil Company, first of the great American trusts, was so powerful that it could intimidate governments and industry alike. This 1904 cartoon reflects the fear that the "octopus" was strangling the public interest. The Supreme Court broke up the oil company's monopoly in 1911 on the grounds that it restricted free trade. Chief Justice Edward D. White's opinion drew a line between trusts that placed "unreasonable" limits on competition and those that monopolized markets through fair competition, a doctrine known as "the rule of reason." *Source: Library of Congress*

uncharacteristic position. Although he usually opposed allowing the federal government to expand its powers, White found himself backing the federal government in the national draft case, in the interests of preserving national security during wartime.

By 1920 Chief Justice White was seventy-five years old, had been on the Court for twenty-six years, and was suffering from cataracts. He came under increasing pressure to retire, especially from Republicans anxious to have an opportunity to make Taft chief justice. White refused to be accommodating, however, and insisted that he would remain on the Court as long as he was able. He was taken ill May 13, 1921, and died six days later in Washington, D.C. As many had predicted, within a month of White's death President Warren G. Harding nominated Taft to fill his seat.

Rufus W. Peckham

1896-1909

RUFUS WHEELER PECKHAM was born in Albany, New York, November 8, 1838. He was the younger of two sons of a distinguished attorney, Rufus Wheeler Peckham, Sr., and Isabella Lacey Peckham. Both parents were from old New York families whose American origins went back to the seventeenth century. His father served as district attorney of Albany County before being elected to a term in Congress in 1852. Rufus Peckham, Sr., served on the New York Supreme Court for ten years and on the court of

appeals, the state's highest tribunal, for three years. His life was cut short in November 1873 when he was lost at sea in a ship collision while traveling abroad.

Young Rufus was given a classical education at the Albany Boys Academy and studied privately in Philadelphia. In 1856 he accompanied his older brother, Wheeler Hazard Peckham, on a year-long tour of Europe, a custom of the time for the privileged class. Two years of studying law followed at his father's firm in Albany, and in 1859 he passed the bar at the age of twenty-one. The same year, his father was elected to the New York Supreme Court, and the fledgling attorney took his place in the distinguished firm of Peckham and Tremain, of which his brother was also a member.

Peckham's practice was successful from the start, and he was soon to become a leading citizen of his community. He attracted prominent clients, including the Albany and Susequehanna Railroad, defending it in its battle against the Erie Railroad, which was led at that time by noted financiers Jim Fiske and Jay Gould. He became a trustee of many local banks and the president of the Albany hospital. Seven years after he entered practice, in November 1866, he married Harriette M. Arnold, the daughter of a wealthy New York City merchant. They were to have two sons.

During this time, Peckham became active in politics, allying himself with the upstate wing of the Democratic party of New York. He was soon a political force in Albany County as an energetic partisan and effective spokesman. In 1869 this combination of qualities brought him the Democratic nomination and election as district attorney for Albany County, like his father before him. His father had been elected to the position in his twenties; the son was thirty-one. During the three years he held the post, Peckham gained additional prominence as a special assistant to the state attorney general in a series of criminal cases. His prosecution of suspects involved in railroad express-car robberies was considered particularly skillful and made him famous. Peckham developed lasting friendships with other upstate Democratic leaders, most notably Grover Cleveland, the former mayor of Buffalo, who was to move from the governorship of New York to the presidency in 1885.

Peckham entered public life again in 1881 as corporation counsel to the city of Albany, but in 1882 lost an attempt to get the Democratic party nomination to the New York Court of Appeals. The following year, however, he gained a seat on the state supreme court and

Rufus Peckham with his wife, Harriette, and his son, daughter-in-law, and grandchildren. Family tradition played a large part in Peckham's career: he had followed in his father's illustrious footsteps as he moved from Albany County attorney to New York Supreme Court judge to appeals court judge. *Source: Collection of the Supreme Court of the United States*

followed it with election to the court of appeals in 1886. This election drew widespread criticism as a blatant partisan effort by President Cleveland to gain control of New York's Democratic party. Commentators were unanimous in their approval of Peckham's professional qualifications and character, but raised doubts about the wisdom of placing an influential Democratic activist on the state's highest court.

The remarkable similarities between Peckham and his father, not only in their names and virtually identical careers but also in their physical appearance and character traits, now became a matter of discussion. Both

During the 1870s "Boss" William Marcy Tweed controlled the corrupt New York City machine that cheerfully defrauded taxpayers out of millions of dollars. Rufus Peckham supported the wing of the state Democratic party intent on smashing the notorious Tweed Ring, but it was his brother, Wheeler Peckham, who successfully prosecuted it. Thomas Nast's devastating caricatures of Tweed, published in *Harper's Weekly,* made his face the most familiar in America after the president's. *Source: American Antiquarian Society*

record entry as in former times seemed pleasurably familiar."

A contemporary noted Peckham's physical resemblance to a portrait of his father that hung in the New York Court of Appeals: "And no one entering the place and simultaneously viewing the painting and the new Peckham on the bench could fail to observe that the latter was to a notable extent a physical replica of his father, as every veteran lawyer who pleaded in the court room recognized that the son was also intellectually a replica." The younger man had strong, distinguished features, and his long wavy hair and full mustache turned silvery gray during his later years.

Peckham wrapped himself in the cloak of judicial neutrality when he moved from bar to bench, but he maintained an interest in political affairs. He was even mentioned from time to time as a potential candidate for high elective office. It was clear, however, from the time of his ascent to the state court of appeals in 1886 that his overriding interest was his service as judge. His opinions generally contained few surprises, and his prose was simple and direct. He demonstrated his judicial nonpartisanship and independence of party influence when he sometimes voted with Republican judges, most notably in 1891 by upholding Republican victories in contested election cases. His ability to separate his judicial responsibilities from his political loyalties was to be an important factor in his appointment to the U.S. Supreme Court.

The roots of the unusual circumstances by which Rufus Peckham, instead of his elder brother, was elevated to the Supreme Court can be found in the long battle for control of the New York Democratic party. The upstate Democrats considered that blocking the corrupt New York City party machine, known as Tammany Hall, from achieving dominance of the state organization was an even more urgent task than defeating Republicans. In the Democratic party's presidential nominating convention of 1876, Peckham was a strong

began public life as Albany County's district attorney at a young age, then were elevated successively to the state supreme court and court of appeals. On the appeals bench, the son filled the very same seat that was vacated by the death of his father only thirteen years earlier. "When the son first appeared on the Supreme bench, lawyers before him seemed to feel that in recalling the sire they needed no introduction to the new incumbent; and the initials R. W. P. signed to an order or

supporter of Samuel J. Tilden, who had been elected governor in 1874 after he had succeeded, as state party chairman, in smashing New York City's notoriously corrupt Tweed Ring in 1871.

Wheeler Peckham, who was respected enough in his profession to be elected president of the New York State Bar, assisted in the successful prosecution of the Tweed Ring. His brother's participation no doubt influenced Rufus in his adamant belief that Tammany Hall "must go down before the Democrats can live." In 1879 he was instrumental in blocking a Tammany Hall effort to prevent renomination of the incumbent governor, and, two years later in the Democratic state convention, he led a successful effort to deny seating to the Tammany Hall delegation. The battle for control of the Democratic party in New York continued, but Rufus Peckham stayed on the sidelines after becoming a judge in 1883. During Cleveland's second term the battle was characterized by a struggle between the president and New York senator David B. Hill. When Justice Samuel Blatchford of New York died in 1893, the efforts to replace him developed into a complicated scenario.

President Cleveland nominated William B. Hornblower, a prominent New York City lawyer to fill the vacancy. Hornblower's confirmation was considered such a certainty that his name was entered in Washington directories and he made plans for the move to the capital. Then Senator Hill announced his opposition, promising to use his senatorial influence to block confirmation. Hill was taking revenge for Hornblower's role in a bar association investigation of a Hill political ally, Isaac Maynard, who, as deputy attorney general of New York, had allegedly tampered with election returns. Cleveland then put forward the name of Wheeler Peckham, but met the same objection from Senator Hill. Wheeler Peckham had been chairman of the New York State Bar Association, which appointed the committee to investigate Maynard. Hill was quoted as saying that if the president had only nominated "the other

Peckham" he would have voted for his confirmation. Cleveland then gave up his effort to fill the vacancy with a New Yorker and instead chose Sen. Edward D. White of Louisiana. White had supported the president in the Hornblower and Wheeler Peckham controversies, but, as a senator himself, was assured of confirmation by his colleagues.

When Justice Howell E. Jackson died in 1895, Cleveland renewed his effort to appoint a New Yorker to the Court. In a tactful letter, he asked Senator Hill whether the younger Peckham would still be acceptable. Hill apparently held no grudge against Rufus Peckham, despite their years on opposite sides of the New York Democratic spectrum, and the president nominated him to the Court December 3, 1895. Unopposed confirmation followed five days later by a voice vote. The appointment raised few public comments; Peckham was generally regarded as an able, sound, and principled jurist.

Peckham was neither greatly surprised nor particularly jubilant over his selection. His friend President Cleveland had repeatedly predicted, "We'll get you down to Washington yet." Apparently Peckham had found more satisfaction in the lower trial courts than the more sedate and scholarly environment of high appellate courts. He commented to a friend soon after the nomination, "If I have got to be put away on the shelf I suppose I might as well be on the top shelf."

Despite his reluctance, he was to give the rest of his life, with almost singular devotion, to his work as an associate justice. Peckham seldom participated in Washington's social life; he accepted few invitations to public gatherings and gave no public addresses. He did not, however, vanish entirely from the political world. A year after taking his seat on the Court Peckham was advising President Cleveland against taking a position on a third term, and only two years before his death he was mentioned as a potential nominee for the New York governorship.

When Joseph Lochner was convicted of violating state maximum working hour laws at his Home Bakery in Utica, New York, he asked the Supreme Court to overturn the law. He argued that the state's need to safeguard public health was not an issue because his bakers could make wholesome bread even if they worked more than ten hours a day. In *Lochner v. New York* (1905), Rufus Peckham wrote that a state maximum working hours law violated the constitutional right of employers to enter freely into contracts with their employees. *Source: From the collection of Joseph Lochner, Jr., by Dante Tranquille*

Peckham believed that the Court's role was to draw strict lines separating the powers of state governments, the rights of the individual, and the authority of the federal government, and then to police those boundaries. He favored government regulation of business only where interstate commerce was directly and substantially affected. He was a strong proponent of the individual's right to freedom of contract as part of his general right to liberty, which he described as the right to "be free in the enjoyment of all his faculties; to be free to use them in all lawful ways; to live and work where he will; to earn his livelihood by any lawful calling; to pursue any livelihood or avocation, and for that purpose to enter into all contracts which may be proper, necessary and essential to his carrying out the purposes above mentioned."

In 1905 he wrote the majority opinion in the landmark case, *Lochner v. New York,* which ruled unconstitutional a New York state law limiting bakery workers to a ten-hour day or sixty-hour workweek. He argued that the state had overstepped its powers in regulating workers' hours and wages because safeguarding the public health was not at issue. "Clean and wholesome bread does not depend upon whether the baker works ten hours per day or 60 hours a week," he wrote. The opinion drew strong dissents from Justices Oliver Wendell Holmes, Jr., and John Marshall Harlan, with Justices William Day and Edward D. White concurring in the dissent. The dissents may have impressed Peckham, for three years later he joined a unanimous Court in a decision upholding a similar law regulating the working hours of women in Oregon.

Like his father before him, Justice Rufus Wheeler Peckham died while serving on the bench. He died October 24, 1909, at the age of seventy-one, in Altamont, New York, near his home city of Albany.

Joseph McKenna
1898-1925

Source: Photo by Harris & Ewing, Collection of the Supreme Court of the United States

THE ACTUAL DATE OF Joseph McKenna's birth is in doubt. Although August 10, 1843, is usually cited, the contemporary record of his baptism lists his birthday as August 14. He was the first child of John McKenna, a baker born in Ireland, and Mary Ann Lucy Johnson McKenna, who had come to the United States as a girl from her native England. The future justice was born in Philadelphia, where his parents operated a small neighborhood bakery in the Irish quarter.

The social climate of mid-century Philadelphia was extremely hostile to immigrants, particularly Irish Catholics. Nativist riots in 1844 burned three Catholic churches, including St. Philip Neri, where Joseph had been christened, and destroyed dozens of houses in the neighborhood. John McKenna's bakery had to be moved five times in ten years, a measure of the instability facing small immigrant-owned businesses. Joseph was enrolled in a local parochial school until his parents decided to move their growing family to a more hospitable environment, away from the economic insecurity and threats of violence.

In 1854 an opportunity arose. Steamship fares dropped dramatically in a price war, and the family packed their meager belongings to move west. The arduous trip took nearly a month. The McKennas set sail in steerage from New York to Panama and crossed the isthmus by train in those pre-canal days. They then sailed up the Pacific coast, finally landing in San Francisco. The family settled a little to the east of the city in the newly established town of Benicia, which was already growing in population and prosperity and had a sizable Irish community.

John McKenna died in 1858, after only four years in California, but his little bakery had prospered enough for him to have some modest investments in real estate. The children helped their mother continue the business by making deliveries and by selling bread on the streets. While not rich, they lived in reasonable security, and Joseph was able to attend parochial schools and, later, to take courses in law at the Benicia Collegiate Institute, graduating in 1864.

McKenna was admitted to the bar the following year and, after only a few months of private practice, he was elected district attorney for Solano County and reelected in 1867. Two years later he returned to private practice and married the German-born Amanda Frances Bornemann, described as "strikingly handsome." The couple had four children who reached adulthood, three daughters and a son.

McKenna remained active in Republican politics. In 1875 he was elected to the state Assembly, where he was something of a reformer in an age of graft and corruption. His law practice grew, and he exhibited a growing

Nativist sentiment against a rising influx of immigrants, particularly Roman Catholics, culminated in 1844 when violent armed clashes in Philadelphia left scores injured and twenty-four dead. After state militia (left) suppressed the riots, the nativists (wearing tall beaver hats) organized the Native American party, which called for barring naturalized citizens from office and extending the waiting period for citizenship to twenty-one years. Joseph McKenna's father moved his business repeatedly because of hostility to Irish Catholics. *Source: Library of Congress*

talent for public speaking. He was quick on his feet, effective in courtroom argument, and adept at cross-examination. Contemporary accounts called him "nimble as a cat" and noted "he is never at a loss and never gets rattled."

After several hard-fought attempts to win a seat in Congress, McKenna was elected to the House of Representatives in 1884 and reelected to three additional terms. In Washington he tended to follow Republican party positions on national issues, especially on tariffs, business regulation, and monetary policy. He was effective in obtaining federal support for local projects and, like most Californians, favored expansion and the railroads. He was also, again like many of his constituents, wary of the growing number of Asians, particularly Chinese, settling on the West Coast, and he backed measures to restrict their freedom. His willingness to support railroad expansion brought him to the attention of California senator Leland Stanford, president of the Southern Pacific and Central Pacific railroads, and the two men became personally close and politically allied.

The tie to Stanford somewhat tarnished McKenna's reputation, however, and the railroad label was difficult to detach later in his career. But McKenna was more than a party hack. He began to forge strong ties within the national leadership of the Republican party, particularly with William McKinley, a powerful member of Congress and chairman of the House Ways and Means Committee. While still relatively new in Congress, McKenna was appointed to that committee and became McKinley's trusted lieutenant and fast friend.

During McKenna's fourth term, a vacancy occurred on the Ninth Circuit Court of Appeals. When the various western political interests could not agree on a candidate to assume the judgeship, Senator Stanford urged President Benjamin Harrison to name McKenna. He was appointed circuit judge in early 1892 and served without marked distinction for five years. To the sur-

While serving in Congress, Rep. Joseph McKenna of California showed strong support for railroad expansion. He became friends with railroad head Leland Stanford when California elected Stanford to the Senate. Stanford, who founded and endowed Stanford University as a memorial to his son in 1885, served railroad interests in the Senate until his death in 1893. *Source: California State Railroad Museum*

prise of his critics, he seemed even-handed in deciding cases involving the railroads. No questions were raised about his impartiality or honesty, and he was characterized as "able" and "painstaking"—this last adjective perhaps a kindly way of saying "slow." McKenna's inadequate education showed most in his writing: syntax and punctuation were always a problem, and he found it difficult to craft a sentence with precision.

After McKinley was elected president in 1896, he was anxious to appoint a Californian to his cabinet, and the name of his old friend Judge McKenna was suggested for secretary of the interior. McKenna discussed that position with the president-elect, candidly pointing out that his Catholic faith would be embarrassing if he headed a department that dealt with Protestant missionary activities on Indian reservations. Instead, McKenna was appointed attorney general. He was the first Californian ever to hold a cabinet office. He served an uneventful nine months in the post, and on December 16, 1897, was nominated associate justice of the Supreme Court, to replace the legendary Stephen J. Field, also a Californian, who was retiring.

Opposition to the nomination was immediate. His railroad connections, his religion, his poor education, his absence of scholarly credentials, his limited legal practice, his mediocre record on the bench all left him open to criticism. Several newspapers called the appointment "weak." Some federal judges from the Northwest wrote to Chief Justice Melville Fuller to protest McKenna's unfitness, and the chief justice brought these letters to the president's attention. Pop-

U.S. marshals destroy worm-infested currants and raisins on a raid of Washington, D.C., bakeries in 1909. Passage of the Pure Food and Drug Act of 1906 increased the police powers of the federal government to regulate on behalf of public health. Writing for a unanimous Supreme Court, Joseph McKenna showed a strong social concern in his opinion upholding the act and gave broad reach to the federal commerce power. *Source: Library of Congress*

ulist senator William V. Allen of Nebraska spoke against the nomination for three hours. But McKenna had strong support in the Senate and was confirmed by voice vote on January 21, 1898, the last justice to take office in the nineteenth century. Aware of his shortcomings, he attended courses at Columbia Law School for several months to improve his legal training before assuming his seat.

McKenna began his tenure with no profound or highly developed judicial philosophy, and neither his education nor his political experience provided the theoretical underpinnings appropriate for service on the Supreme Court. But he was honest and courageous, not doctrinaire, and he grew in depth while serving. "If there was nothing in his past career to justify his appointment," wrote one observer, "there would be considerable in the future to vindicate it." Although he still had to take his time to understand legal complexities and continued to write his assigned opinions slowly, he possessed a sure fund of common sense. His difficulties with English syntax gradually lessened, and it was sometimes amusing, and sometimes annoying, to Justice Oliver Wendell Holmes, Jr., that McKenna was the most persistent critic of Holmes's elegant and trenchant style.

In his twenty-seven years on the Court, McKenna wrote 659 opinions. He was a centrist, perhaps with a mild inclination toward the progressive liberalism of the day. His opinions tended to favor the growth of federal power, particularly in the regulation of business and industry. In anticipation of later positions of Holmes and Louis D. Brandeis, McKenna was very deferential to legislative decisions and tolerant of legislative experimentation. He voted to uphold the constitutionality of the Sherman Antitrust Act, which gave the government power to regulate business monopolies, and he wrote the opinion of the Court in several early antitrust cases. McKenna also wrote the Court's opinion sustaining the Pure Food and Drug Act. He wrote the decision upholding the Mann Act, which gave the federal government enforcement powers over interstate prostitution. He liked patent law and became the Court's expert in that area.

McKenna was usually in the majority and did not write many dissents. While often voting with Holmes, Brandeis, and John Clarke in positions regarded as liberal, in First Amendment cases McKenna was unwilling to read the Free Speech Clause expansively and believed that the Bill of Rights had only limited application. He also believed strongly in property rights, but balanced this view by supporting workers' compensation. Never original, he was open-minded and flexible. Precedent and legal authority were important to his manner of judging, but he was not reactionary. Overall, his approach was cautious and moderate.

Over time, McKenna matured as a jurist, and, if he never developed a profound jurisprudence, he did have his own unique insights. Years after his death, Justice Arthur Goldberg was moved by this passage in a McKenna opinion:

Time works changes, brings into existence new conditions and purposes. Therefore, a principle to be vital must be capable of wider application than the mischief which gave it birth. This is peculiarly true of constitutions. They are not ephemeral enactments, designed to meet passing occasions. They are, to use the words of Chief Justice Marshall, "designed to approach immortality as nearly as human institutions can approach it." The future is their care and provision for events of good and bad tendencies of which no prophecy can be made. In the application of a constitution, therefore, our contemplation cannot be only of what has been but of what may be. Under any other rule a constitution would indeed be as easy of application as it would be deficient in efficacy and power. Its general principles would have little value and be converted by precedent into impotent and lifeless formulas. Rights declared in words might be lost in reality.

McKenna was of medium height, very spare and thin, "birdlike," says one biographer, with a squared-off grayish-white goatee that gave him the look of a New England whaling captain. He loved golf, playing in his younger days with Justice John Marshall Harlan, and later with Justice Joseph Lamar. He was a faithful Catholic, but a severe critic of poor sermons. Although never an avid reader or an intellectual, he was proud of his well-stocked library. He was also the first justice to own a gasoline-powered automobile. McKenna and his wife were family oriented and lived a secluded life. In personal demeanor, he was somewhat formal and austere, perhaps because he was shy.

In 1915 McKenna suffered a slight stroke, and by 1921, when as senior associate justice he administered the oath of office to Chief Justice William H. Taft, his health had failed perceptibly. His last years on the Court were pathetic: his reasoning deserted him, and he became sensitive, easily angered, touchy. On one occasion, completely out of character, he exploded in rage at a conference of the justices. On another occasion, he was assigned an opinion to write and reached a conclusion completely at odds with the vote taken by the Court. The chief justice noted that he could be trusted with only the easiest cases and even then would often miss the point. The justices secretly agreed that they would not allow his vote to be decisive in close decisions. Still, the old man would not retire, despite Taft's urging. "When a man retires," McKenna replied, "he disappears and nobody cares for him." He also resented pressure to leave the Court when he was two years younger than Holmes, whose mental powers were intact.

Finally, Taft insisted that the aged justice retire, and on January 5, 1925, he did. He died nearly two years later on November 21, 1926. On the day of the funeral Holmes wrote to his friend Harold Laski that McKenna was "a truly kind soul" and "a decent gentleman." Laski replied, "I liked him because one always had a sense in his opinions of both growth of mind and a genuine effort to understand."

Oliver Wendell Holmes, Jr.

1902-1932

Source: Library of Congress

OLIVER WENDELL HOLMES, JR., born in Boston, Massachusetts, March 8, 1841, was the first child of Dr. Oliver Wendell Holmes and Amelia Lee Jackson Holmes. A highly regarded medical innovator and professor of anatomy at Harvard Medical School, Dr. Holmes was even better known for his literary essays, which expressed a sophisticated wit and earned him a wide following. He cofounded a distinguished literary journal, *The Atlantic,* and published a collection of his writings under the title *The Autocrat*

of the Breakfast Table, which was extremely popular. Young Holmes's maternal grandfather, Charles Jackson, was a distinguished Boston attorney and associate justice of the Supreme Judicial Court of Massachusetts. Related to many of the city's first families, the future justice grew up in an unusually secure and sophisticated environment, enjoying all the benefits his family's comfortable circumstances and social position could provide.

Upon completion of his preparatory studies at

Dixwell's Private Latin School, Holmes followed the family tradition and enrolled at Harvard College. He graduated in June 1861, having been elected class poet just as his father had in 1829. An unusually serious young man, Holmes studied hard and allowed himself few distractions. In a revealing observation, Dr. Holmes wrote to a friend that his son looked on life "as a solemn show where he is the only spectator."

A staunch abolitionist, Holmes was among the first in his Harvard class to enlist in the Union Army, joining the Twentieth Regiment of Massachusetts Volunteers as a first lieutenant in July 1861. Although his family was not in favor of his enlistment, Holmes went south to join the fighting and served with distinction. By the end of the war Holmes's unit would be among the first half-dozen infantry regiments of the Union Army in the number of men killed or wounded. On October 21, 1861, Holmes was shot in the chest during the battle of Balls Bluff. Returning to his regiment after a period of several months, he was shot again, this time through the neck on September 16, 1862, at the bloody battle of Antietam. On May 2, 1863, at Fredericksburg,

Holmes received a shrapnel wound that almost cost him his leg. Given the state of battlefield medicine during the Civil War, any of these wounds could have been fatal.

Returning to active duty in January 1864, Holmes was assigned as aide-de-camp to Gen. Horatio G. Wright, division commander, army of the Potomac. While serving in this position, Holmes was stationed outside Washington, D.C., the Union capital. One afternoon in the spring of 1864, Holmes reportedly ordered a civilian off an artillery platform, only to discover after barking the blunt command that he was addressing his commander in chief, President Abraham Lincoln. Lincoln interrupted Holmes's apology, remarking that it was reassuring to find at least one Union officer who knew how to speak to civilians. Holding briefly the rank of brevet colonel, Holmes was mustered out of the army July 17, 1864, ending his three-year enlistment with the permanent rank of captain.

Returning to Boston, Holmes entered Harvard Law School in September 1864. Although dissatisfied with

Suffering his second Civil War injury, Oliver Wendell Holmes, Jr., was wounded at Antietam in 1862. The bodies of Confederate soldiers strewn along the Maryland road testify to the carnage of the battle. A third wound later kept Holmes out of the Battle of Gettysburg, where his regiment lost half of its enlisted men and ten of thirteen officers. *Source: Library of Congress*

his courses, he saw the law as a potentially active outlet for his strong scholastic and aristocratic tendencies. He took his degree in June 1866 and then traveled to England and the Continent. Summer trips abroad—especially to England, Scotland, and Ireland—would become in later years an important counterbalance to his relentless commitment to his work.

Returning to Boston in 1867, Holmes was admitted to the Massachusetts bar March 4, only a few days before his twenty-sixth birthday. For the next several years, he practiced law in Boston with his brother, but grew increasingly dissatisfied with the business of his fledgling practice. In 1870 he became coeditor of the *American Law Review,* writing articles on legal history and helping to supervise the publication of the journal. He also lectured on legal history, constitutional law, and jurisprudence at Harvard College. The income from these activities undoubtedly helped supplement his modest revenue from legal fees. More important, they provided Holmes an opportunity to continue his research and writing in legal history and established his reputation as a promising young scholar.

In June 1872 Holmes married Fanny Bowdich Dixwell, the daughter of his childhood schoolmaster. Their marriage lasted fifty-seven years, until Fanny died in 1929 after a long period of invalidism. They had no children. Although he was devoted to his wife, Holmes, who cut a dashing figure, also enjoyed the company of "the ladies" in his circle.

Perhaps as a result of his new family responsibility, Holmes began to practice law more seriously, forming a partnership with two Boston attorneys, George Otis Shattuck and William A. Munroe. For several years the firm enjoyed a growing reputation, but it is unlikely that Holmes had much genuine satisfaction from his law practice or ever viewed it as anything but a means of meeting expenses.

More the result of the success of his writing and editing than of his practice, Holmes was invited by Boston's prestigious Lowell Institute to present the Lowell Lectures on law in 1880. Choosing as his topic the growth and development of the common law, and incorporating and refining ideas from articles he had written for the *American Law Review,* Holmes presented the lectures in November and December. Holmes was encouraged by their favorable reception and had the lectures published as a book, *The Common Law,* in 1881. Now regarded as a classic in the literature of jurisprudence, the book won for Holmes an immediate and enduring reputation as a serious and gifted scholar. Perhaps more significant, it gave "Dr. Holmes's son" a new and independent prominence.

Breaking with the formalism of traditional American jurisprudence, Holmes asserted in *The Common Law* that the law was a living, evolving organism that changed with society's needs. "The life of the law has not been logic; it has been experience," he said, suggesting that "the felt necessities of the time, the prevalent political and moral theories" had more to do with the development of law than logical reasoning. His underlying premise that the law embodied the story of a nation's development focused new attention on the significance of legal history and introduced an entirely new way of thinking about constitutional law and the role of the courts in shaping it. As a result of the critical success of the work, in 1882 Holmes received appointments as a professor of law at Harvard Law School and as associate justice of the Supreme Judicial Court of Massachusetts. He wrote more than 1,000 opinions on that court and became its chief justice in 1899.

In September 1902 a vacancy was created on the U.S. Supreme Court when Justice Horace Gray died. Gray had been chief justice of the Supreme Judicial Court of Massachusetts when he was appointed to the nation's highest court in 1881, and President Theodore Roosevelt most likely viewed Holmes as suitable for the "Massachusetts seat" when he put him on his list of potential candidates. However, despite Holmes's well-established reputation as a legal scholar and outstanding jurist, Roosevelt was concerned about his politics. The president insisted that the eventual nominee be a loyal Republican and an ardent supporter of his progressive politics. Holmes's supporters pointed to his lifelong affiliation as a Republican and his "Boston Brahmin" aristocratic status as evidence of his political philosophy. They also convinced Roosevelt that any man thrice wounded in the service of his country could be trusted on the Court. Holmes was duly nominated December 2, 1902, and confirmed two days later without objection.

Within two years, President Roosevelt came to regret his appointment of Holmes. In March 1904 Justice John Marshall Harlan delivered the Court's opinion in *Northern Securities Co. v. United States,* which had been brought by the government under the Sherman Antitrust Act against a powerful railroad monopoly. Although a majority of the justices supported the government's position, Holmes dissented from the Court's decision to break up the railroad trust. His dissent came as a great surprise to the nation. Roosevelt was furious, denouncing Holmes as a coward and concluding in disgust that he "could carve out of a banana a judge with more backbone!"

During his twenty-nine years on the Court, Holmes would prove Roosevelt's conclusion false, demonstrating his courageous independence in case after case. He tended to take a pragmatic approach to the law, judging each case on its facts rather than with the deliberate intention of producing a particular outcome. Writing some of his greatest opinions in dissent, he was often joined by Justice Louis Brandeis. Holmes's sophisticated approach to the law and unusual eloquence distinguished him as a master of his craft.

His most memorable words are found in *Lochner v. New York* (1905): "A constitution is not intended to embody a particular economic theory. . . . It is made for people of fundamentally different views"; *Abrams v.*

In this 1918 cartoon Uncle Sam rounds up enemies of the United States. During World War I, Congress passed an an amendment to the Espionage Act of 1917, imposing severe penalties on speech that interfered with the prosecution of the war. Oliver Wendell Holmes, Jr., wrote for a unanimous Court in *Schenck v. United States* (1919) that Schenck's words raised a "clear and present danger" and were not protected by the First Amendment. *Source: Library of Congress*

United States (1919): "That at any rate is the theory of our Constitution. It is an experiment as all life is an experiment"; and *Gitlow v. New York* (1925): "Every idea is an incitement. The only difference between the expression of opinion and an incitement . . . is the speaker's enthusiasm for the result. Eloquence may set fire to reason."

In his 1919 opinion for the unanimous *Schenck v. United States* decision, Holmes expressed his firm conviction that the government should not interfere in the right of free speech. He argued that a "remote bad tendency" in a speech or pamphlet was not enough reason to convict a defendant unless there was "a clear and pre-

"The sun streams in the back—and I feel that I am settled for good in a place which is mine," declared Oliver Wendell Holmes, Jr., on moving into his new home in Washington in 1903. He placed his Civil War mementos over a mantelpiece "in the two rooms that make my library, where I have put all the works of my two grandfathers and my father and myself." Holmes died at home in 1935, three years after retiring from the bench at the age of ninety. *Source: Harvard Law Art Collection*

From time to time Holmes was accused of being a cynic or an atheist. He did not believe in organized religion and was convinced that if people concentrated less on helping their neighbors and more on improving themselves everyone would benefit. He also believed that in the absence of personal revelation, there was no way for an individual to prove the superiority of one God, or one set of moral beliefs, over another. As he stated in one of his opinions, "Every year if not every day we wager our salvation upon some prophecy based on imperfect knowledge."

Although capable of expressing in unforgettable language the most fundamental doctrines of democratic political thought, Holmes was not particularly democratic, having little time for those less gifted or accomplished than himself. He had a survival-of-the-fittest view of life and the law and glorified the competition among people and ideas for survival in a free market. Perhaps rightly called "the last Puritan," Holmes celebrated the virtue of work and emphasized the importance of a job well done.

Until his last four years on the Court, Holmes never missed a session and walked to work every day from his home, nearly two miles away. Despite the Court's ruling exempting federal judges from paying income tax, Holmes, like Brandeis, voluntarily paid his share. At the suggestion of Chief Justice Charles Evans Hughes and his colleagues, Holmes retired from the Court January 12, 1932, at age ninety. A widower, he continued to live in Washington and spend his summers at his house in Beverly Farms, Massachusetts.

Holmes died in his Washington home March 6, 1935, and was buried next to his wife in Arlington National Cemetery. As the final act of a life of dedicated service and devotion to his country, Holmes willed his estate to the United States. Ultimately, Congress approved using the funds to finance the *Holmes Devise History of the Supreme Court.*

sent danger" that would justify the government's limiting freedom of speech. Holmes urged that "free trade in ideas" was the best way to discover truth. The Court's holding was that the circular Schenck distributed urging men to resist conscription was not speech protected by the First Amendment.

William R. Day

1903-1922

Source: Library of Congress

WILLIAM RUFUS DAY was born April 17, 1849, to Emily Spaulding Day and Luther Day, in Ravenna, Ohio. The Days were a respected family with New England roots, and young William was heir to small-town values, the Puritan work ethic, and a family legal tradition. His maternal great-grandfather served as chief justice of the Connecticut Supreme Court, while both his maternal grandfather and his father sat on the Ohio Supreme Court, as associate justice and chief justice respectively.

Day graduated from high school at the age of sixteen and entered the class of 1870 at the University of Michigan in Ann Arbor as a literature major. After graduation, he decided to continue the family tradition and returned to Ravenna to clerk in a local judge's law office for a year before entering the University of Michigan Law School. In 1872 Day moved to Canton, Ohio, not far from his hometown, to begin his practice. He would spend the next twenty-five years there as a trial lawyer and a partner in a leading law firm, Lynch and Day.

In campaigning for the presidency in 1896, William McKinley used the "front-porch" method, receiving and addressing delegations at his home in Canton, Ohio. Here he kicks off his campaign by delivering the acceptance speech to the Republican party's notification committee from his porch. As young attorneys active in Canton's Republican party, McKinley and William Rufus Day developed a close friendship that endured until McKinley's death in 1901. *Source: Culver Pictures*

The move to Canton was momentous for Day, and the associations he made there became the most enduring and important of his life.

Day's partner, William S. Lynch, already was a well-established lawyer in Canton and introduced him into the community, providing contacts that enabled Day's career, and the partnership, to prosper. Day specialized in criminal law and gained a reputation as a shrewd advocate, while Lynch pursued corporate law. The firm represented railroads, banks, mines, and utility companies, some of which would grow into companies of national importance.

Lynch also introduced Day to Mary Elizabeth Schaefer, who became his wife in 1875. Their marriage lasted

thirty-seven years, until she died in 1912. They were the parents of four sons, William, Rufus, Stephen, and Luther. According to one of his colleagues, the "domestic relations of Judge Day [were] exceptionally happy. He was a devoted husband and father. He also had many friends, not because he made a conscious effort to gain them, but because he was innately considerate of others and also inspired confidence."

Both Lynch and Day became active in Republican politics. Lynch unsuccessfully challenged Maj. William McKinley, a Civil War hero, for the position of prosecuting attorney of Stark County. In the course of the campaign, Day became well acquainted with McKinley, and they developed a close friendship. Eventually, McKinley came to call upon Day for legal, personal, and political advice and continued to do so throughout his illustrious career. Loyalty was one of Day's strongest traits, and it was apparent in his friendship with McKinley. They remained friends when McKinley served in Congress, the Ohio governor's mansion, and as president of the United States. After McKinley's assassination in 1901, Justice Day observed the anniversary of his friend's birth by distributing carnations to his colleagues on the Supreme Court bench. Day's biographer noted that Justice Louis Brandeis found this to be "a rare loyalty of one man to another, a loyalty that was present in small as well as important matters."

Physically, Day was a slight man with a frail constitution. He suffered from several serious illnesses and needed frequent vacations to renew himself. He was described as "rather above the average height, . . . thin, with a scholar's face and the old-fashioned scholar's shoulders, light complexion, reddish-brown hair and mustache, and [brown] eyes which added to the power in the lines of his face when they were not covered by his eye-glasses. . . . He had a low, but distinct and pleasing voice and a simple and courteous manner; . . . he looked like a gentle old-fashioned professor."

Day's personal habits were modest. His evenings were

spent reading the *Michigan Review* and other serious legal works. He did some bass fishing, played golf occasionally, and enjoyed a polite game of baseball when his health permitted. His principal leisure activity was watching the national pastime. While in Washington, he frequently went directly from the Supreme Court to the ballpark to see a game.

Day's mild manner masked his acute wit and active and able intellect. Many of his opponents found to their dismay that this seemingly frail and harmless man was a formidable opponent. One contemporary told how Day demoralized and defeated a group of lawyers who were attempting to take over an Ohio railway Day represented. After appearing meek and intimidated in the first few days of the trial, "the country lawyer [Day] . . . [left] the lights of the Boston bar in a semi-comatose condition and wondering what had happened to them."

Despite his interest in politics, Day did not wish to become a candidate himself. In 1886 he was drafted by both the Republican and Democrat parties to serve as a judge of the Court of Common Pleas. He resigned his post six months later, citing financial difficulties. In 1889 President Benjamin Harrison nominated Day for a U.S. district court judgeship. Day was confirmed by the Senate, but refused the post due to poor health.

When McKinley won the presidential election of 1896, many thought Day's friendship would be rewarded with a cabinet post, most likely the position of attorney general. Day was nominated to a post in the administration, but only as first assistant secretary of state. The office of secretary was filled by John Sherman, a senator from Ohio, who had resigned from the Senate to take the appointment. Sherman's seat was promptly filled by Marcus Hanna, McKinley's political manager. The public criticized the two appointments as a prearranged political deal, but it soon became apparent that there was a greater reason for concern. Sherman's mental capabilities had deteriorated to the point

that he was not only ineffective, but also a real danger. Day was appointed to assist the ailing Sherman in overseeing the nation's foreign policy. At first, the selection of a man who had no background in diplomacy puzzled Washington officialdom, but Day soon proved his worth.

Day essentially took over Sherman's duties as secretary of state. As such, he was involved in the annexation of Hawaii as a U.S. territory. Day also plunged into negotiations with Spain in an effort to avoid going to war over Cuba. However, after the American battleship *Maine* exploded in Havana Harbor, American sentiment, inflamed by sensationalized newspaper reports, made war inevitable. And so it was the mild-mannered Day who drafted the terms of war against Spain. Once war was declared in April 1898, Sherman's resignation was obtained, and Day was officially appointed secretary of state.

Day favored restraint in dealing with Spain, but public sentiment ran towards expansionism. The "splendid little war" was over in a brief ten weeks, and Day resigned his post September 16, 1898, to head the American delegation negotiating peace terms. Despite his personal feelings, Day carried out his instructions to seek the acquisition of the Philippine Islands, Puerto Rico, and Guam. He is credited with the idea of paying Spain $20 million in compensation for the territories.

At the conclusion of the peace conference, Day returned to private practice in Canton. Only a few months later, however, McKinley appointed Day to the U.S. Court of Appeals for the Sixth Circuit in Cincinnati. Day enjoyed his four years on that bench, especially the company of two other future members of the Supreme Court, William Howard Taft and Horace H. Lurton. Day wrote some eighty opinions as a circuit court judge, mostly having to do with private litigation and rules of procedure.

Day's appointment to the bench ended his involvement in politics, but he remained close to McKinley.

When the president was assassinated in 1901, he was deeply affected by his friend's death and took some time off to grieve. For a while it seemed that Day's influence in Washington had died with McKinley, but on January 29, 1903, McKinley's successor, Theodore Roosevelt, announced he was nominating Day to the Supreme Court. Roosevelt made his intentions known in Canton, where he was attending a memorial service organized by Day to commemorate McKinley's birthday. Taft apparently had been Roosevelt's first choice, but he refused because of his work in the Philippines, and so Roosevelt approached "good Day" to replace Justice George Shiras, who was retiring. Day was sworn in March 2, 1903, beginning two decades of service on the Court.

In 1917 Day wrote for a unanimous Court in *Buchanan v. Warley* that city ordinances that racially segregate neighborhoods are unconstitutional under the Fourteenth Amendment. He said that the law deprived blacks and whites of the right to dispose of their property. An unintended result of this decision was the private covenant, which the Court in 1948 said was unenforceable.

Day's judicial philosophy became most apparent, however, in his interpretation of laws governing commerce. He considered production, transportation, and selling to be separate categories of commerce and believed that each area should be regulated separately. The federal government's role should be relatively small, Day thought, and the states should have greater power to regulate commerce within their own borders. In areas where the two were in conflict, Day usually found in favor of the states. In his majority opinion in *Hammer v. Dagenhart* (1918), Day overturned a federal statute prohibiting the shipment in interstate commerce of goods produced by child labor on the grounds

President William McKinley (far left) appointed his loyal friend William R. Day (seated, center) secretary of state in 1898. Day had served as first assistant to John Sherman, whose mind was so impaired that Day performed all the functions of the office, keeping Sherman away from briefings. This situation led to embarrassing moments, such as when Sherman assured the Japanese minister that the United States had no intention of annexing the Hawaiian Islands, just as the State Department finished its work on the annexation treaty. *Source: Library of Congress*

The young boys working this loom in Macon, Georgia, circa 1912, were hired because they could be paid less than adults and their small hands were more agile. To abolish this practice, Congress passed legislation in 1916 prohibiting articles produced by child labor to be shipped in interstate commerce. William R. Day wrote the opinion for a bitterly divided Court, striking down the law as an unconstitutional intrusion on the power of the states. *Source: National Archives*

that it was an intrastate matter not subject to federal control.

There were some exceptions to Day's view of commerce. Speaking for the Court in *Caminetti v. United States* (1917) and in *Pittsburgh Melting Co. v. Totten* (1918), he ruled that it was appropriate for the federal government to regulate interstate commerce when moral and health hazards were involved.

Day was also opposed to corporations accumulating great wealth. This view was expressed in his dissenting opinion in *United States v. United States Steel Corporation* (1920), in which the Court ruled 4–3 in favor of the steel company. Writing for himself and Justices Mahlon Pitney and John Clarke, Day attacked all giant business combinations, denying that they were inevitable and desirable. He accused U.S. Steel of blatant and open defiance of the law under the Sherman Antitrust Act.

Day was an active member of the Court except when personal problems limited his activity. In 1911 his wife became ill and subsequently died, leaving him unable to work most of the year. He suffered a serious illness in 1915 that kept him off the bench for many months.

Day maintained close ties with his family members and colleagues. His son Rufus served as his law secretary through much of his tenure on the Supreme Court bench and became his constant companion after Mary Day died. His relations with other members of the Court also were warm. Justice Brandeis characterized Day as hard working, a serious scholar, but also a very congenial and charming man. Solicitor General John W. Davis noted that Day's "greatest value probably was in conference. His tact, his personal charm, his knowledge of the law, and his honest-mindedness were of extreme importance in discussions with his brother jurists."

On November 13, 1922, at age seventy-three, Day retired from the Supreme Court. Shortly thereafter, President Warren G. Harding asked him to serve as an umpire on the Mixed Claims Commission, which was set up to resolve claims resulting from World War I. Day was eager to serve, but his poor health forced him to resign in May 1923, ending his career of public service.

That summer Day and his son William vacationed at the family's summer home on Mackinac Island, Michigan. There, on July 9, Day died. He was buried in a simple ceremony in his hometown of Canton, Ohio, joining his wife and his old friend William McKinley.

William H. Moody

1906-1910

WILLIAM HENRY MOODY was a major statesman of the progressive era before becoming Theodore Roosevelt's third and final appointment to the Supreme Court. He was descended from William Moody of Suffolk, England, who, with a small band of Puritans, founded the town of Newbury, Massachusetts, in 1635. The future jurist was born there in the family's 200-year-old homestead December 23, 1853, to Henry L. Moody and Melissa A. Emerson Moody. On the eve of the Civil War, his fa-

ther moved the family to the neighboring town of Danvers, where he ran a large dairy farm. One of Moody's recollections of his boyhood years was wearing an Abraham Lincoln badge in the 1860 presidential election. "From childish impulse," he said, "I was then a Republican."

Moody's early education was in the Danvers public schools. In the fall of 1869 he entered Phillips Academy in Andover to prepare for Harvard College. At Andover, Moody studied classics and was captain of the baseball team; his interest in the sport continued throughout his life. He entered Harvard in 1872, but came close to being dropped at the end of his freshman year for academic deficiencies. To add to his woes, a promising career on the baseball diamond was ended by a leg injury. But matters improved when, as an upper-classman, he came into contact with an eminent historian and inspiring teacher—Henry Adams. Moody wrote his senior thesis under Adams's tutelage and graduated with honors in 1876.

Moody's formal legal education consisted of attending lectures for one term at Harvard Law School and reading law for fifteen months in the Boston office of Richard Henry Dana, a lawyer of international reputation. Moody admitted that his relationship with Dana was not close, but he felt inspired by being "near a man of genius." In April 1878 Moody passed the oral examination for admission to the bar. The examiners, who had been reluctant to hear him because his legal apprenticeship had been shorter than required, declared his performance to be the best they had ever witnessed.

At age twenty-five Moody opened an office in Haverhill, Massachusetts, along the Merrimac River. He soon became a visible presence in the community, serving three years on the school committee. In the mid-1880s he was elected the first president of the New England Baseball League. He became involved in Republican party politics and was voted city solicitor in 1888. Moody's law practice grew steadily after a slow start, and, at the time of his departure for Washington, an editorial in the Haverhill *Evening Gazette* proclaimed, "As an attorney he has but few equals and no superiors in the county."

In 1890 Moody was elected to the first of two terms as district attorney for the eastern district of Massachusetts. He considered these five years to be the best of his life. His name came to national attention for his role as co-prosecutor in the celebrated murder trial of Lizzie Borden, who was accused of the brutal slaying of her fa-

As district attorney for eastern Massachusetts, William H. Moody prosecuted the case of Lizzie Borden, a thirty-two-year-old Sunday school teacher accused of hacking her father and step-mother to death with an ax. Moody drew national acclaim for his deft handling of the prosecution, even though Borden was acquitted. *Source: Fall River Historical Society*

ther and stepmother with an ax. Although she was acquitted by a sympathetic jury, Moody held the prosecution team together and was the most competent lawyer in the case.

This period of Moody's life also provides a footnote to Supreme Court history. A future chief justice of the United States, Harlan Fiske Stone, was then teaching chemistry at Newburyport High School. He later wrote of Moody's influence on his own life. "After a year I left my work and delightful association there with regret. But the law was beckoning to me. Perhaps a friendship I had formed with a brilliant young district attorney who used to attend court at the courthouse on the mall just across from the high school building may have stimulated my interest in the law. His name was Moody, and afterward became Mr. Justice Moody, one of the ablest judges of the United States Supreme Court."

Moody entered national politics in 1895 when he was elected to fill a vacancy in the U.S. House of Representatives. He served four terms in Congress. During his first campaign he met Theodore Roosevelt at a Republican party dinner in Boston. Roosevelt wrote to his friend, Sen. Henry Cabot Lodge, about meeting "that very good young fellow Moody." The two men met again in 1898 in Washington at a Harvard alumni dinner. This meeting, at which they discussed naval affairs, had major consequences for Moody.

The Republicans had large majorities in the House during this period, and party discipline was extraordinarily strong. Moody supported progressive causes such as civil service reform, the eight-hour day for government workers, and direct election of U.S. senators. He also attacked the disenfranchisement of blacks in the southern states and tried unsuccessfully to have voting practices in the South investigated. On the floor and in committee he was noted for his mastery of detail. When Speaker of the House Thomas B. Reed retired in 1899, Moody was mentioned as a possible successor.

Shortly after Roosevelt assumed the presidency in 1901, he named Moody secretary of the Navy, a cabinet position. Moody's two years in this office coincided with Roosevelt's program of naval expansion. In addition to more battleships, Congress voted increases in the number of officers and seamen, and bases were established in Cuba and the Philippines. A reorganization of the department, long advocated by knowledgeable naval officers, began under Moody's direction.

When Philander Knox resigned as attorney general in June 1904, Roosevelt chose Moody to replace him. The president's attack on the monopolies had just begun with the government's victory in a landmark case against the Northern Securities Company. His aggressive antitrust campaign would reach its peak under Moody's direction. Moody recommended that trusts should be prosecuted under the criminal as well as the civil provisions of the Sherman Antitrust Act—something Knox had declined to do. Convictions were secured against the giant paper, coal, and beef trusts. Attorney General Moody personally tried the beef trust case in the lower federal court, and he argued four other cases before the Supreme Court. Justice Oliver Wendell Holmes, Jr., said of his performance, "He made some of the best arguments I have ever listened to for their combination of latent fire, brevity, insight, and point."

During his cabinet years Moody enjoyed a close relationship with his colleagues William Howard Taft and Elihu Root. Roosevelt said Moody was "one of the three or four men with whom I had been in closest touch and on whom I have leaned most heavily during our time of service together." As a bachelor, Moody was also much in demand in Washington social circles.

He was at the point of returning to private practice in Boston when, in June 1906, Justice Henry B. Brown retired from the Supreme Court. After months of indecision the president was on the verge of appointing Horace Lurton, a federal circuit court judge, to replace him. At the last minute he learned that Lurton, with one exception, had decided against the government in every case involving the Commerce Clause of the Constitution. Roosevelt then turned to his attorney general to fill the vacancy. Although his opponents feared he would lack independence because of his closeness to the president, Moody was confirmed by the Senate December 12, 1906. He took his seat next to Justice Holmes five days later. Holmes confided to his legal secretary that Justice Moody kept a box of hard candy at his side and ate from it all day with a sort of methodical persistence.

The Court was pleased with the appointment; all of the justices knew Moody and respected his legal mind. Chief Justice Melville Fuller wrote to a friend in Chicago that he liked the way Moody argued cases. Jus-

The unpopular trusts, which held monopolies over whole markets and had considerable clout over politicians, were the target of President Theodore Roosevelt's progressive reforms. As attorney general, William H. Moody skillfully argued four cases against the trusts before the Supreme Court. Roosevelt and Moody had smashing success in their campaign, obtaining convictions against the Standard Oil trust, and the paper, coal, and beef monopolies. *Source: Library of Congress*

tice William Day told the president that he would be a tower of strength on the bench. Personal relations among the justices were harmonious and relaxed. Moody for his part continued his close association with the president. He wrote important sections of a presidential speech highly critical of conservative judges, and Roosevelt sought his advice occasionally on patronage and other matters.

During his brief four-year tenure, Moody wrote only sixty-seven opinions, including five dissents. He wielded influence, however, in the weekly conference where the justices discussed the cases among themselves. There is evidence that he was often persuasive in winning opposing justices over to his side. His practice of providing concise summaries of his opinions made him a favorite of reporters who covered the Court.

Judicial restraint was the foundation of Moody's legal philosophy. In private correspondence, he complained that too many judges were striking down or narrowly interpreting progressive legislation on the basis of their own prejudices. A liberal nationalist, he believed that Congress had complete power under the Commerce Clause to cope with the social and economic problems of an industrial society. Thus, in the *Employers' Liability Cases* (1908), he dissented when a badly divided majority struck down a federal law holding railroads liable for the injury or death of their employees. He was able to speak for the Court in *St. Louis, Iron Mountain and Southern Railway Company v. Taylor* (1908) in upholding the Safety Appliance Act of 1905, which required railroads to provide safety devices for their equipment. He acknowledged that the act placed a hardship on interstate carriers, but argued that Congress had every

This 1868 depiction of the Angola Railroad disaster shows the rear car jumping from the track. Neither passenger nor employee safety was a great priority in the heady era of railroad expansion. William H. Moody wrote his most important dissent in the *Employers' Liability Cases* (1908), in which the majority struck down a federal law holding employers involved in interstate commerce accountable for the protection of their employees. *Source: Library of Congress*

right to place the blame for injuries resulting from defective equipment on those best able to bear the cost.

Despite his nationalism, Moody recognized that in a federal system some leeway must be left for the states. His best-known opinion illustrates this point. In *Twining v. New Jersey* (1908), a landmark for many years, the Court ruled, over the sole dissent of John Marshall Harlan, that the Bill of Rights guarantee against self-incrimination did not apply in a state trial. States should be free, Moody wrote, to fashion their own codes of criminal procedure, as long as the procedure was fundamentally fair.

In the mid-1920s, when the Court began to selectively incorporate various liberties of the federal Bill of Rights into the Due Process Clause of the Fourteenth Amendment, the *Twining* opinion began to erode, but it was not specifically overturned until 1964. Moody's suggestion in his opinion that some of the Bill of Rights provisions might be enforceable against the states foreshadowed the future course of judicial development.

Moody's opinions are characterized by clarity of expression and logical reasoning. He was at the threshold of an illustrious career on the bench when he became seriously ill. In the spring of 1909 he suffered the beginnings of what resulted in a complete breakdown of the central nervous system, diagnosed as infectious arthritis. He retreated to his home in Haverhill, where he was cared for by his sister. He officially retired from the Court November 20, 1910; a special act of Congress extended him full pension benefits.

The remaining seven years of his life were purgatory, and he referred to himself as one of the "living dead." He followed the Court's work through the opinions sent to him by the justices. Every afternoon a few local friends came to discuss current affairs. Roosevelt and Taft also visited their old friend, as did other state and national political leaders.

He died July 2, 1917. Justice Holmes, who knew Moody from the beginning of his professional life, said, "His work was greatly done."

Horace H. Lurton

1910-1914

Source: Photo by Harris & Ewing, Collection of the Supreme Court of the United States

HORACE HARMON LURTON, at age sixty-five, was the oldest jurist ever to ascend to the Supreme Court; he was also the first southern Democrat to be appointed to the high bench by a Republican president. Lurton was born February 26, 1844, in the town of Newport, Kentucky, across the Ohio River from Cincinnati. His ancestors were English, settling in Virginia in the eighteenth century; some members of the family gradually moved west in the great trans-Appalachian migration. Horace was the son of Sarah Ann Harmon Lurton and Lycurgus Leonidas Lurton, a practicing physician and pharmacist who eventually became an Episcopal minister.

During the 1850s Dr. Lurton uprooted his family to cross Kentucky and live in Tennessee. They settled in Clarksville, a town of about 15,000 inhabitants forty miles north of Nashville on the Cumberland River. Young Horace was educated locally until the age of sixteen, when his family moved to Chicago, and he enrolled at the now defunct Douglas University.

Under the leadership of Gen. John Hunt Morgan, daring Confederate cavalry raiders, including Horace H. Lurton, went behind Union lines to perform acts of sabotage on telegraph lines, bridges, and railroads. On this Virginia railroad, the saboteurs have taken up the track, set the wooden ties aflame, and bent the rails with the heat of the fire. *Source: Library of Congress*

In less than two years his education was interrupted by the shots fired at Fort Sumter, heralding the beginning of the Civil War. Eager to find a way to join the Confederate forces, Lurton gave up his studies. "It is my desire to yet strike a blow in defense of the best of causes—Southern Independence. I would go now if ma would only consent," he wrote to a friend on June 2, 1861. In later years Lurton recalled that he had received a hoopskirt or two, symbol of shirking from military duty, which may have helped overcome his parents' reluctance to return to the South from Illinois.

Lurton enlisted in the Fifth Tennessee Infantry Regiment (later the Thirty-fifth) and by the end of 1861 was a sergeant-major and a seasoned campaigner. A lung infection sidelined him in February 1862, and he returned to Clarksville with a medical discharge and orders to rest. The interruption was very brief; he reenlisted in time to be made prisoner of war with 12,000 other Confederates in Gen. Ulysses S. Grant's taking of Forts Henry and Donelson only a few weeks later. It is unclear whether he escaped or was released, but once free Lurton joined up with the guerrilla band of Gen. John Hunt Morgan, selling a watch his father had given him to buy the required horse. For more than a year Lurton rode with Morgan's daredevil cavalry in a succession of raids, performing acts of sabotage on Union railroads, bridges, and communication stations. But in July 1863, at the end of a long bold campaign, most of Morgan's

2,500 irregulars were captured. Lurton was to spend the next eighteen months of the war in a prison camp on an island in Lake Erie, where he came down with tuberculosis.

Fearing for his health, Lurton, according to a "good character" letter written by his fellow prisoners, apparently took the oath of loyalty to the Union to secure his release. Other reports, notably those circulated by Lurton in later years, describe how his mother traveled to Washington and personally persuaded President Abraham Lincoln to let him go. However the release was accomplished, Lurton returned home full of anti-Union sentiment. "We think a foreign war is rapidly approaching," he wrote to a friend on May 4, 1865, "and if it does then the banner of our invincible Confederacy will again be thrown to the breeze from every house top in our fair Southland. Never despair of so just a cause when supported by such a people."

As he recuperated, Lurton gave up any thought of further undergraduate study; by autumn he was able to enroll in the law school of Cumberland University, a few miles from Nashville. Two years of hard study, much of it at night with days spent working in his father's pharmacy, brought Lurton his law degree and admission to the bar in 1867. In September of that year Lurton married Mary Francis Owen, the daughter of a local physician. Their marriage, which lasted until Lurton's death, produced three sons and two daughters.

Soon after graduation, Lurton became a partner in an influential Clarksville law firm headed by James A. Bailey. A prominent Democratic politician, Bailey would later be appointed to fill the unexpired Senate term of Sen. Andrew Johnson, the former president, upon his death.

Lurton's association with Democratic politics earned him an interim appointment in 1875 as presiding judge of the Sixth Chancery Division (court of equity) of Tennessee. At age thirty-one, Lurton became the youngest chancellor in Tennessee history. A year later his peers on the bench voted unanimously to retain him for a full term.

Financial need drew him back into private practice in 1878, and he entered into a successful eight-year partnership with his predecessor as chancellor, Charles G. Smith. Their association brought Lurton both material rewards and personal prestige. He became president of the largest local bank, a vestryman in the Trinity Episcopal Church, and, in 1882, a trustee of the University of the South.

These assets, combined with a capacity to make friends and a vigorous stump campaign, brought him election, at age forty-two, to the Tennessee Supreme Court in 1886. This position marked the beginning of twenty-eight years on the bench. Once on the court, Lurton began to show an approach to jurisprudence that would stamp his entire career. He became known for his gentleness and civility, his energy, his powers of persuasion, and his great capacity to reconcile opposing arguments. Only rarely did he find it necessary to dissent.

When, after seven years, the office of chief justice was vacated, Lurton's dominant position was so clear that his colleagues voted unanimously for him to take the center chair. Four months later, however, Grover Cleveland, the newly elected president, selected Lurton to sit on the United States Court of Appeals for the Sixth Circuit to replace Howell E. Jackson, who had been appointed to the U.S. Supreme Court. Both Jackson and Lurton were loyal Democrats, Confederate army veterans, and graduates of Cumberland Law School. With a background so similar to Jackson's, Lurton could be expected to continue the existing political and regional balance of the court.

When Lurton arrived in Cincinnati for his new appointment, fate confronted him in the person of the presiding judge of the three-member court of appeals.

William Howard Taft (circa 1891), was presiding judge of the appeals court for the Sixth Circuit when Horace H. Lurton was appointed in 1893. Although a southern Democrat and former Confederate, Lurton impressed Taft so much that when Taft became president he crossed party lines to name Lurton to the Supreme Court. Lurton did not live long enough to see Taft's appointment as chief justice in 1921. *Courtesy of the Cincinnati Historical Society*

The judge was William Howard Taft, only thirty-six years old, a term as solicitor general already behind him, the presidency and chief justiceship of the United States still to come. In 1899, six years after Lurton's arrival, they were joined by William Day, who, like Taft, was an Ohio Republican. The three became fast friends, the political differences between a southern Democrat and two midwestern Republicans giving way to friendship and mutual professional respect. The court was recognized during Lurton's tenure as the ablest of the eight federal appeals courts. Taft later praised Lurton's "industry, his sense of responsibility for the court, his profound knowledge of the law, his wonderful power of reconciliation of the differences in the conference room, and his statesman-like forecast of the principles of the court's decisions." When Taft left to become governor general of the Philippines, Lurton took over as presiding judge.

With his gentle paternal manner, Lurton was the image of the courteous southern gentleman. Short in stature, he was relatively stout and, in keeping with the fashion of his day, had an enormous mustache. According to one observer, Lurton issued "steady-going judgments" and did not "attempt to render startling or sensational decisions." Generally conservative, he used precedent whenever possible to maintain the status quo. Lurton carried his judicial expertise into the classrooms of Vanderbilt University, where he taught constitutional law from 1898 to 1905, before serving as its dean until 1909.

Lurton was nearly appointed to the Supreme Court in 1906 when his friends Taft, now secretary of war, and Day, who had been named to the Court in 1903, persuaded President Theodore Roosevelt that Lurton should succeed Justice Henry B. Brown. But Roosevelt could not overcome the opposition of his fellow Republican, Sen. Henry Cabot Lodge, who pointed out that, with one exception, Lurton had voted against the government in every case involving the Commerce Clause of the Constitution.

The appointment went instead to Attorney General William H. Moody, a Republican of Massachusetts. Lurton's Confederate past, his Democratic affiliation, and his advanced age were all considered strikes against him. However, on December 13, 1909, Taft, now president, brushed aside questions of political partisanship and age to choose his old friend as his first nominee to the high bench. Taft later told him, "The only pleasure of my administration, as I have contemplated it in the past, has been to commission you a Justice of the Supreme Court." The expected partisan opposition in Congress never developed, and Lurton was confirmed a week later.

Lurton felt deeply the historic significance of his appointment. He later wrote about his train journey to Washington to take office, during which he detoured around Cincinnati to take the southern route. "I felt that in appointing me, President Taft, aside from the manifestations of his friendship, had a kindly heart for the South; that he wished to draw the South to him with cords of affection. So, being all a Southerner myself, I determined to go to Washington through the South—every foot of the way."

During his four short years on the high bench, Lurton was influenced by his colleagues to become more progressive. Once on the Court he abandoned his earlier conservatism and voted most frequently with Oliver Wendell Holmes, Jr., joining him in eight dissents. Lurton wrote eighty-seven opinions, none of them groundbreaking or landmark cases, all of them based on solid research and argument. Generally, he went along with a substantial majority of the Court in somewhat enlarging the powers of the federal government. He consistently voted with the majority in upholding the Sherman Antitrust Act, particularly in regard to smaller corporations, but at the same time accepted the concept of "reasonable" monopolies for some corporate giants.

In 1911 Justice Lurton served as a member of the Committee to Revise the Equity Rules in Federal Courts and was apparently so interested in the subject that he went to England that summer to make a special study of English equity practices. He became ill late in the 1913 term, but, after a Florida vacation, Lurton resumed full activity on the bench with the 1914 term. That summer he went with his wife for vacation to Atlantic City, where the genial Tennessean died of a heart attack July 12, 1914.

Charles Evans Hughes

1910-1916, 1930-1941

Source: Photo by Harris & Ewing, Collection of the Supreme Court of the United States

CHARLES EVANS HUGHES, who served non-consecutive Supreme Court terms as associate justice and chief justice, was born April 11, 1862, during the Civil War. His father, David Charles Hughes, was a young Methodist preacher from Wales who landed at New York Harbor in 1855 and found a pulpit in a small community on the Hudson River. Three years later he met and fell in love with Mary Catherine Connelly, a school teacher. To meet the objections of her Baptist parents to marriage outside their faith, Hughes joined the Baptist church and was assigned to a Baptist congregation in Glens Falls, on the upper Hudson River, where Charles was born. He was an only child, brought up under strong religious discipline and moral constraint. Later in life Hughes wrote, "It was the fondest hope of my parents that I would enter the ministry and I was early 'dedicated.' . . . I was constantly warned of the necessity of subduing evil inclinations, lest they grow with my growth and strengthen with my strength."

Sent to a public school at age six, within weeks young Charles found it boring and confining. He submitted to his parents the "Charles E. Hughes' Plan of Study" to continue his education at home. They agreed, with his mother drilling him hard in writing and arithmetic and his father largely directing his reading. By the age of eight he was studying Greek. Shortly before young Hughes turned twelve, the family moved to New York City. Charles was enrolled in a public school, and at age thirteen he received his high school diploma, standing second in his class.

Hughes then enrolled in Madison College (now Colgate University) to prepare for the ministry. At the end of his second year at Madison, Hughes transferred to Brown University, chosen by his parents for its Baptist traditions and by Hughes for its more liberal and cosmopolitan atmosphere. He began to attend the theater, played poker (betting with matchsticks), took up smoking, and became a baseball fan. He earned extra money by ghost writing for fellow students, but did not neglect his studies. Hughes was admitted to the Phi Beta Kappa academic society at the end of his junior year, elected an editor of the student newspaper, and at nineteen, the youngest in a class of forty-three, he graduated in 1881 with third-highest honors.

During the first term of his senior year, he wrote to his mother that he no longer felt a call to the ministry and did not know what he wanted to do after graduation. But by March 1881 he wrote his parents, "The more I think of the future, the more I incline toward the legal profession." Lacking the money to begin law school immediately, Hughes taught Greek, Latin, and algebra for a year at an academy in Delhi, New York, and spent many of his afternoons and evenings reading law in the office of a local lawyer. With his father's support he entered Columbia Law School in the fall of 1882 and graduated with highest honors in 1884. His grade on the New York bar examination was 99.5.

For most of the next twenty years Hughes devoted

himself to the practice of law. He joined the firm of Chamberlin, Carter, and Hornblower, where he had worked summers while at Columbia. Within five years he was made a partner in a reorganized firm, and at age twenty-five he was securely established in the profession. In 1885 he met Antoinette Carter, daughter of one of the senior partners, and three years later they were married in a simple ceremony conducted by Hughes's father. The couple had three daughters and a son who became solicitor general of the United States.

Overworked and in poor health, Hughes broke off this rapid professional and financial ascent in 1891 to accept a full professorship at Cornell University Law School. Although he was happy in teaching, two years later he was persuaded to return to his law firm in New York, continuing for a few years as a special law lecturer at both Cornell University and New York Law School.

Hughes entered public life in 1905 when he was appointed counsel to a New York legislative committee established to investigate gas and electric utility rates. The appointment was greeted with little enthusiasm by the press, but, as Hughes showed his mastery of the case, the commentary turned to praise. "Mr. Hughes is a large man, not burly, but with the appearance of one who is built on big, broad lines," the *New York Evening Mail* reported. "His manner is that of one sure of himself and his position. . . . In his examination and handling of the Consolidated Gas Company officials he has been polite and good natured, but insistent. He has shown a knowledge of the finances and the corporate history of the big gas monopoly superior to that of many of the executive officers, and no obscurities of bookkeeping or intricacies of accounts have disturbed him. He has dug for facts which he knew the books and the witnesses could show, and he has got them." Hughes uncovered hard evidence of corruption, fraud, inflated profits, and adulterated gas, and the result was a huge reduction in gas rates for both the city and individual consumers. Later in the year, this time in the life insurance business, he again exposed widespread financial and political manipulation at the expense of policyholders and small stockholders.

Now a national figure, Hughes emerged as an obvious answer to the New York Republican party's need for a strong candidate for governor in 1906, against the threat posed by William Randolph Hearst. Hughes refused to seek the nomination actively but, partly through the endorsement of President Theodore Roosevelt, was chosen by acclamation at the party convention. In the November election, he was the only statewide Republican candidate to win.

As governor, Hughes insisted upon honesty and efficiency in administration and the appointment of able officials. He persuaded an often reluctant legislature to adopt the nation's first compulsory workmen's compensation laws, safety measures for railway engineers and firemen, an eight-hour day for some railway workers, and the establishment of public service commissions with broad powers over utilities.

As early as 1907 he was being mentioned as a possible Republican candidate for president. He refused to seek the nomination openly, although he permitted efforts on his behalf to continue. The party nominated

William Howard Taft, who asked Hughes to be his running mate, but Hughes declined. Instead, he ran for reelection as governor and won a second term.

President Taft's nomination on April 25, 1910, of Hughes to fill the seat on the Supreme Court vacated by the death of David Brewer, was well received by the Court and the press. Since Taft had earlier told Hughes of his wish to see him become chief justice, he now wrote to his prospective appointee, "Don't misunderstand me as to the Chief Justiceship. I mean that if that office were now open I would offer it to you and it is probable that if it were to become vacant during my term, I should promote you to it; but, of course, conditions change, so that it would not be right for me to say by way of promise what I would do in the future."

Hughes accepted the appointment and was confirmed by the Senate May 2, but before he took his seat, Chief Justice Melville Fuller died. It was widely assumed that Hughes would succeed him. After months of deliberation, however, President Taft elevated Associate Justice Edward D. White to the center seat. Over the next six years, Hughes wrote 151 opinions including 32 dissents. In only nine cases was there dissent from his decisions for the Court. "The youngest member of the

As Warren G. Harding's secretary of state, Charles Evans Hughes negotiated the first successful disarmament treaty in modern history. The 1921 Washington Conference brought together nine naval powers from Europe and the Far East. The resulting treaties not only halted the naval arms race, but also guaranteed Japan power over the Pacific and respected China's independence and territorial integrity, providing peace for a decade. *Source: AP/Wide World Photos*

Court," wrote a biographer, "he contributed energy, practicality, and impressive analytical force to its work."

As the 1916 presidential election approached, Hughes, as he had done twice previously, refused to allow his name to be used in the primary or other selection processes for delegates to the Republican nominating convention. However, he did not go so far as to say he would refuse the nomination if it were offered, and he was chosen on the third ballot. Hughes resigned his post as associate justice immediately, on June 10, and wired his acceptance to the convention. "I have not desired the nomination," he said. "I have wished to remain on the bench. But in this critical period in our nation's history, I recognize that it is your right to summon, and that it is my paramount duty to respond."

The election was one of the closest in history. As the returns came in on election day, the *New York Times,* which had declared its support for Woodrow Wilson, conceded Wilson's defeat. It was not until Friday, with the final returns from California, that the outcome was clear. The electoral vote was 277–254 for Wilson, the popular vote 9,126,300 to 8,546,789. A disappointed Hughes made no effort to continue in Republican politics, but returned to the practice of law in New York City as the senior member of the firm of Hughes, Rounds, Schurman, and Dwight. Over the next four years he represented some of the leading American corporations and appeared in several cases before his former colleagues on the Supreme Court.

The day President Warren G. Harding assumed office, March 4, 1921, he appointed Hughes secretary of state—a post Hughes continued to hold during Calvin Coolidge's administration. Among Hughes's many accomplishments over the next four years were the disarmament treaty of 1922, which froze the international naval arms race for ten years; a four-nation pact promising security for Japan in the Western Pacific; and a nine-nation treaty for multilateral observance of China's open door diplomacy.

Charles Evans Hughes, Jr., (left) was serving as solicitor general in 1930 when President Herbert Hoover appointed his father to be chief justice of the United States. Because the solicitor general argues cases for the government before the Supreme Court, the younger Hughes resigned his position to avoid any appearance of conflict of interest. A third generation of Hughes men is represented here by Stuart Hughes, born in 1916. *Source: Library of Congress*

In 1925 Hughes once again returned to private law practice in an effort to regain his fortunes. Public service had cost him a considerable amount of money in foregone legal fees. But he continued to serve part time in positions of high responsibility, helping the cause of world peace in the late 1920s by serving as judge on the Permanent Court of Arbitration in the Hague and on the Permanent Court of International Justice.

Hughes was the acknowledged leader of the American bar in 1930 when President Herbert Hoover named him chief justice to succeed Taft, the man who had first placed him on the Court. To his surprise and sorrow, unlike his appointment as associate justice in 1910, the nomination drew strong opposition from progressive and southern Democratic senators. After a ten-day de-

Desperate to dilute the conservatism of the Supreme Court, which had been systematically striking down his progressive New Deal legislation, President Franklin D. Roosevelt proposed a plan in 1937 that would allow him to name one justice for every justice over age seventy with ten years service who refused to retire, up to a total of fifteen justices. Chief Justice Charles Evans Hughes persuaded his brethren to uphold some of Roosevelt's reform legislation, blunting the need for a reorganization and helping Congress to defeat the plan. *Source: Library of Congress*

as extensive, as any man ever brought to a seat on the Court, combined with a very powerful and acute mind that could mobilize these vast resources in the conduct of the business of the Court." Chief Justice Hughes took a middle ground between the conservative and liberal camps that formed in the 1930s when the Court was ruling on the constitutionality of innovative legislation intended to help the nation recover from the devastating effects of the Great Depression. Although generally a "swing vote," Hughes voted with the conservatives to strike down much of the New Deal legislation, and he wrote the opinion invalidating the National Industrial Recovery Act.

In 1937 President Franklin D. Roosevelt proposed a plan giving the president the power to appoint an additional member to the Court for each justice over the age of seventy who did not retire. Hughes displayed brilliant political dexterity in persuading the Court to retreat from its adamant opposition to the president's legislation. He skillfully led the Court's turnabout and wrote opinions upholding the constitutionality of the National Labor Relations Act of 1935 and of a law setting minimum wages for women and children workers. The change in the Court's temperament undermined Roosevelt's cry for reform, and Congress defeated the Court-enlargement plan. As chief justice, Hughes helped shape the law to respond to social change during difficult times.

Hughes retired from the Court July 1, 1941, at the age of seventy-nine. He continued to live in Washington until August 17, 1948, when he died of congestive heart failure at his summer cottage on Cape Cod. Justice Oliver Wendell Holmes, Jr., best summed up Hughes's character when he called him "not only a good fellow, experienced and wise, but funny, and with doubts that open vistas through the wall of a non-conformist conscience."

bate in which opponents charged that, because of his career in corporate law, Hughes exemplified "the influence of powerful combinations in the political and financial world," he was confirmed by a vote of 52–26, February 13, 1930. That same day his son, Charles Evans Hughes, Jr., resigned his post as solicitor general in the Hoover administration to avoid a conflict of interest.

Felix Frankfurter, who joined the Court in 1939, later wrote that Hughes took the center seat "with a mastery . . . unparalleled in the history of the Court, a mastery that derived from experience as diversified, as intense,

Willis Van Devanter

1911-1937

Source: Library of Congress

WILLIS VAN DEVANTER, the only justice appointed from the state of Wyoming, was born April 17, 1859, in Marion, Indiana, to Isaac Van Devanter and Violetta Spencer Van Devanter. He was the eldest of eight children, all of whom were reared as Methodists. The earliest of his ancestors to inhabit the New World came from Holland in 1662 and settled in what would become New York State. The family lived in various eastern states before moving to Indiana nine years before Willis's birth.

Bound by his love for the land, Van Devanter found a peaceful satisfaction in farming, but his father, who had a successful career in the law, pressed him to pursue a formal education. The young Van Devanter entered Indiana Asbury (later DePauw) University in 1875. After two years of outstanding work, he was forced to withdraw when his father was stricken with a severe illness. While accompanying him on a convalescent trip to Michigan, Van Devanter met his future bride, Dellice Burhans. They married in 1883 and had two sons.

Spring cattle roundups, such as this 1885 event in Horse Creek, Wyoming, often led to legal wrangles between cattlemen's associations when they convened at railheads to send their herds to market. As a shrewd young Wyoming lawyer,
Willis Van Devanter made a living settling fights over rustling, grazing rights, and unbranded calves. In 1892 he served
as defense attorney for the twenty-three cattlemen accused of organizing rustling raids during the infamous Johnson
County War. *Source: American Heritage Center, University of Wyoming*

Van Devanter's father gradually regained his health,
and the future justice was able to complete his education. He entered Cincinnati Law School in 1879, graduated second in his class in May 1881, and joined his father's law firm, Lacey and Van Devanter. When his father retired in 1884, his law partner, John W. Lacey,
moved to Wyoming, where he had been appointed
chief justice of the Wyoming Territorial Supreme
Court. Willis Van Devanter, anxious for the adventure
and the chance to prove himself, which the Wyoming
Territory offered, followed Lacey to Cheyenne, where
he set up a private practice.

Organized as a territory in 1868 under the auspices of
the Union Pacific Railroad, Wyoming was still rough
and tumble western frontier when Van Devanter arrived. The territory reeled violently from year to year
between economic boom and bust. He profited from
the boom by allying himself with two of the most powerful interest groups in Wyoming at the time: the cattle
ranchers and the railroads. The railroads had opened
the range to ranching, and the ranches, loosely defined,

comprised tens of thousands of acres of unfenced land,
much of which was actually federal reserve, on which
cattlemen's "associations" grazed their herds. At round-
up these herds were brought to the nearest railhead for
shipping, and disputes over rustling, unbranded new-
borns, and land and water rights usually ensued. Not
surprisingly, these disputes accounted for a large portion of Van Devanter's practice.

Van Devanter was also associated with the cattle interests through his father-in-law, who owned a one-
third stake in the sizable Swan Land and Cattle Company. When consecutive harsh winters in 1885 and 1886
destroyed much of the herd and forced the company
into receivership, Van Devanter traveled about the region trying to save the family's investment from bankruptcy, but to no avail. His travels, however, permitted
him to develop numerous political contacts, enabling
him to find benefit even from a disaster.

In 1887 he became law partners with Charles N. Potter, an influential Republican. Their successful partnership lasted two years and counted among its clients the

Burlington Railroad—the first of many legal associations Van Devanter developed with powerful railroad interests. The partnership also marked Van Devanter's establishment in the Republican party apparatus in Wyoming, which he would come to dominate within a decade through personal industry and political skill. Van Devanter was appointed city attorney of Cheyenne in 1887 and, following a vigorous campaign, was elected to the territorial legislature in 1888.

Van Devanter quickly emerged as the leading Republican spokesman in the territorial House of Representatives and was named chairman of the Judiciary Committee despite being a member of the minority party. During his tenure in the House, he drafted a fifty-five-section appropriations bill, which provided for construction of the University of Wyoming at Laramie and a $150,000 addition to the capitol building in Cheyenne. He also codified the territorial laws and statutes, which were voted into effect virtually without debate in 1888. These codes formed the basis of the state constitution when Wyoming gained admission to the Union two years later.

Van Devanter worked tirelessly to promote Republican interests in Wyoming, both on the territorial and national levels. He campaigned hard for Benjamin Harrison's 1888 presidential bid and was rewarded in 1889 with an appointment as chief justice of the Wyoming Territory. Van Devanter's jurisprudence was strongly influenced by his personal beliefs in self-reliance and taking responsibility for one's actions. Following conviction of a thief, he scolded the man that no one physically able to work "need steal in Cheyenne." Years later Van Devanter could recount with some pride that none of his criminal convictions on that court were ever appealed and that none of his civil decisions were ever overturned.

Shortly after Wyoming was admitted as the forty-fourth state, Van Devanter was easily elected to the new state supreme court. He served for only a few days after his confirmation, however, before passing the post on to a fellow Republican and returning to private practice. He formed a highly successful law firm with John Lacey, whom he had followed to Wyoming from Indiana six years before, and who had since become his brother-in-law.

During this period of Van Devanter's private practice, he served as the lead defense attorney for twenty-three cattlemen who were being held by the government for their part in the notorious Johnson County War of 1892. The cattlemen, along with a number of hired guns from Texas, had formed a raiding party in response to losses of their herd to organized rustlers in the north. While instances of rustling had occurred, part of the disputed herd was also claimed by a rival cattlemen's association in Johnson County. The U.S. cavalry arrested members of the raiding party, but Van Devanter eventually managed to secure their acquittal.

One of the few Wyoming attorneys eligible to practice before the Supreme Court of the United States, Van Devanter was called upon by the newly admitted state to represent it in *Ward v. Race Horse* (1896). At issue in Van Devanter's first appearance before the Court was whether Wyoming's statehood voided an Indian treaty that allowed Indians to hunt out of season in violation of state law. The U.S. attorney defending the Indians' treaty rights had prevailed in the U.S. District Court in Cheyenne, but Van Devanter won the case on appeal to the Supreme Court with a 7–1 majority.

Much of Van Devanter's practice involved the legal affairs of his powerful client, the Union Pacific Railroad, including numerous congressional inquiries into the company's land acquisition policies. He also continued to be active in Republican party politics during this period, holding several state and national posts; however, a severe case of typhoid kept him from serving as a delegate to the 1896 national convention.

With his powerful physique and rugged frontier

spirit, Van Devanter had in earlier years hunted grizzly bears with Buffalo Bill in Wyoming's Bighorn Mountains. Yet, throughout the summer and fall of 1896 he lay bedridden and unable to actively campaign for the Republican ticket. Nonetheless, after his election as president, William P. McKinley recognized Van Devanter's service to the party and appointed him assistant attorney general at the Department of the Interior. The post brought Van Devanter to Washington in 1897 and gave him the opportunity to further hone his legal skills in matters relating to public lands and Native Americans. He also brought his expertise to the classroom as a lecturer at Columbian (now George Washington) University.

In 1903 President Theodore Roosevelt appointed Van Devanter to the U.S. Court of Appeals for the Eighth Circuit, where he spent seven years handling numerous cases involving complex technical issues such as jurisdictional questions, land claims, and the rights of railroads. His extensive experience earned him the atten-

Hailed as a "great event," the opening of the Union Pacific Railroad's leg from Omaha to San Francisco in 1869 fulfilled the company's promise of "a railroad from the Atlantic to the Pacific." A longtime attorney for railroad companies, including the powerful Union Pacific, Willis Van Devanter ran into Democratic opposition to his appointment to the Supreme Court. *Source: Union Pacific Museum Collection*

tion of President William Howard Taft, who nominated Van Devanter to the Supreme Court December 12, 1910. Wary of his close ties to the powerful railroad interests, liberals strongly opposed his nomination. Democrat William Jennings Bryan criticized him as "the judge that held that two railroads running parallel to each other for two thousand miles were not competing lines, one of the roads being that of Union Pacific." Nevertheless, his nomination was confirmed by voice vote in the Senate only three days later.

During the twenty-six years Van Devanter served on the Court, he delivered only 346 majority opinions, making him by far the least prolific justice of his time. Probably his most noteworthy majority opinion was in *McGrain v. Daugherty* (1927), in which he affirmed Congress's right to subpoena witnesses. Even though his written output was small, his colleagues regarded his contributions to the weekly conference discussions as vital. Having appointed him to the Court, Taft, now chief justice, said that Van Devanter was "far and away the most valuable man in our court" because of his thoughtful deliberations in the justices' closed conferences. Such praise was shared by Van Devanter's colleagues across the philosophical spectrum. Justice Louis Brandeis once commended Van Devanter as the "master of formulas that decided cases without creating precedents."

While on the Court, Van Devanter was selected to serve on a committee to draft what was later enacted as the Judiciary Act of 1925. He was the chief draftsman of the legislation, which greatly broadened the Court's powers to decide which cases to review. In 1921 the Court had been experiencing a one- to two-year delay between accepting and hearing cases. Van Devanter said, "It is not too much to say that one-third of the business which now comes to the Supreme Court results in no advantage to the litigants." As a result of the Judiciary Act, the Court completely eliminated its backlog by 1929.

In the 1930s the Court found itself increasingly at odds with Congress and President Franklin D. Roosevelt over the constitutionality of legislation designed to combat the devastating effects of the Great Depression. The president, along with his newly elected Democratic majority in Congress, enacted a reform package, commonly known as the New Deal. A majority of the Court's justices, most of whom had been appointed by Roosevelt's Republican predecessors, recognized the problems the nation was facing, but regarded many of the New Deal solutions as dangerous extensions of federal authority beyond what the Constitution allowed.

As the philosophical leader of the so-called Four Horsemen (including Justices Pierce Butler, James McReynolds, and George Sutherland) who made up the Court's consistently conservative wing, Van Devanter played a central role in striking down the president's legislation. After his retirement in 1937 he privately acknowledged that because of ill health he might have stepped down five years earlier were it not for two factors: he sincerely believed Roosevelt's legislation was a threat to the Constitution, and, not being a wealthy man, he depended on his salary as a justice. He waited to retire until June 2, 1937—after Roosevelt signed an act providing increased retirement benefits to justices who had reached age seventy and had at least ten years service.

In retirement, Van Devanter accepted judicial assignments on various New York lower courts. His extraordinary background in legal procedure allowed him to dispose of cases "without sacrifice of fairness or courtesy to litigants, witnesses or counsel" at a rate to which most attorneys appearing before him were unaccustomed. Despite his advancing age, Van Devanter would work on his opinions often past midnight and appear with

Scandals plagued the Harding administration, including the revelation that Attorney General Harry M. Daugherty (above) had failed to prosecute those implicated in the Teapot Dome oil lease fraud. The congressional committee charged with the investigation subpoenaed Daugherty's brother, Mally. He refused to appear, and challenged the Senate's power to compel him to testify. Willis Van Devanter's opinion in *McGrain v. Daugherty* (1927) broadly interpreted Congress's power to secure needed information by compelling private citizens to testify, even without an explicitly stated legislative purpose. *Source: Library of Congress*

decision in hand when court convened the next morning.

In keeping with his love for the land, in 1934 Van Devanter bought a 700-acre tract of land in Maryland, which he farmed. Prior to that he often recuperated from his rigorous schedule on a small island he had purchased in the Great Lakes. Van Devanter died February 8, 1941, in Washington, D.C.

Joseph R. Lamar
1911-1916

JOSEPH RUCKER LAMAR was born October 14, 1857, in Elbert County, Georgia, at Cedar Grove, one of the plantations owned by his maternal grandmother. Both his parents' families had been long established on American soil and were socially prominent in Georgia. Joseph Lamar's first American ancestor on his father's side was a French Huguenot refugee, who in 1665 was granted land in Virginia. Also descended from this ancestor was Joseph's illustrious cousin, Lucius Quintus Cincinnatus Lamar of Missis-sippi, who served on the U.S. Supreme Court from 1888 to 1893.

Joseph's grandfather, Philip Lamar, moved south in 1829 and settled the family on a large tract of land near Columbus, Georgia. Joseph's father, James Lamar, studied law and passed the bar in 1850, but he did not practice law. Rather, influenced by Alexander Campbell, the president of his school, Bethany College, to convert to his new Protestant sect, he become a pastor in the Disciples of Christ church in Augusta.

Joseph was the oldest in his family, which included his brother, Philip, and sister, Mary. The family's harmony was shattered when their mother, Mary Rucker Lamar, died; Joseph was not quite seven years old. Then came the advance of Gen. William Sherman's Union Army through Georgia, which forced the Lamars to take refuge. Late in 1865 James Lamar remarried and returned with his family to Augusta and his pastorate.

The Presbyterian pastorate of Woodrow Wilson's father stood side by side with that of Reverend Lamar, their back yards separated only by a wooden fence. Here the future president and future justice became playmates, in addition to being schoolmates at a private academy. They organized a debating society that met in an attic and played on the same baseball team.

In 1870 the Wilson family moved to South Carolina, and the two Lamar boys were sent for a year to an institute in the small town of Jefferson, Georgia. Their itinerant education continued at the highly respected Richmond Academy in Augusta, then the Penn Lucy Academy in Baltimore, Maryland. In 1874 Joseph entered the University of Georgia in Athens, but his studies were interrupted the following year by illness. Before he could return to the university, his father accepted a call to a pastorate in Louisville, Kentucky, and moved there with his family.

Persuaded by their father to continue their studies at his alma mater, the two brothers completed their undergraduate education at Bethany College, outside Wheeling, West Virginia. Their choice was their own, however, because an inheritance from their grandfather had made them financially independent. Bethany was primarily a theological institution, but nonreligious in its classical and scientific courses. "The boys are juniors in Bethany College—Joe knowing pretty much everything outside the course, and Phil pretty much everything in it," their father wrote at the time. Indeed, Joseph was active in the debating society, pitched for the college baseball team, was a prompter and sometime actor in college theatricals, a member of a Greek letter fraternity, and a regular at most social functions. He was a voracious reader and strong in Latin, but he ignored mathematics so thoroughly that how he passed the examinations was considered a mystery.

Lamar received his B.A. degree in 1877 after two years at Bethany. He enrolled in Washington and Lee University in Lexington, Virginia, to study law, but dropped out after the Christmas holidays and returned to Augusta, where he read law in the office of Henry Clay Foster, a highly respected attorney. Only a few months later Lamar was admitted to the bar.

He returned to Bethany to teach Latin for a year, and perhaps also for sentimental reasons. On January 30, 1879, he married Clarinda Huntington Pendleton, the

Alexander Campbell founded the Disciples of Christ in 1810 with his father, Rev. Thomas Campbell, and other progressive Presbyterians opposed to closed communion. Campbell converted Joseph R. Lamar's father, James, who became a pastor in the new sect's church in Augusta. *Source: Library of Congress*

Clarinda Huntington Pendleton, the daughter of the president of Bethany College, was probably the reason Joseph R. Lamar returned to the school to teach. The couple had a happy marriage and, after her husband's death, Clarinda Lamar wrote *The Life of Joseph Rucker Lamar,* a full-length biography published in 1926. *Source: Courtesy of the Atlanta History Center*

worked hard at his law practice, keeping a law library at home in addition to his office. His record of success in trials, particularly before juries, was such that a young friend asked him, "Mr. Lamar, you only take the cases that you know you are going to win, don't you?" He prepared meticulously and in depth, and remained modest about his successes.

In 1886, at the age of twenty-eight, Lamar ran for the state legislature and was elected against a strong opponent. A representative of Richmond County, he showed particular interest in law reform and wrote legislation that resulted in the more efficient administration of justice in the state. His industry inspired a fellow member to rise during the uncomfortably hot summer session and suggest that the legislature recess indefinitely "and let the Clerk and Joe Lamar finish the business of the session." Although he had stipulated in his campaign that he would serve but one term, friends entered his name for reelection, and Lamar reluctantly accepted a second term.

Before the end of the century, Lamar had become one of the most prominent attorneys in Georgia and one of the most active of Augusta's citizens in positions of public trust. He was a member of the board of Richmond Academy, a trustee of the Medical College, president of the Library Association, president of the city's first lecture bureau, a trustee of his father's former church, and a director of the Orphan Asylum and the Young Men's Christian Association. He became the first president of the Young Men's Business League in 1893 and served it actively for several years. He was also in wide demand as a public speaker.

The governor recognized Lamar's superior talents by appointing him in 1893 to a commission to rewrite the state's law codes. Lamar had a strong feeling for Georgia's heritage and legal traditions, and his research and writings on the state's legal history brought him additional praise. He even traveled to London to examine and copy the voluminous data on Georgia's legal insti-

college president's daughter. They had three children, sons Philip and William and a daughter, Mary, who died in infancy.

Lamar's legal career began in earnest in 1880 when Foster invited him to be his partner. Their association lasted until Foster's death ten years later. The young lawyer's rise was rapid, and the Lamar family acquired a modest house in Augusta, successively enlarged during the twenty-three years they occupied it. It was known as a happy and hospitable home, and Lamar as fun-loving, fond of children, and good at story-telling. He

tutions during the colonial era, which were archived in the British Museum and Lambeth Palace. Lamar claimed to be one of only two men who had examined the colonial records of Georgia "page by page." His nine published papers were judged by historians to be not only great contributions to the legal history of Georgia but also "the best in their field." Some of his public addresses were widely reprinted and circulated, including one on "The Private Soldier of the Confederacy" and another calling for education as a means of productively integrating blacks into the mainstream of American life.

In 1898 the Georgia Supreme Court appointed him to the board examining bar applicants, and he later served as the board's chairman for five years. Then, during a New Year's Eve party in 1902, Gov. Joseph M. Terrell telephoned Lamar to say he had just appointed him to fill out a term on the state supreme court. Earlier in the year, despite the urging of friends and supporters and a known desire to sit one day on the court, he had refused to run for a seat on the bench. He took his place in January, and ran for reelection in 1904, winning easily.

During his two years on the bench in Atlanta, Lamar impressed his colleagues with his concise language and persuasive reasoning. Among several opinions that drew substantial attention was one that, in effect, was later written into federal law. It required the director of a company, who had bought the shares of other stockholders for $110 each, after having contracted to sell the firm's shares for $185 each, to rescind the sale. The court would not allow company executives to benefit from information improperly withheld from shareholders.

Although Lamar enjoyed the work and what he called the "serene atmosphere" of the court, a combination of overwork, ill health, homesickness for Augusta, and possibly financial considerations, led him to resign in April 1905. After he was nearly run down on a busy Atlanta thoroughfare while walking to work from his hotel, he joked that for a man to reside in Atlanta "was contributory negligence."

Lamar returned to private practice and soon drew national attention for his successful appeal to the U.S. Supreme Court of what became known as the *Georgia Railroad Tax Case* (1907). Overruling the state supreme court, the Court accepted Lamar's argument that the Due Process Clause of the Fourteenth Amendment could be applied in a dispute over taxing an out-of-state corporation.

The following year, President William Howard Taft visited Augusta for a postcampaign vacation and played golf with Lamar. In 1910 the president remembered his golfing partner and consulted Georgia senator Augustus O. Bacon about appointing him to the Commerce Court. Bacon suggested that Lamar should be named instead to the Supreme Court to replace William H. Moody, who had retired. The president's further inquiries about him produced extraordinarily strong endorsements from Lamar's peers. "He is the best lawyer in Georgia . . . profound and learned"; "No one better qualified by ability, learning, temperament, personality, and character for service on the highest court"; "If I were called upon to construct a model for a judge, I would take Lamar as he is," were some of the responses.

Notified of his nomination to the high court on December 12, 1910, Lamar immediately expressed fears that as a southerner, a Democrat, and a known defender of railroads he would not be confirmed. His confirmation would make him only the sixth justice ever appointed by a president of another political party. The suspense lasted only three days and ended with unanimous Senate approval.

Lamar had only four active years on the Court, during which he wrote 113 opinions in his clear, logical style. Generally in agreement with his colleagues, he wrote only eight dissents. His most far-reaching decision was probably *United States v. Midwest Oil Company* (1915), in which he upheld the president's right to

Samuel Gompers, the president of the American Federation of Labor, was charged with contempt by the Bucks Stove Company for violating an injunction against a worker-led boycott of the company. Union officials had written the company's name on its "we don't patronize" list, which Gompers claimed was speech protected by the First Amendment. Joseph R. Lamar's 1911 Supreme Court opinion ignored Gompers's arguments, siding with the property rights of business against the free speech rights of labor. *Source: Library of Congress*

withdraw 3 million acres of public lands containing oil deposits from private exploitation in order to preserve oil supplies for the navy.

Lamar's best-known opinion was rendered in the controversial case of *Gompers v. Bucks Stove and Range Company* (1911). In it he discussed how to punish individuals who show contempt of court by obstructing the court's judicial functions, disturbing the peace in the courtroom, or generally being disobedient. Lamar distinguished between civil and criminal contempt and established different punishments for each type, an important legal distinction that has endured. The case had been brought by Samuel Gompers, the president of the American Federation of Labor, to test whether a company had the right to obtain a court injunction to restrain a union from carrying out a boycott or whether such an injunction violated union members' rights to free speech and free expression. Although decided on narrow technical grounds, Lamar's opinion served to uphold the legality of injunctions against boycotts, undermining one of labor's most powerful weapons.

In 1914 he performed a service for his old schoolmate, Woodrow Wilson, who had been elected president in 1912. Lamar joined the commission that successfully negotiated a peaceful settlement of a dispute with Mexico. This extra duty contributed to the stress from overwork he suffered during the 1914 term.

In September 1915 Lamar suffered a paralytic stroke that prevented him from taking his seat at the new term of the Court. Recovery was slow, and on January 2, 1916, he died. The Georgia justice was just two months past his fifty-eighth birthday.

Mahlon Pitney

1912-1922

Source: Photo by W. T. Bather, Collection of the Supreme Court of the United States

MAHLON PITNEY was born February 5, 1858, on his family's farm in Morristown, New Jersey. He was the second of three sons of Henry Cooper Pitney, a successful attorney, and Sarah Louisa Halsted Pitney. Descended from an English buttonmaker named James Pitney who emigrated to America early in the eighteenth century, the future justice traced his ancestry to at least four men who fought in the Revolution, including the great-grandfather for whom young Mahlon was named.

Pitney was educated at private schools and a classical academy in Morristown before entering the College of New Jersey, now Princeton University, in 1875. There, he achieved a measure of success as a debater. Standing six feet tall, he had a slim but athletic build and was adept at sports. As manager of the Princeton baseball team in his senior year, Pitney persuaded a major league player from Philadelphia, Jim Delvin, to come and coach the team, reportedly the first time a professional baseball coach was hired by a college. For much of his college career, Pitney sat opposite a future president, Woodrow Wilson, at their dining club, an acquaintance that served Pitney well in later life.

By his own account, Pitney's decision to make a career in law came before his graduation in 1879. It followed a front-porch conversation with his father, who had achieved a position of leadership at the New Jersey bar and who convinced his son that he had the makings of a successful lawyer. Immediately upon receiving his diploma, he joined his father's law office. Later he was to comment, "I learned my law by absorption. I read and studied, of course, but I got most of it from my father who was a walking encyclopedia of the law." Pitney not only inherited an interest in the law, as did his two brothers, who became lawyers, but also he passed it on to his two sons and one grandson. When he ascended to the Supreme Court, Pitney was the only sitting justice without a law degree (although his alma mater presented him with an honorary LL.B. in 1908). He had found time, however, to obtain a master's degree from Princeton in 1882.

After admission to the bar that same year, he left his father's office to strike out independently in the prosperous little town of Dover, New Jersey. In addition to setting up a legal practice, he became a director of an iron company and helped manage a department store. Seven years later, when his father was appointed a vice chancellor of the state of New Jersey, he returned to manage the family law practice in Morristown. Pitney attracted new clients and developed a reputation as an able and reliable lawyer. He was known to be particularly effective in presenting and arguing cases before appellate courts and in trying cases before a jury.

In November 1891 he married Florence T. Shelton, a New Yorker who had moved to Morristown three years earlier. The couple had three children, two boys and a girl. By then Pitney was pursuing a wide and active range of interests. He was a Freemason and a member of the First Presbyterian Church of Morristown. He

was also a brilliant chess player and in later life drew two matches with world champion Emanuel Lasker. He spent vacation time shooting game in North Carolina and Virginia, sailing off the Rhode Island and Maine coasts, and playing golf everywhere he could. He was said to enjoy good food and to know how to lighten up an after-dinner audience with a joke or humorous topical reference.

Meanwhile, he was emerging as a force in the Republican politics of northern New Jersey, his base of activity being the four-county Fourth Congressional District. In 1894 he was chosen by the state's Republican leadership for the nomination to Congress and ended a twenty-year Democratic monopoly on the seat by winning with a plurality of the vote. He was reelected two years later by a much greater margin, thanks in part to Democratic support for his conservative monetary policies. His platform favored the backing of paper currency with gold and opposed the free coinage of silver advocated by William Jennings Bryan, the radical Democratic and Populist party nominee for president.

Pitney was given influential committee assignments. As a member of the Appropriations Committee, he argued vigorously for fiscal conservatism. His support of corporations was as strong as his fierce opposition to corporate monopoly. Pitney is also remembered for his work on the Foreign Affairs Committee in the Alaskan Boundary dispute, which erupted in 1896 and eventually was settled to U.S. satisfaction.

Political ambition caused Pitney's resignation from Congress in January 1899. Two months before the end of his second term, he was elected to the New Jersey Senate. This state post was not a political demotion, but a move to position himself to run for governor. He was elected minority leader, and, when the Republicans captured the majority in 1900, he became the Senate's president. By then the road to the Republican nomination for governor was wide open; he was the favorite of prominent leaders and considered the likely winner by

Acquaintances since their student days at Princeton University, Woodrow Wilson and Mahlon Pitney both had successful careers in New Jersey politics, although in opposing political parties. As governor of New Jersey, Wilson crossed party lines to back his former classmate's nomination to the Supreme Court. *Source: Library of Congress*

many. But New Jersey's governor, Foster M. Voorhees, was not among them.

Voorhees had his own candidate in mind for the succession and found a way to eliminate the Pitney threat. On February 5, 1901, he appointed Pitney an associate justice of the Supreme Court of New Jersey. Pitney accepted, disappointing his supporters and ending a promising political career at the age of forty-three. In his six years as an associate justice, only 4 of his 166 majority opinions were reversed by the Court of Errors and Appeals, then the state's highest court.

In 1908 the governor appointed Pitney chancellor, the highest position in the New Jersey court system. As chancellor, he presided over the law and equity courts and was administrator of the state's entire judicial sys-

tem. This position made him the chief of a system in which his father had achieved prominence as a vice chancellor. Although his father had formally resigned the previous year, he continued to sit during the first year of his son's tenure, before stepping down to resume his law practice in Morristown. Of all the opinions rendered by Pitney as chancellor, the 1908 case of *Jonas Glass Co. v. Glass Bottle Blowers Association* did the most to earn his reputation as an antilabor judge. Pitney's ruling sustained a lower court's injunction to end a boycott by the association, which was using the boycott to try to unionize the glass bottle plant.

President William Howard Taft's elevation of Pitney from the summit of New Jersey's judiciary to the U.S. Supreme Court was a surprise. Until a week before the

High rates of unemployment made it possible for employers to pay low wages or demand kickbacks from those they hired. The growing trade union movement in the early twentieth century tried to protect workers from such practices as well as dangerous working conditions. On the Supreme Court, Mahlon Pitney wrote several opinions protecting the property rights of business, including the use of the "yellow dog" contract (below), from the growing demands of organized labor. *Source: Library of Congress*

Nº 1241

To Committee of Employee Representatives:
I do hereby promise to return to my regular place of employment at the ----------------- Corporation plant and do further promise to work in harmony and peace with my fellow employees and my employer. In violation of this promise I hereby agree to relinquish my position and leave the Corporation's property at once.

*Signed*_____ *Clock No.*_____

*Interviewed by:*_____

announcement, when Taft was introduced to Pitney at a luncheon in Newark, the favored candidate for the Court vacancy was Pitney's lifelong friend and colleague, Francis J. Swayze. Pitney and Swayze had crammed for the bar examination together thirty years earlier, and Swayze was now an associate justice of the New Jersey Supreme Court. Pitney had discussed his colleague's merits with Taft at the luncheon and was astonished when news of his own nomination reached him on a golf course in Atlantic City.

Of the five associate justices and one chief justice Taft appointed, Pitney was the last and most controversial. His confirmation by the Senate took twenty-three days. His old Princeton classmate, Woodrow Wilson, who was now the governor of New Jersey, crossed party lines to support Pitney's nomination. But liberal senators and union leaders attacked Pitney's record in the New Jersey courts as antilabor and antiprogressive. Feeling compelled to defend himself publicly, Pitney declared, "I am not an enemy to labor." He pointed out that several of the decisions being cited against him had actually been written by his father, and he added that "the public frequently makes the mistake of taking a legal decision based upon a peculiar or individual set of facts and giving it a general, sweeping application neither intended nor implied." Aggressive senators, including progressive Republicans such as Robert M. La Follette, hammered away at the antilabor theme, but with the endorsement of Governor Wilson and William Borah, an influential senator, Pitney was finally confirmed March 13, 1912, by a vote of 50 to 26.

Justice Pitney was a member of the Supreme Court for ten years, delivering 244 majority opinions, nineteen dissents, and five concurring opinions. A tireless worker, he was rarely absent from the bench, participating in all but 19 of 2,412 decisions rendered during his tenure; seven of his absences were due to his final and fatal illness. A 1915 case, *Coppage v. Kansas,* is perhaps the most significant of his high court opinions, reflecting a continued opposition to expanding workers' rights. The case overturned a Kansas law outlawing "yellow dog" contracts, which were agreements employers made with workers requiring total abstention from union membership, present or future, as a condition of employment. Pitney argued that a worker has no right to join a union and remain in the pay of an employer who does not hire union workers. Although he consistently wrote decisions protecting businesses against unions and favoring the application of antitrust law to labor organizations, he also supported workmen's compensation legislation, the stringent application of antitrust law to corporations, and the upholding of a state hour and wage law.

Pitney won the affection and respect of his colleagues, including Justice Oliver Wendell Holmes, Jr., who frequently dissented from Pitney's majority opinions. Holmes endorsed the opinion of his fellow dissenter, Justice Louis Brandeis, who praised Pitney's intellectual honesty and ability to change his mind upon reflection. Holmes added, "When he first came on the bench he used to get on my nerves, as he talked too much from the bench and in conference, but he improved in that and I came to appreciate his great faithfulness to duty, his industry and candor. He had not wings and was not a thunderbolt, but he was a very honest hard working judge and a useful critic."

The stress produced from a decade of overwork on the Court finally caught up to him in August 1922, when he suffered a stroke. Realizing he would not be able to return to the bench, he submitted his resignation, to be effective on December 31 of that year. Five years short of the age required to qualify for retirement benefits, he was granted continuation of his full salary by special act of Congress. The New Jersey jurist died December 9, 1924, at his home in Washington.

James C. McReynolds

1914-1941

Source: Library of Congress

JAMES CLARK MCREYNOLDS was born February 3, 1862, in Elkton, Kentucky, and was raised in a sparsely settled mountain community near the Tennessee border, where self-reliance was more a necessity than a virtue. McReynolds's parents were both members of the fundamentalist Campbellite sect of the Disciples of Christ church and insisted upon a strict moral upbringing for their family. His father, Dr. John McReynolds, was a noted surgeon and wealthy plantation owner of aristocratic Scotch-Irish descent, whose

nickname in the community was "pope" because of his domineering and snobbish nature. Among other reactionary beliefs, John McReynolds opposed public education as too democratic and a financial burden to landowners. His staunchly conservative outlook, which he passed on nearly intact to his son, may explain why James McReynolds suffered increasing isolation as society underwent rapid changes.

Lacking close friends, young McReynolds channeled his energies into the study of plants and birds, which he could examine without leaving the family's estate. At age seventeen he entered Vanderbilt University in Nashville, Tennessee, where he excelled in science. He also became interested in politics, displayed skills in debate, and edited the school paper. His college friends remembered him for his strict study habits, refusal to drink, and lack of interest in sports. In 1882 McReynolds graduated first in his class of nearly 100 students. He began postgraduate work in science, but then left Vanderbilt to study law at the University of Virginia. There he came under the influence of Professor John B. Minor, a strict moralist who taught his students that the law was an unchanging, permanent entity. A willing and enthusiastic student, McReynolds took his degree in only fourteen months under Minor's guidance.

Following graduation in 1884, McReynolds served two years in Washington as an assistant to Sen. Howell E. Jackson, a Tennessee Democrat who later served on the Supreme Court. McReynolds then returned to Nashville and established himself in the practice of law. Primarily representing corporate clients, McReynolds earned a reputation as a careful, meticulous lawyer who, although good at interpreting legal technicalities, was weak as an advocate. He was also known for his arrogance and aloofness, traits that contributed to his defeat, despite Republican support, when he made a bid for Congress in 1896. Four years later, McReynolds was appointed a part-time professor of commercial law at Vanderbilt.

In 1903 McReynolds returned to Washington to serve as an assistant attorney general under Philander Knox, Theodore Roosevelt's attorney general. McReynolds was appointed in part because of personal connections, but mainly because of his suitable political credentials. As a "Gold Democrat" who supported the conservative monetary policy known as the gold standard, he was acceptable to Roosevelt, a progressive Republican. At the Justice Department, McReynolds gained a reputation

for his zealous enforcement of the Sherman Antitrust Act in breaking up business trusts. He regarded monopolies as "essentially wicked" and viewed his prosecution of trusts as a moral crusade. After four years, McReynolds resigned from his position in 1907 to set up a law practice in New York City.

Two years later, President William Howard Taft persuaded him to return to Washington to assist in the final break up of the tobacco trust, a case that McReynolds had avidly pursued in the previous administration. Displaying his independent nature, McReynolds again resigned, this time in protest over Attorney General George Wickersham's compromise in the final settlement with the tobacco monopoly.

McReynolds returned to Democratic party politics in Tennessee, supporting Woodrow Wilson in his successful bid for the presidency in 1912. Although future associate justice Louis Brandeis was widely mentioned for the position of U.S. attorney general, Wilson chose to reward McReynolds's loyalty with an appointment to that post in 1913.

McReynolds's tenure in the cabinet was brief and stormy. Controversies arose over unsubstantiated reports that the Justice Department was spying on federal judges and that the cost of the new Justice Department building far exceeded all reasonable estimates. The most damaging accusations involved McReynolds's attempts to delay prosecution of the son-in-law of a high government official accused of violating the Mann Act, which banned the interstate transport of women for "immoral purposes." Although McReynolds's intent in these matters was above reproach, his violent temper and abrasive nature in dealing with the accusations alienated Congress and caused President Wilson considerable embarrassment. A vacant seat on the Supreme Court remained to be filled after the death in July 1914 of Justice Horace Lurton, a Tennessean. The president saw a perfect opportunity to elevate McReynolds, another Tennessean, to the Court, thereby demonstrating his support for his attorney general and at the same time putting an end to McReynolds's political difficulties. With strong backing from the Democratic party, McReynolds was easily confirmed by the Senate on August 29, 1914, by a vote of 44 to 6.

Once McReynolds was on the Court, his reactionary jurisprudence soon disappointed Wilson. McReynolds also found himself frequently at odds with his fellow justices. Although he sat on the bench for twenty-seven years, McReynolds wrote few majority opinions, mainly taking on cases that involved legal technicalities. He had an appreciation for literature, but avoided the use of literary and classical references in his writing. His opinions were mainly concerned with protecting the rights of business, namely property and contract rights. Some of his decisions in civil liberties cases, however, were surprisingly libertarian. His rulings on education, for example, included striking down a Nebraska law that prohibited the teaching of a foreign language before ninth grade (*Meyer v. Nebraska,* 1923) and overturning a Hawaii statute banning the teaching of the Japanese language (*Farrington v. Tokushiga,* 1927). His dissents often included thinly veiled personal attacks on political and philosophical adversaries.

McReynolds's harshest criticism was reserved for President Franklin D. Roosevelt, whom he once described as an "utter incompetent." During the 1930s, when Roosevelt was trying to pass legislation to pull the country out of the Great Depression, McReynolds banded together with Justices Willis Van Devanter, George Sutherland, and Pierce Butler to fight the president's New Deal programs. They became know as the "Four Horsemen" because of their consistently negative voting pattern. At first, they were extremely successful at striking down Roosevelt's legislation. By 1937, however, Justice Owen Roberts, who had often backed them with his crucial fifth vote, began to side with Chief Justice Charles Evans Hughes and Associate Justices Brandeis, Harlan Fiske Stone, and Benjamin Cardozo in upholding New Deal legislation. The turnaround was due in part to the scare caused by Roosevelt's unsuccessful attempt in 1937 to pass legislation that would have allowed him to increase the number of justices on the Court and dilute the power of the Four Horsemen.

The subsequent shift of the Court reversed some of the previous decisions of the Four Horsemen and forced them into a dissenting role. Van Devanter announced soon thereafter that he was unwilling to continue the struggle, and he retired in June 1937. Sutherland joined him the following year, and Butler's death in 1939 left only one of the four conservatives on the bench. McReynolds clung to his seat, determined to oppose New Deal liberalism as a "lone dissenter."

Young girls from nineteen different countries and ethnic groups proclaim their patriotism at New York's Public School No. 1 in 1926. When the issue of how schools should assimilate immigrant children linguistically came before the Supreme Court in 1923, James C. McReynolds struck down a Nebraska law prohibiting the teaching of modern languages other than English to children who had not passed the eighth grade. *Source: UPI/Bettmann*

Justices James C. McReynolds, Willis Van Devanter, George Sutherland, and Pierce Butler were nicknamed the "Four Horsemen," a double allusion to the Four Horsemen of the Apocalypse and Notre Dame's defensive team, because of their persistent opposition to Franklin D. Roosevelt's New Deal legislation. This 1937 cartoon takes a cynical view of Roosevelt's attempt to weaken the conservative bloc's power by trying to persuade Congress to allow him to appoint up to six new justices to the Supreme Court. *Source: Library of Congress*

Embittered by his growing isolation on the Court and Roosevelt's election to a third term in 1940, McReynolds finally gave up in 1941. Upon leaving office on February 1, the seventy-eight-year-old jurist lamented that he had tried to protect his country but that "any country that elects Roosevelt three times deserves no protection." In the end, McReynolds's narrow interpretation of the Constitution was simply incompatible with the economic and social reforms Roosevelt

and others thought necessary to bring the nation out of the depression. In his impassioned oral dissent in the *Gold Clause Cases* of 1935, McReynolds had complained that the Constitution, as he knew it, was "gone" and that "moral and financial chaos" was fast approaching.

McReynolds's personal behavior during his long tenure on the Court must be addressed. His relations with the two Jewish justices, Brandeis and Benjamin Cardozo, were cool at best. In fact, his dislike for Bran-

Although James C. McReynolds was intolerant of many people, including female attorneys and tobacco smokers, he enjoyed playing golf and duck-hunting with his friends. *Source: Library of Congress*

On one occasion, Justice Stone commented to McReynolds that a particular attorney's brief had been "the dullest argument" he had ever heard. In typical fashion, McReynolds is reported to have replied, "The only duller thing I can think of is to hear you read one of your opinions." He also routinely made negative remarks about women lawyers. When the first woman to be employed in the Office of the Clerk of the Court was installed, she found it best to temporarily absent herself when the tap of McReynolds's cane was heard approaching.

His lack of social graces left the confirmed bachelor a lonely man. McReynolds did, however, have a circle of like-minded friends with whom he felt comfortable and for whom he hosted small dinner parties. He was known to leave others' parties if he felt his status was not properly taken into account in the seating arrangements. McReynolds relaxed by playing golf and duck-hunting.

Although the Tennessee justice's biting sarcasm and rude behavior are well documented, Justice Oliver Wendell Holmes, Jr., once remarked, "Poor McReynolds, is, I think, a man of feeling and of more secret kindliness than he would get the credit for." His colleagues were surprised to learn that McReynolds had supported thirty-three young children victimized by the Nazi blitzkrieg during World War II. He also pledged the first $10,000 in the initial Save the Children Campaign. In his will, McReynolds bequeathed the bulk of his nearly $100,000 estate to charities, among them Children's Hospital in Washington, D.C., and the Salvation Army.

James McReynolds died after a bout of bronchial pneumonia in a Washington hospital August 24, 1946. He was buried in a simple ceremony in Elkton, Kentucky, unaccompanied to his final resting place by the traditional representatives of the Supreme Court.

deis was so strong that for years he would leave the room when Brandeis spoke in conference. No official group photograph was taken of the justices in 1924 because McReynolds refused to sit next to Brandeis, where he then belonged on the basis of seniority. He also declined to speak to John Clarke, whom he considered unequal to the tasks of a Supreme Court justice.

Louis D. Brandeis
1916-1939

Source: Photo by Harris & Ewing, Collection of the Supreme Court of the United States

Louis D. Brandeis was born in Louisville, Kentucky, November 13, 1856. His parents, Adolph Brandeis and Frederika Dembitz Brandeis, were members of three related families that fled to the United States after the failure of the 1848 democratic revolution in the Austro-Hungarian Empire. They had planned to try farming but realized they might have difficulty adapting to agricultural work after their sophisticated, cultured lives in Prague, exemplified by the two pianos and many crates of books they brought with them. Turning instead to commerce, the three families eventually settled in Madison, Wisconsin, where Adolph and Frederika were married. In 1851 they moved to Louisville, where Adolph established a highly successful wholesale grain and produce business.

Louis Brandeis's first memories were of the Union Army camped outside his parents' house and of helping his mother take food and coffee to the soldiers. He, his brother, and two sisters grew up in a prosperous home filled with warmth and culture. Frederika Brandeis raised her children with no knowledge of Jewish rituals but with a lofty sense of morality and public duty, making discussion of public affairs a staple of the family's dinner table. Her brother, Lewis Naphtali Dembitz, a leading lawyer and abolitionist, who was the family's intellectual guide, became young Brandeis's role model, and in his teens Brandeis acknowledged his debt by changing his middle name from David to Dembitz.

Brandeis attended the Louisville Male High School, where his record earned him a gold medal for "pre-eminence in all his studies." In 1872 Adolph, realizing that the country was facing a recession, sold his business and took his family on a long trip to Europe. A year later the sixteen-year-old Louis left his family in Italy and traveled by himself to Dresden, Germany, where he talked the rector of the Annen-Realschule into admitting him without the requisite proof of birth, vaccination certificate, and admission examination. He was an outstanding student of Latin, French, German, literature, mineralogy, geography, physics, chemistry, and mathematics.

The family returned to the United States in 1875, and Brandeis, now eighteen, enrolled at Harvard Law School without a college diploma. He studied the new case method pioneered by Prof. Christopher Columbus Langdell and earned the highest grades the school had ever seen. He remained at Harvard for a year's graduate work, paying his way by tutoring fellow students and proctoring examinations. He then went to work for a St. Louis law firm but, bored by Missouri after the excitement of Cambridge, left after less than a year to begin practice in Boston with a law school classmate, socialite Samuel Warren.

The firm's almost immediate prosperity resulted from a combination of Warren's connections, referrals by Harvard faculty members, the business of Boston's prosperous German-Jewish community, and Brandeis's growing reputation as a brilliant lawyer.

Brandeis had developed an encyclopedic memory at Harvard when difficulties with his eyes forced him to rely on fellow students to read texts to him, but this skill was only part of his attraction as a lawyer. Immersion at Harvard in cases and the common law had taught him that the law was constantly changing and progressing to reflect the necessities of each historical era. To assess his clients' needs, he insisted on understanding not only their immediate problems but also the economic and, occasionally, the political context in which they arose. As he advised a young associate, "Knowledge of the decided cases and of the rules of logic cannot alone make a great lawyer. . . . The controlling force is the deep knowledge of human necessities." He knew that to be able to provide for himself and his family, while retaining the ability to take only cases that interested him and in which he believed his prospective client to be morally correct, he had to make sure he got the clients he wanted. The way to do this fit neatly with his taste for data, and he noted in a memorandum to himself on "The Practice of The Law" that a lawyer was "far more likely to impress clients by knowledge of facts than by knowledge of law." He was successful enough at impressing, retaining, and increasing his clientele of small businessmen to become a millionaire in his forties.

Clients, learning that his abilities went beyond the solving of specific legal problems, called him in as a general adviser. One of the earliest and most important instances was his mediation of a 1902 strike at a shoe factory. The owner was surprised that the workers, usually well paid, refused to take a pay cut when the factory ran into difficulties. Brandeis discovered that, indeed, wages had been good, but seasonal and sporadic, with no work and no pay when orders were not being filled. He devised a method of spacing the work throughout the year so the workers could be assured of a steady income.

The strike brought him into contact with the workers' union, and he realized that the union was crucial if

Women made up the majority of the work force in New England shoe factories in 1906, when the Department of Labor reported that they were "considered more reliable than men." Attorney Louis D. Brandeis helped mediate a strike at a shoe factory in 1902, gaining an appreciation of the importance of labor unions. *Source: Library of Congress*

the employer was not to have unlimited power. This recognition ran counter to the anti-union beliefs of the elite Boston world in which he lived; and it led to his understanding, he said later, that "many things sanctioned by expert opinion and denounced by popular opinion were wrong." His experiences also made him wonder if the concentration of capital and power in the large corporations of the late nineteenth and early twentieth centuries was consistent with democracy. By the time he gave up private practice in 1916, he had begun urging worker ownership and management of business as a more democratic form of industrial development than corporate capitalism.

Brandeis's sense of public responsibility had led to his involvement in public causes, with his first major effort a successful fight from 1893 to 1902 against the attempt of the Boston Elevated Railway to acquire a monopoly over Boston's transportation system. He decided to protect his freedom to suggest the solutions he considered best by not accepting money for certain cases, acting instead pro bono or "for the public good." Later, recognizing that the increasing amount of time he was giving to public service cut into the income of his firm and of the other people dependent on it, he reimbursed the firm for each working hour that he spent on public affairs—roughly half his time. "Some men . . . delight in

automobiles and yachts," Brandeis said. "My luxury is to invest my surplus effort . . . to the pleasure of taking up a problem and solving, or helping to solve it, for the people without receiving any compensation." His zest for public causes and his belief that attorneys had an obligation to work on behalf of the people rather than as employees for wealthy corporations helped create the American pro bono tradition and led to the media's dubbing him the "people's attorney." As such, he redesigned utilities laws for the state of Massachusetts, invented savings bank life insurance, undertook a decade-long war with the monopolistic New Haven Railroad, designed much of President Woodrow Wilson's antitrust policy, advised President Franklin D. Roosevelt to enact unemployment insurance, and advocated legalization of unions, minimum wage and maximum hours laws, public ownership of Alaska's natural resources, and public works projects during the depression of the 1930s.

In 1891 Brandeis married Alice Goldmark, a distant cousin. Their daughter Susan became an attorney who also participated in her father's Zionist activities; their second daughter, Elizabeth, was an economist who helped design the Wisconsin unemployment compensation system, which served as a model for federal legislation. The couple decided as a matter of principle to live frugally, giving money to worthy causes and buying far more books than household goods. They avoided liquor, and Brandeis's only material passion was for ice cream. Judge Julian Mack liked to describe the family's frugality by telling friends that whenever he went to the Brandeis house for dinner, he ate before and afterward.

Another result of his marriage was Brandeis's collaboration with his sister-in-law, Josephine Goldmark, a consumer advocate. In 1908 Brandeis and Goldmark produced what became known as the first "Brandeis brief." Submitted to the United States Supreme Court on behalf of an Oregon law setting maximum hours of work for women, it devoted only 2 pages to legal precedent and more than 100 pages to sociological data

The appointment of Louis D. Brandeis to the Supreme Court in January 1916 set off a four-month confirmation battle, in which conservative forces in industry and finance vigorously fought to keep him off the bench. President Woodrow Wilson and a host of progressive reform groups prevailed, and the Senate confirmed Brandeis, the first Jew appointed to the Court, by a wide margin.
Source: Library of Congress

demonstrating that overlong work days had negative effects on women and their families. It persuaded the Court, then inclined to strike down such welfare legislation, to uphold the law, and it earned Brandeis the rare distinction of being named in the Court's opinion in *Muller v. Oregon.*

Brandeis was a thoroughly assimilated and nonreligious Jew. Nonetheless, in 1914, he accepted the leadership of the American Zionist movement, largely because he envisioned a Jewish state in Palestine that would be small-scale, egalitarian, protective of the rights of Jews and non-Jews alike, hard-working, highly educated, and agrarian, with land and other natural resources held in common. He saw the Palestinian Jewish community as an embodiment of the democratic values he considered vital to the United States, and he maintained his involvement in Zionism for the remainder of his life.

Woodrow Wilson named Brandeis to the Supreme Court January 28, 1916—the first time a Jew was nominated. Although anti-Semitism was a factor in the heated battle over confirmation, the bitterness of the fight was much more a reflection of the business community's fear of a progressive on the Court. Brandeis was nonetheless confirmed June 1, 1916, by a vote of 47 to 22.

Brandeis's creed was reflected in the many opinions he wrote during his twenty-three years on the bench. As one colleague noted, for Brandeis, "Democracy is not a political program. It is a religion." He believed that freedom was endangered by concentration of power, whether in the hands of government or of corporations. He therefore usually favored action by the states over action by the federal government, balancing corporate power with union power, encouraging competition among businesses, and permitting experimentation with laws designed to aid workers.

These positions are reflected in his dissent in *Hitchman Coal and Coke Co. v. Mitchell* (1917), in which he

The Washington Communist Society met in 1930 to plan a demonstration in front of the White House. The police often arrested communist protesters at demonstrations, leading to charges that their First Amendment rights of free speech and free assembly were violated. Louis D. Brandeis, a strong advocate of free speech, saw it as the cornerstone of democracy and "indispensable to the discovery and spread of political truth." *Source: Library of Congress*

criticized the Court for upholding "yellow-dog contracts," which enabled companies to force their employees to agree not to join unions; his dissent in *Quaker City Cab Co. v. Pennsylvania* (1928), in which the Court overturned a state statute taxing corporations more heavily than individually owned businesses and partnerships; his dissent in *Liggett v. Lee* (1933), attacking the Court for overturning a state law imposing heavier license fees on chain stores than on independent shops; his dissent in *Myers v. United States* (1927), in which the Court permitted the president to fire a civil servant, even though a statute required Senate advice and consent before such a dismissal. He insisted that the Court exercise self-restraint and not substitute its opinion for reasonable attempts by legislatures to solve societal problems. But he joined the Court whenever, as in *Schechter Poultry Corp. v. United States* (1935), it struck down what he felt was a level of government

assumption of power not contemplated by the Constitution or inconsistent with democracy.

Brandeis's democratic ideal included not only a fear of power but also, perhaps more important, an insistence on the rights of the individual, particularly as they affected human dignity and the ability of people to participate in the democratic process. In 1928 the Court upheld the government's power to wiretap conversations, arguing that the Constitution did not prohibit it. Brandeis was furious and wrote a dissent insisting that the Founders had included the "right to be let alone" in the Constitution. In later years the Supreme Court came to agree and has repeatedly cited Brandeis in affirming a constitutional right to privacy.

Brandeis considered free speech an absolute necessity if citizens were to have access to ideas and be able to make intelligent choices among them. His opinions in a number of cases went far beyond the doctrine enunciated by Justice Oliver Wendell Holmes, Jr., that the government could suppress speech or printed material it considered to constitute a "clear and present danger" to law and order, particularly in wartime. In Brandeis's view, the right of free speech was the same during wartime as during peacetime, and it existed even if the speech was likely to result in "some violence or . . . destruction of property." Speech could be suppressed only if there was "imminent" danger of "the probability of serious injury to the State." By explaining the role of ideas in a democratic society, Brandeis created the modern jurisprudence of freedom of speech.

Brandeis retired from the Court February 13, 1939, because at eighty-three he felt the burden was too great. He died two years later, on October 5, 1941, following a heart attack. Brandeis left behind a tradition of lawyers contributing their efforts to public service, a jurisprudence based on interpreting the Constitution in light of societal facts, an insistence on privacy and free speech that became the law of the land, and an emphasis on the dignity of the individual.

John H. Clarke

1916-1922

Source: Photo by Harris & Ewing, Collection of the Supreme Court of the United States

JOHN HESSIN CLARKE, the son of Irish Protestants, was born September 18, 1857, in the town of Lisbon, Ohio. His father had immigrated to Lisbon, the county seat, in 1830 and became active in liberal Democratic politics. A successful lawyer, John Clarke, Sr., impressed upon his son the importance of public service. He set an example both as a judge on the county court of common pleas and by establishing an Episcopal parish in the community.

After attending the local high school, Clarke entered Western Reserve College, in Hudson, Ohio. He graduated Phi Beta Kappa in 1877 and received a Master of Arts degree three years later. After making his fortune, Clarke would remember his alma mater in his will with a $1.5 million bequest.

Returning to Lisbon to study law under his father's direction, Clarke passed the bar with honors in 1878. Briefly practicing in his father's law firm, he soon moved to the nearby city of Youngstown in search of greater opportunities. At age twenty-three he opened his own firm, which represented banks, railroads, and other corporate clients.

Clarke bought an interest in the *Vindicator,* the local Democratic paper, and came to love journalism. Under his guidance the paper became a financial success and a prominent voice in progressive politics. He used the newspaper to promote reform, particularly to advocate that all citizens be required to render nonpolitical civil service. His strong support for free local libraries funded by public resources led to his being made a lifetime trustee of the Youngstown Library. In his will he was to leave the library $100,000 to purchase books. Clarke's literary interests extended to giving lectures on Shakespeare and James Russell Lowell at the local literary society, for which he became well known.

He also developed a reputation as a first-rate corporate lawyer, attracting important clients such as the Pennsylvania and Erie railroad companies. In 1897, after seventeen years in Youngstown, Clarke moved to Cleveland to join the firm of Williamson and Cushing. He became a trial lawyer for the Nickel Plate Railroad and the makers of Pullman railroad cars. Yet Clarke continued to support a progressive agenda, even when it conflicted with his clients' interests. He advocated legislation limiting railroad fares and antitrust and antirebate proposals that would also reduce railroad profitability.

Although Clarke's name came up for several important political positions, including governor and congressional representative, he was unwilling to enter Ohio's political arena as a candidate. Nevertheless, he remained influential in Democratic party politics, serving as chairman of the congressional convention for Ohio's Eighteenth District in 1892. He sided with the conservative wing of the Democratic party in 1896 in opposing the populist policies of William Jennings Bryan, who advocated the free coinage of silver. A "gold bug," Clarke represented Ohio at the national convention of Gold Democrats, whose main campaign

issue was a continuance of the gold standard, a policy that linked the dollar's value to a fixed quantity of gold.

Clarke finally ran for office in 1903 as the Democratic candidate for the U.S. Senate. His campaign platform attacked corporate wealth and advocated radical reforms. Many of his proposals, particularly one supporting greater municipal ownership of street railways, clashed with the interests of the clients he represented. He also favored the equalization of taxes, the direct election of senators, workmen's compensation, and disclosure of campaign expenses. Clarke was one of the first Ohio politicians to voluntarily declare his own campaign expenses. Despite his speaking skills and pol-

William Jennings Bryan, who ran three losing campaigns for president, supported the free coinage of silver, a policy he believed would benefit the ordinary person by increasing the supply of money. John H. Clarke represented the opposing wing of the Democratic party. Speaking out against the gold standard at the 1896 party convention, Bryan railed at the monied classes, crying, "You shall not crucify mankind upon a cross of gold," and earned the disapproval of many for using religious symbolism to make his point. *Source: Library of Congress*

ished manner, Clarke lost the race to the more conserv-ative incumbent, Marcus Hanna, a seasoned politician and native of his hometown. Clarke continued to take an active interest in politics, supporting women's voting rights, short electoral ballots, and a national civil service requirement. In 1914 he tried again to run for the Sen-ate, but withdrew when Timothy Hogan, a popular Irish politician, entered the race.

Clarke began his judicial career at the age of fifty-six when President Woodrow Wilson appointed him to a federal judgeship for the northern district of Ohio. An impatient judge, he kept his opinions brief, speeded up court business, and insisted on punctuality. He became known for the receptions he held in the courthouse on the last Friday of each month to welcome aliens who were becoming American citizens. These popular natu-ralization ceremonies featured live music, patriotic songs, and speeches by prominent Cleveland officials.

Two years after appointing Clarke to the Ohio bench, Wilson nominated the silver-haired judge to the U.S. Supreme Court. Influential in promoting him for the seat was an old friend and fellow Ohioan, Newton D. Baker, the secretary of war. Clarke's nomination on July 14, 1916, came shortly after the confirmation of Justice Louis Brandeis, another successful lawyer who had managed the complexities of defending corporations while advocating liberal politics. Wilson intended Clarke to assist Brandeis in tempering the conservative Court with progressivism. Despite criticism from the conservative press, he was confirmed by a voice vote ten days after being nominated.

Clarke did not disappoint Wilson during his six years on the Court. He was a strong supporter of using an-titrust laws to break up business monopolies. When the Court rejected government efforts to convict the U.S. Steel Corporation and the U.S. Shoe Machinery Com-pany of acting as monopolies, Clarke dissented. He managed to muster unanimous support for his opinion in *United States v. Lehigh Valley Railroad* (1920), which held that the railroad had purchased other companies to eliminate competition. He also rallied a majority for his opinion ordering the breakup of the Reading Rail-road's monopoly on the anthracite coal industry. Clarke wrote the decision finding the American Hardwood Manufacturers' Association guilty of trying to fix prices, forcing the government to examine the role of trade as-sociations in encouraging monopolistic behavior.

Clarke also showed his liberalism in strongly support-ing the rights of labor. He upheld restrictions on the number of daily working hours required for industrial and railroad workers and supported a tax on goods made with child labor. He voted against the legality of "yellow dog" contracts, which forced workers to promise not to join unions as a condition for getting or keeping their jobs. With Oliver Wendell Holmes, Jr., he joined in Brandeis's dissent from the Court's ruling that unions are subject to prosecution under antitrust laws if their boycotts restrain a company's commerce.

Although Clarke often agreed with Brandeis and Holmes, he differed from them in the notable First Amendment case of *Abrams v. United States* (1919). He wrote the majority opinion upholding the conviction of Russian-born anarchists and socialists accused of dis-tributing pamphlets urging weapons workers to strike in protest of the U.S. government sending troops to Russia in World War I. Under the Sedition Act of 1918 Clarke found that the intention of the pamphleteers to interfere with the war effort was enough to restrict their speech even if their pamphlets were not persuasive—an interpretation of free speech rights that lasted for sev-eral decades.

Clarke wrote clear opinions that he insisted on keep-ing as short as possible so as not to obscure "the obvious by discussing it." He tried to bring the same efficiency to the Court that he had to the Ohio bench, asking his colleagues to accept only cases that "deal with matters of the greatest public concern." Holmes once com-plained to Chief Justice William Howard Taft that

Clarke sometimes decided cases in advance based on his own political convictions.

To the surprise of the nation, Clarke announced his resignation from the Supreme Court on September 1, 1922, to be effective seventeen days later on his sixty-fifth birthday. He told Brandeis, "I would die happier if I should do all that is possible to promote the entrance of our government into the League of Nations than if I continued to devote my time to determining whether a drunken Indian had been deprived of his land before he died or whether the digging of a ditch in Iowa was constitutional or not."

Although Wilson had originally proposed the creation of the League of Nations, he was disappointed by Clarke's resignation. He told Clarke, "I have been counting on the influence of you and Justice Brandeis to restrain the Court in some measure from [its] extreme reactionary course." Clarke replied that he felt the Court was taking on too many trivial cases and that he and Brandeis "were agreeing less and less."

The press mistakenly suspected that Clarke harbored political ambitions and would return to Ohio to run for president. He had no such intention, but he did have several other reasons for wanting to resign. He was suffering from a loss of hearing and a heart condition. His conservative colleague James McReynolds was openly hostile to him and refused to sign the official letter expressing regret at his resignation. A lifelong bachelor, Clarke was devastated by the deaths of his two sisters, with whom he had been close. He had never seemed as happy in Washington as he had been on the district court in Cleveland, and he expressed great relief at being able to stay home and relax without thinking about Court business.

Above all, as a justice, Clarke felt constrained from speaking out on the issues of the day. He wanted especially to devote his energies to the cause of world peace. Clarke was convinced that it was his duty to "devote what might remain to me of life and health and

John H. Clarke wrote the opinion in *Abrams v. United States* (1919) upholding the conviction on espionage charges of Russian emigres Samuel Lipman, Hyman Lychowsky, Mollie Steimer, and Jacob Abrams. They had thrown leaflets from the windows and roofs of New York City buildings calling for weapons workers to strike. Oliver Wendell Holmes, Jr., and Louis D. Brandeis dissented on the grounds that the "silly" leaflets posed no threat to the war effort against Germany. *Source: From the Collection of Paul Avrich*

strength to doing what I could to cultivate public opinion in our country favorable to having our government take some share in the effort which many other nations are making to devise some rational substitute for irrational war as a means of settling international disputes." He had long believed that the United States, having witnessed the devastation of World War I, should come out of its isolationism and join the League of Nations and the World Court. While still on the Court, he had publicly urged the American government to cancel debts owed by its wartime allies.

After stepping down from the bench, Clarke wrote numerous articles and delivered impassioned speeches across the country urging that peace groups put aside political differences to work together. He became presi-

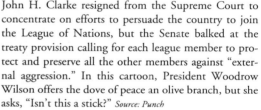

John H. Clarke resigned from the Supreme Court to concentrate on efforts to persuade the country to join the League of Nations, but the Senate balked at the treaty provision calling for each league member to protect and preserve all the other members against "external aggression." In this cartoon, President Woodrow Wilson offers the dove of peace an olive branch, but she asks, "Isn't this a stick?" *Source: Punch*

dent of the League of Nations Non-Partisan Association in 1923 and an active trustee of the World Peace Foundation. He called on ordinary Americans to urge their government to follow other nations in joining the League of Nations. He spent a good deal of his own money on the cause and aggravated his heart condition during the campaigning. By 1930 he realized sadly that Congress did not share his commitment to fostering world cooperation, and he retired to San Diego.

In retirement, Clarke supported the New Deal measures of President Franklin D. Roosevelt. The depression of the 1930s had not diminished his personal wealth, and he advocated paying higher taxes "for a fairer distribution of the good things in life." When Roosevelt announced his 1937 Court-enlargement plan, which would enable him to add new justices to a Court that had been striking down his New Deal legislation, Clarke expressed his support. Roosevelt persuaded the

former justice, age eighty, to endorse the plan publicly. Clarke made a national radio address affirming Congress's constitutional power to change the size of the Supreme Court, as it had done on several occasions in the past. Congress rejected Roosevelt's plan, but Clarke was gratified to see the president have the opportunity to appoint new justices when some of the older members of the Court retired shortly thereafter.

Clarke watched the development of World War II with great sorrow. He told a friend that he "began gravely to doubt the existence of a moral government on this seemingly abandoned planet." The former justice died of a heart attack in San Diego on March 22, 1945, four months before the first atom bomb was dropped on Hiroshima. He did not live to see the conference that created the United Nations, which convened in San Francisco a few weeks after his death.

William Howard Taft

1921-1930

WILLIAM HOWARD TAFT, the only person ever to serve as both chief executive and chief justice of the United States, was born September 15, 1857, in Cincinnati, Ohio. Despite his birthplace, his upbringing was influenced by the Yankee traditions of his forebears. His earliest American Taft ancestor had emigrated from England and settled in Braintree, Massachusetts, in 1675. The Taft family eventually moved to Vermont, where Peter Rawson

Taft, the future chief justice's grandfather, served as a judge on the probate and county courts in Windham County. His son, Alphonso Taft, moved to Cincinnati in 1838. Alphonso Taft was the first member of the family to gain national prominence. He served two terms on the Ohio Superior Court before he was named U.S. attorney general and later secretary of war in the administration of Ulysses S. Grant. President Chester A. Arthur subsequently appointed him ambassador to

William Howard Taft at home with his wife, Helen, and their son Charles. Helen Taft continually tried to scuttle her husband's judicial ambitions in favor of a political career, but he would later write that "the court . . . next to my wife and children, is the nearest thing to my heart in life." *Source: Library of Congress*

Austria-Hungary and then to Russia. Louisa Maria Torrey Taft, his second wife, had five children; the eldest surviving child was William Howard Taft.

Young William was an excellent student and, because of his amiable nature, made friends easily. Indeed, his popularity evoked some concern on his father's part during Taft's undergraduate years at Yale University. On reading his son's report that he had been asked to join Skull and Bones, a prestigious secret society, the elder Taft expressed his doubt that "such popularity was consistent with high scholarship." In fact, Taft's father had little cause for concern. "Bill," as he was known during college, had left none of his family's stern lessons behind on entering his father's alma mater. He never de-

veloped a liking for tobacco or strong drink, and his parents' characteristic frugality saw expression in the detailed records he kept of his expenses. Many of his fellow students consequently came to look upon Taft as a model of gentlemanly manners and behavior. More important, Taft also demonstrated his academic abilities, graduating second in the class of 1878.

In the fall of that year, he began his legal training at Cincinnati Law School and took a part-time position as a reporter of legal affairs for a local newspaper, the *Cincinnati Commercial,* to help pay for his education. Taft gave up his journalistic career upon graduation in 1880 and, after passing the bar, he became assistant prosecuting attorney for Hamilton County, Ohio. The post marked his first direct involvement in Republican party politics, and this position was followed not long after by a two-year tenure as assistant county solicitor.

After several years of courtship, Taft married Helen Herron in 1886. They had a daughter and two sons, one of whom, Robert Alphonso Taft, would follow his father into public service in 1939 by serving several terms as a U.S. senator from Ohio. Less than a year after his marriage, the twenty-nine-year-old lawyer was appointed to the Ohio Superior Court. Although Taft preferred judging, his wife had her eye on the presidency and spent her energies steering him toward a political career.

In 1890 he successfully sought an appointment from President Benjamin Harrison to be solicitor general. Two years later, after Congress had created additional jurisdictions for the federal circuit courts, Taft sought and gained appointment to the U.S. District Court for the Sixth Circuit. He had an immensely satisfying eight-year tenure on the bench, writing 200 opinions and dissenting only once. While a judge, he also held a teaching position at Cincinnati Law School and served as the school's dean.

His early judicial career ended when President William H. McKinley asked him to head a commission to ensure the smooth transition from a military to a civilian government in the Philippines in the aftermath of the Spanish-American War. Reluctantly, Taft accepted the appointment and in 1901 was named governor general of the Philippines protectorate. He quickly demonstrated the diversity of his administrative skills by improving the local economy, building roads and schools, and uniting the island's political factions.

McKinley's death in 1901 brought Theodore Roosevelt and his progressive faction of the Republican party to power. President Roosevelt was an admirer of Taft's abilities and was eager to bring him back to Washington to serve in his administration. Taft rejected Roosevelt's initial offer of a seat on the Supreme Court because he felt he could not leave his post. In 1904 Taft was persuaded, however, to replace Elihu Root as secretary of war because he would continue to be responsible for the administration of the Philippines. He soon became one of Roosevelt's most trusted and respected cabinet advisers as well as his close friend.

As secretary of war, Taft traveled throughout the Caribbean and the Pacific as a foreign policy troubleshooter for the president and oversaw the successful construction of the Panama Canal. Viewing Taft's success as a recommendation for further elevation, President Roosevelt pressed the party to accept him as its next candidate for president. Taft's own conservative political connections in the East, in concert with Roosevelt's progressive supporters in the West, carried Taft to victory in 1908.

During his presidency, Taft had the extraordinary opportunity to elevate Edward D. White to the chief justiceship and to appoint four new justices to the Court—all in one year (a sixth was appointed later in his term). No president since Andrew Jackson had appointed a majority of the Court. Taft's nominations did not follow strict party lines—he appointed three southern Democrats—but were based on competence and integrity. Although many of Taft's nominees were

young, and he hoped they would perpetuate his policies well after he left the White House, for various reasons only Willis Van Devanter and Mahlon Pitney remained on the Court when Taft finally joined it himself in 1921. Of all his accomplishments while chief executive, he was most proud of his Supreme Court appointments.

As president, Taft continued with the antitrust suits against monopolies that had characterized Roosevelt's seven years in office. He also established a postal savings system, a Tariffs Board, and a Children's Bureau to end the evils of child labor. Nevertheless, Taft found himself embroiled in a power struggle with the progressive members of his party, and by 1912 the division had grown beyond repair. An embittered Roosevelt bolted the Republican party to oppose Taft and run under the Bull Moose banner. The split within the party ensured the election of the Democratic candidate, Woodrow Wilson.

Through much of the eight years that followed his

Emilio Aguinaldo led Philippine resistance to American military rule when the United States acquired the Pacific islands as a territory. Aguinaldo was captured in 1901, not long after William H. Taft became governor general of the Philippines and began orchestrating a smooth transition to a civilian government. *Source: Bettmann Archive*

unsuccessful bid for a second term, Taft served as Kent Professor of Constitutional Law at Yale University. Despite the solace he found in those peaceful years on the Yale faculty, Taft was unable to withdraw himself from public life. He served for a year as president of the American Bar Association and was elected president of the League to Enforce Peace in 1915. During World War I he served as joint chairman of the National War Labor Board and actively campaigned to rally American support for the League of Nations.

Long before his presidency, Taft had considered an appointment to the Supreme Court his ultimate goal in life. He held little hope that President Wilson would appoint him, but the election in 1920 of President Warren G. Harding, a Republican, brought a change of fortunes. The president-elect met with Taft shortly after the election to inform him that he would be willing to give him the next available seat on the Court. But losing the presidency in 1912 had deeply wounded Taft's

William Howard Taft realized his greatest ambition in life, surpassing even his election as president, when he signed the oath of office of chief justice of the United States in July 1921. *Source: Bettmann*

pride, and the assaults of his one-time friend Roosevelt had also left their scars. Moreover, the conservative Taft had vigorously opposed Wilson's liberal appointees, particularly Louis Brandeis, and Taft would have been uncomfortable sitting as their equals on the bench. Accordingly, he informed Harding that his only real ambition was to become chief justice.

Taft and his Republican supporters mounted a campaign to guarantee his nomination as chief justice as soon as Edward D. White vacated the post. Taft even went so far as to call upon the aged chief justice, who was known to be in poor health, to ask him to resign. White steadfastly refused, and it was not until his death a year later that Taft gained the long-coveted appointment. He was confirmed by the Senate with only four dissenting votes June 30, 1921.

Chief Justice Taft inherited a strongly divided Court that was far behind in its work. Several of the associate justices were elderly and infirm and no longer able to carry the full weight of their judicial responsibilities. Litigation from World War I was just beginning to find its way onto the Court's docket, and the proliferation of cases arising from the nation's rapid industrialization was swelling the Court's workload as well.

Taft's greatest contribution as chief justice was to address the problem of the burgeoning workload of the Supreme Court and of the judicial court system as a whole. Taft used his personal and political clout—and his connections—to initiate and promote various kinds of judicial reform in an effort to simplify procedures, reduce political patronage, and eliminate the perpetual backlog of pending cases. In 1922 he created what became known as the Judicial Conference of the United States, a body that coordinates, and fosters cooperation among, the federal judiciary's many courts. In going beyond the traditional nineteenth century role of a chief justice and taking on issues outside the Court's immediate domain, Taft became the first "modern" chief justice. He greatly influenced his successors, not only by

Chief Justice William Howard Taft (third from left) and the associate justices admire architect Cass Gilbert's model for a new Supreme Court building in 1929. Taft not only persuaded Congress to fund the building, which would give the Supreme Court its own home for the first time, but he also oversaw its planning and initial construction.
Source: Collection of the Supreme Court of the United States

his administrative reforms, but by expanding and redefining the duties of his office.

From the Court's standpoint, his masterstroke was securing passage of the Judiciary Act of 1925. The act gave the Court greater power to decide which cases it would hear and allowed it to give its prompt attention to constitutional questions. Implementation of these reforms enabled the Court to eliminate its backlog of cases and assume a more effective role at the head of the national judiciary. Taft also successfully campaigned to acquire new quarters for the Court, which had long ago outgrown the cramped confines allotted to it in the Capitol building. By lobbying Congress, he secured funds to construct the first building designed specifically for the Court's use. To ensure that the building would meet the Court's needs, Taft personally supervised its design and the early stages of its construction, although he did not live to see the great marble structure completed in 1935.

Despite his deft personal diplomacy, Taft's leadership came to be threatened by the Court's increasing internal dissent. He was generally successful at massing the Court into a conservative majority, but the critical dissents of Justices Oliver Wendell Holmes and Louis

Brandeis sharply divided the Court, particularly on cases involving labor-management disputes and the prohibition of liquor. The issue of prohibition aroused dissent within Taft's own household as well, as his wife was known to support the repeal of the Eighteenth Amendment, which outlawed the sale of liquor, while the chief justice felt morally and legally obligated to defend its strict enforcement.

As his health began to fail, Taft worried that the conservative ideals he had championed were losing expression on the Court. He felt compelled to remain on the bench despite his growing awareness that he was no longer physically equal to the job. High blood pressure and hardening of the arteries brought a series of crippling strokes, as well as the realization that he would never be able to return to his duties. The man who once called his appointment to the Court "the crowning joy and honor of my life" submitted his resignation February 3, 1930. Confined to his bed, and lapsing in and out of consciousness, Taft lingered long enough to see his close friend Charles Evans Hughes confirmed as his successor. The able Court administrator and architect of the modern judicial system died March 8, 1930.

George Sutherland
1922-1938

Source: Library of Congress

GEORGE SUTHERLAND, the only Supreme Court justice appointed from the state of Utah, was born March 25, 1862, in Buckinghamshire, England. His father, Alexander George Sutherland, was of Scottish descent; his mother, Frances Slater Sutherland, was English.

Sutherland was baptized in the Episcopal church, but sometime in 1862 his father became a convert to the Church of Jesus Christ of Latter-day Saints (the Mormon church), and in the summer of 1863 the Sutherlands left England to join the body of the Mormon church in Utah. The family settled in Springville, Utah, but shortly after their arrival Alexander Sutherland renounced his new-found faith and moved to Montana.

In 1869 the Sutherlands returned to Utah and settled in Provo. The elder Sutherland labored at various jobs. He was a mining prospector, mining recorder, justice of the peace, postmaster, and, ultimately, an attorney.

Life in Utah Territory was harsh. Sutherland later recalled that

the average boy of ten . . . worked very hard. . . . He milked, cut and carried in the night's wood, carried swill to the pigs, curried the horses, hoed the corn, guided the plow or, if not, followed it in the task of picking up potatoes which had been upturned, until his young vertebrae approached dislocation and he was ready to consider a bid to surrender his hopes of salvation in exchange for the comfort of a hinge in the small of his back.

At age twelve young Sutherland became a clerk in a clothing store in Salt Lake City. He later worked in a mining recorder's office and as an agent for the Wells Fargo Company to earn money for college.

In 1879, when Sutherland was seventeen, he entered Brigham Young Academy (now Brigham Young University), where he came under the influence of its strong-willed headmaster, a German immigrant named Karl Maeser. Discussing the Constitution with his students, Maeser, himself a convert to Mormonism, instilled in them the idea that God had guided the Framers. In 1882 Sutherland entered law school at the University of Michigan. There he studied under one of the greatest constitutional scholars of the day, Dean Thomas M. Cooley.

Sutherland did not remain at Michigan to obtain his degree. He was admitted to the Michigan bar in March 1883 before returning to Utah to join his father's law practice and to marry Rosamond Lee, a classmate from Brigham Young Academy. The Sutherlands were married nearly sixty years and had three children, Edith, Emma, and Philip.

Sutherland practiced law in Provo for ten years, first with his father and later with Samuel Thurman, who would serve as chief justice of the Utah Supreme Court, and William King, who would become Sutherland's political opponent. Although not a Mormon, Sutherland maintained good relations with members of the church, even at a time when, politically, he believed he must oppose the Mormon practice of polygamy. Sutherland joined the Liberal party, whose goal it was to deny Utah's admission to the Union until the Mormon church ceased its practice of polygamy. In 1890 Sutherland ran his first campaign for public office, as the Liberal candidate for mayor of Provo. He was soundly defeated. That same year, the Mormon church officially renounced polygamy. The Liberal party disbanded soon after, and Sutherland declared himself a Republican.

In 1892 Sutherland sought the Republican nomination for territorial delegate to Congress. He lost that

UNCLE SAM:——"NOW THERE'S A MERGER THAT WILL STAND LOOKING INTO."

Although not a Mormon, George Sutherland attended what is now Brigham Young University at the behest of his father, briefly a convert to the Mormon church. Sutherland remained on good terms with the church, but he supported the Liberal party, which condemned polygamy and opposed the admission of Utah to the Union until the practice ceased. *Source: Library of Congress*

Women's suffrage marchers, led by Dr. Anna Howard Shaw (in dean's garb), parade down Fifth Avenue in 1912 to publicize their cause. In his two terms as a senator from Utah, George Sutherland was an early champion of the right of women to vote. *Source: Bettmann*

vote, although more narrowly than in his first electoral attempt. The following year he moved his practice to Salt Lake City, where he joined a prominent firm and helped organize the Utah Bar Association. Even at this relatively early stage in his career, Sutherland's views on the role of the judiciary were well developed. In a speech to the bar association in 1895, he said, "Judges do not make laws, but declare them; the rules which govern their deliberations and decisions are to a large extent fixed and permanent . . . [not] to be controlled by temporary considerations or policies." Sutherland said that the judge's role was to stand "as a shield to prevent the exercise of oppressive and arbitrary power on the part of the government."

When Utah was admitted to the Union in 1896, Sutherland was elected to the first state senate, where he served as chairman of the Judiciary Committee. Four years later Sutherland was elected to the U.S. House of Representatives, narrowly defeating King, his former law partner. He served a single term in Congress, preferring to return to law practice in Utah and prepare for a run for a U.S. Senate seat. At that time, the Constitution still provided for selection of U.S. senators by state legislatures. Sutherland won the election and returned to Washington in 1905.

During his two terms in the Senate, Sutherland attained a national reputation for his knowledge of the Constitution and for his ability as an orator, both on and off the Senate floor. He was a vigorous supporter of workmen's compensation, improvements in the working conditions of seamen, and women's suffrage. Although the Nineteenth Amendment, extending the right to vote to women, did not pass until after Sutherland left the Senate, he was one of its early proponents. "Any argument which I may use to justify my own right to vote justifies . . . the right of my wife, sister, mother, and daughter to exercise the same right." He was equally vigorous in opposing what he regarded as regulatory interference by the federal government in the affairs of individuals and businesses, and he opposed the Federal Reserve Act (1913), the Clayton Antitrust Act (1914), and the Federal Trade Commission Act (1914).

In 1913, with Sutherland's support, the Constitution was amended to provide for direct election of senators. In 1916 Sutherland stood for popular election to the Senate, this time losing to King. Sutherland chose not to return to Utah, but remained in Washington to practice law. He was elected president of the American Bar Association in 1916.

The election of Warren Harding as president in 1920 brought Sutherland back into public life. The two men had served in the Senate together, and Sutherland acted as an adviser to Harding during his presidential campaign. In 1921 Sutherland was appointed chairman of the advisory committee of the U.S. delegation to the International Conference on the Limitation of Naval Armaments. The following year he was counsel for the United States in a Norwegian shipping case before the Permanent Court of Arbitration at The Hague. His lectures at Columbia University during this period were published as *Constitutional Power and World Affairs.*

In May 1921 the death of Chief Justice Edward D. White presented President Harding with his first opportunity to name a justice to the Supreme Court. The appointment was complicated by the fact that former president William Howard Taft was quietly but deliberately seeking the position of chief justice. Harding appointed Taft chief justice, but Sutherland did not have to wait long for another vacancy. On September 1, 1922, Justice John Clarke unexpectedly announced he would resign on his sixty-fifth birthday, September 18, to pursue the cause of world peace. Nominated by President Harding September 5, Sutherland was confirmed that same day by the Senate without discussion and without reference to committee—an honor usually reserved only for sitting senators.

Sutherland was well acquainted with the Court and its work. He had known Chief Justice Taft and Justice Willis Van Devanter for many years. Although he frequently disagreed with Oliver Wendell Holmes, Jr., and Louis Brandeis, and had even opposed the latter's nomination to the Court in the Senate, his relations with his fellow justices were warm and congenial. Justice Owen Roberts recalled that at the beginning of conferences, Holmes would approach Sutherland and say, "Sutherland, J., tell us a story." On one occasion, Brandeis, upon reviewing Sutherland's strenuous dissent in a 1934 case in which the majority upheld a Minnesota mortgage moratorium law, returned the dissent to Sutherland inscribed: "My Dear Sutherland: This is perhaps the finest opinion in the history of American constitutional law. Regretfully, I adhere to my error. Brandeis."

Just as Senator Sutherland had been regarded as thoughtful and well-spoken in the Senate, Justice Sutherland was an articulate and forceful voice on the Court. According to Judge Harold Stephens of the U.S. Court of Appeals in Washington, D.C., he was "almost Lincolnian in directness and simplicity." Sutherland quickly formed an intellectual alliance with the conservatives, Van Devanter, James McReynolds, and Pierce Butler. Together, the "Four Horsemen," frequently joined by Taft or Edward Sanford, combined to strike down much regulatory and social legislation. During the nearly sixteen years Sutherland served, the Court invalidated some eighteen acts of Congress; and Sutherland voted with the majority in all but one of these. During the same period, the Court ruled more than 185 state statutes or local ordinances unconstitutional; Sutherland was in dissent only nine times.

In Sutherland's view, the legislative reforms of the New Deal era infringed upon the rights of individuals to determine their own course—their liberty to contract—in violation of the Fifth and Fourteenth amendments. In one of Sutherland's first opinions, in *Adkins v. Children's Hospital* (1923), the Court ruled unconstitutional the District of Columbia's minimum wage law for women. While acknowledging that "freedom of contract may lawfully be subjected to restraint" when legislation is required "in the interest of social justice," Sutherland explained that social well-being ultimately depended on the welfare of individuals. "To sustain the individual freedom of action contemplated by the Constitution, is not to strike down the common good but to exalt it; for surely the good of society as a whole can-

George Sutherland wrote the 1923 decision striking down an act of Congress that set a minimum wage for women working at Children's Hospital and for other employers in the District of Columbia. Sutherland believed that the act, which was intended to prevent inadequate wages from jeopardizing the health and morals of women workers, interfered with women's right to contract and impeded their movement toward equality with men. *Source: Library of Congress*

not be better served than by the preservation against arbitrary restraint of the liberties of its constituent members."

In subsequent cases, Sutherland spoke for the Court to invalidate similar intrusions on the liberties of individuals, for example, a New York law prohibiting the resale of theater tickets at more than fifty cents above the face value of the ticket, a New Jersey statute establishing fees that could be charged by an employment agency, and a Pennsylvania law forbidding corporations to own pharmacies unless all of the stockholders were pharmacists. Many of his opinions, particularly those dealing with the Fifth and Fourteenth amendments, have since been overruled or allowed to slip into disuse. Others, especially those that concern the separation of powers, are as articulate and current as when they were written.

For Sutherland, there was no inconsistency in the fact that the Court so often disagreed with the political branches of government. The Constitution was law, and if it "[stood] in the way of desirable legislation, the blame must rest upon that instrument, and not upon the court for enforcing it according to its terms." He found "a degree of elasticity" in the application but not the meaning of the Constitution, and precisely that "application must expand or contract to meet the new and different conditions." In one of his last dissents, Sutherland warned of the cost of the Court approving the social reforms: "Do the people of this land . . . desire to preserve those [liberties] so carefully protected. . . ? If so, let them withstand all beginnings of encroachment. For the saddest epitaph which can be carved in memory of a vanished liberty is that it was lost because its possessors failed to stretch forth a saving hand while yet there was time."

By 1937 Sutherland was seventy-five, and President Franklin D. Roosevelt, frustrated by the "old men" sitting on the Court and weary of their assault on his New Deal legislation, had proposed a plan to expand the number of justices. Under the plan, the president could appoint an additional justice for each justice over seventy who refused to resign or retire. Sutherland had previously considered retiring, but he was determined to remain on the bench while Roosevelt tried to pack the Court. Roosevelt's plan was defeated in the summer of 1937, and on January 17, 1938, Sutherland retired from the bench. He died four years later, at age eighty, on July 18, 1942, in Stockbridge, Massachusetts.

Pierce Butler

1923-1939

Source: Library of Congress

PIERCE BUTLER was born on St. Patrick's Day, March 17, 1866, in a log cabin in Pine Bend, Minnesota. He was the sixth of eight children born to Patrick and Mary Gaffney Butler, who had emigrated from County Wicklow, Ireland, after the potato famine of 1848. They settled in the riverboat town of Galena, Illinois, where Patrick Butler ran a tavern, before moving to Dakota County, Minnesota, thirty-five miles south of St. Paul, to begin a life of farming on the frontier.

Patrick Butler was an educated, well-traveled man and a staunch Roman Catholic. He had received a degree in civil engineering from Trinity College in Dublin, traveled on the European continent, and taught English in Germany. At dinner each night he supplemented the teaching of the small country school to which young Pierce commuted on horseback, with his own lessons and stories of his travels. In this way, Pierce Butler learned Latin, German, and mathematics. These academic rigors, combined with the morning and evening work on the farm, strengthened him in both mind and body. By age fifteen he stood over six feet tall, was an accomplished wrestler, and had become the teacher at the country school where he had been a student.

In 1881 Butler entered a preparatory program at Carleton College in nearby Northfield. Two years later he was admitted to the college as an undergraduate, earning his tuition by working at a local dairy. At Carleton, Butler was an undistinguished student, earning only a C average. Ironically, one of his lowest marks was in constitutional law. During his college years Butler cemented the strongly conservative opinions and laissez-faire economics that he had absorbed during his early years on his father's farm. He graduated in 1887 with both B.A. and B.S. degrees.

Despite his poor grade in constitutional law, Butler moved to St. Paul to read law at the firm of Pinch and Twohy. At a dinner at the house of his friend and tutor, John Twohy, Butler met Annie Cronin, whom he married in 1891. The couple had eight children.

In 1888, at age twenty-two, Butler was admitted to the bar. Walter Sanborn, a future federal circuit judge who would be instrumental in Butler's nomination to the Supreme Court, approved Butler's admission following oral testing in his court, as was the custom at the time. Butler practiced law for a short time with Stan Donnelly, son of the Populist U.S. representative, Ignatius Donnelly, and in 1891 became assistant to the county attorney for Ramsey County. Two years later, Butler, a Democrat, was elected to the office of county attorney, the only elective office he ever held, achieving in his four-year tenure the highest number of criminal convictions ever for any occupant of the office.

In 1893 Butler also became a senior partner in the firm of How, Butler, and Mitchell, which would establish itself as one of the leading corporate firms in the state during the next thirty years. The firm's major clients were railroads, which were emerging as economic lifelines into the fast-growing Midwest and West. Butler rose quickly to prominence with his skillful settlement of railroad cases. These cases involved "valuation"—determining the worth of railroad property and the appropriate rates the railroad companies could then charge. From 1899 to 1905 Butler worked as general counsel for the Chicago, St. Paul, Minneapolis, and Omaha Railroad, becoming one of the foremost railroad lawyers in the Midwest. In 1908 he was elected president of the Minnesota State Bar Association.

Butler was an expert litigator with an extraordinary ability to absorb and organize the multitude of figures and facts involved in valuation cases. On behalf of his railroad clients, Butler convinced the Interstate Commerce Commission to raise the legal value of railroad properties, allowing them to charge higher rates. He also used his mastery of the facts to fluster witnesses during the brutal cross-examinations for which he became famous. His courtroom demeanor was described as "bullying" and "shredding." One lawyer commented that Butler was "the most ruthless cross-examiner practicing in the courts of that day."

Butler's successes drew the attention of President William Howard Taft's attorney general, George Wickersham, who in 1910 called upon Butler to act as counsel for the federal government in several important antitrust cases. He successfully argued before the district court that several meat-packing companies were guilty of price fixing and conspiracy to eliminate competition. In the "Bleached Flour" cases, Butler invoked the Pure Food and Drug Act and emerged victorious when a jury found a flour company guilty of adulterating and mislabeling its product. Both of these decisions were later overturned in the circuit court of appeals, but Wickersham praised Butler for presenting the government's case "as well as it could be." Wickersham later called Butler "the foremost lawyer in his part of the country."

In 1913 Butler increased his legal stature with his ar-

Pierce Butler was one of Midwest's preeminent railroad lawyers, arguing the *Minnesota Rate Cases* before the Supreme Court. He met former president William Howard Taft at a railroad arbitration, and the two became friends. When Taft became chief justice, he strongly supported Butler's nomination to the Court. *Source: Library of Congress*

gument before the U.S. Supreme Court in the *Minnesota Rate Cases*. Butler became famous for his unflagging defense of the use of "cost of reproduction" of railroad property in determining its value and consequently the appropriate fares. Butler continued his outspoken advocacy of this valuation method as a leading member of the committee of lawyers representing the railroads in proceedings arising from the Federal Railroad Valuation Act of 1913.

Some of Butler's cases concerned Canadian railroads. In 1919 he won a lucrative settlement for the shareholders of a railroad company against the Canadian government. Later he acted as counsel, this time for the Canadian government, in an arbitration in Montreal. Former president Taft served as a mediator and, although he dissented from the board of arbitrators' decision supporting Butler, the two became friends. Butler was serving as counsel in the Toronto Railway Arbitration on November 23, 1922, when he received word that President Warren G. Harding had nominated him to replace William R. Day on the Supreme Court bench.

Butler's nomination was the result of active endorsement by several of his influential acquaintances. San-

born, now a circuit court judge, and Supreme Court justice Willis Van Devanter made strong recommendations to President Harding, with the most vigorous support coming from Taft, who had become chief justice. Taft predicted that if Butler were appointed, he would align himself with Justices Van Devanter, James McReynolds, and George Sutherland to create a conservative majority. Butler's Catholic faith also made him an attractive candidate. Taft, a Protestant, had replaced Chief Justice Edward D. White, a Catholic, and many believed that another Catholic was needed on the Court.

The nomination drew intense resistance, however, from a small but powerful group of liberal senators, primarily George Norris and Robert La Follette, and a senator-elect, Henrik Shipstead. They argued that Butler's strong loyalties to the railroad companies he had represented would prejudice his decisions as a justice. The senators also raised questions regarding Butler's actions at the University of Minnesota, where he served on the Board of Regents from 1907 to 1924. Several liberal professors, most notably William Shaper, head of the Department of Political Science, had been unjustly fired by the board. Shaper had argued for municipal ownership of the street railways, which Butler represented, and subsequently was dismissed from the university because of alleged "pro-German" sentiments during World War I. Shaper claimed that Butler, driven by his opposing political and economic views, had forced his dismissal. Other liberal academics complained that Butler could not tolerate dissent.

Senator La Follette successfully blocked the vote on Butler's nomination until a special congressional session ended December 4, but President Harding promptly renominated Butler the following day. On December 13 the Senate Judiciary Committee sidestepped the controversy and unanimously recommended Butler's confirmation. One week later, with only eight senators voting against him, the fifty-six-year-old Minnesotan was confirmed. A conservative Democrat, Butler was the seventh justice appointed by a president of another party.

Butler served seventeen years on the high bench. As predicted, he frequently voted with Justices Sutherland, McReynolds, and Van Devanter. Together, these so-called Four Horsemen made up a conservative bloc on the Court that consistently overturned much of President Franklin D. Roosevelt's New Deal legislation.

During his tenure, Butler wrote 323 majority opinions, 44 dissenting opinions, and 3 concurring opinions. Butler was not a stylist—he had no flair for an unusual turn of phrase—but his opinions were clearly expressed and demonstrated the same knowledge of pertinent facts that had propelled him throughout his career.

The unwavering faith in laissez-faire economics and the religious values that Butler developed during his early years on the Minnesota farm remained firmly entrenched as he took his seat on the Supreme Court. Justice Oliver Wendell Holmes, Jr., described Butler as a "monolith" with "no seams the frost can get through." Butler had risen from humble beginnings to a seat on America's highest court and was unshaken in his resolve to preserve the rights of the individual to compete freely to improve. Lack of success, Butler reasoned, was through personal fault, not economic disadvantage.

Robert Taft, son of Chief Justice Taft, later said that

A brilliant Minnesota lawyer, Pierce Butler was hired by Attorney General George Wickersham to help prosecute several big antitrust cases in district court. Butler successfully argued in 1911 that several meat companies, such as this Chicago sausage maker, were guilty of price fixing and trying to eliminate competition. *Source: Chicago Historical Society*

Congress created the Tennessee Valley Authority, which built dams and powerhouses on the Tennessee River to restore the region and produce cheap electricity for the farmers who lived in the impoverished area. Pierce Butler dissented in the 1936 case upholding the validity of the act, reasoning that Congress was unconstitutionally overstepping its power and that the government was competing unfairly with private electric companies.
Source: Library of Congress

Butler "was more concerned that the government should keep open channels of individual liberty than he was that the government should extend a paternalistic protection to those who were not so well able, or determined, to succeed through their own efforts." Butler insisted on this philosophy even during the bleak years of the Great Depression.

He categorically opposed social welfare legislation. In 1936 Butler wrote the Court's opinion in *Morehead v. New York ex. rel. Tipaldo,* which struck down a New York law enacting minimum wages for women. He joined McReynolds in a dissent in *Helvering v. Davis* (1937), which upheld the taxing of employers and employees to create old age and unemployment pensions under the Social Security Act of 1935. Butler wrote, "The Constitution grants to the United States no power to pay unemployed persons or to require the states to enact laws . . . for that purpose." Butler also dissented with McReynolds in *Ashwander v. Tennessee Valley Authority* (1936), which dealt with one of the two early New Deal laws the Court declared valid.

Frustrated that the Court kept striking down legislation designed to bring about the country's economic recovery, President Roosevelt lashed out at the aging members of the Court. He complained that the out-

moded "horse and buggy" thinking of "the nine old men" had created "a no man's land" where neither federal nor state government might function. Roosevelt's difficulties with the Court prompted his unsuccessful 1937 reform plan, which would have allowed him to appoint as many as six new justices.

Butler's demeanor while on the Court, as during his earlier years, was aggressive, domineering, and stubborn, especially when he was struggling for what he thought was right. When not working, however, Butler was known as a genial man, a witty story teller, an enthusiastic golfer, and a lover of outdoor life. He was proud of his Irish heritage and described his visit to his parents' homeland in 1934 as one of the happiest episodes of his life. Butler also maintained close ties to his faith by serving on the board of trustees of the Catholic University of America. During his later years, he returned to his rural beginnings, spending his weekends on the 538-acre stock farm he owned in Westminster, Maryland.

Butler died of a bladder ailment November 16, 1939, in Washington, D.C. He was seventy-three. His death left McReynolds the lone Horseman to hold the conservative fort against the new majority of liberal justices appointed by Roosevelt.

Edward T. Sanford

1923-1930

Source: Library of Congress

B ORN IN KNOXVILLE, TENNESSEE, July 23, 1865, only three months after the Confederate Army surrendered at Appomattox, Edward Terry Sanford was the eldest of six children. He grew up in one of the few Republican enclaves of the South and in an area deeply divided by the Civil War. His father, Edward Sanford, Sr., a destitute Connecticut Yankee of colonial heritage, had moved to Tennessee in 1852, where he made a fortune in the construction and lumber business. His mother, Emma Chavannes San-

ford, was the cultivated daughter of French-Swiss parents who had emigrated from Switzerland to Knoxville in 1848.

The elder Sanford took a great interest in his children and was especially eager that they be well educated. Emma Sanford carefully supervised the future justice's preparatory education in private schools. Sanford received the first of several academic degrees in 1883, when, at a precocious eighteen years of age, he graduated from the University of Tennessee at the head of his class with a B.A. and a Ph.B. He proceeded to Harvard University and two years later was class orator at ceremonies where he received his second bachelor's degree.

At Harvard Law School, which he entered in 1886, the year the *Harvard Law Review* was founded, his record was equally brilliant. He was one of the review's first editors and a member of several select societies. In three years he earned two additional degrees, an M.A. magna cum laude and an LL.B. Sanford interrupted his law studies in 1888 long enough to pass the bar examination in Tennessee. A year of postgraduate study of languages in France and Germany ensued, helping him to shed his Tennessee provincialism. He then returned to Knoxville to enter private law practice.

His nearly two decades as a practicing attorney got off to an impressive start when he joined the prestigious law firm of Andrews and Thornburgh. George Andrews had served on the Tennessee Supreme Court and was known as one of the state's ablest lawyers. Jacob M. Thornburgh, who had been a colonel in the Union Army during the Civil War and had served several terms in Congress, was known as a particularly effective trial lawyer. Andrews died in a railway accident a few months after Sanford joined the firm, just as the Tennessee Supreme Court was convening for a term that had a number of Andrews's cases on the docket. Sanford, with little preparation, took over the cases. Applying himself diligently, he soon earned a reputation as an accomplished practitioner.

Sanford practiced law with the firm, the membership of which changed from time to time, until 1907. On January 6, 1891, he married a woman from Knoxville, Lutie Mallory Woodruff, and the couple had two daughters, one predeceasing her father.

As a practicing attorney, Sanford specialized in civil and appellate work. One of his law partners and an intimate friend, James A. Fowler, later wrote that he would have made a highly successful trial lawyer. "He was pleasing in address, quick in his mental processes, ready at repartee, forceful in discussing questions of both fact and law, and he impressed both Courts and Juries with his fairness and sincerity." But, said Fowler, he was extremely cautious, and disliked the unpredictability of trial work before juries. Few lawyers, in Fowler's judgment, were equal to Sanford in his chosen fields. His preparation was meticulous, and he rarely considered a brief or other paper complete until he had submitted it to his associates for criticism.

During these years Sanford began to act on the strong feelings for higher education that he was to demonstrate all his life. He became a trustee of the University of Tennessee in 1897, one of the first of many public service duties he was to undertake. He became a charter member of the board of governors of the Kentucky General Hospital, a member of the board of the East Tennessee Institute, and chairman of the board of the George Peabody College of Teachers. He also served as vice president of the Tennessee Historical Society, president of the alumni associations of both Harvard and the University of Tennessee, vice president of the Harvard Law School Association, and vice president of the American Bar Association, among other similar positions in educational, professional, and charitable groups.

Sanford's rise through the federal judicial hierarchy began in 1905. James McReynolds, an assistant attorney general who was to become a Supreme Court justice in 1914, had begun to prosecute what was known as the fertilizer trust. Much of the activity of the alleged monopoly was in the South, partly in Tennessee. McReynolds knew Sanford and persuaded him to come to Washington as a special assistant to Attorney General William H. Moody (who also later served on the Supreme Court) and help conduct the prosecution of the trust under the Sherman Antitrust Act of 1890.

McReynolds left the Department of Justice at the beginning of 1907, and Sanford was at first hesitant about applying to fill the position he vacated. However, he had expressed to friends a desire for an appointment to the federal bench, and it was suggested to him that the position of assistant attorney general could be a stepping stone. He applied for the appointment, received it, and stayed in the post for seventeen months. He argued a number of cases before the Supreme Court and, significantly, made a favorable impression on President Theodore Roosevelt.

In the spring of 1908 a vacancy occurred on a district court covering eastern and central Tennessee, but Sanford, deciding he would rather stay in Washington, would not let his name be put forward. But Roosevelt had other ideas. When a delegation from Chattanooga called upon him to advocate another candidate, the president said, "I tell you gentlemen, the man I want is Ed Sanford, but he won't take it." Sanford was persuaded to change his mind, and the president sent his name to the Senate immediately. Sanford later related to friends that a conversation with Justice Edward D. White had influenced his decision. White had emphasized the crucial importance of the position in the federal judicial system, saying that the first and real hearing of a case was by the district judge, and he would determine whether justice would be done. Perhaps more persuasive was White's prophecy that Sanford would one day don the robe of a Supreme Court justice himself. White did not live to see his prophecy fulfilled; he died just two years before Sanford joined the Supreme Court.

Whatever his original reservations, Sanford took on his judicial duties with characteristic conscientiousness and exercised them responsibly for fifteen years. Throughout his tenure he continued to pay strict attention to legal detail, to maintaining dignity and civility in his courtroom, to avoiding any personal or professional impropriety, and to expanding his public service activities. He had jurisdiction over two districts and this amount of work, combined with his thorough and deliberate approach, kept him busy.

In 1920 Sanford wrote to his class secretary at Harvard, "My dockets are now crowded, and my work very heavy and done under constant pressure, but, with a bit of vacation now and then and a little golf . . . [I] have kept in excellent health and continue to find enduring satisfaction and contentment in my work." An avid golfer, he owned some two hundred clubs. His secretary once described Judge Sanford as "a man of highly nervous temperament . . . [who] smoked cigars of a small size that could be consumed during a five or ten minute recess at court."

Sanford's friend Fowler, who by then had been appointed assistant attorney general, recorded that Sanford disliked the necessity of imposing punishment on the many offenders who were tried and convicted before him, and that he was considered lenient in sentencing. Sanford preferred to give full consideration to every question he must pass judgment on, rather than ruling immediately on the many points raised in the progress of a trial. Indeed, he sometimes reversed himself in the course of a trial after further consideration of an earlier decision. Sanford had made it clear to friends that he would like an appointment to an appellate court, but they had been unsuccessful in supporting him for appointment to two vacancies that occurred on the Sixth Circuit Court of Appeals.

An unusually close succession of vacancies by death and retirement opened three appointments to the Supreme Court over a period of about a year during Warren G. Harding's short presidency. When a fourth justice, Mahlon Pitney, retired in December 1922, Sanford's friends and supporters swung into action. He had something bordering on unanimous endorsement from his own district: the Republican governor, the state Democratic legislature, and, it was said, every lawyer and every prominent citizen in the districts where he presided backed him. In Washington, his most important advocates were Chief Justice William Howard Taft and Attorney General Harry M. Daugherty. Taft had

Benjamin Gitlow and William Z. Foster, Communist Workers' party candidates for president and vice president in 1928, at Madison Square Garden. Three years earlier the Supreme Court had upheld Gitlow's conviction for publishing an article calling for workers to overthrow capitalism and the government by force. Edward T. Sanford's majority opinion also ruled that states, not just the federal government, must adhere to the First Amendment's "fundamental" provision permitting freedom of speech. *UPI/Bettmann*

met Sanford during his service at the Justice Department, but it was Sanford's effort to mobilize support for the Treaty of Versailles and the League of Nations in the years following World War I that attracted Taft's and Daugherty's attention and praise.

President Harding had received substantial support from the South in his election, including twelve electoral votes from Tennessee, and a southern Republican was considered a reasonable choice for the Court vacancy. Allegations from supporters of other candidates that Chief Justice Taft was "dictating" the selection delayed the appointment somewhat, but on January 24, 1923, Sanford's name went to the Senate, and he was confirmed without difficulty less than a week later.

During his seven years on the high bench, Sanford

delivered the opinion of the Court in 130 cases. Among the most controversial was his 1925 majority opinion in *Gitlow v. New York,* which upheld the conviction of Benjamin Gitlow, under a state criminal anarchy statute. Gitlow a socialist, had published a manifesto urging the overthrow of the government by force. Although it upheld the conviction, Sanford's opinion accepted Gitlow's argument and established "that freedom of speech and of the press . . . are among the fundamental personal rights and 'liberties' protected by the due process clause of the Fourteenth Amendment." This ruling was the first of many holding that the guarantees in the Bill of Rights extend to state, as well as federal, action. Two other cases showed that Sanford was not categorically opposed to denying rights of free

Edward Sanford's majority opinion in the *Pocket Veto Case* (1929) defined the precise circumstances under which the president could exercise the pocket veto power when Congress was not in session. At issue was a bill, passed by Congress but ignored by President Calvin Coolidge (in dark hat) once the legislature adjourned, giving certain Indian tribes the right to file claims in the U.S. Court of Claims. Coolidge posed for this picture with members of the Sioux Indian Republican Club in March 1925. *Source: Library of Congress*

speech to radicals. In one, he reversed a similar conviction; in the other he joined Oliver Wendell Holmes, Jr., in a dissent from a decision that would withhold a U.S. passport from a pacifist.

Sanford consistently favored strict enforcement of antitrust laws regulating business monopolies, and he was often to be found on the side of the public interest. One of his last opinions for the Court, the *Pocket Veto Case* of 1929, was perhaps his most important because it settled an important constitutional issue between the legislative and executive branches that had been unresolved for 140 years. His opinion clarified the rules by which the president could use the pocket veto power to send a bill back to Congress.

Justice Sanford died suddenly March 8, 1930, at age sixty-four. Retired chief justice Taft died only a few hours later, monopolizing the headlines, and the news of Sanford's passing was almost unmarked by the press and the public. Sanford's official Court eulogy remembered him as having "unusual charm" and being "a most gifted speaker." It went on to say, "He was a lover of literature and the arts, was widely read and deeply experienced in law and jurisprudence. He had ardent patriotism and a high sense of duty."

Harlan Fiske Stone

1925-1941, 1941-1946

Source: Library of Congress

HARLAN FISKE STONE was born October 11, 1872, in Chesterfield, New Hampshire. His was the ninth generation in America of the Simon Stone family, which arrived on the *Increase* in 1635 and settled in Watertown, Massachusetts. In 1778 Peter Stone, Harlan's great grandfather, moved his family to Chesterfield. Most of the future justice's American ancestors were rugged hill farmers; and many served as selectmen in their local communities. In 1874, when young Harlan was two years old, the family moved to a farm near Amherst, Massachusetts. There he received his early schooling.

In 1888 he entered the Massachusetts Agricultural College (now the University of Massachusetts) but was expelled for rowdyism in 1890. Despite this black mark on his record, he was admitted to Amherst College the same year after the president was persuaded that his assault on a teacher was a case of mistaken identity and that his scholastic record justified his admission. Stone was moving a pile of horse manure when he received

Harlan Fiske Stone posed with his wife, Agnes, and elder son, Marshall, after his appointment to the Supreme Court. The Stones were engaged for nine years before marrying in 1899, having known each other since childhood summers in New Hampshire. A painter of landscapes, Agnes Stone once exhibited her work at the Corcoran Gallery of Art. *Source: Library of Congress*

football at a high school in Newburyport, Massachusetts. While there he took time to attend sessions of the superior court, where he found a friend in District Attorney William H. Moody, who was later appointed to the Supreme Court by Theodore Roosevelt. What Stone saw in court convinced him that his true calling was the law.

He enrolled in Columbia Law School in New York City, financing his studies by teaching history at a local academy. He graduated in 1898, was admitted to the New York bar, and went to work as a clerk at the prestigious Wall Street firm of Sullivan and Cromwell. At the same time he taught bailments and insurance at Columbia Law School, becoming adjunct professor in 1903.

In 1899, after a nine-year engagement, Stone married his childhood playmate Agnes Harvey. They had two sons. Marshall became a world-class mathematician, and Lauson became a distinguished lawyer. The Stones bought a roomy house in Englewood, New Jersey, to rear their boys. Stone had meanwhile joined another Wall Street law firm, Wilmer and Canfield, which became Wilmer, Canfield, and Stone, and had resigned from the Columbia faculty to devote full time to his law practice. In 1910, however, Columbia's president, Nicholas Murray Butler, persuaded him to return to the law school as dean and professor of law. He remained there until 1923. Under Stone's guidance, the school constantly improved its faculty and its curriculum. Even so, he found time to continue his law practice.

Late in 1923 Stone left Columbia to accept a partnership in Sullivan and Cromwell, heading its litigation department and at last earning enough money to satisfy his yearning for a box at the Metropolitan Opera. Six months later, however, President Calvin Coolidge, a classmate at Amherst and a fellow Republican, appointed him attorney general at an annual salary of $12,000—not even an eighth of what he had been earning. After less than a year in that office, during which

the news. He gave a joyous whoop, tossed the pitchfork aside, and never handled it again. Recalling the incident many years later, he remarked, "Had I realized what I'd be doing later in my career, I'd have hung on to that pitchfork." At Amherst he played football, which cost him a broken nose, joined the Alpha Delta fraternity, and served as president of his class, graduating Phi Beta Kappa in 1894. Three years later Amherst awarded him a master's degree.

In 1894 and 1895 Stone taught natural science (physics, chemistry, botany, and geology) and coached

he cleaned up internal corruption at the Department of Justice and appointed J. Edgar Hoover to head the FBI, Stone was nominated to the Supreme Court by Coolidge. He appeared before the Senate Judiciary Committee—the first Supreme Court nominee to make such an appearance—to deal with questions about his handling of fraud charges against Montana senator Burton K. Wheeler. He was confirmed February 5, 1925 by a 71–6 vote.

One problem that Stone faced when he became a justice was to find adequate office space. At that time the Court staff occupied cramped quarters in the old Senate Office Building along with a number of senators. He and his wife built a house with a roomy two-story wing reserved for his library and chambers, which became a source of great pride.

Physically large and robust, Stone did his best to keep in shape. He was a member of President Herbert Hoover's "medicine ball cabinet," which often exercised together on the White House lawn at 6:30 in the morning. Stone took daily walks of two miles or more, usually accompanied by Agnes or a breathless law clerk.

Soon after his appointment, Stone found an opportunity to criticize a "word game" that had found a place in the Court's opinions. The case was *Metcalf & Eddy v.*

Mitchell (1926), and the question was whether a state tax on income from engineering work for the federal government imposed an impermissible burden on that government. In previous rulings the Court had said that in such cases the outcome depended on whether the tax burden was "direct" or "indirect." Stone objected to these terms because he thought they had no real meaning and were used simply as labels to indicate the result the Court had reached. This concern of Stone's for plain talk continued through the years and was expressed in numerous contexts. He was not inclined to offer easy answers to the difficult issues that came before the Court. Very few of his opinions have needed explanations in later years.

When Chief Justice William Howard Taft resigned in 1930, many expected that Stone would succeed him. Taft, however, fearing that Stone would be unable to "mass" the Court—persuade the justices to join in a single opinion—used his influence against him. Hoover appointed former justice Charles Evans Hughes instead, and Stone's appointment as chief justice was delayed eleven eventful years.

Perhaps the most important problem that confronted the Court during the 1930s related to the scope of its own legitimate power. It had sharply limited the power

In 1923 Harlan Fiske Stone (seated, second from right) left a lucrative partnership in a New York law firm to become attorney general under President Calvin Coolidge (seated, center), his Amherst College classmate. In less than a year Coolidge appointed Stone to the Supreme Court, where he was joined by Secretary of State Charles Evans Hughes (seated, third from left). *Source: National Portrait Gallery*

of Congress and the states to legislate against economic and social evils. It had also interpreted the Tenth Amendment as forbidding Congress to regulate manufacturing, mining, and agriculture because they were deemed local and subject to state, not federal, regulation. Because the states could not effectively regulate the national economy, however, the consequence was that these activities were largely unregulated. As a result, when the Great Depression intensified the need for government regulation, the Court had established the basis to find one after another legislative remedy unconstitutional. The Court's decisions frustrated Congress and the president, who felt that the will of the people, who favored the legislation, was not being served. Stone agreed that the Court had been misinterpreting the Constitution.

He had repeatedly dissented from Court decisions striking down the economic and social legislation of President Franklin D. Roosevelt's New Deal, joining Justices Louis Brandeis and Benjamin Cardozo to form a persistent minority. The three of them adopted the practice of meeting the night before each weekly conference to exchange views—and perhaps also to divide the labor of preparing dissents. In one such dissent, in the 6–3 decision striking down the Agricultural Adjustment Act in 1936, Stone summed up the minority position by accusing the Court of taking on legislative powers. Saying that "the only check upon our own exercise of power is our own sense of self-restraint," he continued, "Courts are not the only agency of government that must be assumed to have capacity to govern."

In the spring of 1937 the Court began to uphold New Deal programs that had seemed doomed to invalidation. This change of heart resulted partly from fear of Roosevelt's proposal to enlarge the Court so he could appoint new justices presumably more sympathetic to his legislation. The plan was rejected by Congress, but a shift in attitude, along with a change of Court personnel due to retirement, suddenly gave Stone and his like-minded colleagues majority support for their views.

An important question remained unsettled. During the years before 1937 the Court had broken new ground for judicial protection of civil liberties. It had struck down statutes impairing the freedoms of expression and religion, had begun to protect racial and religious minorities, and had taken the first steps toward improving the criminal process. Such decisions were often unpopular, and yet the Stone group thought the Constitution required them. Unless the seeming inconsistency was explained in terms of principle, cynics could argue that the Court did not care about the will of the people or about self-government.

Stone took the lead in resolving the inconsistency. His position was that democracy's capacity for correcting its own mistakes is an essential part of it and that the government must therefore tolerate criticism of its actions. Stone also believed that the government is obligated to serve the whole people and that courts should invalidate measures resulting from prejudice against blacks and other minorities. These propositions were articulated in a footnote to Stone's opinion in *United States v. Carolene Products Corp.* (1938). Footnote Four has been called "the most celebrated footnote in constitutional law" and still provides a starting point for analysis of appropriate limits on self-government.

Many of the First Amendment cases involved the Jehovah's Witnesses, an evangelical Christian sect dedicated to spreading the gospel and relentlessly denying the government's authority to control their activities. One fiercely contested claim arose from their belief that saluting the national flag is the same as "bowing down to a graven image" and hence a violation of the Second Commandment. Their children, having been so taught at home, declined to salute the flag at school. Some school districts made daily salutes compulsory and suspended or expelled children who did not comply. In some cases they and their parents were prosecuted in juvenile court. A number of lawsuits resulted.

When school districts made the pledge of allegiance compulsory, Walter Gobitas's children, William and Lillian, Jehovah's Witnesses, were expelled for refusing to salute the flag. In *Minersville School District v. Gobitis* (1940)—the name was misspelled in the Court records—Harlan Fiske Stone wrote a lone dissent arguing that the pledge requirement was a violation of the children's freedom of religion. The Court reversed its ruling three years later, but Stone, now chief justice, assigned Robert Jackson to write it. *Source: UPI/Bettmann*

The first such case to be argued in the Supreme Court was *Minersville School District v. Gobitis* (1940). With World War II under way, it was a poor time for the sect to be questioning the obligation to make a simple gesture of respect to America's symbol of nationhood. Yet, to Stone's credit, he saw the case in true perspective and delivered a noble dissent from the otherwise unanimous Court upholding the flag salute requirement. Three years later, the Court's decision was overruled.

The tremendous expansion of federal regulation during the depression demanded, for effective enforcement, a host of new administrative agencies. Stone led the movement to embrace the administrative process as a positive and necessary aspect of modern law. In recognition of Stone's support of his programs and his policies, and because of his excellent record as associate justice, Roosevelt appointed him chief justice on June 12, 1941. The appointment of a Republican justice by a Democrat was a well-received gesture of unity when the country was poised for war. He was confirmed by voice vote two weeks later. In becoming chief justice, Stone had occupied each one of the nine seats on the Court's bench, which are allotted according to seniority; he was the first justice to do so.

As chief justice, Stone had a difficult time minimizing the sometimes bitter conflicts and disagreements among the brethren during the 1940s, and the Court's efficiency suffered. Moreover, World War II confronted Stone and his Court with wrenchingly difficult questions. Despite the deep and growing concern for fairness to the accused, Stone and most of his colleagues felt compelled to defer to military tribunals and judgments, as the Court had done during the Civil War. In 1943 Stone wrote the unanimous opinion upholding the wartime curfew placed on American citizens of Japanese origin living on the West Coast and in a later case voted to uphold their internment by the government.

On April 22, 1946, while announcing a dissent in a naturalization case, Stone fell forward, stricken by a cerebral hemorrhage. He died that night, abruptly ending twenty-one years of service on the Court.

Owen J. Roberts

1930-1945

Source: Photo by Harris & Ewing, Collection of the Supreme Court of the United States

OWEN JOSEPHUS ROBERTS was born May 2, 1875, in the Germantown section of Philadelphia, to Josephus and Emma Laferty Roberts. His father was the son of Welsh immigrants; his mother was of Scotch-Irish descent. Josephus Roberts had prospered as a hardware merchant and wagon dealer, and young Owen, one of two children and the only son, had the benefit of a private education. He attended Germantown Academy, where he was a member of the debate team. At age sixteen, he entered the University of Pennsylvania.

Roberts excelled academically. He concentrated on Greek and Latin and at one point considered a career teaching Greek. In 1895, at age twenty, he graduated with honors and was elected to Phi Beta Kappa. He then entered the university's law school where, at the end of his first year, he was selected as an editor of the *American Law Register* (now the *University of Pennsylva-*

nia Law Review) and, in his third year, won the prize for the best graduation essay. Roberts graduated from law school in 1898 with highest honors.

He began private practice in Philadelphia, first with the law firm of White and White and later with Roberts, Montgomery, and McKeehan. He also accepted a part-time appointment at the University of Pennsylvania Law School. Between 1898 and 1919 Roberts taught real property, bankruptcy, contracts, and damages, rising from lecturer to full professor. In 1903 he came to the attention of Philadelphia's district attorney, John Bell, who appointed him as first assistant district attorney, a position he held until 1906, when he returned to private practice. In 1904 Roberts married Elizabeth Rogers of Fairfield, Connecticut. They had one child, a daughter.

Known for his diligent preparation and careful oral arguments, Roberts cultivated a successful practice in Philadelphia. At the end of World War I, the U.S. attorney general appointed Roberts as special deputy attorney general to prosecute violations of the Espionage Act in eastern Pennsylvania. Roberts obtained several convictions, including those of the editors and publishers of German and Lithuanian newspapers published in Philadelphia.

In February 1924 Roberts accepted an appointment from President Calvin Coolidge as special counsel to the United States. During the administration of Warren Harding, the Navy had leased certain oil reserves in Elk Hill, California, and Teapot Dome, Wyoming, which it turned out had been fraudulently obtained through bribing the secretary of the interior, Albert B. Fall. Coolidge had already appointed former Democratic senator Atlee Pomerene as special counsel in the matter, and he wished to appoint a Republican. Roberts was summoned to Washington by a former law professor, George Wharton Pepper, since elected to the Senate from Pennsylvania, who introduced Roberts to the

president. Roberts secured the cancellation of the Navy leases and the criminal convictions of Fall and others. His work was highly regarded by Attorney General William Mitchell, and Justice Louis Brandeis confided to Felix Frankfurter, an influential Harvard professor and future Supreme Court justice, that Roberts had made an "uncommonly good impression on our Court."

In March 1930, upon the death of Justice Edward Sanford, President Herbert Hoover nominated John J. Parker, a federal appeals court judge, to fill the vacancy. Judge Parker, a North Carolinian, drew substantial op-

Owen J. Roberts made a name for himself in Washington as a special counsel investigating the Teapot Dome Scandal. The criminal activity of his secretary of the interior, Albert B. Fall, and others so upset President Warren G. Harding that it may have led to his early death. *Source: Library of Congress*

position because of perceptions that he was anti-union and that he opposed the involvement of blacks in politics. The Senate rejected him by two votes in May 1930, and Hoover quickly nominated Roberts. In the wake of the Parker confirmation fight, the president and the Senate were eager to find an acceptable nominee. Roberts drew no opposition from the union front, and he garnered support from the black community when it was learned that he had served as a trustee to the historically black Lincoln University in Pennsylvania. The Senate confirmed Roberts unanimously May 20, 1930.

Roberts joined the Court in the middle of one of the most difficult periods in its history. The Court had struck down numerous state and federal statutes and was increasingly subject to criticism from progressives. Moreover, it was firmly divided philosophically between two groups. One faction, the conservative "Four Horsemen of the Apocalypse," Justices Willis Van Devanter, James McReynolds, George Sutherland, and Pierce Butler, supported laissez-faire economics and felt that the new social legislation of the early 1900s infringed on the rights of the people. The other group, Justices Oliver Wendell Holmes, Jr., Louis Brandeis, and, more recently, Harlan Stone, believed that, without an explicit prohibition, the Constitution permitted the states and the federal government to experiment with innovative social legislation. The conservative group typically had voted as a bloc, looking for the decisive fifth vote from Chief Justice William Howard Taft or Justice Sanford.

Roberts, replacing Sanford, joined the Court only four months after the Senate had confirmed Charles Evans Hughes as Taft's successor. Because they represented the swing votes, both new justices came under extraordinary scrutiny. Frankfurter told Roberts that he would be seen as "a servant neither of a blind traditionalism nor of blind indifference to historic wisdom." He then assured Roberts that although "there is a good deal of loose talk about 'conservative' and 'liberal,' "those labels "hardly describe anybody since we are all a compound of both." Stone wrote to his sons in May 1930 that Roberts "has a good mind. . . . I should expect him to deal in the liberal way with important constitutional problems, because he has the type of mind that would take in all aspects of a problem."

Roberts was indeed "a compound of both" liberal and conservative. He refused to align himself with either camp; in fact, it is often difficult to reconcile Roberts's votes. Early in his service with the Court, he seemed to favor the position of the Four Horsemen. One of the first cases in which he was involved concerned the powers of the Interstate Commerce Commission (ICC) to structure a railroad bankruptcy; a bare majority held that the ICC's actions went beyond its authority. Roberts cast a deciding vote, joining Sutherland's opinion over a dissent by Stone, joined by Holmes and Brandeis. That decision was followed by many others in which Roberts, often along with Hughes, joined the conservatives. In perhaps the most notable of these, *United States v. Butler* (1936), Roberts wrote the majority opinion holding unconstitutional one of the cornerstones of the New Deal, the Agricultural Adjustment Act. The act sought to increase farm prices by paying farmers to decrease their acreage. Roberts wrote that because the Constitution did not delegate to Congress authority to regulate agricultural production directly, it could not do so indirectly by "purchasing" the farmers' compliance.

But any sense that Roberts was voting in the shadow of Sutherland, whom he particularly admired, was quickly dispelled. In one of the important decisions of the era, the Court upheld a Minnesota law, enacted during the Great Depression, authorizing courts to exempt property from foreclosure and to extend mortgage payments. Roberts, along with Brandeis, Stone, and Benjamin Cardozo, who had replaced Holmes, joined the opinion of Chief Justice Hughes in *Home Building and Loan Association v. Blaisdell* (1935). Sutherland led a vigorous dissent for himself, Butler, McReynolds, and Van Devanter. Roberts showed his independence from the conservatives again in a challenge to the authority of New York's Milk Control Board to fix minimum and maximum prices for retail milk sales. In *Nebbia v. New York* (1934) Roberts wrote for the majority, "The Constitution does not guarantee the unrestricted privilege to engage in a business or to conduct it as one pleases." The states might adopt such public programs as they wished, and "with the wisdom of the policy adopted, . . . the courts [would be] both incompetent and unauthorized to deal." This decision marked a significant shift from prior Court decisions holding that such state legislation violated the right to contract; some believed that it heralded the beginning of Roberts's departure from the conservative side of the Court.

His vacillation between the two sides came to national attention in 1937. President Franklin D. Roosevelt was plainly frustrated with what he regarded as Court interference with the progress of the New Deal. The last straw for the president had been the Court's decision in June 1936 striking down New York's minimum wage laws, a decision in which Roberts had provided the necessary fifth vote. In February 1937 Roosevelt proposed a plan that would have given him the power to appoint additional justices to the Supreme Court. But in March 1937 the Court held Washington State's minimum wage law for women constitutional, overruling a prior decision. In *West Coast Hotel Co. v. Parrish,* Roberts, in contrast to his vote of just nine months earlier, voted to uphold the minimum wage law. The steam went out of Roosevelt's proposal, and the "Court-packing plan" went down to defeat in the Senate.

The newspapers assailed Roberts's apparent change of heart as a calculated response to Roosevelt's plan—the "switch in time that saved the Nine"—and they accused the justice of playing politics with his swing vote. After Roberts died, Justice Frankfurter and others concluded

In *United States v. Butler* (1936) Owen J. Roberts wrote the opinion invalidating one of the pillars of the New Deal, the Agricultural Adjustment Act. Congress had passed the law in 1933 to relieve suffering farmers by bringing the prices of farm goods up to pre-World War I levels. To reduce food surpluses, the government paid farmers to produce less and raised the funds to pay them by taxing the first processors of the commodities. *Source: Library of Congress*

that he had voted in the Washington case before Roosevelt's Court-packing announcement and that his previous vote was not inconsistent because of the procedural manner in which the New York case had come before the Court. In any event, the president's conflict with the Court was over. Moreover, within two years Roosevelt had the opportunity to make three appointments to the Court. Van Devanter retired in 1937, and Sutherland the following year. Cardozo died in 1938.

Perhaps Roberts's most enduring opinions dealt with civil rights and liberties. In 1940 he wrote the majority opinion in *Cantwell v. Connecticut,* reversing the convictions of Jehovah's Witnesses, who had been arrested for soliciting religious contributions in violation of a

When greengrocer Leo Nebbia sold two quarts of milk and a loaf of bread for eighteen cents, he was convicted of violating the New York Milk Control Board's order to fix the price of a quart of milk at nine cents, a measure designed to stabilize the market. In 1934 the Supreme Court ruled that the state had a right to adopt such a program and that it did not infringe on Nebbia's constitutional rights. Swing voter Owen J. Roberts aligned himself with the majority in favor of the right of states to regulate business. *Source: Equal Justice Under Law, credit* Rochester Times Union, *Courtesy of Rochester Public Library*

state law. He reasoned, however, that the First Amendment "embraces two concepts—freedom to believe and freedom to act. The first is absolute but, in the nature of things, the second cannot be. Conduct remains subject to regulation for the protection of society." It was the first case in which the Court acknowledged that the Constitution's religion clauses applied to the states as well as to Congress. Roberts also wrote an opinion in

an important case upholding the right of associations to hold outdoor meetings and to distribute literature without securing police permits. And during World War II he dissented forcefully in a controversial case in which the Court upheld the conviction of an American of Japanese descent for violating a military order excluding Japanese-Americans from certain areas on the West Coast. For Roberts, Fred Korematsu was convicted "solely because of his ancestry, without evidence or inquiry concerning his loyalty and good disposition towards the United States. If this be a correct statement of the facts . . . I need hardly labor the conclusion that constitutional rights have been violated."

During his tenure on the Court, Roberts accepted two temporary presidential appointments. In 1932 Hoover selected him to serve as an umpire on the Mixed Claims Commission of the United States and Germany. The commission had before it claims against Germany resulting from explosions on the East Coast, attributed to German agents, before the United States entered World War I. In December 1941 Roosevelt appointed Roberts as head of a committee to investigate and report to Congress on the military's performance at Pearl Harbor.

After fifteen years of service, Roberts resigned from the Court July 31, 1945, to pursue other civic interests. He became involved in the movement to unite free countries in a federation, with an eye to the creation of a world government. He became a member of the National Council of the Boy Scouts of America, president of the Pennsylvania Bar Association, and president of the American Philosophical Society. In the summer of 1948, when the deanship of the University of Pennsylvania became vacant, Roberts accepted the position, serving for three years without pay. He was invited to present the Holmes Lectures at Harvard in 1951; they were later published as *The Court and the Constitution.* Roberts died May 17, 1955, at age eighty, at his farm near Chester Springs, Pennsylvania.

Benjamin N. Cardozo

1932-1938

Source: Photo by Harris & Ewing, Collection of the Supreme Court of the United States

Benjamin Nathan Cardozo and his twin sister, Emily, were born to Albert and Rebecca Nathan Cardozo May 24, 1870, in New York City. The future justice's ancestors were Sephardic Jews of Spain and Portugal who had emigrated to the New World in the mid-eighteenth century. Several members of his family achieved prominence in New York affairs. His first cousin, Michael Hart Cardozo, was nominated to the New York Supreme Court, but died before the election. Another cousin, Emma Lazarus, wrote the verse at the base of the Statue of Liberty. Benjamin's father was elected to the New York Supreme Court, but resigned when charges were lodged against him concerning his involvement in Boss Tweed's corrupt Tammany Hall political machine. Albert Cardozo was accused of using his power to appoint receivers in bankruptcy cases to help his political friends, but he resigned his seat voluntarily before any decision on guilt was reached. Benjamin was only two years old when his father stepped down and returned to private practice.

Seven years later, in 1879, Benjamin's mother died, and his older sister Ellen assumed many of the household responsibilities, including caring for her brothers and sisters. In addition to Benjamin and Emily, these included a brother, Albert, Jr., and two other sisters, Grace and Elizabeth, who was an invalid from childhood. Benjamin and Ellen outlived their siblings and enjoyed a very close relationship throughout their lives. They shared the family home in New York City, neither ever marrying, and Ellen served as Cardozo's chief confidant until her death in 1929.

Young Benjamin was tutored at home by Horatio Alger, a well-known author of children's rags-to-riches stories that emphasized the importance of honesty and industry. He was one of Cardozo's few extrafamilial contacts during his youth. Alger was a popular writer rather than a scholar, but he loved fine literature and imparted that love to his pupil. In later years Cardozo demonstrated an exceptional mastery of language in his opinions and other writings. His literary skills were further complemented by his ability to read classical Greek and a number of other foreign languages from which he would draw allusions.

At the age of fifteen Cardozo entered Columbia College, where he quickly rose to the top of his class and, despite his youth, won the respect of his classmates. He graduated with top honors in 1889 and immediately entered Columbia Law School. During his first year at law school he also studied for a master's degree, which he received in 1891. Cardozo, like many of his classmates, thought that a two-year program had been sufficient for their predecessors, and he decided to skip the

Popular children's author Horatio Alger, right, spun stories about poor boys who attained wealth and power through discipline and industry. With the exception of Benjamin Cardozo's twin, Emily, all the Cardozo children were tutored at home by Alger, who instilled in his pupils a love for great literature. *Source: Library of Congress*

third year of study and prepare for the bar examination without an LL.B. degree. Columbia later "atoned" for not having conferred a law degree on one of its most renowned students by presenting Cardozo with an honorary degree, but not before he had been so honored by nearly every prominent law school in the country.

Cardozo passed the bar in June 1891 and joined the law firm of Donohue, Newcombe, and Cardozo, in which his brother was a partner. He and Albert practiced together for some time under various firm names, and Benjamin Cardozo gained considerable respect among the judges of New York's appellate courts. He was noted for his astonishing memory, which enabled him to cite both volume and page number of relevant precedents years after he had come across them. When Charles Evans Hughes, Jr., was solicitor general, he called Cardozo "a walking encyclopedia of the law."

Cardozo's judicial career began in 1913 with his election to the New York Supreme Court, the state's trial bench. After only one month, Gov. Martin A. Glynn designated Cardozo as one of the supreme court justices assigned to help the New York Court of Appeals clear up its calendar. He was elected to a full term as associate judge on the court of appeals in 1917 and in 1926 became the chief judge. During the six years he presided over the court, it developed a reputation as the leading state court in the nation. Cardozo became renowned for his expertise in common law and for his elegant and persuasive writing.

During this time Cardozo also began to receive wide acclaim as a legal philosopher. In 1920 Yale Law School invited him to deliver the distinguished Storr Lectures, which were published in a highly acclaimed volume entitled *The Nature of the Judicial Process*. Cardozo's description of how judges come to judgment is considered a model of progressive jurisprudence:

What is it that I do when I decide a case? To what sources of information do I appeal for guidance? To what proportion do I permit them to contribute to the result? To

Benjamin Cardozo developed such an outstanding reputation on the New York Court of Appeals that he was widely recognized as the leading state common law judge. He also pioneered new thinking in the area of tort law, making it easier to seek court damages for a harmful wrong. *Source: Photo by Harris & Ewing, Collection of the Supreme Court of the United States*

what proportions ought they to contribute? If a precedent is applicable, when do I refuse to follow it? If no precedent is applicable, how do I reach the rule that will make a precedent for the future? If I am seeking logical consistency, the symmetry of the legal structure, how far shall I seek it? At what point shall the quest be halted by some discrepant custom, by some consideration of the social welfare, by my own or the common standards of justice and morals?

Expanding on his views on the relationship between law and society, Cardozo published two additional lectures, *The Growth of the Law* (1924) and *The Paradoxes*

Cardozo wrote to Oliver Wendell Holmes, Jr., on February 17, 1932, "I know, of course, that I can never fill your place, but it fills me with pride and joy to be told that you are satisfied to have me sit there." Cardozo had been recognized with unprecedented unanimity as the obvious choice to succeed the scholarly liberal. *Source: Harvard Law Art Collection*

of Legal Science (1928), that won him international acclaim.

When vacancies occurred on the U.S. Supreme Court during the 1920s, Cardozo's name was mentioned repeatedly. But Chief Justice William Howard Taft, who wielded considerable influence over Court appointments at the time, consistently vetoed Cardozo's nomination. Taft worried that Cardozo would join with liberal justices Louis Brandeis and Oliver Wendell Holmes, Jr., further dividing the Court and undermining its authority in the public eye. More important, Cardozo was a Democrat, and several successive Republican presidents were reluctant to cross party lines in making nominations to the high court. There was also the traditional concern over regional and religious representation. The state of New York came to be twice represented in 1930, when Justice Harlan F. Stone was joined by the new chief justice, Charles Evans Hughes. The question also arose whether another Jew should join Justice Brandeis on the high court.

When Justice Holmes announced his retirement in 1932, many felt he should be replaced by a liberal intellectual of equal stature. Robert F. Wagner, a Democratic senator from New York, sent Cardozo's name to President Herbert Hoover, and Cardozo's close friends organized a grass-roots campaign to urge his nomination. In an unprecedented show of support, endorsements poured in from judges, law school faculties, bar associations, newspapers, and political leaders across the country. Reluctant to leave New York, Cardozo tried to dissuade friends from campaigning on his behalf for such a demanding office. Despite the silver-haired bachelor's striking appearance, his health was extremely frail. By 1930 Cardozo had suffered the first of a series of heart attacks and had already outlived his five siblings, which no doubt made him keenly aware of his own mortality.

Justice Stone offered to resign his "New York" seat to make a place for Cardozo on the bench, but was turned down. Pressure from within his own party, notably by Attorney General William Mitchell, helped persuade President Hoover, a conservative Republican, to nominate Cardozo. Driven by patriotic duty and respect for the high honor, Cardozo accepted the nomination and was confirmed by the Senate on February 24, 1932, without debate.

The transition to Washington life proved difficult for Cardozo. A gentle, sensitive man, he had cherished his close friendships with his New York colleagues. The deep philosophical divisions that affected the Supreme Court during his tenure, as well as the tradition of independence between chambers at the Court, contributed to his sense of isolation. Although he was on cordial terms with his fellow liberal justices, Stone and Brandeis, and was good friends with Chief Justice Hughes, Cardozo missed the camaraderie of his brethren in Albany. He was also the target of the open anti-Semitism of conservative justice James McReynolds, who had conspicuously ignored the proceedings at Cardozo's swearing in by reading a newspaper on the bench. Cardozo rarely had a harsh word for anyone and was effusive with compliments and praise, particularly to his clerks. His graciousness was exceeded only by his extraordinary tact and diplomacy. Despite these attributes, he avoided much of Washington's social scene and looked forward to vacations in New York.

Although he served less than six years, Cardozo wrote more than 100 opinions for the Court. In *Steward Machine Company v. Davis* and *Helvering v. Davis* (both 1937), he upheld the constitutionality of provisions of the Social Security Act of 1935, which established unemployment compensation and old age benefits. He interpreted the taxing and spending clauses in the Constitution, which allow for Congress to "lay and collect" taxes to provide for the "General Welfare," as justification for the Social Security provisions. Also in 1937 Cardozo wrote the decision in *Palko v. Connecticut,* outlining criteria for determining which provisions of the Bill of Rights should be incorporated into the Fourteenth Amendment and applied to the states. Specifically, he held that the Fifth Amendment's provision against double jeopardy should not be incorporated into the Fourteenth Amendment's due process guarantees on the state level, because only those rights that "represented the very essence of ordered liberty" should be so applied. The *Palko* case was part of an important new doctrine interpreting the boundaries of state and federal power as concurrent and overlapping.

Joining the Court in an era dominated by a conservative majority, Cardozo mostly voted with the liberal minority and was therefore rarely assigned to write opinions in landmark cases. His dissents, however, like those of his predecessor, Holmes, whom he deeply admired, have become an important legacy of eloquent, well-reasoned judicial philosophy. His keen insight and literary craftsmanship assured his opinions' enduring historical prominence. In explaining his approach to writing opinions, Cardozo once remarked: "Form alone takes, and holds and preserves substance, saves it from the welter of helpless verbiage that we swim in as in a sea of tasteless tepid pudding." Hughes said his writings constituted "a mighty arsenal of forensic weapons."

Cardozo saw "justice, morals, and social welfare" as important forces in shaping constitutional law. His vigorous support of liberal views on social and economic issues anticipated the Court's movement during President Franklin D. Roosevelt's New Deal era toward a more progressive judicial philosophy. Sadly, he lived to see only the beginning of this transition. Cardozo was bedridden throughout the summer of 1935, barely recovering sufficiently to return to the bench that fall. At the end of the 1936 term, he asked his law clerk to return for a second year because he lacked the stamina to break in a new clerk. In January 1938 Cardozo suffered a paralyzing stroke; he died six months later, on July 9. Judge Learned Hand, a renowned member of the Second Circuit Court of Appeals, later said of his friend:

He was wise because his spirit was uncontaminated, because he knew no violence, or hatred, or envy, or jealousy, or ill will. I believe that it was this purity that chiefly made him the judge we so much revere; more than his learning, his acuteness, and his fabulous industry. In this America of ours where the passion for publicity is a disease . . . it was a rare good fortune that brought to such eminence a man so reserved, so unassuming, so retiring, so gracious to high and low, and so serene."

Hugo L. Black
1937-1971

Source: Collection of the Supreme Court of the United States

HUGO LAFAYETTE BLACK was born February 27, 1886, in the hill country of Clay County, Alabama, the baby in a family of eight children. His parents were William Lafayette Black, who came from a merchant family, and Martha Ardella Toland Black, who came from a landholding family. Rough and primitive living conditions prevailed in rural Alabama, even for people like the Blacks and Tolands.

Black's boyhood was much like that of all boys in country villages. His home life was happy except for his father's occasional drinking sprees. Black early developed an ear for music; he played all the country music instruments—fiddle, organ, piano, guitar, and harmonica—all with the same rollicking country rhythm. But, unlike the typical country boy, he read everything he could get his hands on, from Fred Fearnot detective stories to Charles Dickens. He devoured the Bible, not because he was especially devout, but because he enjoyed the common sense and wisdom.

As a boy, he hung out at the courthouse on the town square. He would go down to listen to the candidates for political offices and declared himself a Democrat almost before he could pronounce the word. When the circuit court came to Ashland, the county seat of Clay County, young Black attended frequently, observing the character traits of the lawyers and judges and noting (sometimes critically) the trial strategies. While the circuit court worked elsewhere, he kept an eye on the semiprofessional checkers and domino competitions among the old men at the courthouse, prevailing on them to teach him their skills and, finally, to admit him to their competitions.

Black was schooled at Ashland College, a statewide institution supported by private and public funds, which taught every level from primary to college. He excelled in both mathematical and language subjects and was proceeding through with distinction until an incident occurred that ended his secondary education: he broke the switches his professor lashed at him for intervening in a disciplinary episode involving the professor and Black's sister.

Instead of finishing high school, Black, at age seventeen, enrolled in the Birmingham Medical School for the 1903 school year, hoping to follow in the footsteps of his brother Orlando, a medical doctor, whom he admired. Black completed two full years of medical schooling in one year. Despite this achievement, the courtroom scenes and political speeches he had witnessed as a boy beckoned him. Black entered the University of Alabama Law School in 1904. He excelled in his courses and graduated with honors.

At age twenty Black opened up a law office across the street from the courthouse in Ashland. After one year of country law practice, his law office, full of books and practice tools, burned down. Always ambitious, Black determined to open up anew in a place with more opportunity. He considered moving to some far western and thinly populated state such as Wyoming or Montana where one could move into high political position while still young, but instead decided to open a practice in Alabama's big city—Birmingham. He sought maximum exposure, joining and usually becoming president of every lodge and civic club that would accept him. He became the teacher of the Adult Sunday School men's class at the First Baptist Church, and before long more than 1,000 people were coming each Sunday to hear him apply the wisdom and common sense of the Bible to everyday problems. Whenever he met new people, he would note down their names, addresses, family connections, and the circumstances of his meeting with them. He would review these notes just before going into any geographical area for a speech or a meeting to be sure he would not forget anyone.

Black oriented his practice toward working people and the unions that sought to get them a better deal. He counted the United Mine Workers and the Fraternal Order of Police among his clients. He quickly established a place as the top personal injury lawyer in the state, coaxing high verdicts from juries by a combination of charm, fiery presentations, detailed knowledge of the facts, including the medical facts, and his growing contacts. He also served as a part-time police court judge in 1910 and 1911.

In 1914 he made his first political move by persuading the voters of Jefferson County to elect him county solicitor (public prosecutor). When he left the solicitor's post in 1917 to join the World War I effort, Black had succeeded in emptying a docket that had once held as many as 3,000 pending cases. He served during the war as a captain in the field artillery of the army, but never left the United States.

In 1921, two years after his return to civilian life in Birmingham, Black married Josephine Foster, a beautiful and popular woman who was a descendant of a prominent southern Alabama family and of one of Ten-

Hugo Black married Josephine Foster in 1921. Six years after her death in 1951, Black wed Elizabeth Seay DeMerritte. *Source: Photo by Harris & Ewing, Collection of the Supreme Court of the United States*

nessee's most renowned political families. The Blacks had three children—Hugo, Jr., Sterling, and Josephine. Black's law practice flourished, partially because of his trial skills and partially because of the contacts he had cultivated. In 1923 Black joined one organization too many: the Ku Klux Klan. Although he resigned two years later, his brief affiliation would haunt him the rest of his life.

By 1925 Black's practice had brought him wealth enough to last a lifetime, and he was ready for new challenges. He announced his candidacy for the U.S. Senate against a strong field of candidates, including the son of a former senator, a former governor, and the wealthiest coal mine magnate in Alabama. Black's campaign revolved around the theme of economic justice for the poor, the weak, and the helpless. He brought off his upset victory by his unique ability to attract crowds wherever he spoke, an effective grass-roots organization, the good feelings generated by the music that he brought out of fiddles, pianos, and harmonicas, and the respect he generated by showing strongly against the best checkers and domino players in each community.

When he entered the Senate in 1927, he found for the first time in his career, away from his constituents in Alabama, that he had time on his hands. With his senatorial privileges, he commandeered a study room in the basement of the Capitol building and, with educational programs and books ordered from the Library of Congress, acquired the liberal arts education he had missed.

Meanwhile, he served the Democratic party and its leadership in the Senate loyally and tirelessly. He risked almost certain defeat in 1928 when he supported the Democratic presidential candidate, Al Smith, who was a Catholic, against the Republican candidate, Herbert Hoover. In doing so Black resisted the pressure of Alabama's senior senator, Tom Heflin, and his anti-Catholic friends, who had talked him into joining the Ku Klux Klan. After the campaign, Black spearheaded a successful movement to get Heflin and the disloyal Democrats out of the party, which resulted in Heflin's defeat by John Bankhead, Black's principal opponent in the 1926 election.

Although the voters of Alabama reelected Black in the tragic depression year of 1932, he suffered as most Americans when he lost the fortune he had accumulated as a trial lawyer. From then on, he lived only on his salary and expenses as a public servant and prided himself on his ability to live within his limited means.

In his second term, Black zealously championed legislation and senatorial investigations aimed at a more equal division of wealth between the rich and powerful and the poor and powerless. In his job as Democratic whip of the Senate, he pushed through most of President Franklin D. Roosevelt's New Deal legislation, rounding up the Democratic senators for crucial votes. He sponsored the minimum wage and maximum hours laws in effect today. Through congressional investigation, he exposed misappropriation of government subsidies by shipping and airline companies and corrupt lobbying practices by notables such as press baron William Randolph Hearst.

Black resented the striking down of much of the New Deal legislation by the conservative Supreme Court. He felt that the Court had intruded on Congress's functions by using invented constitutional doctrine to invalidate laws Congress had passed. He supported President Roosevelt's unsuccessful attempt in 1937 to reverse this process by packing the Court with additional justices.

On August 12, 1937, Roosevelt chose Black to fill the first Supreme Court vacancy that occurred during his presidency. The Senate confirmed him five days later with a vote of 63–16. Before Black took his seat, however, the Hearst newspapers discovered and exposed his former membership in the Ku Klux Klan. Not trusting the newspapers, Justice Black went on national radio and stated that he had joined and later resigned from the Klan. He denied ever harboring any prejudice against any race or religion. Nevertheless, a petition was filed in the Supreme Court requesting that the Court deny him his seat. The Court promptly denied the request. Chief Justice Charles Evans Hughes administered the oath of office to Black as pickets paraded outside the Supreme Court building.

Immediately on taking his seat, Black undertook to turn the Court around and move it in a direction more consistent with his vision of the spirit of the writers of the Constitution and its amendments. Toward this end, he began to write dissenting opinions crafted with flawless logic and solid research in language that an ordinary citizen could understand. He filed dissent after dissent, at first alone, then joined by others as old justices retired and were replaced by new, more liberal justices. In those dissents, he seeded the ground with principles that came to full flower during the Warren Court era. Among other things, his dissents opened the door to the termination of forced segregation of races, to the application of the Bill of Rights to the states, to the abolition of the use of forced confessions, to the provision of counsel at public expense for poor people charged with serious crimes, and to voting systems guaranteeing that one person's vote counts as much as another's.

He summed up the judicial philosophy that guided these dissents in *Chambers v. Florida* (1940) early in his Supreme Court career. "Under our Constitutional system, courts stand against any winds that blow as havens of refuge for those who might otherwise suffer because they are helpless, weak, outnumbered, or because they

Attorney General Homer Cummings discusses with Uncle Sam Hugo L. Black's affiliation with the Ku Klux Klan. Black had belonged to the Klan briefly in the 1920s when the white supremacist organization dominated politics in several southern states, including Alabama. The revelation, which came after his confirmation in 1937, caused a stir, but Black's nationwide radio address reassured most Americans that he was not prejudiced. *Source: Library of Congress*

are non-conforming victims of prejudice and public excitement."

But he reserved his strongest passion for the freedoms of speech and religion guaranteed by the First Amendment. He interpreted the text of the amendment— "Congress shall make no law . . . abridging the freedom of speech, or of the press; or the right of people peaceably to assemble"—literally, frequently proclaiming in opinions, on television, at lectures in law schools, and in meetings of judges that "no law *means* no law abridging these rights—*no law,*" tapping for emphasis a ten-cent pocket-sized copy of the Constitution that he pulled out of his right coat pocket. He particularly opposed the application of any "balancing test" to First Amendment freedoms, writing in his *In re Anastopolo* (1961) dissent, "This Court should not permit governmental action that plainly abridges constitutionally protected rights of the People merely because a majority believes that on 'balance' it is better, or 'wiser,' to abridge those rights than to leave them free."

Black was careful, however, not to push his *Chambers* philosophy beyond what could be solidly justified by the text of the Constitution or unstrained historical interpretation of the intent of its architects. Hence in later years he departed from his brethren who shared his *Chambers* philosophy when they supported the right to privacy, the protection of "symbolic speech," and other doctrines he could not find in the text of the Constitution. Depending on the commentator, these views of Black's have been described either as "the conservatism of old age" or as a mark of his solid judgment.

Not all of Black's considerable influence on the philosophy of the Supreme Court in the twentieth century, however, can be attributed to his energy, judgment, and collegial and rhetorical skills. He served on the Court for thirty-four years, under five chief justices, most of them as senior justice. Because of this seniority, he exercised the functions and powers of chief justice in intervals between the retirement or death of one chief justice and the ascension of the next. The right to assign cases to particular justices fell to Black during these intervals, and also when Black voted with the majority and the sitting chief justice was in the minority.

Although Black's opinion production was prolific, he always found time for his family. With Josephine, he established a compound in 1937 in the Old Town section of Alexandria, Virginia. They refurbished a house dating back to the colonial era, replanted the surrounding grounds, remodeled an old barn into an artist's studio for Josephine, and built a tennis court for Black that he would use until he became disabled by his last illness.

Black was devastated by Josephine's unexpected death in 1951. He found consolation in his clerks and his children, consciously trying to infuse in them a sustaining philosophy of life as well as his political and constitutional philosophy. He taught that health and success would most likely come to one who worked mind and body hard, practiced self-discipline, cultivated a sense of fun, and sought what he called the "golden mean." He married his secretary, Elizabeth Seay DeMerritte, in his seventy-second year. They had a fun-filled, joyous relationship the rest of his life. Like Josephine, Elizabeth pulled Black away from his desk and encouraged his sociable and fun side.

Justice Black retired from the Court after suffering an impairing stroke September 17, 1971. He died eight days later and was interred with ten-cent Constitutions in his pocket.

Stanley F. Reed

1938-1957

Source: Library of Congress

STANLEY FORMAN REED was born December 31, 1884, in the small town of Minerva in Mason County, Kentucky. His father, John R. Reed, was a practicing physician; his mother was Frances Forman Reed. Stanley's family lived comfortably, and his parents were active socially. A good student, he completed preparatory school and received a degree from Kentucky Wesleyan College before the age of eighteen. He then entered Yale University, where he won the Bennett American History Prize and received a second bachelor's degree in 1906.

After spending one year at the University of Virginia Law School, Stanley returned to Kentucky. He married Winifred Elgin of Maysville, the county seat of Mason County, on May 11, 1908. That fall he returned to law school at Columbia University, but he did not complete his degree. Rather, at the end of the academic year the Reeds sailed for France, where he studied civil and international law for a year at the Sorbonne.

They returned in 1910 to Maysville, then a town of 6,500 in a tobacco-rich area. Reed read law for a brief period in the office of a local lawyer before being admitted to the Kentucky bar. He then hung out his shingle and, while waiting for clients to seek his services, he became active in politics. Elected to serve as a representative to the Kentucky General Assembly from 1912 to 1916, he became president of the Kentucky Young Democrats and supported Woodrow Wilson in his 1916 presidential bid. When the United States entered World War I, Reed sought and received a commission as a lieutenant in an army intelligence unit and closed his practice during his tour of duty in 1918.

The following year Reed joined the firm of Worthington, Cochran, Browning, and Reed—later called Browning, Reed, and Ziegler. Among the firm's major clients were the Chesapeake and Ohio Railroad and the Burley Tobacco Growers Cooperative Association. During the next decade, Reed helped organize the tobacco cooperative and ultimately became its primary legal adviser. In 1929 a former president of the cooperative recommended that Reed be named general counsel to the Federal Farm Board, an organization created at the suggestion of President Herbert Hoover to deal with agricultural problems resulting from the Great Depression.

With their two sons, Stanley and John, the Reeds moved to Washington and settled into quarters at the Mayflower Hotel, where they continued to reside during their long stay in Washington. Winifred Reed became active in the National Society of Daughters of the American Revolution, serving as registrar general from 1932 to 1935. In December 1932, near the end of the Hoover administration, Reed was promoted to general counsel of the Reconstruction Finance Corporation (RFC), an organization designed to combat the severe economic depression by making loans to banks, businesses, and agricultural enterprises. Reed kept the position when Franklin D. Roosevelt assumed office in 1933.

Stanley and Winifred Reed stroll to the Supreme Court after the justice's appointment in 1938. *Source: Collection of the Supreme Court of the United States*

While Reed participated in many newsworthy activities at the RFC, the most critical to his career was the successful litigation of the *Gold Clause Cases*. To raise domestic commodity prices, the Roosevelt administration advocated reducing the gold content of the dollar. The government also maintained it had the right to annul clauses in contracts with private companies requiring payment in gold. When the litigation reached the Supreme Court, Reed was made special assistant to Attorney General Homer Cummings and helped him argue the government's case. They achieved a notable

As solicitor general, Stanley Reed argued the government's case in a number of landmark cases testing the constitutionality of progressive New Deal legislation. He lost in *Schechter Poultry Corp. v. United States* (1935), in which the Supreme Court ruled on the validity of the National Industrial Recovery Act. The Schechter brothers hoist their lawyer in celebration of the Court's decision that the Live Poultry Code of Fair Competition, which they had violated, was unconstitutional. *Source: Bettmann*

victory for New Deal monetary policy and established a lifelong friendship.

Upon Cummings's recommendation, President Roosevelt named Reed to be solicitor general on March 18, 1935. Reed had been offered a choice between becoming the government's chief advocate or a lower-level federal judge, and he chose to be solicitor general even though the annual salary was $2,500 lower. During his three years in the post, Reed battled the country's top lawyers before the Supreme Court to defend the constitutionality of the New Deal's experimental legislation. At the beginning of his term, the government suffered a series of major defeats: in *Schechter Poultry Corp. v. United States* (1935) the National Industrial Recovery Act was declared unconstitutional; in *Humphrey's Executor v. United States* (1935) the president's power to remove a member of the Federal Trade Commission was denied; and in *United States v. Butler* (1936) the Agricultural Adjustment Act was invalidated.

After the *Butler* decision, the Roosevelt administration proposed a controversial plan under which the president would be authorized to add one justice to the

Court for each member who reached the age of seventy but failed to retire, up to an overall total of fifteen. Reed's involvement in the so-called "Court-packing" plan was not publicized, and he was largely successful in avoiding the contentious political battle that led to its defeat. As the judicial tide turned during the final year of Reed's tenure as solicitor general, the administration won some important victories, including decisions upholding the National Labor Relations Board and the Tennessee Valley Authority Act. The shock of the Court reorganization plan and the retirement in early 1937 of Justice Willis Van Devanter, which gave Roosevelt his first chance to appoint a justice, were both factors in changing the Court's temperament.

In January 1938 Justice George Sutherland announced his retirement, and Roosevelt had his second opportunity. His first appointee, Hugo Black, had proven highly controversial, and the president sought to avoid another confirmation battle by appointing Reed who, although also a liberal Democrat, was generally respected for his legal acumen, experience, and judicious demeanor. On January 25, 1938, only ten days

Long lines of black voters in Cobb County, Georgia, casting ballots for the 1946 Democratic primary elections showed that when the government removed obstacles to voting, blacks turned up at the polls in large numbers. Two years earlier Stanley Reed had written the opinion in *Smith v. Allwright,* finding unconstitutional state primary elections open only to whites, a system that had effectively disenfranchised blacks in the one-party South. *Source: Bettmann*

after his nomination, fifty-three-year-old Reed was unanimously confirmed by the Senate.

During his nineteen years on the Court, Reed wrote 339 opinions, 231 for the majority, 20 concurring, and 88 dissenting. Writing opinions did not come easily to him, and he worked long hours, taking home a briefcase loaded with reading most evenings and weekends. A contemporary said Reed displayed "unusual degrees of friendliness, serenity and generosity." Chief Justice Warren E. Burger once remarked that "he exemplified the virtues of the true 18th century gentleman, the epitome of civility." However, "his large bald pate, massive jowls, pince-nez and stern composure" made him seem daunting to at least one commentator.

Reed's opinions continued to reflect his belief in big government, social welfare programs, and the government's right to regulate the economy. During the first full term of his tenure, he had the satisfaction of upholding in *United States v. Rock Royal Cooperative* (1939) the constitutionality of the Agricultural Marketing Act, essentially reversing the *Butler* decision that he had lost as solicitor general. He wrote the opinion in *United States v. Appalachian Electric Power Co.* (1940), which greatly expanded federal authority over the nation's inland waterways. He also voted with the majority in the landmark decision that overruled *Hammer v. Dagenhart,* a 1918 decision limiting the power of Congress to act under the Commerce Clause.

Reed was highly deferential toward the powers of the executive branch, and he supported judicial restraint.

This tendency showed itself dramatically in 1952 when he joined Chief Justice Fred Vinson in strenuously dissenting from the majority opinion holding President Harry S. Truman's seizure of the steel mills during the Korean War to be invalid. Reed was equally cautious about challenging the legislature's power.

The Kentucky justice extended his consistent support for the government's position into cases involving civil liberties. He sided with the government in its efforts to prosecute alleged communists for subversive activities. He upheld the Hatch Act against claims that, by prohibiting federal civil servants from political activities, the Act constituted an invasion of their rights of free speech. He also said he was "opposed to broadening the possibilities of defendants escaping punishment by these more rigorous technical requirements in the administration of justice."

Reed, however, did not side with those who supported segregation. He played a strong role in the Court's move toward constitutional protection of racial equality and civil rights. Despite his southern upbringing, Reed joined the majority in the line of decisions opening up graduate and law schools to black applicants. He also wrote the landmark decision in 1944 holding the southern institution of a "white primary" to choose electoral candidates invalid, the 1945 decision preventing a labor union from avoiding application of state antidiscrimination laws, and the 1946 decision declaring racial segregation on motor carriers in interstate commerce unconstitutional. His greatest impact came in the watershed case of *Brown v. Board of Education of Topeka* (1954), when, despite misgivings about the Court's role in desegregating public schools, he ultimately abandoned a dissent so the Court could issue its ground-breaking decision unanimously.

Justice Reed retired February 25, 1957, at age seventy-two. He was still in good health and continued to maintain an office in the Court building and be active in judicial affairs. He accepted President Dwight D. Eisenhower's offer to be chairman of the Civil Rights Commission, which was established by the Civil Rights Act of 1957. Although he had served from 1939 to 1941 as chairman of Roosevelt's Committee on Civil Service Improvement, Reed was unprepared for the political dimensions and magnitude of his responsibilities at the new commission. As a federal judge still subject to judicial assignments, he also questioned the propriety of his involvement in the commission and shortly submitted his resignation.

As permitted by statute, Reed accepted several hundred assignments to sit on panels of judges hearing cases in the Court of Claims and the Court of Appeals of the District of Columbia. To those panels he contributed not only his long judicial experience, but also his share of opinions, producing more than forty majority opinions for those courts before he resigned his duties in 1970. He also accepted appointment in 1958 by the Supreme Court as special master in a case between Virginia and Maryland involving fishing rights.

After moving to a nursing home in New York, Reed died April 2, 1980, at age ninety-five. He was buried in Maysville, where for most of his life he had maintained a 300-acre tobacco and dairy farm that he visited nearly every summer.

Felix Frankfurter
1939-1962

Source: Photo by Harris & Ewing, Collection of the Supreme Court of the United States

FELIX FRANKFURTER was born November 15, 1882, in Vienna, Austria. At the age of twelve he immigrated with his parents to the United States and settled on the Lower East Side of New York. He would become the sixth, and to date the last, foreign-born Supreme Court justice. He would also become the third justice of Jewish extraction to join the Court, although he did not practice his religion.

As a youth, Frankfurter began a lifelong habit of reading many newspapers each day. In him the press had its most ardent supporter and most severe critic; he believed that freedom also meant responsibility. He quickly mastered English and attended the College of the City of New York, graduating in 1902. He took a year to earn some money in the city's Tenement Department and, after a false start toward other law schools, was persuaded to enter Harvard to satisfy his doctor's recommendation for the country life.

He was first in his class in all three of his years at Harvard Law School. When he graduated in 1906, he helped edit a volume of Prof. John Chipman Gray's *Property Cases* and accepted a position at a lavish $1,000 annual salary with a firm in New York—one of the first Jews to be hired by a top rank New York law firm. But he soon became Henry L. Stimson's assistant in the U.S. Attorney's Office in New York at $750 a year, as part of a reform movement for federal law enforcement under President Theodore Roosevelt.

In 1909 Stimson ran for governor of New York, with Frankfurter as his primary campaign aide. More interested in resolving the issues than in popularizing them, they lost. When Stimson became secretary of war in William Howard Taft's cabinet in 1911, Frankfurter went with him as general factotum carrying the title of law officer in the Bureau of Insular Affairs of the War Department.

In Washington he was at the center of a circle of energetic, industrious, and ambitious young men, who would later rise as statesmen. But Washington meant Frankfurter's introduction not only to the machinery of national government but also to the role of Supreme Court advocate, in which he apparently excelled. The world was his oyster, and he had found the pearl. He used Professor Gray's introduction to begin a friendship with Justice Oliver Wendell Holmes, Jr. He also got to know Louis Brandeis, who was probably the only one of his great friends, including Holmes, Roosevelt, and Stimson, who recommended that he accept an offer of a professorship from Harvard Law School. Holmes told him, "Academic life is but half life—it is withdrawal from the fight in order to utter smart things that cost you nothing except the thinking them from a cloister." Despite the warning, Frankfurter began his teaching career in 1914.

At Harvard, Frankfurter would prove Holmes wrong by uniting the law school world with the public battles for justice that made his name cursed in Boston society. He picked up the National Consumers League minimum wage and maximum working hours cases from

Brandeis, who had been preparing to argue them in the Supreme Court before he was appointed to that bench in 1916. Frankfurter also became active in the Zionist movement at this time and helped found the *New Republic* magazine with Herbert Croly and Walter Lippmann.

Frankfurter had been commissioned a major in the reserves of the Judge Advocate General's Office in 1914. When the United States entered World War I, he returned to Washington to work for Newton D. Baker, former head of the National Consumers League, who now, as secretary of war, was in charge of labor relations. Frankfurter was appointed secretary and counsel to the President's Mediation Commission on labor problems. As such he investigated the case of Tom Mooney, who allegedly planted a bomb at San Francisco's Preparedness Day Parade, and the Bisbee, Arizona, case in which 1,100 striking miners were forced out of their labor camps and deported to a deserted town in New Mexico. In both cases Frankfurter found that violations of individual rights had occurred. In 1918 Frankfurter was named chairman of the War Labor Policies Board, the aim of which was to mediate the interests of industry and labor. In that position he first met Franklin D. Roosevelt who, as assistant secretary of the navy, also served on the board.

When the war ended, Frankfurter went to the Paris Peace Conference, not as an American official but on behalf of the American Zionist movement. Upon his return to Harvard, he found time to court and win the beautiful Marion A. Denman, the love of his life. Their wedding was performed December 20, 1919, by Judge Benjamin Cardozo of the New York Court of Appeals, later Frankfurter's predecessor on the Supreme Court. Marion Frankfurter was an astonishingly bright woman, every bit her husband's intellectual equal, with more refined tastes in art and literature, and a will of iron. She was housebound and then bedridden during most of his tenure on the Supreme Court, and he sel-

Felix Frankfurter and his wife, Marion, at the time of his appointment to the Supreme Court in 1939 to replace Benjamin
Cardozo. As a friend and judge on the New York Court of Appeals, Cardozo had performed their wedding ceremony in 1919.
Source: Library of Congress

dom attended mixed social gatherings because she
could not.

In the early 1920s Frankfurter helped defend victims
of Attorney General A. Mitchell Palmer's raids on alleged communists during the "red scares." In the late
1920s came his almost surgical dissection of the record
in the controversial Sacco-Venzetti case, which showed
the lack of due process in their trial. His aid and comfort to the National Association for the Advancement
of Colored People and his founding membership in the
American Civil Liberties Union further confirmed his

"radical nature" in the minds of many Americans, including the Harvard "Establishment."

Frankfurter's "radicalism" was also to be found in the
classroom. He had his students dissect cases, examine
the circumstances that produced them, and understand
the sociological and economic as well as the legal envi-
ronments in which they occurred. The number of cases
covered in the course of a term were few, but the material was superabundant. The best of Frankfurter's professional writings appeared in the *Harvard Law Review*
and in books made of his lectures; his casebooks in administrative law and in federal jurisdiction were pioneering efforts. His study with Roscoe Pound of
"Criminal Justice in Cleveland" was an early precursor
of much "legal sociology."

During this time, Frankfurter became one of the
most controversial public figures in the United States.
He had no hesitation in giving advice to government
officials, but, more important, they had no hesitation
in asking for it. With an army of friends and former
students to call on, he successfully suggested nominees
for important posts in the Roosevelt administration. In
1932 Frankfurter refused a nomination to the Supreme
Judicial Court of Massachusetts made by Gov. Richard
Ely. He also told Roosevelt, who was forming his cabinet in 1932, that he did not want to become solicitor
general, even if that was, as the president suggested, a
necessary condition to a Supreme Court nomination. It
was not that he had a distaste for power, but rather that
he had a clearer conception of the realities of government than most. In the long run a "mere" professor
might be better able to influence government through
private advice and public declamations than a high official.

In any event, he was scheduled to teach at Oxford
University for the 1933–1934 school year and was a sufficiently devoted Anglophile not to let that chance go by.
At Oxford he met physicist Niels Bohr, and as a result
of their meeting Frankfurter became one of the few

nonscientists to learn about the discovery of the atomic bomb. When this story became known, it just added to the myth that Frankfurter knew even the most intimate secrets of the U.S. government.

Frankfurter devoted his life to mastering the two areas that contribute most to the abilities of a justice: lawyering and statecraft. While mastery of the law and philosophy might be adequate to a justice's ability to perform his tasks well, the broader-gauged the jurist in terms of statesmanship as well as law, the greater the comprehension of what is truly at stake in the great issues brought before the Court. This is not to suggest that Frankfurter's mind was limited by law and politics; all social sciences and humanities came within his range.

There was perhaps no man in America better versed in the lore of the institution than Frankfurter when Roosevelt appointed him to the Supreme Court on January 5, 1939. His familiarity with its history and judgments, with its personnel and their habits, with its problems and needs, was unmatched. His close association with Brandeis and Holmes gave him a window into the world of the nine justices, and his diligent study of the cases, the briefs and arguments, and the business of the Court made him a natural choice to succeed Justice Cardozo. Roosevelt hoped Frankfurter would join his first two Court appointees, Hugo Black and Stanley Reed, in setting the Court back on a proper course after years of opinions striking down his New Deal legislation. Frankfurter was unanimously confirmed by the Senate on January 17.

Because of his expertise, Frankfurter may have been

Felix Frankfurter believed, as did a great many Americans, that Nicola Sacco and Bartolomeo Vanzetti, center, had not received a fair trial because they were Italian-born immigrants and anarchists. Frankfurter's public relations efforts were unsuccessful at winning them a new trial, and they were executed in 1927 despite scant evidence of their involvement in the crime of which they were accused—a holdup and shootings at a Massachusetts shoe factory.
Source: Library of Congress

the Court's best problem-solver had he been able to act alone, but he had to exercise his authority in committee. And he was better at addressing issues than at convincing his colleagues how to do so. Except for his rejection of absolutes, his faith in reason, and his requiring a full comprehension of the facts in a case, it is hard to assign Frankfurter a judicial doctrine. Those who would sum up his judicial efforts in a phrase label him a devotee of "judicial restraint."

His belief in that doctrine is reflected in a speech he made at Harvard in which he opposed the idea that certain provisions in the Constitution were intended to adjust to "the social arrangements and beliefs of a particular epoch." Although "like all legal provisions without a fixed technical meaning, [the provisions] are ambulant, adaptable to the changes of time," he did not believe that their "vagueness" gave the Court authority to overturn acts by the legislative and executive branches. "Holding democracy in judicial tutelage is not the most promising way to foster disciplined responsibility in a people," he argued. When it was not a government's legislative actions that were called in question, however, Frankfurter frequently recognized the obligation of the Court to impose restraints on acts by the executive, especially police actions that violated the Bill of Rights, including the Due Process Clause.

As early as 1912 he had told Morris Cohen, the famed philosopher, who had been his roommate at Harvard, "Precedents, not underlying philosophic principles, form our legal habit of thought. It is the case system, which is the empiric, scientific method, that gave us the necessary data and method, first, for a historic, and then for a sociological basis of law." He later expressed the difficulty a judge faces in ruling on "grave and complex problems . . . that excite the public interest" when they "present legal issues inextricably and deeply bound up in emotional reactions to sharply conflicting economic, social, and political views." He contended that "it is not the duty of judges to express their personal at-

titudes on such issues, deep as their individual convictions may be. The opposite is the truth; it is their duty not to act merely on personal views."

None of his opinions demonstrates the incisiveness, or what he called the "aperçus," of Holmes's writings. The opinions tended to be overwritten, and none stands out as particularly momentous or dramatic, unless it is his dissent in *Board of Education v. Barnette* (1943), in which he would have sustained a law compelling a religious minority to salute the flag even against their beliefs, or his separate opinion in *Cooper v. Aaron* (1958), in which he stated the reasons why government must be bound by the rule of law. His opinions tended to be professorial, although not pedantic, solidly built arguments for his conclusions, which generally adhered to precedents or gave extensive reasons for departing from it. He belonged to no jurisprudential coterie of the Court. At times he was to be found in the judicial company of Robert Jackson and then John M. Harlan, but, to use Holmes's phrase, he often "flocked alone."

Frankfurter was not a modest man. He took to heart the advice his mother gave him early on: "Hold yourself dear." It does not demean him to say that he was almost as talented as he believed himself to be. Frankfurter's principal occupation in life was communicating with others, with presidents and workers, with professors and pupils, but mostly with friends. His friendships were legion, not only in law, academia, and government, but also in theater, music, literature, and publishing.

A heart attack brought on by a cerebral stroke forced him to retire August 28, 1962. Even near the end, he continued to write letters in his almost illegible handwriting, which became more and more difficult to comprehend. He remained a follower of Holmes's dictum: "to live is to function"—to function is to live. Frankfurter died in Washington, D.C., on February 22, 1965.

William O. Douglas

1939-1975

Source: Library of Congress

BORN IN MAINE, Minnesota, October 16, 1898, William Orville Douglas was the second of three children of Rev. William Douglas and Julia Bickford Fisk Douglas. In 1904 Douglas's father, a Presbyterian minister who had recently moved his wife and children to a new pastorate in Washington State, died, leaving them impoverished. William had contracted a near fatal case of infantile paralysis at the age of three, and he had a difficult childhood in Yakima,

Washington. However, through the loving care and intellectual encouragement of his strong-willed mother and his determined efforts to strengthen his weakened legs through hiking, he overcame his handicap and graduated from Yakima High School in 1916 as valedictorian. The love of the outdoors that he developed in his early years played a vital role in shaping his adult personality.

With the help of a tuition scholarship, Douglas entered Whitman College in Walla Walla, Washington. He lived in a tent for a while and financed his studies with a variety of odd jobs. He spent summers as a migrant worker and was exposed to radical union doctrines, but he remained unconverted by them. After graduating Phi Beta Kappa from Whitman in 1920, he accepted a position teaching English and Latin at Yakima High School, hoping to put aside money for law school.

Unable to save enough from his meager teaching salary, Douglas left Washington in 1922 for New York with plans to work his way through Columbia Law School. At Columbia, Douglas tutored, wrote correspondence courses, and worked as a research assistant for Prof. Underhill Moore. He encouraged Douglas to examine the relationships between law and business by introducing him to the ideas of Louis Brandeis. The emphasis Brandeis placed on the public responsibility of business gave Douglas a broadened perspective about the uses of law beyond the narrow focus of his specializations in corporate bankruptcy, reorganization, and receivership.

In 1925 Douglas graduated second in his class at Columbia and accepted a position with Cravath and partners, a prestigious Wall Street law firm. There he gained two years of practical experience and an intense dislike for corporate practice. After a frustrating attempt to establish a private practice in Yakima, Douglas returned to New York in 1927 and accepted a full-time teaching position at Columbia Law School. The following year the ambitious young professor was hired by Yale Law School. The five years Douglas spent at Yale were, in many respects, the happiest of his life, surrounded as he was with good intellectual company, his growing family, and the comforts provided by a decent salary.

By the late 1920s, the sandy-haired professor had established a considerable reputation. His research and his popular course at Yale on financial law, in which he used actual cases rather than theory, earned him

renown. The stock market crash and ensuing Great Depression created a tremendous interest in his areas of expertise. From 1929 to 1932 Douglas collaborated in the Business Failures Project sponsored by the U.S. Commerce Department. Yale recognized his growing reputation by appointing him to its prestigious Sterling Chair of Commercial and Corporate Law in 1932. With the advent of the New Deal, he came to the attention of Joseph P. Kennedy, the acting head of the newly created Securities and Exchange Commission (SEC), who was recruiting staff to write regulations for the nation's stricken banks, financial markets, and securities industries. From 1934 to 1936, Douglas directed the SEC's Protective Study Committee, probing the reasons why the rights of small investors, in contrast to those of corporate officers and bankers, were so poorly protected in reorganization actions.

Douglas found himself at home among the New Deal's elite. His wit and conversational skills served him well, making him a welcome guest at President Franklin D. Roosevelt's poker parties. In 1936 he was appointed a commissioner of the SEC, and the following year, at age thirty-eight, he was named its chairman. During his two-year tenure he pushed aggressively to bring more public responsibility into the securities industry with calls for self-regulation reinforced by SEC regulations. While Douglas was contemplating resigning from the SEC and entering private practice to better support his family, the president appointed him to the Supreme Court on March 20, 1939. Confirmed two weeks later by a 62–4 vote, Douglas assumed the seat recently vacated by his hero, Louis Brandeis, and began what, at thirty-six years and seven months, proved to be the longest tenure of any justice.

Douglas's early decisions, written during World War II, gave few hints that he was to evolve from a pro-New Deal realist, who applied a balancing approach to cases dealing with civil liberties, to a result-oriented activist. Most of them dealt with the business-govern-

Julius and Ethel Rosenberg, photographed in a patrol car after their conviction for atomic espionage in 1951. William O. Douglas was unable to persuade his brethren to stay their death sentence on procedural grounds, and they were executed. This attempt, and Douglas's dissent in the Supreme Court's conviction of leaders of the American Communist party in 1952, drew criticism during the cold war. *Source: Bettmann*

ment relationship and, like his opinion in *United States v. Socony-Vacuum Oil Co.* (1940), they upheld the regulatory powers of the federal government. A strong supporter of the World War II effort, Douglas concurred in the Court's approval of sweeping federal wartime powers, including the internment of Japanese-American citizens, although he expressed private reservations at the time. Subsequently, he held in *Ex parte Endo* (1944) that the government had no right to hold or even set parole for those of undoubted loyalty. Douglas wrote his initial First Amendment opinion in *Teamsters Local 802 v. Wohl* (1942). In it he applied a balancing approach, holding that because picketing was something more than mere speech it could be regulated to ensure its peaceful application.

The death of President Roosevelt, the end of World War II, and the crystallization of his own philosophy combined to remove any obligation Douglas had to restrain his civil libertarian beliefs. To an even greater degree than Justice Brandeis, he found it impossible to develop a judicial personality separate from his role as an involved citizen. His opinions relied increasingly on his observations about the state of the country and less upon legal principles from past decisions.

During Fred Vinson's tenure as chief justice from 1946 to 1953, Douglas joined fellow justice Hugo L. Black in advocating that First Amendment freedoms deserved a preferred position in relation to other freedoms guaranteed by the Bill of Rights. As a result, he dissented sharply on the grounds of freedom of expression and association when the Court upheld the conviction of leaders of the American Communist party in *Dennis v. United States* (1951). This stance, and an abortive attempt in 1953 to stay, on procedural grounds, the execution of convicted spies Julius and Ethel Rosenberg, made him the target of much conservative criticism during the cold war.

Douglas found a relatively comfortable niche for himself as a member of the activist majority of the liberal Court led by Earl Warren. He ardently supported the sweeping decisions dealing with school desegregation, reapportionment, criminal justice procedure, and religion in the schools that the Warren Court used as instruments of reform. During those years Douglas completed his journey to absolutism, the belief that many of the rights guaranteed in the Bill of Rights, such as freedom of expression, are simply beyond the power of government to regulate. His opinion in *Griswold v. Connecticut* (1965), in which the Court struck down a law forbidding the sale of birth control devices to married people, was a high-water mark in the evolution of what he hoped, in pursuit of Brandeis's earlier thoughts, would become a distinct doctrine of privacy anchored in the "penumbra" of several of the amendments in the Bill of Rights.

His closing years on the Court saw him often dissent vigorously, as in *Johnson v. Louisiana* (1972), in which he condemned the idea that a state could permit convictions in criminal cases with a non-unanimous jury. Such departures, he felt, were encroachments on important procedural protections of the Bill of Rights by an increasingly conservative Court.

The postwar years also witnessed an explosion of literary activity on Douglas's part. In addition to two au-

Estelle Griswold, left, opened a birth control clinic in New Haven in violation of an 1879 Connecticut law prohibiting the use of contraceptives. William O. Douglas wrote the 1965 Supreme Court decision striking down the law and establishing a constitutional right to privacy. *Source: UPI/Bettmann*

tobiographical volumes and some 800 Court opinions written between 1946 and his retirement in 1975, Douglas produced speeches, articles, and books on civil liberties, wilderness preservation and conservation, and foreign policy. All were aimed at challenging his readers to action. His writings on civil liberties paralleled his movement toward judicial activism on the Court. In five books and numerous articles, Douglas used his considerable descriptive powers and personal anecdotes to praise nature's beauty and warn of the dangers of its desecration. In his 1965 work, *A Wilderness Bill of Rights,* he advocated the creation of a right to sue on behalf of nature preservation and statutory protection for wilderness areas, positions that delighted conservationists and drew sharp criticism from developers. In his eleven books on foreign policy he issued warnings far in advance of many American experts about revolutions in developing countries generated by nationalism, poverty, and exploitation. Rejecting the American containment position, he called for a foreign policy based on peaceful economic competition with the Soviet Union and a "bit by bit" construction of world law.

Douglas's increasingly outspoken beliefs both on and off the Court drew criticism. Some charged that he lacked a proper judicial attitude because he shunned dignified silence in favor of judicial activism and outspoken stances on public questions. Others, including fellow justices, charged that his strong beliefs and public advocacy prejudiced him toward cases that came before the Court. None of this criticism seemed to have had any appreciable effect on Douglas. When, for example, many conservatives called for his impeachment in 1951 after he had urged the admission of mainland China to the United Nations, he simply ignored them. He could not, however, disregard a 1970 investigation—fueled by conservatives critical of the Court's liberal bent and of the Senate's rejection of two Republican Supreme Court nominees—of his ties to the Parvin Foundation, which received money from gambling interests. A special House Judiciary Subcommittee found no grounds for impeachment.

Four marriages, the last two to women one-third his age, added to his controversial reputation. These troubled relationships may have stemmed from Douglas's tendency to measure women against his mother, who had been both supportive and overly protective, and find them wanting. Documents reveal that his alimony and support payments put him under considerable financial pressure. In 1923 he married Mildred Riddle, an English teacher he had met while teaching in Yakima. He appeared to be a distant, stern, and demanding father to his two children, who came to resent his decreasing attention as his career in Washington soared. Citing incompatibility, Douglas's first wife divorced him in 1953, and in 1954 he married Mercedes Hester Davison, an extroverted Washington socialite and divorcée who had been his traveling companion on a number of his world journeys. She divorced him in 1963, and a few months later he married Joan Martin, a twenty-four-year-old student he had met while lecturing at Allegheny College. She found it impossible to adapt to the limelight of Washington society, and they were divorced in 1966. That same year, he married Cathleen Ann Heffernan, a twenty-three-year-old college student who refused to be dominated; she became a lawyer and offered Douglas love and intellectually fulfilling companionship in his last years.

On December 31, 1974, Douglas suffered a stroke that left him partially paralyzed and somewhat mentally impaired. Intense pain forced him to retire from the Court on November 12, 1975. Although physically weakened, he managed to attend the 1977 dedication ceremonies for the Chesapeake and Ohio National Historic Trail Park that he had worked so long to establish, and he continued work on the second volume of his autobiography. Douglas died at the Walter Reed Army Medical Center January 19, 1980, at the age of eighty-one.

An ardent outdoorsman and conservationist, William O. Douglas spent most of his leisure time hiking in wilderness areas all over the world. He published several books on nature preservation and on his travels. *Source: Will Thompson, Yakima Valley Museum*

Although not the greatest legal technician or the greatest intellect to sit on the Supreme Court, Douglas could be matched by few in his passion for justice. Writing in 1973, the editor of the *Nation* characterized Douglas's contribution to the American constitutional tradition: "His great merit is that, as a vigorous judicial activist, he has specialized over the years in the defense of the Bill of Rights, whose provisions are under recurrent attack because they always conflict with the special interests of the moment." It is the utter consistency of this stance and his willingness to create precedents permitting what he described as "the adjustment of the Constitution to the needs of the time," that made his judicial career memorable.

Frank Murphy

1940-1949

Source: Photo by Harris & Ewing, Collection of the Supreme Court of the United States

FRANK MURPHY was born April 13, 1890, in Sand Beach (later Harbor Beach), Michigan. Baptized William Francis Murphy, he was the third of four children of John F. Murphy, a country lawyer who was active in Democratic politics, and Mary Brennan Murphy. Murphy attended public school in his hometown and then enrolled in the University of Michigan, receiving an LL.B in 1914. He joined a Detroit law firm, Monaghan and Monaghan, and taught law in night school.

When the United States declared war on Germany in April 1917, Murphy applied for officer's training, was commissioned a lieutenant in the infantry, and served briefly in France and Germany at the war's end. Before returning home, he enrolled for short sessions of legal study at Lincoln's Inn, London, and Trinity College, Dublin. Three days after his discharge from the army, Murphy, a Democrat, was sworn in as first assistant U.S. attorney for the Eastern District of Michigan.

Public service was to occupy Murphy for the remain-

Gov. Frank Murphy reviews the local constabulary soon after his arrival in the Philippines in 1933. He became high commissioner of the islands when they attained commonwealth status in 1935. *Source: Bettmann*

der of his life except for a brief period in private law practice in 1922 and 1923. As a public servant, he was a consistent supporter of fiscal integrity, the welfare state, organized labor, and civil liberties. He served as a judge on the Recorder's Court, Detroit's unified criminal court, from 1924 to 1930. A superb campaigner, Murphy was elected Detroit's mayor in 1930 following the recall of the incumbent. As mayor, he made a valiant effort to cope with the city's massive unemployment, caused by the Great Depression, and he was responsible for the creation of the U.S. Conference of Mayors.

In recognition for his support in the 1932 presidential campaign, Franklin D. Roosevelt selected Murphy in 1933 to be the governor-general of the Philippine Islands. When the Philippines attained commonwealth status in 1935, Roosevelt named Murphy the first high commissioner. Murphy helped bring New Deal-style reforms to the Philippines and was an ardent supporter of Philippine independence. Roosevelt brought Murphy back to Michigan in 1936, mistakenly believing that he needed him to carry the state in the 1936 presidential election.

Elected Michigan's governor in 1936, Murphy

presided over one of the few state "little" New Deals, and he helped to settle the great General Motors sitdown strike. He was defeated for reelection in 1938 in what was then a Republican state.

Roosevelt selected Murphy to be the nation's attorney general in 1939, and he served a notable year in that position. He created what is now the Civil Rights Division of the Department of Justice and successfully crusaded against crime and corruption, prosecuting such figures as Kansas City's Democratic boss, Tom Pendergast, and newspaper publisher Moses Annenberg.

Ambitious and self-centered, Murphy avoided alcohol and tobacco and exercised regularly because he regarded physical fitness as essential to political success. He early came to enjoy the company of the rich and the well-born, but he had genuine compassion for the afflicted and unfortunate. Although unusually attractive to women, he never married. He was always his own man, but he was, in his fashion, a devout Catholic, and he was influenced by Catholic social thought.

It is not entirely clear why President Roosevelt selected Murphy to replace Justice Pierce Butler, who died in 1939. The appointment, to be sure, perfectly fit

In 1936 employees at a General Motors plant in Flint, Michigan, sat down by their machines in the nation's first sit-down strike. Gov. Frank Murphy negotiated an end to the strike, which forced the company to recognize the workers' new union, the United Auto Workers. The Supreme Court declared sit-down strikes illegal in 1939 because they prevented the company from continuing operations by hiring strikebreakers. *Source: Library of Congress*

the prescription for a successor to Butler, a Catholic from the Midwest, just as it met Roosevelt's general criteria for selecting Supreme Court justices: loyalty to the New Deal, "a libertarian and egalitarian philosophy of government under law," and, with war looming, support for the president's "war aims." It may be, however, that Roosevelt wished to rid himself of an attorney general whose successful prosecution of city bosses and threatened prosecution of others posed a threat to the president's third-term ambitions. Murphy was unanimously confirmed by the Senate January 16, 1940, and took his judicial oath February 5.

Murphy joined the Court with a great deal of reluctance; he had misgivings about his qualifications for the job, and he was disinclined to give up the active life of a politician for the contemplative life of a justice. After the attack on Pearl Harbor, he would have liked to resign from the Court to command troops in the field, but he was told he was too old for such an assignment. He had to content himself, as a lieutenant on inactive status, with participation in army training during the Court recess in 1942. He begged the president in 1943 and 1944 for an assignment that would take him into or near the Philippines, but it was not to be. Instead, he served as chairman of Philippine War Relief and as chairman of the National Committee against Nazi Persecution and Extermination of the Jews.

After two terms of indecision on the Court, during which he took his cues largely from the Court's prevailing tendencies, Murphy decided what his particular role as a justice should be. In a self-conscious statement in 1941, he observed that a seat on the Court gave a justice "the rarest of all opportunities to evangelize for tolerance and all things that are just, that sweeten this life for men." Although he wavered on occasion, Murphy had charted the course he would follow on the Court. It is doubtful that he took offense at the remark that began making the rounds in 1944: "The Supreme Court tempers justice with Murphy."

In appraising the facts in a case, Murphy tended to rely on his own considerable experience in public life. He was also influenced by his conception of what best served the public interest. And what best served the public interest, as he saw it, was "to enlarge men's freedoms and make them content with justice," to provide "security and equal justice to the inarticulate" and the "humblest," and "to sweeten life that has been burdensome." "I write the law as my conscience bids me," he unashamedly remarked in 1946. The principles that guided him, the role that he defined for himself, led Murphy to be more concerned with results than with legal craftsmanship. He was not unique among justices in this respect, but he was more obvious than most in exposing his preferences.

Although Murphy did not ignore precedent in deciding cases, the freedom of the individual and a just result ranked higher in his scale of values than the cases of yesteryear. While on the Court, he was a member of the majority in twenty-one of the twenty-five cases in which precedents were overruled. Aware that he could express his views in a relatively uninhibited fashion when writing in dissent, whereas he might have to accommodate to others in writing for the Court, Murphy appeared to take increasing pleasure in the role of the dissenter. Along with his 130 Court opinions and 20 concurrences, he wrote 69 dissents.

Murphy's most important substantive contributions as a justice were in the areas of labor law, the rights of defendants in criminal cases, and civil rights and civil liberties. He wrote more opinions concerning labor, with which he had considerable experience before joining the Court, than on any other subject. In his first opinion, *Thornhill v. Alabama* (1940), Murphy equated peaceful picketing with freedom of speech and declared invalid a statute that prohibited all picketing at the scene of a labor dispute. After *Thornhill*, a state government could no longer legally prohibit all picketing, and peaceful picketing of the sort involved in the case enjoyed constitutional protection even if the picketed party had suffered some injury.

While on the Court, Murphy wrote more opinions than any other justice in cases involving interpretation of the Fair Labor Standards Act (FLSA). Committed to the worker's cause, he was inclined to resolve doubts regarding the statute in favor of the employees, recognizing, as he wrote in one such case, that the Court was "dealing with human beings and with a statute . . . intended to secure to them the fruits of their toil and exertion." In three of his most significant FLSA opinions, Murphy ruled that workers must be paid for travel time in iron ore mines, underground travel in coal mines and walking time on the employer's premises at a pottery company.

Murphy was as solicitous for the rights of defendants as he was for workers. Speaking for the Court in *Trupiano v. United States* (1948), Murphy proclaimed a new rule to govern federal searches and seizures, namely, that "in seizing goods and articles, law enforcement agents must secure and use search warrants wherever reasonably practicable." He dissented when the Court, in *Wolf v. Colorado* (1949), decided that the rule excluding evidence obtained from illegal searches and seizures in federal cases did not apply in state cases. He consistently held that indigent defendants in state criminal cases were entitled to counsel not only in capital cases, as the Court had ruled before he joined it, but in noncapital cases as well, a position the Court did not accept until after Murphy's death.

Murphy believed the First Amendment enjoyed a "preferred place" in the constitutional spectrum, but among the freedoms, religious freedom, for him, was more "preferred" than others. This belief became evident in the opinions he wrote defending the right of Jehovah's Witnesses to practice and propagate their faith by whatever means they chose. Whether the case involved licensing taxes, door-to-door distribution of literature, the flag salute, child labor, or conscientious objection to military service, the Catholic Murphy sided with the Witnesses.

Murphy also became the Court's expert in Native American cases, mindful always of the "moral and political responsibilities" the nation had incurred toward

In 1944 the Supreme Court upheld the constitutionality of interring Japanese-Americans on the West Coast in detention centers as a military necessity during World War II. Frank Murphy wrote a powerful dissent against the policy, which he viewed as a "legalization of racism." He argued that Japanese-Americans should have been judged on an individual basis to determine their loyalty, the way persons of German and Italian ancestry were treated. *Source: AP/Wide World Photos*

Native Americans. Sensitive to the wickedness of racism, he became the first justice to hold that union discrimination against a minority group whom it represented violated constitutional guarantees. In a Court conference in 1948, he declared his opposition to the "separate but equal" doctrine legitimizing racial segregation six years before the Court came to the same conclusion.

Murphy strongly defended civil liberties during World War II, contending that for the Court to follow any other course would rob the war of its meaning. In *Schneiderman v. United States* (1943) he held that to prove a naturalized citizen, in this case a communist, had procured his citizenship illegally, the government had to provide evidence that was "clear, unequivocal, and convincing." In *Hirabayashi v. United States* (1943) Murphy concurred with great reluctance when a unanimous Court upheld the military's curfew order as applied to Japanese-American citizens on the West Coast.

When the majority in *Korematsu v. United States* (1944) upheld the exclusion of Japanese-American citizens from the West Coast, Murphy, in a notable and deeply felt dissent, wrote that the action went beyond "the very brink of constitutional power" and fell into "the ugly abyss of racism."

Although Murphy claimed that his opinions had enlarged freedom of speech, press, religion, and thought, and had provided protection for the indigent and inarticulate, his close friend and fellow justice, Wiley B. Rutledge, once remarked that Murphy's voice was "crying too often in the wilderness" on the 1940s Court. Many of Murphy's dissents, however, became Court doctrine during the years of the Warren Court.

Murphy experienced heart trouble in 1942, and he was hospitalized off and on with a variety of ailments during his last three years on the Court. He died in Detroit of a coronary thrombosis on July 19, 1949, at the age of fifty-nine.

James F. Byrnes

1941-1942

JAMES FRANCIS BYRNES was a grandson of Irish-Catholic immigrants to the United States. He was born in Charleston, South Carolina, May 2, 1882, six weeks after his father, James, a municipal clerk in the police department, died of consumption. Young James's mother, Elizabeth McSweeney Byrnes, supported him and his older sister, Leonore, by making dresses in the working-class neighborhood where they lived.

Byrnes's formal education was limited. He completed six years of parochial and one subsequent year of public school in Charleston. To relieve some of his mother's financial burdens, he quit school at age fourteen and took a job as an office boy in the law firm of Benjamin H. Rutledge, Jr., a Charleston aristocrat who traced his lineage back to John Rutledge, an early justice of the Supreme Court. After hours, Rutledge guided Byrnes through an extensive reading program that did much to compensate for his lack of a high school education. In 1900 Rutledge also helped Byrnes, whose mother had

Rep. James Byrnes of South Carolina during an unsuccessful campaign for a Senate seat in 1924. In 1930 he ran again, this time winning his race. *Source: Library of Congress*

taught him the skills to become an accomplished stenographer, to win the job of official reporter for South Carolina's second judicial circuit, headquartered at Aiken.

Byrnes rose rapidly in the society of his new town. During his first year as a court reporter, he read law under the district's chief judge, James A. Aldrich. In 1903 he was admitted to the South Carolina bar as a practicing attorney. The next year he also became co-owner and editor of the town's newspaper, the *Journal and Review*. While working at those three different occupations, Byrnes married Maude Perkins Busch, the daughter of a prominent Aiken businessman, in 1906. Byrnes left the Catholic church and joined the Episcopal church of which his wife was a member. Two years

later, he was elected solicitor (prosecuting attorney) of the second district. Based on his success in that office, Byrnes, at age twenty-eight, was elected to the U.S. House of Representatives as a Democrat in 1910.

The slender Byrnes wore clothes "that a small town dude would give his elk's tooth to own" and moved with "quick, nervous mannerisms" that one person later compared to "Jimmy Cagney doing an impersonation of George M. Cohan." He also impressed nearly everyone he met as a man with an uncommonly quick mind, an ingratiating charm, an uncanny ability to form an acceptable compromise out of conflicting points of view, and a burning ambition to succeed at whatever he did.

Byrnes was a southern progressive intent on improving the post-Reconstruction South's standard of living and restoring it to national leadership without sacrificing the most cherished traditions of middle-class, white southerners. On the one hand, such a program called for seeking federal assistance to regulate the conduct of large national corporations and improve the welfare of farmers and other historically disadvantaged groups among the white population. On the other hand, it called for resisting any federal attempt to undermine either racial segregation or the large supply of cheap, non-union labor that gave the South a competitive advantage over the rest of the country in attracting labor-intensive industries such as textiles.

Byrnes pursued that philosophy as a member of Congress from 1911 to 1925. He supported virtually all the domestic and foreign policy reforms initiated by President Woodrow Wilson. After Wilson left office, Byrnes opposed with equal vigor the more conservative policies of the Republican presidents of the early 1920s.

In 1924 Byrnes ran for a seat in the U.S. Senate. He was defeated in a close election by Coleman L. Blease. Byrnes then moved to Spartanburg, South Carolina, where for the next six years he practiced law in the firm of Nichols, Wyche, and Byrnes. In 1930 he ran for the

Senate again and this time defeated Blease in another close election.

As a senator Byrnes began to win widespread national attention. A close friend of Franklin D. Roosevelt, whom he he had met during the Wilson administration, Byrnes served as a major political adviser during Roosevelt's successful presidential campaign of 1932. After the election, Byrnes quickly earned a reputation as Roosevelt's favorite senator and the de facto Democratic whip in the Senate. From 1933 through 1936, he supported all major pieces of New Deal legislation and played a pivotal role in passing many of them. Along the way, said one historian, he became "the most influential southern member of Congress between John Calhoun and Lyndon Johnson."

After the elections of 1936, Byrnes used his influence in different ways. He opposed most of the more liberal labor, welfare, and racial policies advocated by New Dealers during Roosevelt's second administration. That opposition helped to bring the New Deal to a close in 1939. Over the next two years, however, Byrnes played a major role in adopting all of the president's national security legislation aimed at leading the United States away from isolation toward active opposition to Nazi Germany and other fascist powers. On matters of foreign policy and defense, said columnist Joseph Alsop in early 1941, "There are few men in Washington [the president] owes more to than Mr. Byrnes." On June 12, 1941, Roosevelt repaid the debt by nominating Byrnes to a vacancy on the Supreme Court. That same day, the Senate waived confirmation hearings and approved the nomination by a voice vote.

As a general rule, Byrnes believed that a justice should exercise "judicial restraint." By that, he meant that the Court should defer to the will of Congress whenever possible and try to avoid staking out broad constitutional ground when interpreting the law. Some of his colleagues, notably Justices Harlan F. Stone and Felix Frankfurter, tended to agree, but others were in-

clined to embrace a "judicial activism" that was more willing to override the legislative branch and blaze new constitutional frontiers to promote what they perceived as desirable social results.

Those trends were evident in the first, and perhaps best known, opinion that Byrnes wrote for the Court. The case, *Edwards v. California* (1941), originated as a challenge to a California law that made it illegal to transport indigents from other states into the state of California. All of the justices believed that the law was unconstitutional, but they disagreed on the reasons why. Speaking for the Court, Byrnes chose the well-trodden ground provided by many past decisions under the Commerce Clause of the Constitution. Any attempt by one state to prevent free movement across its borders, he argued, "imposes an unconstitutional bur-

As victims of the Dust Bowl poured into California in the 1930s, the state passed a law prohibiting the transportation of nonresident indigents into the state. The Supreme Court overturned the so-called "Okie law" in 1941. James F. Byrnes's opinion in *Edwards v. California* recognized a constitutional right to interstate travel and made it harder to pass laws discriminating against the poor. *Source: Library of Congress*

den upon interstate commerce." "It is unnecessary," he added, to decide whether such a law "is repugnant to other sections of the Constitution."

Justice William O. Douglas wrote a concurring opinion that argued that the case called for breaking new constitutional ground and asserting a more fundamental right under the Fourteenth Amendment. Surely the individual liberties of human beings, Douglas wrote, ought to enjoy "a more protected position in our constitutional system than does the movement of cattle . . . across state lines. . . . The right to move freely from state to state is an incident of national citizenship protected by the privileges and immunities clause of the Fourteenth Amendment against State interference." The different approaches taken by the two camps, said the *Wall Street Journal,* suggested that the "traditional liberalism" of the older justices who had united behind Byrnes might soon be "left behind as the Young New Dealers" on the Court "step out with a new brand of liberalism."

The divergent points of view were especially evident in a large number of cases that addressed the extent of a citizen's civil liberties under the Bill of Rights. On many occasions, Byrnes opposed an expansion of those liberties; on others, he supported them. He also had a mixed voting record on the many cases that addressed the relationship between state government and the federal government, although he tended to support the rights of the states. On balance, Byrnes's voting record on these two kinds of cases was liberal in comparison to the records of most of the justices who had served on earlier Courts, but to the right of center of those who served with him.

During his brief sixteen-month tenure on the Court, Byrnes wrote sixteen opinions, a figure that surpassed the total of most of his colleagues in the same time period. His most notable decisions placed limitations on the enforcement of the national minimum wage law, prohibited sailors from engaging in a sit-down strike on board a ship docked at port, invalidated a tenant farming law that violated the Thirteenth Amendment, overturned the murder conviction of a black man who had been physically coerced into making a confession, and exempted the Teamsters Union from prosecution under the federal Anti-Racketeering Act of 1934.

While on the Court, Byrnes worked for greater unity among the justices. He never wrote a dissenting opinion himself and, on several occasions, tried to persuade his colleagues not to write them either. In that regard he was unsuccessful, for the Court, under Chief Justice Stone, produced what at that time was a record high percentage of dissenting and concurring opinions. But if Byrnes was unable to mute the justices' philosophical differences, he did seem to promote more personal congeniality among the members of the Court, and he was noted for his warmth and gaiety.

Justice Frankfurter thought that Byrnes would have made great contributions if he had elected to stay on the Court for a longer time. Byrnes had an "excellent and quick brain," "uncommon sagacity," and "the real judicial temper," Frankfurter said. Indeed, he asserted, "there was no man on the Court who was truly more judicial-minded than Jim Byrnes—and hardly any as much."

After the Japanese attack on Pearl Harbor, however, Byrnes became increasingly restless on the Court. "My country's at war," he said, "and I want to be in it. I don't think I can stand the abstractions of jurisprudence at a time like this." Aware of Byrnes's feelings and of the fact that his much-heralded political skills could be of great use to the war effort, the president quietly gave him a series of "extracurricular" tasks to perform while he still sat on the bench. For several months, Byrnes covertly advised the administration and served as its liaison man with important members of Congress on a wide range of executive and legislative matters pertaining to the war. Sensitive to the possible impropriety of such actions, Byrnes resigned from the Court in the

Secretary of State James F. Byrnes briefs President Harry S. Truman in 1946 on the progress of the Paris Peace Conference. The negotiations ultimately broke down because of growing tension with the Soviet Union. *Source: Collection of the Supreme Court of the United States*

fall of 1942 to accept appointment as the director of the newly created Office of Economic Stabilization.

After six months, he was promoted to the directorship of the Office of War Mobilization (OWM). There, he was known as the "assistant president" because he supervised virtually every aspect of the domestic war effort while exercising powers second only to Roosevelt's. In 1944 Byrnes made a bid for the Democratic vice presidential nomination but was rejected because of the strong opposition of blacks and organized labor. Deeply hurt by the incident and having finished most of the job, he resigned as head of the OWM ahead of schedule in March 1945. After Roosevelt died, Byrnes returned to Washington in July to serve as President Harry Truman's secretary of state. He supervised American foreign policy during the last phases of World War II and the first phases of the cold war with the Soviet Union. A combination of physical fatigue and differences with the Truman administration led Byrnes to resign from the State Department in January 1947. For the next

four years, he practiced law with the Washington firm of Hogan and Hartson.

Byrnes reentered politics in 1950 when he was elected governor of South Carolina. In that office, he spearheaded campaigns to attract industrial development, curb the violence of the Ku Klux Klan, and improve schools for blacks. But he also strongly opposed the liberal domestic policies of Truman's "Fair Deal," orchestrated regional resistance to school desegregation, and led a movement to establish a South that was politically independent from the national Democratic party. After he left office in 1955, Byrnes vigorously criticized the decisions of the Warren Court, railed against the racial reforms of the "Second Reconstruction," and opposed every Democratic presidential candidate until his death from a heart attack on April 9, 1972. At the time, Byrnes was more remembered for fighting a rear-guard action against desegregation during the 1950s than for the far more constructive roles he had earlier played in American government.

Robert H. Jackson

1941-1954

ROBERT HOUGHWOUT JACKSON, one of the few justices selected by a president to represent the United States in negotiations with other world powers, was born in Spring Creek, Pennsylvania, February 13, 1892. Raised on a farm near Frewsburg and Jamestown, New York, Jackson was of Scotch and Dutch ancestry. His mother was Angelina Houghwout Jackson, and his father, William Eldred Jackson, was a farmer, lumberman, and stock breeder. Both sides of Jackson's family had a rugged, independent character.

Early in his career, Robert Jackson lived up to those traditions of independence and self-reliance. After graduating from Jamestown High School in 1911, he declined his father's advice to become a doctor. Instead, he "read law" with a local attorney, finished a two-year course at Albany Law School in one year, observed arguments in the New York Court of Appeals, and was admitted to the New York Bar in 1913 at the age of twenty-one. Except for the one year of law school, Jackson had no formal education after high school; but he

Robert H. Jackson served as solicitor general and attorney general to Franklin D. Roosevelt. The president intended to promote Jackson to chief justice after he served a few terms on the Court, but Roosevelt died before the promotion could be made. *Source: Collection of the Supreme Court of the United States*

was a voracious reader of the classics, biography, and history, which no doubt contributed to his breadth of view and his exceptional writing ability.

Jackson's financial success as a lawyer permitted him to buy a house in Jamestown, a pleasure boat, and a farm where he could raise and ride horses and enjoy the outdoors. In 1916 he married Irene Alice Gerhardt, daughter of a builder in nearby Kingston. The Jacksons had a son and a daughter. Their son, William Eldred Jackson, became a lawyer and served as his father's personal aide at the Nuremberg trials.

Although he was an active Democrat, Jackson's professional abilities were so highly regarded that the Republican-dominated Jamestown government named

him acting corporation counsel. And Democrat though he was, banks, utilities, and other businesses retained him as counsel and as a director. At the same time, he had individual clients, both rich and poor. Even before he was admitted to the bar, he was permitted to represent union workers indicted in connection with a streetcar strike, and they were acquitted.

Jackson was active in the organized bar, serving as president of the Jamestown bar, president of the Federation of Bar Associations of Western New York, and chairman of the National Conference of American Bar Association Delegates. In these activities he became friends with Charles Evans Hughes. In later years, Jackson, as solicitor general and attorney general of the

United States, would appear many times before Chief Justice Hughes.

Jackson's first post in Washington was with the Bureau of Internal Revenue. President Franklin D. Roosevelt was familiar with Jackson's work in his behalf when he was governor of New York. Roosevelt persuaded a reluctant Jackson to come to Washington in 1934 as general counsel to the bureau, which needed rejuvenation. After a successful stint there, he moved to the Justice Department as assistant attorney general in charge of the Tax Division and then the Antitrust Division. All the while he continued as a close friend and personal adviser to President Roosevelt.

In 1937 Jackson told Roosevelt that he wished to resign from the government and return to private practice, but the president rejected that idea and made him solicitor general in March 1938. In that advocate's position, which he loved, Jackson argued and won many cases for the government before the Supreme Court. Justice Louis Brandeis said Jackson should be solicitor general for life. In 1940 President Roosevelt appointed Jackson U.S. attorney general. One of his assignments was to advise the president whether he had the authority, without seeking the approval of Congress, to conclude an executive agreement with Great Britain. The United States proposed transferring to the British fifty over-age destroyers, which England desperately needed to combat German submarines, in exchange for naval and air bases on British possessions in the Western Hemisphere. Jackson's favorable opinion provided a strong underpinning for that vital transaction.

President Roosevelt had informed Jackson of his plan to appoint him chief justice when Hughes retired. However, when that event occurred, the three of them agreed that it would be best for the Court and for Jackson if he were to serve first as an associate justice under Harlan Fiske Stone, who was then elevated to chief justice. Jackson's appointment was made June 12, 1941, and was confirmed by the Senate July 7. During his thirteen years of service on the high bench, Jackson delivered 148 opinions for the Court, 46 concurrences, and 115 dissents. His style was clear, direct, and persuasive, so that his opinions were easily understood. In his concurrences and dissents, he felt free to use forceful language, sometimes punctuated by sarcasm or cynicism and sometimes spiced with humor. "We are not final because we are infallible, but we are infallible because we are final," he once said about the Court.

The first Jackson opinion that aroused public interest was his majority decision in *Board of Education v. Barnette* (1943), which overruled *Minersville School District v. Gobitis* (1940). In his often-cited opinion, holding that a school board could not constitutionally compel an unwilling school child to salute the flag and recite the oath of allegiance, Jackson said, "The very purpose of the Bill of Rights was to withdraw certain subjects from the vicissitudes of political controversy, to place them beyond the reach of majorities and officials and establish them as legal principles to be applied by courts. One's right to life, liberty, and property, to free speech, a free press, freedom of worship and assembly, and other fundamental rights, may not be submitted to vote; they depend on the outcome of no elections."

The next year, in his dissent in *Korematsu v. United States,* Jackson expressed disapproval of the wartime confinement of American citizens in "relocation camps" strictly because of their Japanese ancestry. "Now, if any fundamental assumption underlies our system, it is that guilt is personal and not inheritable" he said. Almost fifty years later, Congress adopted Jackson's view that the confinement was unlawful and awarded damages to internees like Fred Korematsu.

Jackson's opinions reflected strong support for individual rights and a revulsion for arbitrary government action at any level. He was vigorous in his support for the right of Congress to regulate interstate commerce and to enact strict antitrust laws. He believed in fair treatment and fair trials, with the right to counsel, for

Justice Robert H. Jackson took leave from the Supreme Court to serve as the chief counsel of the United States at the Nuremberg trials. He listens to evidence of Nazi war crimes with Russian Uri Pokrovski (right) in this October 1946 photograph. *Source: UPI/Bettmann*

persons accused of crime, but thought that at times the Court was too ready to overturn factual findings by state courts. He criticized as unfair the Immigration Service's use of secret evidence on "security" grounds and prosecutors' abuse of the conspiracy argument to obtain admission of prejudicial and otherwise inadmissible evidence.

In April 1945 Justice Jackson acceded to President Harry S. Truman's request that he become the chief U.S. prosecutor against the leaders of Nazi Germany for their wars of aggression and war crimes and the atrocities they ordered or permitted. This assignment involved the difficult job of negotiating an agreement among the United States, Soviet Russia, England, and France, all with different legal and judicial systems, to establish an international tribunal. Outstanding advocates, including John W. Davis, agreed that Justice Jackson's opening statement, outlining the charges

against the Nazi defendants, and his closing argument were two of the greatest examples of advocacy of all time. The reason Jackson believed that "the long months at Nuremberg were well spent in the most important, enduring and constructive work of my life," is made clear in his opening remarks:

The privilege of opening the first trial in history for crimes against the peace of the world imposes a grave responsibility. The wrongs which we seek to condemn and punish have been so calculated, so malignant, and so devastating, that civilization cannot tolerate their being ignored because it cannot survive their being repeated. That four great nations, flushed with victory and stung with injury, stay the hands of vengeance and voluntarily submit their captive enemies to the judgment of the law is one of the most significant tributes that Power ever has paid to Reason."

After the Nazi defendants had been convicted and sentenced, Jackson resumed his Court duties during the

1946 term. His return dispelled rumors that he would not come back because of tension among the justices and because of President Truman's failure to honor the commitment President Roosevelt had made that Jackson would be named chief justice upon Stone's retirement.   Despite these difficulties, Jackson maintained good relations with his colleagues and managed to produce some of his greatest opinions. In his concurrence in *Youngstown Sheet & Tube Co. v. Sawyer* (1952), usu-

Robert H. Jackson wrote a concurring opinion in *Youngstown Sheet & Tube Co. v. Sawyer*, also known as the *Steel Seizure Case*. The Court said presidential authority did not extend to seizing private steel mills, even if the purpose was to keep them operating during a war. *Source: Library of Congress*

ally called the Steel Seizure case, which invalidated President Truman's attempted seizure of private steel mills during the Korean War to prevent a strike, Jackson produced a thoughtful explanation of the basic constitutional doctrine of separation of powers that the Court found helpful in the Watergate case many years later. His delineation in the case of the limits of presidential authority is often cited: "The Constitution did not contemplate that the title of Commander-in-Chief *of the Army and Navy* will constitute him also Commander-in-Chief of the country, its industries, and its inhabitants."

In 1954, at the request of Harvard University, Jackson undertook preparation of the Godkin Lectures for delivery in 1955. The three lectures, published posthumously and entitled *The Supreme Court in the American System of Government,* have been widely recognized as a revealing study and analysis of the Court by one who was closely associated with it as both a participant and an outside observer.

Jackson suffered a heart attack March 30, 1954, and was advised that he could look forward to a relatively long life if he curtailed his activities, but that a continuation would represent a risk of death at almost any time. He characteristically chose the latter course and left the hospital on May 17 to be on the bench when the Court's unanimous antisegregation decision in *Brown v. Board of Education* was announced.

The self-styled "country lawyer" died suddenly October 9. The official Court eulogy noted his outstanding career as a lawyer and a judge but also emphasized his charming personality and his engaging humor. Charles S. Desmond, chief judge of the New York Court of Appeals, said that his friend Bob Jackson would be "wryly amused" to be remembered as a shining example of the American success story, but "would rather be remembered as a lawyer of his time and place who by obeying his code lived a useful, happy life and died an honored citizen."

Wiley B. Rutledge

1943-1949

WILEY BLOUNT RUTLEDGE was born in Cloverport, Kentucky, July 20, 1894. Rutledge's father was a circuit-riding Baptist preacher. Rutledge's mother contracted tuberculosis in 1901, and the young family left Kentucky in search of a more favorable environment—settling first in Texas, next in Louisiana, and then in North Carolina. In 1903, when Rutledge was nine, his mother died. Soon thereafter, the widower-preacher moved his three children to pulpits in Kentucky and Tennessee, settling finally in Marysville, not far from Knoxville. Although he was brought up in his father's fundamentalist Baptist faith, Rutledge later became a Unitarian.

In Marysville, Rutledge finished high school and started college. An ancient languages major, he completed his undergraduate studies at the University of Wisconsin, at Madison, in 1914. Because he could not afford the law school at Madison, Rutledge became a high school teacher in Bloomington, Indiana, and concurrently enrolled at Indiana University's law school.

Within a year Rutledge fell gravely ill of the disease that had killed his mother. By 1917 Rutledge had recovered sufficiently to marry Annabel Person, who had been his Greek teacher at Marysville College. They would have two daughters and one son.

Drawn by the climate, the young couple moved to Albuquerque, New Mexico. After three years, they moved again, to Boulder, Colorado. There Rutledge repeated the Bloomington experiment, simultaneously teaching high school and studying law. This time, however, he stayed healthy and in 1922 graduated from the University of Colorado Law School. After two years of practice in Boulder, Rutledge accepted a call to return to the law school as a member of the faculty. His two vocations—teaching and law—were joined.

Rutledge taught at Boulder for two years. Then, in 1926, he accepted an invitation to join the law faculty of Washington University in St. Louis. He was to remain there for nine years—the last five of them, 1930 to 1935, as dean. Rutledge then became dean of the University of Iowa College of Law.

Dean Rutledge was greatly beloved by his students and by his faculty colleagues. Willard Wirtz—a junior colleague who was later to become secretary of labor—described the way Rutledge taught. Rutledge insisted on

treating his students as human beings, getting to know them as individuals. He did this, seemingly oblivious to the other demands upon his time, by opening his office door and his home, inviting the students in singly and in groups of two or three, and then sitting and talking with them. The conversation would be personal at first, as teacher and student found out what underlay the other's reactions. Then it would broaden out, proceeding with an awareness of assumptions, predilections and biases. Now the human heart of the subject matter of the day's lecture could be taken up intelligently, and that of the morning's headlines. The subject would become not just a particular case or a news story but how a decent, honest, intelligent man approaches any subject coming within the professional competence and obligation of the lawyer. For an hour or so the

law would be taught as it was a hundred years ago when the neophyte learned his profession in the office of an established member of the bar. "Reading law" they called it. But it was so much more than that. It was the transmission of a tradition of professional service, the handing on perhaps less of information than of a spirit and a whole quality of professional competence and responsibility.

The "reading law" teaching method was, as Wirtz said it, the dean's way of countering "the hollowness of curricula and courses in which the value elements inherent in sound legal concepts emerge only incidentally. . . . We train artisans, [Rutledge] said, while a democratic society pleads for architects."

Beginning in 1933 Rutledge became an increasingly forceful voice of criticism of the spate of Supreme Court decisions invalidating economic reform legislation, including major elements of President Franklin D. Roosevelt's New Deal. In 1937 he emerged as one of the few leaders of the American legal community (politicians aside) to give public support to Roosevelt's ill-fated "Court-packing" plan, which would have allowed the president to appoint additional justices to the Supreme Court. Rutledge's support for the unpopular plan drew the wrath of Iowa legislators, who threatened to withhold salary raises at the university. Two years later, in March 1939, Roosevelt selected Rutledge to serve on the U.S. Court of Appeals for the District of Columbia.

Rutledge savored his four years on the court of appeals. Closest to him philosophically was Henry Edgerton, a pacifist and civil libertarian who was also a former law teacher. Another good friend—who would again be his colleague on the Supreme Court—was Fred Vinson. Recalling their years together on the court of appeals, Chief Justice Vinson noted that Rutledge found particular professional fulfillment in addressing the issues of local District of Columbia law, which were then a major ingredient of the court's docket. "Like the late Justice [Benjamin] Cardozo, he derived much satisfaction and renown from his treatment of problems which are usually the concern of state courts." But Vinson also observed that even on the court of appeals Rutledge "manifested that concern for individual rights and freedom of thought, speech and religion which was to bring him great tribute."

On January 11, 1943, Roosevelt nominated Rutledge, age forty-eight, to the Supreme Court. The president told him that his Iowa affiliation had been an important factor. "Wiley, we had a number of candidates for the Court who were highly qualified, but they didn't have geography—you have that." Rutledge was confirmed by the Senate February 8, becoming the last of Roosevelt's appointees.

As a member of the Supreme Court, Rutledge had little further occasion to address the local law problems that had engaged him on the court of appeals. The 171 majority, concurring, and dissenting opinions—almost 30 a year—that he wrote during his six industrious years on the Court covered the gamut of federal statutory and constitutional issues. Among his most notable decisions was *Thomas v. Collins* (1945), which showed his sympathy for the rights of labor. Rutledge's opinion invalidated a Texas statute that required "labor union organizers to acquire an 'organizer's card' from the Texas secretary of state before soliciting any members." In *Prince v. Massachusetts* (1944) he wrote the opinion sustaining the conviction for violation of a Massachusetts child labor law of a Jehovah's Witness who, with her nine-year-old niece, sold evangelical literature on the streets of Brockton. His opinion in *Prince* surprised many Court watchers because Rutledge's usual stance in Jehovah's Witness cases, on both the court of appeals and the Supreme Court, was one of great concern for a religious sect that he perceived as having been harassed by a variety of government restraints.

Although Rutledge often wrote for the Court in matters of considerable constitutional consequence, he made his mark chiefly in powerful dissents—particularly in certain of the major civil liberties cases that

came before the Court in the 1940s. Two of his most celebrated dissents, in *Everson v. Board of Education* (1947) and in *In re Yamashita* (1946), are representative.

Everson was one of this century's most important tests of the relationship of church and state, in the context of the First Amendment's Establishment Clause. In *Everson,* Justice Hugo Black, writing for a five-justice majority that included Chief Justice Vinson, and Justices Stanley Reed, William O. Douglas, and Frank Murphy, adopted Thomas Jefferson's "wall of separation" formula to draw the line between church and state matters, but nonetheless sustained New Jersey's program of funding bus transportation for parochial school students. Rutledge, speaking for himself, Justices Felix Frankfurter, Robert Jackson, and Harold Burton, drew on James Madison's "Memorial and Remonstrance Against Religious Assessments" to demonstrate that the judgment of the Court was invalid.

In Rutledge's view:

Two great drives are constantly in motion to abridge, in the name of education, the complete division of religion and civil authority which our forefathers made. One is to introduce religious education and observances into the public schools. The other, to obtain public funds for the aid and support of various private religious schools. . . . In my opinion both avenues were closed by the Constitution. Neither should be opened by this Court. The matter is not one of quantity, to be measured by the amount of money expended. Now as in Madison's day it is one of principle, to keep separate the separate spheres as the First Amendment drew them; to prevent the first experiment upon our liberties; and to keep the question from becoming entangled in corrosive precedents. We should not be less strict to keep strong and untarnished the one side of the shield of religious freedom than we have been of the other.

Fifteen years after *Everson,* Douglas, one of the five members of the *Everson* majority, acknowledged that Rutledge's dissent had "stated . . . durable First Amendment philosophy" and that *Everson* "seems in retrospect to be out of line with the First Amendment." Nearly five decades after it was written, Rutledge's dissent con-

The Sacred Heart Elementary School of Pittsburgh, considered a model school, was photographed in 1947, the same year the Court decided *Everson v. Board of Education*. Justice Wiley Rutledge dissented from the Court's opinion, which found that a New Jersey plan to reimburse parents for children's bus transportation to parochial schools did not violate the First Amendment's Establishment Clause. *Source: AP/Wide World Photos*

tinues to be one of the defining documents in the ongoing debate over the religious clauses of the Constitution.

In his magisterial dissent in *Yamashita,* Rutledge articulated what he conceived to be America's commitment to equal justice for even the most despised criminal. Gen. Tamoyuki Yamashita was the Japanese commander in the Philippines during World War II. After the Japanese surrender, Yamashita was tried by a military tribunal for myriad crimes, against both civilians and prisoners of war, committed by troops at least nominally under the general's command. He was convicted and sentenced to death. The Supreme Court declined to hear a petition that alleged a host of failures

by the military tribunal to observe minimal forms of fair judicial procedure. The majority of the justices, speaking through Chief Justice Stone, felt it sufficient that the tribunal was duly authorized to try Yamashita. Two justices—Rutledge and Murphy—dissented. Rutledge said:

More is at stake than General Yamashita's fate. There could be no possible sympathy for him if he is guilty of the atrocities for which his death is sought. But there can be and should be justice administered according to law. In this stage of war's aftermath it is too early for Lincoln's great spirit, best lighted in the Second Inaugural, to have wide hold for the treatment of foes. It is not too early, it is never too early, for the nation steadfastly to follow its great constitutional traditions, none older or more universally pro-

Gen. Tamoyuki Yamashita, the commander of the Japanese forces in the Philippines accused of overseeing atrocities during World War II, prepares his legal defense in 1945. Wiley Rutledge and Frank Murphy dissented from what they considered a breach in fairness procedures committed by the military tribunal that sentenced Yamashita to death. *Source: Library of Congress*

tective against unbridled power than due process of law in the trial and punishment of men, that is, of all men, whether citizens, aliens, alien enemies or enemy belligerents. It can become too late.

Rutledge died September 10, 1949, following a massive stroke. Only fifty-five years old, he had served but six years on the Court and was at the height of his powers. Rutledge left the Court and the nation a dual and abiding legacy. There is his constitutional jurisprudence, embodied in his opinions and other writings. And, infusing that jurisprudence, there is a latter-day Lincolnian dedication to democratic principles rooted in America's heartland.

Rutledge was a modest man who had a simple and straightforward civic faith. At the memorial services honoring the justice, his fellow dean-turned-judge, Charles E. Clark of Yale and the Second Circuit, spoke of Rutledge's "greatness as a judge and his nobility as a human being." Clark added:

I regard him as one of the most consistent exemplifiers of a way of life, of a belief in morality and character, of any of the Justices who have ever served upon the court. That is certainly high tribute; I make it deliberately because I think it not only amply deserved, but one which history will freely yield.

Harold H. Burton

1945-1958

HAROLD HITZ BURTON was born in Jamaica Plain, Massachusetts, June 22, 1888. His father, Alfred Burton, had family roots in Maine and served as the dean of faculty at the Massachusetts Institute of Technology for twenty years. His mother, Gertrude Hitz Burton, was the granddaughter of the first Swiss consul general to the United States.

Burton spent his early childhood in Switzerland with his mother because of her ill health. As a result, he was fluent in French as well as English and developed a life-long interest in Switzerland. His mother died when he was seven, and Burton returned to the United States to live with his father. Alfred Burton raised him with the traditional Republican and Unitarian values that his family had long held.

Following in his father's footsteps, Burton enrolled in Maine's Bowdoin College. Active in sports, he was a pole-vaulter for the track team and the quarterback of the football team. He also won a college mathematics prize and was elected to Phi Beta Kappa. After gradua-

416

tion in 1909 he made the pilgrimage to Cambridge, Massachusetts, with some of his classmates to enter Harvard Law School. Burton received his LL.B. in 1912 and married Selma Florence Smith in June of the same year. They had a happy marriage and were the parents of two sons and two daughters.

In the belief that distancing himself from the East Coast would provide greater opportunities to practice law, Burton and his wife settled in Cleveland, Ohio. Two years later, that same belief sent them farther west, to Idaho and Utah, where Burton worked as legal counsel for a series of public utilities. The First World War temporarily halted Burton's legal career; he enlisted in the 361st Infantry, United States Army. He achieved the rank of captain and was awarded the Purple Heart and the Belgian Croix de Guerre.

After the war the Burtons returned to Cleveland, where the future justice established a private practice.

He also taught corporate law at nearby Western Reserve University Law School. Burton quickly became involved in community activities, serving as president of the First Unitarian Church of Cleveland. He was active in veterans' affairs through the American Legion. His interest in politics also became apparent during this time.

Generally, Burton's approach to politics was middle of the road, and he received the support of members of both parties. During the Great Depression, this bipartisan support became especially important for relief efforts to succeed. In 1928 he was elected to one term as a Republican in the Ohio legislature. He also served as the city's director of law from 1929 to 1932. When Cleveland abolished its hired city manager system and moved to an elected mayoralty in 1931, Burton served as acting mayor for several months. In 1935 Burton was elected mayor on a reform platform, promising to run

Harold H. Burton poses in the Supreme Court building with his son, Lt. Robert S. Burton; daughter, Mrs. Charles Weidmer; grandson, "Skippy" Weidmer; and wife, Selma Smith Burton, shortly after being sworn in as associate justice in 1945. *Source: Library of Congress*

gangsters out of the city. He supported New Deal relief efforts in spite of their origin in the Democratic party of President Franklin D. Roosevelt. The "Boy Scout Mayor" was reelected twice by the largest majorities in the city's history. The success of his political career took its toll on his family, however; Burton was so busy with his duties as mayor that his children would make appointments with his office to see him.

In 1940 he was elected to the U.S. Senate and took the oath of office with a former college roommate, Ralph Owen Brewster, a Republican from Maine. Burton became involved in the war effort, serving on the Senate Committee on the Conduct of the War, known as the Truman Committee, which investigated fraudulent claims against the government. He also served as one of four sponsors of the Ball-Burton-Hill-Hatch resolution (known as B²H²), which provided for U.S. participation in a postwar international peace group. His work on the resolution in spite of isolationist sentiment laid the ground work for the United States to join the United Nations after the war.

His close association with Harry S. Truman on the committee would serve him well after Truman became president. On July 31, 1945, Justice Owen Roberts resigned, and Truman had his first Supreme Court vacancy to fill. Truman, a Democrat, selected Burton for a number of reasons. Their close working association was a factor, as was the lack of any Republican associate justices on the Court. By appointing a Republican, Truman hoped he would improve relations with Republican leaders in Congress. Chief Justice Harlan F. Stone gave his advance approval of Burton, believing his legislative experience would be helpful in establishing legislative intent in many cases. Truman also expected that the Democratic governor of Ohio, Frank Lausche, would appoint a Democrat to the Senate to replace Burton.

Also under consideration for the vacant seat was Florence E. Allen of Ohio, the first woman to be seriously considered for a seat on the Court. Allen was the first woman to serve as a judge on a state supreme court. Burton was nominated September 19, 1945, and confirmed by a voice vote the same day, becoming the first Republican appointed an associate justice by a Democratic president. Burton would later describe his transition from the Senate to the Court as going from "a circus to a monastery."

Clevelanders held the new justice in high regard. One friend, Dilworth Lupton, said of him: "He will bring to the office a sportsmanship that will win him the respect of both adherents and opponents; a plodding intellectual penetration that will search out the heart of great issues; a faculty for creative listening that is a prime requisite of a judicial mind; and a sense of quiet humor that marks a matured man. And he will bring to the office a spirit of dedication to external principles—a dedication that few men possess."

In his thirteen years on the Court, Burton wrote ninety-six majority, fifty dissenting, and fifteen concurring opinions. His writing was direct, simple, and unremarkable in style. He wanted his opinions to be quickly and clearly understood. As expected, he relied heavily on legislative history, and his thoroughness required a tremendous amount of research by the justice and his clerks. His voting pattern was generally more conservative than not, and he often sided with Chief Justice Fred Vinson. After Earl Warren was appointed chief justice, Burton became more aligned with Stanley Reed, Sherman Minton, and John Marshall Harlan. One of his major contributions on the Court was keeping tensions among the justices, particularly on the Vinson Court, to a minimum. His interest in maintaining order helped to reduce strife.

Justice Burton supported the government in anticommunist cases. In *Beilan v. Board of Public Education* (1958) he was part of a 5–4 majority that upheld the validity of a Pennsylvania law allowing the school board to dismiss employees who could not prove they were unaware of the subversive nature of organizations of which they were members. Among these employees was a Philadelphia teacher who refused to answer questions from his superintendent about membership in a communist political association. Burton saw the law as reasonable since the teacher's refusal brought his "fitness to serve as a public school teacher" into question.

He went along with the Court in questions of race relations on a narrow free-flow-of-commerce argument rather than personal beliefs. In *Henderson v. United States* (1950) he concluded that all people are to be treated without discrimination on racial or other grounds in the operation of a carrier, in this case a train, regulated by federal statutes. He supported the overturning of the "separate but equal" doctrine in the landmark case of *Brown v. Board of Education* (1954).

Burton and another Truman appointee, Tom Clark, angered the president in 1952 with their votes in the *Steel Seizure Case.* The Court ruled that Truman did not have the authority to seize the nation's steel mills in the face of a threatened strike. In spite of this disagreement, Burton and Truman maintained a close friendship. Burton also established close ties to President Dwight D. Eisenhower and advised him on lower court appointments and on selecting his own successor, Potter Stewart.

Burton dissented in *Toolson v. New York Yankees* (1953), a case in which the Court reaffirmed the antitrust exemption that major league baseball enjoyed. Burton believed that baseball was a big business and should be treated as such, subject to the same antitrust laws as other businesses. He was not antibaseball. He was a Cleveland Indians fan and, while serving as mayor, he would practice in advance of opening day to ensure that his opening pitch was up to par. He believed in the Indians enough to bet a dime on their World Series chances.

Although Burton generally sided with the states in criminal cases, in one important case he came down

Although a baseball fan, Harold H. Burton dissented in *Toolson v. New York Yankees* (1953), which exempted major league baseball from the antitrust rules applied to other big businesses. In 1953 the Yankees had another cause to celebrate: Mickey Mantle's grand slam home run during the World Series. *Source: National Baseball Library, Cooperstown, N.Y.*

against them. Louisiana had tried to electrocute Willie Francis, but the chair malfunctioned and he survived. The Court ruled that it was neither double jeopardy nor cruel and unusual punishment to try to execute him again. Burton angrily dissented, pointing out that repeated attempts to electrocute a prisoner would be considered cruel if the failures were intentional. Why, he asked, should there be a distinction for unintentional failures?

In labor cases Burton tended to uphold the rights of states to limit the picketing activities of unions. In a 1950 case, *International Brotherhood of Teamsters v. Hanke,* Burton joined Justice Felix Frankfurter's opin-

Seventeen-year-old Willie Francis reads his prayer book in his Louisiana jail cell after surviving an electric chair malfunction at his execution in 1946. Harold H. Burton dissented from the Supreme Court's ruling that it would be neither double jeopardy nor cruel and unusual punishment to try to execute him again.
Source: Bettmann

ion that the picketing by teamsters of an independent business to force the owner to join the union interfered with the rights of the community. Picketing, they reasoned, was not protected as freedom of expression. In *Local Plumbers Union No. 10 v. Graham* (1953), Burton and six others held that the state of Virginia could en-

join the picketing of a non-union labor site on the grounds that the picketing infringed on Virginia's right-to-work laws.

In addition to his judicial duties, Burton wrote a number of articles on Court history, Chief Justice John Marshall, and the Supreme Court building. His respect for the Court was so great that he never entered the building without first removing his hat. Burton especially enjoyed giving tours of the Supreme Court, including one for Edward R. Murrow's "Person to Person" television show with his wife, Selma, at his side.

Chief Justice William Rehnquist, then law clerk to Justice Robert Jackson, likened Burton to a "supremely cultured English butler one might see in a movie." His primary pleasures were bird watching, daily exercise, his work on the Court, and his research into its history. Although the media portrayed him as an inveterate party-goer, Burton preferred the quiet stay-at-home life and went to parties because his wife liked them.

He resigned October 13, 1958. Suffering from Parkinson's disease, he took his doctor's advice that the strain of the Court's workload could be making him worse. His colleagues on the bench wrote in appreciation of his service that he "has regarded his position on the court as a trusteeship, and has dedicated himself to it wholly and without stint." Justice Frankfurter wrote to him, "No member of the Supreme Court deserves admiration more than you for exercising with exquisite and unqualified fidelity the judicial powers entrusted to the members of the Court."

After his retirement he was able to continue working for a while. He helped the District of Columbia Court of Appeals with its caseload until the Parkinson's finally progressed too far. Burton died in Washington, D.C., October 28, 1964.

Fred M. Vinson

1946-1953

Source: Photo by Bachrach, Collection of the Supreme Court of the United States

FREDERICK MOORE VINSON, the second son of James Vinson and Virginia Ferguson Vinson, was born January 22, 1890, in the small town of Louisa, Kentucky. In later years he delighted in recounting that he "had been born in jail," neglecting to explain that his father was the town and county jailer and that his birth had taken place in the jailer's comfortable quarters and not in a cell block. Of Anglo-Saxon origin, his paternal great-grandfather had first arrived on the Appalachian frontier around 1800.

As a youngster Fred Vinson did not have an attractive appearance: he was thin, gawky, asthmatic, with pipe stem legs, and features badly scarred by acne. In later years he filled out to stand over six feet tall and developed the sagging jowls and sad eyes under a high brow that identified him throughout his public career.

His deep intellectual strength became apparent at an early age, but it also led to arrogance and made him a difficult child and a trying student to his teachers. He graduated from his hometown's Kentucky Normal College at the top of his class in 1908. In those days the so-called "normal" schools operated at the high school-junior college level, and their main output was teachers for one-room country schools. However, aware of Vinson's intellectual promise, his Kentucky Normal professors arranged for his admission to Centre College in Danville, Kentucky, as a probationary member of its senior class.

His parents were moderately wealthy for the times and could have supported him at college, but Vinson insisted on doing it on his own. He borrowed $750 on a cosigned note from his cousin's bank to partially finance his education. Academic scholarships and part-time work enabled him to complete three years at Centre, including two years in the Centre Law School. After receiving his A.B. degree in 1909, Vinson set an academic record at the law school with a ninety-eight average. "Vins," as he was known to his classmates, was credited with the ability to memorize textbooks and quote them back from page number references. He could also add columns of six-digit numbers in his head with unfailing accuracy. In college he began to cultivate the fiction—so useful during his political campaigns—that he was a "poor struggling boy from the hills," despite the comfortable affluence of his childhood.

Vinson had a great love for baseball and continued to play it even after he was elected to Congress. At Centre, he led the Praying Colonels to three successful seasons while also playing some semiprofessional games. He seriously considered a career in baseball on graduation from law school and tried out for the majors. Failure to gain a place with the Cincinnati Reds convinced him of the correctness of his family's wishes that he seek his fortune in the law.

Barely twenty-one years old when he graduated from law school in 1911, Vinson returned to Louisa to pass the bar exam and enter practice with an older partner. He practiced law for seventeen years, but neither his firm nor his sideline business ventures in banking,

milling, and grocery enterprises were ever big money-makers. In 1923 he married Roberta Dixson of Louisa, and they had two sons. Fred, Jr., followed in his father's footsteps and became a federal government attorney, and James Robert became a businessman in eastern Kentucky.

Instead of rushing to arms during World War I, Vinson waited for the draft board in Louisa to call him. He never saw overseas duty or combat and was in officer training school at Camp Pike, Arkansas, when the war ended. On demobilization and return to Louisa, he reopened his law practice and became active in local veteran activities, which later provided him an excellent avenue into politics.

Vinson won his first elective political office, the minor post of commonwealth attorney for the Thirty-second Judicial District of Kentucky, in 1921. Three years later he was elected as a Democrat to the U.S. House of Representatives to fill an unexpired term and, with only a one-term interruption, remained there until his resignation in 1938. Vinson served on the Pensions, Flood Control, Public Lands, Military Affairs, and Appropriations committees. Ultimately, he was assigned to the powerful Ways and Means Committee, which is responsible for writing tax legislation. Here he developed the mastery of government finance that was to earn him renown.

His first five years in Congress were not distinguished for their legislative output. Finally, after outgrowing the comic role of country bumpkin, Vinson had eight years that were quietly spectacular. During this period he made the transition from county courthouse politician to national statesman. Defeated in the 1928 Republican landslide, he spent the next two years in Ashland, Kentucky, nominally practicing law but actually perfecting the political organization that maintained him in Congress for the next eight years and continued to do his bidding long afterwards. His congressional colleagues joked that taxes on tobacco and domestic oil were the only taxes that Fred Vinson ever voted against: both were important to his constituency.

Vinson's basic conservatism endeared him to the leadership of the southern Democrats, but his open admiration of President Franklin D. Roosevelt made him welcome in the ranks of the New Deal. Although he differed with the president on treatment of America's war veterans and helped override a presidential veto of a bonus payment to World War I veterans, in all other matters, he faithfully followed the White House. Vinson figured prominently in establishing the New Deal Agricultural Adjustment Act and the Social Security system, and he was also active in coal and revenue matters. His main work, however, was with the Ways and Means Committee. The reforms Vinson helped force into the American tax structure were long overdue and have endured.

In 1937 Roosevelt rewarded Vinson for faithful service by appointing him a judge on the U.S. District Court of Appeals for the District of Columbia. From the beginning Vinson's decisions demonstrated his faith in the ability of the American people to guide their national destiny and a strong belief in the necessity of a powerful executive to cope with the problems of a great world power, especially in time of war. He always sought to learn the "intent of Congress" by studying the hearings and floor debates that produced legislation pertinent to the litigation before him. His decisions generally favored the government and took a less sympathetic view of the individual. His personal knowledge of much that had transpired in Congress and his phenomenal memory produced decisions that were usually upheld on appeal to the Supreme Court.

In March 1942 Chief Justice Harlan F. Stone designated Vinson for extra duty as chief judge of the U.S. Emergency Court of Appeals, which had been created to cope with a backlog of war-related cases. Vinson served on both courts until his resignation in May 1943 to become Roosevelt's director of the Office of Eco-

As director of President Roosevelt's Office of Economic Stabilization from 1943 to 1945, Fred Vinson pursued a policy of wage controls unpopular with many members of Congress. *Source: Library of Congress*

nomic Stabilization—his first post in the executive branch. As director he was responsible for controlling inflation in the booming war economy. Vinson's success made him an effective but unpopular member of the Roosevelt administration. His knowledge of tax matters and his ties with Congress made him highly qualified for the post, as well as for the other executive branch positions that soon followed.

Vinson became administrator of the Federal Loan Agency in March 1945 and a month later was promoted to be director of the Office of War Mobilization and Reconversion. The job had been held by James F. Byrnes, a former member of Congress and former Supreme Court justice. When Harry S. Truman became president upon Roosevelt's death in 1945, he realized he would need experienced advisers. Vinson's skills as fiscal manager, political organizer, and congressional liaison for Roosevelt made him even more valuable to his friend Truman, who appointed him secretary of the Treasury July 23, 1945. At Treasury, Vinson administered the last of the war bond drives, firmly fixed U.S. primacy in international finance, and recommended the Revenue Act of 1945 to raise taxes.

Long before Chief Justice Stone's death in 1946, the Supreme Court was suffering deep philosophical divisions and was split on many issues. Hoping that Vinson might provide the leadership to unite and redefine the Court's role in the federal government, Truman appointed him chief justice June 6, 1946. The appointment was confirmed by voice vote two weeks later. Truman recognized in his friend and adviser an unabashed belief in strong government by the executive and a more deferential role for the judiciary.

As chief justice, Vinson generally supported presidential authority in controversial decisions involving labor issues and the national security measures Truman implemented because of the threat of world communism. Vinson wrote the Court's opinion in *Dennis v. United States* (1951) upholding the conviction of eleven leaders of the U.S. Communist party, thereby finding constitutional an act of Congress that made it illegal to belong

to a subversive organization. He was often forced, however, to vote with the minority. Most notably, Vinson dissented in *Youngstown Sheet & Tube Co. v. Sawyer* (1952), in which the Court struck down a presidential order to seize private steel mills to avoid a strike and the disruption of steel production during the Korean War. Unlike the majority, Vinson found that the president had not overreached the limits of his constitutional powers.

Vinson served only seven years on the Court, half the average length of a chief justice's tenure. During that time tensions on the Court relaxed, but this change was due more to the Court's new personnel than to Vinson's leadership. He cut back the justices' workload by accepting jurisdiction only in cases of clear national importance, despite the loud outcries of indignation that followed. He also reduced the chief justice's personal burdens by increasing his law clerks to three. At best, he achieved only modest success in uniting the impossibly divided Court.

On race relations and civil rights, however, his suc-

Eleven leaders of the American Communist party were arrested and jailed in 1951 after Congress passed the Smith Act, which made it illegal to belong to a subversive organization. In *Dennis v. United States* (1951) Chief Justice Fred Vinson upheld the act by reason that the threat of communism justified a restriction on the rights of free expression. *Source: Library of Congress*

J. D and Ethel Lee Shelley and their children in their St. Louis home. Chief Justice Fred Vinson wrote the Court's unanimous opinion that the state of Missouri could not enforce a restrictive covenant, an agreement among home owners that they would not sell or rent to a non-Caucasian. *Source: George Harris*

cess was measurable. He wrote the Court's unanimous opinions in *Shelley v. Kraemer* (1948), which stated that racially restrictive covenants are unenforceable; *McLaurin v. Oklahoma State Regents* (1950), which ruled that once admitted to a state university blacks may use all the facilities; and *Sweatt v. Painter* (1950), which held that a state may not deny a black admission to law school even if there is a "black" law school available. These decisions did not go so far as to overturn the separate-but-equal doctrine of *Plessy v. Ferguson* (1896), but set the stage for the Court to do so in 1954.

President Truman thought so highly of Vinson that he hoped he would succeed him in office. The Democratic party was badly split during the Truman years, and the president thought that Vinson might unite the party to retain the White House in 1952. His rise in the federal power structure was steady and showed many signs of culminating in the presidency. Vinson, however, had no presidential ambitions.

He died of a heart attack September 8, 1953, in his Washington hotel apartment. When probated, his estate showed net assets including insurance of less than $1,000. He had no source of income except his public office salary throughout his national career. No survivor benefit pensions were provided for wives of Supreme Court members at the time, and his death left Roberta Vinson impoverished. Only through the dedicated efforts of some friends was a modest pension of $5,000 a year created for her. Although Vinson's decisions routinely affected the fate of billions of dollars, his service to the nation had been totally without thought of personal gain. Vinson remains the only member of the Supreme Court ever to have served in all three branches of government prior to his appointment.

Tom C. Clark

1949–1967

THOMAS CAMPBELL CLARK was born September 23, 1899, in Dallas, Texas, the seventh of ten children. He later came to prefer the less formal "Tom C. Clark" over his given name and used that form throughout his life. His parents, William Clark and Virginia Falls Clark, had moved to Texas from Mississippi; both were from distinguished southern families. A well-respected lawyer in Dallas, William Clark was the youngest man, up to that time,

to have been elected president of the Texas Bar Association.

Young Tom was educated in local public schools, where he excelled at debating and received an award for oratory in his senior year. After graduating from high school in 1917, he attended Virginia Military Institute in Lexington, Virginia. Financial difficulties forced him home after a year, and he decided to join the World War I effort. Because he was underweight, he could not enlist in the regular army, but instead joined the national guard and became a top sergeant.

A few months later the war was over, and Clark returned to college—this time enrolling at the University of Texas in Austin. He received his A.B. in 1921 and his LL.B. the following year. While at the university he met his future wife, Mary Ramsey, a fellow student. Her father, William Ramsey, was a banker who had been a judge on the Court of Criminal Appeals and on the Texas Supreme Court. The two were married on November 8, 1924, and had three children: Thomas Campbell, Jr., William Ramsey, and Mildred, who was called "Mimi." Tom, Jr., born in 1925, died at the age of six from meningitis.

Upon graduation Clark began practicing law with his father and brother in their Dallas law firm. William Clark's strong connections to the Democratic party in Texas helped his son develop good relationships with many of the party's leaders. After five years, Tom Clark left the firm to serve as assistant district attorney for Dallas County, handling civil litigation. He made several thousand dollars each year for the county by recovering delinquent taxes and performed other tasks such as advising the court, defending actions against county officers, and handling condemnation proceedings for road construction. He never lost a case as assistant district attorney.

Clark became close friends with District Attorney William McCraw, and the two opened up a private law practice in 1932. When McCraw left the firm to run for attorney general of Texas two years later, Clark served as campaign manager in his successful race.

Clark left a prosperous and growing private practice in 1937 when Sen. Tom Connally invited him to come to Washington to work for the Justice Department. He was made a special assistant in the War Risk Insurance Office, scheduling for trial some 3,000 backlogged claims by servicemen demanding compensation for war-related injuries. A year later he transferred to the Antitrust Division and was sent to New Orleans for six months. Louisiana was awash in federal investigations and indictments connected with the late Huey Long's terms as a U.S. senator and governor. Clark was responsible for cases involving antitrust violations by the building and lumber industries.

In 1940 Clark was appointed head of the Antitrust Division's offices on the West Coast. He and his family were living in Beverly Hills, California, when the Japanese bombed Pearl Harbor. One month later, Attorney General Francis Biddle appointed Clark civilian coordinator of alien enemy control for the Western Defense Command. When the government decided to remove all people of Japanese ancestry from strategic areas on the West Coast, Clark was assigned to supervise the evacuation of Japanese-American citizens to relocation camps. Although at the time he believed that the evacuation was necessary for security reasons, Clark later described his involvement as "the biggest mistake of my life."

Back in Washington in 1942, Clark's life was profoundly affected by close contact with a junior senator from Missouri, Harry S. Truman. At that time Truman chaired the Senate War Investigating Committee, and Clark's new assignment was to investigate people or businesses trying to defraud the government during the war. When he found a record unclear or needed further investigation, Clark would ask Truman for help. The following year Clark was promoted to assistant attorney general for the Antitrust Division, and in 1944 he became head of the Criminal Division.

Clark supported Truman in his successful 1944 bid for the Democratic nomination for vice president. When Franklin D. Roosevelt died in 1945 and Truman became president, he asked Clark to be his attorney general. Clark was an active attorney general, exercising his full powers and personally arguing several cases before the Supreme Court. During his four-year tenure, Clark initiated programs reflecting his personal concerns. He continued to be a strong advocate for antitrust laws, and he began a campaign against juvenile delinquency. To promote knowledge of American history, he organized the Freedom Train, which traveled around the country carrying the nation's major historic documents.

Clark served as attorney general during the early years of the cold war when national security and communist subversion were major concerns. As such, he was vigorous in investigating and prosecuting American communist leaders and other alleged subversives. Clark persuaded Truman to appoint a presidential commission to investigate employee loyalty in 1947, and he urged the president to deport aliens who adhered to foreign governments or their principles. While in

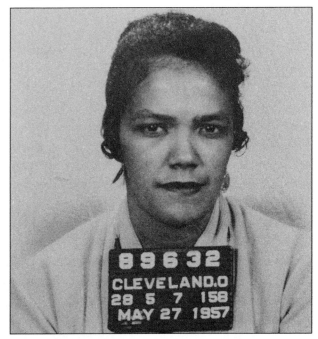

When the police searched for a fugitive in Dollree Mapp's home without a warrant, they found obscene materials and arrested her. In *Mapp v. Ohio* (1961) the Supreme Court reversed her conviction, ruling that evidence obtained through an unconstitutional search could not be admitted in court. *Source:* The Plain Dealer, *Cleveland, Ohio*

charge of the Justice Department's Criminal Division, Clark had worked closely with FBI director J. Edgar Hoover, and, as attorney general, he supported expanding the investigatory power of the FBI to give it greater wiretapping powers. Clark testified before the House Un-American Activities Committee (HUAC) on the difficulties of drafting anticommunist legislation and thought a good start would be to force organizations to label themselves and their propaganda as communist. The practice of publishing an attorney general's list of subversive political organizations began under his administration.

Clark became disillusioned with HUAC's tactics, and in the 1948 presidential campaign he and Truman accused the committee of irresponsibly trying to inflate the communist danger for political purposes. During that same campaign, Truman found it necessary to point to the Justice Department's zealous internal security program to show that his administration had not been "soft on communism" as conservatives had accused.

On August 2, 1949, President Truman again rewarded his friend, this time by naming him to fill the seat on the Supreme Court vacated by the death of Frank Murphy. Clark's nomination ran into minor opposition by labor, civil rights, and civil liberties groups, as well as those who thought Murphy, who had been the only Roman Catholic on the bench, should be replaced by another Catholic, instead of Clark, a Presbyterian. With backing by the American Bar Association and Texas senators Connally and Lyndon B. Johnson, Clark was confirmed August 18 by a Senate vote of 73–8.

Truman expected Clark's voting record on the high court to be similar to that of Chief Justice Fred Vinson, and his appointment was seen as a way of strengthening Vinson's power on the Court. At first Clark voted consistently with Vinson and issued almost as few dissents as the chief justice. In 1952 he showed surprising independence, however, by voting with the majority, against

As the civil rights movement gained strength, demonstrators demanding service at whites-only lunch counters were not only arrested and convicted but also ill-treated by private citizens, as in this 1963 incident in Jackson, Mississippi. Justice Tom C. Clark's opinion in *Hamm v. Rock Hill* (1964) made it possible to overturn the convictions of those arrested for sitting in before passage of the Civil Rights Act of 1964. *Source: AP/Wide World Photos*

the chief justice (and the president), in ruling that Truman's seizure of private steel mines during the Korean War was unconstitutional. Three years after Earl Warren became chief justice in 1953, Clark began to dissent more frequently, particularly in decisions on civil liberties cases that sustained individual freedoms against the power of government. His dissents often reflected his experiences on national security and loyalty issues as attorney general.

In the 1960s the number of national security cases subsided, and Clark adopted a more moderate position on the Court. In 1961 he wrote the opinion in *Mapp v. Ohio,* a major criminal justice case. It involved state officials using illegally seized evidence to convict an individual of possessing obscene materials. Clark, writing for the Court, reversed the conviction and held that states were bound by the exclusionary rule, meaning they cannot use illegally seized evidence in the courtroom. He felt it meaningless to give people the right to be free from unreasonable searches and seizures and

then use illegal evidence to convict. If the government is a lawbreaker, the public will become likewise, he reasoned.

He wrote the majority opinion in an important church-state case in 1963, *School District of Abington v. Schempp.* His ruling overturned a state law that required a Bible reading at the start of each day in the public schools. He called the practice a devotional exercise and therefore a violation of the separation of church and state. Two years later, in *United States v. Seeger,* he held that to be classified as a conscientious objector and be exempted from the draft, an individual did not have to believe in God in the traditional sense as long as he demonstrated a sincere belief that paralleled the belief others had in God.

Clark consistently supported the Court's decisions to improve the legal standing of blacks. In the 1964 companion cases of *Heart of Atlanta Motel v. United States* and *Katzenbach v. McClung,* he upheld the 1964 Civil Rights Act, which outlawed segregation in hotels, mo-

Ramsey Clark being sworn in as attorney general by his father, Tom C. Clark, in 1967. Justice Clark resigned his seat on the Supreme Court to avoid having to rule on cases his son prosecuted for the government. *Source: National Archives*

tels, and restaurants involved in interstate commerce. In these particular cases he found both a motel and a restaurant to be significantly connected to interstate commerce so as to warrant coming under federal law. That same year Clark held in *Hamm v. Rock Hill* that the Civil Rights Act implied that persons who had tried to integrate lunch counters by "sitting in" and asking for service would have been doing nothing illegal if the law had been in effect at that time. Therefore, he argued, there was no reason to prosecute those who had been arrested at earlier sit-ins, and all those prosecutions had to stop. Thousands of convictions were overturned as a result of Clark's ruling.

When he decided to leave the high court at age sixty-seven, Clark did so because his son Ramsey had been nominated to be attorney general in February 1967. Because many of the Court's cases came from the Justice Department, Clark would have had to vote on his son's cases. Justice Clark resigned his seat on June 12, 1967, to avoid even the appearance of a conflict of interest.

Still energetic and active, Clark accepted invitations to sit on federal courts in all the judicial circuits in the country, to help with their overburdened caseloads. He

had become actively involved in the reform of judicial administration while still on the Supreme Court and had helped found the National Judicial College, established to train new judges and provide continuing education for federal judges throughout the nation.

A likable, friendly man with silver hair, a slender frame, and a trademark bow tie, Clark traveled around the country speaking to judges and members of the bar about how to improve judicial administration. He was instrumental in urging that Congress fund the Federal Judicial Center, which was created in 1967 to explore ways to improve and modernize the administration of the federal court system. He served as its first director until 1970. When the Supreme Court Historical Society was organized in 1974, Clark became the first chairman of the board of trustees.

Clark died in his sleep from heart failure on June 13, 1977, in New York City, while there to help with the workload of the Court of Appeals for the Second Circuit. There was an outpouring of grief for the man who had done so much to improve the administration of justice.

Sherman Minton
1949-1956

Source: *Photo by Harris & Ewing, Collection of the Supreme Court of the United States*

SHERMAN MINTON was born October 20, 1890, on a farm near Georgetown, Indiana, in the southern part of the state. About eight miles away was New Albany, which he was to call home much of his life. His father, John Evans Minton, was a marginal farmer who sometimes worked as a laborer on the Air Line Railroad. His mother, Emma Lyvers Minton, died from cancer when Sherman was only nine years old.

Young "Shay" held jobs from the age of eight and saved his wages until he could enroll at Indiana University. In college he excelled at sports, particularly football and baseball, and was in a class that included future Republican presidential candidate Wendell L. Willkie and future Democratic governor Paul V. McNutt. He continued his education at Indiana School of Law, where he graduated summa cum laude in 1915, ranking first in his class.

He then received a scholarship that made it possible for him to attend the Yale Law School, where he received a Master of Laws in 1916. At Yale he confronted one of his teachers, former president William Howard Taft, in a classroom exchange. When Minton told Taft the Supreme Court was wrong to have decided a certain case the way it had, Taft replied, "I am afraid, Mr. Minton, that if you don't like the way the law is interpreted, you will have to get on the Supreme Court and change it." Years later Minton regretted his instruction under Taft; he told Justice Felix Frankfurter that Taft held to the "bird dog" school, which meant one should "first find what the Court has said and stick to it." "I think my training and practice were too much in that school," Minton concluded. "I did believe a great deal in stability, which was a fetish with Taft."

A much happier circumstance was his marriage to

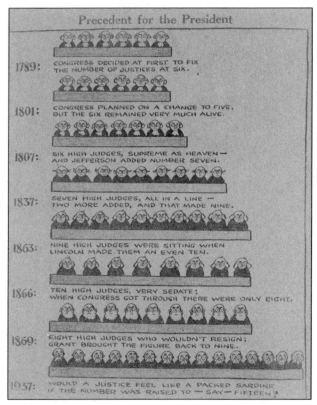

Precedent for the President

1789: CONGRESS DECIDED AT FIRST TO FIX THE NUMBER OF JUSTICES AT SIX.

1801: CONGRESS PLANNED ON A CHANGE TO FIVE, BUT THE SIX REMAINED VERY MUCH ALIVE.

1807: SIX HIGH JUDGES, SUPREME AS HEAVEN — AND JEFFERSON ADDED NUMBER SEVEN.

1837: SEVEN HIGH JUDGES, ALL IN A LINE — TWO MORE ADDED, AND THAT MADE NINE.

1863: NINE HIGH JUDGES WERE SITTING WHEN LINCOLN MADE THEM AN EVEN TEN.

1866: TEN HIGH JUDGES, VERY SEDATE; WHEN CONGRESS GOT THROUGH THERE WERE ONLY EIGHT.

1869: EIGHT HIGH JUDGES WHO WOULDN'T RESIGN; GRANT BROUGHT THE FIGURE BACK TO NINE.

1937: WOULD A JUSTICE FEEL LIKE A PACKED SARDINE IF THE NUMBER WAS RAISED TO — SAY — FIFTEEN?

This famous Herblock cartoon lampoons President Franklin D. Roosevelt's proposal to enlarge the Supreme Court's membership to offset the anti-New Deal majority. Sen. Sherman Minton of Indiana backed the president's plan, earning his gratitude and, eventually, a White House job. *A copyright 1937 cartoon by Herblock*

Gertrude Gurtz on August 11, 1917. They had two sons, Sherman and John, and a daughter, Mary Anne. The year they married, the United States entered World War I, and Minton became an army captain. While stationed in Paris, he took the opportunity to enroll at the Sorbonne, where he studied international law, Roman law, and jurisprudence.

Back in Indiana after the war, Minton ran unsuccessfully for Congress in 1920 and 1930. His political fortunes changed when Paul McNutt was elected governor in 1932. McNutt appointed him a public counselor of the Public Service Commission in 1933. Utility rates went down, which helped Minton run a successful Senate campaign the following year. In the midst of the Great Depression, he ran as a populist, with the slogan "You can't offer a hungry man the Constitution!" In the Senate, Minton was an enthusiastic New Dealer. He became the assistant Democratic whip and forged friendships with the other freshman senators, particularly Harry S. Truman.

Frustrated at having his New Deal legislation negated by the Supreme Court, in 1937 President Franklin D. Roosevelt attempted to change its personnel by increasing the number of justices. Senator Minton strongly supported this "Court-packing" plan. He even introduced legislation designed to make it more difficult for the Court to invalidate government legislation. His proposal would have required seven votes before legislation could be declared unconstitutional. Minton's backing of all aspects of President Roosevelt's program did not go unnoticed in the White House. There is strong reason to believe Minton was considered for a seat on the Court in 1937, but his associate, Sen. Hugo L. Black of Alabama, was chosen instead.

Minton campaigned for reelection in 1940 on the New Deal record and on his support of the politically popular Alien Registration Act banning subversive activity. But he also favored military preparedness and the draft, which was not popular in Indiana. His major obstacle was Willkie's presidential candidacy; Minton could not overcome the Republican's home state popularity and the strength of his party, and he lost the election. This defeat closed the period of his public life that he enjoyed the most. Years later when he reflected on his Senate experience, he said, "We were in a revolution, and I was close to the throne."

Roosevelt asked Minton to work in the White House in 1941, a position he soon found uncomfortable because their personal relationship was not close. Nonetheless, as the adviser in charge of coordinating military agencies, Minton mobilized White House support for Senator Truman's resolution to investigate defense activities, which made possible the Truman Defense Committee and provided Truman a degree of national visibility he had previously lacked. Minton mentioned to Truman that "your old seat mate was batting for you when he was down at the White House." Years later, Minton liked to recount this incident to his law clerks and would tell them, "That's how Vice-Presidents are made." Then, after a pause, he would add, "And that's how Supreme Court Justices are made."

Later in 1941 Roosevelt appointed Minton to the Court of Appeals for the Seventh Circuit, where he stayed until his appointment to the Supreme Court in 1949. When Justice Wiley Rutledge died unexpectedly in September of that year, Truman, now president, did not hesitate. On the day of the memorial service, five days after Rutledge's death, the president called Minton in New Albany and offered his old friend the seat. Minton immediately accepted.

In an unusual move, Minton declined to appear before the Senate Judiciary Committee to testify, on the grounds that he was a sitting judge. His actual reason for not appearing was that he feared a heated confrontation over the question of his "judicial temperament." Because Minton had acquired a reputation as a strong partisan while a senator, Justice Frankfurter cautioned him against testifying. At the confirmation hear-

ings his temperament was explored at length, as were his policy preferences—he was viewed by everyone as a liberal—and his health. He had suffered a mild heart attack in 1945; also, since 1943 he had been treated for pernicious anemia (a vitamin deficiency that can result in fatigue, depression, confusion, memory loss, or heart palpitations). But he had sat regularly on the bench of the court of appeals during the preceding three years. The Senate confirmed him by a 48–16 vote on October 4, 1949.

Although some may have expected Minton to vote with the liberal bloc because of his voting record as a senator, his experience in the 1930s when the Supreme Court struck down New Deal legislation he had helped draft in Congress gave him a dim view of judicial activism. He thought the Court should be deferential toward decisions made by the executive and legislative branches, and his view of precedent meant that he was disinclined to stray from past Court decisions. Had he been on the Court in the 1930s, his antipathy toward an aggressive use of judicial power would have been consistent with the liberal views of the day, but by the time he got to the Court the pendulum had swung to the right.

In the 1950s Minton continued to believe the Court should refrain from overturning legislation, and he joined the other Truman appointees in a conservative coalition that supported the government's positions. If it came to a choice between upholding the power of the legislature and that of the executive, he favored the latter. This preference became apparent when he joined Chief Justice Fred Vinson's dissent in the *Steel Seizure Case* of 1952, in which a majority ruled unconstitutional President Truman's seizure of private steel mills during the Korean War.

During the high-profile national security cases of the cold war era, Minton was invariably on the government's side. He was disinclined to overturn legislation made by Congress, and litigants carried a heavy burden

Ellen Knauff, a German-born woman who married a U.S. soldier, celebrates her release from Ellis Island in 1951. She was detained there for nearly three years on suspicion that she had spied for Czechoslovakia. In a decision written by Sherman Minton, the Supreme Court had ruled in 1950 that the government had the right to deny due process to a nonresident alien. *Source: UPI/Bettmann*

when they argued before him. In *United States ex. rel. Knauff v. Shaughnessy* (1950), Minton wrote the opinion upholding an order to exclude the German-born wife of an American veteran. She had been declared an "undesirable alien" by the Department of Justice without a hearing, a denial of the right to due process accorded by the Fifth Amendment. The Court—following precedent—concluded that a nonresident alien is not entitled to due process.

Another result of the cold war was the widespread use of loyalty oaths that teachers and school administrators were expected to swear if they wanted to keep their jobs. In *Adler v. Board of Education* (1952) Minton wrote in support of New York's Feinberg Law, which made it grounds for discharge to belong to any organization designated subversive. His opinion upheld New York's use of loyalty oaths as a prerequisite for employment as a teacher; it also found an individual's associations to be relevant to the question of whether one was disloyal. In another case, involving the relationship between a state and the nation, *Pennsylvania v. Nelson* (1956), Minton agreed with Justice Stanley Reed's dissent that state antisubversion legislation was constitutional. The dissenters did not believe that antisubversion legislation on the national level had superseded it.

Minton usually resolved criminal procedure cases in favor of the government, as in the majority opinion he wrote in *United States v. Rabinowitz* (1950). He found that it was not a violation of the Fourth Amendment's prohibition against unreasonable searches and seizures for the police to conduct a warrantless search, in a lawful arrest, of the area within the suspect's control. Although he supported the power of the government to restrict individual civil liberties, he did not believe the government had the right to discriminate on the basis of race. Minton's was one of the four votes needed to bring the landmark school desegregation case of *Brown v. Board of Education* (1954) before the Court. From the beginning, he was in favor of reversing the "separate but equal" doctrine in race relations.

Inside the Court, Minton's folksy, gregarious ways made him popular with his colleagues. His unpretentious personal style was plain and earthy. Justice John Marshall Harlan called him "Rabelaisian," and Justice Tom Clark remarked on his tendency to be "naturally salty." He was one member of the Court who was welcome in everyone's office. However, as his health deteriorated during his later years on the Court (he continued to suffer from pernicious anemia) he began to appear forbidding to many of the law clerks. One described him as "somewhat emaciated, disdainfully using

In 1950 Sen. Joseph McCarthy of Wisconsin began a frenzied crusade against communism in America, charging that government agencies were riddled with subversives. Fear of Soviet spies caused several states to pass laws requiring loyalty oaths for their employees. Sherman Minton voted to uphold several antisubversive statutes. *Source: UPI/Bettmann*

a cane, almost arrogant." Following a luncheon with the Court's clerks, however, Minton reversed the initial impression by "charming them right out of their eye teeth."

Despite his formal education, which was more extensive than that of anyone else on the Court, he was not regarded as an intellectual. Nonetheless, as one of his clerks remarked, he was "smart and sharp." Minton did not anguish over the cases or over the writing of the opinions, which he saw as shorthand expressions for group decisions, not as opportunities for the expression of personal views. Because of his health, it was difficult for him to sit through long oral arguments, and he infrequently asked questions from the bench.

It was during oral argument that he first sensed a decline in his powers of concentration. Minton had always held the view that public officials have a tendency to hold on to their positions too long (he was even critical of President Roosevelt on this score) and he did not want that to happen to him. "But for my feeling of inadequacy and decrepitude and the embarrassment which comes from this deferential treatment accorded my 'senility' I would stay on," he wrote to Frankfurter. Consequently, he choose to retire on October 15, 1956, even though doing so gave a Republican president the opportunity to replace him. "There will be more interest in who will succeed me than in my passing," he told reporters that same day. "I'm an echo."

Minton returned to New Albany and lived another nine years. In retirement he converted to Catholicism, which was also his wife's religion. He told his daughter he wondered why he had not done so years earlier. He died April 9, 1965, at age seventy-five.

Earl Warren

1953-1969

EARL WARREN was born March 19, 1891, in Los Angeles. His parents, Methias and Chrystal Warren, were born in Scandinavia and brought as young children to America. Methias Warren worked for the Southern Pacific Railroad and moved his family to Bakersfield so that he could work in the railroad yards there. The family had very little money. His father once joked, "My boy, when you were born I was too poor to give you a middle name."

Warren lived in Bakersfield until 1908, when he went to Berkeley to attend the University of California. In 1912 he became one of the first students from his high school to receive a college diploma—thanks in large part to the encouragement and financial aid of his father. Although, in his own words, his "scholarship was fair but in no sense outstanding" in college, Warren went on to study at the University's newly opened law school. He obtained his degree in 1914 and worked briefly for an oil company and a law firm. In 1917 he enlisted in the Army hoping to fight overseas, but he was stationed instead in training camps in the United States.

Discharged a year later, Warren worked as a legislative and municipal aide and in 1920 became a deputy on the staff of the Alameda County district attorney. Five years later, he became district attorney and held that position until 1938. He developed a reputation as a tough, incorruptible prosecutor who enforced prohibition and corruption laws and crusaded against vice and violent crime. A 1931 survey declared that Warren was "the best district attorney in the United States."

Soon after he was appointed district attorney, Warren married Swedish-born Nina Palmquist Meyers, a widow with a small son. By 1935, when Warren was in his last term as Alameda district attorney, they had six attractive children, giving Warren what rival politicians used to term his "unbeatable family." The importance of Nina and the family to Warren and his career cannot be overstated. Justice Potter Stewart once remarked that if Chief Justice Warren looked at cases in terms of "those eternal, rather bromidic, platitudes," such as home, family, and country, it was only that they were "platitudes in which he sincerely believed." Warren's

home and family life provided the foundation for his scale of values throughout his professional life.

In 1938 Warren was elected attorney general of California, having secured the nominations of the Democratic and Progressive parties in addition to his own Republican party. Warren's tenure as attorney general was blemished by his role in securing the exclusion of those of Japanese ancestry from the West Coast after the invasion of Pearl Harbor. He later wrote that he deeply regretted his action, and he told Justice Arthur Goldberg, "In retrospect, that's one of the worst things I ever did."

Warren was elected governor in 1942. He reorganized the state government and secured major reform legislation—notably, measures for modernizing the state's hospital system, improving its prisons and its correctional system, creating an extensive highway program, and increasing old-age and unemployment benefits. Warren proved an able administrator and was the only governor of his state to be elected to three terms. In the 1946 gubernatorial election he won both the Democratic and Republican nominations, and in the 1950 election he defeated President Franklin D. Roosevelt's son James by an almost two-to-one margin.

Earl Warren's handsome family was not only a great asset in his political campaigns but also provided the foundation for his sense of values. This photograph, taken when Warren was attorney general of California, was used in his successful 1942 gubernatorial campaign. From the left, Robert, Nina (Honeybear), Dorothy, Earl, Jr., Virginia, James, and their parents.
Source: Bancroft Library, University of California at Berkeley

Linda Brown, at age nine in 1952, gained national prominence when her father charged that the segregated schools in Kansas were inherently discriminatory. The watershed decision in *Brown v. Board of Education* (1954) striking down school segregation was unanimous thanks to Chief Justice Earl Warren's efforts at persuading his colleagues to join in his opinion. *Source: AP/Wide World Photos*

Warren had started his career as an orthodox Republican. By the time he was governor, he was a leader of the party's progressive wing, both in the state and the nation. Indeed, according to his successor, Edmund G. Brown, "I as a Democrat and he as a Republican thought pretty much alike." Brown also called Warren "the best Governor that California ever had."

Warren was a serious contender for the presidency in 1948 and 1952. He failed to secure the nomination both times, although he was the Republican candidate for vice president in 1948. After he threw his support to Dwight D. Eisenhower's successful 1952 bid for the presidency, Warren was promised the first Supreme Court vacancy, which occurred when Chief Justice Fred Vinson died unexpectedly in September 1953. Warren

was confirmed by the Senate on March 1, 1954, although, as a recess appointment, he had joined the Court on opening day of the 1953 term.

Warren may not have been a profound legal scholar, but his leadership abilities and skill as a statesman made him one of the most effective chief justices in the Court's history. Justices who served with him stressed Warren's leadership abilities, particularly his skill in conducting their weekly conference to decide the cases. "It was incredible," said Justice William J. Brennan, Jr., just after Warren's retirement, "how efficiently the Chief would conduct the Friday conferences, leading the discussion of every case on the agenda, with a knowledge of each case at his fingertips."

At conference, Warren rarely contradicted the other justices and made sure that each of them had his full say. Most important, he stated the issues in a simple way, reaching the heart of the matter while stripping it of legal technicalities. As a newspaper noted, "Warren helped steer cases from the moment they were first discussed simply by the way he framed the issues."

In his first conference on the school desegregation case, *Brown v. Board of Education* (1954), Warren presented the question before the Court in terms of racial inferiority. He told the justices that segregation could be justified only by belief in the inherent inferiority of blacks and, if the cases upholding segregation were to be followed, it had to be upon that basis. Warren's simple words went straight to the ultimate human values involved. In the face of such an approach, arguments based on legal scholarship would have seemed inappropriate, almost trivial.

Brown was the Warren Court's most important decision and in many ways the watershed case of the century. When *Brown* struck down school segregation, it signaled the beginning of effective civil rights enforcement in American law. *Brown* also clearly illustrates Warren's leadership of his Court. When the justices first discussed the case under his predecessor, Chief Justice

Vinson, they were sharply divided. Under Warren, they ruled unanimously that school segregation was unconstitutional, a crucial show of solidarity necessary to persuade southern states to accept the decision. The unanimous decision was a direct result of Warren's considerable efforts.

In his discussion of the case, Vinson had stressed the legislature's failure to outlaw segregation. To Warren, that fact could scarcely justify the legal sanction of a immoral and unconstitutional practice. On the contrary, the years of legislative inaction, coupled with the unlikelihood that Congress would attempt to correct the situation in the foreseeable future, made it necessary for the Court to intervene. The alternative would leave untouched a practice that flagrantly violated both the Constitution and the ultimate human values involved. The chief justice found that alternative unacceptable. Because the other branches had defaulted in their responsibility, the Court had to ensure enforcement of the prohibition against segregation by the state.

Next to *Brown*, the most significant Warren Court case was *Baker v. Carr* (1962). The decision there led to a drastic shift in political power throughout the nation. Through its "one person, one vote" principle, the Warren Court ultimately worked an electoral reform to correct unfair distribution of voters among legislative districts.

In addition to racial and political equality, Warren sought equality in criminal justice. The landmark here was the 1963 *Gideon v. Wainwright* case, which required counsel for indigent defendants. Warren's emphasis on fairness in criminal proceedings also led to the 1961 *Mapp v. Ohio* decision, barring illegally seized evidence from being introduced at a defendant's trial, and the 1966 *Miranda v. Arizona* decision, requiring that arrested persons be told of their right to remain silent, to have a lawyer present when they are questioned, and to have the court appoint an attorney for those who cannot afford to pay.

Miranda in particular was a direct result of the insights Warren gained during his tenure as a district attorney. Methods of arrest, questioning of suspects, and police conduct in the station house were matters that the chief justice intimately understood from his years as prosecutor in California. Above all, he recognized the problem of police abuses and the lack of effective methods to deal with them.

Earlier courts had stressed property rights. A movement in the other direction, emphasizing the rights of individuals, had begun under Chief Justices Harlan Stone and Fred Vinson. Under Warren, the Court firmly placed individual rights, particularly First Amendment rights, in a preferred constitutional posi-

Clarence Earl Gideon, a penniless convict who had not been able to afford a defense attorney, sent a handwritten petition from prison to the Supreme Court to hear his case. In 1963 the Supreme Court ruled unanimously that every state must provide counsel to an indigent charged with a felony. *Source: National Archives*

tion. Freedom of expression protection was extended to civil rights demonstrators and those who criticized public officials, and the power to restrain publication on obscenity grounds was limited. The Court also recognized new personal rights, notably a constitutional right of privacy.

As a judge, Warren does not rank with the leading legal craftsmen, nor will he be noted for his mastery of the common law. But he never pretended to be a judicial technician. Instead he was a "result-oriented" judge, who used his power to secure the outcome he deemed right in the cases before his Court. Using his authority to the utmost, he never hesitated to do whatever he thought necessary to translate his own conceptions of fairness and justice into the law of the land.

For Chief Justice Warren, the technical issues traditionally fought over in constitutional cases always seemed to merge into larger questions of fairness. His great concern was expressed in the question he so often asked when the cases were argued before the Court: "But was it fair?" His conception of fairness was the key to most of the Warren criminal law decisions. When government lawyers tried to justify decisions by traditional legal arguments, Warren would interject, "Why did you treat him this way?" When the chief justice concluded that an individual had been treated in an unfair manner, he would not let legal rules stand in the way in his effort to remedy the situation.

In reaching what he considered the fair result, Warren was not restrained by the demands of precedent, for he considered principle more important. The major decisions of the Warren Court overruled decisions of earlier Courts. Those precedents had left the enforcement of constitutional rights to the political branches. If they failed to act, in Warren's view, this situation left the Court with the choice either to follow precedent or do what it believed was right. For him, the choice was clear.

Because Warren used straightforward language, his important opinions have a simple power of their own. Perhaps the *Brown* opinion did not articulate the juristic bases of its decision in as scholarly a manner as it could have, but, as Warren wrote in his memorandum transmitting the *Brown* draft, the opinion was "prepared on the theory that [it] should be short, readable by the lay public, non-rhetorical, unemotional and, above all, non-accusatory." The decision in *Brown* emerged from a typical Warren moral judgment, with which few today would disagree. When all is said and done, Warren's place in the legal pantheon rests, not upon his opinions, but upon his decisions.

While serving as chief justice, Warren also chaired the commission that investigated the assassination of President John F. Kennedy in 1963. He worked until midnight every night for ten months straight to meet the tight deadline imposed by President Lyndon B. Johnson.

Warren expressed disappointment that he had never become president. Yet, as chief justice, he was able to accomplish more than most presidents. He led his Court to what Justice Abe Fortas once termed "the most profound and pervasive revolution ever achieved by substantially peaceful means." The Warren Court decisions giving wider effect to constitutional rights worked a transformation in both the law and the society that can be compared only with that brought about by political revolution or military conflict.

Warren retired from the Court June 23, 1969, after his successor, Warren E. Burger, had been appointed. He continued to take an interest in the Court, expressing opposition to a proposal to set up a new court of appeals to screen petitions for review in the Supreme Court. An avid sportsman, he also pursued his favorite pastimes, hunting and fishing. Warren suffered a fatal heart attack July 9, 1974.

John Marshall Harlan

1955-1971

JOHN MARSHALL HARLAN was born in Chicago May 20, 1899, to John Maynard Harlan and Elizabeth Palmer Harlan. His father was a prominent attorney in Chicago who served as alderman and twice ran unsuccessfully as the Republican candidate for mayor. The Harlans named their only son after his grandfather, an associate justice of the Supreme Court who had already completed twenty-two of the thirty-four years he would spend on the high bench by the time his namesake was born.

Harlan's early education was at the Appleby School in Oakville, Ontario, and at the Lake Placid School in New York. In 1916 he began Princeton University, where, at slightly over six feet tall, he cut an imposing figure. He quickly became a student leader: he was elected class president for three years, editor of the daily *Princetonian,* and chairman of the Senior Council.

In 1920 Harlan received his A.B. degree and proceeded to Balliol College in Oxford, England, as a Rhodes scholar. During his three years at Oxford he

While heading the Prohibition Division of the U. S. Attorney's Office for the Southern District of New York, John Marshall Harlan successfully prosecuted Earl Carroll (pictured) on perjury charges. Producer of the Broadway musical "Vanities," Carroll was accused of displaying a nude chorus girl in a bathtub of champagne at an after-hours party at his theater. *Source: Library of Congress*

was in the top 5 percent of his class and earned B.A. and M.A. degrees in jurisprudence.

Harlan came to New York in 1923 and took a job with the distinguished law firm of Root, Clark, Buckner, and Howland. Partner Emory R. Buckner, who was to become Harlan's mentor, told him immediately that he had "better go to law school" in the United States, and Harlan enrolled at New York Law School. He attended classes in the afternoons while working at the law firm and received his LL.B. degree in one year.

When Buckner was appointed U.S. attorney for the Southern District of New York (the chief federal prosecutor for Manhattan, the Bronx, and Long Island) in March 1925, he took his young protege with him into federal service. During his tenure Buckner recruited several dozen young gifted lawyers who became known as "Buckner's Boy Scouts."

In the fall of 1925 Harlan was selected to head the office's Prohibition Division, which gave the twenty-six-year-old responsibility for the most difficult and politically sensitive prosecutions. Although Buckner did not agree with the prohibition laws, he felt duty-bound to enforce them. Under Buckner's direction, Harlan

brought a highly publicized perjury prosecution against Earl Carroll, producer of the flashy musical, "Vanities." Carroll had held a party at his theater where, in the wee hours of the morning, a nude chorus girl bathed in a tub filled with champagne. Publicity over the party resulted in a federal investigation, during which Carroll testified before the grand jury that no alcohol was served at the party and that there was no champagne in the tub. Carroll was convicted in 1926, and the court of appeals upheld the conviction, with Harlan writing the government's brief.

When Buckner returned to his law firm in April 1927, Harlan went with him and continued to excel at trial work as a prosecutor. He also developed an expertise in appeals, and Buckner relied on him to write the briefs for appellate courts. By December 1927, however, Harlan was back in public service. Buckner had agreed to the request of Gov. Alfred E. Smith of New York to investigate graft in municipal sewer construction. He appointed Harlan as his principal assistant. The investigation led to the indictment and conviction of the Queens borough president. Harlan again wrote the appellate brief, and the conviction was affirmed.

Harlan's duties as a special assistant attorney general were briefly interrupted in November 1928 for his marriage to Ethel Andrews, the daughter of a Yale history professor and sister of another associate at Buckner's law firm. The Harlans had one daughter, Eve, and five grandchildren.

Harlan resumed work at the law firm in 1930 and became a partner in 1931. He spent the next decade building a reputation as one of New York's leading litigators. He specialized in complex trials, the most famous of which concerned a $40 million estate that had been left to charity but was claimed by hundreds of purported relatives of the deceased. Assisted by Henry J. Friendly, who was later to become a highly respected federal appellate judge, Harlan succeeded in refuting most of the private claims so that the estate went to bona fide relatives and the charities that were his clients.

When the United States entered World War II, Harlan became chief of the Operational Analysis Section of the Eighth Air Force. The section's mission was to provide technical advice on bombing operations, and it consisted of selected civilians in the fields of mathematics, physics, electronics, architecture, and law. Harlan served in London until 1945, volunteering in 1943 for a daylight bombing raid in which he sat as a waist gunner. For his military contributions, Harlan won the U.S. Legion of Merit as well as the Croix de Guerre of France and of Belgium. He was most proud of these wartime accomplishments and later displayed photographs on the walls of his Supreme Court chambers depicting bombers delivering their payloads.

Public service called him again in 1951, when he became chief counsel to the New York State Crime Commission. The commission conducted hearings into the influence of organized crime on state government. Its reports led to the establishment of the Waterfront Commission of New York Harbor.

Harlan gained national renown as a practicing lawyer in the postwar years. He argued important Supreme Court cases and represented the Du Pont Corporation in major antitrust and commercial litigation. He also volunteered as a director of the Legal Aid Society and, for the Association of the Bar of the City of New York, served as chairman of the Committee on Ethics, chairman of the Committee on the Judiciary, and vice president. He became a name partner of his law firm.

In January 1954 President Dwight D. Eisenhower nominated Harlan, a politically inactive Republican, to the U.S. Court of Appeals for the Second Circuit. He was confirmed without delay by the Senate and took his seat on the bench on March 6, 1954. He had served only eight months when Supreme Court justice Robert H. Jackson of New York died suddenly. President Eisenhower quickly announced his intention to name Harlan to the seat.

The nomination was applauded by the press as nonpartisan. Congress, however, delayed hearings because southern senators were angry at the Supreme Court's recent school desegregation decision. Moreover, some senators feared that Harlan's studies at Oxford had made him a "one-worlder" who would surrender American sovereignty to "world government." The president resubmitted the nomination January 10, 1955, and hearings were held the following month. The Senate confirmed the nomination by a 71–11 vote March 16, and Harlan took his seat twelve days later.

Justice Harlan did not share the activist views of the Warren Court majority in the 1960s. In criminal cases he usually sided with the prosecution, and he was reluctant to invalidate legislation on constitutional grounds. Early in his tenure Harlan formed a close friendship, as well as an ideological and intellectual alliance, with Justice Felix Frankfurter. They agreed in more than 80 percent of the cases they heard together.

Harlan was a staunch believer in federalism. He felt strongly that the Constitution assigned different powers to, and set different limitations upon, the federal government and state and local governments. He viewed state governments as subject to rules of "fundamental fairness," which justified limited application of the protections of the Bill of Rights to the states. Even when dealing with freedom of speech, Harlan permitted greater latitude for local regulation of expression than for federal limitations on speech.

Harlan also advocated caution when the Court expanded its jurisdiction to areas that had not previously been the subjects of litigation. He agreed with Frankfurter, for example, that courts should not enter the "political thicket" of unfair apportionment of legislative districts, and in 1964 he dissented from the Warren Court's adoption of a constitutional rule requiring "one man, one vote" in state legislatures. His legal and constitutional conclusions supported his philosophy of government—that courts should not lead the way in political reform. He said that it was a "mistaken view of the Constitution and the constitutional function" of the Supreme Court to believe "that every major social ill in this country can find its cure in some constitutional principle, and that this Court should take the lead in promoting reform when other branches of government fail to act."

Harlan was not, however, a doctrinaire conservative. He judged each case on its own merits, and in some areas he was surprisingly liberal. When dealing with police searches and seizures of evidence, for example, Harlan set strict standards for government agents and even permitted private lawsuits for damages against federal employees who violated constitutional rights. He was also an early proponent of the right of privacy in the marital bedroom, objecting on that ground to a state law that prohibited the use of contraceptives.

Harlan showed concern for protecting the rights of free speech and association. Relatively early in his Supreme Court tenure, he upheld the right of the National Association for the Advancement of Colored People to keep its Alabama membership list confidential. Several years later, when an early civil rights "sit-in" case came before the Court, he voted to uphold the rights of blacks to desegregate lunch counters in the South on the ground, which he alone advocated, that their sit-in was a form of constitutionally protected expression. At the end of his Court tenure, he wrote the majority opinion in *Cohen v. California* (1971) ruling that the constitutional protection for speech extended

Daisy Bates (center), head of the Arkansas chapter of the National Association for the Advancement of Colored People (NAACP), was arrested in 1957 for refusing to make her membership lists public. John Marshall Harlan wrote the Supreme Court opinion overturning her conviction as a violation of the right to freedom of association, which he said was protected by the First and Fourteenth Amendments. *Source: Thomas McAvoy,* Life *Magazine, copyright Time Warner Inc.*

to an offensive slogan written on a jacket worn into a local courthouse. He said that "the constitutional right of free expression is powerful medicine" and that "verbal tumult, discord, and even offensive utterance" are part of "the broader enduring values which the process of open debate permits us to achieve."

Justice Harlan's relationship with his colleagues—even those with whom he disagreed strongly—was very close. He tried to persuade them gently with written legal memoranda. His genial demeanor and his sincere consideration for the feelings of others made him the most personally respected member of the Court. After Harlan's death, Justice Potter Stewart said of him, "What truly set him apart was his character, not his scholarship. His generous and gallant spirit, his selfless courage, his freedom from all guile, his total decency."

He believed that federal judges should meet exceptionally high standards of integrity and nonpartisanship. He thought judges should not even vote for candidates for public office, and he refrained from voting once he was appointed. Harlan also refused, on grounds of constitutional principle, to attend the president's annual State of the Union speech delivered to Congress.

Harlan is remembered as the ultimate professional whose opinions are models of clarity that later judges have tried to emulate. If he could not agree with the reasoning of a majority opinion in a case, even if he joined in the outcome, he went to great pains to articulate precisely why he reached his own particular result. This practice accounts, in part, for the extraordinary number of opinions he wrote. In the years between 1963 and 1967—when he was often a dissenter from the liberal rulings of the Court—he wrote an average of forty-three opinions each Court term. He wrote almost half again as many opinions as William O. Douglas, the second most prolific justice.

In 1963 Harlan's eyesight began to fail. He had to use strong lights and heavy magnifying lenses to read. To

Protests against the Vietnam War had become heated by 1971, when the Supreme Court ruled on *Cohen v. California,* a case involving the right to wear a jacket inscribed with vulgar language protesting the draft in a state courthouse building. John Marshall Harlan wrote the widely cited decision upholding the right under the First Amendment. *Source: Library of Congress*

the very end, however, he insisted on writing opinions by hand. Briefs, petitions, and draft opinions of other justices would be read to him by his law clerks. Calling on an extraordinary memory, he was able to recall earlier Supreme Court decisions, and his output never slackened even though he was functionally blind for the last six years of his service on the Court. He announced opinions in public sessions from memory, recalling relevant facts and constitutional principles.

During the summer of 1971, Harlan was disabled by a bad back, which was ultimately diagnosed as cancer of the spine. On September 23 he submitted his retirement letter. Harlan continued to see visitors at his hospital bed and was clear-minded enough to discuss with them the legal issues that were, to him, "the most fascinating of intellectual pursuits," until he died on December 29.

William J. Brennan, Jr.
1956–1990

Source: Library of Congress

WILLIAM JOSEPH BRENNAN, JR., was born in Newark, New Jersey, April 25, 1906, the second of eight children and the first son of William Joseph Brennan and Agnes McDermott Brennan. His parents had emigrated separately from Ireland just before the turn of the century and met and married in the United States in 1903.

Brennan's father stoked a coal-fired furnace at the Ballantine brewery in Newark, but the home in which Brennan grew up was not the typical working-class environment. His father rose through the ranks to become a local union leader and fought long and hard for the legitimacy of organized labor. His labor activities propelled him into local politics as the workers' candidate. Popular and respected, he was elected four times, beginning in 1917, to the Newark Board of Commissioners, the city's governing body. As commissioner of the Department of Public Safety, he was in charge of the police and fire departments.

Although his parents had little formal education,

they were both avid readers, from newspapers to the classics, and the Brennan household was alive with discussion of politics and public affairs. Young Brennan excelled in the local public schools and kept himself supplied with pocket money by working odd jobs: delivering milk for a local dairy, working at a gas station, and making change for the trolley in downtown Newark.

He also helped his father campaign. His first real exposure to politics was enough to convince him that he wanted no part of it. But his father's values left an indelible mark. His campaign message—"A square deal for all, special privileges to none"—was reflected in Justice Brennan's often-stated concern that law and constitutional interpretation be marked by fairness and a commitment to human dignity. Moreover, as director of public safety, the senior Brennan was credited with changing police procedures to curb unprovoked beatings and threatening interrogations. Many cases concerning this type of police practice came before the Supreme Court in the 1960s while Brennan served under Chief Justice Earl Warren.

Brennan's father initially steered him toward a career in business and finance. He attended the University of Pennsylvania's Wharton School of Finance for his undergraduate education, but friends persuaded his father that Brennan could make more of a mark on Wall Street as a lawyer, and so Brennan enrolled in Harvard Law School.

Before he graduated from Penn in 1928, however, Brennan secretly married Marjorie Leonard of Orange, New Jersey, whom he had met at a Christmas dance and dated for two years. Brennan said they married secretly because it was unseemly in that time for a man to marry a woman he could not support. Marjorie had a job with a local insurance company and could not afford to give it up to move to Boston. Their marriage was not disclosed even to their families until 1931, when Brennan finished law school.

At Harvard, Brennan studied under Felix Frankfurter. They later served together on the Supreme Court and frequently differed. Frankfurter remarked, in Brennan's presence, that he felt successful as a professor when his students thought for themselves, "but Brennan's carrying it too far." When his father died suddenly of pneumonia before his third year of law school, Brennan was forced to get a scholarship from Harvard. He finished in the top 10 percent of his class and was a member of the Harvard Legal Aid Bureau, an honor society.

After law school, Brennan returned to New Jersey and joined Pitney, Hardin, and Skinner, a prominent Newark firm with a corporate practice. He developed a reputation as a quick thinker and a tireless worker, helping with major clients by handling labor relations disputes. It was strange for Brennan to find himself representing management in labor disputes, but he worked hard at being fair and commanded the respect of the unions, due in part to his father's background. By 1938, settled in a house he bought in South Orange, Brennan became a partner in the firm.

The first of the Brennans' children, William III, was born in 1933, and the second, Hugh, in 1936. Their daughter, Nancy, was born in 1949. Bill III became a prominent lawyer in Princeton, Hugh became a high-ranking administrator at the Commerce Department, and Nancy, the executive director of Baltimore's city life museums.

In 1942 Brennan joined the Army for the duration of World War II, moving his family to Washington, D.C., and for a time to Los Angeles. Rising to the rank of colonel, he specialized in resolving labor and manpower difficulties that arose from converting American companies to wartime production.

When he returned to Newark after the war, he was quickly made a name partner in the firm. His expertise and reputation in labor law continued to grow, and he was in constant demand to represent companies in their union problems. However, the long hours away from his family and the gulf between his representation of management and his labor heritage made him increasingly uncomfortable.

At the same time, Brennan became involved in a successful reform of the New Jersey court system to eliminate delays, inefficiency, and corruption. In 1949 Republican governor Alfred Driscoll appointed Brennan, a Democrat, a judge on the newly reorganized superior court. Brennan quickly became a trusted lieutenant to New Jersey's chief justice, Arthur Vanderbilt. In 1950 Brennan was elevated to the appellate division of the superior court.

Two years later, Brennan was appointed to the New Jersey Supreme Court. Because of the need for geographic distribution on the court, he moved from

William J. Brennan, Jr., became Chief Justice Arthur Vanderbilt's right-hand man on the New Jersey Supreme Court. Although they did not always agree on specific issues, Vanderbilt (above) endorsed President Dwight D. Eisenhower's selection of Brennan for a seat on the U.S. Supreme Court. *Source: Bettmann*

South Orange to Rumson, near the coast. He continued his efforts at court reform to eliminate unfair delays and cemented his relationship as Vanderbilt's right-hand man. The success of this affiliation was a tribute to Brennan's personal skills because the two disagreed on many court decisions.

Brennan's determination to find an element of compassion in the law was apparent from some of his decisions in New Jersey, but was not nearly as pronounced as it became later. It was his reputation as a court reformer that brought him to the attention of the Republican Dwight D. Eisenhower administration.

In May 1956 Brennan addressed a Justice Department conference on efforts to improve efficiency and reduce delays in the courts. Three months later, when Justice Sherman Minton announced plans to retire from the U.S. Supreme Court, Eisenhower told Attorney General Herbert Brownell that he wanted to consider a Democrat, to demonstrate, shortly before the November presidential election, that he could be bipartisan. He said that they should consider state court judges and that it had been too long since there had been a Catholic on the Court. Already known to Justice Department officials because of the May conference (and with the endorsement of Vanderbilt, whom Eisenhower admired), Brennan became a logical choice.

On October 16, 1956, Brennan took his place on the Supreme Court bench without Senate confirmation, appointed by the president during a congressional recess. He was confirmed by the Senate March 19, 1957, with the only dissent shouted audibly by Sen. Joseph McCarthy during a voice vote.

In his thirty-four-year tenure Brennan sat with twenty-two other justices and wrote more than 1,250 published opinions, including at least 450 majority opinions and 400 dissents. Upon joining the high court, Brennan developed a rapport with Chief Justice Warren and became his lieutenant, much as he had been to Vanderbilt. Brennan helped to pave the way for a legal development that he considered a virtual revolution—the application, through the Fourteenth Amendment guarantee of due process, of many of the provisions of the Bill of Rights as a check on the exercise of authority by state and local governments, not merely to curb federal power.

On the Warren Court, Brennan was most often in the liberal majority. Indeed, one year he wrote no dissenting opinions. His decisions included *New York Times v. Sullivan* (1964), which provided greater protection for free speech by making it more difficult for public officials to win damages from the news media for libel. His ruling in *Baker v. Carr* (1962) that federal courts should consider cases of disproportionate voting districts led to the principle of one person, one vote and was later praised by Chief Justice Warren as the "most important" of his tenure.

In *Fay v. Noia* (1963), overruled in 1991, Brennan helped to establish an important role for federal courts in reviewing the fairness of state court criminal convictions. In 1968 a Brennan decision warned the states that it was time to stop dragging their feet on school desegregation. And in 1970 Brennan wrote for the Court in *Goldberg v. Kelly* that government benefits, such as welfare, were a form of property that could not be taken away or denied without due process.

During the chief justiceships of Warren Burger and William Rehnquist, the Court grew more conservative, and Brennan found himself more often in dissent. Even then, his victories were significant. In *Craig v. Boren* (1976) he led the Court in raising the level of justification that governments must have for policies that discriminate based on sex. And, in a series of subsequent decisions spanning the next fourteen years, he established the constitutional legitimacy of many affirmative action programs that sought to compensate for past discrimination.

He also wrote a line of decisions making government accountable to the people for damage caused by gov-

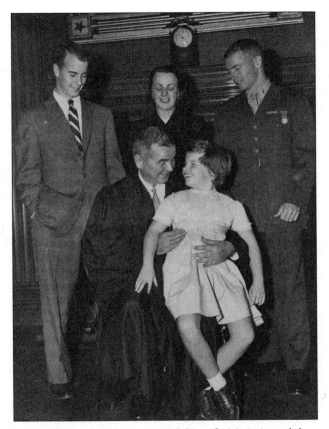

Justice William J. Brennan, Jr., with his wife, Marjorie, and three children, Hugh, Nancy, and Lt. William J. Brennan III, on October 16, 1956, the day of his investiture. *Source: UPI/Bettmann*

ernment officials, laying to rest, at least partially, the adage that you can't fight city hall. He capped his career with decisions in *Texas v. Johnson* (1989) and *United States v. Eichman* (1990) that burning an American flag as a form of protest is a type of free speech that is protected by the First Amendment, no matter how offensive it may be to some people.

Brennan is a slight man, about five feet, eight inches tall, but he is long on personal skills. His considerable charm and easy, unassuming manner carried over to his discussions with other justices about how to decide cases and when to make changes or compromise on an opinion, making him extraordinarily persuasive during the Court's deliberations. His "personal warmth," wrote

L. B. Sullivan (second from right), the police and fire commissioner of Montgomery, Alabama, celebrates a $500,000 libel suit victory against the *New York Times* with his attorneys. His case called slanderous a full-page advertisement endorsing the civil rights movement and blaming southern law enforcement officials for acts of intimidation and "terror." Justice William J. Brennan, Jr., wrote the Supreme Court opinion overturning the decision in 1964, stating that public officials are held to a higher standard than private citizens when proving libel. *Source: Bettmann*

Gregory Johnson, convicted of burning the American flag in a demonstration in Dallas, unfurls the flag as another protester sets it on fire. William J. Brennan, Jr., wrote the 1989 opinion for the Supreme Court, which ruled that the act was a form of "speech" and therefore protected by the First Amendment. *Source: Bill Pierce*

his colleague Byron White, "contributed a great deal to his effectiveness as a justice."

But many people never saw this gregarious side of Brennan because he had little visibility off the bench for more than one-third of his Court tenure. From 1969 until her death in 1982, Marjorie Brennan struggled with throat cancer and other forms of the disease, and Brennan spent much of his time caring for her. In 1983 he married Mary Fowler, his secretary since 1957, and reemerged as a popular public speaker.

Brennan always maintained that the role of law and the courts was to better the lot of mankind. The judge, he said, should always function with "a sparkling vision of the supremacy of the human dignity of every individual." Nowhere was this view more prevalent than in his assertion, beginning in 1972, that the death penalty was cruel and unusual punishment that violated the Constitution.

Throughout his tenure, he was criticized for usurping the role of the legislature or substituting his preferences for the language of laws and of the Constitution. In the 1980s this criticism grew as conservatives gained political power and began to occupy the judiciary. Brennan never wavered from his belief that the courts had to interpret for the times. The Constitution's "genius . . . rests not in any static meaning it might have had in a world that is dead and gone, but in the adaptability of its great principles to cope with current problems and current needs," he said in 1985.

A stroke forced Brennan to retire on July 20, 1990. In 1966, while they were still sitting together, Chief Justice Warren paid Brennan a tribute that also fits his last years on the Court. Warren wrote, "He administers the Constitution as a sacred trust, and interprets the Bill of Rights as the heart and life blood of that great charter of freedom. His belief in the dignity of human beings—all human beings—is unbounded. He also believes that without such dignity men cannot be free."

Charles E. Whittaker

1957-1962

Source: Photo by Ackad, Collection of the Supreme Court of the United States

CHARLES EVANS WHITTAKER was born to Charles and Ida Miller Whittaker February 22, 1901, on a farm in northeastern Kansas, six miles from the small town of Troy. He attended nine grades of school at a little white schoolhouse adjacent to his father's farm. At night, he did his homework and received his inspiration by reading the stories of Horatio Alger, whose heroes always rose from modest origins to achieve riches and respectability.

For a year and a half he went to high school in Troy, commuting by pony. While attending school, he heard about a sensational murder trial taking place in St. Joseph, Missouri, sixteen miles to the east. Whittaker decided then that he was going to be a lawyer, and his evening reading switched from Horatio Alger to books about great trials and famous lawyers. On his sixteenth birthday, Whittaker's mother died. Devastated, he quit high school and spent the next three years working on the farm for his father. Young Charles supplemented the family's income by tracking game on the Kansas plains and by selling the pelts of small animals he caught in traps.

His ambition to become a lawyer persisted, however, and at age nineteen, over his father's objections, Whittaker, armed with $700 he had saved over the three years of work, headed for Kansas City, Missouri, to pursue a legal career. He found a job as office boy in a leading Kansas City law firm, Watson, Gage, and Ess, applied for admission to the Kansas City School of Law, a private night law school, and was admitted on the condition that he simultaneously complete his high school education.

Disciplined and determined, Whittaker started work as an office boy at eight o'clock in the morning, attended law school and completed his high school studies in the late afternoon and evening, and did his homework until midnight. He had little time for relaxation and fun. In 1923, three years after arriving in Kansas City and one year before he graduated from law school, he passed the Missouri bar examination and became a lawyer at the firm where he had been the office boy.

As a practicing lawyer, Whittaker was nervous, impatient, and hardworking, and yet, at the same time, gentle, modest, and considerate. He paid incredible attention to detail and strove for perfection. He often worked six days a week, twelve to fifteen hours a day. Whittaker had little time for socializing, vacations, hobbies, or expanding his limited knowledge of the broader social, political, or economic issues. He practiced general litigation and was eminently successful. In 1928 he married Winifred R. Pugh of Kansas City, and they eventually had three sons. He became a full partner in his law firm in 1932, and the firm name was changed to Watson, Ess, Groner, Barnett, and Whittaker.

In the early 1950s Whittaker moved away from trial practice and toward corporate counseling and business transactions for companies such as Montgomery Ward and Union Pacific Railroad. He also involved himself in general community and professional service, becoming active at his Methodist church, the Chamber of Commerce, and the Missouri Bar Association, of which he became president. A Republican, he made small annual contributions to the party but was not particularly active in politics.

Political forces swirling around him, however, were creating circumstances that led to Whittaker's meteoric and unprecedented rise through the federal judiciary system. One of his clients was the local newspaper, the *Kansas City Star*. The paper was controlled by Roy Roberts, who admired Whittaker's legal ability and the manner in which he had represented the *Star* in the courtroom. He and Whittaker became friends. Roberts was also a close friend and political supporter of Gen. Dwight D. Eisenhower and a charter member of the Republican "Draft Eisenhower" movement in 1952.

On March 1, 1954, a vacancy opened in the Federal District Court for the Western District of Missouri, and Whittaker decided he wanted the job. He placed a phone call to Roberts, the only call he said he ever had to make to obtain any of his three judicial posts. Roberts gave his enthusiastic support, and President Eisenhower appointed Whittaker to the district court bench July 5.

On the bench, Whittaker continued to be thorough, attentive, and hardworking, but also restless and anxious. He paid particular attention to the factual details of each case, believing that once he had mastered them he would be able to apply the facts to existing law and reach a just result. In less than a year, he cleaned up a congested docket. The two years he spent as a district court trial judge were the happiest of his life.

In December 1955 Judge John Caskie Collet of the federal Court of Appeals for the Eighth Circuit died. He was the only Missourian on that court, and Whittaker was the lone Eisenhower district court judge from

Missouri. Whittaker's name was put forward for the vacancy, and on June 22, 1956, he assumed his new duties. He was there a brief nine months, during which he participated in thirty-three cases, wrote eleven opinions, and dissented once. It was, for Whittaker, a drab, reclusive existence; he missed the stimulation of jury trials.

In early 1957 Justice Stanley Reed of Kentucky retired. Eisenhower wanted to replace him with a conservative with judicial experience. At the time, there was no one on the Court who came from a state between Ohio and California, and Whittaker was one of the few federal Republican appellate judges from the Midwest. Moreover, like Eisenhower, Whittaker had been raised in Kansas, and he had the backing of Roberts, who had a direct line to the White House. On March 2, 1957, the president nominated Whittaker to the Supreme Court, and the Senate confirmed him unanimously seventeen days later. He became the first Missourian and the first native Kansan to become a member of the high court. In less than three years Whittaker had gone from the district court to the Supreme Court, causing Justice Felix Frankfurter to quip that the Court could get a judge from the district court faster than it could get a case.

Whittaker plunged into his new job with his usual vigor and determination. He attempted to apply his district court prescription for a good judge: put aside all political, social, and economic leanings; master the facts of the particular case; "find the applicable law without predilection to prejudices"; and apply the facts to that law so as to reach a true and just conclusion. But the task of a Supreme Court justice is vastly different from that of a trial court judge. At the trial level, it may be possible to master the facts of a case and then find the law that applies to those facts to reach a just result. At the Supreme Court level, there are too many complex cases with facts to be mastered, and the applicable law often must be made, not discovered. Indeed, within a few months after taking his seat, Whittaker confided to

Roy Roberts, the owner of the *Kansas City Star,* with his friend Gen. Dwight D. Eisenhower, whose successful presidential campaign he faithfully supported from the start. Roberts recommended that President Eisenhower appoint Charles E. Whittaker, an attorney who had represented the *Star,* to a district judgeship in Missouri. *Source:* Kansas City Star

one of his law clerks that he had made a serious mistake leaving the district court bench in Kansas City, where he enjoyed presiding over jury and judge-tried cases.

As a justice, Whittaker found himself the swing man on the nine-man court. Chief Justice Earl Warren and Justices Hugo L. Black, William O. Douglas, and William J. Brennan, Jr., represented the liberal wing of the Court, while Justices Frankfurter, Harold Burton, Tom C. Clark, and John Marshall Harlan comprised the more conservative point of view. There were many 4–4 votes at conference, with Whittaker, the junior justice, who by custom votes last, obliged to cast the crucial deciding vote.

Although courted by justices from both philosophical wings during his first two years on the Court, Whittaker set aside political points of view. Depending on his view of the facts of a particular case, he sided sometimes with the liberals, particularly in emotional cases involving individual liberty, and sometimes with the conservatives. His liberal vote was crucial in *Green v. United States* (1957), in which the Court voted 5-4 that a man tried for first degree murder, but found guilty of second degree murder, could not later be retried for the more serious charge without violating the Constitution's Double Jeopardy Clause. In *Moore v. Michigan* (1957) he again sided with the four liberals to hold that a young, uneducated black man had not knowingly waived his right to the benefit of counsel. In *Trop v. Dulles* (1958) he cast the deciding vote to strike down a

section of the Nationality Act of 1940, which provided that a wartime deserter could be stripped of his citizenship. Indeed, he found the government's position wanting in two other cases that challenged the Nationality Act.

Yet the conservatives found Whittaker on their side on at least an equal number of 5–4 decisions. He cast the decisive vote in another case called *Green v. United States* (1958), in which the Court upheld a contempt sentence against two Communist party officials for disobeying an order to surrender to federal marshals. In *Thomas v. Arizona* and *Crooker v. California* (1958) he joined the four conservatives to uphold state convictions of defendants who claimed their confessions had been coerced. In *Beilan v. Board of Education* (1958) the Court, with Whittaker casting the deciding vote, held that a public school teacher could be dismissed for refusing to answer questions about possible past communist affiliations. In *Gore v. United States* (1958) he voted with the conservatives that consecutive sentences could

Justice Charles E. Whittaker and his family stroll in Washington in March 1957, shortly before he took his seat on the Supreme Court. Left to right, sons Gary and Kent, Mrs. Whittaker, Justice Whittaker, daughter-in-law, and son Dr. Keith Whittaker. *Source: AP/Wide World Photos*

Charles E. Whittaker joined a Supreme Court that was often split between the liberal wing led by Chief Justice Earl Warren and the more conservative wing led by Felix Frankfurter. As the junior justice, Whittaker found himself in the position of casting the deciding vote at conference.
Source: Photo by Ackad, Collection of the Supreme Court of the United States

be imposed for three separate violations of narcotics laws arising out of a single narcotics sale.

As time went on, however, Whittaker sided more often with the conservatives. He felt particularly close to the conservative Justice Harlan, a man of warmth and understanding, and had a deep respect for his constitutional scholarship. He described Harlan as one of "God's anointed souls." A conservative by upbringing, temperament, and training, Whittaker undoubtedly felt more comfortable with that wing of the Court. But he never felt a slackening of the pressure created by his need to master the facts and law of every case, his inability to delegate any significant authority to his law clerks, and his feelings of inadequacy because his academic credentials did not measure up to those of some of the other justices.

Early in 1962, after five years on the Court, Whittaker was physically, mentally, and emotionally exhausted. Not only was he working six to seven days a week, but also he was putting in seventeen hours a day. Anxiety prevented him from sleeping the other seven. He lost his appetite and suffered from deep depression.

He could not concentrate and found it difficult to write a simple sentence. The stress of the job had broken him. On March 6, 1962, he entered Walter Reed Army Medical Center, suffering from a nervous breakdown. The medical verdict was that he must retire to regain his health. On March 29, almost five years to the day after he took office, he followed his doctors' advice. It was another year and a half before he returned to normal health.

Following his retirement, Whittaker did not resume the full-time practice of law, nor was he active in public life. He became an arbitrator for General Motors in disputes between the auto company and its dealers. In 1966 he was asked by the Senate Committee on Standards and Conduct to devise a code of ethical conduct for senators. In addition, he spoke out in favor of channeling grievances through the court system after becoming troubled by the increase in civil disobedience on campuses and in the streets during the late 1960s. Whittaker died of a ruptured aneurysm in the abdominal aorta November 26, 1973, in Kansas City.

Potter Stewart
1958-1981

Source: Photo by Harris & Ewing, Collection of the Supreme Court of the United States

ORN IN THE HOME of his maternal grandfather in Jackson, Michigan, January 23, 1915, Potter Stewart was the second of three children of a prosperous and well-established Cincinnati family. His father, James Garfield Stewart, was a prominent trial lawyer and popular Republican politician who won successive elections to the Cincinnati City Council, was the city's mayor for nine years, and later served as a justice of the Ohio Supreme Court. Because James

Stewart was so well known in Cincinnati, everybody stopped to talk to him, and many mistakenly referred to young Potter as "Jimmy." At the family dinner table, his father would enliven the conversation with tales of the day's adventures in court. As Stewart recalled many years later, "I . . . grew up assuming that I would be a lawyer."

Although his father was an early influence on his career choice and later facilitated advancement in that career, Potter's closest relationship was with his mother. Harriet Potter Stewart was also active in Cincinnati's political life as president of the League of Women Voters and as a leader of the movement to reform Cincinnati's city government. Her energies and strong personality were directed, however, largely to her children—Potter, his older sister, Irene, and his younger brother, Zeph.

As a youth Stewart enjoyed an affluent lifestyle with trips to Europe, summers in Wyoming, and private schooling. His sense of humor and natural abilities as an actor and mimic were frequently turned to the amusement of his friends. He could be ingenious in devising practical jokes, which he would execute with skill. In prep school, these talents earned him the title of class wit. He also channeled his youthful energy into more serious pursuits. He was a good student—first at the University School in Cincinnati and later at the prestigious Hotchkiss School in Connecticut. When the Great Depression inflicted unaccustomed financial hardship on the Stewart family, scholarship aid allowed him to continue at Hotchkiss, from which he graduated in 1933.

That same year Stewart enrolled in Yale College with a scholarship supplemented by earnings from his own work, including summer employment as a reporter for a Cincinnati newspaper. At Yale, he majored in English literature, was named class orator, and was elected to Phi Beta Kappa. In his senior year, he took charge of the *Yale Daily News* and, to the surprise of his Republican father and the conservative Yale community, declared the paper's editorial support for President Franklin D. Roosevelt's New Deal. He graduated cum laude in 1937 and was awarded a fellowship for a year's study at Cambridge University in England.

Returning to the United States in 1938, Stewart enrolled in Yale Law School. His academic excellence there earned him a coveted position as an editor of the *Yale Law Journal* and membership in the Order of the Coif, a legal honor society. He also won the moot court competition, effectively demonstrating his mastery of the skill of oral advocacy. He graduated with honors in 1941.

Stewart joined a corporate law firm in New York City rather than returning to Cincinnati to begin his career. Perhaps recalling the boyhood experience of being called by his father's name, he, as he put it, "wanted to be regarded as more than just my father's son." After the attack on Pearl Harbor a few months later, he began active duty as a naval officer on fuel transport ships operating in the Atlantic and Mediterranean. During the war years Stewart met Mary Ann Bertles, his future wife and lifelong companion. Their courtship was accelerated by the war and, while Stewart's ship was in port, they were married in Williamsburg, Virginia, April 24, 1943. Two days later, Stewart departed for additional sea duty.

When he was discharged from the navy in 1945, he returned briefly to New York, but soon accepted an offer from a leading law firm in his hometown. As a skilled trial lawyer, Stewart earned the high regard of his professional colleagues. Returning to his Republican roots, he ventured into politics and was elected to the Cincinnati City Council in 1949 and 1951. When Stewart's second term on the city council ended in 1953, he decided to devote his attention to his law practice and to his three young children—Harriet, Potter, Jr., and David.

Upon the recommendation of Republican senator John W. Bricker of Ohio, President Dwight D. Eisenhower appointed Stewart to fill a vacancy on the Sixth Circuit Court of Appeals in 1954. At the age of thirty-nine, he became the youngest judge serving in the federal judiciary. Clarity, brevity, and careful reasoning characterized his appellate opinions. He was particularly skillful in capturing the essence of a case in a com-

Sen. John W. Bricker, R-Ohio, recommended Potter Stewart (above) for a seat on the Sixth Circuit Court of Appeals. Appointed by President Dwight D. Eisenhower in 1954, Stewart, at thirty-nine, became the youngest judge serving in the federal judiciary. *Source: Photo by Peter Ehrenhaft, Collection of the Supreme Court of the United States*

pact phrase. Dissenting from his court's refusal to set aside the conviction of a man who was arrested, tried, and sentenced on the same day, Judge Stewart observed that "swift justice demands more than just swiftness."

When Attorney General William Rogers asked Stewart to come to Washington in October 1958, Stewart assumed that the request concerned his work for a committee on the administration of the federal courts. Upon his arrival in Washington, however, Rogers told Stewart that the president wanted to nominate him to the Supreme Court to replace Harold Burton, who was retiring. The next day Eisenhower announced the appointment. One week later, on October 14, 1958, Stew-

art took his seat on the Supreme Court. At age forty-three he was the second youngest justice since the Civil War.

Because the Senate was in recess when he was appointed to the Court, Stewart faced Senate confirmation hearings while he was deciding cases and writing opinions. When the hearings began in early April 1959, much of the questioning concerned his view of the Court's 1954 decision in *Brown v. Board of Education*, requiring the desegregation of public schools. Stewart responded that the inquiring senators should not vote for his confirmation on the assumption that he favored overruling *Brown*. The Senate confirmed the nomination May 5, 1959, by a 70–17 vote, with all the negative votes cast by senators representing southern states.

The Court he joined was sharply divided between liberals and conservatives. Both factions competed for Stewart's vote, placing him in what Justice Felix Frankfurter described as an "intellectual traffic jam." Stewart refused to be identified with either faction and followed a cautiously independent course, at times voting with the liberals and at other times with the conservatives. As a result, he was described as a "swing justice"—one who moved between the two factions and whose vote could therefore be decisive in close cases. For the same reasons that he rejected the simplistic labels of "liberal" and "conservative," Stewart considered the characterization of swing justice to be meaningless. His independent voting record was not the product of a shifting political ideology, but the result of how he viewed his judicial responsibilities. He believed that a judge should remove from his judicial work his own political, religious, and moral beliefs and decide cases only on the basis of the law and the Constitution.

Because of his keen appreciation of the difference between personal beliefs and the commands of the Constitution, Stewart often voted to uphold the constitutionality of statutes that he would not favor as a legislator. He voted to uphold some death penalty statutes, but after his retirement he revealed that he opposed capital punishment as a citizen and would vote against it were he a legislator. Dissenting in *Griswold v. Connecticut* (1965), the Court's invalidation of a state ban on contraceptive devices, he wrote that the statute was "an uncommonly silly law," but not unconstitutional.

Stewart's approach to constitutional law was cautious and restrained. For the most part, he refused to adopt inflexible rules that would unduly restrict the power of government to address complex social and economic problems. He preferred narrow decisions reaching only as far as required to decide the particular case and pro-

tect constitutional rights. There were some exceptions to this incremental approach. For example, he endorsed a more absolutist rule prohibiting government decisions based on race. He first expressed this view in cases involving statutes prohibiting interracial cohabitation or marriage, which he voted to overturn, and later held to it in voting to invalidate affirmative action programs designed to remedy the effects of discrimination.

Stewart drafted his opinions in longhand, often working at home during the late evening and into the night. His concise, clear, and graceful writing style is evident in his more than 600 Supreme Court opinions. Prominent among Stewart's contributions to con-

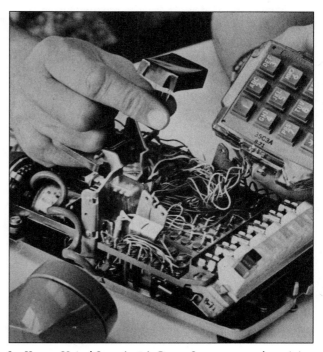

In *Katz v. United States* (1967), Potter Stewart wrote the opinion changing what constitutes a legal police search under the Fourth Amendment's protections. He ruled that a police tap on telephone wires in a phone booth for the purposes of eavesdropping and recording a conversation violates a defendant's right to privacy even though technically no "search" of the phone booth had been made. *Source: Copyright* Washington Post. *Reprinted by permission of the District of Columbia Public Library*

stitutional law are his many opinions on the Fourth Amendment law of search and seizure, including a landmark decision, *Katz v. United States* (1967), extending the amendment's protection to the interception of telephone conversations by law enforcement officials. Other major contributions include his strong support of the First Amendment freedoms of speech and press.

His talent for the memorable phrase is evident in many of his opinions. In an early death penalty case he wrote that random imposition of the death penalty is "cruel and unusual in the way that being struck by lightening is cruel and unusual." He characterized the Court's upholding of fees that excluded indigent persons from bankruptcy courts as permitting "Congress to say that some of the poor are too poor even to go bankrupt."

Stewart was admired by his friends and colleagues as a man of integrity, intelligence, and diligence. The responsibilities of his office tempered but did not eclipse his lively sense of humor. His often self-effacing wit, gracious manner, and unfailing consideration of others earned him the respect and affection of most of his brethren during his twenty-three years on the Court. He thoroughly enjoyed his judicial duties but sought neither public recognition nor higher office. When there was speculation that President Richard M. Nixon might appoint him chief justice, he met discreetly with the president and withdrew his name from consideration. When the Court's term concluded each summer, he would leave what he once called "the marble palace in Washington" for the family summer home in New Hampshire. There he enjoyed life's ordinary pleasures of fishing, visiting with his children, and closely following the progress of the Cincinnati Reds baseball team.

Justice Stewart retired from the Supreme Court July 3, 1981. One of the primary reasons for his decision to retire at the relatively young age of sixty-six was to have more time with his family. He was also aware that throughout the history of the Court the tenure of some justices had exceeded their good health and vitality. With characteristic wit, he noted that "it's better to go too soon than to stay too long."

He remained active in the years after his retirement, accepting appointments to two presidential commissions and making extended academic visits to Yale and other law schools. With his deep, mellifluous voice, he recorded legal texts for the blind and provided thoughtful commentary for the television series "The Constitution: That Delicate Balance." He also continued his work as a judge on selected cases in the courts of appeals and as chairman of an international arbitration commission.

While visiting his daughter in Vermont during the Thanksgiving holidays in 1985, Stewart suffered a severe stroke. He died December 7, 1985, in Hanover, New Hampshire, at the age of seventy. The legacy of his years on the Court includes not only the many important opinions he wrote, but also his recognition that no generation of judges has a monopoly on the meaning of the Constitution. For Potter Stewart, the law was "always an unfinished tapestry the weaving of which is never done."

Byron R. White
1962-1993

BYRON RAYMOND WHITE was born in Fort Collins, Colorado, June 8, 1917, but grew up in the sugar-beet farming community of Wellington to the northeast. His father, A. Albert White, managed the local outlet of a lumber supply company. Wellington was hit hard by the Great Depression, and White recalled, shortly after his appointment to the Supreme Court, that "by the normal standards of today we were all quite poor, although we didn't necessarily feel poor because everyone was more or less the same.

Everybody worked for a living. Everybody. Everybody." For young White, work included manual labor in the beet fields after school and during summers, as well as section work for the Colorado and Southern Railroad.

The strongest personal influence on White was undoubtedly his brother, Clayton S. (Sam) White, five years his senior. Although neither of his parents had attended high school, Sam White graduated first in his class and earned the state scholarship that was awarded to all valedictorians. At the University of Colorado he

461

A versatile and talented athlete, Byron White was voted All American in football at the University of Colorado. After graduation in 1938 he played a season of professional football for the Pittsburgh Pirates (now the Steelers). Nicknamed "Whizzer," he led the league in rushing and was the highest paid player in the sport. *Source: Collection of the Supreme Court of the United States*

starred in football, won a Rhodes scholarship to Oxford University, and studied medicine.

Not to be outdone, Byron White won the same scholarship. He was a junior Phi Beta Kappa (first in his 267-person class), student body president his senior year, a three-sport star with three letters in football, four in basketball, and three in baseball, and a football All American on Colorado's 1937 Cotton Bowl team. He, too, won a Rhodes scholarship to Oxford, but he was also offered a professional football contract with the old Pittsburgh Pirates. He sat out his senior baseball season to mull over his choices before he learned that he could play for the Pirates and postpone his matriculation at Oxford by one term. "Whizzer," as he was called, led the league in rushing and, at $15,000, was the highest-paid player of the day. In 1954 he was named to the Collegiate Hall of Fame.

White went to Oxford in January 1939, but stayed only two terms because American students were sent home in September when World War II broke out. During his nine months abroad, White twice met John F. Kennedy, whose father was the U.S. ambassador to the Court of St. James's (Great Britain). White returned to enter Yale Law School, simultaneously playing football on weekends during the 1940 and 1941 seasons for the Detroit Lions team, which had purchased his contract from Pittsburgh.

After Pearl Harbor, White tried to join the marines but was rejected because of colorblindness. He successfully enlisted in the navy and became an intelligence officer in the Pacific Theater, where he encountered John Kennedy again. White was responsible for preparing the report of the sinking of Kennedy's PT-109. White was awarded a Bronze Star and discharged as a lieutenant commander.

After the war, he returned to Yale—"the most stimulating intellectual experience I had up to that time." He was named to the Order of the Coif, a legal honor society, and graduated magna cum laude, with the Cullen Prize for high academic grades. He clerked for the chief justice of the United States, Fred Vinson, in 1946 and married Marion Stearns, a daughter of the president of the University of Colorado, the same year. He then returned to Colorado to practice law in Denver with the firm that is now Davis, Graham, and Stubbs.

For nearly fourteen years, he engaged in a diverse general practice. As he later recalled, "I had a good, satisfactory practice and a pretty decent life." An intensely, even ferociously private man, he enjoyed his work and his family, which included a son and a daughter. His hobbies were those of solitude. An accomplished alpine skier and a passionate dry-fly fisherman, White preferred the Colorado mountains for the former and western Montana for the latter.

Despite his penchant for privacy, White was always active in local politics, primarily at the grass-roots level. Indeed, his judicial philosophy may have been shaped largely by his faith in the political process and his corresponding skepticism of the legitimacy of public policy created by unelected judges. Shortly after his appointment to the Supreme Court, he told an interviewer, "Everyone in this country has an obligation to take part in politics. That's the foundation, the most important principle, on which our system is built. If our system is to work, people must intelligently elect their representatives in the legislatures and the Congress and their local government. And the best way to do it is to get their feet wet in politics."

Despite his involvement in Democratic party politics, White encountered John Kennedy only once be-

tween 1947, when Kennedy was a freshman member of Congress and White was clerking for Vinson, and the 1960 presidential race. Before the Democratic convention that year, White organized the Colorado Committee for Kennedy; after the convention, the candidate's brother, Robert Kennedy, asked White to head the National Citizens for Kennedy Committee, which was designed as a nonpartisan appeal.

After the election, White was named Robert Kennedy's deputy attorney general and enjoyed mixed success in the number two position at the Department of Justice. He was widely praised for helping to recruit a uniformly talented and energetic team of young assistant attorneys general, many of whom went on to distinguished careers in both government and the private sector. He also was recognized for his courage and icy calm in personally addressing the riots that grew out of the "freedom rides" from Birmingham to Montgomery, Alabama, in the spring of 1961. He was criticized for not working harder to prevent the nomination of some federal district judges who later became intransigent obstacles to civil rights. As deputy, White was responsi-

White greeting Sen. John F. Kennedy on his arrival in Denver in November 1959. White organized Colorado support for Kennedy's 1960 presidential race. After the election, Attorney General Robert Kennedy hired White as his deputy. *Source: UPI/Bettmann*

ble for overseeing the vetting of more than 100 judicial appointments, more than had ever been made in such a short period of time. President Kennedy's own political vulnerability due to a paper-thin election victory, an entrenched seniority system in the Senate, and cronyism made White's task more difficult than some critics conceded.

When Charles E. Whittaker retired in 1962 after only five years on the Supreme Court, President Kennedy took a week to choose his successor. He finally narrowed the field to three: Harvard law professor Paul Freund, Secretary of Labor Arthur Goldberg, and federal appeals judge William Hastie, the only nonwhite of the three. Kennedy told Arthur Schlesinger, Jr., "But I didn't want to start off with a Harvard man and a professor; we've taken so many Harvard men that it's damn hard to appoint another. And we couldn't do Hastie this time; it was just too early." Nor was Kennedy eager to lose Goldberg from the cabinet, and, in any event, he anticipated making several more appointments to the Court. Nicholas Katzenbach, who would eventually succeed White as deputy attorney general, has reported that he suggested White's name to Robert Kennedy; others have told how the president was taken with the idea of the model "New Frontier" judge—the man of great ability and achievement who had no ambition for the office. Twelve days after being nominated, on April 11, 1962, White was confirmed by the Senate by a voice vote. He took his seat five days later.

Unlike the three justices appointed just before him, White had no prior judicial experience, nor had he held elective office. Of his personal manner, White's old friend Erwin Griswold has conceded, in an otherwise admiring essay, that White "can give the appearance of brusqueness." Griswold also acknowledges that White developed an aggressive style of questioning on the bench, but explains both traits on the ground that "his mind is so clear and quick."

White joined a Court in transition. Justice Felix Frankfurter suffered a disabling stroke in April 1962 and was replaced in the fall by Goldberg, who joined Chief Justice Earl Warren and Justices Hugo Black, William O. Douglas, and William J. Brennan, Jr., to form a solid voting bloc in many areas of the Court's docket, especially civil rights. White attracted notoriety early in his career with sharply worded, even caustic, dissents to decisions identifying novel constitutional rights. For example, only months after White took his seat, the Court decided *Robinson v. California* (1962), which held that drug addiction was an illness and punishment of it was therefore unconstitutional. White said the majority was writing "into the Constitution [their] own abstract notions of how best to handle the narcotics problem." In 1966 he lambasted the majority in the famous criminal procedure case of *Miranda v. Arizona* for inventing a rule that he foresaw having a "corrosive effect on the criminal law," "return[ing] a killer, rapist or other criminal to the streets . . . to repeat his crime whenever it pleases him," and thus achieving "not a gain, but a loss, in human dignity." His most famous and scorching dissent was to the 1973 abortion decision, *Roe v. Wade,* in which he condemned the Court for acting illegitimately and declared that the decision could be justified only as an exercise of "raw judicial power."

White's importance to the Court, however, is not as a dissenter. He has written a number of important majority opinions in a variety of fields, from labor law to antitrust, as well as in the more publicly recognized areas of criminal procedure and race—most notably *Washington v. Davis* (1976), which established that a certain standard of intent to discriminate needed to be demonstrated for a violation of the Equal Protection Clause of the Fourteenth Amendment. Although sharply criticized by many political interest groups, the opinion reflected White's own attempt to mediate between aggressive enforcement of equal rights, which he earlier championed at the Justice Department, and his view that the

Ernesto Miranda, right, with his defense attorney John L. Flynn, was convicted of kidnapping and rape after he confessed while in police custody. Byron White dissented in the landmark *Miranda v. Arizona* (1966) decision, which set Miranda free because he had not been told that he had the right to remain silent and to have an attorney with him during interrogation or that his statements in custody could be used against him. *Source: UPI/Bettmann*

Constitution is not an empty vessel into which judges may pour any social policy they see fit. He best expressed the latter view in his opinion in *Moore v. City of East Cleveland* (1977), a concise and eloquent essay on the Court's role in developing the proper scope of the Due Process Clause.

White wrote important opinions concerning freedom of the press, including decisions denying constitutional protection to the identity of journalists' sources or their workplaces. He also urged the Court to marshal its resources more effectively to resolve conflicting interpretations of federal statutes and other important issues.

White's style in writing opinions is—like the author—precise, unpretentious, and impatient to finish the job. He wastes no time measuring competing views or amplifying abstract theories. Katzenbach has explained:

It is my belief that to a large degree his opinions reflect his character and personality as well as his view of the role of the Court. As to the latter, he has strong views as to the predominant role of the political branches in our governmental system and deplores the tendency for justices to believe the Constitution embodies their personal views of what is good for society. As to the former, he has a professional practitioner's view, a belief that hard work and determination can lead to success, and a lack of sympathy for those who abuse power and privilege as well as those who whine about bad luck. These views tend to make him tough on those in government or out who don't respect and comply with law.

Justice White remains a puzzle to many. More than one scholar has expressed perplexity over the perceived dissonance between White's voting record on the Court and President Kennedy's "own often expressed concepts in civil liberties and human dignity." A thoughtful examination of the record will suggest, on the contrary, that the observation rests on a misapprehension of both Kennedy and White and on an erroneous assumption about presidential ability to know or dictate judicial behavior, especially over time.

Justice White announced March 19, 1993, that he would retire at the end of the term. Serving more than three decades on the Court, White showed himself to be his own man, not part of a bloc or a negotiating team. He treated his job very pragmatically, not as an academic seminar for theorists. Most important, he viewed his judicial oath as a trust and not as an estate.

Arthur J. Goldberg
1962-1965

Source: Photo by Harris & Ewing, Collection of the Supreme Court of the United States

ARTHUR JOSEPH GOLDBERG'S origins were humble, and his is the classic story of a poor child of immigrants making his fame and fortune in America. He was born August 8, 1908, the youngest of eight surviving children of Joseph and Rebecca Goldberg. Both of his parents were Russian Jews who had immigrated to the United States and settled in Chicago. Goldberg's father, who died when Arthur was eight, sold produce to hotels from a wagon pulled by a blind horse. The family moved every year to get one month's free rent. Arthur held several jobs in his youth, including delivery boy at a shoe factory, shoe salesman, fish wrapper, and suit packer.

Despite the financial hardships of his childhood, Goldberg completed high school at age fifteen. He then began attending Crane Junior College by day and De Paul University by night. He subsequently entered Northwestern University, where he graduated first in his class in 1929 with a B.S.L degree and took his J.D. degree, summa cum laude, the following year.

Goldberg was only twenty when Illinois admitted him to the bar. He first worked for a firm doing mortgage foreclosures, but quit because he found such work distasteful during the Great Depression. In 1931 he married Dorothy Kurgans, and they had two children, Barbara and Robert. Dorothy Goldberg was a painter and a writer who in later years became known for her activism on women's issues.

After clerking for a Chicago law firm, Pritzker and Pritzker, Goldberg opened his own practice. His involvement in President Franklin D. Roosevelt's 1936 reelection campaign sparked a concern for the plight of the worker, and he devoted more of his time to labor law. One of Goldberg's first major labor clients was the American Newspaper Guild, which was embroiled in a successful strike against a Chicago newspaper owned by press baron William Randolph Hearst.

When the United States entered World War II, Goldberg served as a special assistant in the Office of Strategic Services, which was responsible for military intelligence. He was assigned to be chief of the labor division in Europe and supervised espionage of labor groups for purposes of sabotage.

After the war, Goldberg continued his practice of labor law. The United Steelworkers of America named him general counsel in 1948. He also represented the Congress of Industrial Organizations (CIO), which sought to unionize major industries. Because of his work with these and other clients, Goldberg played an important part in the historic merger in 1955 of the American Federation of Labor (AFL) and the CIO, and he wrote the constitution of the new AFL-CIO. In 1959 he represented the steelworkers in a strike that lasted more than 100 days and ended in a significant victory for labor. He continued to work for the AFL-CIO as a special counsel until 1961.

When he cooperated in 1957 with congressional committees investigating corruption in organized labor, Goldberg met Robert F. Kennedy, who was the chief counsel for the Senate Select Committee on Improper Activities in the Labor or Management Field. Goldberg's relationship with the Kennedys was strengthened

An expert on labor law, Arthur J. Goldberg served as general counsel of the United Steelworkers of America (USW). Here Goldberg (left) poses with other USW leaders and steel company officials outside the White House after a bargaining session in 1952. *Source: Library of Congress*

in 1958 when he supported labor reform legislation that Sen. John F. Kennedy had proposed. Goldberg was instrumental in obtaining the support of organized labor groups for John Kennedy's 1960 presidential campaign. It was not a surprise, therefore, when Kennedy nominated Goldberg secretary of labor in his cabinet in 1961. Goldberg was confirmed unanimously by the Senate and praised by Republican senator Barry Goldwater as "the most outstanding choice" in the new cabinet.

Twenty-four hours after Goldberg was sworn in, he was on his way to New York to help mediate a tugboat strike. During his tenure, Goldberg called upon his wide experience in labor law to arbitrate a number of disputes. The most significant of these involved the U.S. Steel Corporation. President Kennedy was committed to holding down the cost of steel so as not to disrupt the economy at a time when the nation was undergoing a period of recovery. Goldberg worked to resolve the dispute between labor and management, proposing only modest increases in wages that would not result in raising the price of steel. The two sides agreed to his proposal, but three days later U.S. Steel executives announced a price increase. Representing an angry Kennedy, Goldberg went back to U.S. Steel to demand a recision. After significant pressure was brought to bear against the company, its executives finally relented.

As secretary of labor, Goldberg was also involved in creating procedures to reduce strikes at missile construction sites so that national security would not be threatened. He helped persuade Congress to pass an increase in the minimum wage and undertook the reorganization of the Office of Manpower Administration, which oversaw employment and job training initiatives. Goldberg's advice to President Kennedy often went beyond issues related to the Labor Department to include such areas as federal aid to the arts, Social Security benefits, and foreign policy.

Goldberg served only fifteen months as secretary of labor. On August 28, 1962, Felix Frankfurter retired from the Supreme Court. The following day, Kennedy nominated Goldberg to fill the vacancy. He was confirmed by the Senate nearly a month later, on September 25, by voice vote. He took over what many called the "Jewish seat" because it had been held by Benjamin Cardozo from 1932 to 1938 and by Frankfurter since 1939.

In a speech before the American Bar Association in 1963, Goldberg spoke about the differences he experienced when he left the cabinet to become a member of the Court: "The Secretary continually worries about what the President and an unpredictable Congress will do to his carefully formulated legislative proposals; the President, the Congress and the Secretary wonder what the Justice will do to theirs." He also noted that "the Secretary's phone rings all the time, the Justice's phone never rings."

Goldberg approached his work on the Court with characteristic energy. He continued to apply the philosophy that had dominated his earlier endeavors, that while there are difficult problems in the world, solutions to them can be found. Although he served only three terms on the Court, from October 1962 through June 1965, he wrote a number of significant majority opinions dealing with important constitutional issues. Moreover, his appointment provided the crucial fifth vote to give the liberal wing of the Court led by Chief Justice Earl Warren a majority.

Goldberg's opinions show that he was a strong advocate of individual rights. In his majority opinion in *Kennedy v. Mendoza-Martinez* (1963), he struck down the section of the immigration law that revoked the citizenship of anyone who left or remained outside the country to evade military service. In *Watson v. City of Memphis* (1963), which concerned the pace at which desegregation of public parks and other municipal facilities was implemented, Goldberg made clear that the Court would not tolerate delay. "The basic guarantees of our Constitution are warrants for the here and now and, unless there is an overwhelmingly compelling reason, they are to be promptly filled," he wrote.

Goldberg's most notable opinion was in *Escobedo v. Illinois* (1964). The case involved Danny Escobedo, an Illinois man charged with murder. Escobedo repeatedly asked to consult his lawyer during interrogation by the police, but his requests were denied. He was eventually convicted on the basis of incriminating statements he made to the police during interrogation. Escobedo challenged the conviction because he had been denied his right to an attorney, and the Court overturned the conviction—but on different grounds. Goldberg's reasoning focused on the fact that Escobedo had not been informed of his constitutional right to remain silent rather than make statements that might later be used against him. The *Escobedo* opinion, a 5–4 decision, set an important precedent in criminal procedure cases.

In July 1965 President Lyndon B. Johnson asked Goldberg to leave the Court and become the U.S. ambassador to the United Nations. Citing the difficulties of the Vietnam War and the need to have a distinguished person replace Adlai Stevenson as ambassador, Johnson persuaded Goldberg that his special negotiating talents would be invaluable. There is speculation that Johnson's real motivation in asking Goldberg to resign was Johnson's desire to appoint his friend and adviser, Abe Fortas, to the Supreme Court. Whatever the rationale, Johnson did, in fact, nominate Fortas to fill Goldberg's seat. When Goldberg accepted the appointment to the United Nations, he told Johnson, "I shall not, Mr. President, conceal the pain with which I leave the Court after three years of service. It has been the richest and most satisfying period of my career." He told reporters on July 20, the day he was named to his new post, "In all candor, I would rather the President had not asked me to undertake this duty. But it appears perhaps I can at this stage of our national life make a contribution, I hope, in this area of foreign affairs."

Convicted for murdering his brother-in-law in 1960, Danny Escobedo appealed his case because he had not been allowed to consult a lawyer during police interrogation. Arthur J. Goldberg's 1964 decision expanded constitutional protections for criminal defendants. This photo of Escobedo, taken after the Supreme Court's landmark ruling, shows him awaiting processing for a burglary charge. *Source: UPI/Bettmann*

Goldberg resigned from the Court five days later and moved to New York City to take up his new duties. At his request, he would continue to be called "Mr. Justice" for the rest of his life.

Goldberg's tenure as ambassador to the United Nations had its successes. In response to the Arab-Israeli war of June 1967, he was influential in negotiating a realistic solution to the Middle East conflict. It called for the Arab states to recognize the state of Israel, which in turn would pull back to its pre-1967 borders. He showed particular skill in obtaining the support of the Soviet ambassador for the resolution, although peace remained exclusive.

Johnson had emphasized that Goldberg's negotiating

At the request of Lyndon B. Johnson, Arthur J. Goldberg (left) resigned from the Supreme Court in 1965 to become the ambassador to the United Nations. Johnson said he needed Goldberg's skills as a negotiator to bring an end to the Vietnam War, but the war continued.
Source: AP/Wide World Photos

skills and reputation would perhaps lead to a settlement of the Vietnam War. This was not the case, however; the difficult goal of resolving the Vietnam conflict eluded him. In the meantime, Goldberg and Johnson held different views on how the war in Vietnam should be conducted, and their relations deteriorated over the years. By the end of Goldberg's tenure at the UN, insiders reported that Johnson took exception to his frequent telephone calls and memoranda calling for American de-escalation of the war.

A frustrated and disappointed Goldberg resigned his post in June 1968 and returned to the practice of law, remaining in New York City. In 1970 he ran for governor of New York on the Liberal-Democratic ticket against Nelson A. Rockefeller, the Republican incumbent. It was not a successful experience, and Goldberg was not tempted by elective politics again.

In 1971 Goldberg returned to Washington, where he practiced law and lectured at various colleges and universities. Drawing on his experiences on the Supreme Court, in 1971 he wrote a book entitled *Equal Justice:*

The Warren Era of the Supreme Court. He had previously published several other works, including *AFL-CIO Labor United* (1956) and *The Defenses of Freedom* (1966). During the 1970s, Goldberg was often called in to work on international arbitration cases, and from 1977 to 1978 he served as a U.S. ambassador-at-large for President Jimmy Carter. In that role he became a vocal critic of eastern-bloc nations for their human rights violations and an equally vocal advocate of resolving problems through negotiation. Carter awarded him the Presidential Medal of Freedom in 1978.

Outside his professional life, Goldberg enjoyed hiking, swimming, and watching football. He and his wife often retreated to their house in the Virgin Islands. Goldberg continued to practice law in Washington, D.C., and pursue his many extralegal interests until his death from heart disease on January 19, 1990. In his memoirs, President Johnson aptly praised Goldberg for his legal and negotiating abilities, calling him "a skilled arbiter and a fair-minded man."

Abe Fortas
1965-1969

Source: Library of Congress

BORN IN MEMPHIS, Tennessee, June 9, 1910, Abe Fortas was the youngest of five children of William Fortas and Ray Berson Fortas, Orthodox Jews who had emigrated from England. A cabinetmaker by training, William Fortas operated a small shop with his wife in one of the poorer sections of Memphis. Young Abe attended the local public schools and contributed to the family finances by working in a shoe store at night. Encouraged by his father, he studied music and showed a considerable talent for playing the violin. He formed a jazz band and performed at local dances and parties to earn money. Fortas attended Southwestern College in Memphis on an academic scholarship, graduating first in his class in 1930. Because of his remarkable skills as a debater, he decided on a career in the law.

Fortas entered Yale Law School, where he met William O. Douglas, a young professor who had already made his name as a leading expert on financial law. The poor Jewish southerner and the westerner of humble origins had something in common: both were outsiders to the East Coast establishment. Douglas quickly recognized his new student's talent and stimulated his interest in business law. Fortas became a member of the Order of the Coif, a legal honor society, and editor-in-chief of the prestigious *Yale Law Journal*. He graduated second in his class in 1933.

Upon graduation, he was offered a position on the Yale Law School faculty, but before long was commuting between New Haven and Washington, D.C., where he collaborated intermittently on several of the government's New Deal programs designed to combat the effects of the Great Depression. His first job was with the Agricultural Adjustment Administration (AAA), whose goal was to raise agricultural values by regulating production. While working summers and part time at the AAA, Fortas met an economist named Carolyn Eugenia Agger, whom he married in July 1935. He encouraged his wife to enroll in law school at Yale, and she eventually established herself as one of the nation's leading tax attorneys.

In 1934 Douglas hired his friend and former student away from the AAA to work for him at the Securities and Exchange Commission (SEC), a newly created government agency designed to regulate stock exchanges and trading practices. While continuing to teach, Fortas assisted Douglas on a study of business failures until 1937 when, again through his former professor's influence, he was hired to be the assistant director of the SEC's public utilities division.

Lured by the excitement and challenge of Franklin D. Roosevelt's New Deal programs and tired of what he perceived as the petty politics and low pay of academia, Fortas quit teaching business law at Yale for good in 1939. Douglas, now appointed to the Supreme Court, helped Fortas secure the post of general counsel of the Public Works Administration (PWA), an organization intended to increase employment and business activity through the construction of roads, public buildings,

and other public works projects. A few months later, realizing that the PWA would soon be shut down, Fortas transferred to become counsel of the Bituminous Coal Division.

In 1941 Fortas was appointed director of the Division of Power at the Department of the Interior and the following year, at age thirty-two, the rising young bureaucrat was promoted to be the department's undersecretary. As such, he served as assistant to Harold Ickes, the colorful and influential secretary of the interior. Fortas wielded enormous power at Interior; *Newsweek* called him "Ickes' Field Marshal" and "the man on whom Ickes relies for counsel, information and guidance." Biographers have noted that Fortas's devoted service to the government was more as an ambitious technician than as a crusader for the liberal New Deal ideology.

In 1946 Fortas left the government to go into private practice with Thurman Arnold, another former law school teacher, who had come to Washington to work in the Justice Department's Antitrust Division and had since become an appeals court judge. Together with Paul Porter, Arnold and Fortas founded what quickly became one of Washington's leading corporate law firms.

During the next twenty years, Fortas developed a reputation as a skilled corporate lawyer as well as a courageous advocate. While his firm's clientele included many of the country's corporate giants, Fortas also volunteered to litigate on behalf of the underdog in cases involving civil and individual rights. During the 1950s, when McCarthyism was at its height and suspected communists were vigorously prosecuted, Fortas successfully defended Owen Lattimore, a policy expert on China and Mongolia who was accused of disloyalty to his country. Fortas also represented Monte Durham in a precedent-setting District of Columbia case in 1954, winning his client a decision that significantly broadened the modern insanity defense. In another landmark case, the Supreme Court appointed Fortas in 1962 to represent Clarence Earl Gideon, an indigent Florida inmate who had challenged the constitutionality of his robbery conviction in a handwritten petition. Fortas's argument helped the Court establish the right of an individual accused of a serious criminal offense to be represented by an attorney at trial, even if counsel must be appointed at public expense.

It was during his early years in Washington that Fortas first met Lyndon B. Johnson, then an obscure member of Congress from Texas. Johnson solicited Fortas's help on a dam project of considerable importance to his constituents and was impressed by the young man's talents. In 1948, when Johnson won the Democratic senatorial primary of Texas by less than 100 votes, his opponents accused him of stuffing the ballot box in one of the precincts and persuaded a federal judge to take Johnson's name off the ballot. Called in again to perform a favor for his friend, Fortas won a stay from Justice Hugo Black. Johnson's name was restored to the ballot, giving him the Democratic nomination and, inevitably, the Senate seat. As Johnson gained power and prestige in the Senate and eventually became vice president and president, Fortas became one of his most trusted advisers. The contrast between the two friends was striking: Fortas was fine-boned, polite, soft-spoken, and had refined tastes, whereas Johnson was big, talkative, and rather rough. Their unlikely relationship would continue even after Fortas took his place on the Supreme Court, with the president regularly calling on him for extrajudicial advice, notably on Vietnam War policy.

In July 1965 President Johnson persuaded Justice Arthur Goldberg to resign from the Supreme Court and accept an appointment as U.S. ambassador to the United Nations. Although Johnson claimed he needed Goldberg's negotiating skills to mediate an end to the Vietnam War, many believe that Johnson wanted to create a vacancy on the Court so he could appoint his old friend and confidant. Johnson offered the post in-

Abe Fortas's close friendship with Lyndon B. Johnson began when Fortas was a Washington attorney and Johnson a little-known representative from Texas. The advisory relationship continued throughout Fortas's tenure on the Supreme Court. Here Fortas is subjected to a friendly dose of the well-known Johnson "treatment." *Source: LBJ Library*

formally to Fortas, who declined because he was reluctant to abandon the responsibilities and income of his lucrative practice. Besides, he was happy with his independent role of confidential adviser to the president. (On similar grounds, Fortas had already turned down Johnson's offer a year earlier to become attorney general.) Nevertheless, an insistent president nominated Fortas, without securing his acceptance, on July 28, barely three days after receiving Goldberg's resignation. The Senate confirmed Fortas's appointment by voice vote August 11, and Fortas, without ever giving his formal consent to the president, joined the Court in October.

Lacking experience as a judge, Fortas was more comfortable in the role of advocate than in applying theoretical doctrines to specific cases. In his brief four years on the Court, he proved to be a supporter of measures that broadened the constitutional rights of criminal defendants. He provided the decisive fifth vote for Chief Justice Earl Warren's majority opinion in *Miranda v. Arizona* (1966), the landmark case that required law enforcement officers to inform suspects of their constitutional rights prior to questioning. Fortas was particularly concerned with expanding the rights of juveniles. Writing for the Court in 1967, he held in *In re Gault* that the privilege against self-incrimination and the right to counsel extended to juvenile court proceedings. He insisted that "under our Constitution, the condition of being a boy does not justify a kangaroo court."

In one of his last and most famous opinions, *Tinker v. Des Moines Independent Community School District* (1969), Fortas wrote that the wearing of black armbands by students protesting the Vietnam War was "closely akin" to the "pure speech" protected by the First Amendment. Consequently, such public expression of opinion was entitled to constitutional protection as a form of peaceful and nondisruptive "symbolic" speech as long as it did not violate the rights of others. However, in another important freedom of speech case, he advocated a need for realistic limits on slander and defended the right of public officials to be protected from "shotgun attacks in virtually unlimited open season."

Drawing on his experiences as a corporate lawyer, Fortas took the lead role on the Court in business cases. Openly pro-business, he dissented in several antitrust cases striking down corporate mergers. Either in dissent or while speaking for the Court, Fortas wrote persuasive opinions in his clear, eloquent style. He continued to exhibit a strong interest in the relationship between psychology and law, a subject on which he had frequently published.

In 1968 Chief Justice Warren indicated to President

Mary Beth Tinker and her brother John display the black armbands they wore to school to protest the Vietnam War. Their action got them suspended from school in 1965. Abe Fortas wrote the 1969 Supreme Court opinion ruling that the armbands were "symbolic" speech protected by the First Amendment and that the children's suspensions were unconstitutional.
Source: Bettmann

Johnson his intention to retire at the end of the Court's spring term. The president quickly sent Fortas's name to the Senate for confirmation as chief justice, but the nomination was doomed because of Johnson's growing unpopularity. Amid charges of "cronyism" and political manipulation, Republicans and conservative southern Democrats criticized the president, who had announced he would not seek reelection, for attempting to "pack" the Court before he left office. In addition, a disclosure that Fortas had been paid $15,000 for teaching a seminar at a local law school brought charges of extrajudicial impropriety and further fanned the flames of opposition. In the face of mounting criticism, Johnson was braced to withdraw the nomination after a Senate vote failed to end a filibuster that had prevented the nomination from reaching the floor. On October 3, at Fortas's request, the nomination was withdrawn and he remained on the Court as an associate justice.

The following May *Life* magazine dropped a bombshell when it published an article about Fortas's involvement with an indicted stock manipulator, Louis E. Wolfson. The article revealed that Fortas had received $20,000 from Wolfson's charitable foundation in 1966, after he had joined the Court, but that he had returned the sum eleven months later. Although it was clear that Fortas had been interested in helping the charity develop its civil rights projects, he had also given informal advice to Wolfson about his legal troubles. After initially denying the relationship, Fortas resigned from the Court on May 14, 1969, in the face of public condemnation and talk of impeachment. In a letter to Chief Justice Warren, he denied any wrongdoing but explained that he wanted to let the Court "proceed with its vital work free from extraneous stress." His resignation ended the tradition of the "Jewish seat" in which a

Music was an important part of Justice Abe Fortas's life since boyhood. An accomplished violinist, Fortas (right) played in a semiprofessional string quartet while serving on the Supreme Court and following his resignation. *Source: Collection of the Supreme Court of the United States*

series of Jewish justices had sat in unbroken succession since 1932.

With his reputation shattered, a saddened Fortas resumed the private practice of law in partnership with another attorney in Washington. An accomplished violinist, he continued to play regularly in a semiprofessional string quartet—as he had while sitting on the Court. His love of music led him to become a board member of the Kennedy Center for the Performing Arts and of Carnegie Hall International.

The former justice returned to the Supreme Court thirteen years after his resignation to present an oral argument in a case involving Puerto Rico, whose interests Fortas had long supported. It was his last appearance. He died two weeks later, on April 5, 1982, of a heart attack in his Georgetown home.

Thurgood Marshall
1967-1991

Source: Library of Congress

THURGOOD MARSHALL, the first African-American to serve on the Supreme Court, was born July 2, 1908, in Baltimore, Maryland. Named for his grandfather, Thoroughgood Marshall, a freed slave, he was the second son of William Canfield Marshall, a dining car waiter and later chief steward at a private club, and Norma Arica Marshall, a teacher in a segregated elementary school.

After graduating from high school in 1925, Marshall went to Lincoln University in Pennsylvania, the nation's oldest black college. There, his strong oratorical skills led the debating team to a string of impressive victories. He also began what was to become a lifelong struggle fighting segregation. In a nearby movie theater, Marshall and his friends refused to sit in the balcony—the so-called "nigger heaven"—sitting instead in the "whites only" orchestra section.

During college, Marshall met Vivian ("Buster") Burey, a University of Pennsylvania undergraduate. They married in 1929. Marshall's part-time job as a

476

bellhop and Buster's secretarial work supported them through college, and in 1930 Marshall graduated with honors. His interest in debating and in improving society led him to reject his mother's suggestion that he become a dentist and to choose law instead.

Marshall considered attending the University of Maryland Law School, but, knowing it was an all-white institution that would not admit him, he opted for Howard University. Although he had to commute from his parents' house in Baltimore and work part time, Marshall graduated first in his class in 1933. His impressive performance attracted the attention of two faculty members who became his mentors, Prof. William Hastie and Dean Charles Houston. Their goal was to teach law students to be "social engineers" who would use the law to improve the community, and they were eager to enlist this outstanding student to work with the National Association for the Advancement of Colored People (NAACP) in its efforts to challenge segregation.

After graduation, Marshall opened his own law office in Baltimore, but volunteered much of his time to the local branch of the NAACP. One of his first, and probably more satisfying, efforts was his suit against Maryland's law school. Representing a young black man denied admission, Marshall and Houston convinced the state courts that maintaining a law school for whites only and none for blacks violated the "separate but equal" doctrine that was then the law of the land, and was therefore unconstitutional. In addition to fighting segregation, Marshall challenged the legality of the common practice of paying black school teachers less than comparably qualified whites.

In 1936 Houston, by then special counsel to the NAACP in New York, invited Marshall to be his assistant. He accepted despite Houston's warning that the job would be frustrating and dangerous. One of their early efforts was to use the Maryland strategy to challenge the constitutionality of Missouri's all-white law school. The result was a landmark case, *Missouri ex rel. Gaines v. Canada* (1938), in which the Supreme Court ordered the university to admit the black plaintiff.

When Houston resigned as NAACP special counsel in 1938, Marshall, at age thirty, replaced him. One year later, the NAACP created the Legal Defense and Educational Fund, Inc., to provide free legal aid to blacks who suffered from race discrimination, and Marshall became its director-counsel. In a series of cases that eventually wound up in the Supreme Court, Marshall and his colleagues successfully challenged the constitutionality of "whites only" primaries that effectively denied blacks any vote, the practice of segregated interstate transportation, and the enforcement of racially restrictive covenants in private residences. With ten years of successful litigation behind him, Marshall earned the nickname "Mr. Civil Rights."

Segregated education continued to be one of Marshall's high-priority targets. When Texas sought to

In 1936 Charles Houston, former dean of Howard University Law School, recruited Thurgood Marshall to work as his assistant at the NAACP's Manhattan headquarters. Marshall masterminded twenty-nine victories before the Supreme Court, striking down racial discrimination in areas such as education, housing, transportation, electoral politics, and criminal justice. *Source: Library of Congress*

comply with the separate but equal requirement by creating a black law school consisting of two rented rooms
and two part-time instructors, Marshall persuaded the
Supreme Court that this school was clearly inferior to
the all-white University of Texas Law School. In *Sweatt
v. Painter* (1950) the university was ordered to admit the
black plaintiff. Marshall also challenged Oklahoma's
method of dealing with the separate but equal doctrine.
When a district court ordered the University of Oklahoma to admit George McLaurin, a sixty-eight-year-old
black college professor, to a doctoral program available
only at the university, officials admitted him but on a
"segregated basis." McLaurin could listen to lectures
only from outside the classroom, received a screened-off
desk in the library, and was allowed in the cafeteria only
when white students were not eating. The Supreme
Court agreed that these restrictions failed to provide
McLaurin with equal facilities and ordered their elimination.

Armed with these precedents, Marshall decided it
was time to attack segregation in the primary and secondary public schools. As chief strategist, he coordi-
nated suits in South Carolina, Delaware, Kansas, Virginia, and the District of Columbia. Primarily responsible for the challenge brought in Clarendon County,
South Carolina, where the facilities for blacks were
clearly inferior, Marshall was unwilling to accept the
defense's strategy of conceding the inequality and
promising to improve the blacks' facilities. He opted for
the riskier approach of attacking segregation head-on,
arguing that separate education was inherently unequal.
Relying on sociological data, he sought to prove that
segregation psychologically damaged black children,
but the district court rejected his argument. The
Supreme Court agreed to hear the case, combining it
with the NAACP school cases in the four other jurisdictions. This time, Marshall's arguments prevailed.
On May 17, 1954, a unanimous Court issued its landmark *Brown v. Board of Education of Topeka* decision

Future justice Thurgood Marshall, fourth from right, and other
NAACP Legal Defense and Educational Fund attorneys for the
plaintiffs in the landmark school desegregation decision, *Brown v.
Board of Education* (1954), congratulate each other on their monu-
mental victory. *Courtesy NAACP Public Relations*

declaring segregation inherently unequal and therefore
unconstitutional.

Marshall could not celebrate his victory for long.
Shortly after the *Brown* decision, he learned that Buster
was dying of cancer. Devastated by the news, he spent
the fall and winter caring for her. She died in February
1955.

Marshall had to go on. The Court had scheduled arguments on the remedy in *Brown* and in May 1955 announced that states must end school segregation "with
all deliberate speed." Marshall was disappointed because he wanted a specific deadline, accurately foreseeing that this indeterminate phrase would permit states
to stall. Encountering enormous resistance, Marshall
spent the next several years trying to get states to comply with *Brown.*

But Marshall wanted to do more than to implement
Brown; he sought to extend its principle beyond education. In a series of cases, Marshall persuaded the
Supreme Court that separate but equal was unconstitutional in every public forum—public housing, recreational facilities, beaches, transportation, and sports
arenas. He also succeeded in defending the NAACP

against Alabama's attempt to ban it from the state. In his last Supreme Court argument as a private litigant—and his twenty-ninth victory in the Court—Marshall convinced the justices to overturn the conviction of sixteen black students arrested in Baton Rouge, Louisiana, for peacefully "sitting in" at a segregated lunch counter.

During this period, Marshall's personal life improved as well. In December 1955 he married Cecilia ("Cissy") Suyat, an NAACP colleague. In the next few years, they had two sons, Thurgood, Jr., and John William.

By 1961 Mr. Civil Rights had become the most successful African-American lawyer in history. Impressed by Marshall's skills, President John F. Kennedy nominated him for a judgeship on the Second Circuit Court of Appeals. With several southern senators on the Judiciary Committee opposed to the appointment, the hostile, protracted confirmation process took more than eleven months.

In his four years on the court of appeals, Marshall wrote 118 opinions on a wide variety of subjects. His success rate was unbeatable; none of his ninety-eight majority opinions was reversed by the Supreme Court, an accomplishment that did not go unnoticed. In July 1965 President Lyndon B. Johnson asked Marshall to become solicitor general of the United States.

This time Marshall was quickly confirmed, becoming the first African-American to serve in the post. It was a significant time to be the government's chief legal advocate. The Civil Rights Act of 1964 and the Voting Rights Act of 1965 had just been passed, and the Twenty-fourth Amendment (prohibiting poll taxes in federal elections) had just been ratified. As solicitor general, Marshall would have significant power in shaping the implementation of these new laws. Here, too, his success record was outstanding—he won fourteen of nineteen cases.

On June 13, 1967, President Johnson nominated Marshall to the Supreme Court, declaring it "the right thing to do, the right time to do it, the right man and the

right place." No prior nominee had had such an extensive and successful record of arguments before the Court. Despite this record, it took another round of protracted questioning before Marshall was confirmed by a vote of 69–11 on August 30.

Joining the Court's liberal majority, Marshall was able to write majority opinions supporting an expansive view of the Constitution and individual rights. In his first few years, for example, he wrote several significant First Amendment opinions, notably *Stanley v. Georgia* (1969), which held that the Constitution protects a person's right to read anything in the privacy of his home, including obscene materials. Another First Amendment case was *Police Department of Chicago v. Mosely* (1972), forbidding the government from favoring some speech over others in permitting picketing. In addition, he wrote important criminal procedure decisions, including *Benton v. Maryland* (1969), holding that the Double Jeopardy Clause, which prohibits trying an individual twice for the same crime, applies not only to the federal government but also to the states.

Justice Hugo L. Black (right) swears in the new solicitor general of the United States, Thurgood Marshall, August 24, 1965, as President Lyndon B. Johnson, Marshall's wife, Cecilia, and their two sons look on. The first African-American to serve as solicitor general, Marshall was also the first African-American appointed to the Supreme Court. *Source: LBJ Library*

Within a few years of Marshall's arrival, however, the Court's personnel changed, and Marshall found it necessary to make his contributions through powerful dissents. He often criticized his colleagues' use of legal formalisms that could obscure the real world and the real people affected by their decisions. In the field of equal protection, for example, he preferred a more flexible approach over what he regarded as an unduly formal, rigid analysis adopted by the Court's majority. When the Court upheld the constitutionality of a mandatory fifty dollar fee to file in bankruptcy court, assuming that a poor person could simply pay the fee in weekly installments, Marshall dissented. Chastising the majority's failure to appreciate "how close to the margin of survival" many poor people are, he concluded, "It is perfectly proper for judges to disagree about what the Constitution requires. But it is disgraceful for an interpretation of the Constitution to be premised upon unfounded assumptions about how people live."

Marshall's real world experience also led him to adamantly oppose capital punishment. Having defended many facing the death penalty, he decried its finality and often unjust applications. In 1972, when the Court agreed that the death penalty was being implemented in too arbitrary a manner, in violation of the Eighth Amendment's prohibition of cruel and unusual punishment, Marshall was pleased. Four years later, however, the Court modified this view and upheld the use of capital punishment. At that point, Marshall and his colleague William Brennan began their practice, which they continued for their whole tenure, of dissenting in every case that upheld the death penalty.

Always the realist, Marshall reminded those celebrating the Constitution's bicentennial that, because it condoned slavery, the Constitution was "defective from the start. . . . 'We the People' no longer enslave, but the credit belongs not to the framers. It belongs to those who refused to acquiesce in outdated notions of 'liberty,' 'justice,' and 'equality,' and who strived to better them. . . . *The true miracle was not the birth of the Constitution, but its life."* Marshall declared his intention to celebrate the bicentennial of the Constitution "as a living document, including the Bill of Rights and the other amendments protecting individual freedoms and human rights."

On June 27, 1991, at the age of eighty-two, Marshall announced his retirement. While his colleagues on the Court did not always agree with him, they respected his convictions, accomplishments, and fierce candor. As Justice Byron White noted, Marshall told them "the way it was. . . . He characteristically would tell us things that we knew but would rather forget, and he told us much that we did not know due to the limitations of our own experiences." William Brennan fondly praised Marshall's "special voice."

His was a voice of authority: he spoke from first-hand knowledge of the law's failure to fulfill its promised protections for so many Americans. It was also the voice of reason, for Justice Marshall had spent half a lifetime using the tools of legal argument to close the gap between constitutional ideal and reality. And it was a voice with an unwavering message: that the Constitution's protection must not be denied to anyone and that the Court must give its constitutional doctrine the scope and sensitivity needed to assure the result. Justice Marshall's voice was often persuasive, but whether or not he prevailed in a given instance, he always had an impact . . . [speaking] for those who might otherwise be forgotten.

Marshall died of heart failure on January 24, 1993. Thousands—all ages, all races—spent hours waiting in the cold to pay their respects to this hero as he lay in state in the Supreme Court. Thousands more came the next day to the National Cathedral to honor him for his work as an advocate for reform and a symbol of hope. He was warmly eulogized by the simple words that had frequently buoyed the hopes of his downtrodden clients: "The lawyer's coming."

Warren E. Burger
1969-1986

WARREN EARL BURGER, who served longer in the post of chief justice than all but three of his fourteen predecessors, was born September 17, Constitution Day, in 1907. He was the fourth of seven children of Charles and Catherine Burger. The family lived in a frame house in a working-class district of St. Paul, Minnesota. His Swiss-Austrian-German grandparents had come to the Midwest before the Civil War, and his grandfather won the Congressional Medal of Honor in an isolated engagement with overwhelmingly superior Confederate troops.

From the time he was able to pick tomatoes on a thirty-acre family truck farm near St. Paul, young Burger knew the meaning of work. By the age of eleven, he had acquired a daily newspaper route, and among the additional odd jobs he picked up on Saturdays was helping a maker of theatrical backdrops. He was greatly motivated by his mother, a strong, practical woman whose adages Burger still quotes: "The time to fix the cracks in the plaster is when you first move into a house. Later on you don't pay any attention to them."

In school Burger was drawn to journalism and became editor of the high school weekly paper. He showed talent at drawing and sculpting, digging clay from the banks of the nearby Mississippi River for his early efforts at sculpture. One, a head of Benjamin Franklin that Burger made at age fifteen, was reproduced in 1987 by the Franklin Mint and sold to benefit the Commission on the Bicentennial of the U.S. Constitution.

Burger was awarded a scholarship to Princeton University, but he could not accept it because it meant he could not continue contributing to the family finances. He decided to study law, and night school was the only way open. He worked full time as an accountant for an insurance company, advancing, as he later joked, to senior accountant of a staff of two.

From 1925 to 1927 he attended University of Minnesota pre-law classes at night and graduated from St. Paul College of Law (since renamed William Mitchell College of Law) in 1931. On receiving his LL.B. magna cum laude, Burger was appointed to the faculty of his alma mater and taught there for seventeen years as an adjunct professor of contracts. That same year he joined an established law firm where he practiced for the next twenty-one years.

In 1933 Burger married Elvera Stromberg, a schoolteacher he had met when they were both attending the University of Minnesota night school. Future Supreme Court justice Harry A. Blackmun, a fellow Minnesotan and close friend, served as best man at their wedding. A son and a daughter were born to the couple.

Burger and the firm prospered even in the Great Depression years. His legal work covered a wide range of practice, and he developed a reputation as a skilled advocate. During these years, Burger also participated in the civic life of his hometown. Among other activities,

he served as president of the city's Junior Chamber of Commerce and organized the first St. Paul Council on Human Relations to fight racial discrimination. When Japanese-Americans were forced to leave the West Coast during World War II, the council created a special committee to find housing and employment for those who came to St. Paul. Burger also played a leading role in reforming a notoriously corrupt police department, by making the police chief a career position and giving special training to police officers in dealing with minorities.

In the late 1930s Burger joined in an effort, largely sparked by Harold E. Stassen, to revitalize the state's Republican party, long out of power, as a vehicle to replace an inefficient and corrupt state government. It succeeded in 1938 with the election of Stassen as governor. Burger also played a critical role in the victory of Dwight D. Eisenhower at the 1952 Republican convention, delivering some important southern delegates and the deciding vote of the Minnesota delegation.

Eisenhower invited him to Washington in 1953 to serve as assistant attorney general for the Civil Division at the Justice Department. There he successfully prosecuted a civil case against wealthy Greek ship owners for a huge restitution claim growing out of their illegal acquisition of war surplus American ships. His quick mastery of maritime law earned him the nickname "Admiral" from his colleagues.

In 1955, just as Burger was preparing to return to his St. Paul partnership, a vacancy occurred on the U.S. Court of Appeals for the District of Columbia Circuit, and Eisenhower offered Burger the seat. The appeals court in Washington, D.C., is sometimes called the "little Supreme Court" because of the significance of the litigation it handles. Judge Burger delved deeply into constitutional questions and also into criminal law.

During his thirteen years on the court of appeals, one of Burger's activities was to study the courts and penal institutions of Europe, seeking better solutions to

America's stubborn problems of crime and corrections. In 1957 he helped to establish the Appellate Judges' Seminar at New York University and served on its faculty for more than a dozen years. He later co-chaired a comprehensive eight-year study for the American Bar Association (ABA) on standards of criminal justice.

At this time Burger began speaking out on the growing problems of the American judicial system: inefficient management of the courts, the overload of cases, long delays in hearing and resolution, and inadequacies in the administration of the prison system. He advocated improving legal education with emphasis on practical skills and ethics. A widely reprinted 1967 speech expressed his dissatisfaction with a judicial system that was "not working" and caused "decent people" to experience "a suppressed rage, frustration, and bitterness, [while criminals] feel that they can 'get by' with anything."

President Richard Nixon nominated Burger to be chief justice on May 21, 1969, after President Lyndon B. Johnson's efforts to elevate Associate Justice Abe Fortas to fill the seat vacated by Earl Warren had failed. On June 9 Burger was easily confirmed by the Senate in a 74–3 vote.

As chief justice, Burger lost no time in moving to repair the cracks he perceived in the nation's judicial structure. Some repairs were designed to deal more efficiently with the staggering increase in cases seeking Supreme Court review. Oral arguments were reduced to one hour per case from two hours; attorneys seeking admission to the Supreme Court Bar could choose to complete the process by mail rather than by personal appearance, saving the Court from administering the oath to each of the 5,000 lawyers who apply each year; complete opinions, with few exceptions, were no longer read from the bench (which sometimes had consumed half a day), but instead were summarized from the bench and the full text released in print; word processors and copying machines turned out the drafts and

memoranda that formerly had been typed with eight carbon copies.

Burger's initiatives effected changes at every level of the judicial system, state and federal, all of which were suffering from a staggering overload. Case filings in the federal trial courts had more than doubled in twenty years, and there was at least a corresponding increase in appeals, a "litigation explosion." Delays were enormous; it took some cases as much as five years to come to trial.

Within weeks after taking office in August 1969, Burger appeared informally at the annual ABA convention to propose a study on prisons and corrections. He also called for the appointment of professionally trained administrators to relieve district and appellate judges of time-consuming administrative chores. At another meeting he discussed improvements in the education and training of lawyers. The Institute for Court Management was created and operating within six months, and the graduates assigned to district and appellate courts at the rate of thirty-five or forty a year. Case dispositions by federal judges rose by a third in the decade that followed.

Burger had long recommended six-person juries in civil cases, shortening the trial process and saving millions of dollars annually. The smaller jury was soon adopted in most federal jurisdictions. He persuaded the chief justices of forty states to create state-federal judicial councils, which have eliminated parallel trials of multiple disaster cases with the same issues in more than one court and conflicts in jury verdicts. He convinced the Federal Bureau of Prisons to establish ways of registering grievances throughout the correctional system, reducing prisoner petitions to the federal courts by a third. He urged the fifty states, with their similar problems but often isolated judiciaries, to pool their experience and ideas in the National Center for State Courts, established in 1971. A 1986 resolution adopted by the Conference of State Chief Justices and State

Court Administrators said that Burger had done "more than any person in history to improve the operation of all our nation's courts."

In addition to his activities as chief justice, Burger wrote as many majority opinions as any of his colleagues on the Court. Almost always on the side with the greater consensus, he voted with the majority in 80 percent of cases decided in his first thirteen terms. Under his leadership, the Court cut back some of the more extreme liberal positions of the Warren Court. His opinion in *Miller v. California* (1973) redefined the law of obscenity under the First Amendment and gave

Pat Nixon says goodbye to Gerald and Betty Ford as the Nixons prepare to board the helicopter that will fly them from the White House. In 1974 Warren E. Burger wrote the Supreme Court decision directing President Richard Nixon to turn over the tapes of White House conversations that had been subpoenaed in the Watergate conspiracy trial. The unanimous decision led to Nixon's resignation a few weeks later. *Source: Nixon Project, National Archives*

more authority to local communities. In a series of cases involving religious freedom, he championed an "accommodationist" approach to the First Amendment guarantees of free exercise of religion, reasoning that the Constitution does not "require complete separation of church and state; it affirmatively mandates accommodation, not merely tolerance, of all religions, and forbids hostility toward any." On matters of criminal justice and the rights of the accused, his opinions gave greater weight to law enforcement than had the Warren Court.

In a historic irony, Burger delivered the unanimous opinion in a 1974 case that led to the resignation of the president who had appointed him. In *United States v. Nixon* (1974) the Court ruled that the president must surrender tapes of recorded conversations, which had been subpoenaed in a criminal conspiracy trial. Burger reasoned that a broad claim of executive privilege, while rooted in the separation of powers, must yield to the demands of justice and a fair trial. Seventeen days after the opinion was announced, Nixon became the first president in American history to resign. In another notable separation of powers case, *Immigration and Naturalization Service v. Chadha* (1983), Burger struck down Congress's one-house vetoes of decisions made by federal agencies.

Throughout Burger's tenure, the Court confronted the vexing question of court-ordered busing to achieve school desegregation. In *Swann v. Charlotte-Mecklenburg County Board of Education* (1971) Burger wrote the ruling that permitted busing, and in *Milliken v. Bradley* (1974) he limited busing to intradistrict integration plans. Burger also announced the Court's ruling in *Fullilove v. Klutznick* (1980), upholding Congress's power to adopt minority-based affirmative action programs for awarding government contracts. His opinions generally took each case on its own merits, paid close attention to the facts, and were narrowly crafted to the issues at hand. His judicial record thus cannot be en-

The Supreme Court under Chief Justice Warren E. Burger was asked to rule on several cases involving the constitutionality of court-ordered busing to achieve school integration. *Source: AP/Wide World Photos*

capsulated as simply either "liberal" or "conservative," but rather as moderate, balanced, and pragmatic.

While he was chief justice, Burger enjoyed horseback riding, gardening, and taking long walks near his home in Virginia. Because of his keen interest in art, antiques, and history, Burger was particularly active as chairman of the board of the National Gallery of Art and as chancellor of the Smithsonian Institution, positions he held by virtue of being chief justice.

Accepting President Ronald Reagan's offer to become chairman of the Bicentennial Commission, Burger

stepped down from the Court September 26, 1986, to take over direction of the five-year observance and "to give ourselves a history and civics lesson." He directed a huge program of activities, including projects in schools and colleges, major judicial gatherings, publication of books and pamphlets, massive distribution of copies of the Constitution, and the creation and preparation of television documentaries.

Burger died of congestive heart failure June 25, 1995, roughly a year after the death of his wife, Elvera.

Harry A. Blackmun
1970-1994

Source: National Geographic Society

Harry Andrew Blackmun was born in Nashville, Illinois, November 12, 1908. He grew up in St. Paul, Minnesota, where his father owned a grocery and hardware store. His family was of modest means, but, looking back on those years, Blackmun has suggested that their circumstances "didn't do me any harm at all."

The Harvard Club of Minnesota selected Blackmun to receive a tuition scholarship. To cover his expenses at Harvard College, he worked at odd jobs ranging from delivering milk to grading math papers. He majored in mathematics, receiving his A.B. summa cum laude and election to Phi Beta Kappa in 1929.

Blackmun at first considered becoming a physician, but ultimately decided on a career in law and received his LL.B. degree from Harvard Law School in 1932. Among his law professors was Felix Frankfurter, whom Blackmun did not admire much at the time but whom he later came to regard as a great teacher and a formative influence.

486

After law school, Blackmun clerked for John B. Sanborn, a judge on the U.S. circuit court in St. Paul, for a year and a half. He then spent sixteen years in private practice in Minneapolis with Dorsey, Colman, Barker, Scott, and Barber, specializing in the "characteristically precise fields" of taxation, trusts and estates, and civil litigation. During that time he taught real property and tax courses at the St. Paul College of Law and then at the University of Minnesota Law School. In 1941 Blackmun married Dorothy Clark, and they eventually had three daughters—Nancy, Sally, and Susan.

In 1950 Blackmun became the first resident counsel at the Mayo Clinic, the world-renowned medical center in Rochester, Minnesota. He remained in that post until 1959, a period he subsequently described as the "happiest decade" in his life, largely because it gave him "a foot in both camps—law and medicine." Blackmun's association with the Mayo Clinic enhanced his reputation as a serious, hard-working, and capable attorney, and prompted President Dwight D. Eisenhower to nominate him to the U.S. Court of Appeals for the Eighth Circuit. Blackmun joined the court November 4, 1959, replacing his former mentor, Judge Sanborn. Blackmun established himself as the most studious member of the Court and was generally labeled a conservative.

A substantial percentage of Blackmun's opinions on the Eighth Circuit concerned taxation, but he also wrote notable opinions on other subjects. For example, in perhaps the first appellate opinion declaring brutal treatment of prisoners to be illegal, Blackmun wrote in *Jackson v. Bishop* (1968) that disciplining prisoners by lashing them was cruel and unusual punishment. Blackmun later expressed pride in the *Jackson* decision and in the role such cases have played in improving conditions in the nation's prisons.

In a 1967 case Blackmun held that because of binding precedent his court could not prohibit a private homeowner from refusing to sell his home to a black. Invit-

ing the Supreme Court to rethink the precedents, Blackmun suggested several approaches for finding such discrimination unlawful, and he was pleased when the Supreme Court accepted his invitation and reversed its position.

On April 14, 1970, Blackmun was nominated to the Supreme Court in President Richard Nixon's third attempt to fill the seat vacated by Abe Fortas. The Senate had rebuffed Nixon's attempts to place a conservative southerner on the Court by rejecting the nominations of judges Clement F. Haynsworth, Jr., and G. Harrold Carswell. Chief Justice Warren E. Burger recommended Blackmun for the post. Burger had known Blackmun since they were children in St. Paul. Blackmun had been best man at Burger's wedding.

Harry A. Blackmun served as the first resident counsel of the prestigious Mayo Clinic in Rochester, Minnesota, from 1950 to 1959. He became an expert on the relationship between law and medicine during his affiliation with the medical center. *Source: Mayo Clinic News Bureau*

Norma McCorvey was the real "Jane Roe" behind the Supreme Court's controversial 1973 abortion decision, *Roe v. Wade*, written by Harry A. Blackmun. She is pictured here in 1989, more than fifteen years after she challenged Texas's anti-abortion statute.
Source: Bettmann

The Senate unanimously confirmed "Old No. 3" (Blackmun's self-deprecating term) May 12, 1970. Derided initially as one of the "Minnesota Twins" because of his ties to Burger and their similar voting pattern, Blackmun and Burger soon diverged, both professionally and personally.

Blackmun established himself as a justice who preferred to focus on the pragmatic aspects of each case rather than the theoretical. He showed a populist concern for the "little guy," the person who would be affected by the decision and whose modest circumstances may be foreign to many members of the Court.

There are many examples of Blackmun's insistence that the Court stay grounded in the real world. A consistent supporter of race-conscious affirmative action programs, Blackmun asked the Court in *University of California Regents v. Bakke* (1978) to accept the reality that "in order to get beyond racism, we must first take account of race. There is no other way." Dissenting from upholding limits on government funding of abortions, Blackmun wrote, "There truly is another world out there, the existence of which the Court, I suspect, either chooses to ignore, or fears to realize." Blackmun later challenged the "comfortable perspective" from which the Court decreed that the effect of a regulation increasing the cost of an abortion by forty dollars was insignificant.

Blackmun found himself (except in some criminal procedure matters) regularly aligned with the Court's liberals and against the Court's right wing. Many saw a pronounced leftward shift on Blackmun's part, but he, while conceding a conscious effort to "hold the center," insisted, as did other observers, that it was the Court that had swung to the right. In any event, Blackmun's evolution showed a greater comfort with his role on the nation's highest court and an increased willingness to allow his personal character and his concern for fairness to influence his decision making.

Blackmun showed his growing independence in the decision that remains his best known and most controversial, *Roe v. Wade* (1973). In *Roe* a seven-member majority struck down a Texas statute that prohibited women from having—and doctors from performing—most abortions. Blackmun's opinion held that the constitutional right to privacy recognized in earlier decisions was "broad enough to encompass a woman's decision whether or not to terminate her pregnancy." After weeks of medical and historical research at the Mayo Clinic, Blackmun wrote that, until a fetus is viable (capable of surviving with medical help outside the womb), the state may regulate abortion only to protect the woman's health. After viability, the state's compelling interest in the fetus' potential life would permit a complete ban on abortion, except where necessary to protect the mother's life or health.

Roe v. Wade illustrates two recurrent interests and themes in Blackmun's work: the right to privacy and the interplay between medical and legal issues. Some commentators have noted that portions of *Roe* read as if the interest being protected belonged to the doctor as much as the patient. In later abortion cases, Blackmun focused more directly on the woman's privacy interests. In 1986, for example, Blackmun's opinion for the Court invalidated provisions of a state law that sought to "intimidate women into continuing pregnancies." Blackmun concluded, "Few decisions are more personal and intimate, more properly private, or more basic to individual dignity and autonomy, than a woman's decision—with the guidance of her physician and within the limits specified in *Roe*—whether to end her pregnancy. A woman's right to make that choice freely is fundamental."

Blackmun expressed his views on the right to privacy most forcefully in his 1986 dissent in *Bowers v. Hardwick.* The majority upheld, by a 5–4 vote, Georgia's arrest of a homosexual for private, consensual sexual activity. Blackmun noted that the case concerned not "a fundamental right to engage in homosexual sodomy," but the "most valued" of rights, "the right to be let alone." He wrote, "The fact that individuals define themselves in a significant way through their intimate sexual relationships with others suggests, in a Nation as diverse as ours, that there may be many 'right' ways of conducting those relationships, and that much of the richness of a relationship will come from the freedom an individual has to choose the form and nature of these intensely personal bonds." "Tolerance of nonconformity," Blackmun said, was far less threatening than interference with consensual intimate behavior that occurs at home.

Blackmun's contributions on other medical-legal is-

sues include his exploration of the state's duties to those it commits to mental institutions. In *Jackson v. Indiana* (1972), he wrote for the Court that a retarded deaf mute arrested for petty theft, but found by psychiatrists to be incompetent to stand trial, could not be warehoused indefinitely in a mental institution that provided no treatment. "At the least, due process requires that the nature and duration of commitment bear some reasonable relation to the purpose for which the individual is committed." A decade later, Blackmun suggested that a severely retarded man committed by the state against his will might be constitutionally entitled to treatment aimed at preserving the basic skills, such as dressing himself, he had upon entering the institution.

His aptitude on medical issues likewise sparked Blackmun's dissent from the Court's 1983 *Barefoot v. Estelle* decision, which upheld the practice in capital punishment cases of allowing the jury to rely on a psychiatrist's prediction of the defendant's future dangerousness. Both at the Eighth Circuit and on the Supreme Court, Blackmun had put aside personal misgivings about the death penalty in voting to uphold its constitutionality. But for Blackmun, imposing the death penalty because of predictions that the American Psychiatric Association had shown to have no scientific validity, was too much. Indeed, during the next decade he became increasingly convinced that "both fairness and rationality cannot be achieved in the administration of the death penalty." Before retiring in 1994 he declared capital punishment unconstitutional "as currently administered."

Blackmun's tenure on the Court produced contributions in a number of other fields as well. In the late 1970s, he wrote three major decisions establishing that commercial speech— advertising and other speech with a business purpose—is protected by the First Amendment to the Constitution. In these cases he found that a state could not prohibit truthful advertising about legal

Michael Hardwick was arrested in 1982 for violating the Georgia antisodomy statute. Although the state did not prosecute Hardwick, it did not drop the charge. Hardwick's appeal to the Supreme Court was aimed at overturning the law, but the Court decided, 5–4, against him. Justice Harry A. Blackmun wrote the sharply worded dissent in which he called for "tolerance of nonconformity." *Source: AP/Wide World Photo*

abortions, the prices of prescription drugs, or fees for routine legal services.

In religion cases, Blackmun generally resisted efforts to erode the wall between church and state. In *Lynch v. Donnelly* (1984) Blackmun's dissent noted the harm religion suffers when the wall is lowered. *Lynch* condoned government sponsorship of a multifaceted Christmas display that included a nativity scene, reasoning that the crèche was part of the city's secular celebration of the Christmas season. Blackmun noted the irony of "a setting where Christians feel constrained in acknowledging [the crèche's] symbolic meaning and non-Christians feel alienated by its presence." Blackmun refused to join the Court "in denying . . . the sacred message that is at the core of the crèche." In a subsequent case, Blackmun's opinion for the Court held that by displaying a crèche standing alone on public property, the government was conveying an impermissible religious message.

Another Blackmun opinion worth noting is *Flood v. Kuhn* (1972), which reaffirmed that the antitrust laws do not apply to professional baseball. The opinion is best remembered for an introductory section in which Blackmun indulged his love of the national pastime by recalling some baseball lore and listing the game's immortals. Blackmun was mortified when he realized, too late, that he inadvertently had left Giants outfielder Mel Ott off the list.

Blackmun's humility and self-effacing humor prompted radio personality Garrison Keillor, a fellow Minnesotan, to label him "the shy person's justice." Although sometimes chided for working too hard and too slowly and agonizing too much over decisions, he often revealed a mischievous streak. Examples include Blackmun's silence when his hearing aid beeped during the justices' secret conference, leading one justice to fear the room was bugged, and his delight in arriving at White House functions, behind black limousines, in his old blue Volkswagen.

During the 1980s Blackmun co-moderated an annual summer seminar on justice and society at the Aspen Institute. He enjoyed speaking at universities, often reading from his Supreme Court mail and discussing his goal of keeping the Court from drifting too far to the right. A history buff, he represented the judicial branch on the National Historical Publications and Records Commission.

The eighty-five-year-old justice stepped down on July 29, 1994, after twenty-four terms on the Court. In announcing his retirement, he said he wanted to be known "as a good worker in the vineyard who held his own and contributed generally to the advancement of the law."

Lewis F. Powell, Jr.
1972-1987

LEWIS FRANKLIN POWELL, JR., was born in Suffolk, Virginia, September 19, 1907. He grew up in Richmond, where his father owned and ran a small business. Powell's family was prosperous, though not rich, and he attended private schools until he was ready for college. Both his mother and the headmaster of his high school wanted Powell to attend the University of Virginia, but he chose Washington and Lee University in Lexington, Virginia, instead, partly because the baseball coach had led Powell to believe he could

make the team there. The coach was wrong; Powell did not even make the freshman baseball squad, although he became the quarterback on the football team.

Powell earned his B.S. degree and election to Phi Beta Kappa in 1929 and stayed at Washington and Lee two more years to obtain a law degree. The decision to go into law was a natural one for him. Long afterward he noted, "I was interested in history, and it seemed clear to me that soldiers and lawyers made most of the history. I entertained no ambition for a military career, and so for me the only choice was the law." After finishing his legal studies, Powell passed the Virginia bar exam, and prepared to begin practice. At his father's urging, however, he placed his career on hold for another year of schooling, this time in the master of law program at Harvard. There, Powell studied under several well-known professors such as Roscoe Pound (then the dean) and Felix Frankfurter, soon to take a seat on the Supreme Court.

Powell finished his Harvard studies in 1932. Although the country was in the midst of the Great Depression, Powell had a number of job possibilities. He turned down an offer of $150 per month from Davis, Polk, and Wardwell, a New York firm led by former Democratic presidential candidate John W. Davis, to take a position for a third as much money from Christian, Barton, and Parker, one of the leading firms in Richmond. Later, when he had risen to the top ranks of the legal profession, Powell would advise promising law students to shun the bright lights of New York or Washington, D.C., and return to their hometowns where they could more easily play a substantial role in community affairs. As his legal career commenced in the mid-1930s, Powell prepared to do just that.

Shortly after he began practice, Powell entered into two relationships that would define much of his adult life. In 1934 he left Christian, Barton to join the firm of Hunton, Williams, Anderson, Gay, and Moore, then (and now) the largest law firm in Richmond. Powell eventually became a senior partner, and the firm remained his professional home until his appointment to the Supreme Court thirty-seven years later. In 1936 he married Josephine Rucker, the daughter of a prominent Richmond doctor.

By the time the attack on Pearl Harbor thrust the United States into World War II, the Powells had two young daughters, and consequently he was exempt from the draft. He nevertheless decided to enlist. After a failed eye examination kept him out of the navy, he joined the Army Air Corps' intelligence unit. This decision led to one of Powell's most important jobs, which had nothing to do with the law. For roughly the last half of the war, Powell was the chief of operational intelligence on the staff of Gen. Carl Spaatz, who commanded the U.S. bomber forces in Europe. In that capacity, Powell became one of the leading figures in the ULTRA project—the Allies' code-breaking operation that successfully deciphered German military messages. As Powell has described it, he was responsible for "blending ULTRA intelligence with other information in ways that concealed the source," so as to avoid tipping off the Germans. He took great pride in the operation, justifiably claiming it "shortened the war and saved thousands of lives."

After the war, the Powells had a third daughter and a son, and Lewis Powell settled down again to law practice in Richmond. He did some work as a litigator, but his primary focus was on counseling business clients. He helped some of Richmond's expanding businesses buy other companies and served as counsel for, among others, Philip Morris and the United Virginia Bank. At the same time, he became ever more involved in local government. He chaired a commission that drafted a new city charter, joined the boards of various charitable organizations, and was elected by the city council to the Richmond School Board, which he chaired from 1952 to 1961, a period of tremendous turmoil. In 1954 the Supreme Court declared public school segregation unconstitutional, and many parts of the South reacted with defiance. In Virginia a powerful political movement urged "massive resistance" to racial integration; a number of localities closed their public schools altogether to avoid integrating them. Due in part to Powell's efforts, Richmond's schools remained open throughout the 1950s, but they also remained racially segregated.

During this time Powell achieved national stature in the legal profession. From 1964 to 1965, he served a

Richard Nixon congratulates his Supreme Court nominee, Lewis F. Powell, Jr., at a ceremony attended by members of Powell's family. Nixon crossed party lines in choosing the Virginia Democrat, whom he admired for his tough stance on crime issues. *Source: White House Photographer, Collection of the Supreme Court of the United States*

term as president of the American Bar Association (ABA). Powell's tenure was unusually active. He began the ABA's effort to set forth uniform standards for the criminal justice system, a project that has influenced the law of criminal procedure. At his urging, the ABA endorsed government-funded legal aid for the poor, prompting the creation of the Legal Services Corporation. At the close of his ABA presidency, Powell took up other public duties. In the late 1960s he served on presidential commissions on crime and defense policy and on a commission to revise Virginia's constitution.

Powell thus had had a long and full career when President Richard Nixon nominated him to the Supreme Court on October 22, 1971, to replace Justice Hugo L. Black. Although Powell was a lifelong Democrat, he had expressed sympathy with some of the views of the Republican administration, particularly on crime issues. Perhaps more important, he was a southerner, and Nixon already had twice sought to name a southerner to the Court. Both nominees were rejected by the Sen-

ate after heated battles. The administration believed Powell would fare better in the Senate.

He initially resisted when asked if he would serve, pointing out that at sixty-four he would be among the oldest justices ever nominated. But an appeal from the president, and the advice of his family and friends, convinced him to accept. Powell's confirmation, as Nixon had guessed, was speedy and virtually unanimous. He was confirmed December 6, 1971, with only a single senator voting against him.

Powell wasted no time making his mark, writing a number of important opinions early in his career on the Court. In *San Antonio Independent School District v. Rodriguez* (1973), his majority opinion denied an equal protection challenge to the way government funds were allocated to different school districts in Texas. This decision gave broad authority to state and local officials in administering public schools, a position Powell, as a former school board member, found natural. But Powell did not always side with the government in constitu-

Lewis F. Powell, Jr. wrote the Supreme Court decision in 1973 upholding the Texas public school financing system that gave broad authority to state and local authorities in administering the schools. Demetrio Rodriguez (pictured) and other Mexican-American parents had challenged the system as being discriminatory on the basis of economic status. *Source: Institute of Texas Cultures*

tional disputes. One of his earliest opinions was *United States v. United States District Court* (1972), in which he limited the power of the president to authorize searches to protect national security.

As these opinions show, Powell did not fit neatly into any political or ideological category. "The truth is," he told one of his first law clerks, "I do not regard myself as conservative or liberal." Rather, he had different instincts in different types of cases. He voted fairly consistently with the conservatives on criminal procedure is-

sues. He joined in a series of decisions that limited the exclusionary rule, which bars the use of illegally seized evidence at trial. He also voted to relax restrictions on police interrogation of suspects. These decisions reflected Powell's view that the criminal justice system ought to focus on the defendant's innocence or guilt and not on what he saw as collateral issues, such as whether the police had behaved properly or not.

On the other hand, Powell could be a strong defender of free speech and other civil liberties claims. He wrote opinions extending free speech rights to businesses and protecting movie theaters that showed potentially offensive films. And he joined in the Court's controversial decision to recognize a woman's constitutional right to an abortion.

Above all, Powell valued moderation. He avoided extreme positions on either side of most issues, which often placed him squarely in the middle, as the crucial swing vote, of a divided Supreme Court. In *University of California Regents v. Bakke* (1978), a case challenging a racial quota in a California medical school's admissions policy, four of the justices voted to declare all such affirmative action programs illegal, while another four voted to permit them virtually across the board. Powell took a middle position striking down the medical school's quota as too rigid, but explicitly upholding more moderate affirmative action policies. From then on Powell was always in the majority in the Court's affirmative action decisions and always stuck to his initial position: race-conscious action was permissible, but rigid quotas were not.

The same pattern appeared in the Court's death penalty decisions. In Powell's first year as a justice, the Court struck down all the nation's death penalty statutes, with the nine justices writing nine separate opinions explaining their various positions. Powell dissented from this decision. Four years later Powell, Potter Stewart, and John Paul Stevens collaborated on a series of joint opinions that upheld the death penalty as a

Allan Bakke, twice denied admission to medical school in Davis, California, filed suit challenging an admission policy that reserved a certain number of places for minorities. Justice Lewis F. Powell, Jr., wrote the decision in *University of California Regents v. Bakke* (1978), the Court's first major statement on the constitutionality of affirmative action programs. Bakke received his medical degree from the university in 1982.
Source: AP/Wide World Photo

general matter, but created a detailed series of restrictions on its use. This framework still survives.

Powell's time on the Court seems to have been happy, but it was not easy. He told one of his clerks, "I've found my health is better when I work only a six-and-a-half-day week." He never left the office without a briefcase bulging with evening reading. But if the job was hard on Powell, he was anything but hard on those with whom he worked. Sandra Day O'Connor, who served with Powell for six years, said of him:

I have known no one in my lifetime who is kinder or more courteous than he. If at times he was unhappy or frustrated with one of us, he never expressed a harsh thought or criticism. Instead, he would smile and say, in his soft Southern accent, something like: "Now, I would be pleased to have any of you join me. And I would be happy to hear any of your suggestions."

Ironically, the retirement of this courtly, well-mannered justice on June 26, 1987, prompted a political tempest. Robert Bork, President Ronald Reagan's nominee to succeed Powell, was defeated by the Senate after a heated battle. Under pressure, Douglas Ginsburg withdrew his name before he was even officially nominated. Powell avoided any public comment on the controversy and busied himself hearing cases with the Fourth Circuit Court of Appeals in Richmond.

In addition to pinch-hitting for other federal judges, Powell has, since his retirement, taught for brief periods at both the Washington and Lee and University of Virginia law schools. As they have done since he became a justice in 1972, Powell and his wife continue to live in Washington most of the year, but spend their summers in Richmond, where Powell keeps an office at the federal courthouse. When in Richmond and not working, he is usually to be found at the family's longtime home overlooking the James River.

William H. Rehnquist

1972-1986, 1986-

Source: Photo by National Geographic Society, Collection of the Supreme Court of the United States

WILLIAM HUBBS REHNQUIST was born in Milwaukee, Wisconsin, October 1, 1924. He grew up in the suburb of Shorewood, the son of a paper salesman. Rehnquist's strongly conservative views can be traced directly to his childhood. According to a *Washington Post* report, the political heroes in the Rehnquist household were "Republican standard bearers such as Alf Landon, Wendell Willkie and Herbert Hoover." When Rehnquist was asked (during the Democratic administration of Franklin D. Roosevelt) by his elementary teacher about his career plans, he replied, "I'm going to change the government."

He served in the Army Air Corps during World War II as a weather observer in North Africa. Following the war, he attended college on the GI Bill, earning both a B.A. (Phi Beta Kappa) and M.A. in political science at Stanford University in 1948. Rehnquist received a second M.A., in government, from Harvard two years later. He then entered Stanford Law School, where he graduated first in his class in 1952. (The student who ranked third was Sandra Day, who later joined him on the Supreme Court.) Rehnquist was described by one of his instructors as "the outstanding student of his law school generation." He also had the reputation among his classmates as a formidable advocate of the conservative point of view on political issues.

Rehnquist met Justice Robert Jackson when he came to Stanford to dedicate the new law school building in the summer of 1951. An interview for a possible clerkship with him was arranged by a professor who was a former Jackson clerk. Despite Rehnquist's feeling, following the interview, that Jackson "had written me off as a total loss," he was offered the highly coveted position. Jackson, a moderate, does not appear to have had any influence on Rehnquist's already well-developed political or judicial philosophies. Indeed, in his book on the Supreme Court, Rehnquist speaks well of Jackson, but no such influence is noted. Justice Felix Frankfurter seems to have made more of an impression; Rehnquist describes Frankfurter as a "magnetic" personality to whom he was "tremendously drawn . . . by

his willingness to discuss and argue while asking no quarter by reason of his position or eminence."

What Rehnquist considered to be the too-liberal views of his fellow law clerks certainly made a strong impression on him, and in 1957 he published an article in *U.S. News and World Report* criticizing their "extreme solicitude for the claims of Communists and other criminal defendants, expansion of federal power at the expense of State power, great sympathy toward any government regulation of business—in short, the political philosophy now espoused by the Court under Chief Justice [Earl] Warren." Rehnquist contended that this political bias on the part of the clerks might have some influence over which cases the Court chose to decide, but not over the way any justice voted in a particular case.

In 1953, following his clerkship, he married Natalie ("Nan") Cornell, whom he had met at Stanford, and the couple had a son and two daughters. Rehnquist went to work for a law firm in Phoenix, choosing that city for its climate, both meteorological and political. He followed advice that Justice Frankfurter had given

The Stanford Law Class of 1952 class boasted two future Supreme Court justices: William H. Rehnquist (back row, far left) and Sandra Day, who became Sandra Day O'Connor (first row, second from left). *Source: UPI/Bettmann*

Richard Nixon presents certificates of office to his two Supreme Court nominees, Lewis F. Powell, Jr., and William H. Rehnquist, in 1971. They both joined the Court on January 7 the following year.
Source: UPI/Bettmann

him "that conservatives as well as liberals ought to get active on the political scene." He became a Republican party official and an outspoken opponent of liberal legislative initiatives such as busing to achieve school integration. While campaigning for Republican presidential candidate Barry Goldwater in 1964, Rehnquist became friendly with Richard Kleindienst, another Phoenix attorney. Kleindienst was appointed deputy attorney general in Richard Nixon's administration and arranged for Rehnquist to become assistant attorney general for the Justice Department's Office of Legal Counsel.

One of Rehnquist's principal functions in this job was to screen, along with Kleindienst and Attorney General John Mitchell, candidates for potential Supreme Court positions. When attempts to find a suitable candidate to replace retiring justice John Marshall Harlan had reached an impasse, Mitchell informed Rehnquist that they had settled on someone—Rehnquist himself. Despite his relative youth (he was forty-seven), inexperience, and political views that diverged from those of many senators, his nomination was confirmed, 68-26, December 10, 1971. He joined

the Court on January 7, 1972, the same day as Justice Lewis F. Powell, Jr.

Rehnquist summarized his vision of the nation's constitutional structure in a speech at the University of Texas a few years later:

It is almost impossible . . . to conclude that the [Founders] intended the Constitution itself to suggest answers to the manifold problems that they knew would confront succeeding generations. The Constitution that they drafted was intended to endure indefinitely, but the reason for this well-founded hope was the general language by which national authority was granted to Congress and the Presidency. These two branches were to furnish the motive power within the federal system, which was in turn to coexist with the state governments; the elements of government having a popular constituency were looked to for the solution of the numerous and varied problems that the future would bring.

During his early years on the Court, despite the presence of three other Republican appointees, Rehnquist was often the only dissenter, espousing a view of states' rights and limited federal judicial power that many regarded as outmoded. He resisted the view of the other eight members of the Court that the Equal Protection

Clause of the Fourteenth Amendment applied to, and required heightened scrutiny of, state-sponsored discrimination against illegitimate children, resident aliens, and women. Indeed, he insisted that the Equal Protection Clause had only marginal application beyond cases of racial discrimination. In the area of criminal procedure, Rehnquist urged the Court to overturn *Mapp v. Ohio* (1961), which made the rule excluding illegally seized evidence from admission in a trial applicable to the states. Rehnquist also seemed hostile to *Miranda v. Arizona* (1966), which guaranteed that suspects in police custody be informed of their rights before interrogation, although he never directly argued that it should be reversed.

Still, even in his early years on the Court, Rehnquist was less likely to be in dissent than liberal justices William O. Douglas, William J. Brennan, Jr., and Thurgood Marshall. The ideas expressed in some of Rehnquist's early dissents became influential in later majority opinions. As Harvard law professor Laurence Tribe observed, "Even in lone dissent, he has helped define a new range of what is possible."

When dissenting, Rehnquist has made his most telling points in opposition to the majority's efforts to enact "desirable" social policy with little support from the constitutional or statutory provisions they are supposed to be interpreting. An example is *United Steel Workers of America v. Weber* (1979). This case involved an affirmative action plan devised by the Kaiser Aluminum and Chemical Company and the United Steelworkers. The "voluntary" plan reserved for blacks half of available positions in an on-the-job training program. Brian Weber, excluded solely because he was white, filed suit based on Title VII of the Civil Rights Act of 1964, which provides that "it shall be unlawful for an employer . . . to fail or refuse to hire . . . any individual . . . because of such individual's race." The statute goes on to say that its provisions are not to be interpreted "to require any employer . . . to grant pref-

erential treatment to any individual or group." Nevertheless, a 5–2 majority reversed the lower courts, finding that the discrimination against whites was not against the "spirit" of Title VII and consequently not prohibited. In a bitter dissent, Rehnquist concluded that "close examination of what the Court proffers as the spirit of the Act reveals it as the spirit of the present majority, not the 88th Congress."

Rehnquist also dissented in *Roe v. Wade* (1973), in which the majority based a woman's right to an abortion on a constitutional right of privacy that arose not from the terms but from the "penumbras" of the Bill of Rights. He wrote, "To reach its result, the Court necessarily has had to find within the scope of the Fourteenth Amendment a right that was apparently completely unknown to the drafters of the Amendment."

The 1975 term saw Rehnquist come into his own as the leader of the ever-shifting conservative wing of the Court. He wrote several majority opinions that cut back the power of the federal government vis-à-vis the

When Brian Weber (above) applied for admittance to an apprenticeship-training program at his company, Kaiser Aluminum and Chemicals, he was turned down. He took the company to court for discrimination against whites, challenging its policy of reserving half the openings in the program for minority applicants. Calling affirmative action programs unconstitutional, William H. Rehnquist dissented from the Supreme Court's 1979 decision that ruled against Weber. *Source: AP/Wide World Photos*

states. The most notable of these was *National League of Cities v. Usery*, in which Rehnquist used an expansive reading of the Tenth Amendment to strike down a federal statute that regulated the wages and hours of state government employees, although such regulation was within Congress's commerce power. The opinion showed that if faced with a choice between judicial restraint and states' rights, doctrines he generally supported, Rehnquist was prepared to defend states' rights more aggressively.

When Warren Burger announced his resignation as chief justice and President Ronald Reagan nominated Rehnquist as his replacement June 20, 1986, there was a firestorm of protest among liberals. Sen. Edward Kennedy denounced Rehnquist as having an "appalling record on race," and liberal columnists branded him a right-wing extremist. A concerted effort was undertaken to find something in his past that might provide a basis for defeating the nomination. Assorted allegations were raised concerning harassment of black voters when he was a Republican party official in Phoenix, the handling of a family trust, a memo he had written to Justice Jackson as a law clerk urging that the "separate but equal" doctrine not be overruled in *Brown v. Board of Education* (1954), and racially restrictive covenants in the deeds to his Phoenix house and summer home in Vermont. The Senate perceived that these allegations were either unproven or, if true, were "ancient history" and irrelevant to his fitness for the post of chief justice. Significantly, no serious charge of misconduct was alleged as to Rehnquist's nearly fifteen years as an associate justice. After much controversy, he was confirmed September 17 by a 65–33 vote.

If the 1975 term saw Rehnquist become a major force on the Court, it was the 1987 term, his second year as chief justice, that saw him mature in that position. In a speech he gave in 1976 Rehnquist had discussed the role of chief justice, citing Charles Evans Hughes as his model. "Hughes believed that unanimity of decision contributed to public confidence in the Court. . . . Except in cases involving matters of high principle he willingly acquiesced in silence rather than expose his dissenting views. . . . Hughes was also willing to modify his own opinions to hold or increase his majority."

Following that advice, in the 1987 term he achieved a high level of agreement with his fellow justices, ranging from 57.6 percent with Thurgood Marshall to 83.1 percent with Anthony Kennedy. His managerial abilities in the 1987 term won the praise of Justice Harry Blackmun, who deemed him a "splendid administrator in conference." For the first time in years, the Court concluded its work prior to July 1, in part because it had taken on fewer cases.

During the 1987 term, Rehnquist also showed that he could be flexible, joining with the more liberal justices to subject the dismissal of a homosexual CIA agent to judicial review and to support the freedom of speech claims of *Hustler* magazine to direct off-color ridicule at a public figure. Most significant, in *Morrison v. Olson* (1988) Rehnquist wrote the majority opinion upholding Congress's right to appoint independent counsels to investigate and prosecute high government officials, a right that was challenged by the Reagan administration.

Rehnquist continues to be an effective manager whose humor and fairness have contributed to the cordial relations among the justices. He enjoys a variety of hobbies, including oil painting, singing, stamp collecting, theater-going, and poker. He has written two popular books on the Court's history: *The Supreme Court: How It Was, How It Is* (1988) and *Grand Inquests: The Historic Impeachments of Justice Samuel Chase and President Andrew Johnson* (1992). The chief justice has been a widower since his wife died in October 1991.

John Paul Stevens

1975-

Source: Photo by National Geographic Society, Collection of the Supreme Court of the United States

JOHN PAUL STEVENS was born in Chicago April 20, 1920, the youngest of four children, all sons, of Ernest James Stevens and Elizabeth Street Stevens. His father made a fortune in hotels and insurance and for a time owned and managed the Stevens Hotel, now the Chicago Hilton. The family home was adjacent to the University of Chicago. Stevens attended high school in the university's laboratory school.

He continued in college at the University of Chicago, his father's alma mater, joining Psi Upsilon, his father's fraternity. He majored in English, edited the school paper, won the university's highest honors for scholarship and campus activities, and graduated Phi Beta Kappa in 1941. The next year he married Elizabeth Jane Sheeren, with whom he had a son and three daughters. They divorced in 1979, and he married Maryan Mulholland Simon the following year.

Stevens considered becoming a teacher before joining the World War II effort. A naval officer assigned to a code-breaking team from 1942 to 1945, he was awarded

John Paul Stevens (right) with Chief Justice Warren E. Burger and President Gerald Ford on December 19, 1975, the day of his investiture. Ford considered his appointment of Stevens, a political moderate, as a step toward healing the nation after the divisive Watergate scandal. *Source: Gerald R. Ford Library*

the Bronze Star. After the war, encouraged by one of his brothers, an attorney, he studied law at Northwestern University, as had his father. Stevens became editor-in-chief of the law review and in 1947 graduated first in his class with the highest grades in the law school's history. He then served as clerk to Wiley Rutledge, a liberal Supreme Court justice.

Returning to Chicago, Stevens joined a prominent law firm that specialized in antitrust law. He earned a solid reputation as an antitrust lawyer and formed his own law firm in 1951. He also taught antitrust law at the Northwestern University and University of Chicago law schools. Stevens served as associate counsel of a House of Representatives subcommittee studying monopoly power in 1951, and from 1953 to 1955 as a member of the attorney general's committee to study antitrust laws. Because of his competence and integrity, he was named general counsel to an Illinois commission investigating the conduct of state supreme court justices in 1969. In 1970 President Richard Nixon appointed him to the Seventh Circuit Court of Appeals.

In his years on the court of appeals, Stevens gained distinction as a legal craftsman. When William O. Douglas retired from the Supreme Court in 1975, Stevens was one of eleven candidates (including future nominee Robert Bork) considered by Attorney General

Edward Levi, a former law dean and president of the University of Chicago. There was consensus within the legal community that Stevens was an unusually able jurist. Although a registered Republican, he had never been active in party politics. As Sen. Charles Percy of Illinois said in his supporting statement, he was a "lawyer's lawyer" when named to the court of appeals and was now a "judge's judge." President Gerald Ford hoped that the nomination of a moderate who had been given the American Bar Association's highest rating would help restore confidence in government in the wake of the Watergate scandals. The Senate confirmed Stevens December 17, 1975, 98–0, and he took the oath of office two days later at the age of fifty-five.

On the Supreme Court Stevens has been practical and down-to-earth rather than ideological, and he has continued to be as independent minded as he was on the court of appeals. This approach has set him apart from the other justices, most of whom have been either habitually liberal, particularly in supporting the rights of the individual, or conservative, supporting the authority of the government. Stevens has been the least predictable member of the Court, although in recent years he appeared more liberal as the Court moved to the right with each Reagan and Bush appointment.

Independent-minded pragmatists like Stevens are not often appointed to the Court because presidents usually want justices who will vote reliably and not oppose their programs. If they are wise in the ways of the Court, presidents know that justices do not bow down to them; yet presidents hope for some ideological compatibility. Stevens, however, is a justice without a social agenda. As judge and justice he has seen himself as a problem solver, not a crusader. His constitutional theory is about deciding individual cases well, one by one.

His ways of judging have differed from those of the more consistent liberals and conservatives on the Court in two basic respects. The first is a cluster of mutually reinforcing tendencies: an appetite for facts, sensitivity to a variety of values, and a search for balance among them. The second is an inclination to defer to other institutions when it can be done in good conscience and, when it cannot, an insistence that the Court decide thoughtfully, without shortcuts. Stevens hungers for facts about the behavior of the people in each case and about others in society with similar problems who will be affected by the Court's decision. To make a decision without understanding both the case and its social context is often to miss the point. Facts cast light on the stakes: Who gains? Who is hurt? How? How much? The challenge, for Stevens, is to weigh and balance the conflicting values that come to mind as he explores the details of a case.

An openness to experience and to the interplay of facts and values is evident throughout Stevens' opinions. A good example is his opinion for the majority in *Federal Communications Commission v. Pacifica Foundation* (1978), upholding an administrative decision to accept a father's complaint against a radio station for broadcasting a monologue entitled "Filthy Words," inadvertently tuned in while he was driving with his son. Rather than deal with freedom of speech as an abstraction, as some of his colleagues did, Stevens explored a series of facts in the case, each of which illuminates important personal or societal interests.

· It was a radio broadcast, intruding upon "the privacy of the home, where the individual's right to be left alone plainly outweighs the First Amendment rights of an intruder," not a book or a theater production. "Outside the home, the balance between the offensive speaker and the unwilling audience may sometimes tip in favor of the speaker, requiring the offended listener to turn away." A radio broadcast, however, is also available to children, in whose well-being the government has a legitimate interest and over whom parents have a claim of authority. It was heard by a young child, and

Stand-up comic George Carlin was arrested in 1972 on a disorderly conduct and profanity charge for delivering his monologue, "The Seven Words You Can't Say on TV." The monologue, which the Pacifica network broadcast at two o'clock one afternoon, was the catalyst for a First Amendment test. In 1978 John Paul Stevens wrote the Supreme Court opinion in *FCC v. Pacifica,* ruling that the government could regulate the repetitious use of indecent words on the air because broadcast signals intrude on the privacy of the home, but that the government may not ban such language altogether. *Source: UPI/Bettmann*

young children are more apt to be adversely affected than older children. The monologue was broadcast in the afternoon, when the very young are more likely to listen, rather than at night. Its plain language also affected its accessibility. For contrast, Stevens quoted a passage from the *Canterbury Tales* at least as lewd as anything in the monologue but relatively obscure and less likely to turn up uninvited in anyone's house. That it was spoken rather than written made it available even to children too young to read. This broadcast, he said, "could well have enlarged a child's vocabulary in a minute."

Further, the explicit language was spoken during regular programming, not in a telecast of an Elizabethan comedy, for example, to which a different kind of audience would be tuned. To support his view of the monologue as speech of relatively little importance, Stevens

appended it in full to his opinion, (where it now sits, in law libraries across the country, safely inaccessible to all but callous adults). Last, he deliberately did not decide that this broadcast would justify a criminal prosecution (in which other basic rights would be invoked). Fact-gathering is Stevens's way of discovering how a case will affect people and their constitutional rights and responsibilities. It is an exercise in which, as he says, "one's initial impression of a novel issue is frequently different from his final evaluation," and balancing is his way of deciding which values shall prevail. In this case, had it been high comedy, for example, or a willing adult audience, Stevens's balance might have tipped the other way, protecting the performance and rejecting the complaint.

Stevens argues that one who is close to the facts is in the best position to make intelligent decisions. Appellate courts, including the Supreme Court, are handicapped by limited, secondhand information and often, too, by a lack of technical expertise. If sounder judgments can be made by specialists on the scene, such as administrators, parents, and trial judges, Stevens's inclination is to let their decisions stand. It is toward Congress that he is most respectful, because of its exceptional political insight, access to information, and constitutional authority. Typically he studies the language and the legislative history of a statute before the Court to discover the lawmakers' will. Yet if an honest search turns up no coherent legislative purpose, or simply an absence of serious discussion, he is far less deferential.

For example, dissenting in *Delaware Tribal Business Committee v. Weeks* (1977), he found "manifestly unjust and arbitrary" an act of Congress that, in settling a claim by the Indian Claims Commission, provided funds for all but one of the dispersed groups of Delaware Indians covered by the commission's award, without explaining the exception. Stevens concluded that the exception was unintentional. "There is no reason to believe that the discrimination is the product of an actual legislative choice," he wrote. In a dissent to *Fullilove v. Klutznick* (1980) he called a public works law allocating 10 percent of appropriated funds to minority contractors "slapdash." Congress, he said, "for the first time in the Nation's history, has created a broad legislative classification for entitlement to benefits based solely on racial characteristics, . . ." but it "was not the subject of any testimony or inquiry in a legislative hearing. . . . It is true that there was a brief discussion on the floor of the House as well as in the Senate on two different days, but only a handful of legislators spoke and there was virtually no debate." The evident purpose, he concluded, was to give certain congressional constituents "a piece of the action." In other words, if Congress wants to test the limits of the Constitution, it should do so with care.

Stevens also defers to lower court decisions and to Supreme Court precedent, but, again, not if they are badly done. He has found fault with the Court's complex (and in his view hopelessly confusing) definitions of obscenity and establishment of religion, for example. He has also criticized summary judgments—cases decided without oral argument when the justices are content with the initial written arguments—because they are decisions based on incomplete information.

Some of Stevens's critics believe his emphasis on fact, context, and balance sabotages the higher calling of the Court of providing principled, moral leadership for the legal system and the nation—"legitimizing nascent aspirations [and] reinvigorating dormant ideals," as one put it. Further, his irrepressible habit of writing more concurring and dissenting opinions than anyone else on the Court, most years, has disturbed those who favor Court unity. They cite cases such as *Brown v. Board of Education* (1954), in which the members of the Court set differences aside and joined in support of one plain, powerful statement in defense of school desegregation. To Stevens's admirers, the independence of mind, the rooting for facts and meaning, the imaginative insights, and the assumption that neither life nor law is simple, offer a fresh look at society's problems as an alternative to old legal labels and familiar solutions.

The man himself, it is agreed, is quiet and mild-mannered. At one time or another he has played serious squash, bridge, tennis, and golf and flown his own small airplane. He possesses a puckishness that now and then finds its way into his opinions—particularly his concurrences and dissents. Justice Stevens has a fondness for bow ties, which, too, in its way is a dissenting opinion.

Sandra Day O'Connor
1981-

Source: Photo by National Geographic Society, Collection of the Supreme Court of the United States

SANDRA DAY O'CONNOR, the first woman appointed to the Supreme Court, was born March 26, 1930, to Harry A. Day and Ada Mae Wilkey Day in El Paso, Texas. She grew up on the Lazy B Ranch, 198,000 acres of land with more than 2,000 cattle, twenty-five miles from the town of Duncan in southeastern Arizona. Her grandfather, Henry Clay Day, had founded the ranch in the early 1880s, some thirty years before Arizona gained statehood. The ranch house, a simple, four-room adobe building, had neither running water nor electricity until Sandra Day was seven. In the drought years of the Great Depression, her family confronted real hardship, but the ranch eventually prospered.

Day's sister and brother, Ann and Alan, were born in 1938 and 1939; she therefore spent her first eight years as an only child, and most of these years on a remote ranch. Her early childhood friends were her parents, ranch hands, a bobcat, and a few javelina hogs. She learned to entertain herself and to find diversion in books. Her mother spent hours reading to her from the *Wall Street Journal,* the *Los Angeles Times,* the *New Yorker,* and the *Saturday Evening Post.* By the age of eight, she was also mending fences, riding with the cowboys, firing her own .22 rifle, and driving a truck.

At age five, Sandra Day began to spend the school months with her maternal grandmother, Mamie Wilkey, in El Paso in order to attend Radford School, a private establishment for girls. She spent each summer at the ranch. Day lived with her grandmother from kindergarten through high school, with a one-year interruption at age thirteen, when homesickness impelled her to return to Arizona. During her years in El Paso, she was deeply influenced by her grandmother's strong will and high expectations.

Day graduated from high school at sixteen and entered Stanford University. She earned a degree in economics magna cum laude in 1950. In her senior year she began to study law and then continued at Stanford Law School. There she served on the *Stanford Law Review* and won membership in the Order of the Coif, a legal honor society. She graduated in 1952, third in her law school class of 102 students. That same year Sandra Day

married John Jay O'Connor III, whom she had met while working on the law review.

O'Connor set out to find a job as a lawyer but was repeatedly turned down by firms that would not hire women. The one job offer she received was for a position as a legal secretary. Ironically, almost thirty years later, Attorney General William French Smith, who had been a senior member of the firm that made the offer, would be instrumental in O'Connor's appointment to the U.S. Supreme Court. Instead of becoming a secretary, O'Connor accepted a position as a deputy county attorney in San Mateo, California. She recalls how that job "influenced the balance of my life because it demonstrated how much I did enjoy public service."

John O'Connor graduated a year after his wife and joined the U.S. Army Judge Advocate General Corps, in which he served for three years in Frankfurt, Germany. While overseas, Sandra Day O'Connor worked as a civilian lawyer for the Quartermaster Corps. The couple returned to the United States in 1957 and moved to Maricopa County, Arizona. In the next six years they had three sons, Scott, Brian, and Jay.

In 1958, after the birth of her first child, O'Connor

Sandra Day (patting bull) with her parents and a friend. Day grew up on her family's nearly 200,000-acre ranch in southeastern Arizona. *Source: Chelsea House Publishers with permission of Justice Sandra Day O'Connor*

Ronald Reagan fulfilled a campaign promise to name a woman to the Supreme Court by appointing Sandra Day O'Connor in 1981. She was confirmed unanimously by the Senate. *Source: AP/Wide World Photos*

opened her own firm with a partner, Tom Tobin. She stopped working, however, after Brian's birth. From 1960 to 1965, besides being a full-time mother, O'Connor did a variety of volunteer work. She wrote questions for the Arizona bar exam, helped start the state bar's lawyer referral service, sat on the local zoning commission, and served as a member of the Maricopa County Board of Adjustments and Appeals. In 1965 she served as a member of the Governor's Committee on Marriage and Family, worked as an administrative assistant of the Arizona State Hospital and acted as an adviser to the Salvation Army, and volunteered in a school for blacks and Hispanics. During these years, O'Connor also became actively involved in Republican politics. She worked as a county precinct officer for the party from 1960 to 1965, and as district chairman from 1962 to 1965. "Two things were clear to me from the onset," O'Connor has remarked about that period in her life. "One is, I wanted a family and the second was that I wanted to work—and I love to work."

O'Connor returned to regular employment in 1965, as an assistant state attorney general, while also contin-

uing her volunteer work. In 1969, when Isabel A. Burgess resigned from her seat in the Arizona Senate to accept an appointment in Washington, D.C., Gov. Jack Williams appointed O'Connor as her replacement. O'Connor won reelection to the state Senate in two successive terms. She was elected majority leader in 1972, the first woman to hold such office anywhere in the United States. Among her Republican colleagues, her voting record was moderate to conservative, although she differed with some of them on issues such as discrimination and in her support of the Equal Rights Amendment. In addition, she served as co-chair of the state committee to elect Richard Nixon to the presidency.

In 1974 O'Connor won a hard-fought election to a state judgeship on the Maricopa County Superior Court, on which she served for the next five years. Republican leaders encouraged her to run for governor in 1978, but she declined. In 1979 the Democratic governor selected O'Connor as his first appointee to the Arizona Court of Appeals. There, she decided appeals on subjects spanning workmen's compensation, divorce, criminal convictions, torts, and real property. Twenty-one months later, on August 19, 1981, President Ronald Reagan fulfilled a campaign promise to appoint a woman to the U.S. Supreme Court and nominated O'Connor to the seat vacated by Justice Potter Stewart.

In her Senate confirmation hearings, O'Connor expressed cautiously conservative views on capital punishment, the rule excluding illegally obtained evidence from trials, and busing for desegregation, while declining to be pinned down on the question of abortion. When asked how she wanted to be remembered, O'Connor replied: "Ah, the tombstone question. I hope it says, 'Here lies a good judge.' " On September 15, 1981, seventeen of the eighteen members of the Judiciary Committee recommended her approval. One voted "present" because O'Connor had declined to condemn the Supreme Court's 1973 abortion decision, *Roe v. Wade*. The Senate confirmed her appointment 99–0, and O'Connor took the oath of office September 26, 1981. When she began her first term in October, O'Connor brought to the Court experience from service in all three branches of government and was the only sitting justice who had been elected to public office.

At this point, O'Connor was considered very conservative. *Time* magazine labeled her Justice William H. Rehnquist's "Arizona twin"; indeed, in her first term the two voted together on twenty-seven of the thirty-one decisions decided by 5–4 votes. In her first five terms, O'Connor was often aligned with the conservative faction of the Court. Nevertheless, in her best-known opinion of her first term, O'Connor was joined by the liberal wing of the Court in a 5–4 ruling that a state-supported university in Mississippi could not constitutionally exclude men from its school of nursing. By the end of the 1984 term, O'Connor had come to be identified as a restrained jurist, a strong supporter of federalism, and a cautious interpreter of the Constitution.

In subsequent terms, O'Connor often voted with the centrist Lewis F. Powell, Jr., and the two were in the majority on 5–4 rulings more often than any other justices. While O'Connor generally sided with her conservative colleagues, she frequently wrote her own, narrower concurrence. "It has become almost commonplace for 5–4 rulings by the Court's conservative bloc to be embroidered—and often limited—by an O'Connor concurrence," one observer commented in 1989. "Even though none of the other justices agree completely with her views, they in effect become the law because of her position near the center of the Court's ideological spectrum." O'Connor came under increasing scrutiny as the swing vote on a Court often sharply divided over issues such as affirmative action, the death penalty, and abortion. "As O'Connor goes, so goes the Court," another observer would declare in 1990. When David Souter joined the Court that fall, O'Connor and he voted the same way in every 5–4 decision during his first term.

Among O'Connor's noted opinions are those dealing with issues of religious freedom. A concurring opinion she wrote in *Lynch v. Donnelly* (1984) on the constitutionality of a government-sponsored nativity scene has subsequently established the legal standard for determining when such displays violate the Constitution's prohibition on government establishment of religion. A year later, another O'Connor concurrence was important in outlining the constitutional bounds on a state-prescribed "voluntary moment of silence" for school children. According to O'Connor, the challenged law was unconstitutional in that its purpose was to encourage prayer, but might have passed muster had it not favored "the child who chooses to pray . . . over the child who chooses to meditate or reflect."

In other opinions, O'Connor has endorsed affirmative action for minorities if "narrowly tailored" to correct a demonstrated wrong, but not otherwise. In a landmark 1989 opinion, *City of Richmond v. J. A. Croson Co.,* O'Connor's opinion for the Court concluded that

Sandra Day O'Connor wrote a concurring opinion in *Lynch v. Donnelly* (1984) that established the legal standard for determining the constitutionality of a government-sponsored nativity scene. When the subject came up again in *County of Allegheny v. ACLU* (1989), the Court used the standard to rule that the crèche, used alone and in a public building, violated the Establishment Clause, while a combined Christmas tree and menorah display did not. *Sources: Thomas Ondrey; (bottom) Andy Starnes*

government programs setting aside a fixed percentage of public contracts for minority businesses violate equal protection. On the highly charged issue of abortion, O'Connor searched for a middle ground in a series of decisions in the 1980s and ultimately found one in 1992. In *Planned Parenthood of Southeastern Pennsylvania v. Casey*, O'Connor and Justice Anthony Kennedy joined a controversial plurality opinion by Justice Souter that criticized the constitutional foundation

for—yet declined to overturn—the Court's original 1973 recognition of the right to abortion. Consistent with her own tenures as a state legislator and state judge, O'Connor has favored limiting intrusions by federal courts on state powers, especially in criminal matters. She has taken a similarly restrained view of federal judicial power with respect to the legislative and executive branches.

Legal scholars have had difficulty categorizing O'Connor's jurisprudence. Her opinions are conservative and attentive to detail, but also open-minded; they reflect no profound ideology and rarely contain any sweeping rhetoric. Critics say that her opinions have no passion, no lofty vision, and lack a personal tone. O'Connor has been compared to Justices Powell and John Marshall Harlan, "whose careers were distinguished by a devotion to pragmatic resolution of the issues before them." She is described as a justice "who looks to resolve each case and no more, one with no overarching philosophy that might preordain a result."

O'Connor is a tall, striking woman, with glittering eyes and an unflinching gaze. She speaks with quiet, confident authority. Her former law clerks describe her as very much in control, committed, intense, a perfectionist—but also warm, down-to-earth, and irrepressibly upbeat. Shortly after taking her seat, O'Connor established a morning exercise class in the Court gym for the women employees. Her chambers are noted for long hours and sometimes seven-day work weeks, punctuated with popcorn, Mexican brunches, or mandatory outings to the Smithsonian or to go whitewater rafting. In the fall of 1988 O'Connor was diagnosed with breast cancer; the day before her surgery she fulfilled a speaking engagement at Washington and Lee University, and she was back on the bench ten days later, without missing an oral argument.

Antonin Scalia
1986-

Source: Photo by National Geographic Society, Collection of the Supreme Court of the United States

ANTONIN SCALIA was born March 11, 1936, in Trenton, New Jersey, the only child of S. Eugene Scalia and Catherine Scalia. His father, who was born in Sicily and emigrated to the United States as a young man, was a professor of Romance languages. His mother, born to immigrant Italian parents, was a schoolteacher. As the first American of Italian heritage appointed to the Supreme Court, Scalia's ascent to the pinnacle of his profession was proclaimed by many as an example of the American dream.

When Scalia—"Nino" to his friends—was five years old, his father became a professor at Brooklyn College, and the family moved to Elmhurst, a section of Queens, New York. Growing up in New York was stimulating and challenging, particularly when Scalia carried the French horn he played in band to and from school on the subway during rush hour. He was a good student, first in public school in Queens and later at St. Francis Xavier, a military prep school in Manhattan, where he graduated first in his class. He received his

A.B. summa cum laude in history in 1957 from George-town University and was the class valedictorian. At Harvard Law School, where he received his LL.B. magna cum laude, Scalia served as note editor of the *Harvard Law Review*. Following graduation, he spent a year traveling in Europe, including Eastern Europe, as a Sheldon Fellow of Harvard.

While at Harvard, Scalia met and became engaged to Maureen McCarthy, an English major at Radcliffe College and the daughter of a Massachusetts physician. The couple married in September 1960 and have nine children. The Scalias have enjoyed a strong and mutually supportive relationship, enriched by their deep faith in Catholicism. She has done volunteer work wherever they lived, including working with hospitalized children, helping retarded young adults, and teaching in the Sunday school at their parish church. He has maintained his interest in travel and music (he prefers classical music, especially opera, and sings tenor), and he plays an aggressive game of tennis.

Scalia began his legal career in 1961 as an associate at the law firm of Jones, Day, Cockley, and Reavis in Cleveland, Ohio. Colleagues at the firm remember him as a "brash, instantly likable" fellow who impressed them with his legal abilities and warm, gregarious personality, often engaging other lawyers in spirited debates over legal issues. Scalia worked in a number of different areas, including real estate, corporate financing, labor, and antitrust. In 1967 he decided to go into teaching and became a law professor at the University of Virginia.

Four years later, Scalia took a leave from Virginia to begin a distinguished career in government service. He served first as general counsel, Office of Telecommunications Policy, in the administration of President Richard Nixon and played a leading role in negotiating a compromise among industry groups to set the framework for the growth of cable television. In 1972 and for the next two years, he served as chairman of the Ad-ministrative Conference of the United States, an independent agency charged with the task of improving the effectiveness and efficiency of the administrative process. From 1974 to 1977 he served President Gerald Ford as assistant attorney general for the Office of Legal Counsel at the Justice Department. It was in this position, as legal adviser for the executive branch, that Scalia began to articulate his deep respect for the presidency as an institution—a respect that would later mark his judicial writings.

After he left government, Scalia returned to teaching law, briefly at the Georgetown University Law Center, then at the University of Chicago from 1977 to 1982. While at Chicago, he took leave to teach at Stanford University. From 1981 to 1982 he served as chairman of the American Bar Association's section on administrative law and was chairman of the Conference of Section Chairs—a recognition by his peers of his leadership abilities.

In 1982 President Ronald Reagan appointed Scalia to the U.S. Court of Appeals for the District of Columbia Circuit. He served on this court, considered second in importance only to the Supreme Court, for four years. He was regarded by those who argued before him as a well-prepared judge, who genuinely enjoyed using oral arguments as an opportunity to probe, to challenge, and to engage in dialogue with responsive counsel. Scalia also earned the reputation of being collegial—able and willing to work with the other judges on the court to produce agreement or, if not agreement, a clear statement of the differences for others to tackle. As in his previous positions, his judicial colleagues, whether liberal or conservative, became his friends, and he was admired for his legal intellect, earthy wit, and "mean piano."

On the court of appeals, Scalia began to expound on his longstanding belief that courts and judges have a limited role in the three-branch system of government established by the Framers of the Constitution. He

Sens. Ernest Hollings, D-S.C., Phil Gramm, R-Texas, and Warren Rudman, R-N.H., display T-shirts promoting their deficit reduction bill in 1985. As an appeals judge for the District of Columbia circuit, Antonin Scalia presided over a three-judge panel that ruled that the Gramm-Rudman-Hollings statute violated the Constitution's rule separating the powers of the three branches of government. *Source: AP/Wide World Photos*

wrote opinions taking a restrictive view of "standing"—that is, holding that people challenging government action had to have suffered a "personal hurt" by the action before they could be heard by a court. He also made clear that when judges hear cases challenging legislation on its face or challenging its application to particular facts, they should not substitute their own view of what is proper for the view of the legislature or the agency charged with implementing or enforcing the legislation. This philosophy does not mean that Scalia thinks judges are powerless; to the contrary, he sees them as the guardians of the allocation of power among the three branches.

In one of the more visible cases in which he was involved, Scalia presided over a three-judge panel that invalidated, on separation of powers grounds, the Gramm-Rudman-Hollings budget-balancing statute. The panel held that the statute unlawfully delegated to the comptroller general, an officer removable by Congress, the power to enforce budget ceilings—a function of the executive branch. This decision was appealed to the Supreme Court and, like most of the Scalia opinions reviewed by the Court, it was affirmed.

On June 17, 1986, President Reagan nominated Scalia to the Supreme Court, to fill the seat left vacant by the elevation of William Rehnquist to chief justice. In his testimony before the Senate Judiciary Committee, Scalia said that he considered the most important part of the Constitution to be the system of "checks and balances among the three branches, . . . so that no one of them is able to 'run roughshod' over the liberties of the people." Scalia was confirmed unanimously (98–0) by the Senate September 17.

From the beginning of his tenure on the Court, Scalia has continued to express, often in a lone concurring or dissenting opinion, his conviction that the judicial branch is the protector of the separation of powers crafted by the Founders. One of the more important cases that arose during his early years was *Morrison v. Olson* (1988), a suit challenging the constitutionality of the independent counsel, an individual selected by the judiciary to investigate senior officials of the executive

Justice Antonin Scalia with his wife, Maureen, and several of their nine children on the day of his investiture. *Source: Photo by Dane Penland, Smithsonian Institution, Collection of the Supreme Court of the United States*

branch. The Court upheld the legislation creating the post, but Scalia wrote a forceful dissent, arguing that Congress had impermissibly vested at least some of the traditional executive power to prosecute in the hands of someone not fully within the supervision and control of the president—an arrangement that had no support in the Constitution. Scalia asked, "Once we depart from the text of the Constitution, just where short of that do we stop?"

Scalia's "textualist" approach to interpreting the Constitution and statutes is reflected in his skepticism about the utility of legislative history materials, such as committee reports or the remarks of members of Congress on the House or Senate floor, to determine the meaning of a statute. Scalia thinks that the only legitimate interpretive guide is the text of the statute or related provisions of enacted law that shed light on the

meaning of the disputed text. In a March 1992 opinion concurring in the Court's more lenient reading of an ambiguous criminal statute, he sternly rejected the majority's reliance on the statute's legislative history. "The only thing that was authoritatively adopted *for sure* was the text of the enactment; the rest is *necessarily* speculative," he wrote.

Scalia's adherence to the text before him makes him unwilling to find constitutional rights that are not plainly set forth in the language of the Constitution or firmly grounded in American tradition. In two notable cases, *Webster v. Reproductive Health Services* (1989) and *Cruzan v. Director, Missouri Department of Health* (1990), he has rejected any constitutional basis for a right to an abortion or a right to refuse life-sustaining treatment. Adhering to his view of the limited role of the judiciary, he has said that such issues are essentially "political" and should be decided by elected legislators, not life-tenured judges. Some applaud Scalia's view; others believe that the Constitution is a "living document" that has more to it than the mere words with which it was written.

While Scalia is often said to be the most consistently conservative justice, his textual approach has sometimes produced alliances with the more liberal members of the Court in defense of rights that he considers explicit in the Constitution or rooted in longstanding tradition. One example is his support for the Court's holding that flag burning is a form of political expression protected under the First Amendment, despite his deep personal contempt for flag burners. Another example is his dissent from the majority of the Court when it upheld the validity of a mandatory drug-testing program for customs employees, explaining that in his view it violated the Fourth Amendment's prohibition against unreasonable searches and seizures. Likewise, he dissented in *Maryland v. Craig* (1990), a decision that permitted children testifying in abuse cases to do so by closed-circuit television on the ground that it was inconsistent with the Sixth Amendment, which protects the right of the accused to confront his or her accuser.

From his opinions, it is clear that Scalia believes that the American legal system is best served when the Court articulates clear rules of decision, not when it engages in subjective balancing tests. He appears to be willing to draw lines and would adhere to them even if it sometimes means overruling long-established precedents.

Not surprisingly, Scalia has attracted his share of admirers and critics alike. His opinions, which reflect a strong personal style and obvious passion, often confront a fellow justice's thinking on an issue. Described as "verbal hand grenades," his opinions are also widely considered to be well-written and to make good reading.

Although Scalia's views are not endorsed by a majority of the Court, he is having an effect—as in the Court's more circumspect use of legislative history. Given the force of his personality, the disarming quality of his humor, his strong intellectual and analytical abilities, and his conviction of the correctness of his position, Scalia is a strong presence on the bench.

Antonin Scalia dissented in the Supreme Court's 1990 decision permitting children to testify in abuse cases on closed circuit television. A textualist, he argued that the Sixth Amendment plainly spells out the right of the defendant to confront his or her accuser. *Source: Photo Researchers, Inc.*

Anthony M. Kennedy

1988-

Source: Photo by National Geographic Society, Collection of the Supreme Court of the United States

ANTHONY MCLEOD KENNEDY was born July 23, 1936, in Sacramento, California, and lived there nearly all his life before being appointed to the Supreme Court. His father, Anthony J. Kennedy, had worked on the docks and put himself through the University of California, graduating from law school in 1927. He moved to Sacramento to take his first job as executive secretary to Gov. James Rolph. After working in state government for several years, he began a private

law practice. A typical part of a Sacramento law practice in those days was lobbying the state legislature; however, it was only in session a few months of the year, and most of the elder Kennedy's practice involved conventional legal work.

Kennedy's mother, Gladys McLeod Kennedy, known by her childhood nickname "Sis," graduated from Stanford University in 1928 and taught school in San Francisco for two years before moving to Sacramento to take a job as a secretary in the California Senate. There she met her future husband, whom she married in 1932. The best man at the wedding was the groom's law school classmate Roger Traynor, who later became a highly influential chief justice of California. Throughout her long life, Sis Kennedy was a leader in Sacramento civic activities.

Young Anthony was the middle of three children. In those days Sacramento and its legal community were fairly small. Through his father, Kennedy grew up knowing Earl Warren, the future chief justice of the United States, and other prominent California politicians. Starting at age eleven and continuing for five years, Kennedy held a job after school as a page boy for the state Senate. He later worked in his father's law office, proofreading wills and sitting at counsel table while his father tried cases.

After graduating from high school, Kennedy went to Stanford University, where he was elected to Phi Beta Kappa and received an A.B. in 1958. He spent his final undergraduate year at the London School of Economics and to this day remains something of an Anglophile. He attended Harvard Law School, where he served on the board of student advisers, and received a J.D. cum laude in 1961.

Kennedy began his law practice as an associate of the San Francisco law firm Thelen, Marrin, Johnson, and Bridges, which then had twenty-two lawyers. He took a leave of absence during his first year to serve on active duty in the Army National Guard. In 1963 his father died suddenly, and Kennedy returned to Sacramento to take over the practice. For the next twelve years, he pursued a general law practice, including litigation and corporate work for small businesses, as well as lobbying and state administrative practice.

In 1963 Kennedy married Mary Davis, a Sacramento native he had known since childhood. Davis received her undergraduate degree from the University of Cali-

fornia and a masters degree in education from Stanford University. For many years she worked as a teacher and librarian in the Sacramento public schools. The Kennedys have three children, Justin, Gregory, and Kristin, all of whom attended Stanford. Gregory is also a graduate of Stanford Law School.

Starting in 1965 Kennedy taught constitutional law on a part-time basis at the McGeorge School of Law of the University of the Pacific. He was a popular instructor, and his three-hour Monday night classes were well-subscribed. His approach to teaching constitutional law was largely historical, and he devoted a substantial part of the course to cases decided under the Commerce Clause of the Constitution.

After Ronald Reagan was elected governor in 1966, Kennedy came to know him in the course of doing personal legal work for members of his staff. Reagan asked Kennedy to draft an amendment to the state constitution to impose permanent limits on the taxing and spending powers of the state government. Kennedy worked closely with the governor in developing and promoting this proposal, which was submitted in 1973 as a ballot initiative known as "Proposition 1." Although this initiative was defeated, it paved the way for the later success of the "Proposition 13" tax limitation initiative.

In 1974 an opening occurred on the U.S. Court of Appeals for the Ninth Circuit. Kennedy was recommended for the job by Reagan and selected by President Gerald Ford at a time when Ford still hoped to dissuade Reagan from a Republican primary challenge. Even though Reagan continued his fight for the nomination, Ford did not withdraw Kennedy's nomination. Kennedy was confirmed by the Senate in April 1975. At thirty-eight, he was the youngest federal appeals judge in the country when appointed to the bench.

At the time Kennedy joined the court, the Ninth Circuit had thirteen active judges. He maintained his

Fifteen passengers died in an Amtrack crash in 1987 as a result of the engineer's substance abuse. In 1989 Anthony Kennedy wrote the opinion for the Supreme Court upholding the Federal Railroad Administration's right to test railroad workers for drug and alcohol abuse after accidents without first obtaining a warrant. *Source: Marty Katz/Gamma-Liaison*

chambers in Sacramento, but traveled often to San Francisco, Los Angeles, and other cities to hear cases. During President Jimmy Carter's administration the Ninth Circuit was expanded to twenty-three judges and dominated by liberal appointees. Kennedy became a leader of the conservative judges, but he also developed friendly relations with the new appointees.

Kennedy's record as a Ninth Circuit judge was conservative but not confrontational. His opinions were written narrowly and avoided sweeping pronouncements on constitutional or political theory. Among his most significant opinions was *Chadha v. Immigration and Naturalization Service* (1980), which held unconstitutional a one-house legislative veto provision under

which Congress asserted the power to overturn an executive branch decision to suspend the deportation of an alien. The U.S. Supreme Court upheld the ruling three years later on much broader grounds, effectively overturning in one stroke more provisions in more federal laws than it had invalidated in its entire history. *American Federation of State, County, and Municipal Employees v. State of Washington* (1985) was the first major case on the theory of "comparable worth." Kennedy's opinion rejected the argument that federal law required employers to pay the same for jobs predominantly held by women as for different jobs involving "comparable" qualifications that were held predominantly by men. In *Beller v. Middendorf* (1980) his opinion upheld navy regulations prohibiting homosexual conduct. Kennedy's opinion did not reject the idea that the Constitution could provide some protection for sexual privacy in other contexts.

By 1987 Kennedy's mentor, Ronald Reagan, was president, and Justice Lewis F. Powell, Jr., had retired. The Senate had just rejected Judge Robert Bork, after one of the most contentious confirmation fights in U.S. history. Kennedy was at the top of a short list of potential nominees, as a conservative jurist who had not made enemies or written the sort of controversial opinions and articles that had been used against Bork. At the last minute, however, the president was persuaded by a group of hard-core Bork partisans in the Senate to nominate Douglas Ginsburg, a former Harvard law professor and Justice Department official who had recently been appointed to the Court of Appeals for the District of Columbia Circuit. The Ginsburg nomination lasted nine days and was withdrawn after various controversies arose, including revelations about past marijuana use.

Thus, by November the short list was down to one name, and on November 30, 1987, Reagan nominated Kennedy. His confirmation hearings were an amicable contrast to the combative Bork hearings. The senators did not ask the same sort of probing questions, and they allowed Kennedy to answer with soothing generalities. Many Bork critics spoke favorably about Kennedy, apparently to assure the public that they were not reflexively anti-conservative. He was perceived by liberals and moderates as more pragmatic and open-minded and less ideological than Bork. Ironically, his toughest inquisitor proved to be conservative Republican senator Gordon Humphrey. Kennedy was confirmed by a unanimous vote of the Senate February 3, 1988.

An experienced federal judge, Kennedy was immediately comfortable with the work of the Supreme Court. His opinions there are generally consistent with the record he compiled on the court of appeals. Among his significant early opinions were those upholding the constitutionality of workplace drug testing. In *Skinner v. Railway Labor Executives Association* (1989), he found constitutional the Federal Railroad Administration's requirement that railroad workers be tested for drug and alcohol use after major accidents, on the grounds that the government has a compelling interest in public safety and does not need a warrant for this type of "search." The same year, he wrote the opinion in *National Treasury Employees Union v. Von Raab* upholding the U.S. Customs Service's requirement that its employees be tested for drug use when they apply for promotions to jobs that involve drug-interdiction activities or require them to carry firearms. Such a "search" without a warrant or any particularized suspicion of an employee was justified, he reasoned, by the government's interest in the integrity of the law enforcement process.

It surprised some conservatives when Kennedy (along with Justice Antonin Scalia) joined the opinion of Justice William J. Brennan, Jr., in *Texas v. Johnson* (1989), which held that flag burning is symbolic speech protected by the First Amendment. On the touchy subject of abortion, Kennedy—along with Sandra Day O'Connor and David Souter—appears to be carving out a middle ground. The three wrote the Court's opinion in *Planned Parenthood of Southeastern Pennsylvania v. Casey* (1992), which upheld a woman's right to an abortion while permitting certain state regulations. However, Kennedy generally has participated in the Supreme Court's conservative trend, particularly on criminal law issues. For example, he wrote a significant opinion restricting prisoner abuse of federal habeas corpus petitions in *McCleskey v. Zant* (1991).

Kennedy's tenure on the Court thus far suggests that his mild, friendly manner is a potent tool for building majorities. His tendency to eschew broad, dramatic interpretations of the law also has attracted adherents to

Justice Anthony Kennedy surprised Court observers by joining with Justices Sandra Day O'Connor and David Souter to write the opinion in *Planned Parenthood of Southeastern Pennsylvania v. Casey* (1992), in which the Court upheld the right to an abortion, while permitting some state restrictions. This demonstration in front of the Supreme Court building occurred the day the decision was announced. *Source: R. Michael Jenkins*

his opinions, notably the more liberal Harry Blackmun in the drug-testing cases. Chief Justice William Rehnquist has appeared to use Kennedy as a bridge-builder often enough to win him the appellation "Rehnquist's lieutenant."

Through his friendly disposition, Kennedy has made the Supreme Court a more pleasant place for its staff and visitors. He has earned the reputation as a down-to-earth, accessible justice who takes his staff out to see Shakespeare plays and has photographed tourists (who may or may not have recognized him) in front of the Court. One former clerk attributes Kennedy's charm to his "utter lack of pretentiousness." Despite his reputation for sobriety and seriousness, Kennedy once dis-

played his sense of humor by delivering a speech on the Constitution before the Federal Bar Association dressed as James Madison.

When he is not performing the time-consuming tasks of his office, Kennedy enjoys reading books of all kinds, particularly history and English literature. He also displays a strong interest in Supreme Court history and frequently quizzed Justice Brennan about the distinguished jurists he served with during his long tenure. Kennedy remains a devout adherent to the Roman Catholic faith in which he was raised. He enjoys a variety of recreational sports, including tennis, golf, swimming, jogging, and bicycling, but he is not particularly avid about any of them.

David H. Souter

1990-

Source: Photo by National Geographic Society, Collection of the Supreme Court of the United States

DAVID HACKETT SOUTER was born in Melrose, Massachusetts, September 17, 1939, the only child of Joseph A. Souter and Helen Hackett Souter. Although he lived with his parents in Massachusetts, Souter spent much of his youth, including most summers, at his maternal grandparents' farmhouse in Weare, a small New Hampshire town twenty miles southwest of Concord, the state capital.

After his grandparents had passed away, Souter, age eleven, and his family moved to the farmhouse. His fa-

ther was a banker with the New Hampshire Savings Bank in Concord. He died in 1976, but Souter's mother still lives near the family farmhouse in a retirement community.

Souter has called Weare, which borders Hopkinton Lake, "a town large in geography [and] small in population," where everybody "knew everybody else's business or at least thought they did. And we were, in a very true sense, intimately aware of other lives. We were aware of lives that were easy and lives that were very hard." It is, indeed, a typical small town in rural New England, still governed by a town meeting. Souter learned many "lessons in practical government" by sitting in the back bench of the Weare Town Hall and watching the town meetings.

Souter attended the local public school and was immediately recognized as a student of great promise. One of his teachers later observed that the small school could not contain his "bounding intelligence." Souter's parents sent him to Concord High School, where he excelled academically. He graduated in 1957 and was voted "most sophisticated" and "most likely to succeed" by his classmates.

He continued his education at Harvard, where he majored in philosophy and wrote his senior honors thesis on the jurisprudence of Justice Oliver Wendell Holmes, Jr. Souter was elected to Phi Beta Kappa and graduated magna cum laude in 1961. Awarded a Rhodes scholarship to attend Oxford University for two years, he studied jurisprudence at Magdalen College, where he received bachelor's and master's degrees.

In 1963 Souter returned to Harvard to study law. Despite the demands of his legal curriculum, Souter also served as proctor for an undergraduate dormitory. This role required him to be "on call" twenty-four hours a day to counsel thirty Harvard freshmen, who presented him with the wide variety of problems and challenges young students face in adjusting to college and life away from home.

Souter had no interest in practicing law anywhere other than New Hampshire. When he graduated in 1966 he accepted a position as an associate with a prominent Concord law firm, Orr and Reno, where he had worked as a summer law clerk. He had a general legal practice that included matters of corporate law and taxation, real estate law, and general litigation. A portion of his practice was pro bono, representing clients who could not afford to pay the usual fees charged by the firm. It was on behalf of one of these clients, a woman who had lost custody of her children and was trying to get them back, that Souter first appeared in court.

Even after only a brief period in private practice, a colleague at Orr and Reno suggested that Souter "would seem to be a natural judge." He was too young for such an appointment, but he was nonetheless interested in public service. A partner at the firm observed that Souter "wanted to break out, to be in charge of something, to be responsible for his own outcomes." When the attorney general of New Hampshire offered Souter a position in 1968, he accepted immediately.

Souter began his career in public service as an assistant attorney general in the criminal division. He was assigned to cases at both the trial and appellate levels. He also performed special assignments for the attorney general and deputy attorney general. His major cases included a murder prosecution arising out of a gangland killing and a dispute between the Atlantic coast states and the federal government over title to under-sea resources outside the three-mile territorial limit.

When Warren B. Rudman became attorney general of New Hampshire in 1971, he selected Souter as his deputy. Rudman, who later became a U.S. senator, recalls his promotion of Souter. "I could see how brilliant he was, how valuable to the work of the office." A close and enduring friendship developed between the two men during the five years Souter served as deputy attorney general. Together, they built the attorney general's office into an extremely effective legal office. Souter's responsibilities included supervising the work of other lawyers in the office and counseling senior government officials.

Gov. Meldrin Thompson, impressed with Souter's work, appointed him attorney general in 1976 when Rudman resigned to enter private practice. Among the major issues in which Souter was involved was a vigorous and successful campaign to prevent legalized casino gambling in New Hampshire. He also participated in the prosecution of more than 1,000 protesters who had occupied the Seabrook nuclear power plant in 1977.

Although a Republican, Souter was never active in party politics. He devoted all of his energies to his legal practice, taking time out only to attend his Episcopal church and to pursue hobbies such as mountain climbing, classical music, and reading. His civic activities included fourteen years' service on the Board of Trustees of Concord Hospital, of which he was president from 1978 to 1984. A history buff, he has also served as vice president of the New Hampshire Historical Society.

In 1978, after two years as attorney general, Souter was appointed associate justice of the New Hampshire Superior Court, the state's trial court of general jurisdiction. The justices of the superior court do not have chambers or a courtroom in any particular county; rather, they travel from county to county trying cases. Thus, during his service on this court, Souter "rode the circuit" of New Hampshire's ten counties, presiding in the courthouses of Berlin, Laconia, Dover, Keene, Manchester, and Concord. As Souter later described it, he presided over every type of case imaginable and "saw every sort and condition of the people of my State that a trial court of general jurisdiction is exposed to. I saw litigants in international commercial litigation for millions, and I saw children who were the unwitting victims of domestic disputes and custody fights."

A substantial number of cases over which Souter presided were criminal prosecutions, and he acquired a reputation as a tough but fair judge with criminal defendants. A former public defender in New Hampshire who tried numerous cases before Souter has stated, "He was an excellent trial judge, although he was the kind of judge you knew was really going to hammer people at sentencing." Souter developed a keen interest in and respect for the jury system. He had a practice of meeting with the members of the jury after a case to discuss their participation in the legal system. One lawyer who appeared frequently before Souter observed that,

Thomas D. Rath, left, David Souter, center, and Warren Rudman, right, three successive attorneys general of New Hampshire, posed together in 1977, the year after Souter took over the post from Rudman. Rath followed Souter, who became a superior court judge. *Source:* Concord Monitor

as a result of his solicitous treatment, "juries loved him."

Looking back on his service as a trial judge, Souter believes he learned two important lessons about judging that remain with him. First, "whether we are on a trial court or an appellate court, at the end of our task some human being is going to be affected." Second, "if, indeed, we are going to be trial judges, whose rulings will affect the lives of other people and who are going to change their lives by what we do, we had better use every power of our minds and our hearts and our beings to get those rulings right."

Souter took those lessons with him to the Supreme

Court of New Hampshire when Gov. John Sununu appointed him an associate justice in 1983. Administering the oath of office, Sununu remarked, "When I'm old and gray, people will say, 'This is one of the greatest things you did as governor.' " During his seven years on the state supreme court, Souter developed a reputation as a scholarly, tough-minded intellectual with a deep respect for precedent and history. "He really raised the level of an already fine court," one litigator before that court noted. "He dominated oral arguments, and he resurrected cases and jurists that had been ignored for years."

Souter not only brought a broad historical perspective to the New Hampshire Supreme Court, but also he demonstrated a fierce independence on matters of principle. In *State v. Koppel* (1987) he dissented from a decision holding that random checkpoints to catch drunk drivers were unconstitutional under the New Hampshire Constitution. Subsequently, the U.S. Supreme Court has held that such checkpoints are legal under the federal Constitution.

Souter's reputation as a jurist soon extended beyond New Hampshire. President Ronald Reagan seriously considered him as a nominee to the Supreme Court in 1987. In April 1990 President George Bush named Souter to the U.S. Court of Appeals for the First Circuit. Three months later, Justice William J. Brennan, Jr., retired from the Supreme Court, and Senator Rudman recommended that the president appoint Souter to fill the seat.

On July 23, 1990, three days after Brennan's retirement, Bush announced his intention to nominate Souter to the Court. Having served only a few months as a federal judge, Souter was not a well-known na-

The justices of the U.S. Supreme Court, with David Souter, then the newest member, in the center. *Source: Photo by Ken Heinen, Collection of the Supreme Court of the United States*

tional figure. The press investigated the conservative, hard-working bachelor's past, but could find nothing controversial. When his confirmation hearings began, as one newspaper reported, Souter "cast aside the silence that had clothed his nomination to the United States Supreme Court to reveal intelligence, poise—and a sense of humor." The chairman of the Judiciary Committee, Sen. Joseph Biden, told Souter at the conclusion of his testimony, "I . . . have been impressed with your knowledge. I have been impressed with your ability to articulate your position. I have been impressed with the ease with which you were able to make clear the purpose behind . . . a number of decisions, including even referring to the sense within those opinions that most would spend time in a law library having to look up. And you have done it off the top of your head."

Souter was confirmed October 2, 1990, by a 90–9 vote, and took his seat on the Court a week later. He has since emerged as the intellectual leader of the Court's centrist coalition, often carving out a middle ground for other justices to join. A moderate pragmatist, Souter shows a strong respect for precedent. This tendency was reflected in his first major opinion, *Planned Parenthood of Southeastern Pennsylvania v. Casey* (1992), which, in an unusual move, he wrote with Justices Sandra Day O'Connor and Anthony Kennedy. The Court's opinion permitted several state regulations of abortion to stand, but declined to overturn *Roe v. Wade.*

Souter has written on a wide variety of subjects. He dissented on First Amendment free speech grounds from a decision allowing a person to sue a newspaper for its failure to honor a promise of confidentiality. In *Cohen v. Cowles Media Co.* (1991) he found the state's interest in enforcing a newspaper's promise of confidentiality did not outweigh the public's interest in the unfettered publication of information. In 1992 he wrote the opinion for the Court in *Norman v. Reed,* invalidating on constitutional grounds portions of the Illinois election law that unduly burdened access to the ballot

Dan Cohen beams after winning his Supreme Court case in 1991 against both daily newspapers in the Twin Cities. Cohen had provided them with information during the 1982 gubernatorial campaign under conditions of confidentiality, but the newspapers later revealed his name. David Souter dissented, saying that the public's interest in unfettered information outweighed the promise of confidentiality. *Source: AP/Wide World Photos*

by new political parties. And in a forceful concurring opinion in a capital case, Souter joined the majority in concluding that information about a murder victim may be presented to a sentencing jury.

Souter has developed a reputation as a charming wit with a wry sense of humor who delights in entertaining colleagues and visitors with tall tales. Despite his move to Washington, D.C., Souter retains the traits of a rugged, individualistic New Englander. He refuses to wear an overcoat, even on the coldest days, and he brings his lunch to work (usually an apple and yogurt). At night, after work, he will often go for a long run. During the summer, he returns to his home in Weare and climbs the tallest peaks of the nearby White Mountains.

Clarence Thomas

1991-

Source: Photo by National Geographic Society, Collection of the Supreme Court of the United States

CLARENCE THOMAS was born June 23, 1948, in Pin Point, Georgia, an enclave of 500 inhabitants south of Savannah on the Moon River. Named after the plantation that once stood on the land, Pin Point had been divided up after the Civil War and given to the former slaves. In that marshy, dirt-poor community, which had neither sewers nor paved roads, most people worked for a few cents a day cleaning crabs and shucking oysters.

Young Clarence was the second child and first son of Leola Williams and M. C. Thomas. Clarence's father abandoned the family when he was two and his mother was pregnant with her third child. She managed to keep the family together by working as a maid, clothing her children in hand-me-downs donated to their Baptist church. After the wooden house they lived in burned down and their mother remarried, Clarence and his brother went to live with their grandfather, Myers Anderson, in Savannah.

An ardent Catholic, loyal Democrat, and active

member of the National Association for the Advancement of Colored People (NAACP), Anderson had a profound influence on Thomas's upbringing and character. In a time when African-Americans were forced to the backs of buses, banned from restaurants, and denied employment opportunities, Anderson decided the only way to beat racism was to work for himself. He developed a flourishing business delivering wood, coal, ice, and heating oil from the back of a pick-up truck. As a result, he was able to provide his grandsons with a comfortable home, including things most people take for granted, such as three meals a day and indoor plumbing.

A strict but loving man, Anderson admonished his grandsons to work hard in school. He enrolled them in St. Benedict the Moor, an all-black grammar school run by white nuns. The nuns were strict disciplinarians who pushed their students to achieve their greatest potential. After school Thomas and his brother worked for their grandfather making fuel deliveries. Thomas later recalled how his grandparents had impressed on him that "school, discipline, hard work and 'right-from-wrong' were of the highest priority."

Because his grandfather wanted him to become a priest, Thomas left his black parochial high school after two years to attend a Catholic boarding school just outside Savannah. The only African-American in his class at St. John Vianney Minor Seminary, Thomas suffered from the bigotry of many students, but managed to excel academically. At lights out a classmate would tease, "Smile, Clarence, so we can see you," he later recalled. In 1967 Thomas entered Immaculate Conception Seminary in northwestern Missouri to prepare for the priesthood. The prejudice he encountered there convinced him to quit a school that did not practice what it preached. The last straw was a fellow student's delight at hearing the news that Rev. Martin Luther King, Jr., had been slain.

Thomas worked for a while before making his way in 1968 to Holy Cross, a Jesuit college in Worcester, Massachusetts. Holy Cross had begun an ambitious black recruitment program in the wake of the King assassination and attracted more than a few black students that year. Thomas helped found the Black Student Union, which decided in its second year that its members should live together in one dormitory. Thomas was the lone dissenter in the vote, preferring, as he later explained, to "profit from the experience by learning to associate [with] and understand the white majority." Thomas gave in, but brought his white roommate from the previous year to live with him. During college Thomas participated in a free breakfast program for local schoolchildren and was a Black Panthers sympathizer.

Thomas graduated ninth in his class in 1971 with an English honors degree. The day following graduation he married Kathy Grace Ambush, a student at a nearby Catholic women's college. Two years later she gave birth to their son, Jamal. By then Thomas was enrolled at Yale Law School, having been accepted, in part, under

Clarence Thomas was the only black student in his graduating class at the Catholic boarding school he attended outside Savannah, Georgia. *Source: Catholic Diocese of Savannah, Georgia*

an affirmative action plan to recruit qualified minorities. It troubled Thomas that he was the beneficiary of such a plan. He later explained, "You had to prove yourself every day because the presumption was that you were dumb and didn't deserve to be there on merit." He sat in the back row in his classes so as not to be given special treatment because of his race. To prove his abilities outside the sphere of traditional black issues, he took courses in tax and antitrust law instead of civil rights and constitutional law.

Graduating in 1974, Thomas joined the staff of the attorney general of Missouri, John Danforth, a young Republican who would become his political mentor. The only African-American in the office, Thomas requested to work in tax law, not civil rights. When Danforth was elected to the Senate in 1977, Thomas took a job in the private sector, at Monsanto, a St. Louis chemical company. His work there primarily consisted of shepherding pesticides through government registration.

After two and a half years Thomas decided to go to Washington and work in politics. He joined Senator Danforth's staff as a legislative assistant in charge of energy and environmental projects, once again purposefully staying clear of black issues. At the same time, Thomas became active in the black conservative movement, which believes that welfare, busing, affirmative action programs, and government set-asides make African-Americans dependent on government charity and do more harm than good. He did not view integration as a solution. Instead, he reasoned, African-Americans should help themselves through education, enterprise, work, and self-reliance.

In 1981 the new administration of President Ronald Reagan took notice of the rising young conservative and appointed him assistant secretary for civil rights in the Education Department. Thomas said in a 1987 speech, "I had, initially, resisted and declined taking the position of assistant secretary for civil rights simply be-

cause my career was not in civil rights and I had no intention of moving into this area. . . . I always found it curious that even though my background was in energy, taxation, and general corporate regulatory matters, that I was not seriously sought after to move into one of these areas." After only ten months in the job, Reagan promoted him to be the director of the Equal Employment Opportunity Commission (EEOC).

As the head enforcer of federal laws against discrimination in the workplace, Thomas did not have an easy time. At first, the Reagan administration found him too independent-minded, but in the course of his nearly eight years on the job he generally supported the administration's opposition to the use of numerical goals and timetables for bringing suits against companies that did not hire enough minorities. Democrats and civil rights groups attacked the EEOC's move away from these traditional remedies to discrimination. Defending the administration's position, Thomas once asked a congressional committee whether anyone would ever suggest that primarily white Georgetown University should be made to recruit white basketball players. He privately argued that, although racial preference programs enable a few qualified African-Americans to achieve, they do not help the majority.

In keeping with its reluctance to enforce goals and timetables, the EEOC under Thomas also largely abandoned the use of class action suits that relied on statistical evidence to prove widespread discrimination at corporations, preferring to focus on individual suits instead. Many credit Thomas with improving morale at the agency and making it more efficient. Others criticize him for letting 9,000 age discrimination complaints lapse, an inaction he has admitted was the "single most devastating event" of his tenure.

During this time he had personal difficulties as well. His grandfather died in 1983. Two years earlier Thomas and his wife had separated. They were divorced in 1984,

Clarence Thomas and his wife Virginia were joined by three nuns from his grammar school, St. Benedict the Moor, at Thomas's swearing in as a judge on the U.S. District Court of Appeals in 1990. *Source: Sister Mary Virgilius Reidy*

and he kept custody of his son. At a conference in 1986 Thomas met Virginia Lamp, a spokesperson for the U.S. Chamber of Commerce. They were married five months later at a ceremony in her native Nebraska; Jamal was his father's best man. Long active in Republican politics, Virginia Thomas is a senior aide to Rep. Dick Armey, the House majority leader.

Given his quick rise through the ranks of government in the 1980s, few were surprised when Thomas was appointed in 1990 to be a judge on the U.S. Court of Appeals for the District of Columbia. In his brief eighteen months as an appeals judge, Thomas did not develop a comprehensive judicial philosophy. He wrote a revealing opinion for the court in an affirmative action case he heard in January 1991, but it was not released until after he had taken his seat on the Supreme Court. The decision held that the federal government may not give preferential treatment to women in awarding broadcast licenses, even though it does so for other

minority groups. Because studies could not show that women's ownership of broadcast licenses increased programming designed for women, Thomas reasoned that the government could not demonstrate that the sex-preference policy would promote greater diversity on the airwaves, as it had for minority-owned franchises.

On July 1, 1991, George Bush selected Thomas to replace Thurgood Marshall, the first African-American member of the Supreme Court. Many civil rights groups, notably the NAACP and the Congressional Black Caucus, declared that they would not support Thomas because of his opposition to the traditional civil rights agenda. His endorsement by African-American conservatives focused increased attention, however, on the diversity of African-American politics.

As the full Senate was about to vote on Thomas's confirmation, a sensational story broke. The press was leaked information regarding an FBI report, which the Judiciary Committee had been shown, alleging that

Thomas had sexually harassed a former employee at the EEOC. University of Oklahoma law professor Anita Hill, who had made the allegation, was brought in for questioning by the Judiciary Committee, and the hearings were reopened amid a flurry of controversy. Hill, also an African-American and a Yale Law School graduate, outlined her allegations in detail in nationally televised hearings. Thomas categorically denied the charges, calling the ordeal "a high-tech lynching for uppity blacks." The Senate voted to confirm Thomas on October 15, 1991, by a vote of 52 to 48, the closest confirmation vote in this century's history.

Thomas has expressed support for a limited role for the Court and a narrow reach of constitutional guarantees. When the Court ruled in *Hudson v. McMillian* (1992) that excessive force used by a prison guard may violate the Constitution even if it does not result in serious injury to a prisoner, Thomas dissented. He argued that the Eighth Amendment's prohibition against cruel and unusual punishment "should not be turned into a national code of prison regulation." He cautioned that the majority opinion was "yet another manifestation of the pervasive view that the federal constitution must address all ills in our society." In a death penalty case, Thomas wrote a separate concurring opinion that emphasized the irrelevance of a prisoner's poor background and troubled upbringing. He warned that consideration of such handicaps by judges could lead to arbitrary leniency and might result in discrimination against black defendants. In a 1994 case challenging the Voting Rights Act, *Holder v. Hall*, Thomas criticized the notion that race defines political interest and that minority groups all think alike on political matters.

Age forty-three when appointed, Thomas is the youngest member of the Court. Gregarious, with a

A Louisiana prison inmate, beaten by guards while he was handcuffed and shackled, brought a lawsuit, even though his injuries resulted in no permanent damage. Clarence Thomas dissented from the majority decision that excessive force by a prison guard may violate the Eighth Amendment protection against "cruel and unusual punishment," even if it does not result in serious injury.
Source: American Correctional Association

hearty laugh, Thomas enjoys lifting weights, watching basketball, and smoking cigars. Although born a Baptist and raised a Catholic, he now regularly attends an Episcopal church.

Ruth Bader Ginsburg
1993-

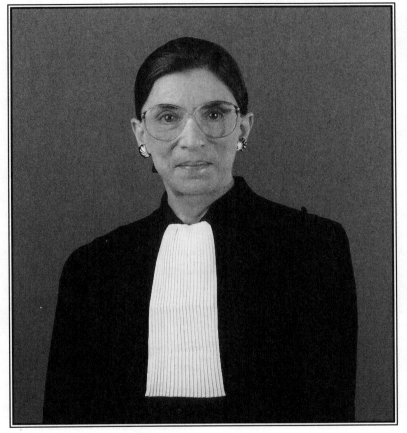

Source: Collection of the Supreme Court of the United States

RUTH BADER GINSBURG was born Joan Ruth Bader on March 15, 1933, in Brooklyn, New York. Her parents, Nathan Bader and Celia Amster Bader, were Jewish Americans whose families had immigrated to the United States—Celia's from central Europe four months before she was born and Nathan's from Russia when he was thirteen. An older sister, Marilyn, died at the age of eight, so Ruth Bader grew up as an only child, in the Flatbush section of Brooklyn. Her father worked first as a furrier and later, as a haberdasher.

Celia Bader played a critical role in her daughter's intellectual development. She took Ruth on frequent trips to the library and saved money to enable her daughter to attend college. Ruth excelled in high school, winning scholarships that would pay her way through college without dipping deeply into her mother's savings. Sadly, Celia struggled with cancer

Celia Amster Bader graduated from high school at age fifteen with top grades. She then went to work in New York's garment district and gave part of her earnings to her family to enable her older brother to attend college. Before her tragic early death, Celia strongly impressed upon her daughter Ruth the importance of education and achievement. *Source: Photo by Harcourt-Harris Studios, New York, Collection of the Supreme Court of the United States*

throughout Ruth's high school years and died the day before graduation.

Ruth Bader continued to fulfill her mother's hopes in college at Cornell University, where she was elected to Phi Beta Kappa and graduated first among the women in her class. At Cornell she met Martin Ginsburg, whom she married following her graduation in 1954. Together they decided to pursue careers in the law.

Ruth Bader Ginsburg entered Harvard Law School a year behind her husband, following two years in Fort Sill, Oklahoma, where he served in the army. Their daughter, Jane, was still a baby, and the two law stu-

dents shared child care duties and household chores. Harvard Law School was less than welcoming to the nine women in its class of 1959, providing no room for them in its main dormitories. Despite the chilly atmosphere and the extra demands of her young family, Ginsburg excelled in her classes and won a spot on the law review.

During her second year at Harvard, Martin Ginsburg was diagnosed with cancer. While he underwent massive surgery and radical radiation treatments for a condition doctors told him few had ever survived, Ruth covered her husband's classes as well as her own, copying notes for him and typing his third-year paper. Martin recovered and was able to complete his course work and graduate on time. When he accepted a job as an associate with a New York City law firm, Ruth transferred to Columbia Law School so that the family could remain together. There she made law review again and graduated tied for first in her class.

Although she had superior academic credentials, Ginsburg received no job offers from New York law firms, nor was she able to obtain a clerkship interview with a Supreme Court justice. As she has recalled, her status as "a woman, a Jew, and a mother to boot" was "a bit much" for prospective employers in those days. One enlightened district court judge in New York, Edmund L. Palmieri, finally hired Ginsburg as a law clerk. Twenty years later, he rated her as among the best clerks he had ever employed.

Following her clerkship, Ginsburg took part in a comparative law project sponsored by Columbia Law School. As the prime part of her work for the project, she coauthored a book on judicial procedure in Sweden. After almost daily tutoring in Swedish for several months, she traveled to Sweden to observe Swedish courts in operation. In years immediately prior to her Supreme Court appointment, Ginsburg spent some of her spare time assisting in the translation of the Swedish Code of Judicial Procedure into English.

In 1963, she became the second woman to join the law faculty of Rutgers University in New Jersey. While at Rutgers, Ginsburg became pregnant with her second child, James. Worried about retaining her nontenured position, she hid her pregnancy from her employers during the school year by wearing clothes borrowed from her ever supportive, one-size-larger mother-in-law.

Her personal encounter with the special obstacles faced by women attempting to combine career and family coincided with a professional awakening. In the early 1960s, prompted in part by her reading of Simone de Beauvoir's *The Second Sex,* Ginsburg recognized that the second-class treatment she had experienced was a symptom of a larger problem—social conditions that denied women choices and opportunities open to men. The law, she believed, should aid in redressing these inequities. While continuing to teach at Rutgers, Ginsburg assisted the New Jersey affiliate of the American Civil Liberties Union in litigating sex discrimination cases, prime among them, cases on behalf of school teachers who were forced to forfeit their jobs when they became pregnant. Asked by her Rutgers students to teach a course on sex-based discrimination, Ginsburg was surprised to discover how little had been written on that subject.

The Supreme Court had upheld a series of laws that treated women differently from men—for example, by preventing women from working as bartenders or lawyers under the rationale that women, as members of "the gentler sex," were in need of special protection from life's hardships. Ginsburg believed that such sex stereotyping, although ostensibly benign, demeaned women and unfairly limited their opportunities. In her view, the equal protection principle stated in the Fourteenth Amendment to the U.S. Constitution, which prohibits discrimination based on race, should bar gender-based discrimination as well. But in the 1960s and early 1970s, Ginsburg found that promoting this viewpoint was an uphill battle. As she recalled at her confirmation hearings: "Race discrimination was immediately perceived as evil, odious, and intolerable. But the response I got when I talked about sex-based discrimination was 'What are you talking about? Women are treated ever so much better than men.' I was talking to an audience that thought . . . I was somehow critical about the way they treated their wives . . . [and] their daughters."

Changing these views—and the law that reflected them—could not be accomplished overnight. Victory would require persuading a majority of the Supreme Court that sex-based legal classifications should be scrutinized much more closely by the courts than other government choices. Ginsburg, like Thurgood Marshall in his battle against racial discrimination, recognized that a cautious, incremental approach would be the surest method of achieving enduring change in the law. In her words, "[t]he courts needed to be educated. That requires patience: it may mean holding back a case until the way has been paved for it."

Ginsburg launched her campaign by joining forces with the ACLU's national office. She helped to write the ACLU's brief in a key Supreme Court sex discrimination case, *Reed v. Reed* (1971), which struck down a state law that preferred men over women as administrators of decedents' estates. However, because the Court reached its decision without explicitly adopting a heightened standard of review, the ruling did not guarantee similar results in other cases.

The ACLU established a Women's Rights Project in 1972 and placed Ginsburg at the helm. Over the next eight years, she sought to persuade a majority of the Supreme Court that sex-based legal distinctions should trigger some form of heightened judicial scrutiny.

To execute this strategy, Ginsburg selected cases that would allow her to make her point on behalf of women's rights without appearing strident or radical. Her objective was to convince the Court that gender-based stereotyping harmed not only women, but all of society. Often the plaintiffs in Ginsburg's cases were men, and the well-being of families was at stake. For example, in *Weinberger v. Wiesenfeld* (1975), a widower whose wife had died in childbirth wanted to stay home to take care of his infant son. If his wife had survived him, she automatically would have been entitled to Social Security benefits based on his salary; however, Wiesenfeld could not receive those benefits. In effect, his wife had paid her Social Security taxes at the same rate as a man, but had not obtained an equivalent measure of protection for her family. This discrepancy arose, Ginsburg argued, from society's inaccurate—and damaging—preconception that husbands are always the wage-earners and wives the dependent caregivers. A unanimous Supreme Court held the exclusion of fathers like Wiesenfeld unconstitutional, although again without explicitly applying a heightened standard of review.

Between 1972 and 1978, Ginsburg argued six cases before the Court involving sex-role stereotyping and won five. In *Craig v. Boren* (1976), the Court finally accepted Ginsburg's view (expressed in a "friend-of-the-court" brief) that gender-based legal distinctions deserved heightened scrutiny.

A later generation of feminist legal scholars has criticized Ginsburg's equal protection theories. They argue that her approach failed to take account of the real differences between the sexes that may sometimes warrant laws giving women preferential treatment. Critics and admirers agree, however, that Ginsburg's work in the 1970s fundamentally altered the legal and social landscape, creating unprecedented personal and professional opportunities for women.

In 1972, Ginsburg left Rutgers to teach at Columbia Law School, where she became the first tenured woman law professor. Her distinguished teaching career and ACLU achievements won her a national reputation and prompted President Jimmy Carter to appoint her to the U.S. Court of Appeals for the District of Columbia Circuit in 1980. Martin Ginsburg moved with his wife

Stephen Wiesenfeld and his son, Jason, became the center of an important Supreme Court case, *Weinberger v. Wiesenfeld* (1975). After the death of his wife, who had been the principal wage-earner in the family, Wiesenfeld applied for survivors' benefits for himself and his son. A provision of the Social Security Act stated that a widow with children was entitled to benefits based on the earnings of her deceased husband, but a widower in similar circumstances was excluded from the benefits his wife had earned. Arguing on behalf of Wiesenfeld, Ginsburg questioned the law's assumption that husbands are always the wage-earners and wives the dependent caregivers. In a unanimous decision, the Court struck down the challenged provision as unconstitutional. *Source: AP/Wide World Photos*

to Washington, D.C., leaving his New York tax practice and chair at Columbia Law School to become a professor at Georgetown University Law Center.

As a judge, Ginsburg garnered respect with her clear thinking, careful reasoning, and assiduous preparation for every case. Her prompt drafting of each opinion she was assigned and her scrupulous attention to the details of each case stemmed from her appreciation that the court's rulings would change the lives or practices of persons affected by judicial decisions. This sensitivity to the real-world effects of her decisions led her to take her law clerks on periodic tours of the local prisons in which some of the defendants in the court's criminal cases were incarcerated.

While serving on the D.C. Circuit, Ginsburg dissented in a challenge to a statute allowing the judiciary to appoint independent counsel to investigate allegations of wrongdoing by senior executive officers. A panel of the appeals court struck down the law as an unconstitutional infringement of the separation of powers, reasoning that only the executive branch is empowered to appoint prosecutors. Ginsburg rejected this approach as excessively formalistic. She found the majority's holding ironic, because the purpose of the independent counsel law was to maintain the balance of power among the various branches of government by curbing abuses of executive authority. In *Morrison v. Olson* (1988), the Supreme Court upheld the constitutionality of the statute.

The resignation of Justice Byron White in the spring of 1993 afforded President Bill Clinton the opportunity to become the first Democratic president in twenty-six years to make a Supreme Court appointment. Clinton announced that he was looking for a nominee with "a fine mind, good judgment, wide experience in the law and in the problems of real people, and somebody with a big heart." Calling Ginsburg "the Thurgood Marshall of gender equality law," he concluded that she possessed the requisite intellectual and emotional stature for the job.

Much of the initial resistance to Ginsburg's nomination came from within the feminist movement because she had expressed reservations about the reasoning of the Supreme Court's decision in *Roe v. Wade* (1973)

upholding a woman's right to choose an abortion. Ginsburg would have preferred a more measured approach—an opinion that invited gradual liberalization of state abortion laws, one that might avoid a political backlash. At her confirmation hearings, however, Ginsburg dispelled any doubts about her commitment to a woman's reproductive choice. She characterized a woman's right to choose an abortion as "something central to a woman's life, to her dignity. . . . And when government controls that decision for her, she's being treated as less than a full adult human being responsible for her own choices."

The Senate voted 97–3 to confirm Ginsburg's nomination, and she took the oath of office on August 10, 1993. Ginsburg's second major opinion on the Supreme Court displayed her characteristic tendency to approach legal questions in terms of real-world experience. In *Ratzlaf v. United States* (1994), Ginsburg wrote the Court's opinion reversing a criminal conviction for "willfully violating" a prohibition on "structuring" cash transactions so as to avoid a reporting requirement applicable to transactions involving more than $10,000. A majority of the Court concluded that the prosecution had to prove the defendant knew of not only the reporting requirement, but also the prohibition on breaking up transactions to evade it. The government had argued that the very act of structuring suggested an involvement in criminal activity, such as money laundering or tax evasion, and thereby demonstrated the necessary bad intent. In rejecting this argument, Ginsburg listed several innocent reasons that might motivate an ordinary citizen to break up cash deposits into small sums, such as a fear of burglary resulting from the bank's reports.

Ginsburg is known as a ruthless editor with a keen eye for detail. Her soft voice and reserved manner hide great perceptiveness and a warm interest in people. She is an opera devotee who has appeared in full period costume—complete with wig and fan—as an extra in a Washington Opera production.

Stephen G. Breyer
1994-

Source: Photo by Richard W. Strauss, Smithsonian Institution. Courtesy of the Supreme Court Historical Society

STEPHEN GERALD BREYER was born August 15, 1938, in San Francisco, to Irving Breyer, a lawyer and administrator for the city school system, and Anne Breyer, the daughter of East Prussian immigrants. The commitment to good government that would characterize Stephen Breyer's later career began developing in his earliest years. His father brought him along on trips to the voting booth and helped him develop what Breyer later described as "a trust in, almost a love for the possibilities of a democracy" and a belief that "with trust and cooperation and participation, people can work through their government to improve their lives." His mother was active in local Democratic politics, the League of Women Voters, and a United Nations program that brought foreign visitors to their home. "She was the one who made absolutely clear to me that whatever intellectual ability I have means nothing . . . unless I can work with other people and use whatever talents I have to help them. So I joined the Boy Scouts, I did work as a delivery boy, I [dug] ditches for the Pacific Gas and Electric Company, and I mixed salads up in the city's summer camp."

Breyer attended Lowell High School, the elite flagship of the public school system, where he excelled early and often. An accomplished member of the debating team, he was voted most likely to succeed by his class. Breyer's love of learning and his curiosity about his Jewish identity persuaded him to attend religious school on Sundays. In college he continued his religious involvement by teaching younger students at a local synagogue.

Fearing that Harvard University might lead their son to become too bookish, his parents convinced him to attend Stanford University instead. Graduating with highest honors in 1959, Breyer traveled to Oxford University on a Marshall Scholarship. There, he received a B.A. with first-class honors in 1961 for his study of philosophy, politics, and economics.

Breyer completed his education in 1964 with an LL.B. magna cum laude from Harvard Law School. He was elected articles editor of the *Harvard Law Review* and wrote his required independent work on pragmatism, exploring the philosophies of Charles S. Peirce, William James, and Willard Quine. His thesis—that judges should make decisions by carefully considering how their conclusions would effect people's social, political, and legal circumstances—foreshadowed his orientation as a judge twenty years later.

Breyer went to Washington after graduation to clerk for Associate Justice Arthur J. Goldberg. He wrote the first draft of Goldberg's famous opinion in *Griswold v. Connecticut* (1965), which established the constitutional right to privacy. Over the next thirty years Breyer would again and again exchange the academic environment of Boston for the public law challenges of the nation's capital. His practice of applying his scholarly skills to the real world issues of federal regulatory law became a hallmark of his career.

From 1965 to 1967 Breyer worked in the U.S. Department of Justice as a special assistant to Assistant Attorney General Donald F. Turner, a Harvard law professor who significantly influenced the development of antitrust regulation.

During this period Breyer met Joanna Freda Hare, the daughter of Lord John Blakenham, an influential Tory politician and leader of Britain's Conservative Party. Their marriage in 1967 brought him into a wealthy and elite English family and allowed him frequent occasions to revisit the country he had come to love as a student. Also an Oxford graduate, Joanna Breyer went on to earn a doctorate in clinical psychology from Harvard University, and began working with young cancer patients and their families at the Dana-Farber Cancer Institute in Boston. Identifying his wife's work as a sobering and affecting influence, Breyer became a trustee of the institute.

Shortly after their marriage, Breyer returned to Cambridge to begin his academic career at Harvard Law School. He specialized in federal administrative law, broadening his inquiry beyond antitrust to include the burgeoning challenges of the regulatory regime in the post-New Deal state. Over the next twenty years, Breyer developed a sophisticated yet pragmatic theory of the regulatory state that complemented his lifelong commitment to good government.

Breyer believes that a pro-competitive approach to economic regulation appropriately maximizes the benefits available from the free market and, at the same time, reduces the burdens that flow from unnecessary regulation. For example, in his early scholarship he argued that the courts should not penalize "the honest monopolist" by equating injury to a competitor caused by "skill, foresight, and industry"—or indeed by accident—with the injury to competition prohibited by antitrust laws. In addition, his work has included a searching critique of counterproductive regulation, such as laws that require the complete elimination of slight health risks at costs that make impossible other, more compelling reforms.

On the other hand, Breyer holds that a strong regulatory regime is essential in precisely those areas, like health and safety, in which economically driven arguments cannot supply the medical and scientific decisions, let alone the moral valuations, that are necessary. Ultimately, Breyer's arguments point to a vital role for government in maintaining that level of regulatory control that is productive. He favors reforming and reshaping government regulatory structures so that they operate more constructively. For example, Breyer has advocated the creation of an elite corps of civil servants who would evaluate risk assessments justifying various federal regulations in order to determine overall costs and benefits.

Breyer returned to Washington, D.C., in 1973 as an assistant special prosecutor in the Watergate investigation. He stayed on for the following two years as special counsel to the Administrative Practices Subcommittee of the Senate Judiciary Committee. During that time, he critiqued the government's management of the airline industry, concluding that it had limited competition and handicapped the industry's growth. He later used the tools of economic analysis to help design and engineer the controversial airline deregulation of 1978. Breyer's most dramatic strategy was the careful orchestration of public hearings which he effectively used to swing congressional opinion to his model. Whether the deregulatory experiment was a necessary remedy for an inefficient industry or a disruptive force in a delicately balanced business is still in dispute. Allies and opponents both point to the wave of airline bankruptcies, fare reductions, and industry dislocations that followed deregulation to support their views.

Breyer's work on airline deregulation demonstrated not only his determination to tackle difficult regulatory tangles; it also showcased an exceptional capacity to build bipartisan consensus on politically divisive issues. That talent proved essential to his effectiveness in his next Washington job—a two-year stint as chief counsel of the Senate Judiciary Committee. There, he repeatedly brokered compromises over sensitive issues such as the release of material on low-level public corruption investigations in the Carter administration. Though a life-long Democrat working under Sen. Edward Kennedy, a renowned liberal, Breyer gained credibility with Republicans as someone with a fair, balanced approach.

In late 1980, President Jimmy Carter nominated Breyer for a seat on the U.S. Court of Appeals for the First Circuit. While Republicans, anticipating their party's victory that fall, repeatedly stalled other Democratic appointees, Breyer's bipartisan charm eased his confirmation and he became the last Carter choice to be elevated to the federal bench.

During his tenure on the court of appeals, Breyer continued teaching at Harvard Law School. In 1992 he delivered the prestigious Oliver Wendell Holmes lectures that ultimately would become the foundation for his influential book on the regulatory system, *Breaking the Vicious Cycle: Towards Effective Risk and Regulation.*

In 1985 Breyer was appointed to serve on the U.S. Sentencing Commission. The commission, an independent establishment within the judicial branch, was charged with rationalizing and reforming federal criminal sentencing procedures, since penalties varied widely and unfairly under the existing system. The commission's task was enormously difficult and politically sensitive for a number of reasons. It required ranking the "punishable merit" of a great variety of crimes, which in turn involved weighing different theories of punishment, such as rehabilitation and retribution. In addition, sentencing was an area in which judges jealously guarded their long-standing discretion.

Working from a statistical compilation of average prison sentences, Breyer created a complicated grid that federal judges were required to use to guide further sentencing. Many praised this solution for standardizing rather than rethinking sentencing, and for showing re-

While serving as special counsel to the Administrative Practices Subcommittee of the Senate Judiciary Committee from 1973 to 1975, Breyer concluded that government regulations had handicapped the growth of the airline industry. He won congressional support for the controversial airline deregulation of 1978 by staging public hearings and arguing for increased competition and greater fare flexibility. *Source: Black Star/ Andy Levin*

straint appropriate to a judicial effort. Others complained that "average" sentences inaccurately reflected the range of considerations that led judges to impose much shorter or longer prison terms. All agreed, however, that the effort confirmed Breyer's ability to build consensus and his commitment to rationalizing regulatory solutions. In 1989 the Supreme Court registered its own approval by upholding the constitutionality of the U.S. Sentencing Commission in the landmark separation of powers case, *Mistretta v. United States.*

Though tremendously demanding, Breyer's many roles seemed only to energize him and to inform his activities on the bench. He became renowned as a coalition builder on the First Circuit who ranked achieving a unified opinion more highly than articulating his own opinion in detail. He became known as well for his incisive and thorough knowledge of the cases—and their frequently bulky records. His intelligence and dedication established his reputation as one of the leading jurists of his generation.

Breyer's interest in balancing private incentives and market advantages with the strengths of the regulatory state quickly asserted itself in his opinions. For example, in a series of antitrust cases (including *Concord v.*

Boston Edison Co. (1990) and *Kartell v. Blue Shield of Massachusetts, Inc.* (1984)), he emphasized the competition-inducing goals of antitrust law to avoid formulaic solutions. His record in a wide variety of other areas demonstrated the same practical approach. As Breyer himself once described the effort of judging:

I assume that law itself is a human institution, serving basic human or societal needs. It is therefore properly subject to praise, or to criticism, in terms of certain pragmatic values, including both formal values, such as coherence and workability, and widely shared substantive values, such as helping to achieve justice by interpreting the law in accordance with the "reasonable expectations of those to whom it applies."

As a judge, Breyer exhibited the same dry wit that colleagues had appreciated in his previous posts. Asked once by a *Harvard Law Bulletin* reporter to categorize his own legal philosophy, Breyer declined, but added jokingly: "Roscoe Pound said once, 'That judge is so stupid, he doesn't know if he's a member of the historical epistemological school or the sociological functional school of jurisprudence.'"

After coming agonizingly close to a Supreme Court nomination in 1993, Breyer was President Bill Clinton's

Appointed to the U.S. Sentencing Commission in 1985, Breyer helped develop sentencing guidelines for federal judges. Pictured here are the members of the original commission: (front row, left to right) Ilene H. Nagel, William W. Wilkins, Jr. (chair), Helen G. Corrothers; (back row, left to right) George E. MacKinnon, Breyer, Michael K. Block, Paul H. Robinson. *Source: U.S. Sentencing Commission*

choice on May 14, 1994, for the seat vacated by Justice Harry A. Blackmun. True to form, Breyer easily won confirmation, 87–9, in the Senate. The discussion focused not on whether he would be confirmed, but on what kind of justice he would be.

Almost all agreed that Breyer's ability to build consensus, his intelligence, energy, and wit would be welcome contributions to the Court. Practitioners in a wide range of regulatory law fields, such as antitrust, environmental, and administrative law, eagerly anticipated his expert consideration of their concerns. Some observers worried that his pragmatism made him unpredictable, but most saw only virtue in the flexibility, realism, and sophistication of his approach. Indeed, many hoped his pragmatism would make a good counterbalance to Justice Antonin Scalia's powerful but more formalistic theories. Finally, most wondered what effect Stephen Breyer would have on the political balance of the Court.

Within his first term, Breyer had established his presence on the Court with characteristic force. He immediately broke with Supreme Court tradition by joining in the questioning at his first oral argument and by writing a dissent as his first opinion. He energetically took issue with Justice Scalia, differing as often on method as on substance. Thus, in *Plaut v. Spendthrift Farm, Inc.* (1995), Scalia, writing for the majority, invalidated a federal statute on grounds that cast separation of powers concerns in categorical and structural terms. Breyer concurred on far narrower grounds, listing a combination of factors that persuaded him to accept the majority's conclusion in the specific circumstances of the case.

Breyer also repeatedly joined the more liberal wing of the Court, rejecting the reasoning of the more conservative majority in a series of important constitutional cases. Thus, in *U.S. v. Lopez* (1995), Breyer authored a stinging dissent, joined by Justices John Paul Stevens, David Souter, and Ruth Bader Ginsburg, defending Congress's power to regulate the possession of guns in school zones across the nation as within federal authority over interstate commerce. And, in *Sandin v. Conner* (1995), Breyer in dissent defended a broader approach to the due process protections accorded the liberty interests of prisoners than that taken by the majority.

The Breyers both enjoy camping, bicycling, and keeping up with world events. They have three children: Chloe, Nell, and Michael.

Members of the Supreme Court of the United States

Name	State Appointed From	Appointed by President	To Replace	Date Nominated†	Date Senate Confirmed	Judicial Oath Taken+	Date Service Terminated	Years of Service >#
CHIEF JUSTICES								
Jay	N.Y.	Washington	New seat	9/24/1789	9/26/1789	10/19/1789	6/29/1795	6
Rutledge, J.	S.C.	Washington	Jay	7/1/1795†	12/15/1795 Rej.	8/12/1795	12/15/1795	1
Ellsworth	Conn.	Washington	Rutledge, J.	3/3/1796	3/4/1796	3/8/1796	12/15/1800	4
Marshall, J.	Va.	Adams, J.	Ellsworth	1/20/1801	1/27/1801	2/4/1801	7/6/1835	34
Taney	Md.	Jackson	Marshall, J.	12/28/1835	3/15/1836	3/28/1836	10/12/1864	28
Chase, S. P.	Ohio	Lincoln	Taney	12/6/1864	12/6/1864	12/15/1864	5/7/1873	8
Waite	Ohio	Grant	Chase, S. P.	1/19/1794	1/21/1874	3/4/1874	3/23/1888	14
Fuller	Ill.	Cleveland	Waite	4/30/1888	7/20/1888	10/8/1888	7/4/1910	22
White, E.	La.	Taft	Fuller	12/12/1910	12/12/1910	12/19/1910	5/19/1921	10
Taft	Conn.	Harding	White, E.	6/21/1921	6/30/1921	7/11/1921	2/3/1930	8
Hughes	N.Y.	Hoover	Taft	2/3/1930	3/13/1930	2/24/1930	5/30/1941	11
Stone	N.Y.	Roosevelt, F.	Hughes	6/12/1941	6/27/1941	7/3/1941	4/22/1946	5
Vinson	Ky.	Truman	Stone	6/6/1946	6/20/1946	6/24/1946	9/8/1953	7
Warren	Calif.	Eisenhower	Vinson	9/30/1953†	3/1/1954	10/5/1953	6/23/1969	15
Burger	Va.	Nixon	Warren	5/21/1969	6/9/1969	6/23/1969	9/26/1986	17
Rehnquist	Va.	Reagan	Burger	6/20/1986	9/17/1986	9/26/1986		

† Recess appointment.
+ According to best authority available.
* Promoted.
> Length of service is calculated from the day of Senate confirmation and is rounded up.
\# Length of service for associate justices who also served as chief justices is listed separately in the two sections. To calculate the total length of the member's tenure on the Court, combine the two sums.

Name	State Appointed From	Appointed by President	To Replace	Date Nominated†	Date Senate Confirmed	Judicial Oath Taken+	Date Service Terminated	Years of Service >#
ASSOCIATE JUSTICES								
Cushing	Mass.	Washington	New seat	9/24/1789	9/26/1789	2/2/1790	9/13/1810	21
Rutledge, J.	S.C.	Washington	New seat	9/24/1789	9/26/1789	2/15/1790	3/5/1791	1
Wilson	Pa.	Washington	New seat	9/24/1789	9/26/1789	10/5/1789	8/21/1798	9
Blair	Va.	Washington	New seat	9/24/1789	9/26/1789	2/2/1790	1/27/1796	6
Iredell	N.C.	Washington	New seat	2/8/1790	2/10/1790	5/12/1790	10/20/1799	9
Johnson, T.	Md.	Washington	Rutledge, J.	11/1/1791	11/7/1791†	8/6/1792	1/16/1793	1
Paterson	N.J.	Washington	Johnson, T.	3/4/1793	3/4/1793	3/11/1793	9/9/1806	13
Chase, S.	Md.	Washington	Blair	1/26/1796	1/27/1796	2/4/1796	6/19/1811	15
Washington	Va.	Adams, J.	Wilson	12/19/1798†	12/20/1798	2/4/1799	11/26/1829	31
Moore	N.C.	Adams, J.	Iredell	12/4/1799	12/10/1799	4/21/1800	1/26/1804	4
Johnson, W.	S.C.	Jefferson	Moore	3/22/1804	3/24/1804	5/7/1804	8/4/1834	30
Livingston	N.Y.	Jefferson	Paterson	12/13/1806	12/18/1806	1/20/1807	3/18/1823	16
Todd	Ky.	Jefferson	New seat	2/28/1807	3/3/1807	5/4/1807	2/7/1826	19
Duvall	Md.	Madison	Chase, S.	11/15/1811	11/18/1811	11/23/1811	1/14/1835	23
Story	Md.	Madison	Cushing	11/15/1811	11/18/1811	2/3/1812	9/10/1845	34
Thompson	N.Y.	Monroe	Livingston	12/8/1823†	12/19/1823	2/10/1823	12/18/1843	20
Trimble	Ky.	Adams, J. Q.	Todd	4/11/1826	5/9/1826	6/16/1826	8/25/1828	2
McLean	Ohio	Jackson	Trimble	3/7/1829	3/7/1829	1/11/1830	4/4/1861	32
Baldwin	Pa.	Jackson	Washington	1/4/1830	1/6/1830	1/18/1830	4/21/1844	14
Wayne	Ga.	Jackson	Johnson, W.	1/6/1835	1/9/1835	1/14/1835	7/5/1867	32
Barbour	Va.	Jackson	Duvall	12/28/1835	3/15/1836	5/12/1836	2/25/1841	5
Catron	Tenn.	Van Buren	New seat	3/3/1837	3/8/1837	5/1/1837	5/30/1865	28
McKinley	Ala.	Van Buren	New seat	9/18/1837	9/25/1837	1/9/1838	7/19/1852	15
Daniel	Va.	Van Buren	Barbour	2/27/1841	3/2/1841	1/10/1842	5/31/1860	19
Nelson	N.Y.	Tyler	Thompson	2/4/1845	2/14/1845	2/27/1845	11/28/1872	27
Woodbury	N.H.	Polk	Story	12/23/1845†	1/3/1846	9/23/1845	9/4/1851	5
Grier	Pa.	Polk	Baldwin	8/3/1846	8/4/1846	8/10/1846	1/31/1870	23
Curtis	Mass.	Fillmore	Woodbury	12/11/1851	12/20/1851	10/10/1851	9/30/1857	5
Campbell	Ala.	Pierce	McKinley	3/21/1853	3/25/1853	4/11/1853	4/30/1861	8
Clifford	Maine	Buchanan	Curtis	12/9/1857	1/12/1858	1/21/1858	7/25/1881	23
Swayne	Ohio	Lincoln	McLean	1/21/1862	1/24/1862	1/27/1862	1/24/1881	19
Miller	Iowa	Lincoln	Daniel	7/16/1862	7/16/1862	7/21/1862	10/13/1890	28
Davis	Ill.	Lincoln	Campbell	12/1/1862	12/8/1862	12/10/1862	3/4/1877	14
Field	Calif.	Lincoln	New seat	3/6/1863	3/10/1863	5/20/1863	12/1/1897	34
Strong	Pa.	Grant	Grier	2/7/1870	2/18/1870	3/14/1870	12/14/1880	10

Name	State Appointed From	Appointed by President	To Replace	Date Nominated†	Date Senate Confirmed	Judicial Oath Taken+	Date Service Terminated	Years of Service >#
Bradley	N.J.	Grant	New seat	2/7/1870	3/21/1870	3/23/1870	1/22/1892	21
Hunt	N.Y.	Grant	Nelson	12/3/1872	12/11/1872	1/9/1873	1/27/1882	9
Harlan (I)	Ky.	Hayes	Davis	10/16/1877	11/29/1877	12/10/1877	10/14/1911	34
Woods	Ga.	Hayes	Strong	12/15/1880	12/21/1880	1/5/1881	5/14/1887	6
Matthews	Ohio	Garfield	Swayne	3/14/1881	5/12/1881	5/17/1881	3/22/1889	7
Gray	Mass.	Arthur	Clifford	12/19/1881	12/20/1881	1/9/1882	9/15/1902	20
Blatchford	N.Y.	Arthur	Hunt	3/13/1882	3/27/1882	4/3/1882	7/7/1893	11
Lamar, L.	Miss.	Cleveland	Woods	12/6/1887	1/16/1888	1/18/1888	1/23/1893	5
Brewer	Kan.	Harrison, B.	Matthews	12/4/1889	12/18/1889	1/6/1890	3/28/1910	20
Brown	Mich.	Harrison, B.	Miller	12/23/1890	12/29/1890	1/5/1891	5/28/1906	15
Shiras	Pa.	Harrison, B.	Bradley	7/19/1892	7/26/1892	10/10/1892	2/23/1903	10
Jackson, H.	Tenn.	Harrison, B.	Lamar, L.	2/2/1893	2/18/1893	3/4/1893	8/8/1895	2
White, E.	La.	Cleveland	Blatchford	2/19/1894	2/19/1894	3/12/1894	12/18/1910*	17
Peckham	N.Y.	Cleveland	Jackson, H.	12/3/1895	12/8/1895	1/6/1896	10/24/1909	13
McKenna	Calif.	McKinley	Field	12/16/1897	1/21/1898	1/26/1898	1/5/1925	26
Holmes	Mass.	Roosevelt, T.	Gray	12/2/1902	12/4/1902	12/8/1902	1/12/1932	29
Day	Ohio	Roosevelt, T.	Shiras	1/29/1903	2/23/1903	3/2/1903	11/13/1922	19
Moody	Mass.	Roosevelt, T.	Brown	12/3/1906	12/12/1906	12/17/1906	11/20/1910	3
Lurton	Tenn.	Taft	Peckham	12/13/1909	12/20/1909	1/3/1910	7/12/1914	4
Hughes	N.Y.	Taft	Brewer	4/25/1910	5/2/1910	10/10/1910	6/10/1916	6
Van Devanter	Wyo.	Taft	White, E.	12/12/1910	12/15/1910	1/3/1911	6/21/1937	26
Lamar, J.	Ga.	Taft	Moody	12/12/1910	12/15/1910	1/3/1911	1/2/1916	5
Pitney	N.J.	Taft	Harlan (I)	2/19/1912	3/13/1912	3/18/1912	12/31/1922	10
McReynolds	Tenn.	Wilson	Lurton	8/19/1914	8/29/1914	10/12/1914	1/31/1941	26
Brandeis	Mass.	Wilson	Lamar, J.	1/28/1916	6/1/1916	6/5/1916	2/13/1939	22
Clarke	Ohio	Wilson	Hughes	7/14/1916	7/24/1916	10/9/1916	9/18/1922	6
Sutherland	Utah	Harding	Clarke	9/5/1922	9/5/1922	10/2/1922	1/17/1938	15
Butler	Minn.	Harding	Day	11/23/1922	12/21/1922	1/2/1923	11/16/1939	17
Sanford	Tenn.	Harding	Pitney	1/24/1923	1/29/1923	2/19/1923	3/8/1930	7
Stone	N.Y.	Coolidge	McKenna	1/5/1925	2/5/1925	3/2/1925	7/2/1941*	16
Roberts	Pa.	Hoover	Sanford	5/9/1930	5/20/1930	6/2/1930	7/31/1945	15
Cardozo	N.Y.	Hoover	Holmes	2/15/1932	2/24/1932	3/14/1932	7/9/1938	6
Black	Ala.	Roosevelt, F.	Van Devanter	8/12/1937	8/17/1937	8/19/1937	9/17/1971	34

† Recess appointment.
+ According to best authority available.
* Promoted.
> Length of service is calculated from the day of Senate confirmation and is rounded up.
Length of service for associate justices who also served as chief justices is listed separately in the two sections. To calculate the total length of the member's tenure on the Court, combine the two sums.

Name	State Appointed From	Appointed by President	To Replace	Date Nominated†	Date Senate Confirmed	Judicial Oath Taken+	Date Service Terminated	Years of Service >#
Reed	Ky.	Roosevelt, F.	Sutherland	1/15/1938	1/25/1938	1/31/1938	2/25/1957	19
Frankfurter	Mass.	Roosevelt, F.	Cardozo	1/5/1939	1/17/1939	1/30/1939	8/28/1962	23
Douglas	Conn.	Roosevelt, F.	Brandeis	3/20/1939	4/4/1939	4/17/1939	11/12/1975	36
Murphy	Mich.	Roosevelt, F.	Butler	1/4/1940	1/16/1940	2/5/1940	7/19/1949	9
Byrnes	S.C.	Roosevelt, F.	McReynolds	6/12/1941	6/12/1941	7/8/1941	10/3/1942	1
Jackson, R.	N.Y.	Roosevelt, F.	Stone	6/12/1941	7/7/1941	7/11/1941	10/9/1954	13
Rutledge, W.	Iowa	Roosevelt, F.	Byrnes	1/11/1943	2/8/1943	2/15/1943	9/10/1949	6
Burton	Ohio	Truman	Roberts	9/19/1945	9/19/1945	10/1/1945	10/13/1958	13
Clark	Texas	Truman	Murphy	8/2/1949	8/18/1949	8/24/1949	6/12/1967	18
Minton	Ind.	Truman	Rutledge, W.	9/15/1949	10/4/1949	10/12/1949	10/15/1956	7
Harlan (II)	N.Y.	Eisenhower	Jackson, R.	1/10/1955	3/16/1955	3/28/1955	9/23/1971	16
Brennan	N.J.	Eisenhower	Minton	10/15/1956†	3/19/1957	10/16/1956	7/20/1990	34
Whittaker	Mo.	Eisenhower	Reed	3/2/1957	3/19/1957	3/25/1957	3/31/1962	5
Stewart	Ohio	Eisenhower	Burton	10/14/1958†	5/5/1959	10/14/1958	7/3/1981	22
White, B.	Colo.	Kennedy	Whittaker	3/30/1962	4/11/1962	4/16/1962	3/19/1993	30
Goldberg	Ill.	Kennedy	Frankfurter	8/29/1962	9/25/1962	10/1/1962	7/25/1965	3
Fortas	Tenn.	Johnson, L.	Goldberg	7/28/1965	8/11/1965	10/4/1965	5/14/1969	4
Marshall, T.	N.Y.	Johnson, L.	Clark	6/13/1967	8/30/1967	10/2/1967	6/27/1991	24
Blackmun	Minn.	Nixon	Fortas	4/14/1970	5/12/1970	6/9/1970	7/29/1994	24
Powell	Va.	Nixon	Black	10/22/1971	12/6/1971	1/6/1972	6/26/1987	16
Rehnquist	Ariz.	Nixon	Harlan (II)	10/21/1971	12/10/1971	1/7/1972	9/26/1986*	14
Stevens	Ill.	Ford	Douglas	11/28/1975	12/17/1975	12/19/1975		
O'Connor	Ariz.	Reagan	Stewart	8/19/1981	9/21/1981	9/26/1981		
Scalia	Va.	Reagan	Rehnquist	6/17/1986	9/17/1986	9/26/1986		
Kennedy	Calif.	Reagan	Powell	11/30/1987	2/3/1988	2/18/1988		
Souter	N.H.	Bush	Brennan	7/23/1990	10/2/1990	10/9/1990		
Thomas	Va.	Bush	Marshall, T.	7/1/1991	10/15/1991	10/23/1991		
Ginsburg	N.Y.	Clinton	White, B.	6/14/1993	8/3/1993	8/10/1993		
Breyer	Mass.	Clinton	Blackmun	5/13/1994	7/29/1994	8/3/1994		

† Recess appointment.
+ According to best authority available.
* Promoted.
> Length of service is calculated from the day of Senate confirmation and is rounded up.
Length of service for associate justices who also served as chief justices is listed separately in the two sections. To calculate the total length of the member's tenure on the Court, combine the two sums.

Bibliography

General Sources on the Supreme Court and the Justices

Abraham, Henry Julian. *Justices and Presidents: A Political History of Appointments to the Supreme Court.* 3d ed. New York: Oxford University Press, 1992.

Barnes, William Horatio. *Illustrated Cyclopedia of the American Government.* n.p.: 1875.

Blandford, Linda A., and Patricia R. Evans, eds. *Supreme Court of the United States, 1789–1980: An Index to Opinions Arranged by Justice.* Millwood, N.Y.: Kraus International Publications, 1983; Supplement 1980–1990, 1994.

Blaustein, Albert P., and Roy M. Mersky. *The First One Hundred Justices: Statistical Studies on the Supreme Court of the United States.* Hamden, Conn.: Archon Books, 1978.

Burger, Warren E. *It Is So Ordered: A Constitution Unfolds.* New York: William Morrow, 1995.

Campbell, Tom Walter. *Four Score Forgotten Men; Sketches of the Justices of the U.S. Supreme Court.* Little Rock: Pioneer Publishing, 1950.

Carson, Hampton Lawrence. *The History of the Supreme Court of the United States, With Biographies of All the Chief and Associate Justices.* 1902. Reprint. New York: B. Franklin, 1971.

Choper, Jesse H., ed. *The Supreme Court and Its Justices.* Chicago: American Bar Association, 1987.

Cushman, Clare, ed. *The Supreme Court Justices: Illustrated Biographies, 1789–1995.* 2d ed. Washington, D.C.: Congressional Quarterly, 1995.

Dunham, Allison, and Philip B. Kurland, eds. *Mr. Justice.* Chicago: University of Chicago Press, 1964.

Flanders, Henry. *The Lives and Times of the Chief Justices of the Supreme Court of the United States.* 1881. Reprint. Buffalo: W. S. Hein, 1972.

Friedman, Leon, and Fred L. Israel, eds. *The Justices of the United States Supreme Court: Their Lives and Major Opinions.* Vols. 1–5. New York: Chelsea House, 1995.

Hall, Kermit L., editor in chief. *The Oxford Companion to the Supreme Court of the United States.* New York: Oxford University Press, 1992.

Harrell, Mary Anne, and Burnett Anderson. *Equal Justice Under Law: The Supreme Court in American Life.* 6th ed. Washington, D.C.: Supreme Court Historical Society, with National Geographic Society, 1994.

History of the Supreme Court of the United States (The Oliver Wendell Holmes Devise). New York: Macmillan, 1971–.

Jacobs, Roger F., comp. *Memorials of the Justices of the Supreme Court of the United States.* Littleton, Colo.: Fred B. Rothman, 1981.

Lamb, Charles M., and Stephen C. Halpern, eds. *The Burger Court: Political and Judicial Profiles.* Champaign: University of Illinois Press, 1991.

Lankevich, George J., ed. *Supreme Court in American Life.* Millwood, N.Y.: Associated Faculty Press, 1986–.

Lerner, Max. *Nine Scorpions in a Bottle: Great Judges and Cases of the Supreme Court.* Edited by Richard Cummings. New York: Arcade Publishing, 1994.

Lewis, William Draper, ed. *Great American Lawyers.* Philadelphia: John C. Winston, 1907–1909.

Marcus, Maeva, ed. *The Documentary History of the Supreme Court of the United States, 1789–1800.* New York: Columbia University Press, 1985–.

Martin, Fenton S. *How to Research the Supreme Court.* Washington, D.C.: Congressional Quarterly, 1992.

Mason, Alpheus Thomas. *The Supreme Court From Taft to Burger.* Baton Rouge: Louisiana State University Press, 1979.

Mersky, Roy M., comp. *The Supreme Court of the United States: Hearings and Reports on Successful and Unsuccessful Nominations of Supreme Court Justices by the Senate Judiciary Committee, 1916–1995.* Buffalo: W. S. Hein, 1977–.

O'Brien, David M. *Storm Center: The Supreme Court in American Politics.* 3d ed. New York: W. W. Norton, 1993.

Schwartz, Bernard. *A History of the Supreme Court.* New York: Oxford University Press, 1993.

Shnayerson, Robert. *The Illustrated History of the Supreme Court of the United States.* New York: Henry N. Abrams in association with the Supreme Court Historical Society, 1986.

"Special Issue." *American Bar Association Journal* (June 15, 1986): 5–64.

Supreme Court Historical Society. *Journal of Supreme Court History.* Annual. Washington, D.C.: Supreme Court Historical Society, 1990–.

———. *Yearbook.* Annual. Washington, D.C.: Supreme Court Historical Society, 1976–1989.

The Supreme Court of the United States: Its Beginnings & Its Justices, 1790–1991. Washington, D.C.: Commission on the Bicentennial of the United States Constitution, 1992.

Tribe, Laurence H. *God Save This Honorable Court: How the Choice of Supreme Court Justices Shapes Our History.* New York: Random House, 1985.

Umbreit, Kenneth Bernard. *Our Eleven Chief Justices; A History of the Supreme Court in Terms of Their Personalities.* 1938. Reprint. Port Washington, N.Y.: Kennikat Press, 1969.

Urofsky, Melvin I., ed. *The Supreme Court Justices: A Biographical Dictionary.* New York: Garland Publishing, 1994.

Van Santvoord, George. *Sketches of the Lives and Judicial Services of the Chief-Justices of the Supreme Court of the United States.* New York: C. Scribner, 1854.

Warren, Charles. *The Supreme Court in United States History.* 1926. Reprint. Littleton, Colo.: Fred B. Rothman, 1987.

Westin, Alan F., ed. *An Autobiography of the Supreme Court: Off-the-Bench Commentary by the Justices.* 1963. Reprint. Westport, Conn.: Greenwood Press, 1978.

Witt, Elder. *Guide to the U.S. Supreme Court.* 2d ed. Washington, D.C.: Congressional Quarterly, 1990.

Sources on Individual Justices

HENRY BALDWIN

Baldwin, Henry. *A General View of the Origin and Nature of the Constitution and Government of the United States.* 1837. Reprint. New York: Da Capo Press, 1970.

Taylor, Flavia M. "The Political and Civil Career of Henry Baldwin." *Western Pennsylvania Historical Magazine* 24 (March 1941): 37–50.

PHILIP P. BARBOUR

Cynn, Paul P. "Philip Pendleton Barbour." *John P. Branch Historical Papers of Randolph-Macon College* 4 (1913): 67–77.

Story, Joseph. "Eulogy." *United States Reports* (15 Peters), v–vii. Washington, D.C., 1841.

HUGO L. BLACK

Ball, Howard. *The Vision and the Dream of Justice Hugo L. Black: An Examination of a Judicial Philosophy.* University: University of Alabama Press, 1975.

Black, Hugo LaFayette. *Mr. Justice and Mrs. Black: The Memoirs of Hugo L. Black and Elizabeth Black.* New York: Random House, 1986.

Black, Hugo, Jr. *My Father, A Remembrance.* New York: Random House, 1975.

Dunne, Gerald T. *Hugo Black and the Judicial Revolution.* New York: Simon and Schuster, 1977.

Freyer, Tony Allan. *Hugo L. Black and the Dilemma of American Liberalism.* Glenview, Ill.: Scott, Foresman, 1989.

———, ed. *Justice Hugo Black and Modern America.* Tuscaloosa: University of Alabama Press, 1990.

Hamilton, Virginia Van der Veer. *Hugo Black: The Alabama Years.* Baton Rouge: Louisiana State University Press, 1972.

Magee, James J. *Mr. Justice Black, Absolutist on the Court.* Charlottesville: University Press of Virginia, 1979.

Meador, Daniel John. *Mr. Justice Black and His Books.* Charlottesville: University Press of Virginia, 1974.

Newman, Roger K. *Hugo Black: A Biography.* New York: Pantheon, 1994.

Simon, James F. *The Antagonists: Hugo Black, Felix Frankfurter and Civil Liberties in Modern America.* New York: Simon and Schuster, 1989.

Yarbrough, Tinsley E. *Mr. Justice Black and His Critics.* Durham, N.C.: Duke University Press, 1988.

Yoder, Edwin M., Jr. "Black v. Jackson: A Study in Judicial Enmity." In *The Unmaking of a Whig* by Edwin Yoder, 3–104. Washington, D.C.: Georgetown University Press, 1990.

HARRY A. BLACKMUN

"Dedication and Tribute: Honorable Harry A. Blackmun, Associate Justice, United States Supreme Court." *Annual Survey of American Law* (1990): ix–xlv.

"Dedication to Justice Harry A. Blackmun on the Occasion of His Twenty-Fifth Year as a Federal Judge." *Hamline Law Review* 8 (January 1985): 1–149.

Jenkins, John A. "A Candid Talk With Justice Blackmun." *New York Times Magazine,* February 20, 1983.

"Justice Harry A. Blackmun." *North Dakota Law Review* 71 (1995): 1–185.

Koh, Harold Hongju. "The Justice Who Grew." *Journal of Supreme Court History* 1994: 5–8.

Lazarus, Edward. "Breakfast With Harry Blackmun." *The Washington Post,* April 7, 1994: A27.

"A Tribute to Justice Harry A. Blackmun." *Harvard Law Review* 108 (November 1994): 1–22.

"A Tribute to Justice Harry A. Blackmun: 'The Kind Voice of Friends.'" *American University Law Review* 43 (Spring 1994): 687–753.

JOHN BLAIR, JR.

Drinard, J. Elliott. "John Blair." *Proceedings of the Virginia State Bar Association* 39 (1927): 436–449.

SAMUEL BLATCHFORD

Blatchford, Harriet Wickes, ed. *The Blatchford Memorial.* New York: n.p., 1871.

Hall, A. Oakey. "Justice Samuel Blatchford." *Green Bag* 5 (November 1893): 489–492.

"Honors to the Memory of Mr. Justice Blatchford." *Albany Law Journal* 48 (November 18, 1893): 415–416.

JOSEPH P. BRADLEY

Bradley, Charles, comp. *Miscellaneous Writings of the Late Hon. Joseph P. Bradley, Associate Justice of the Supreme Court of the United States.* 1901. Reprint. Littleton, Colo: Fred B. Rothman, 1986.

Fairman, Charles. "The Education of a Justice: Justice Bradley and Some of His Colleagues." *Stanford Law Review* 1 (January 1949): 217–255.

———. "Mr. Justice Bradley." In *Mr. Justice,* edited by Allison Dunham and Philip B. Kurland, 65–91. Chicago: University of Chicago Press, 1964.

———. "What Makes a Great Justice: Mr. Justice Bradley and the Supreme Court, 1870–1892." *Boston University Law Review* 30 (January 1950): 423–485.

Lurie, Jonathan. "Mr. Justice Bradley: A Reassessment." *Seton Hall Law Review* 16 (1986): 343–375.

Parker, Cortland. "Joseph P. Bradley." *American Law Review* 28 (July/August 1984): 481–509.

Whiteside, Ruth A. "Justice Joseph Bradley and the Reconstruction Amendments." Ph.D. diss., Rice University, 1981.

LOUIS D. BRANDEIS

Baker, Leonard. *Brandeis and Frankfurter: A Dual Biography.* New York: New York University Press, 1986.

Baskerville, Stephen W. *Of Laws and Limitations: An Intellectual Portrait of Louis Dembitz Brandeis.* Cranbury, N.J.: Associated University Presses, 1994.

Frankfurter, Felix, ed. *Mr. Justice Brandeis.* 1932. Reprint. New York: Da Capo Press, 1972.

Gal, Allon. *Brandeis of Boston.* Cambridge: Harvard University Press, 1980.

Mason, Alpheus Thomas. *Brandeis, A Free Man's Life.* New York: Viking Press, 1946.

Paper, Lewis J. *Brandeis.* Englewood Cliffs, N.J.: Prentice Hall, 1983.

Strum, Philippa. *Brandeis: Beyond Progressivism.* Lawrence: University Press of Kansas, 1993.

Strum, Philippa. *Louis D. Brandeis: Justice for the People.* New York: Schocken Books, 1984.

Urofsky, Melvin I. *Louis D. Brandeis and the Progressive Tradition.* Boston: Little, Brown, 1981.

———. *A Mind of One Piece: Brandeis and American Reform.* New York: Scribner, 1971.

WILLIAM J. BRENNAN, JR.

Brennan, William Joseph. *William Brennan, Supreme Court Justice.* Washington, D.C.: National Public Radio, 1987. Sound cassette. Interview with Justice Brennan, originally broadcast on NPR's "All Things Considered."

Clark, Hunter R. *Justice Brennan: The Great Conciliator.* Secaucus, N.J.: Carol Publishing Group, 1995.

Friedman, Stephen J., ed. *An Affair With Freedom: Justice William J. Brennan, Jr.* New York: Atheneum, 1967.

Goldman, Roger, with David Gallen. *Justice William J. Brennan, Jr.* New York: Carroll and Graf, 1994.

Post, Robert C. "Justice William J. Brennan and the Warren Court." *Constitutional Commentary* 8 (Winter 1991): 11–25.

"Reason, Passion, and Justice Brennan: A Symposium." *Cardozo Law Review* 10 (October/November 1988): 3–234.

"Special Issue Dedicated to Justice William J. Brennan." *John Marshall Law Review* 20 (Fall 1986): 1–199.

Wermiel, Stephen J. "The Nomination of Justice Brennan: Eisenhower's Mistake? A Look at the Historical Record." *Constitutional Commentary* 11 (Winter 1994/1995): 515–537.

DAVID J. BREWER

Bergan, Francis. "Mr. Justice Brewer: A Perspective of a Century." *Albany Law Review* 25 (June 1961): 191–202.

Brodhead, Michael J. *David J. Brewer: The Life of a Supreme Court Justice, 1837–1910.* Carbondale: Southern Illinois University Press, 1994.

Eitzen, D. Stanley. *David J. Brewer, 1837–1910: A Kansan on the United States Supreme Court.* Emporia: Kansas State Teacher's College, 1964.

Hylton, Joseph Gordon. "David Josiah Brewer: A Conservative Justice Reconsidered." *Journal of Supreme Court History* 1994: 45–64.

Moline, Brian. "David Josiah Brewer, Kansas Jurist." *Kansas Bar Association Journal* 55 (January/February 1986): 7–11.

STEPHEN G. BREYER

"The Breyer Nomination." *Legal Times* 17 (May 23, 1994): whole issue.

"Judge Breyer's Life," "Breyer: Pragmatic Leader." *The Washington Post,* June 26–27, 1994: two articles, A-1.

"Justice Stephen Breyer's Contribution to Administrative Law: Symposium." *Administrative Law Journal of the American University* 8 (Winter 1995): 713–787.

HENRY B. BROWN

Brown, Henry Billings. *Memoir of Henry Billings Brown: Late Justice of the Supreme Court of the United States: Consisting of An Autobiographical Sketch With Additions to His Life by Charles A. Kent.* New York: Duffield and Company, 1915.

Butler, Charles H. "Mr. Justice Brown." *Green Bag* 18 (June 1906): 321–330.

Glennon, Robert J., Jr. "Justice Henry Billings Brown: Values in Tension." *Univ. of Colorado Law Review* 44 (1973): 553–604.

Warner, Robert M. "Detroit's First Supreme Court Justice." *Detroit Historical Society Bulletin* 13 (May 1957): 8–13.

WARREN E. BURGER

Burger, Warren E. *Delivery of Justice.* St. Paul: West Publishing Co., 1990.

"Excerpts From Interview With Chief Justice Burger on Role of the Supreme Court." *New York Times,* July 4, 1971, 24.

Gazell, James A. "Chief Justice Burger's Quest for Judicial Administrative Efficiency." *Detroit College of Law Review* 1977 (Fall 1977): 455–497.

"New Ways to Speed Up Justice: Interview With Chief Justice Warren E. Burger." *U.S. News & World Report,* August 21, 1972, 38–46.

"A Professional for the High Court." *Time,* May 30, 1969, 16–20.

"Q. & A. With the Chief Justice." *American Bar Association Journal* 71 (January 1985): 91–94.

Sanders, Donald. "Chief Justice As Painter, Sculptor." *Washington Star,* August 24, 1975, F–3.

"Symposium: The Jurisprudence of Chief Justice Warren E. Burger." *Oklahoma Law Review* 45 (Spring 1992): 1–168.

"A Tribute to Chief Justice Warren E. Burger." *Harvard Law Review* 100 (March 1987): 969–1001.

HAROLD H. BURTON

Atkinson, David N. "Justice Harold H. Burton and the Work of the Supreme Court." *Cleveland State Law Review* 27 (1978): 69–84.

Berry, Mary Frances. *Stability, Security, and Continuity: Mr. Justice Burton and Decision-Making in the Supreme Court.* Westport, Conn.: Greenwood Press, 1978.

Hudon, Edward G., ed. *The Occasional Papers of Mr. Justice Burton.* Brunswick, Maine: Bowdoin College, 1969.

Marquardt, Ronald G. "The Judicial Justice: Mr. Justice Burton and the Supreme Court." Ph.D. diss., University of Missouri, 1973.

PIERCE BUTLER

Danelski, David Joseph. *A Supreme Court Justice Is Appointed.* 1964. Reprint. Westport, Conn.: Greenwood Press, 1980.

Sikes, Lewright B. "The Public Life of Pierce Butler." Ph.D. diss., University of Tennessee, 1973.

JAMES F. BYRNES

Burns, Ronald D. *James F. Byrnes.* New York: McGraw-Hill, 1961.

Byrnes, James F. *All in One Lifetime.* New York: Harper, 1958.

Messer, Robert L. *The End of an Alliance: James F. Byrnes, Roosevelt, Truman, and the Origins of the Cold War.* Chapel Hill: University of North Carolina Press, 1982.

Moore, Winfred Bobo. "New South Statesman: The Political Career of James Francis Byrnes, 1911–1941." Ph.D. diss., Duke University, 1975.

JOHN A. CAMPBELL

Connor, Henry Groves. *John Archibald Campbell, Associate Justice of the United States Supreme Court, 1853–1861.* 1920. New York: Da Capo Press, 1971.

Holt, Thad, Jr. "The Resignation of Mr. Justice Campbell." *Alabama Review* 12 (1959): 105–118.

Jordan, Christine. "Last of the Jacksonians." 78–88. *Supreme Court Historical Society Yearbook, 1980.* Washington, D.C.: Supreme Court Historical Society, 1980.

Mann, Justine S. "The Political and Constitutional Thought of John Archibald Campbell." Ph.D. diss., University of Alabama, 1966.

McPherson, James P. "The Career of John Archibald Campbell: A Study in Politics and the Law." *Alabama Review* 19 (1966): 53–63.

Murphy, James. "Justice John Archibald Campbell on Secession." *Alabama Review* 28 (1975): 48–58.

Skult, Ronald. "John Archibald Campbell, A Study in Divided Loyalties." *Alabama Lawyer* 20 (July 1959): 233–264.

BENJAMIN N. CARDOZO

Hellman, George Sidney. *Benjamin N. Cardozo, American Judge.* 1940. Reprint. New York: Russell and Russell, 1969.

Levy, Beryl Harold. *Cardozo and Frontiers of Legal Thinking.* Rev. ed. Cleveland: Press of Case Western Reserve University, 1969.

Noonan, John Thomas. *Persons and Masks of the Law: Cardozo, Holmes, Jefferson, and Wythe as Makers of the Masks.* New York: Farrar, Straus and Giroux, 1976.

Pollard, Joseph Percival. *Mr. Justice Cardozo; a Liberal Mind in Action.* 1935. Reprint. Westport, Conn.: Greenwood Press, 1970.

Posner, Richard A. *Cardozo: A Study in Reputation.* Chicago: University of Chicago Press, 1990.

Shientag, Bernard Lloyd. *Moulders of Legal Thought.* New York: Viking Press, 1943.

JOHN CATRON

Caldwell, Joshua William. *Sketches of the Bench and Bar of Tennessee.* Knoxville: Odgen Brothers, 1898.

Chandler, Walter. *The Centenary of Associate Justice John Catron of the United States Supreme Court.* Washington, D.C.: U.S. Government Printing Office, 1937.

Livingston, John. "Biographical Letter from Justice Catron." In *Portraits of Eminent Americans Now Living,* by John Livingston, 73–81. New York: R. Craighead, Printer, 1854.

SALMON P. CHASE

Belden, Thomas G., and Marva R. Belden. *So Fell the Angels.* Boston: Little, Brown, 1956.

Blue, Frederick J. *Salmon P. Chase, A Life in Politics.* Kent, Ohio: Kent State University Press, 1987.

Chase, Salmon Portland. *Inside Lincoln's Cabinet; the Civil War Diaries of Salmon P. Chase.* Edited by David Donald. New York: Longmans, Green, 1954.

Hart, Albert Bushnell. *Salmon P. Chase.* 1899. Reprint. New York: Chelsea House, 1980.

Middleton, Stephen. *Ohio and the Antislavery Activities of Attorney Salmon Portland Chase, 1830–1849.* New York: Garland Publishing, 1990.

Niven, John. *Salmon P. Chase: A Biography.* New York: Oxford University Press, 1995.

Schuckers, Jacob W. *The Life and Public Services of Salmon Portland Chase.* 1874. Reprint. New York: Da Capo Press, 1970.

Smith, Donnal Vore. *Chase and Civil War Politics.* 1930. Reprint. Freeport, N.Y.: Books for Libraries Press, 1972.

"A Symposium on Salmon P. Chase and the Chase Court: Perspectives in Law and History." *Northern Kentucky Law Review* 21 (Fall 1993): 1–252.

SAMUEL CHASE

Chase, Samuel, defendant. *Trial of Samuel Chase.* 1805. Reprint. New York: Da Capo Press, 1970.

Elsmere, Jane Shaffer. *Justice Samuel Chase.* Muncie, Ind.: Janevar Publishing, 1980.

Haw, James A., et al. *Stormy Patriot: The Life of Samuel Chase.* Baltimore: Maryland Historical Society, 1980.

Rehnquist, William H. *Grand Inquests: The Historic Impeachments of Justice Samuel Chase and President Andrew Johnson.* New York: Morrow, 1992.

TOM C. CLARK

Frank, John Paul. "Tom Clark." In *The Warren Court,* 77–96. New York: Macmillan, 1964.

Gazell, James A. "Justice Tom C. Clark as Judicial Reformer." *Houston Law Review* 15 (January 1978): 307–330.

Rudko, Frances H. *Truman's Court: A Study in Judicial Restraint.* Westport, Conn.: Greenwood Press, 1988.

A Symposium on the Tom C. Clark Papers. Austin, Texas: Tarlton Law Library Publications, 1987.

Temple, Larry. "Mr. Justice Clark: A Tribute." *American Journal of Criminal Law* 5 (October 1977): 271–274.

JOHN H. CLARKE

Levitan, David Maurice. "The Jurisprudence of Mr. Justice Clarke." *Miami Law Review* 7 (December 1952): 44–72.

Warner, Hoyt Landon. *The Life of Mr. Justice Clarke: A Testament to the Power of Liberal Dissent in America.* Cleveland: Western Reserve University, 1959.

Wittke, Carl. "Mr. Justice Clarke in Retirement." *Western Reserve Law Review* 1 (June 1949): 28–48.

NATHAN CLIFFORD

Barnes, William Horatio. "Nathan Clifford, Associate Justice." In *The Supreme Court of the United States,* by W. Barnes, 73–78.

Part II of Barnes's *Illustrated Cyclopedia of the American Government.* n.p.: 1875.

Chandler, Walter. "Nathan Clifford: A Triumph of Untiring Effort." *American Bar Association Journal* 11 (January 1925): 57–60.

Clifford, Philip Greely. *Nathan Clifford, Democrat, 1803–1881.* New York: Putnam's, 1922.

BENJAMIN R. CURTIS

Curtis, Benjamin Robbins. *Jurisdiction, Practice, and Peculiar Jurisprudence of the Courts of the United States.* Edited, with notes, by George Ticknor Curtis and Benjamin R. Curtis. 1880. Reprint. Littleton, Colo.: Fred B. Rothman, 1989.

Curtis, Benjamin Robbins, ed. *A Memoir of Benjamin Robbins Curtis, LL.D., with Some of His Professional and Miscellaneous Writings.* 1879. Reprint. New York: Da Capo Press, 1970.

Leach, Richard H. "Benjamin R. Curtis: Case Study of a Supreme Court Justice." Ph.D. diss., Princeton University, 1951.

WILLIAM CUSHING

Cushing, John D. "A Revolutionary Conservative: The Public Life of William Cushing, 1732–1810." Ph.D. diss., Clark University, 1959.

Cushing, William. "Letters from William Cushing." *Massachusetts Historical Society Proceedings* 61 (1927/28): 69–71.

Jones, Francis R. "William Cushing." *Green Bag* 13 (September 1901): 415–417.

"Letters Relative to his Appointment to the Supreme Court and Return of his Commission as Chief Justice." *Massachusetts Historical Society Proceedings* 44 (1910/11): 526–527.

O'Brien, F. W. "The Pre-Marshall Court and the Role of William Cushing." *Massachusetts Law Quarterly* 43 (March 1958).

Rugg, Arthur Prentice. "William Cushing." *Yale Law Journal* 30 (1920): 128–144.

PETER V. DANIEL

Burnette, Lawrence. "Peter V. Daniel: Agrarian Justice." *Virginia Magazine of History and Biography* 62 (July 1954): 289–305.

Daniel, Peter Vivian. Letter, "Travel to Cincinnati in 1853." Edited by William D. Hoyt, Jr. *Ohio State Archaeological and Historical Quarterly* 51 (January–March 1942): 62–64.

Frank, John Paul. *Justice Daniel Dissenting; A Biography of Peter V. Daniel, 1784–1860.* Cambridge: Harvard University Press, 1964.

DAVID DAVIS

Barnes, William Horatio. "David Davis, Associate Justice." In *The Supreme Court of the United States,* by W. Barnes, 89–94. Part II of Barnes's *Illustrated Cyclopedia of the American Government.* n.p.: 1875.

Dent, Thomas. "David Davis of Illinois: A Sketch." *American Law Review* 53 (July/August 1919): 535–560.

King, Willard Leroy. *Lincoln's Manager, David Davis.* Cambridge: Harvard University Press, 1960.

Pratt, Harry Edward. "David Davis, 1815–1856." Ph.D. diss., University of Illinois, 1930.

WILLIAM R. DAY

"Character of Mr. Justice Day." *American Law Review* 37 (May/June 1903): 402–403.

Duncan, George W. "The Diplomatic Career of William Rufus Day, 1897–1898." Ph.D. diss., Case Western Reserve University, 1976.

McLean, Joseph E. *William Rufus Day: Supreme Court Justice from Ohio.* Baltimore: The Johns Hopkins University Press, 1946.

Roelofs, Vernon W. "William R. Day: A Study in Constitutional History." Ph.D. diss., University of Michigan, 1942.

WILLIAM O. DOUGLAS

Ball, Howard, and Phillip J. Cooper. *Of Power and Right: Hugo Black, William O. Douglas, and America's Constitutional Revolution.* New York: Oxford University Press, 1992.

Douglas, William Orville. *The Court Years, 1939–1975. The Autobiography of William O. Douglas.* New York: Random House, 1980.

———. *Go East, Young Man: The Early Years. The Autobiography of William O. Douglas.* New York: Random House, 1974.

———. *Of Men and Mountains.* 1950. San Francisco: Chronicle Books, 1990.

Duram, James C. *Justice William O. Douglas.* Boston: Twayne, 1981.

Simon, James F. *Independent Journey: The Life of William O. Douglas.* New York: Harper and Row, 1990.

Stone, Cathleen Douglas. "Looking Back While Stepping Forward." *Gonzaga Law Review* 25 (1989/1990): 1–8.

Urofsky, Melvin I., ed. *The Douglas Letters: Selection from the Private Papers of Justice William O. Douglas.* Bethesda, Md.: Adler and Adler, 1987.

Wasby, Stephen L., ed. *"He Shall Not Pass This Way Again": The Legacy of Justice William O. Douglas.* Pittsburgh: University of Pittsburgh Press, 1990.

GABRIEL DUVALL

Dilliard, Irving. "Gabriel Duvall." In *Dictionary of American Biography,* supp. 1, 272–274. New York: Charles Scribner's Sons, 1944.

OLIVER ELLSWORTH

Brown, William Garrott. *The Life of Oliver Ellsworth.* 1905. Reprint. New York: Da Capo Press, 1970.

Buchanan, James M. "Oliver Ellsworth, Third Chief Justice." *Supreme Court Historical Society Yearbook, 1991.* Washington, D.C.: Supreme Court Historical Society, 1991, 20–26.

Jones, Francis R. "Oliver Ellsworth." *Green Bag* 13 (November 1901): 503–508.

Lettieri, Ronald John. *Connecticut's Young Man of the Revolution: Oliver Ellsworth.* Hartford: American Revolution Bicentennial Commission of Connecticut, 1978.

STEPHEN J. FIELD

Bergan, Philip J., Owen M. Fiss, and Charles W. McCurdy. *The Fields and the Law: Essays.* San Francisco: United States District Court for the Northern District of California Historical Society, 1986.

Black, Chauncey Forward, and Samuel B. Smith, eds. *Some Account of the Work of Stephen J. Field, as Legislator, State Judge, and Justice of the Supreme Court of the United States.* New York: S. B. Smith, 1895.

Field, Stephen Johnson. *Personal Reminiscences of Early Days in California.* 1893. Reprint. New York: Da Capo Press, 1968.

Swisher, Carl Brent. *Stephen J. Field, Craftsman of the Law.* 1930. Reprint. Chicago: University of Chicago Press, 1969.

ABE FORTAS

Kalman, Laura. *Abe Fortas: A Biography.* New Haven: Yale University Press, 1990.

Lewis, Anthony. *Gideon's Trumpet.* New York: Random House, 1964.

Mason, Alpheus Thomas. "Pyrrhic Victory: The Defeat of Abe Fortas." *Virginia Quarterly Review* 45 (Winter 1969): 19–29.

Murphy, Bruce Allen. *Fortas: The Rise and Ruin of a Supreme Court Justice.* New York: Morrow, 1988.

FELIX FRANKFURTER

Baker, Leonard. *Brandeis and Frankfurter: A Dual Biography.* New York: New York University Press, 1984.

Baker, Liva. *Felix Frankfurter.* New York: Coward-McCann, 1969.

Burt, Robert. *Two Jewish Justices: Outcasts in the Promised Land.* Berkeley: University of California Press, 1988.

Frankfurter, Felix. *Felix Frankfurter Reminisces: Recorded in Talks with Harlan B. Phillips.* 1960. Reprint. Westport, Conn.: Greenwood Press, 1978.

Hirsch, H. N. *The Enigma of Felix Frankfurter.* New York: Basic Books, 1981.

Lash, Joseph P., and Jonathan Lash. *From the Diaries of Felix Frankfurter.* New York: Norton, 1975.

Murphy, Bruce Allen. *The Brandeis/Frankfurter Connection: The Secret Political Activities of Two Supreme Court Justices.* New York: Oxford University Press, 1982.

Parrish, Michael E. *Felix Frankfurter and His Times.* New York: Free Press, 1982.

Simon, James F. *The Antagonists: Hugo Black, Felix Frankfurter and Civil Liberties in Modern America.* New York: Simon and Schuster, 1989.

Urofsky, Melvin I. *Felix Frankfurter: Judicial Restraint and Individual Liberties.* Boston: Twayne Publishers, 1991.

MELVILLE W. FULLER

Furer, Howard B. *The Fuller Court, 1888–1910.* Millwood, N.Y.: Associated Faculty Press, 1986.

King, Willard Leroy. *Melville Weston Fuller, Chief Justice of the United States, 1888–1910.* Chicago: University of Chicago Press, 1967.

RUTH BADER GINSBURG

Markowitz, Deborah L. "In Pursuit of Equality: One Woman's Work to Change the Law." *Women's Rights Law Reporter* 14 (Spring/Fall 1992): 335–359.

"Ruth Bader Ginsburg: Her Life and Her Law." *The Washington Post,* July 18–20, 1993: three articles, section A.

"The Ginsburg Nomination." *Legal Times* 16 (June 21, 1993): whole issue.

ARTHUR J. GOLDBERG

Carmen, Ira H. "One Civil Libertarian Among Many: The Case of Mr. Justice Goldberg." *Michigan Law Review* 65 (December 1966): 301–336.

Goldberg, Dorothy Kurgans. *A Private View of a Public Life.* New York: Charterhouse, 1975.

"In Memoriam: Arthur J. Goldberg, 1908–1990." *Northwestern University Law Review* 84 (Spring/Summer 1990): 807–831.

Lasky, Victor. *Arthur J. Goldberg, the Old and the New.* New Rochelle, N.Y.: Arlington House, 1970.

Moynihan, Daniel P., ed. *The Defenses of Freedom: The Public Papers of Arthur J. Goldberg.* New York: Harper and Row, 1966.

Rubin, Eva. "The Judicial Apprenticeship of Arthur J. Goldberg, 1962–1965." Ph.D. diss., Johns Hopkins University, 1967.

"Stripping Away the Fictions: Interview With Mr. Justice Arthur J. Goldberg." *Nova Law Journal* 6 (Summer 1982): 553–571.

HORACE GRAY

Davis, Elbridge B., and Harold A. Davis. "Mr. Justice Horace Gray: Some Aspects of His Judicial Career." *American Bar Association Journal* 41 (May 1955): 421–424, 468–471.

Hoar, George F. "Memoir of Horace Gray." *Massachusetts Historical Society Proceedings* 18 (January 1904): 155–187.

Mitchell, Stephen R. "Mr. Justice Horace Gray." Ph.D. diss., University of Wisconsin, 1961.

Spector, Robert M. "Legal Historian on the United States Supreme Court: Justice Horace Gray, Jr., and the Historical Method." *American Journal of Legal History* 12 (July 1968): 181–210.

Storey, Moorfield. "Horace Gray." In *Later Years of the Saturday Club, 1870–1920,* edited by M. A. DeWolfe Howe, 49–53. Boston: Houghton Mifflin, 1927.

Williston, Samuel. "Horace Gray." In *Great American Lawyers,* vol. 8, edited by William D. Lewis, 137–188. Philadelphia: J. C. Winston Company, 1907–1909.

ROBERT C. GRIER

Brown, David Paul. "Robert Cooper Grier, LL.D." In *The Forum,* vol. 2, edited by David P. Brown, 91–101. Philadelphia: R. H. Small, 1856.

Jones, Francis R. "Robert Cooper Grier." *Green Bag* 16 (April 1904): 221–224.

Livingston, John. "Honorable Robert C. Grier." In *Portraits of Eminent Americans Now Living,* by John Livingston, 67–71. New York: R. Craighead, Printer, 1854.

JOHN MARSHALL HARLAN (1877–1911)

Beth, Loren P. *John Marshall Harlan: The Last Whig Justice.* Lexington: University Press of Kentucky, 1992.

Beth, Loren P. "Justice Harlan and the Uses of Dissent." *American Political Science Review* 49 (December 1955): 1085–1104.

Clark, Floyd Barzilia. *The Constitutional Doctrines of Justice Harlan.* 1915. Reprint. New York: Da Capo Press, 1969.

Owen, Thomas Louis. "The Pre-Court Career of John Marshall Harlan." Ph.D. diss., University of Louisville, 1970.

Westin, Alan F. "The First Justice Harlan: A Self-Portrait from His Private Papers." *Kentucky Law Journal* 46 (Spring 1958): 321–366.

Yarbrough, Tinsley E. *Judicial Enigma: The First Justice Harlan.* New York: Oxford University Press, 1995.

JOHN MARSHALL HARLAN (1955–1971)

Ballantine, Arthur A. "John M. Harlan for the Supreme Court." *Iowa Law Review* 40 (Spring 1955): 391–399.

"Centennial Conference in Honor of Justice John Marshall Harlan." *New York Law School Law Review* 36 (1991): 1–286.

Shapiro, David L., ed. *The Evolution of a Judicial Philosophy: Selected Opinions and Papers of Justice John M. Harlan.* Cambridge: Harvard University Press, 1969.

Wilkinson, J. Harvie. "Justice John Marshall Harlan and the Values of Federalism." *Virginia Law Review* 57 (October 1971): 1185–1221.

Yarbrough, Tinsley E. *John Marshall Harlan: Great Dissenter of the Warren Court.* New York: Oxford University Press, 1992.

OLIVER WENDELL HOLMES, JR.

Aichele, Gary Jan. *Oliver Wendell Holmes, Jr.—Soldier, Scholar, Judge.* Boston: Twayne Publishers, 1989.

Baker, Liva. *The Justice from Beacon Hill: The Life and Times of Oliver Wendell Holmes.* New York: HarperCollins, 1991.

Biddle, Francis. *Mr. Justice Holmes.* 1942. Reprint. Westport, Conn.: Greenwood Press, 1986.

Bowen, Catherine Drinker. *Yankee from Olympus.* Boston: Little, Brown, 1944.

Holmes and the Common Law: A Century Later. Three lectures by Benjamin Kaplan, Patrick Atiyah, Jan Vetter. Cambridge: Harvard Law School, 1983.

Howe, Mark De Wolfe. *Justice Oliver Wendell Holmes: The Shaping Years, 1841–1870; The Proving Years, 1870–1882.* Cambridge: Belknap Press of Harvard University Press, 1957–1962.

Kellogg, Frederic Rogers. *The Formative Essays of Justice Holmes: The Making of an American Legal Philosophy.* Westport, Conn.: Greenwood Press, 1984.

Konefsky, Samuel Joseph. *The Legacy of Holmes and Brandeis: A Study in the Influence of Ideas.* 1956. Reprint. New York: Da Capo Press, 1974.

The Mind and Faith of Justice Holmes: His Speeches, Essays, Letters, and Judicial Opinions. Selected and edited by Max Lerner. 1943. Reprint. New Brunswick, N.J.: Transaction, 1989.

Monagan, John S. *The Grand Panjandrum: Mellow Years of Justice Holmes.* Lanham, Md.: University Press of America, 1988.

Novick, Sheldon M. *Honorable Justice: The Life of Oliver Wendell Holmes.* Boston: Little, Brown, 1989.

White, Edward G. *Justice Oliver Wendell Holmes: Law and the Inner Self.* New York: Oxford University Press, 1993.

CHARLES EVANS HUGHES

Glad, Betty. *Charles Evans Hughes and the Illusions of Innocence: A Study in American Diplomacy.* Urbana: University of Illinois Press, 1966.

Hendel, Samuel. *Charles Evans Hughes and the Supreme Court.* 1951. Reprint. New York: Russell and Russell, 1968.

Hughes, Charles Evans. *The Autobiographical Notes of Charles Evans Hughes.* Edited by David J. Danelski and Joseph S. Tulchin. Cambridge: Harvard University Press, 1973.

Perkins, Dexter. *Charles Evans Hughes and American Democratic Statesmanship.* 1956. Reprint. Westport, Conn.: Greenwood Press, 1978.

Pusey, Merlo John. *Charles Evans Hughes.* 1951. Reprint. New York: Garland, 1979.

WARD HUNT

Barnes, William Horatio. "Ward Hunt, Associate Justice." In *The Supreme Court of the United States,* by W. Barnes, 113–116. Part II of Barnes's *Illustrated Cyclopedia of the American Government.* n.p.: 1875.

"The Old Judge and the New: Mr. Justice Nelson and his Successor, Ward Hunt." *Albany Law Journal* 6 (December 14, 1872): 400–401.

JAMES IREDELL

Graebe, Christopher T. "The Federalism of James Iredell in Historical Context." *North Carolina Law Review* 69 (November 1990): 251–272.

Harrison, Helen Dortch, comp. *Life and Correspondence of James Iredell, Index.* Chapel Hill: University of North Carolina Library, 1955.

Iredell, James. *The Papers of James Iredell.* Edited by Don Higginbotham. Raleigh: North Carolina Division of Archives and History, 1976.

McRee, Griffith John. *Life and Correspondence of James Iredell, One of the Associate Justices of the Supreme Court of the United States.* New York: D. Appleton, 1857.

Waldrup, John Charles. "James Iredell and the Practice of Law in Revolutionary Era North Carolina." Ph.D. diss., University of North Carolina at Chapel Hill, 1985.

HOWELL E. JACKSON

Calvani, Terry. "The Early Career of Howell Jackson." *Vanderbilt Law Review* 30 (January 1977): 39–72.

Doak, Henry M. "Howell Edmunds Jackson." *Green Bag* 5 (May 1893): 209–215.

Green, John W. "Judge Howell E. Jackson." In *Law and Lawyers; Sketches of the Federal Judges of Tennessee* by John W. Green, 43–48. Jackson, Tenn.: McCowat-Mercer Press, 1950.

Hardaway, Roger D. "Howell Edmunds Jackson: Tennessee Legislator and Jurist." *West Tennessee Historical Society Papers* 30 (1976): 104–119.

ROBERT H. JACKSON

Desmond, Charles S., et al. *Mr. Justice Jackson; Four Lectures in His Honor.* New York: Columbia University Press, 1969.

Gerhard, Eugene C. *America's Advocate: Robert H. Jackson.* Indianapolis: Bobbs-Merrill, 1958.

———. *Supreme Court Justice Jackson: Lawyer's Judge.* Albany, N.Y.: Q Corporation, 1961.

Prettyman, E. Barrett, Jr. "Robert H. Jackson: 'Solicitor General for Life.'" *Journal of Supreme Court History* 1992: 75–85.

Steamer, Robert Julius. "The Constitutional Doctrines of Mr. Justice Robert H. Jackson." Ph.D. diss., Cornell University, 1954.

Yoder, Edwin. "Black v. Jackson: A Study in Judicial Enmity." In *The Unmaking of a Whig* by Edwin Yoder. Washington, D.C.: Georgetown University Press, 1990, 3–104.

JOHN JAY

Jay, William. *The Life of John Jay: With Selections from his Correspondence and Miscellaneous Papers.* 1833. Reprint. Freeport, N.Y.: Books for Libraries Press, 1972.

Johnson, Herbert Alan. *John Jay, Colonial Lawyer.* New York: Garland Publishing, 1989.

Johnson, Herbert Alan. *John Jay, 1745–1829.* Albany: Office of State History, 1970.

Monaghan, Frank. *John Jay.* New York: Bobbs-Merrill, 1935.

Morris, Richard B. *John Jay, the Nation, and the Court.* Boston: Boston University Press, 1967.

Pellew, George. *John Jay.* 1890. Reprint. New York: Chelsea House, 1980.

THOMAS JOHNSON

Arnebeck, Bob. *Through a Fiery Trial; Building Washington 1790–1800.* Lanham, Md.: Madison Books, 1991.

Delaplaine, Edward S. *The Life of Thomas Johnson: Member of the Continental Congress, First Governor of the State of Maryland, and Associate Justice of the United States Supreme Court.* New York: F. H. Hitchcock, 1927.

Offutt, T. Scott. "Thomas Johnson and Constitutional Government." *Constitutional Review* 13 (October 1929): 204–211.

WILLIAM JOHNSON

Morgan, Donald Grant. *Justice William Johnson, the First Dissenter: The Career and Constitutional Philosophy of a Jeffersonian Judge.* Columbia: University of South Carolina Press, 1954.

———. "The Origin of Supreme Court Dissent." *William and Mary Quarterly* 10, 3d series (July 1953): 353–377.

Schroeder, Oliver. "The Life and Judicial Work of Justice William Johnson, Jr." *University of Pennsylvania Law Review* 95 (December 1946): 164–201; (February 1947): 344–386.

ANTHONY M. KENNEDY

Jehl, Douglas. "Judge Kennedy's Roots in Sacramento Go Deep." *Los Angeles Times,* December 14, 1987, 1.

Melone, Albert P. "Revisiting the Freshman Effect Hypothesis: The First Two Terms of Justice Anthony Kennedy." *Judicature* 74 (June–July, 1990): 6–13.

Williams, Charles F. "The Opinions of Anthony Kennedy: No Time For Ideology." *American Bar Association Journal* 74 (March 1, 1988): 56–61.

JOSEPH RUCKER LAMAR

Gilbert, S. Price. "The Lamars of Georgia: L.Q.C., Mirabeau B., and Joseph R. Lamar." *American Bar Association Journal* 34 (December 1948): 1100–1102, 1156–1158.

Lamar, Clarinda Huntington (Pendleton). *The Life of Joseph Rucker Lamar, 1857–1916.* New York: Putnam, 1926.

Sibley, Samuel H. *Georgia's Contribution to Law: The Lamars.* New York: Newcomen Society of England, American Branch, 1948.

LUCIUS Q.C. LAMAR

Cate, Wirt Armistead. *Lamar and the Frontier-Hypothesis.* Baton Rouge: Franklin Press, 1935.

———. *Lucius Q. C. Lamar, Secession and Reunion.* Chapel Hill: University of North Carolina Press, 1935.

"Dedication to the Memory of L. Q. C. Lamar." *Mississippi Law Journal* 63 (Fall 1993): 1–127.

Murphy, James B. *L. Q. C. Lamar: Pragmatic Patriot.* Baton Rouge: Louisiana State University Press, 1973.

HENRY BROCKHOLST LIVINGSTON

Dangerfield, George. *Chancellor Robert R. Livingston of New York.* [H. B. Livingston's cousin.] New York: Harcourt, Brace, 1960.

Dunne, Gerald T. "The Story-Livingston Correspondence (1812–1822)." *American Journal of Legal History* 10 (July 1966): 224–236.

Livingston, Edwin Brockholst. *The Livingstons of Livingston Manor.* New York: The Knickerbocker Press, 1910.

HORACE H. LURTON

Green, John W. "Judge Horace H. Lurton." In *Law and Lawyers: Sketches of the Federal Judges of Tennessee, Sketches of the Attorneys General of Tennessee, Legal Miscellany, Reminiscences by John W. Green,* 79–84. Jackson, Tenn.: McCowat-Mercer Press, 1950.

Tucker, David M. "Justice Horace Harmon Lurton: The Shaping of a National Progressive." *American Journal of Legal History* 13 (July 1969): 223–232.

Williams, Samuel C. "Judge Horace H. Lurton." *Tennessee Law Review* 18 (April 1944): 242–250.

JOHN MARSHALL

Adams, John Stokes, ed. *An Autobiographical Sketch by John Marshall.* 1937. Reprint. New York: Da Capo Press, 1973.

Baker, Leonard. *John Marshall: A Life in Law.* New York: Collier Books, 1974, 1981.

Beveridge, Albert Jeremiah. *The Life of John Marshall.* Boston and New York: Houghton Mifflin, 1919.

Faulkner, Robert Kenneth. *The Jurisprudence of John Marshall.* 1968. Reprint. Westport, Conn.: Greenwood Press, 1980.

Jones, William Melville, ed. *Chief Justice John Marshall: A Reappraisal.* 1956. Reprint. New York: Da Capo Press, 1971.

Loth, David Goldsmith. *Chief Justice: John Marshall and the Growth of the Republic.* 1949. Reprint. New York: Greenwood Press, 1970.

Magruder, Allan Bowie. *John Marshall.* 1898. Reprint. New York: AMS Press, 1972.

Mason, Frances Norton. *My Dearest Polly: Letters of Chief Justice John Marshall to His Wife, With Their Background, Political and Domestic, 1779–1831.* Richmond: Garrett and Massie, 1961.

Stites, Francis N. *John Marshall, Defender of the Constitution.* Boston: Little, Brown, 1981.

Surrency, Erwin C., ed. *The Marshall Reader: The Life and Contributions of Chief Justice John Marshall.* New York: Oceana Publications, 1955.

Thayer, James Bradley. *John Marshall.* 1901. Reprint. New York: Da Capo Press, 1974.

White, G. Edward. *The Marshall Court and Cultural Change, 1815–1835.* Abridged ed. New York: Oxford University Press, 1991.

THURGOOD MARSHALL

Bland, Randall Walton. *Private Pressure on Public Law: The Legal Career of Justice Thurgood Marshall, 1934–1991.* Revised ed. Lanham, Md.: University Press of America, 1993.

Davis, Michael D., and Hunter R. Clark. *Thurgood Marshall: Warrior at the Bar, Rebel on the Bench.* Secaucus, N.J.: Carol Publishing Group, 1992.

"Dedication to Mr. Justice Thurgood Marshall." *Black Law Journal* 6 (1978): 1–147.

Goldman, Roger, with David Gallen. *Thurgood Marshall: Justice For All.* New York: Carroll and Graf, 1992.

"Justice Thurgood Marshall: Reflections on a Life Well-Spent." *American Bar Association Journal* 78 (June 1992): 56–76, 118.

"Justice Thurgood Marshall Symposium." *Arkansas Law Review* (1987): 661–855.

Kluger, Richard. *Simple Justice: The History of Brown v. Board of Education and Black America's Struggle for Equality.* New York: Knopf, 1975.

Redding, J. Saunders. *The Lonesome Road; The Story of the Negro's Part in America.* New York: Doubleday, 1958, 315–334.

Rowan, Carl T. *Dream Makers, Dream Breakers: The World of Justice Thurgood Marshall.* Boston: Little, Brown, 1993.

"Symposium Honoring Justice Thurgood Marshall." *Georgetown Law Journal* 80 (August 1992): 2003–2130.

"Thurgood Marshall Commemorative Issue." *Howard Law Journal* 35 (Fall 1991): 1–114.

"A Tribute to Justice Marshall." *Harvard Blackletter Journal* 6 (Spring 1989): 1–140.

"A Tribute to Justice Thurgood Marshall." *Stanford Law Review* 44 (Summer 1992): 1213–1299.

"Tributes." *Yale Law Journal* 101 (October 1991): 1–29.

Tushnet, Mark V. *Making Civil Rights Law: Thurgood Marshall and the Supreme Court, 1936–1961.* New York: Oxford University Press, 1994.

STANLEY MATTHEWS

Chase, Salmon Portland. "Some Letters of Salmon P. Chase, 1848–1865." [Written to Stanley Matthews.] *American Historical Review* 34 (April 1929): 536–555.

Greve, Charles Theodore. "Stanley Matthews." In *Great American Lawyers,* vol. 7, 395–427. Edited by William Draper Lewis. Philadelphia: J. C. Winston Company, 1907–1909.

Helfman, Harold M. "The Contested Confirmation of Stanley Matthews to the United States Supreme Court." *Historical and Philosophical Society of Ohio* 8 (July 1958): 154–170.

JOSEPH MCKENNA

"Attorney-General McKenna." *Green Bag* 9 (July 1897): 289–290.

McDevitt, Matthew. *Joseph McKenna: Associate Justice of the United States.* 1946. Reprint. New York: Da Capo Press, 1974.

JOHN MCKINLEY

Hicks, Jimmie. "Associate Justice John McKinley: A Sketch." *Alabama Review* 18 (July 1965): 227–233.

Levin, H. "John McKinley." In *The Lawyers and Law Makers of Kentucky,* by H. Levin, 150. Chicago: Lewis Publishing Company, 1897.

Whatley, George C. "Justice John McKinley." *North Alabama History Association Bulletin* 4 (1959): 15–18.

JOHN MCLEAN

Kahn, Michael A. "The Appointment of John McLean to the Supreme Court: Practical Presidential Politics in the Jacksonian Era." *Journal of Supreme Court History* 1993: 59–72.

Letters of John McLean to John Teesdale. Oberlin, Ohio: Bibliotheca Sacra, 1899.

Veritas, pseud. *A Sketch of the Life of John McLean, of Ohio.* Washington, D.C.: n.p., 1846.

Weisenburger, Francis Phelps. *The Life of John McLean, a Politician on the United States Supreme Court.* 1937. Reprint. New York: Da Capo Press, 1971.

JAMES C. MCREYNOLDS

Bond, James E. *I Dissent: The Legacy of Chief Justice James Clark McReynolds.* Fairfax, Va.: George Mason University Press, 1992.

Fletcher, R. V. "Mr. Justice McReynolds: An Appreciation." *Vanderbilt Law Review* 2 (December 1948): 35–46.

Jones, Calvin P. "Kentucky's Irascible Conservative: Supreme Court Justice James Clark McReynolds." *Filson Club History Quarterly* 57 (January 1983): 20–30.

Knox, John. *My Experiences as Law Clerk to Mr. Justice James C. McReynolds of the Supreme Court of the United States During the Year That President Franklin D. Roosevelt Attempted to "Pack" the Court.* Oak Park, Ill.: n.p., 1978.

Schimmel, Barbara B. "The Judicial Policy of Mr. Justice McReynolds." Ph.D. diss., Yale University, 1964.

SAMUEL F. MILLER

Barnes, William Horatio. "Samuel F. Miller, Associate Justice." In *The Supreme Court of the United States,* by W. Barnes, 83–88. Part II of Barnes's *Illustrated Cyclopedia of the American Government.* n.p.: 1875.

Fairman, Charles. *Mr. Justice Miller and the Supreme Court, 1862–1890.* Cambridge: Harvard University Press, 1939.

Gregory, Charles Noble. *Samuel Freeman Miller.* Iowa City: State Historical Society of Iowa, 1907.

Swinford, Mac. "Mr. Justice Samuel Freeman Miller (1816–1873)." *Filson Club History Quarterly* 34 (January 1960): 35–44.

SHERMAN MINTON

Atkinson, David N. "Mr. Justice Minton and the Supreme Court, 1949–1956." Ph.D. diss., University of Iowa, 1970.

Hull, Elizabeth Anne. "Sherman Minton and the Cold War Court." Ph.D. diss., New School for Social Research, 1977.

Wallace, Harry L. "Mr. Justice Minton, Hoosier Justice on the Supreme Court." *Indiana Law Journal* 34 (1959): 145–205, 377–424.

WILLIAM H. MOODY

Heffron, Paul T. "Profile of a Public Man." *Supreme Court Historical Society Yearbook, 1980.* Washington, D.C.: Supreme Court Historical Society, 1980, 30–31, 48.

———. "Theodore Roosevelt and the Appointment of Mr. Justice Moody." *Vanderbilt Law Review* 18 (March 1965): 545–568.

McDonough, Judith R. "William Henry Moody." Ph.D. diss., Auburn University, 1983.

Representative Men of Massachusetts, 1890–1900. Everett, Mass.: Massachusetts Publishing Co., 1898, 154–156.

Weiner, Frederick B. *The Life and Career of William Henry Moody.* Cambridge: Harvard University Press, 1937.

Whitelock, George. "Mr. Justice Moody, Lately Attorney General." *Green Bag* 21 (June 1909): 263–266.

ALFRED MOORE

Davis, Junius. *Alfred Moore and James Iredell, Revolutionary Patriots.* Raleigh: North Carolina Society of the Sons of the Revolution, 1899.

Mason, Robert. *Namesake: Alfred Moore 1755–1810, Soldier and Jurist.* Southern Pines, S.C.: Moore County Historical Association, 1989.

FRANK MURPHY

Fine, Sidney. *Frank Murphy.* Vol. 1, *The Detroit Years.* Vol. 2, *The New Deal Years.* Chicago: University of Chicago Press, 1979. Vol. 3, *The Washington Years.* Ann Arbor: University of Michigan Press, 1975–1984.

Howard, J. Woodford. *Mr. Justice Murphy; A Political Biography.* Princeton: Princeton University Press, 1968.

Lunt, Richard D. *The High Ministry of Government: The Political Career of Frank Murphy.* Detroit: Wayne State University Press, 1965.

SAMUEL NELSON

"Biographical Sketch of Justice Samuel Nelson." *Central Law Journal* 1 (January 1, 1874): 2–3.

Countryman, Edwin. "Samuel Nelson." *Green Bag* 19 (June 1907): 329–334.

Leach, Richard H. "Rediscovery of Samuel Nelson." *New York History* 34 (January 1953): 64–71.

"The Old Judge and the New." *Albany Law Journal* 6 (December 14, 1872): 400–401.

SANDRA DAY O'CONNOR

"The Jurisprudence of Justice Sandra Day O'Connor." *Women's Rights Law Reporter* 13 (Summer/Fall 1991): whole issue.

Marie, Joan S. "Her Honor: The Rancher's Daughter." *Saturday Evening Post,* September 1985, 42–47+.

Smith, Betsy Covington. "Sandra Day O'Connor." In *Breakthrough: Women in Law* by Betsy Covington Smith, 117–137. New York: Walker, 1984.

Spaeth, Harold J. "Justice Sandra Day O'Connor: An Assessment." In *An Essential Safeguard: Essays on the United States Supreme Court and Its Justices,* edited by D. Grier Stephenson, Jr., 81–98. New York: Greenwood Press, 1991.

WILLIAM PATERSON

Boyd, Julian Parks. "William Paterson, Forerunner of John Marshall." In *Lives of Eighteen from Princeton,* edited by Willard Thorp, 194–196. Princeton: Princeton University Press, 1946.

Degnan, Daniel A. "Justice William Paterson: Founder." *Seton Hall Law Review* 16 (1986): 313–338.

Haskett, Richard C. "William Paterson, Counsellor at Law." Ph.D. diss., Princeton University, 1952.

Hickox, Charles F. III, and Andrew C. Laviano. "William Paterson." *Journal of Supreme Court History* 1992: 53–61.

O'Connor, John E. *William Paterson: Lawyer and Statesman, 1745–1806.* New Brunswick, N.J.: Rutgers University Press, 1979.

Wood, Gertrude Sceery. *William Paterson of New Jersey, 1745–1806.* Fair Lawn, N.J.: Fair Lawn Press, 1933.

RUFUS W. PECKHAM

Duker, William F. "Mr. Justice Rufus W. Peckham and the Case of *Ex Parte Young: Lochner*izing *Munn v. Illinois.*" *Brigham Young University Law Review* (1980): 539–558.

Hall, A. Oakey. "The New Supreme Court Justice." *Green Bag* 8 (January 1896): 1–4.

Proceedings of the Bar and Officers of the Supreme Court of the United States in Memory of Rufus Wheeler Peckham, December 18, 1909. Washington, D.C.: n.p., 1910.

Proctor, L. B. "Rufus W. Peckham." *Albany Law Journal* 55 (May 1, 1897): 286–288.

MAHLON PITNEY

Belknap, Michael R. "Mr. Justice Pitney and Progressivism." *Seton Hall Law Review* 16 (1986): 381–423.

Breed, Alan R. "Mahlon Pitney: His Life and Career, Political and Judicial." Senior thesis, Princeton University, 1932.

Levitan, David Maurice. "Mahlon Pitney, Labor Judge." *Virginia Law Review* 40 (1954): 733–770.

Stenzel, Robert David. "An Approach to Individuality, Liberty, and Equality: the Jurisprudence of Mr. Justice Pitney." 2 vols. Thesis, New School for Social Research, 1975.

LEWIS F. POWELL, JR.

Freeman, Anne Hobson. *The Style of a Law Firm: Eight Gentlemen of Virginia.* Chapel Hill: Algonquin Books, 1989.

Gunther, Gerald. "In Search of Judicial Quality on a Changing

Court: The Case of Justice Powell." *Stanford Law Review* 24 (June 1972): 1001–35.

Jeffries, John Calvin, Jr. *Justice Lewis F. Powell, Jr.* New York: C. Scribner, 1994.

Kahn, Paul W. "The Court, the Community and the Judicial Balance: The Jurisprudence of Justice Powell." *Yale Law Journal* 97 (November 1987): 1–60.

Putney, Diane T., ed. *ULTRA and the Army Air Forces in World War II: An Interview With Associate Justice of the U.S. Supreme Court Lewis F. Powell, Jr.* Washington, D.C.: Government Printing Office, 1987.

"A Tribute to Justice Lewis F. Powell, Jr." *Harvard Law Review* 101 (December 1987): 395–420.

"Tribute to Justice Lewis F. Powell, Jr." *Virginia Law Review* 68 (February 1982): 161–332.

Wilkinson, J. Harvie. *Serving Justice: A Supreme Court Clerk's View.* New York: Charterhouse, 1974.

STANLEY REED

Boskey, Bennett. "Justice Reed and His Family of Law Clerks." *Kentucky Law Journal* 69 (1980–1981): 869–876.

Fassett, John D. *New Deal Justice: The Life of Stanley Reed of Kentucky.* New York: Vantage Press, 1994.

Fitzgerald, Mark James. "Justice Reed: A Study of a Center Judge." Ph.D. diss., University of Chicago, 1950.

O'Brien, Francis William. *Justice Reed and the First Amendment: The Religion Clauses.* Washington, D.C.: Georgetown University Press, 1958.

Prickett, Morgan D. S. "Stanley Forman Reed: Perspectives on a Judicial Epitaph." *Hastings Constitutional Law Quarterly* 8 (Winter 1981): 343–369.

"Stanley Reed: Tributes by Warren Burger, William Brennan, Potter Stewart." *Kentucky Law Journal* 69 (1980–1981): 711–720.

WILLIAM H. REHNQUIST

Boles, Donald Edward. *Mr. Justice Rehnquist, Judicial Activist: The Early Years.* Ames: Iowa State University Press, 1987.

Davis, Sue. *Justice Rehnquist and the Constitution.* Princeton: Princeton University Press, 1989.

Jenkins, John A. "The Partisan: A Talk With Justice Rehnquist." *New York Times Magazine,* March 3, 1985.

"Reagan's Mr. Right." *Time,* June 30, 1986.

Rehnquist, William H. *The Supreme Court; How It Was; How It Is.* New York: William Morrow, 1987.

Savage, David G. *Turning Right: The Making of the Rehnquist Supreme Court.* New York: Wiley, 1993.

Weaver, Warren, Jr. "Mr. Justice Rehnquist, Dissenting." *New York Times Magazine,* October 13, 1974.

OWEN J. ROBERTS

Leonard, Charles A. *A Search for a Judicial Philosophy: Mr. Justice Roberts and the Constitutional Revolution of 1937.* Port Washington, N.Y.: Kennikat Press, 1971.

"Owen J. Roberts: In Memoriam." *University of Pennsylvania Law Review* 104 (December 1955): 311–379.

Pusey, Merlo J. "Justice Roberts' 1937 Turnaround." *Supreme Court Historical Society Yearbook, 1983.* Washington, D.C.: Supreme Court Historical Society, 1983, 102–107.

JOHN RUTLEDGE

Barnwell, Robert W. "Rutledge, 'The Dictator.'" *Journal of Southern History* 7 (May 1941): 215–224.

Barry, Richard Hayes. *Mr. Rutledge of South Carolina.* New York: Duell, Sloan and Pearce, 1942.

Jones, Francis R. "John Rutledge." *Green Bag* 13 (July 1901): 325–331.

WILEY B. RUTLEDGE

Harper, Fowler Vincent. *Justice Rutledge and the Bright Constellation.* Indianapolis: Bobbs-Merrill, 1965.

Pollak, Louis H. "W. B. R.: Some Reflections." *Yale Law Journal* 71 (July 1962): 1451–58.

Stevens, John Paul. "Mr. Justice Rutledge." In *Mr. Justice,* edited by Allison Dunham and Philip B. Kurland, 177–202. Chicago: University of Chicago Press, 1964.

"A Symposium to the Memory of Wiley B. Rutledge." *Iowa Law Review* 35 (Summer 1950): 541–692; *Indiana Law Journal* 25 (Summer 1950): 421–559.

EDWARD T. SANFORD

Cook, Stanley A. "Path to the High Bench: The Pre-Supreme Court Career of Justice Edward Terry Sanford." Ph.D. diss., University of Tennessee, 1977.

Fowler, James A. "Mr. Justice Edward Terry Sanford." *American Bar Association Journal* 17 (April 1931): 229–233.

Green, John W. "Judge Edward T. Sanford." In *Law and Lawyers: Sketches of the Federal Judges of Tennessee, Sketches of the Attorneys General of Tennessee, Legal Miscellany, Reminiscences* by John W. Green. Jackson, Tenn.: McCowat-Mercer Press, 1950, 64–69.

ANTONIN SCALIA

Adler, Stephen J. "Live Wire on the D. C. Circuit." *American Lawyer* (March 1985): 86–93.

Bronner, Ethan. "Bulldog Justice." *Washingtonian,* December 1990, 138–139, 245–248.

"The Jurisprudence of Justice Antonin Scalia." *Cardozo Law Review* 12 (June 1991): 1583–1867.

Kannar, George. "The Constitutional Catechism of Antonin Scalia." *Yale Law Journal* 99 (April 1990): 1297–1357.

GEORGE SHIRAS, JR.

Shiras, George III. *Justice George Shiras, Jr., of Pittsburgh, Associate Justice of the United States Supreme Court, 1892–1903; A Chronicle of His Family, Life, and Times.* Edited and completed by Winfield Shiras. Pittsburgh: University of Pittsburgh Press, 1953.

DAVID H. SOUTER

Carlson, Margaret. "An 18th Century Man." *Time,* August 6, 1990, 19–22.

"David H. Souter." *Current Biography Yearbook, 1991.* New York: Wilson, 1991, 543–547.

Lacayo, Richard. "A Blank Slate." *Time,* August 6, 1990, 16–18.

JOHN PAUL STEVENS

Kramer, Victor H. "The Case of Justice Stevens: How to Select, Nominate and Confirm a Justice of the United States Supreme Court." *Constitutional Commentary* 7 (Summer 1990): 325–340.

O'Brien, David M. "Filling Justice William O. Douglas's Seat: President Gerald R. Ford's Appointment of Justice John Paul Stevens." *Supreme Court Historical Society Yearbook, 1989.* Washington, D.C.: Supreme Court Historical Society, 1989, 20–39.

Popkin, William D. "A Common Law Lawyer on the Supreme Court: The Opinions of Justice Stevens." *Duke Law Journal* (November 1989): 1087–1161.

Sickels, Robert J. *John Paul Stevens and the Constitution: The Search for Balance.* University Park: Pennsylvania State University Press, 1988.

POTTER STEWART

Barnett, Helaine Meresman, and Kenneth Levine. "Mr. Justice Potter Stewart." *New York University Law Review* 40 (May 1965): 526–562.

Bendiner, Robert. "The Law and Potter Stewart: An Interview with Justice Potter Stewart." *American Heritage,* December 1983, 98–104.

Binion, Gayle. "Justice Potter Stewart: The *Unpredictable* Vote." *Journal of Supreme Court History* 1992: 99–108.

Frank, John Paul. "Potter Stewart." In *The Warren Court,* 133–148. New York: Macmillan, 1964.

Marsel, Robert S. "The Constitutional Jurisprudence of Justice Potter Stewart: Reflections on a Life of Public Service." *Tennessee Law Review* 55 (Fall 1987): 1–20.

"A Retirement Press Conference." *Tennessee Law Review* 55 (Fall 1987): 21–39.

HARLAN FISKE STONE

Danelski, David Joseph. "The Chief Justice and the Supreme Court." Ph.D. diss., University of Chicago, 1985.

Konefsky, Samuel Joseph. *Chief Justice Stone and the Supreme Court.* 1945. Reprint. New York: Hafner, 1971.

Mason, Alpheus Thomas. *Harlan Fiske Stone: Pillar of the Law.* 1956. Reprint. Hamden, Conn.: Archon Books, 1968.

Stone, Lauson H. "My Father the Chief Justice: Harlan F. Stone." *Supreme Court Historical Society Yearbook, 1978.* Washington, D.C.: Supreme Court Historical Society, 1978, 7–17.

JOSEPH STORY

Commager, Henry Steele. "Joseph Story." In Gasper G. Bacon, *Lectures on the Constitution of the United States, 1940–1950.* [Delivered March 31; April 2, 4, 1941.] Boston: Boston University Press, 1953.

Dunne, Gerald T. *Justice Joseph Story and the Rise of the Supreme Court.* New York: Simon and Schuster, 1970.

Eisgruber, Christopher L. M. "Justice Story, Slavery, and the Natural Law Foundations of American Constitutionalism." *University of Chicago Law Review* 55 (1988): 273–327.

McClellan, James. *Joseph Story and the American Constitution: A Study in Political and Legal Thought with Selected Writings.* Norman: University of Oklahoma Press, 1971.

Newmyer, R. Kent. *Supreme Court Justice Joseph Story: Statesman of the Old Republic.* Chapel Hill: University of North Carolina Press, 1985.

Schwartz, Mortimer D., and John C. Hogan, eds. *Joseph Story: A Collection of Writings by and about an Eminent American.* New York: Oceana Publications, 1959.

Story, William W., ed. *Life and Letters of Joseph Story.* 1851. Reprint. Freeport, N.Y.: Books for Libraries Press, 1971.

———. *The Miscellaneous Writings of Joseph Story.* 1852. Reprint. New York: DaCapo Press, 1972.

Sutherland, Arthur E. *The Law at Harvard: A History of Ideas and Men, 1817–1967.* Cambridge: Belknap Press of Harvard University Press, 1967.

WILLIAM STRONG

Barnes, William Horatio. "William Strong, Associate Justice." In *The Supreme Court of the United States,* by W. Barnes, 101–106. Part II of Barnes's *Illustrated Cyclopedia of the American Government.* n.p.: 1875.

"Retirement of William J. Strong." *American Law Review* 15 (February 1881): 130–131.

Strong, Daniel Gerald. "Supreme Court Justice William Strong, 1808–1895." Ph.D. diss., Kent State University, 1985.

Strong, William. "The Needs of the Supreme Court." *North American Review* 132 (May 1881): 437–450.

———. "Relief for the Supreme Court." *North American Review* 151 (November 1890): 567–575.

GEORGE SUTHERLAND

Arkes, Hadley. *The Return of George Sutherland: Restoring a Jurisprudence of Natural Rights.* Princeton, N.J.: Princeton University Press, 1994.

Mason, Alpheus Thomas. "The Conservative World of Mr. Justice Sutherland, 1883–1910." *American Political Science Review* 32 (June 1938): 443–477.

Paschal, Joel Francis. *Mr. Justice Sutherland: A Man Against the State.* Princeton, N.J.: Princeton University Press, 1951.

Saks, J. Benson. "Mr. Justice Sutherland." Ph.D. diss., Johns Hopkins University, 1940.

NOAH H. SWAYNE

Barnes, William Horatio. "Noah H. Swayne, Associate Justice." In *The Supreme Court of the United States,* by W. Barnes, 79–82. Part II of Barnes's *Illustrated Cyclopedia of the American Government.* n.p.: 1875.

Magrath, C. Peter. *Morrison R. Waite: The Triumph of Character.* New York: Macmillan, 1963.

Silver, David Mayer. *Lincoln's Supreme Court.* Urbana: University of Illinois Press, 1956.

WILLIAM HOWARD TAFT

Anderson, Judith Icke. *William Howard Taft: An Intimate History.* New York: Norton, 1981.

Mason, Alpheus Thomas. *William Howard Taft, Chief Justice.* 1965. Reprint. Lanham, Md.: University Press of America, 1983.

Pringle, Henry Fowles. *The Life and Times of William Howard Taft: A Biography.* 1939. Reprint. Norwalk, Conn.: Easton Press, 1986.

Ross, Ishbel. *An American Family: The Tafts, 1678 to 1964.* 1964. Reprint. Westport, Conn.: Greenwood Press, 1977.

Taft, Helen Herron. *Recollections of Full Years, by Mrs. William Howard Taft.* New York: Dodd, Mead and Company, 1914.

ROGER B. TANEY

Lewis, Walker. *Without Fear or Favor: A Biography of Chief Justice Roger Brooke Taney.* Boston: Houghton Mifflin, 1965.

Newmyer, R. Kent. *The Supreme Court Under Marshall and Taney.* 1968. Reprint. Arlington Heights, Ill.: Harlan Davidson, 1986.

Palmer, Benjamin Whipple. *Marshall and Taney: Statesmen of the Law.* 1939. Reprint. New York: Russell and Russell, 1966.

Smith, Charles William, Jr. *Roger B. Taney: Jacksonian Jurist.* 1936. Reprint. New York: Da Capo Press, 1973.

Steiner, Bernard Christian. *Life of Roger Brooke Taney, Chief Justice of the United States Supreme Court.* 1922. Reprint. Westport, Conn.: Greenwood Press, 1970.

Swisher, Carl Brent. *Roger B. Taney.* New York: Macmillan Company, 1935.

Tyler, Samuel. *Memoir of Roger Brooke Taney, LL.D., Chief Justice of the Supreme Court of the United States.* 1872. Reprint. New York: Da Capo Press, 1970.

CLARENCE THOMAS

"Clarence Thomas." *Current Biography.* New York: Wilson, April 1992, 49–54.

Gerber, Scott D. "The Jurisprudence of Clarence Thomas." *Journal of Law and Politics* 8 (Fall 1991): 107–141.

Kaplan, David A. "Supreme Mystery." *Newsweek,* September 16, 1991.

McCaughey, Elizabeth P. "Clarence Thomas's Record as a Judge." *Presidential Studies Quarterly* 21 (Fall 1991): 833–835.

Williams, Juan. "A Question of Fairness." *Atlantic Monthly,* February 1987, 70–75, 78–82.

SMITH THOMPSON

Hammond, J. *The History of Political Parties in the State of New York.* Albany: n.p., 1842.

Lobingier, Charles S. "The Judicial Opinions of Mr. Justice Thompson." *Nebraska Bar Bulletin* 12 (May 1924): 421–426.

Roper, Donald Malcolm. *Mr. Justice Thompson and the Constitution.* 1963. Reprint. New York: Garland, 1987.

THOMAS TODD

Gardner, Woodford L., Jr. "Kentucky Justices on the U.S. Supreme Court." *Register of the Kentucky Historical Society* 70 (1972): 121–142.

"Letters of Judge Thomas Todd of Kentucky to His Son at College." *William and Mary Quarterly* 22 (1913): 20.

Levin, H. "Thomas Todd." In *The Lawyers and Law Makers of Kentucky* by H. Levin, 149. Chicago: Lewis Publishing Company, 1897.

O'Rear, Edward C. "Justice Thomas Todd." *Kentucky State Historical Society Register* 38 (February 1940): 112–119.

"Supreme Court Tribute to Justice Todd." *United States Reports* (13 Peters), iii–viii. Washington, D.C., 1839.

ROBERT TRIMBLE

Goff, John S. "Mr. Justice Trimble of the United States Supreme Court." *Kentucky Historical Society Register* 58 (January 1960): 6–28.

Levin, H. "Robert Trimble." In *The Lawyers and Lawmakers of Kentucky,* by H. Levin, 149–150. 1897. Reprint. Easley, S.C.: Southern Historical Press, 1982.

Schneider, Alan N. "Robert Trimble: A Kentucky Justice on the Supreme Court." *Kentucky State Bar Journal* 12 (December 1947): 21–30.

WILLIS VAN DEVANTER

Gould, Lewis L. "Willis Van Devanter in Wyoming Politics, 1884–1897." Ph.D. diss., Yale University, 1966.

Holsinger, M. Paul. "The Appointment of Supreme Court Justice Van Devanter: A Study of Political Preferment." *American Journal of Legal History* 12 (October 1968): 324–335.

———. "Willis Van Devanter: The Early Years, 1859–1911." Ph.D. diss., University of Denver, 1964.

———. "Willis Van Devanter: Wyoming Leader, 1884–1897." *Annals of Wyoming* 37 (October 1965): 170–206.

Nelson, Daniel A. "The Supreme Court Appointment of Willis Van Devanter." *Annals of Wyoming* 53 (Fall 1981): 2–11.

FRED M. VINSON

Bolner, James. "Mr. Chief Justice Vinson: His Politics and His Constitutional Law." Ph.D. diss., University of Virginia, 1962.

Frank, John Paul. "Fred Vinson and the Chief Justiceship." *University of Chicago Law Review* 21 (Winter 1954): 212–246.

Hatcher, John Henry. "Fred Vinson, Congressman From Kentucky: A Political Biography, 1890–1938." Ph.D. diss., University of Cincinnati, 1967.

Palmer, Jan S. *The Vinson Court Era: The Supreme Court's Conference Votes.* New York: AMS Press, 1990.

Pritchett, Herman C. *Civil Liberties and the Vinson Court.* Chicago: University of Chicago Press, 1954.

MORRISON R. WAITE

Barnes, William Horatio. "Morrison R. Waite, Chief Justice." In *The Supreme Court of the United States,* by W. Barnes, 65–72. Part II of Barnes's *Illustrated Cyclopedia of the American Government.* n.p.: 1875.

Magrath, C. Peter. *Morrison R. Waite: The Triumph of Character.* New York: Macmillan, 1963.

Morris, Jeffrey Brandon. "Morrison Waite's Court." *Supreme Court Historical Society Yearbook, 1980.* Washington, D.C.: Supreme Court Historical Society, 1980, 38–48.

Stephenson, D. Grier, Jr. "The Chief Justice as Leader: The Case of Morrison Remick Waite." *William and Mary Law Review* 14 (Summer 1973): 899–927.

Trimble, Bruce Raymond. *Chief Justice Waite, Defender of the Public Interest.* 1938. Reprint. New York: Russell and Russell, 1970.

EARL WARREN

"Chief Justice Warren." *Harvard Law Review* 88 (November 1974): 1–12.

Schwartz, Bernard. "Earl Warren as Judge." *Hastings Constitutional Law Quarterly* 12 (Winter 1985): 179–200.

———. *Super Chief: Earl Warren and His Supreme Court—A Judicial Biography.* New York: New York University Press, 1983.

Warren, Earl. *The Memoirs of Earl Warren.* Garden City, N.Y.: Doubleday, 1977.

———. *The Public Papers of Chief Justice Earl Warren.* Edited by Henry M. Christman. New York: Simon and Schuster, 1959.

White, G. Edward. *Earl Warren, A Public Life.* New York: Oxford University Press, 1982.

BUSHROD WASHINGTON

Annis, David Leslie. "Mr. Bushrod Washington, Supreme Court Justice on the Marshall Court." Ph.D. diss., University of Notre Dame, 1974.

Custer, Lawrence B. "Bushrod Washington and John Marshall: A Preliminary Inquiry." *American Journal of Legal History* 4 (January 1960): 34–48.

Dunne, Gerald T. "Bushrod Washington and the Mount Vernon Slaves." *Supreme Court Historical Society Yearbook, 1980.* Washington, D.C.: Supreme Court Historical Society, 1980, 25–29.

McDorman, J. Steven. "The Late Mr. Justice Bushrod Washington." *Green Bag* 9 (August 1897): 329–335.

JAMES M. WAYNE

Battle, George G. "James Moore Wayne: Southern Unionist." *Fordham Urban Law Journal* 14 (March 1964): 42–59.

Lawrence, Alexander A. *James Moore Wayne, Southern Unionist.* 1943. Reprint. Westport, Conn.: Greenwood Press, 1970.

BYRON R. WHITE

Hutchinson, Dennis J. "The Man Who Once Was Whizzer White." *Yale Law Journal* 103 (October 1993): 43–55.

"Justice Byron R. White: Tribute." *Brigham Young University Law Review* 1994: 209–368.

Liebman, Lance. "Swing Man on the Supreme Court." *New York Times Magazine,* October 8, 1972.

Savage, David G. "Byron White: Color Him Constant." *Los Angeles Times,* May 31, 1988, 1, 12.

"Special Issue: Justice Byron R. White: On the Twenty-Fifth Anniversary of His Accession to the Supreme Court of the United States." *University of Colorado Law Review* 58 (Summer 1987): 339–514.

Weyand, Alexander M. *Football Immortals.* New York: Macmillan, 1962, 204–207.

White, Byron R. "Some Current Debates." *Judicature* 73 (October–November 1989): 155–161.

Wright, Alfred. "A Modest All-American Who Sits on the Highest Bench." *Sports Illustrated,* December 12, 1962, 85–98.

EDWARD DOUGLASS WHITE

Carter, Newman. "Edward D. White in Personal Retrospect." *Supreme Court Historical Society Yearbook, 1979.* Washington, D.C.: Supreme Court Historical Society, 1979, 5–7.

Cassidy, Lewis C. *The Catholic Ancestry of Chief Justice White.* Philadelphia: Patterson and White, 1927.

Highsaw, Robert Baker. *Edward Douglass White: Defender of the Conservative Faith.* Baton Rouge: Louisiana State University Press, 1981.

Klinkhamer, Marie Carolyn. *Edward Douglass White, Chief Justice of the United States.* Washington, D.C.: Catholic University of America Press, 1943.

Morris, Jeffrey B. "Chief Justice Edward Douglass White and President Taft's Court." *Supreme Court Historical Society Yearbook, 1982.* Washington, D.C.: Supreme Court Historical Society, 1982, 27–45.

CHARLES E. WHITTAKER

Christensen, Barbara B. "Mister Justice Whittaker: The Man on the Right." *Santa Clara Law Review* 19 (1979): 1039–1062.

Cole, Judith. "Mr. Justice Charles Evans Whittaker: A Case Study in Judicial Recruitment and Behavior." Thesis, University of Missouri-Kansas City, 1972.

Lashly, Jacob M. "Mr. Justice Whittaker." *American Bar Association Journal* 43 (June 1957): 526–527.

Rehnquist, William H. "The Making of a Supreme Court Justice." *Harvard Law Record* 29 (October 8, 1959): 7–10.

Volz, Marlin M. "Charles Evans Whittaker—a Biographical Sketch." *Texas Law Review* 40 (June 1962): 742–743.

JAMES WILSON

Goodrich, Charles A. "James Wilson." In *Lives of the Signers of the Declaration of Independence,* by Charles A. Goodrich, 300–309. New York: W. Reed and Company, 1829.

Harlan, John Marshall. "James Wilson and the Formation of the Constitution." *American Law Review* 34 (July–August 1900): 481–504.

Maxey, David W. "The Translation of James Wilson." *Journal of Supreme Court History* 1990: 29–43.

Pascal, Jean-Marc. *The Political Ideas of James Wilson, 1742–1798.* New York: Garland, 1991.

Seed, Geoffrey. *James Wilson.* Millwood, N.Y.: KTO Press, 1978.

Smith, Page. *James Wilson, Founding Father, 1742–1798.* 1956. Reprint. Westport, Conn.: Greenwood Press, 1973.

LEVI WOODBURY

Bader, William D., Henry J. Abraham, and James B. Staab. "The Jurisprudence of Levi Woodbury." *Vermont Law Review* 18 (Winter 1994): 261–312.

Capowski, Vincent Julian. "The Making of a Jacksonian Democrat, Levi Woodbury, 1789–1831." Thesis, Fordham University, 1966.

Cole, Donald B. *Jacksonian Democracy in New Hampshire, 1800–1851.* Cambridge: Harvard University Press, 1970.

Wheaton, Philip D. "Levi Woodbury: Jacksonian Financier." Ph.D. diss., University of Maryland, 1955.

Woodbury, Charles Levi. *Memoir of Honorable Levi Woodbury, LL.D.* Boston: David Clapp and Son, 1894.

Woodbury, Levi. *Writings of Levi Woodbury, LL.D., Political, Judicial and Literary.* Boston: Little, Brown, 1852.

WILLIAM B. WOODS

Baynes, Thomas E. "A Search for Justice Woods: Yankee from Georgia." *Supreme Court Historical Society Yearbook, 1978.* Washington, D.C.: Supreme Court Historical Society, 1978, 31–42.

Brister, Edwin M. P. *Centennial History of the City of Newark and Licking County, Ohio.* 1909. Reprint. Defiance, Ohio: Hubbard, 1982.

Reid, Whitelaw. *Ohio in the War: Her Statement, Generals and Soldiers.* Columbus: Eclectic Publishing, 1893.

Smith, Joseph Patterson. *History of the Republican Party in Ohio.* Chicago: Lewis Publishing, 1898.

Books About the Supreme Court for Young Readers

Aaseng, Nathan. *Great Justices of the Supreme Court.* Minneapolis: Olive Press, 1992.

Bains, Rae. *The Supreme Court.* Mahwah, N.J.: Troll Associates, 1985.

Bernstein, Richard B. *Into the Third Century: The Supreme Court.* New York: Walker, 1989.

Coy, Harold. *The Supreme Court.* Revised by Lorna Greenberg. New York: F. Watts, 1981.

Friedman, Leon. *The Supreme Court.* New York: Chelsea House, 1987.

Goode, Stephen. *The Controversial Court: Supreme Court Influences on American Life.* New York: Messner, 1982.

Greene, Carol. *The Supreme Court.* Chicago: Childrens Press, 1985.

Latham, Frank Brown. *FDR and the Supreme Court Fight, 1937: A President Tries to Reorganize the Federal Judiciary.* New York: F. Watts, 1972.

Lieberman, Jethro Koller. *Free Speech, Free Press, and the Law.* New York: Lothrop, Lee and Shepard Books, 1980.

Rierden, Anne B. *Reshaping the Supreme Court: New Justices, New Directions.* New York: F. Watts, 1988.

Stein, R. Conrad. *The Story of the Powers of the Supreme Court.* Chicago: Childrens Press, 1989.

Weiss, Ann E. *The Supreme Court.* Hillside, N.J.: Enslow Publishers, 1987.

Books About Supreme Court Justices for Young Readers

RUTH BADER GINSBURG

Ayer, Eleanor H. *Ruth Bader Ginsburg: Fire and Steel on the Supreme Court.* New York: Dillon Press, 1994.

Henry, Christopher E. *Ruth Bader Ginsburg: Associate Justice of the United States Supreme Court.* New York: Franklin Watts, 1994.

JOHN MARSHALL HARLAN (1877–1911)

Latham, Frank Brown. *The Great Dissenter, John Marshall Harlan, 1833–1911.* New York: Cowles Book Company, 1970.

Stiller, Richard. *The White Minority: Pioneers for Racial Equality.* New York: Harcourt Brace Jovanovich, 1977.

OLIVER WENDELL HOLMES, JR.

Dunham, Montrew. *Oliver Wendell Holmes, Jr. Boy of Justice.* Indianapolis: Bobbs-Merrill, 1961.

JOHN JAY

Smith, Donald Lewis. *John Jay: Founder of a State and Nation.* New York: Teachers College Press, Columbia University, 1968.

JOHN MARSHALL

Brown, Richard Carl. *John Marshall.* Morristown, N.J.: Silver Burdett, 1968.

Cook, Fred J. *Fighting for Justice.* Chicago: Kingston House, 1961.

Martin, Patricia Miles. *John Marshall.* New York: Putnam, 1967.

Martini, Teri. *John Marshall.* Philadelphia: Westminster Press, 1974.

Monsell, Helen Albee. *John Marshall, Boy of America.* [Fiction] Indianapolis: Bobbs-Merrill, 1962.

Steinberg, Alfred. *John Marshall.* New York: Putnam, 1962.

Tucker, Caroline. *John Marshall, the Great Chief Justice.* New York: Ariel Books, 1962.

THURGOOD MARSHALL

Aldred, Lisa. *Thurgood Marshall.* New York: Chelsea House, 1990.

Bains, Rae. *Thurgood Marshall: Fight for Justice.* Mahwah, N.J.: Troll Associates, 1993.

Cavan, Seamus. *Thurgood Marshall and Equal Rights.* Brookfield, Conn.: Millbrook Press, 1993.

Fenderson, Lewis H. *Thurgood Marshall: Fighter for Justice.* New York: McGraw-Hill, 1969.

Greene, Carol. *Thurgood Marshall: First African-American Supreme Court Justice.* Chicago: Childrens Press, 1991.

Haskins, James. *Thurgood Marshall: A Life for Justice.* New York: Henry Holt, 1992.

Hess, Debra. *Thurgood Marshall: The Fight for Equal Justice.* Englewood Cliffs, N.J.: Silver Burdett Press, 1990.

Krug, Elisabeth. *Thurgood Marshall: Champion of Civil Rights.* New York: Fawcett Columbine, 1993.

Prentzas, G. S. *Thurgood Marshall.* New York: Chelsea Juniors, 1994.

Young, Margaret B. *The Picture Life of Thurgood Marshall.* New York: Watts, 1971.

SANDRA DAY O'CONNOR

Bentley, Judith. *Justice Sandra Day O'Connor.* New York: J. Messner, 1983.

Berwald, Beverly. *Sandra Day O'Connor, a New Justice, a New Voice.* New York: Fawcett Columbine, 1991.

Fox, Mary Virginia. *Justice Sandra Day O'Connor.* Hillside, N.J.: Enslow Publishers, 1983.

Gherman, Beverly. *Sandra Day O'Connor: Justice for All.* New York: Puffin, 1993.

Greene, Carol. *Sandra Day O'Connor: First Woman on the Supreme Court.* Chicago: Childrens Press, 1982.

Henry, Christopher E. *Sandra Day O'Connor.* New York: Franklin Watts, 1994.

Huber, Peter William. *Sandra Day O'Connor.* New York: Chelsea House, 1990.

Macht, Norman Lee. *Sandra Day O'Connor.* New York: Chelsea Juniors, 1992.

Woods, Harold. *Equal Justice: A Biography of Sandra Day O'Connor.* Minneapolis: Dillon Press, 1985.

WILLIAM HOWARD TAFT

Casey, Jane Clark. *William Howard Taft: Twenty-Seventh President of the United States.* Chicago: Childrens Press, 1989.

Falkof, Lucille. *William H. Taft, 27th President of the United States.* Ada, Okla: Garrett Educational Corporation, 1990.

Myers, Elisabeth P. *William Howard Taft.* Chicago: Reilly and Lee, 1970.

Severn, Bill. *William Howard Taft, the President Who Became Chief Justice.* New York: McKay, 1970.

ROGER BROOKE TANEY

Flavius, Brother. *The Pride of Our Nation: A Story of Chief Justice Roger Brooke Taney.* Notre Dame, Ind.: Dujarie Press, 1961.

CLARENCE THOMAS

Halliburton, Warren J. *Clarence Thomas: Supreme Court Justice.* Hillside, N.J.: Enslow Publishers, 1993.

EDWARD DOUGLASS WHITE

Hagemann, Gerard. *The Man on the Bench; A Story of Chief Justice Edward Douglass White.* Notre Dame, Ind.: Dujarie Press, 1962.

Author Affiliations

Gary J. Aichele, former executive director, Supreme Court Historical Society

David N. Atkinson, professor of political science and law, University of Missouri-Kansas City

Thomas E. Baynes Jr., judge, U.S. Bankruptcy Court, Middle District of Florida

Loren P. Beth, professor emeritus of political science, University of Georgia

Hugo L. Black, Jr., attorney, Kelly, Black, Black et al., Miami

Susan Low Bloch, professor of law, Georgetown University Law Center

Craig M. Bradley, professor of law, Charles L. Whistler Faculty Fellow, School of Law, Indiana University

James Buchanan, Training Specialist, Court Education Division, The Federal Judicial Center

Jay S. Bybee, assistant professor, Louisiana State University Law Center

Vincent J. Capowski, professor, Department of History, Saint Anselm College

Christine Desan, assistant professor of law, Harvard Law School

James C. Duram, professor, Department of History, Wichita State University

Sidney Fine, Andrew Dickson White Distinguished Professor of History, University of Michigan

John P. Frank, attorney, Lewis and Roca, Phoenix

John S. Goff, professor, Department of History, Phoenix College

James Haw, associate professor of history, Indiana University-Purdue University at Fort Wayne

Paul T. Heffron, former assistant chief of the Manuscript Division, Library of Congress

Charles F. Hickox III, assistant professor of business law, University of Rhode Island

Peter Huber, attorney, Kellogg, Huber, Hansen & Todd, Washington, D.C.

Dennis J. Hutchinson, associate professor and senior lecturer in law, University of Chicago Law School

Robert D. Ilisevich, librarian, Crawford County Historical Society

Herbert A. Johnson, Hollings Professor of Constitutional Law, University of South Carolina School of Law

Judith Johnson, assistant professor of history, Wichita State University

Sally Katzen, administrator, Office of Information and Regulatory Affairs, Office of Management and Budget

Alan C. Kohn, attorney, Kohn, Shands, Elbert, Gianoulakis, and Giljum, St. Louis

Gil Kujovich, professor of law, Vermont Law School

Philip B. Kurland, William R. Kenan, Jr., Distinguished Service Professor Emeritus, University of Chicago Law School

Robert W. Langran, professor of political science, Villanova University

Andrew C. Laviano, professor of business law, University of Rhode Island

Nathan Lewin, attorney, Miller, Cassidy, Larroca, and Lewin, Washington, D.C.

Jonathan Lurie, professor of history and adjunct professor of law, Rutgers University

Louis Lusky, Betts Professor of Law Emeritus, Columbia University School of Law

Alan S. Madans, attorney, Rothschild, Barry, and Myers, Chicago

James M. Marsh, counsel, Hecker Brown Sherry and Johnson, Philadelphia

Roy M. Mersky, Hyder Centennial Professor of Law

and director of research, Tarlton Law Library, University of Texas at Austin

F. Thornton Miller, assistant professor, Department of History, Southwest Missouri State University

Brian J. Moline, attorney, Kansas City

Danny Moody, founder, North Carolina Supreme Court Historical Society

Winfred B. Moore, Jr., professor, Department of History, The Citadel, Military College of South Carolina

Leonard M. Niehoff, attorney, Butzel Long, Detroit, and adjunct professor, Wayne State University Law School

James O'Hara, Department of Law, Loyola College of Maryland

Louis H. Pollak, U.S. District Court judge, Eastern District of Pennsylvania

Edith Lampson Roberts, staff attorney, Environmental Law Institute

Donald Roper, associate professor of history, State University of New York, New Paltz

Bernard Schwartz, Chapman Distinguished Professor of Law, University of Tulsa

Robert J. Sickels, professor emeritus, Department of Political Science, University of New Mexico

Philippa Strum, professor, Department of Political Science, Brooklyn College of The City University of New York

William J. Stuntz, E. James Kelly, Jr., Research Professor of Law, School of Law, University of Virginia

John J. Sullivan, attorney, Mayer, Brown & Platt, Washington, D.C.

Robert Warner, dean, School of Information and Library Studies, University of Michigan

Stephen Wermiel, associate professor of law, Georgia State University College of Law

Richard K. Willard, attorney, Steptoe and Johnson, Washington, D.C.

Index